Kirtley Library
Columbia College
8th and Rogers
Columbia, MO. 65201

*DUKE UNIVERSITY PUBLICATIONS*

TRANSITIONS
IN
AMERICAN LITERARY HISTORY

# *Transitions in* AMERICAN LITERARY HISTORY

EDITED BY
HARRY HAYDEN CLARK
*for the* AMERICAN LITERATURE GROUP *of the*
Modern Language Association

OCTAGON BOOKS

A DIVISION OF FARRAR, STRAUS AND GIROUX

New York    1975

Copyright, 1954, Duke University Press

*Reprinted 1967*
*by special arrangement with Duke University Press*

*Second Octagon printing 1975*

OCTAGON BOOKS
A DIVISION OF FARRAR, STRAUS & GIROUX, INC.
19 Union Square West
New York, N.Y. 10003

LIBRARY OF CONGRESS CATALOG CARD NUMBER: 67-18758
ISBN 0-374-91672-1

Manufactured by Braun-Brumfield, Inc.
Ann Arbor, Michigan

Printed in the United States of America

# Introduction

# Introduction

MORE than two decades have elapsed since a group of scholars wrote "for the American Literature Group of the Modern Language Association" the book entitled *The Reinterpretation of American Literature* (edited by Norman Foerster), which sought to contribute to "the understanding of its historical development" by defining the principal factors involved as the Puritan tradition, the frontier spirit, romanticism, and realism. During these two decades a vast amount of analytical scholarship has been published which has greatly illuminated our literary history and the major spokesmen of these four movements at their peak. However, if scholarship develops most fruitfully by alternating analysis with synthesis, it seems desirable that the American Literature Group should experiment once more by devoting itself to at least one cooperative and synthetic program.[1] After considerable discussion it was decided that the problem which seems especially in need of elucidation (and which emerges directly out of *The Reinterpretation*) is the problem of how and especially why American literature did change historically from one center of emphasis to another. Most of our universities offer excellent courses on "periods" and "movements," but comparatively little attention seems to have

[1] We are grateful to Professor Perry Miller for taking part in the program of 1948 and addressing the Group on the subject of why Transcendentalism arose. Subsequent commitments prevented him from contributing to the present book, however, and Professor Alexander Kern graciously accepted our invitation to cover this topic.

been devoted in the way of synthesis to the obvious and fascinating problem of transitions.

Naturally there can be and has been endless quibbling about these movements if they are considered as "absolutes," and naturally some scholars have become discouraged and suggested that we drop all such terms as puritanism, neoclassicism, and romanticism or find new terms. However, no other terms appear to have won any wide acceptance, and the adoption of an organization based on merely political history (such as Colonialism, the Revolution, and Unionism) fails to focus attention on elements which are distinctive in literary craftsmanship. To surrender all attempts at distinguishing centers of emphasis and merely to add together biographies, summaries, and appraisals without any concern for the logical articulation of ideas or the rise and fall of major movements has obvious disadvantages and invites the familiar censure of courses in literary history as "shotgun" courses in purposeless chaos. Since much of the scholarship devoted to the literature of England and other countries is organized on the basis of the periods or patterns of ideas and craftsmanship mentioned, it would seem that, granting the difficulties, our practice as teachers of literature would be smoother, especially in the case of cross references to parallels in other literatures, if we accept the historically established terminology. Such an eminent scholar of English literature as Ronald Crane does not hesitate to focus his work upon "neoclassicism," and scholars such as René Wellek are now defending the essential consistency of "romanticism."[2] In the present work we have used such terms not as representing anything static or absolute but rather as representing somewhat flexible centers of emphasis with widening circles of departure from such centers. It is noteworthy that René Wellek and Austin Warren, who tend to subordinate literary history to critical value-judgments, conclude:

[2] See Mr. Crane's summary of "Neoclassical Criticism" in the *Dictionary of World Criticism*, edited by J. T. Shipley (New York, 1943), pp. 192-203; René Wellek, "The Concept of 'Romanticism' in Literary History," in *Comparative Literature*, I (1949), 1-23; 147-172; Morse Peckham, "Toward a Theory of Romanticism," *Publications of the Modern Language Association*, LXVI (March, 1951), 5-23; R. P. Adams, "Romanticism and the American Renaissance," *American Literature*, XXII (Jan., 1952), 419-433.

It should be frankly realized that a period is not an ideal type or an abstract pattern or a series of class concepts, but a time section, dominated by a whole system of norms, which no work of art will ever realize in its entirety. *The history* of a period will consist in tracing of the changes from one *system of norms to another*. While a period is thus a section of time to which some sort of unity is ascribed, it is obvious that this unity can be only relative. It merely means that during this period a certain scheme of norms has been realized most fully. If the unity of any one period were absolute, the periods would lie next to each other like blocks of stone, without continuity of development. Thus the survival of a preceding scheme of norms and the anticipations of a following scheme are inevitable, as a period is historical only if every event is considered as a result of the whole preceding past and if its effects can be traced into the whole future.[3]

Thus considering the successive periods or movements as relative and as merely centers of emphasis with many gradations, it has seemed best to concern ourselves in this series of essays not with the periods at the time of their most typical development but with the "in-between" periods and to concentrate on "tracing the changes" in something like a cause-and-effect sequence from one period to another.

While I fancy most of the contributors to the present discussion would disclaim both complete determinism and any complete biological or evolutionary approach to literary history as an "organism," it should be obvious that literary history does involve continuity and sequence. Perhaps if any one metaphor is to be adopted, it should be one which figures literary history not as one self-conscious "organism" or as like the Mississippi River whose sections are united, but as "convention and revolt," involving a vast variety of often fortuitous factors. For example, changes in the emphasis of our literary history are caused by such obvious matters as the rise and decline of gifted personalities whose birth or death could not be predicted; the variety of changing environments to which they try to adapt their writing; the unique and unpredictable sequence of the reading of each, involving as it does many foreign influences; the topical timeliness of various themes in relation to

---

[3] *The Theory of Literature* (New York, 1949), p. 278. The quotation is used with the courteous permission of the publishers, Harcourt, Brace and Company. The italics are mine.

economic crises, literary fashions, etc.; the changing emphasis in education which conditions the taste of the reading public and hence the demand which conditions the literary supply; the rise and fall of magazines as the "outlet" for writers; and both inertia and revolt bred by boredom with the reiteration of ideas and artistic devices which were once vital and fresh. Our approach is not in any way incompatible with that of those who prefer to disregard a time sequence and to concentrate upon the exhaustive explication of individual poems or other forms. We are merely experimenting with trying to put together the main sequence of our literary history and trying to account for changes in this sequence and in emphasis.

It is hoped that the work may have practical usefulness in two ways. If there are signs that other approaches to literature have tended to lessen student interest in the "survey" course and in literary history, it is hoped that the present stress on *why* our literary history developed as it did, why the emphases changed from period to period, will help to rescue such courses from the dull handbook listing of biographies and titles and summaries and to encourage teachers to present the changes in our literary history as a genuinely mature challenge offering a fertile field for explanation. For the convenience of busy teachers who wish to get the "gist" of each paper quickly, each has been provided with a succinct summary of the main lines of argument. Second, even if some readers dislike to think in terms of the rise and fall of the movements designated— puritanism, neoclassicism, romanticism, and realism—and prefer an "atomic" approach in terms of isolated individuals or books, it is hoped that the present essays may provide considerable stimulation for scholarly investigation and co-operative seminar work by placing the spotlight on each of the somewhat neglected "valleys" between the better known peaks of our literary history. The writers of these essays will not be seriously troubled if the question of terminology is disregarded and readers are led to investigate more carefully the writings which appeared *between* the age of Edwards, the age of Franklin, the age of Irving, the age of Emerson, and the age of Howells. To this end the contributors have tried to avoid the arrogance of unsupported or subjective assertions, and the findings of the book are buttressed by nearly eleven hundred notes giving precise references to the evidence used for the generalizations. Thus scholars who wish to extend the investigations can begin on a solid footing where the present essays end. Incidentally, we have ended with 1891 (the date of Howells's full-length elucidation of realism) mainly because the present essays filled our program and one book; it is hoped that if the present experiment seems to have merits some other group will continue and deal with the transitions during the last sixty years. Finally, it would be helpful if those who use the book as a springboard for further advanced research would co-operate with our brethren in the field of English literature in producing books (comparable to W. J. Bate's excellent *From Classic to Romantic*) devoted to explaining the reasons for the transitions in English literary history. For until such English transitions are fully clarified students of American literature deserve to be treated with tolerance if some of their findings are tentative.

Perhaps as editor I ought to remark that since the plan of dealing with the decline of certain ideas and the rise of others within the same periods involves separate papers, some little overlapping and repetition of evidence (usually from opposite sides) are inevitable. Since each contributor was free to develop his own interpretation in an integrated way, some diversity of views is also inevitable; but it is hoped that such diversity will stimulate further study.

Grateful acknowledgment is made of the fact that the present papers were read (in the order printed) by Professors Norman Pearson, Lewis Leary, Arlin Turner, Grant C. Knight, René Wellek and Henry Pochmann, E. E. Leisy, and Robert Spiller. Their many constructive suggestions are much appreciated. Warm thanks are also due to Dr. William Parker, the Secretary of the Modern Language Association, for helping us arrange the program and for authorizing the publication of the book as for the Association. We are also grateful to Professor J. B. Hubbell for reading the manuscript for the Duke University Press, and to Mr. Ashbel Brice, the Director, for his courteous and painstaking assistance.

HARRY HAYDEN CLARK
*Chairman of the American Literature Group
of the Modern Language Association for 1948*

## Contents

| | PAGE |
|---|---|
| INTRODUCTION<br>*Harry Hayden Clark* | v |
| I. THE DECLINE OF PURITANISM<br>*Clarence H. Faust* | 1 |
| II. THE LATE EIGHTEENTH CENTURY:<br>AN AGE OF CONTRADICTIONS<br>*Leon Howard* | 49 |
| III. THE DECLINE OF NEOCLASSICISM, 1801-1848<br>*M. F. Heiser* | 91 |
| IV. THE RISE OF ROMANTICISM, 1805-1855<br>*G. Harrison Orians* | 161 |
| V. THE RISE OF TRANSCENDENTALISM, 1815-1860<br>*Alexander Kern* | 245 |
| VI. THE DECLINE OF ROMANTIC IDEALISM, 1855-1871<br>*Floyd Stovall* | 315 |
| VII. THE RISE OF REALISM, 1871-1891<br>*Robert Falk* | 379 |
| INDEX | 443 |

# Transitions
## in
# American Literary History

# The Decline of Puritanism

# The Decline of Puritanism

❦

### CLARENCE H. FAUST
THE FUND FOR THE ADVANCEMENT OF EDUCATION

PURITANISM as exemplified in the New England colonies of Plymouth and Massachusetts Bay during the seventeenth and early eighteenth centuries was an all-embracing system of beliefs and practices. Puritan life and theory were not compartmentalized. The organization and operation of the civil community, economic activity, social life, and scientific investigation, as well as religion and ethics, found a place, or were carefully fitted into place, as parts of a theoretic and practical whole. As Perry Miller has remarked, "Puritanism was not only a religious creed, it was a philosophy and a metaphysic; it was an organization of man's whole life, emotional and intellectual, to a degree which has not been sustained by any denomination stemming from it."[1] The unity of Puritanism was achieved, not by preoccupation with theology and disregard for other sciences, but by a synthesis of the sciences in relation to theology. John Cotton could quote with approval "what Mr. Perkins hath, in one of his prefatory pages to his golden chaine. that the word, and scriptures of God doe conteyne a short *upoluposis*, or platforme, not onely of theology, but also of other sacred sciences, (as he calleth them) attendants, and handmaids thereonto, which he maketh ethicks, eoconomicks, politicks, church-government, prophecy, academy."

[1] Perry Miller and Thomas Johnson, *The Puritans* (New York, 1938), p. 4.

It is very suitable to gods all-sufficient wisdome, and to the fulness and perfection of Holy Scriptures, not only to prescribe perfect rules for the right ordering of a private mans soule to everlasting blessedness with himselfe, but also for the right ordering of a mans family, yea, of the commonwealth too. . . . Gods institutions (such as the government of church and of commonwealth be) may be close and compact, and co-ordinate one to another, and yet not confounded.[2]

In this view of the matter, even the natural sciences were not expected to be in opposition to religion or theology. "I have often wished," wrote Increase Mather in 1683, "that the Natural History of New-England might be written and published to the world; the rules and method described by that learned excellent person Robert Boyle, Esq., being duely observed therein," and he cited in support of his endeavor to make an accurate collection of "Things Rare and Wonderful, both in the Works of Creation and Providence" the resolutions drawn up in support of this enterprise at a "General meeting" of the ministers of the Colony on May 12, 1681.[3] His son Cotton encouraged young ministers, "to spend much more Time in the Study" of "what we call Natural Philosophy," and added that "as thorough an Insight as you can get in the *Principles* of our *Perpetual Dictator*, the Incomparable Sr. *Isaac Newton*, is what I mightily commend unto you."[4]

As Puritanism undertook to embrace all sciences, so it undertook to direct all human institutions and activities. In the Puritan view, church and state were closely related enterprises. "The worke wee have in hand," said John Winthrop to his fellow passengers on board the *Arabella* bound for New England in 1630, "it is by a mutuall consent, through a speciall overvaluing [overruling] providence, and a more than an ordinary approbation of the Churches of Christ, to seeke out a place of Cohabitation and Consorteshipp under a due forme of Government both civill and ecclesiasticall."[5] Few Puritans were prepared to go as far as John Eliot, who contended in *The Christian Commonwealth* that God as monarch of

[2] "Copy of a letter from Mr. Cotton to Lord say and seal in the year 1636," *The Puritans* (New York, 1938), p. 209.
[3] Preface for *Remarkable Providences* (London, 1856).
[4] Cotton Mather, *Manductio ad Ministerium: Directories for a Candidate of the Ministry* (Boston, 1726), pp. 47-50.
[5] *A Modell of Christian Charity, Collections of the Massachusetts Historical Society,* VII (3rd ser.), 45.

the universe had not only promulgated in the Scriptures the law to which all men were in all instances subject, but had specified precisely the form of civil polity under which they should live, and who was prepared to assert that "Christ is the right Heir of the Crown of England."[6] But the framers of the Cambridge Platform of 1648 insisted that

It is the duty of the Magistrate, to take care of matters of religion, & to improve his civil authority for the observing of the duties commanded in the first, as well as for the duties commanded in the second table. They are called Gods. The end of the magistrate's office, is not only the quiet & peaceful life of the subject, in matters of righteousness & honesty, but also in matters of Godliness, yea of all Godliness.

By matters of religion, the Cambridge Assembly explained, "We understand indefinitely, whether those of Doctrine or Discipline, of faith or practice."

[The civil magistrate's] power is not limited to such matters of Religion onely, which are against the light of nature, or against the Law of Nations, or against the fundamentalls of Religion; Therefore we say not barely thus "In matters of the first table" but joyn therewith "In matters of Religion" that all ambiguity may be avoided, and that it may be understood as well of matters which are purely Evangelicall ... and we say "commanded or forbidden in the word" meaning of the whole word, both of Old and New Testament: exception being made onely of those things which are meerly Ceremoniall ... and cleered to be abolished in the New Testament.[7]

Nor was a man's business or vocation separated from religion. "Not onely my spirituall life," wrote John Cotton in *The Way of Life*, "but even my Civill life in this world, all the life I live, is by the faith of the Son of God."

He exempts no life from the agency of his faith, whether he live as a Christian man, or as a member of this or that Church, or Commonwealth, he doth it all by the faith of the Son of God.

Now for the opening of this point let me shew you what are those severall acts of faith which it puts forth about our occasions, and vocations, that so we may live in God's sight therein.

[6] *The Christian Commonwealth: or, The Civil Polity of the Rising Kingdom of Jesus Christ* (1659), *Collections of the Massachusetts Historical Society*, IX (3rd ser.), 133.
[7] Williston Walker, *The Creeds and Platforms of Congregationalism* (New York, 1893), pp. 189, 236.

We live, according to Cotton, both an inward and an outward temporal life. The latter is "either a Civill, or a naturall life."

Civill life is that whereby we live, as members of this or that City, or Town, or Commonwealth, in this or that particular vocation and calling.

Naturall life I call that, by which we doe live this bodily life, I meane by which we live a life of sense, by which we eate and drinke, by which we goe through all conditions, from our birth to our grave. . . . And now both these a justified person lives by faith. . . . *A true beleeving Christian, a justified person, hee lives in his vocation by his faith.*[8]

It was upon this aspect of Puritan belief that Max Weber fixed when he ascribed the rise of capitalism to Puritan theology in *The Protestant Ethic and the Spirit of Capitalism;* and R. H. Tawney concluded for the same reason in *Religion and the Rise of Capitalism* that "to the Puritan, a contemner of vain shows of sacramentalism, mundane toil becomes a kind of sacrament."[9]

Puritans like Cotton Mather undertook to order all their activities to a single, religious end. Mather reminded his readers in the *Manductio ad Ministerium* that they had been taught from "Infancy, to Glorify God and Enjoy Him Forever," and proceeded to apply this principle to every aspect of life, not only to religious worship and to study and learning, but to social and economic pursuits, to marriage and conversation, and even to eating, sleeping, and dress.

When I am a Married Man, I am doing my *Duty to God*, in conforming to the *Ninth* of *Ecclesiastes* and *Ninth*.

*Why do I* Trim, Cleanse, Adorn my *Body?*

Lord, I desire to Recommend my self unto them, unto whom I would be *Acceptable* in my *Endeavors* to convey something of *Thee* unto them.

*Why do I suffer my self to be perswaded into any brief Diversions?*

Lord, I desire, that by a little unbending of my *Bowe*, and Remitting of the Intenseness of my *Essays to do Good*, I may the more harden it into a *Bowe of Steel;* and Return with more vigour to the Work of my God.[10]

[8] *The Puritans*, p. 319.
[9] R. H. Tawney, *Religion and the Rise of Capitalism* (New York, 1947), p. 166.
[10] *Manductio ad Ministerium*, pp. 4-14.

Ideally at least, the Puritan was to order all of his activities to "the work of the Lord" and, as part of this effort, he was to interweave all sciences on the woof of theology. When John Cotton preached the farewell sermon at Southhampton in 1630 to the colonists setting out for Massachusetts Bay, he treated the religious, the political, the economic, the social, and the intellectual aspects of the enterprise as all of a piece. His text was the scriptural promise to David: "Moreover I will appoint a place for my people Israell, and I will plant them, that they may dwell in a place of their owne, and move no more." Herein God promises, he said, both "the designment of a place for his people" and "a plantation of them in that place." Among the blessings which he found the text to imply when properly interpreted was the assurance that God's people shall dwell on the land thus acquired "like Free-holders in a place of their owne," possessing their lands absolutely, not simply by legal right, but by divine appointment. Cotton then asked how "this worke of God . . . in appointing a place for a people" is accomplished. It may be managed, he answered, by casting out "the enemies of a people before them by lawfull warre with the inhabitants"; or by giving "a forreigne people favour in the eyes of any native people to come and sit downe with them either by way of purchase, as *Abraham* did obtaine the field of Machpelah; or else when they give it in courtesie, as *Pharaoh* did the land of *Goshen* under the sons of *Jacob*." In short, warfare, purchase, and diplomatic negotiation are on the basis of the Scriptures and under the conditions therein specified, legitimate methods of colonization. Finally, God may plant a people by making "a Countrey though not altogether void of inhabitants, yet void in that place where they reside. Where there is a vacant place," Cotton explained, "there is liberty for the sonne of *Adam* or *Noah* to come and inhabite, though they neither buy it, nor aske their leaves"; and he supported his point by full citations from biblical history. In effect he thus gave a religious and theological justification based upon principles drawn from "the work of God" for what would in later generations, by the followers of Locke in America, for example, be represented as a natural right, that of man's making use of any means of subsistence not already appropriated by others. Cotton concluded this part of his sermon with an admonition to consider the places in which we dwell in the light of God's provisions for our appointment to them.

This may teach us all where wee doe now dwell, or where after wee may dwell, be sure you looke at every place appointed to you, from the hand of God: wee may not rush into any place and never say to God, By your leave; but we must discern how God appoints us this place. There is poore comfort in sitting down in any place, that you cannot say, This place is appointed me of God. Canst thou say that God spied out this place for thee, and there hath setled thee above all hindrances? Didst thou finde out that God made roome for thee either by lawfull descent, or purchase, or gift, or other warrantable right? Why then this is the place God hath appointed thee; here hee hath made roome for thee, he hath place thee in *Rehoboth*, in a peacable place: This we must discern; or els we are but intruders upon God.

With respect to the question "How shall I know whether God hath appointed me such a place?" Cotton is detailed and specific in drawing out principles from the Scriptures. He listed "foure or five good things, for procurement of any of which I may remove." In this list emigration for religious liberty stands fifth. Before mentioning it Cotton adduced reasons for believing that a man may move to a new country with confidence that he is doing so by divine appointment when he emigrates for the purpose of gaining knowledge, or "for merchandize and gaine-saik," or for the purpose of settling "a City or commonwealth elsewhere," or when he "may employ his Talents and gift better elsewhere." As Cotton represented the matter, knowledge, commerce, politics, and personal development are not extrareligious justifications for immigration; they are instruments of God's purpose. Cotton took special pains to make this clear with respect to business enterprise, arguing that "our Saviour approveth travails for Merchants, Math. 13.45,46. when hee compareth a Christian to a Merchantman seeking pearles: For he never fetcheth the comparison for an unlawfull thing to illustrate a thing lawfull." He recognized the obvious objection to this argument that in the New Testament the Christian is compared with the unjust steward and the thief in the night, but argued that this is not really a likeness of things unlawful to things lawful, because what is compared is not "the injustice of the one, or the theft of the other; but the wisdome of the one and the sodainesse of the other; which in themselves are not unlawfull."

With the same almost painful care in interpreting Scripture, he justified removal to a new country for political purposes, as a matter of divine appointment.

> Wee may remove ... to plant a colony, that is, a company that agree together to remove out of their own Country, and Settle a City or Commonwealth elsewhere.... So when the hive of the Commonwealth is so full, that Tradesmen cannot live one by another, but eate up one another, in this case it is lawfull to remove.[11]

Thus all aspects of the great adventure upon which Cotton's audience was about to embark were given religious significance. All of its problems were set into a theological context, and satisfying answers to them might be expected from a properly disciplined scrutiny of the Scriptures. Politics, economics, ethics, science, and religion were not discrete; and man's activities in all of these areas could be directly related to God's purposes and thus given cosmic justification and significance.

Puritan histories, like Puritan sermons, illustrate this trait of Puritanism. Puritan historians undertook the task Cotton Mather set for himself in the *Magnalia*, to "write the wonders of the Christian religion, flying from the depravations of Europe to the American strand"; and believed themselves "assisted by the holy author of that religion ... [to] report the wonderful displays of His infinite power, wisdom, goodness, and faithfulness, wherewith His divine providence hath irradiated an Indian wilderness."[12] As Captain Edward Johnson put it in his *History of New England*, or *The Wonder-Working Providence of Sions Saviour in New England:* "Oh yes! Oh yes! Oh yes! All you the people of Christ that are here Oppressed, Imprisoned and scurrilously derided, gather yourselves together, your wifes and little ones, and answer to your severall Names as you shall be shipped for your service, in the Westerne World, and more especially for planting the united Collonies of new England.... Know this is the place where the Lord will create a new Heaven, and a new Earth and new Churches, and a new Commonwealth together."[13] Puritan accounts such as these,

---

[11] "Gods Promise to His Plantations," *Old South Leaflets*, No. 53, pp. 4-15.
[12] "A General Introduction," *Magnalia Christi Americana* (Hartford, 1853).
[13] Quoted by Herbert W. Schneider, *The Puritan Mind* (New York, 1930), p. 8.

of the establishment and growth of the little settlements in Massachusetts, assumed through the relation of all aspects of their development to the ultimate purposes of the universe, an impressive scope, which the accounts of the settlement of Virginia, however stirringly Captain John Smith presents them in his *Description of New England*, or *The General History of Virginia*, do not possess. The founding of New England was a part of the grand reformation of religion in the world, which was itself a glorious continuation of the history of God's dealings with man as recorded in the Old and New Testaments. Mather thinks it not improper to compare himself with the great historians of the ancients, referring in his general introduction to the *Magnalia* to Polybius, Tacitus, Josephus, and Livy.[14]

The system of beliefs which made the Puritan unification possible had in its amazing completeness and in its logical consistency a kind of magnificence. Even in the middle of the nineteenth century, when it had disintegrated as a consequence of the crumbling of key concepts under the impact of both theoretical and practical objections, its consistency and fulness were admitted by such critics as Joseph Henry Allen.

It seems to be very complete and full; to have an answer ready for every exigency; to deal with things in a systematic and orderly method; to comprehend the entire circle of providential action, so far as we are concerned in it; and so to give a precise, clear, and consistent account of every relation between God, man, and the future world, in which we can possibly be placed. I do not say it is satisfactory; but it is certainly consistent with itself. Its merits in this regard are very great. It has herein a great advantage over its opponents. Like a disciplined and compact body of troops, it can bear up long against the uncertain and irregular force of a vastly greater number, having no defined system of operation and no common end in view.[15]

When this comprehensive system of theology which had built politics and ethics, natural science and economics into itself began to disintegrate, it was under the simultaneous operation of two forces. It suffered from the impact of political, social, economic, and scientific developments in American life, which produced and

[14] *Ibid.*
[15] Joseph Henry Allen, *Ten Discourses on Orthodoxy* (Boston, 1849), p. 23.

fostered activities and institutions out of harmony with those Puritanism had produced and nourished; and it began to crumble internally through the dislocation of key elements in the synthesis it had achieved and the disruption of its internal balances. Certain aspects of the Puritan conception of God, for example "God's justice and His mercy": and certain principles of knowledge, such as "reason" and "revelation," which Puritans like the theologian Shepard and the poet Edward Taylor had labored to reconcile and had managed intellectually and imaginatively to hold in delicate balance, seemed incapable of reconciliation to later generations of New England ministers and laity, who were perhaps less pious or less intellectual, and whose philosophy rested, in any case, on other bases than the Puritan's. Certain principles, moreover, which Puritan theology had appropriated from the sciences it had engulfed, and which it had exploited in making such sciences as politics and economics its "attendants and handmaids," came obstreperously to occupy key positions in the Puritan intellectual system and helped eventually to revolutionize it. The conception of God as "Monarch of the Universe," for example, which the Puritan poet Wigglesworth and the Puritan theologian Bellamy had elaborated with the aid of political theory, became difficult if not impossible to maintain in the light of the evolution of political principles during the eighteenth century. Thus the picture of God as an "Absolute Monarch" became progressively less convincing as the principle of absolute monarchy in human affairs became, with the events leading up to the American Revolution, increasingly unpopular.[16]

As the historians of Puritanism have always pointed out and as indeed Puritans themselves repeatedly asserted, the Puritan system of ideas and activities was theocentric. The aspects of the Puritan

---

[16] See, for example, Jonathan Mayhew, *Two Sermons on the Extent and Perfection of the Divine Goodness* (Boston, 1762), pp. 26, 50. God is called King, said Mayhew, but "It ought not to be inferred from hence, that he is an arbitrary being, in that ill sense, in which the word arbitrary is used respecting tyrants." "If I were to form my conceptions of God's moral character, by such discourses as I have sometimes heard and read, and such as were by many, thought to be truly *evangelical;* instead of thinking Him really 'good to All.' . . . I could not but conclude Him to be *infinitely* more *unjust* and *cruel,* than any other being in the Universe."

conception of the Deity which provided the basis for the theological revolution of the eighteenth and nineteenth centuries may be conveniently illustrated from the works of Thomas Shepard, whose eloquent expositions of Puritan theology were among the most frequently quoted religious works of the seventeenth and early eighteenth centuries. When Shepard undertook in his *Sincere Convert* to prove the existence of God, he employed three lines of argument. The first involved a conception of God as the great workman and architect:

When we see a stately house, although we see not the man that built it, yet will we conclude thus, surely some wise artificer had been working here; can we, when we behold the stately theater of Heaven and Earth, conclude other, than that the finger, arms, and wisdom of God hath been here, although we see not the time when he began to build?

To this view of God as the wise workman, the great artificer, Shepard added in his second line of argument for the existence of the deity a conception of God as the creator, able not only to change and arrange what already existed in order to achieve his purposes, but able also to bring things into existence. We infer the existence of God, Shepard said, from the existence of "the Creatures begotten of God." These are evidence of a power able to give life, a power able to bring something out of nothing, not merely to contrive something from existing materials. We are assured of God's existence, he said, from the things which must have had a creator.

Shepard's final line of proof is drawn from the conscience of man, which is taken as evidence of the existence of a divine judge and governor. Especially in the day of death, wrote Shepard, when men "are near God's Tribunal, do they acknowledge him clearly." Often, moreover, even in the midst of life does conscience "like a hangman torment man; ergo, there is some strange Judge that gave it that command."[17] In the treatment of any important theological problem Shepard had recourse, then, to three conceptions of God: God as the great artificer, or contriver, or workman, whose relation to men, the instruments and materials for his workmanship, could be understood in terms of analogies drawn from the arts and crafts involving the distinction of means and ends; second,

[17] Thomas Shepard, *Sincere Convert* (London, 1655), p. 9.

God as the great creator, whose relation to mankind could be understood in terms of eternal being, and the temporal existences begotten by it, often presented in the analogy of a father and his children; third, God as the great king, law-giver, and judge, whose relation to mankind, his subjects, could be understood in terms of political and legal analogies.

Thus for Shepard the evil of the fall of Adam had a triple aspect as viewed from a threefold conception of God as contriver, as creator, and as king. The fall of Adam involved, for one thing, the failure of man to perform his function as an instrument or "contrivance" of the deity. Man was created, according to Shepard, as a "temple of God." By the sin of Adam that temple was damaged and stands in need of repair. Secondly, as a consequence of Adam's sin, men are spiritually dead. Originally created with inward principles or sources of spiritual life, man has now "no more good in him (whatsoever he thinks) than a dead carrion hath. . . . Our bodies are but living coffins to carry a dead soul in." Shepard elaborated this point with something like the ingenuity of his contemporary John Donne. As "a dead man hath his worms gnawing him," he wrote, "so natural man hath the worm of conscience breeding now: which will be gnawing him shortly." Adam's fall involved a violation of the divine law, a flaunting of the sovereignty of the monarch of the universe. By it, Adam became, to use Shepard's own phrase, "a traitor" to God's government, and thus came to merit, together with his descendants, the punishment which God as judge had decreed, a part of which conscience as a hangman had already been appointed to execute. In this passage conscience, which, in the analogy viewing man as the offspring of eternal being is represented as a "worm" gnawing the dead soul, becomes, in the analogy viewing man as subject to a divine ruler, an executioner in the divine government of men.[18]

As the fall of Adam was a threefold evil, a violation of the laws of the king of heaven, a failure of man as an instrument of the universal workman, and the death of principles originally imparted to the soul by creation, so the recovery of virtue had a threefold aspect. Man must yield himself as an instrument to the divine pur-

[18] *Ibid.*

poses, must have re-created within him principles or foundations of virtuous action, in the possession of which he becomes a "new creature,"[19] and must submit to the government and laws of God.

Shepard took pains to insist upon the inadequacy of the terms which he employed in describing the Deity. The nature of God is not definable, he said, in human terms. It is above the grasp of finite intelligence. When Moses desired to see God face to face he was instructed to be content with a view of God's "backward parts." Men must not suppose that even the clearest views they have of the divine nature are complete or that they may be refined and elaborated to constitute a perfect definition. In so far as Shepard's warning was effective it prevented the treatment of analogies respecting the character of God in a rigidly literal way. The balance and interplay of analogies concerning God's nature and relations with men gave Shepard's theology both a certain richness and a considerable scope.

Other Puritans, however, preoccupied with some one of the conceptions of God current among them, and exploiting it literally, developed more precise but more limited and ultimately more vulnerable doctrines on this subject. Michael Wigglesworth's *Day of Doom* is a case in point. Wigglesworth's notorious work is a roughshod, poetic elaboration of the conception of God as the Ruler and Judge of the Universe.

> The Judge draws nigh, exalted high upon a lofty throne,
> Amidst the throng of angels strong, lo, Israel's Holy One!
> The excellence of whose presence and awful majesty
> Amazeth Nature, and every Creature, doth more than terrify.[20]
>
> . . . . . . . . . . .
>
> Thus all men's pleas the judge with ease doth answer and confute,
> Until that all, both great and small, are silencèd and mute.
> Vain hopes are cropt, all mouths are stopt, sinners have naught to say,
> But that 'tis just and equal most they should be damned for aye.[21]

The far richer poetical talent of Edward Taylor employs itself in *God's Determinations Touching His Elect* with the same con-

[19] *Ibid.*
[20] William Rose Benét and Norman Holmes Pearson (eds.), *Oxford Anthology of American Literature* (New York, 1938), p. 48.
[21] *Ibid.*, p. 52.

cept of God. The opening section of the poem deals with "The Effects of Mans Apostasy" and the second section opens with a description of the fashion in which "Offended Justice comes in fiery Rage."

> Out rebell, out (saith Justice), to the Wrack,
>     Which every joynt unjoynts, doth streatch and strain,
> Where Sinews tortur'de are untill they Crack,
>     And Flesh is torn asunder grain by grain.
>     What! Spit thy Venom in my Face? Come out
>     To handy gripes, seeing thou art so stoute.[22]

But whereas Wigglesworth had been preoccupied with the ineffectual pleas of sinners brought to justice before the great Judge on the day of doom, Taylor is concerned in the long dialogue of the second section of the poem with the problem of "justice" and "mercy," and he finds in God's determination to exercise "grace" to mankind so as to satisfy both mercy and justice the ground for "an ecstacy of joy" which reaches its climax in the final group of stanzas in the poem:

> In Heaven souring up, I dropt an Eare
>     On Earth: and Oh! sweet Melody!
> And listening, found it was the Saints who were
>     Encroacht for Heaven that sang for Joy.
>     For in Christs Coach they sweetly sing,
>     As they to Glory ride therein.[23]

In his concern for the problem of justice in God's relationship to men, Taylor does not forget, as Wigglesworth seems to, the other aspects of the divine nature. In the preface to the poem he admires the creative power of the deity:

> Infinity, when all things it beheld,
> In Nothing, and of Nothing all did build.
> . . . . . . . . .
> Who spake all things from nothing; and with ease
> Can speake all things to nothing, if he please.[24]

And in what are perhaps the finest lines in the poem, he admires the workmanship of the contriver of the universe:

---

[22] Thomas Johnson (ed.), *The Poetical Works of Edward Taylor* (New York, 1939), p. 36.
[23] *Ibid.*, p. 109.   [24] *Ibid.*, p. 31.

> Upon what Base was fixt the Lath, wherein
> He turn'd this Globe, and rigalld it so trim?
> Who blew the Bellows of his Furnace Vast?
> Or held the Mould wherein the world was Cast?
> Who laid its Corner Stone? Or whose command?
> Where stand the Pillars upon which it stands?
> Who Lac'de and Fillitted the earth so fine,
> With Rivers like green Ribbons Smaragdine?
> Who made the Sea's its Selvedge, and its locks
> Like a Quilt Ball within a Silver Box?
> Who spread its Canopy? Or Curtains Spun?
> Who in this Bowling Alley bowld the Sun?
> . . . . . . . . . .
> Who? who did this? or who is he? Why, know
> It's Onely Might Almighty this did doe.
> His hand hath made this noble worke which Stands
> His Glorious Handywork not made by hand.[25]

The literal, detailed, and inflexible elaboration of the idea of God as King and Judge in *The Day of Doom*, rather than Shepard's or Taylor's broader view, came to represent the Puritan theology in the minds of many later New Englanders. Such doctrines as "the damnation of infants," which Wigglesworth had versified (though he represented the stern Judge on the Day of Doom as assigning to infants "the easiest room in hell") were the basis for much of the revulsion against Calvinism in New England during the early nineteenth century.[26]

That despite the disclaimers of the orthodox, Wigglesworth's poem represented an important strain at least in New England Puritanism, is clear from the work of Joseph Bellamy, whose *True Religion Delineated*, published in 1750, was one of the most influential theological writings of the eighteenth century. Bellamy was a disciple of Jonathan Edwards, but it is doubtful whether any of Edwards's works, except, perhaps, his *Life of Brainard*, secured so wide a reading at the time. Published by subscription, it came out with the support, as Harriet Beecher Stowe observed in an illuminating chapter devoted to it in her novel *Old Town Folks*,

---

[25] *Ibid.*
[26] See George E. Ellis, *A Half Century of Unitarian Controversy* (Boston, 1857), pp. 83-85; also *Autobiography, Correspondence, Etc. of Lyman Beecher, D.D.*, ed. Charles Beecher (New York, 1865), II, 137-143.

of "almost every good old Massachusetts or Connecticut family," including "the Emersons, the Adams, the Brattles of Brattle Street . . . the Cottons . . . the Hookers, with many more names of families yet continuing to hold influence in New England." Mrs. Stowe believed that "It was heedfully and earnestly read in every good family of New England," and that "its propositions were discussed everywhere."[27]

According to Bellamy, God could best be conceived as "the Monarch of the Universe" and men as "rebellious subjects" who had been incited to revolt by the traitorous angel, Satan. Religion thus became for Bellamy fundamentally a matter of obedience to the divine law, and salvation involved the satisfaction of that law through the vicarious punishment of "the Prince of Righteousness." In the opening sentence of the book true religion is defined as consisting "in a conformity to the law of God, and in a compliance with the gospel of Christ." The first half of the work then specified the nature of the lawgiver whom man has offended, and the law which man has broken. Adam, according to Bellamy, was the legal representative of mankind, and "by divine appointment, he stood and acted as our public head . . . a representative in the room of all posterity." Adam's defection had rendered all mankind "legally guilty and liable to be dealt with accordingly." The second half of the work dealt with "the New Covenant" established when Christ, "the Prince of Heaven," satisfied the demands of the divine law which Adam had violated. Pardon can come to man only as he again becomes a dutiful subject of the King of Heaven. A knowledge of theology was the first step in this direction. When we see what God is, Bellamy wrote, "We begin to see why he assumes the character of most high God, supreme Lord and Sovereign Governor of the whole world," and we then "resign the throne to Him and become His willing subjects."

The significance of God's creative activity and of His providential operations, that is the significance of God as creator and workman, consists in Bellamy's view in the establishment, by means of these activities, of God's right to rule what He has made and upholds. If God "brought all things out of nothing into being, and holds up all things in being every moment; then all things are

[27] Harriet Beecher Stowe, *Old Town Folks* (Boston, 1880), p. 373.

absolutely and entirely his, by original, independent right. And, if all things are his, He has a natural right of government over all; and it becomes Him to take the throne, and to be King in his own world."[28]

For Bellamy, then, God was to be understood basically as the King of the Universe. Harriet Beecher Stowe, observing this trait of Bellamy's work and mistakenly ascribing it to the New England theology as a whole, remarked in her chapter on "My Grandmother's Blue Book" (Bellamy's *True Religion Delineated*) in *Old Town Folks* that "If any should ever be so curious as to read this old treatise, as well as most of the writings of Jonathan Edwards, they will perceive with singular plainness how inevitably monarchial and aristocratic institutions influenced theology." This system of belief, she pointed out, assumes that "the King can do no wrong,—that the subject does everything to the King, and the King nothing to the subject, that the King's first duty is to take care of himself, keep up state, splendor, majesty, royalty, and that it is the people's duty to give themselves up, body and soul without murmuring to keep up this state, splendor, and royalty."[29]

Bellamy's approach to theology was not, however, the only one in favor among Puritans. More widely held, though equally limited in conceptual structure, was the formulation of the Puritan theology in terms of God as the manager of the universe, the great workman or "contriver."

Perhaps the fullest statement of the Puritan theology as it was developed by several generations of New England divines is to be found in Samuel Willard's *Compleat Body of Divinity*, published with a long and impressive list of subscribers as a magnificent nine-hundred-page double-column volume in 1726. Willard was graduated from Harvard College in 1659, ten years after Shepard's death, and became in 1678 minister of the Old South Church in Boston. In 1701 he became in addition Vice President of Harvard, the position he had until his death. His lengthy and learned commentary on the Westminster catechism, posthumously published in

---

[28] Thomas Bellamy, *True Religion Delineated*, *Works* (Boston, 1811-1812) I, 53, 96, 301-312, 459.
[29] *Op. cit.*, p. 373.

1726, was the first folio volume of theology produced in this country, and the largest book which had been published in America on any subject up to the time of its appearance.

The threefold conception of the nature of God and of his relation to mankind, on which Shepard had developed his theological views, was familiar to Willard. He would in any case have found the suggestion for it in the Westminster catechism, on which the 250 lectures composing his complete body of divinity were an item-by-item commentary, and in the Cambridge Platform of 1646.[30]

Willard employed all three of these conceptions of the deity in his commentary on the catechism, though he systematically translated the references to God as creator and as king into terms of God's providential operations; that is to say, he conceived of God fundamentally as the great "workman" or "artificer." In his hands, consequently, the Puritan theology as Shepard had presented it suffered an elaborate warping into a quite different system. For one thing, Willard, unlike Shepard, framed his arguments for the existence of God primarily as inferences from the workings of providence, finding in the course of affairs, as well as in human consciousness, evidence of the existence of a supreme agent, pursuing universal ends by irresistible means. In answer to question four of the catechism, "What is God?," he offers proof for the existence of the deity under three heads: "the works of creation," "the works of providence," and the internal "witness in every man," especially that of conscience. These topics parallel Shepard's threefold conception of God as creator, as artificer, and as judge or ruler. In Shepard the consideration of God as original being, as the manager of means to suitable ends, and as the head of the universal government of things, involves sharply separate sets of terms. Willard, however, interprets the divine creative activity, the divine government, and the divine art so as to telescope all three in the last. Creation and government are analyzed in terms of the art of adopting means to ends, and become thus only aspects of the activity of the divine workman. The creation points for Willard not

---

[30] Samuel Willard, *A Compleat Body of Divinity in Two Hundred and Fifty Expository Lectures on the Assemblies Shorter Catechism* (Boston, 1726).

to an eternal being, but to "an exquisite workman" and though Willard refers to the testimony of natural conscience as evidence for the existence of a divine ruler, he defines a law or rule as a guide used by a workman in adopting means to the accomplishment of his task. "A rule," he earlier had explained, "is nothing else *but that whereby a man is guided* to do his work, and to sute it to the Ends and Use for which he doth it; and the reason of it is, because he may else miss, and so lose his Labour. There is necessarily a requisite Sutableness between the *Means* and the *End*. The right suting of them, 'tis the nature of a Rule to discover." By means of this shift in the meaning of the term "law," Willard translates questions concerning the divine law and government into questions concerning the divine means and ends. For him the divine law is fundamentally not a legal pronouncement by the monarch of the universe, but a rule of achieving the divine ends. His analysis of the government of the universe is consequently shaped, not in terms drawn from the analogy of politics, but in terms drawn from the analogy of workmanship or art.

With respect, moreover, to the creative power of God, Willard not only describes it in terms of workmanship, rather than in terms of the relationship of being and becoming or creator and creatures, but points out that it is inferior to God's providential power. To bring good out of an existing evil requires greater power, he argues, than to bring something out of nothing. To produce something out of nothing requires only the establishment of the negative contrary, while to produce good out of evil requires the establishment of the positive contrary of the thing. "In *Creation*," he says, "God Made something out of Nothing: Thus the world was produced from a *Negative* Contrary, and that was Wonderful. But in Providence, God brings *Good* out of *Evil*, from a Positive Contrary which is more Wonderful." In short, for Willard the glory of God is more fully evident in His providential workmanship than in His strictly creative activities.

In Willard's terms, then, the fall of Adam and the consequent corruption of mankind are to be understood as failure of men to perform the function which God had intended them to perform, that is to serve as instruments of the divine purposes. The fall of man is called an apostasy, he points out, because by it "man left the place which God had set him in." There was a station to which he was appointed, but he deserted it: God commanded him to serve Him; and to Make His glory the utlimate scope of his whole life, and all his actions.

The fall was also called an offense, because an offense signifies a *falling beside ones Aim or Mark* which he should have gone to: And this was the very Nature of the Apostasy; for in it Man fell beside his Rule, which should have guided him to his End, and so he mist of that: he declined from the Law which God gave him to direct him to his Happiness, and so he fell quite beside it.[31]

This conception of God as the great artificer or workman or contriver Willard shared with many other Puritans, including his famous contemporary Cotton Mather, who in *The Christian Philosopher* undertook to summarize systematically the results of contemporary natural philosophy, so as to exhibit "the works of the glorious God," "the contrivance of our most glorious Creator," which he declared "cannot be wisely observed without admiration and astonishment."[32] This aspect of Puritanism has been emphasized by Herbert Schneider in his *History of American Philosophy:*

> The theory of nature and the philosophy of history were unified for the New England Puritans by their Christian Platonism. They defined nature as the art (technē) of God. . . .
> God Himself is interpreted as "art," and the discipline of the human mind is the attempt at ordered understanding of the divine wisdom. There is no secular science: the so-called "secondary causes" are intelligible, not merely as secondary, but as intrinsic instrumentalities of God's "economy of redemption." Technology is thus sanctified. . . .
> The *eupraxia*, or skill, exhibited in the works (*euprasomena*) of God or man was the basic category of plutosophic analysis and enabled the Puritans to interpret their arts and crafts, including the most mercantile and menial, in the perspective of God's will.[33]

And it also enabled the Puritans, it may be observed, to interpret the character and activities of the diety in terms of human arts and crafts.

We do the numerous New Englanders of the school Willard represents a serious injustice when we describe them in the com-

[31] *Ibid.*, pp. 11, 37, 39-40, 134, 142-145, 156, 177, 209.
[32] Cotton Mather, *The Christian Philosopher* (London, 1721), pp. 1, 122.
[33] Herbert Schneider, *A History of American Philosophy* (New York, 1946), pp. 7-9.

mon, contemporary meaning of the term Puritan, as men preoccupied with absurdly legalistic and elaborately unimportant prohibitions, supposed to have divine sanction, against not only what may be still regarded as ethically wrong, but against anything that gives pleasure. Puritans like Mather and Willard did not think of themselves as hedged round by arbitrary rules against this and that innocent thing. They are not to be supposed to have looked in constant fear toward the great day of judgment, when the Monarch of the Universe would review the records of their lives in the light of His formidable laws and consign those who had violated His statutes to eternal punishment. We should come nearer the truth if we supposed that such men conceived of the universe as a magnificent contrivance designed for ends far outreaching man's own little existence and aims—ends to which men might adjust themselves and with respect to which they might even find places of glory as instruments of infinite purposes. They believed themselves peculiarly favored in having an insight into the plans of a universal architect and workman and into their own possibilities as well as weaknesses. Failure held its terrors, to be sure, but they were not the terrors of a narrow, blue-law morality. They were the terrors of men who felt they might fail to fit into universal purposes too high to be apprehended or stated beyond the point of saying that man's chief end was to serve the great Architect and Artist of the Universe and to enjoy Him forever.

Yet despite a certain magnificence which was achieved in this kind of Puritanism, preoccupation with the concept of God as "workman," "contriver," "artist" involved Puritanism in difficulties. If God planned and managed everything for His own high and inscrutable purposes, man was not only denied freedom of will, but relieved of responsibility for sin and failure. Nothing could be more ingenious than the philosophic devices by which the Puritans endeavored to avoid denying either the sovereignty of God or the moral responsibility of man. The great achievement of Jonathan Edwards in his *Inquiry Concerning Freedom of Will* (1754) seems to have failed chiefly because of its metaphysical subtlety. Edwards expressed the hope that he had once and for all refuted the objection of Arminians to the Calvinist position by proving that men have a large area of freedom to do as they please, though no freedom to determine what will please them, and thus are both wholly dependent on God and morally accountable for their actions; but his position was very generally misunderstood as sheer determinism, or dismissed as metaphysical hairsplitting, or condemned as disingenuous.[34] The Puritan position in this respect came to be understood and rejected on the grounds indicated in the jingle popular in Boston in the early nineteenth century:

> You can and you can't.
> You will and you won't.
> You'll be damned if you do.
> And be damned if you don't.

Each aspect, indeed, of the threefold conception of the Deity which early Puritans entertained presented a serious moral problem when literally and exclusively developed. If God was conceived of as king of the universe, rather than as its workman or artist, and men were regarded as His rebellious subjects, the difficulty of justifying the ways of God to man lay in defending the idea of God as an Absolute Monarch who promulgated laws and executed judgments simply for the sake of His own glory. This was the view against which Channing thundered in his famous review entitled "The Moral Argument against Calvinism."[35] On the other hand, the representation of God as the great workman or contriver, the arranger of all that comes to pass in the universe, involved the Puritans in equally difficult ethical problems. In this view of religion God seemed to be made the author of evil as well as good, and man seemed relieved of moral responsibility.

The third aspect of the Puritan's view of the deity also had its difficulties. To those descendants of the Puritans who resolved the problems of God's moral government in the universe and His control of all its processes by reference to God as Eternal Being, the source from which finite existences flow, another danger opened itself. It was possible in this view to make virtue not a matter of obedience to a divine law, or of yielding to divine ends and purposes, but of identification with eternal being. The virtuous man was not merely an obedient subject, or an efficient instrument of

[34] G. E. Ellis, *A Half Century of the Unitarian Controversy* (Boston, 1857), pp. 95-103.
[35] *The Works of William Ellery Channing* (Boston, 1872), I, 221-231.

the divine operations, but a mind whose ideas and purposes had been so harmonized with the thought and intentions of God, that, to use Edwards's phrase, he was "infinitely, nearly, and closely united to God."[36] Edwards, to whom in his youth the doctrines of Calvinism had seemed horrible, found it possible to embrace them in this form with satisfaction and even with ecstasy. But the conception of the human soul as an emanation from Eternal Being opened possibilities which the earlier Puritans had regarded with peculiar horror. In this form Puritanism could easily be converted into something which to Puritans resembled pantheism. It was, indeed, just such a dislocation of Puritan ideas that Emerson accomplished three-quarters of a century after Edwards. And it is no accident that Emerson's "Divinity School Address" was labeled pantheism by orthodox divines, nor that in reply Emerson's followers should point out a resemblance between Transcendentalism and Edwardeanism.[37] Edwards himself had made much of "a supernatural light immediately imparted to the soul," and reoriented to another metaphysical base this doctrine strongly resembling Emerson's doctrine of reason and intuition. Edwards himself would, of course, have rejected the connection, for his insistence upon the absolute chasm between the finite and the infinite would have precluded anything resembling Emerson's doctrine of the "Oversoul."

The power and sweep of the early Puritan theology were very largely a consequence of the complexity and elaboration with which Puritan theologians had worked into a coherent and plausible system ideas concerning the nature and processes of the universe and ideas concerning the nature and operations of man, which out of the context of that system would appear paradoxical or even contradictory. But this very trait of Puritanism rendered it less stable than a more naïve and simpler theology would have been. Its internal collapse was consequently accomplished chiefly through simplifications in which one of the several aspects of the Deity which men like Shepard had discussed was taken to be the whole

---

[36] Jonathan Edwards, *Dissertation concerning the End for which God Created the World*, in *Representative Selections* (Cincinnati, 1935), p. 347.
[37] Ralph Waldo Emerson, *Representative Selections*, ed. Frederick I. Carpenter (Cincinnati, 1934), p. 10.

of the matter. In any one of these simpler versions Puritanism can easily be made to appear ridiculous, and the contemporary reader of Michael Wigglesworth's *Day of Doom* wonders how any group of men could have given serious assent to such a system.

A second equally important line of development in New England thought undermined the theology of the founding fathers of Plymouth and Massachusetts Bay. It involved a sequence of shifts in the location of basic certainty in philosophy. Every philosophy must begin somewhere, must start from what is certain or better known, to deal with what is uncertain or unexplained. Puritans began with the nature of God. The starting point for the speculations of the most metaphysical of them, Jonathan Edwards, was the conviction that something must always have existed, and that what had always existed must be the infinite and eternal mind of God.

That there should be absolutely nothing at all is utterly impossible, the mind can never [, ] Let it stretch its conceptions ever so much bring it self to conceive of a state of Perfect nothing . . . it is the greatest Contradiction and the Aggregate of all Contradictions . . . so that we see it is necessary some being should Eternally be and tis a more palpable Contradiction still to say that there must be being somewhere and not otherwise . . . so that we see this necessary eternal being must be infinite and Omnipresent. . . .
. . . and how Doth it Grate upon the mind to thin[k] that something should be from all Eternity, and nothing all the while Conscious of it . . . yea it is Really impossible it should be that Anything should be and nothing know it. . . . Certainly it [the universe] exists no where but in the Divine mind.[38]

Certain of Eternal Being, Edwards was troubled about the status and character of temporal things. "In treating of Human Nature," he instructed himself in his notebooks, "treat first of Being in General, and show what is in Human Nature, necessarily existing from the nature of Entity.[39] He delighted, he said, to contemplate uncreated and absolute being, and he must labor to discover the bases for the existence of the natural world and of man, and to uncover the relations of these to eternal being and to each other.

[38] Jonathan Edwards, *Representative Selections*, pp. 18-23.
[39] *Works of Jonathan Edwards*, ed. Sereno Dwight (New York, 1829). I, 664-665.

His great treatises had therefore to do with questions of free will of so dependent a creature as man (*A Careful and Strict Enquiry into . . . Freedom of Will*), the origin of sin in a universe produced by a self-existent, all-powerful, perfect being (*Original Sin*), and the possibilities of excellence for finite and temporal creatures (*The Nature of True Virtue*); and he was led finally in his greatest philosophic achievement, the *Dissertation Concerning the End for Which God Created the World*, to ask Why should there have been a creation at all? What end could it serve? And why should an Eternal Being have desired the existence of creatures?

Channing, who repudiated Puritanism as raising false questions and providing unsatisfactory answers, was certain, not about the being and nature of God as the Puritans had been, but about the nature of man, and confident of the trustworthiness of man's faculties, both intellectual and moral.

> We must start in religion from our own souls. In these is the fountain of all divine truth. . . . There are, indeed, philosophical schools of the present day, which tell us, that we are to start in all our speculations from the Absolute, the Infinite. But we rise to these conceptions from the contemplation of our own nature; and even if this were not so, of what avail would be the notion that Absolute, Infinite existence, and Uncaused Entity if stripped of all those intellectual and moral attributes which we learn only from our own souls.[40]

What required explanation for Channing, consequently, was the nature and character of the Deity. How could God be constituted as three persons in one? Could His chief concern be as Puritans declared the achievement of His own glory? Could He be supposed, as Puritans further insisted, to decree in accordance with His arbitrary good pleasure that some men should enjoy salvation, while others were eternally damned? "We are presumptuous, we are told, in judging of our creator," wrote Channing, "but He Himself has made this our duty, in giving us a moral faculty; and to decline it is to violate the primary law of our nature."[41] The step from Edwards to Channing is in one respect short and easy. Edwards had been certain of an Infinite Being, because to deny such

[40] *Works* (Boston, 1841), I, xviii.
[41] "The Moral Argument against Calvinism" (1809), *Works*, I, 232; "Unitarian Christianity" (1819), *ibid.*, III, 69-92; "Christianity a Rational Religion," *ibid.*, IV, 58-65.

being involved contradictions and "put the mind into mere Convulsion and Confusion."[42] Channing's position was that if this method of human reasoning were valid, if it established conclusively the existence of infinite being, then finite mind and its operations were the proper starting points of theology.

The swing from Puritanism becomes complete with Emerson, whose dissatisfaction with the theology which had solved Channing's problems led him to resign the pulpit of the Second Unitarian Church in Boston. Emerson turned to nature for basic insights as Channing had to man. He read extensively in natural science, planned lectures on natural history, and informed his brother that he was tempted to "have an observatory and a telescope and a laboratory and a battery."[43] His first important publication was entitled *Nature*, and in the "Introduction" to it, he proposes to interrogate nature in the certainty that we have no questions nature cannot answer.

Undoubtedly we have no questions to ask which are unanswerable. We must trust the perfection of the creation so far as to believe that whatever curiosity the order of things has awakened in our minds, the order of things can satisfy. Every man's condition is a solution in hieroglyphics to those inquiries he would put. He acts it as life, before he apprehends it as truth. In like manner, nature is already, in its forms and tendencies, describing its own design. Let us interrogate the great apparition that shines so peacefully around us.[44]

The elaborate system of the Puritan theology was, then, not only weakened by the oversimplification of its complex view of the Deity, but it was undermined by the shifting of basic principles from God to man to nature. It is perhaps one of the chief marks of such a shift that it involves a recognition of an element of the mysterious in what comes to be regarded as basic, coupled with an unwillingness to countenance a mysterious aspect in what had been taken as a certain base of speculation. Confident of the validity of modern science, we do not insist that the contemporary physicist's conception of the nature of the atom be wholly understandable

---

[42] Jonathan Edwards, *Representative Selections*, p. 18.

[43] *Letters*, ed. Ralph L. Rusk (New York, 1939), I, 343, 397. See also Professor Rusk's summary of Emerson's interest in natural science, *ibid.*, I, lxii-lxiii.

[44] Ralph Waldo Emerson, *Representative Selections*, p. 10.

or even wholly intelligible to us. The Puritan, confident of the existence of God as the proper foundation of all thought, likewise did not insist that the nature of God be wholly intelligible, or that all paradoxes concerning it be resolved. That the Trinity should be a mystery did not trouble him, though it greatly troubled the Unitarian who believed that we must begin all our speculations with human nature. The readiness of the Puritan to believe in what he could not wholly understand seemed to Unitarians wholly naïve, just as to many twentieth-century minds Channing's confidence in the goodness of human nature and in the trustworthiness of man's moral faculties, coupled with his acknowledgment that much in the operations of the human mind was mysterious and incomprehensible, appears a simple-minded optimism. Future generations may perhaps view with wonder the confidence men in our own time exhibit in accepting the pronouncements of our natural scientists concerning the constitution of a four-dimensional universe and the behavior of its unseen atoms, while not pretending that these matters are clear to us.

The Puritan's view of the nature of truth and of the means for acquiring it, like his view of the nature of God, were useful instruments in establishing and maintaining the comprehensive system of the sciences he held, while at the same time involving, like the Puritan conception of the Deity, a nice adjustment and balance of ideas wherein, by even slight shifts of emphasis or apparently minor dislocations, new philosophic positions, horrendously erroneous from the Puritan point of view, could easily arise. Reason and revelation were not opposed as the Puritans saw the matter, nor were they independent avenues to truth. John Wise in vindicating the government of the New England churches in 1717 found it justified both by "the Royal assent of the supream Monarch of the Churches," while at the same time so admirable "under the brightest Light of Nature, there is no greater Example of natural Wisdom in any settlement on Earth." Looking at it in both ways, he said, "It is agreeable that we attribute it to God whether we receive it nextly from Reason or Revelation, for that each is equally an Emanation of his Wisdom." God has hung out many lights to guide man through a dark world.

This admirable Effect of Christs Creating Power in hanging out so many Lights to guide man through a dark World, is as Applicable to the Light of Reason, as to that of Revelation. For that the Light of Reason as a Law and Rule of Right, is an Effect of Christ's Goodness, care, and creating Power, as well as of Revelation; though Revelation is Nature's Law in a fairer and brighter Edition. This is granted by the *London* Ministers P.8.C.3. "That, that which is evident by, and consonant to the true Light of Nature, or Natural Reason, is to be accounted, *Jure Divino*, in matters of Religion."[45]

It was one consequence of this view that the Puritans thought it proper to apply the most rigorous reasoning to the interpretation of the Scriptures. The care and detail with which Puritans analyzed the Bible, compared passage with passage, dissected scriptural propositions, and reconciled apparent contradictions by the employment of nice distinctions, and then boldly projected inferences from the biblical text into every area and almost into every corner of every area of life makes it impossible to regard them as antirationalists. At the same time they were saved by one important consideration from falling into what they would have regarded as the dangerous error of dependence upon natural reason. As Perry Miller has pointed out, the Puritans found natural reason insufficient in the present depraved state of mankind. Had man retained the innocence with which he came from the hands of his Creator, natural reason unaided by revelation might have been sufficient, but it was one important consequence of the fall of our first parents that natural reason had been rendered untrustworthy. Puritans like John Cotton were convinced of "the depravation of nature, in the blindnesse of our minds: who are so far from discerning spiritual things ... that we cannot rightly judge of moral or civil things." All this, as Miller observes, did not lead the Puritan to "deny that truth can be discovered in nature, poetry, right reason, and the consent of nations. He does not deny that these things are emanations of God's wisdom, and that from them men may gain all manner of valuable instruction.... What the Puritan does insist on is that the natural man, if left to himself, will not read the lessons of nature and reason correctly."[46]

[45] John Wise, *Vindication of the Government of the New England Churches* (1717), in *The Puritans*, pp. 257-258.
[46] *The Puritans*, pp. 50-52.

Puritans, from Shepard to Edwards, were led consequently to distinguish between two kinds of truth—"real" and "notional." A man may in a sense perceive the truth, said Shepard, without fully sensing its reality. He may arrange ideas properly, and in a sense be convinced of the validity of a true argument. His notions may be correct, and yet his perceptions imperfect. The difference, Shepard says, is like that between seeing a lion painted upon a wall and actually being confronted by a real lion.

In a "Treatise of Ineffectual Hearing of the Word," he makes the distinction in terms of a painted and a real sun:

1. Quest. How did the Jewes hear, and yet not hear God speaking? 2. Answ. There is a two fold work, or rather a double declaration of the same work. 1. There is Gods externall or outward word, containing letters and syllables, and this is his externall voice. 2. There is God[s] internal work and voice, which secretly speaks to the heart. . . . As 'tis with a painted sun on the wall, you see the Sun and Stars, but there is a difference between seeing this and the Sun and Starres themselves, wherein is an admirable glory: go to a painted Sun, it gives you no heat, nor cherisheth you not; so it is here.

This inward work is double. 1. Ineffectual, (though inward.) 2. Effectual. 1. Ineffectual, is that which hath some inward operation upon the heart, but it attains not Gods end to bring a man to a state of life.[47]

Real knowledge is more than the product of impeccable logic, more even than a correct perception emotionally moving. It is a state of being of the soul involving such response of the passions and the will as restores man to a right relationship with God. Almost a century later Edwards made the same point in his sermon *A Divine and Supernatural Light Imparted to the Soul*. The light, he explained, does not consist of new ideas or new truths, but rather it gives the soul a new view of the truth, or to use Edwards's own phrase, a new "relish" for it. The "doctrine" of the sermon as Edwards states it, is "that there is such a thing as a Spiritual and Divine light, immediately imparted to the soul by God, of a different nature from anything that is obtained by natural means." This light is not to be confused with natural conscience or reason which "will, by meer nature, make a man sensible of guilt, and will ac-

---

[47] Thomas Shepard, *Subjection to Christ . . . Together with a Treatise of Ineffectual Hearing of the Word* (London, 1757), pp. 89-90.

cuse and condemn him when he has done amiss." God, it is true, may assist natural conscience "but in the renewing and sanctifying work of the Holy Ghost, those things are wrought in the soul that are above nature, and of which there is nothing of the like kind in the soul by nature." God acts very differently in these two cases. "He may indeed act upon the mind of a natural man; but he acts in the mind of a saint as an indwelling vital principle. He acts upon the mind of an unregenerate person as an extrinsic occasional agent; for in acting upon them he doth not unite himself to them, for notwithstanding all of his influences that they may be the subjects of, they are still sensual, having not the spirit." "There is," Edwards explains, "a two-fold understanding or knowledge of good of that God has made the mind of man capable of."

The first, that which is meerly speculative and notional: as when a person only speculatively judges that anything is, which speculative by the agreement of mankind, is called good or excellent.... And the other is that which consists in a sense of the heart: as when there is a sense of the beauty, amiableness, or sweetness of a thing; so that the heart is sensible of pleasure and delight in the presence of the idea of it....

Thus there is a great difference between having an opinion, that God is holy and gracious, and having a sense of the loveliness and beauty of that holiness and grace. There is a difference between having a rational judgment that honey is sweet, and having a sense of its sweetness.[48]

The difference does not lie for Edwards in men's being moved or remaining unmoved by religious truths. Men's natural feelings may respond to a notional knowledge. "Men by mere principles of nature are capable of being affected with things that have a special relation to religion as well as other things. A person by mere nature, for instance, may be liable to be affected with the story of Jesus Christ, and the sufferings he underwent, as well as by any other tragical story." The difference is a difference of kind, with respect both to ideas and emotions, traceable to a difference in the constitution of the soul, which in the case of natural man, operates solely from those principles which men possess merely by virtue of their humanity, whereas in the case of regenerate man, new principles of knowledge and feeling have by divine agency

[48] Jonathan Edwards, *Representative Selections*, pp. 103-107.

been instituted, so as to constitute the elect as a new creature. The elect and the nonelect thus belong strictly speaking to different species. An animal or plant behaves regularly in accordance with a set of natural principles as established foundations of behavior. These constitute it a member of its species, which may then be defined by reference to them. The elect and the nonelect behave regularly and differently on the basis of a radically different constitutional equipment and belong therefore to different species.

The spirit of God, in those convictions which unregenerate men sometime have, assists conscience to do this work in a further degree than it would do if they were left to themselves.... But in the renewing and sanctifying work of the Holy Ghost, those things are wrought in the soul that are above nature, and of which there is nothing of the like kind in the soul by nature: and they are caused to exist in the soul habitually, and according to such a stated constitution or law that lays such a foundation for exercises in a continued course, as is called a principle of nature. Not only are remaining principles assisted to do their work more freely and fully, but those principles are restored that were utterly destroyed by the fall; and the mind thenceforth habitually exerts those acts that the dominion of sin had made it wholly destitute of, as a dead body is of vital acts.[49]

This view of knowledge gave the Puritans who held it a powerful controversial weapon. If the truths they enunciated and defended, the truths they found glorious and entertained with relish, seemed to their opponents erroneous and distasteful, the explanation lay near at hand. Nothing more could be expected of the nonelect than that they should reject with disdain and distaste what the Puritans, enjoying the blessed advantage of divinely reconstituted minds or souls, found overwhelmingly convincing and completely satisfying. As Shepard puts it, "There is a state of light to which God calls his people only; or rather there is a spirit of light, illumination, or revelation let into the mind, which is peculiar to the beloved of Christ."[50] And he warns those who find "gospel truth" unconvincing and unmoving that "when God hath an intent to harden a man's heart and to damn him ... there is a secret loathing of truth, in regard of the commands of it." God "hardens, and

---

[49] *Ibid.*, p. 103.
[50] Thomas Shepard, *Parable of the Ten Virgins* (Falkirk, 1797), I, 419, 267, 315.

blinds, and prepares for eternal ruin, all the men in the world by this means."[51]

But potent and reassuring as this conception of knowledge was, it provided an opening for a serious embarrassment and difficulty to the Puritans. How were they to meet the arguments of one convinced like themselves of the possession of divine light? How could they reject the doctrines of one who insisted that he had experienced regeneration? How, in short, were they to deal with Ann Hutchinson? The difficulty of this question for the Puritans is revealed in John Winthrop's account of the attempt of colonial ministers to correct Mrs. Hutchinson. One of Mrs. Hutchinson's "two dangerous errors," according to Winthrop, was "That the person of the Holy Ghost dwells in a justified person"; the other was "That no sanctification can help to evidence to us our justification," or in less theological language, that leading a sober, righteous, and Godly life was no evidence of that change of heart in which true religion consisted. The danger of the second error in the view of the Puritan clergy lay in its disregard of morality in favor of a fanatical religious enthusiasm. Concerned that religion should be represented as more than merely good behavior, they were equally concerned that it should be more than private emotional experience. They laid themselves open consequently to Mrs. Hutchinson's charge that they were making religion a mere "covenant of works," rather than an inward experience. The first of Mrs. Hutchinson's errors included the present possibility of supernatural revelation. The question was whether the elect were infallibly preserved from error by personal union with God's spirit. Mrs. Hutchinson believed that she had been led to the position she took by the teachings of John Cotton himself, and although Cotton eventually participated in her condemnation, there is ample evidence that a slight distortion of Cotton's views could produce Mrs. Hutchinson's doctrines. When Cotton met with "the other ministers in the way," he cleared himself with respect to what Winthrop had called the second of Mrs. Hutchinson's errors by announcing his belief "that sanctification did help to evidence justification." On the other hand, he was less

---

[51] Thomas Shepard, *Subjection to Christ . . . Together with a Treatise of Ineffectual Hearing of the Word*, p. 107.

sure that Mrs. Hutchinson was in error when she held "that the person of the Holy Ghost dwells in a justified person," though he believed that a distinction between himself and Mrs. Hutchinson might be made: "but, for the indwelling of the person of the Holy Ghost, he held that still, as some others of the ministers did, but not union with the person of the Holy Ghost (as Mrs. Hutchinson and others did) so as to amount to a personal union." Three weeks later, Winthrop reports, a general agreement was reached "in the chief matter of substance, viz. that the Holy Ghost is God, and that he doth dwell in the believers, (as the Father and Son both are said also to do,) but whether by his gifts and power only, or by any other manner of presence, seeing the Scripture does not declare it,—it was earnestly desired, that the word person might be forborn, being a term of human invention and tending to doubtful disputation in this case." The distinctions by means of which the parties were separated became indeed so fine that Winthrop observed a few months later that "no man could tell (except some few, who knew the bottom of the matter) where any difference was."[52]

It was a nice and difficult balance which Puritans tried to maintain. The elect were capable of a new kind of apprehension of truth. This apprehension did not include the private discovery of new truth, and Winthrop can refer scornfully to the way in which Mrs. Hutchinson "vented her revelations" before the general court, and Edwards could insist in discussing the divine and supernatural light immediately imparted to the soul, that this light "is not the suggesting of any new truths of propositions not contained in the word of God."

This suggesting of new truths or doctrines to the mind, independent of any antecedent revelations of those propositions, either in word or writing, is inspiration; such as the prophets and apostles had, and such as some enthusiasts pretend to. But this spiritual light that I am speaking of, is quite a different thing from inspiration: it reveals no new doctrine, it suggests no new proposition to the mind, it teaches no new thing of God, or Christ, or another world, not taught in the Bible; but only gives a due apprehension of those things that are taught in the word of God.[53]

[52] *The Puritans*, pp. 129-132.
[53] Jonathan Edwards, *Representative Selections*, p. 105.

Neither Winthrop nor Edwards believed, furthermore, that the religious enlightenment of the elect was a matter of heightened feelings.[54] The mind of the elect was moved to joy in the truth of the gospel, but not every expression of religious feeling was valid. The cause of true religious enlightenment was God acting in a supernatural way upon the mind in such a manner that the divine spirit might be said to "dwell" in the believer, but not in such a fashion that the personal traits of the believer were assimilated into the personality of God, or could be regarded as completely the expressions of the divine spirit.

This carefully balanced doctrine could easily be upset, and indeed was upset, in two ways. By throwing the emphasis upon the feelings and ideas of the individual believer, as Mrs. Hutchinson had done, it produced early in the Puritan experience in New England the Antinomian movement of which she was head, and could culminate in the "self-reliance" of Ralph Waldo Emerson. On the other hand, by emphasis upon the devices Winthrop had employed to resolve the difficulties raised by Mrs. Hutchinson, that is, the calling of a "synod" for the purpose of verifying issues, debating the merits of positions, and reaching reasoned general conclusions on the basis of the interpretation of scripture, it opened the way for that rationalizing of religion which exhibits itself in Charles Chauncey's attack on the Great Awakening, and which culminates in William Ellery Channing's "rational Christianity."[55]

The ambitious attempt of the Puritans to unify science around theology and to order human activities about religion achieved its very considerable measure of success at the very necessary expense of a considerable degree of complexity. Careful distinctions rigorously applied were its chief instrument. The Puritans were aware that such a system could not be maintained by an ignorant ministry, or among unthinking laymen. They early provided for a college; and far from regarding treatment of theological subjects in the pulpit as improper, they looked upon the theological education of the laity as one of the chief functions of the Church. Oversimplification of the doctrine of the nature of God, or the doctrine concern-

---

[54] *Ibid.*, pp. 105-106.
[55] *Ibid.*, xviii; "Christianity a Rational Religion," *Works of William E. Channing* (Boston, 1872), IV, 31 ff.

ing the process of sanctification, or the nature of truth and the ways of acquiring it, could affect the Puritan system of ideas disastrously. To think of God simply as the monarch and lawgiver of the universe would lead to mere legalism (and it is in this oversimplified fashion that Puritanism is represented in popular, present-day definitions of it). To conceive of God simply as the great manager and contriver of affairs in the world could easily lead to a conception of man as simply a tool or instrument for the attainment of God's glory and could thus undermine, as Channing was quick to point out, the character of the Deity. To conceive of God as infinite being from which all finite existences emanate could easily lead to pantheism. And, finally, to suppose that a good man, as especially elected by God, received supernatural assistance to virtue and to knowledge, could easily lead to the assertion of the validity of individual moods and opinions, while the corrective of such individualism by appeals to what men find generally reasonable could easily lead to rationalism and to the rejection of the supernatural authority of the scriptures and of the church. In a sense, then, the Puritan system held within itself the explosives which demolished it.

It was weakened, furthermore, by reason of its methods for achieving comprehensiveness, in another way. Embracing politics, economics, ethics, and natural science, it absorbed into itself concepts and principles from these sciences and then found itself obliged to recognize and employ them in theology itself. Some of the most striking and ultimately some of the most subversive of these intruders came from economics and political science. In an admirable paper on "The Marrow of Puritan Divinity" Perry Miller has traced the history and pointed out some of the consequences of the introduction into Puritan theology of the covenant doctrine, which "holds that man hath not only been in relation to God as creature to creator, subject to lord, but more definitely through a succession of explicit agreements or contracts, as between two partners in a business enterprise."[56]

The Covenant theology is briefly described in *The Confession of Faith Owned and Consented unto by the Eldors and Messengers*

[56] *Publications of the Colonial Society of Massachusetts*, XXXII (1938), 260-261.

*of the Churches Assembled at Boston in New England, May 12, 1680:*

The distance between God and the Creature is so great, that although reasonable creatures do owe obedience unto him as their Creator, yet they could never have attained the reward of life, but by some voluntary condecension on Gods part, which he hath been pleased to express by way of Covenant.
 II. The first Covenant made with man, was a Covenant of Works, wherein life was promised to Adam, and in him to his posterity, upon condition of perfect and personal obedience.
 III. Man by his fall having made himself uncapable of life by that Covenant, the Lord was pleased to make a second, commonly called the Covenant of Grace: wherein he freely offereth unto sinners life and salvation by Jesus Christ, requiring of them faith in him that they may be saved, and promising to give unto all those that are ordained unto life, his holy Spirit, to make them willing and able to believe.
 IV. This Covenant of Grace is frequently set forth in the Scripture by the name of a Testament, in reference to the death of Jesus Christ the Testator, and to the everlasting Inheritance, with all things belonging to it, therein bequeathed.
 V. Although this Covenant hath been differently and variously administered in respect of Ordinances and Institutions in the time of the Law, and since the coming of Christ in the flesh; yet for the substance and efficacy of it, to all its spiritual and saving ends, it is one and the same; upon the account of which various dispensations, it is called the Old and New Testament.[57]

The doctrine of compact or covenant was therefore one of the devices by means of which the Puritan system of beliefs achieved its comprehensiveness. The relationships of man and wife in the family, or of minister and laity in the church, of rulers and subjects in the state, of the individual soul to God, and indeed of families, churches, and states as social groups to God, were formulated in terms of mutually binding agreements. This is the background of John Winthrop's oft-quoted statement in *A Modell of Christian Charity written on board the Arrabella, on the Attlantick Ocean.*

For the worke wee have in hand, it is by a mutuall consent, through a special overruleing providence, and a more then an ordinary approbation of the Churches of Christ to seeke out a place of Cohabitation and Consorteshipp under a due forme of Government both civill and ecclesiasticall. . . .

[57] Walker, *Creeds and Platforms of Congregationalism*, pp. 374-375, 439.

Thus stands the cause betweene God and us, wee are entered into Covenant with him for this worke, wee have taken out a Commission, the Lord hath given us leave to drawe our owne Articles wee have professed to enterprise these Accions upon these and these ends, wee have hereupon besought him of favour and blessing: Now if the Lord shall please to hear us, and bring us in peace to the place wee desire, than hath he ratified this Covenant and sealed our Commission, [and] will expect a strickt performance of the Articles contained in it, but if wee shall neglect the observacion of these Articles which are the ends wee have propounded, and dissembling with our God, shall fall to embrace this present world and prosecute our carnall intencions seekeing greate things for ourselves and our posterity, the Lord will surely breake out in wrathe against us be revenged of such a periured people and make us knowe the price of the breache of such a Covenant.[58]

The theory of covenants also provides the background of Winthrop's equally famous speech to the general court on July 3, 1645, concerning "the great questions that have troubled the country ... about the authority of the magistrates and the liberty of the people." Having been acquitted in impeachment proceedings instituted by the lower house of the general court because of his intervention in an election dispute in the town of Hingham, Winthrop rose to clarify what he regarded as a confusion about liberty. There was, he said, "a two-fold liberty, natural (I mean as our nature is now corrupt) and civil or federal." The first was the liberty which man in common with the beasts had to do as he pleased. It is, said Winthrop, "a liberty to evil as well as good." Civil or federal liberty might, he said, "also be termed moral, in reference to the covenant between God and man, in the moral law, and the politic covenants and constitutions, amongst men themselves."

This liberty is maintained and exercised in a way of subjection to authority; it is of the same kind of liberty wherewith Christ hath made us free. The woman's own choice makes such a man her husband; yet being so chosen, he is her lord, and she is to be subject to him, yet in a way of liberty, not of bondage; and a true wife accounts her subjection, her honor, and freedom, and would not think her condition safe and free, but in her subjection to her husband's authority. Such is the liberty of the church under the authority of Christ, her king and husband. . . . Even so, brethren, it will be between you and your magistrates. If you stand for your natural corrupt liberties, and will do what is good in

[58] *The Puritans*, pp. 197-198.

your own eyes, you will not endure the least weight of authority, but will murmur, and oppose, and be always striving to shake off that yoke; but if you will be satisfied to enjoy such civil and lawful liberties, such as Christ allows you, then will you quietly and cheerfully submit unto that authority which is set over you, in all the administrations of it, for your good.[59]

In Winthrop's view then, the moral law, the family, the church, and the commonwealth rested upon compact and mutual agreement; and his speech illustrates the manner in which ethics, politics, ecclesiastical polity, and religion were strung like beads on the doctrine of the covenant. All this makes another passage in Winthrop's speech of special interest. In arguing that good subjects must not contend for what he has called natural liberty, but must yield to the authority of the magistrates, he reveals the source of the covenant doctrine in social theory:

We account him a good servant who breaks not his covenant. The covenant between you and us is the oath you have taken of us, which is to this purpose, that we shall govern you, and judge your causes by the rules of God's laws and our own, according to our best skill. When you agree with the workman to build you a ship or house, etc., he undertakes as well for his skill as for his faithfulness, for it is his profession, and you pay him for both.[60]

The principle of covenants belongs basically to business and to social arrangements. It was not developed in theology and applied to economics and politics; it was borrowed from these fields by theology as a means of reformulating theological problems realistically and solving them convincingly. As Herbert Schneider has remarked in his *History of American Philosophy*, "The covenant theory of the church was really the ecclesiastical aspect of 'social contract' theory, and its basic aim was to transform the 'status' of the elect of Calvinistic theory into a 'contract' relationship of voluntary obligation. The theory was welcomed chiefly in middle-class and mercantile circles and was part of the general movement away from feudal and towards commercial conceptions of authority and government."[61] It was a useful importation. It brought into harmony the theological view of God as ruler or lord and the

[59] *Ibid.*, p. 207.
[60] *Ibid.*, p. 206.
[61] Herbert Schneider, *History of American Philosophy*, p. 4.

doctrine of justification by faith. It aided in synthesizing theology, politics, economics, and sociology. It made it possible to reformulate Calvinistic theology in what must have seemed to the contemporaries of Ames and Preston, of Shepard and Hooker and Cotton, common sense terms. But it was a dangerous importation into Puritanism, a Trojan horse within its citadel, for as the conceptions of the nature and proper ends of the agreements upon which governments are founded moved increasingly toward a "democratic" theory, revised principles of government were inevitably applied to theology. This is another aspect of the significance of Harriet Beecher Stowe's analysis of the decline of the Puritan doctrine of God as "Monarch of the Universe," cited above.

Thomas Shepard's formulation of the doctrine of the "imputation of Adam's sin to his descendants" may serve to illustrate the point. The theological problem is that of the punishable guilt of all men as a consequence of the fall of Adam in the Garden of Eden. Shepard explains it in terms of the covenant theology by saying that Adam was our representative duly appointed to stand in our place, and duly authorized to act for us. Since he sinned as our agent, we share part of his guilt. To the objection that we did not elect Adam as our representative, Shepard replies that God elected him, and that since God is wiser than we would have been, no better representative could be supposed.[62] Whether this explanation fully satisfied Shepard's Puritan hearers we have no way of knowing, but it is easy to guess how it would have struck the generation of New Englanders of 1776, to whom the theory of "virtual representation" in Parliament was wholly unacceptable. There can be little doubt about the response which many members of that generation would have made to the suggestion that the British crown designate a representative of the colonies in Parliament. To us as inheritors of the ideas of that generation, Shepard's formulation of the doctrine of imputation must seem quaint, and we may take our judgment of it as illustrating one consequence of the importation into Calvinistic theology of the covenant theory.

The objections to Puritanism which accumulated with greater and greater weight through the eighteenth century were often of this kind. The distinguishing mark of such objections is the oft-

[62] Thomas Shepard, *The Sound Believer* (London, 1645), p. 31.

repeated declaration that we cannot regard as goodness in God traits which we should regard as evil in men. This is the basic premise, for instance, of Charles Chauncey's *The Benevolence of the Deity*, published in 1784. Some there are, he said, who "pretend, that the goodness, and other moral attributes of *God*, are not only different in *degree*, but in *kind* likewise, from the moral qualities in creatures." But these must be in error, for the idea of moral goodness is applicable "to men, or angels, or any created intelligences whatsoever; or even to the Supreme Being Himself." On any other supposition we make the goodness of God inconceivable and unintelligible and must "worship an unknown God, if we worship him at all." On this premise, Chauncey argued that since we regard a man as morally good only when he shows concern for the happiness of others, we must when we speak of the goodness of God mean "a natural disposition in the Deity, moving him to the communication of happiness."[63] To argue as Jonathan Edwards had that "God's chief end in the creation is His own glory" was then, in Chauncey's view, to deny the goodness of the Deity. Channing later argued with more specific reference to New England Puritans that no conception of God which shocks our moral sense can possibly be true, and Tom Paine, with whom Puritans like Lyman Beecher were in the habit of comparing Channing, had asserted that "any system of religion that has anything in it that shocks the mind of a child cannot be a true system."[64]

This position, that the standards of conduct for men and the ideas of goodness which men generally entertain are applicable to the Deity was more than an aspect of the shift in the location of certainty mentioned above; it was a reasonable consequence of the importation into theology of principles developed for the judgment of human conduct, such as those used in the formulation of Covenant Doctrines. In so far as the Puritan synthesis was accomplished by introducing into theology concepts and principles from economics and politics, the way was prepared for a revolution in which the Puritan queen of the sciences should be cast from her throne and retained as a handmaid of ethics and politics. In Benjamin

[63] Charles Chauncey, *The Benevolence of the Diety* (1784), pp. 14-17.
[64] Thomas Paine, *Age of Reason*, in *Representative Selections*, ed. Harry Hayden Clark (Cincinnati, 1944), p. 275.

Franklin the revolution is complete. When Franklin drew up his proposals for an English School in 1749, he assigned to religion a place which would have horrified his Puritan ancestors. In outlining the curriculum he had urged an important place for history, by means of which "almost all kinds of useful knowledge" may be "introduced to advantage, and with pleasure to the students." Among other things, he said, "history will afford frequent opportunities of showing the necessity of a public religion, from its usefulness to the public; the advantage of a religious character among private persons, the mischiefs of superstition and so forth, and the excellency of the Christian religion above all others ancient or modern."[65] To Franklin, in short, religion was useful to society and to individuals, whereas for Puritans like John Cotton, politics and ethics were "handmaids" of religion.

What is true of the relationship of politics or social theory to theology in the Puritan system, as illustrated in the development of the covenant theory, is true in somewhat different respects of the relationships between natural science and Puritanism. It is now generally recognized that the Puritans, far from opposing natural science, were hospitable to it, and it is less necessary than it was when Samuel Morison wrote *The Puritan Pronaos*, to correct the "common notion that the New England puritans were hostile or indifferent to science, while nourishing and coddling various pseudoscientific superstitions, such as astrology, demonology, and witchcraft."[66] To the Puritans no aspects of life and no range of natural phenomena were irrelevant for theology, and theology in its turn bore upon them all. They were consequently assiduously attentive to the whole range of natural events. Earthquakes and disasters at sea were interpreted as signs of God's displeasure; escapes from disaster and favorable seasons, as signs and marks of his favor. Miracles were hardly a problem, since by the distinction between "common providence" and "special providence," that is, between God's regular arrangement of natural events and unusual instances

---

[65] Benjamin Franklin, "Proposals Relating to the Education of Youth in Pensilvania," in *Representative Selections*, ed. Frank Luther Mott and Chester E. Jurgenson (Cincinnati, 1936), p. 203.

[66] Samuel E. Morison, *The Puritan Pronaos: Studies in the Intellectual Life of New England in the Seventeenth Century* (New York, 1936), pp. 234 ff.

of divine activity on special occasions, Puritans could inquire carefully into the natural law while prepared to expect the miraculous.[67] Mather's ecstatic description of the construction of plants as evidences of the divine "contrivance" of the natural world is, if not invariable among Puritans, at least not out of harmony with Puritan theology.

> The Contrivance of our most Glorious Creator, in the Vegetables growing upon this Globe, cannot be wisely observed without Admiration and Astonishment. . . .
> The *Anatomy of Plants*, as it has been exhibited by the incomparable Curiosity of Dr. *Grew*, what a vast *Field of Wonders* does it lead us into!
> The most inimitable *Structure* of the Parts!
> The particular Canals, and most adapted ones, for the conveyance of the lymphatic and essential Juices!
> The Air-Vessels in all their curious Coylings!
> The *Coverings* which befriend them, a Work unspeakably more curious in reality than in appearance!
> The strange Texture of the *Leaves*, the angular or circular, but always most orderly position of their Fibers; the various *Foldings*, with a *Duplicature*, a *Multiplicature*, the *Fore-rowl*, the *Back-rowl*, the *Tre-rowl*; the noble Guard of the Films interposed!
> The *Flowers*, their Gaiety and Fragrance. . . .![68]

Nor is it correct to suppose, as we sometimes have, that the Puritans who interested themselves in natural science were inclining toward deism. The principal line of attack on revelation as it was developed by such deists as Thomas Blount, Charles Gilden, Thomas Chubb, and Matthew Tindal rested upon the premise that the Creator was omnipotent, omniscient, and benevolent. Since He was all good, he must, so deists argued, desire the happiness of mankind; since He was all wise, He must be fully aware of what was requisite to this end; since He was all powerful, He must be able to provide the means for achieving it. It followed, as deists saw the matter, that God must have furnished all men in all ages, even those

---

[67] Cotton Mather opens *The Christian Philosopher*, a summary of contemporary science, with the remark that "The Essays now before us will demonstrate that *Philosophy* [natural philosophy] is no *Enemy*, but a mighty and wondrous *Incentive* to Religion." Yet Mather was constantly on the lookout for "remarkable providences."

[68] Cotton Mather, *The Christian Philosopher* (London 1721), pp. 122, 127.

of the meanest capacities, both with the means of knowing what was essential to their felicity, and with the capacity of attaining it. The writers who employed this line of argument seemed to have been fully aware that its conclusions depended upon the validity of the assumptions which underlay it, the assumption mainly that God was necessarily good, that His command did not originate simply in His arbitrary pleasure, but that the divine will was determined, as they put it, by the moral fitness or reason of things.[69] In resisting the deistic attack on the supernatural authority of the Scriptures, the defenders of orthodoxy insisted, for one thing, that the feebleness of human reason, at least since the fall of Adam, rendered it inadequate for the full discovery of the nature of things, and second, that there was an area of divine activity to which the rule of moral fitness was inapplicable, an area that was therefore inaccessible to reason, even at its best. Besides those actions which are morally necessary for the Deity, and those which are morally impossible to Him, said Samuel Clarke in the Boyle lectures of 1704, there are still others which are morally indifferent, and with respect to these, discovery by reference to moral criteria is plainly impossible. Right or wrong in such matters must depend wholly upon God's willing pleasure, and are therefore discoverable only through special revelation.[70] These positions were related to a difference in method between the deist and the orthodox divine. To put the matter very generally, the deist almost invariably developed his position from general principles presented as self-evident or as universally granted, the contradiction of which was inconceivable. The defenders of revealed religion, on the other hand, rested their case upon "experience," "history," "fact," as providing a decisive weight of evidence for their tenets. As Thomas Halyburton put it in *Natural Religion Insufficient*, when a conclusion from general and abstract principles runs counter "to what we most certainly know and have experience of . . . we have

[69] Charles Blount, *Miscellaneous Works of Charles Blount, Esq.* (1695), pp. 180-181. Thomas Chubb, *Vindication of the Moral Character of God, Collection of Tracts* (London, 1730), pp. 10-16, 251. Matthew Tindal, *Christianity as Old as the Creation* (London, 1731), pp. 335-345.

[70] Samuel Clarke, *The Being and Attributes of God, the Obligations of Natural Religion and the Truth and Certainty of the Christian Revelation* (London, 1705-1706).

reason to conclude that there lies certainly a fallacy or mistake" in our argument.[71]

This difference between arguing self-evident general truths as over against arguing from experience and historical evidence parallels the difference between Cartesian and Newtonian scientists in the seventeenth century. Roger Coates in his preface to the second edition of Newton's *Principia* (1714) contrasted the followers of Descartes, who according to him attempted to explain natural phenomena on the base of invented hypothesis, with the Newtonians, who refused to make hypotheses and insisted rigorously upon the experimental method. God's will as the basis of natural phenomena could not, he said, be made out by man's hypothesizing. It must be discovered through careful observation of the actual course of events.[72] When orthodox divines invoked the evidence of experience and history to meet the arguments of the deists that an all-good, all-powerful, and all-wise Being could neither have desired to leave any of His creatures in ignorance concerning His will nor have been unable to make it clear to them, and that consequently men, even those of the "meanest capacities," must be able to discover all that was essential with regard to religion and morality from the operations of their own minds without the aid of supernatural revelation, they regarded themselves as employing the method of the great Sir Isaac. It is this view of the matter which lies behind Cotton Mather's well-known advice to candidates for New England pulpits:

What we call Natural Philosophy, is what I must encourage you to spend much more time in the study of ... when I said Natural Philosophy, you may be sure, I did not mean, the Peripetetic ... nor the hypotheses ... too justly called Philosophical Romances. ... And therefore as thorough an insight as you can get into the principles of our *Perpetual Dictator*, the Incomparable Sir Isaac Newton, is what I mightily commend to you. Be sure, *The Experimental Philosophy* is that, in which alone your mind can be at all established.[73]

---

[71] P. 252. See also John Conybeare, *A Defense of Reveal'd Religion* (London, 1732), pp. 154-161.
[72] *Sir Isaac Newton's Mathematical Principles of Natural Philosophy and His System of the World* (Berkeley, California, 1946), pp. xx-xxxiii.
[73] Cotton Mather, *Manductio and Ministerium* (Boston, 1726), pp. 47, 50.

At this point then, as in the case of the covenant theory, Puritan theologians borrowed shrewdly. To the objections against the doctrine of the depravity of natural man they brought the evidence of history and experience; and Jonathan Edwards argued in *The Great Christian Doctrine of Original Sin Defended*, that the constant and unvarying appearance of sin, generation after generation among men, could be explained only by tracing it to a cause in the nature of men.[74] Having made the appeal to experience, they were vulnerable, however, to the new form of deism exemplified in Hume and Tom Paine which rose about the middle of the eighteenth century. Hume's attack on miracles is based upon the argument from experience, and Tom Paine in *The Age of Reason* makes natural science the opponent of orthodoxy, and undertakes to explain historically the imposition of revealed religion, as well as to trace historically the career of deism.

That which is now called natural philosophy, embracing the whole circle of science of which astronomy occupies the chief place, is the study of the works of God, and of the power and wisdom of God and his works, and is the true theology.

As to the theology that is now studied in its place, it is the study of human opinions and of human fancies concerning God. It is not the study of God himself in the works that he has made, but in the writings that man has made; and it is not among the least mischiefs that the Christian system has done in the world that it has abandoned the original and beautiful system of theology, like a beautiful innocent, to distress and reproach, to make room for the bag of superstition.

Contending that "the study of the dead languages" has been unfortunately substituted for the study of the sciences, Paine proposed "to compare, or rather to confront, the evidence that the structure of the universe affords with the Christian system of religion."[75] Once, again, in short, the Puritan synthesis, though it achieved a temporary success by borrowing principles from a field it had undertaken to assimilate, provided for its own eventual disruption. In relation to each of its basic concepts of the Deity, its assimilation of natural science led to difficulties. In terms of God as ruler of the universe, the principles of natural phenomena were seen as natural

---

[74] Jonathan Edwards, *Representative Selections*, pp. 316-323.
[75] Thomas Paine, *Representative Selections*, ed. Harry Hayden Clark (Cincinnati, 1944), pp. 263, 273.

law. In terms of God as the great contriver, natural phenomena were seen as providential operations. In terms of God as infinite being, they were dependent finite existences. The first view made it difficult to insist upon the necessity of revelation; the second made it difficult, except by the most arbitrary wrenching, to establish the divine goodness; and the third opened the door to pantheism, or at least to that replacing of admiration for the Deity by admiration for the natural, which has been repeatedly exhibited in American literature from Walt Whitman to William Saroyan.

Whether in the decline of Puritanism such events as the separation of church and state and the halfway covenant are causes or effects seems difficult to determine. Were these events consequences of the decline of Puritanism, or were they the basis of its decline? This much seems clear—that the powerful and precarious unity of Puritanism gradually crumbled instead of giving way suddenly like Holmes's one-horse shay which has been taken as a symbol of it. During the second quarter of the eighteenth century Jonathan Edwards made heroic efforts to arrest its decay by reinterpreting Calvinistic theology in the terms current in late seventeenth- and early eighteenth-century philosophy, though his work involved a sharp limitation of the scope of theology so that politics was left out of the new unity he contrived. Despite Edwards's efforts the decline went on, as nicely adjusted relationships of ideas within the system itself fell out of balance; as principles imported into Puritan theology from other sciences asserted themselves; and as the system, thus weakened, was battered by political, economic, and social developments in America. Preoccupation with business and commerce in the flourishing new republic, the emergence of what the Puritan leaders would have regarded as dangerous democratic tendencies in government, the humanitarian concern with social reform—all these if not the progeny of Puritanism, as has sometimes been suggested, were at least to some extent indebted to it, and each of them had repaid its debt by weakening some parts of the ambitious and impressive structure of thoughts and activity which Puritan minds and hands had erected.

# The Late Eighteenth Century:
## An Age of Contradictions

# The Late Eighteenth Century: An Age of Contradictions

*LEON HOWARD*
UNIVERSITY OF CALIFORNIA, LOS ANGELES

I

THE LATE EIGHTEENTH century either is or—in our present state of knowledge—appears to be the most complex period in American intellectual and literary history. Its pervading temper was humanistic. For the old Puritan preoccupation with the relationship between man and God it substituted an equally acute concern for the ways of man to man. The major subject matter of its literature became politics rather than religion. And when its poets looked into the future they had visions of a millennium of peace on earth instead of a day of doom and eternal judgment. They expected the rising glory of America to culminate in an era of good will for all the world in which the spirit of partisanship was unknown and men were united in a happy fellowship of commerce and prosperity.[1] Yet the men who dreamed these dreams not only engaged in civil war but quarreled so violently among themselves afterward that they established a pattern of political dissension which has survived

---

[1] Representative poems on the "rising glory of America" theme are: Philip Freneau and Hugh Henry Brackenridge, *The Rising Glory of America*, read at the Princeton commencement exercises of 1771; the poetic conclusion to John Trumbull's *Essay on the Use and Advantages of the Fine Arts* (New Haven, 1770); Timothy Dwight, *America, or a Poem on the Settlement of the British Colonies* (New Haven, 178-?); Joel Barlow, *The Vision of Columbus* (Hartford, 1787).

to the present day. One of the most striking contradictions evident to a student of the period is the contrast between an ideal of peace and the reality of a contentiousness so deeply rooted that it has had a lasting effect upon American culture.

Its dominant intellectual quality was that of enlightenment. From the time John Dickinson began writing his *Letters from a Farmer in Pennsylvania*, while Tom Paine appealed to the "Common Sense" of the colonists and wrote his later papers in the time of the "Crisis," during the Federalists' support of the Constitution, and through some of the best partisan writings of the last decade of the century, the most vigorous and often remembered literature of the period appealed to men who were willing to raise their minds above their immediate material interests and contemplate the effects of their acts upon the distant future. In the midst of passionate controversy many men were willing to profess a disinterested search for wisdom and make an appeal to rational judgments. Yet these seekers after the truth admitted the existence of three entirely different kinds of truth, disagreed over the relative values of each, and held contrary opinions concerning the way each type of truth could be achieved. Thus another striking contradiction of the time may be observed in the contrast between the widespread spirit of enlightenment and the lack of clarity in men's philosophical beliefs.

If any strain in the philosophical beliefs of the age can be designated as significantly new in the intellectual history of America, it is that of the revolt against empiricism. The great Mr. Locke had dominated the minds of Americans during the first half of the century, and his influence was pervasive in the second, instructing them in the ways of knowing, defining their political beliefs, and having a quiet but genuine effect upon their theories of education.[2] But by the end of the century few men were willing to accept his doctrines without reservations. In particular, they refused to believe that their minds were originally blank tablets on which experience and reflection impressed the sum total of their ideas. Instead, they welcomed arguments designed to prove that the great ideas by which man lived were derived from some source other than ex-

[2] For a summary of Locke's influence, see Merle Curti, "The Great Mr. Locke, America's Philosopher, 1783-1861," *Huntington Library Bulletin*, No. 11 (1937), pp. 107-151.

perience and were common to all people in all ages and in all lands. Yet they showed a peculiar intellectual susceptibility to the empirical forces of their own particular environment, and they were quick to bring abstract philosophical ideas to the judgment of experience and treat that as the final court of appeal. The sharp contradiction between their denial of empiricism and their persistently empirical habits of thinking provides a still further problem in the analysis of an age in which Americans acquired by experience and presented as realities certain attitudes and ideas which Europeans held in defiance of experience and later called "romantic."

Finally, the late eighteenth century was a period in which scores of young Americans, in the enthusiasm of their youth, directed their ambitions toward the creation of a new literature which would bear witness to the original genius of their new country. They read the latest works of criticism and designed great epics. They studied the best of the old and most of the new English poets and exhibited a sensitive recognition of the new interests which were to provide subject matter for the romantic revolution in English verse. Yet the products of their enthusiasm, study, and sensitivity are generally imitative in form, neoclassic in style, and deadly in their effect upon sensitive later readers. The contradiction implicit in a literature which was original in intent yet imitative in effect, romantic in substance yet neoclassic in form, is a fourth obstacle to the satisfactory description of this period in the conventional terminology of literary history.

In a sense, these contradictions are not very startling after all. To yearn for peace in the midst of contentiousness, to step high and wide upon flimsy philosophical stilts, to violate theory with practice, and to reach beyond one's grasp are all common characteristics of what we choose to call human nature; and they are to be found displayed in the total literature of any period in any country whose citizens were expressive enough to record the variety of their opinions. The late eighteenth century in America may appear chaotic only because it failed to produce any great literary landmarks which would serve as points of reference for a survey. Yet unless one subscribes to the eighteenth-century theory of original genius and the optimistic notion that "genius will out" in a sort of spiritual victory of mind over matter, some explanation must be sought in the conditions of the time for the peculiar contrast between this undefinable period and the age of dominant puritanism which preceded it and the age of formal romanticism which followed. Its literature, which should provide the clues to such an explanation, is relatively unknown; and much of the scholarship that has been devoted to it has been directed by points of view which are irreconcilable. Hence an effort to grapple with the period as a whole, especially to search for general causes, may be simple foolhardiness. But it should be possible to survey the ground and perhaps suggest a course for future—and more conclusive—investigations.

## II

First, with respect to the political controversies of the late eighteenth century, we can say with assurance that the American revolution was not an ideological revolution but a civil war of interests, although the warring factions, of course, used ideas as weapons of attack and defense. The great body of controversial literature preceding, including, and immediately following the Declaration of Independence was propaganda in the modern sense of the word,[3] ingeniously contrived to support causes whose opposition was deeply rooted in the principles of English mercantilism, the current financial difficulties of the United Kingdom, and the character of American society. The basic assumptions made by this propaganda and the fascination it exercised upon the minds of men after it had served its immediate purpose are matters of interest in another connection, but the division between Patriot and Tory was not a basic division in American life. If we are willing to forget—as most Americans have forgotten—the ruthless injustice of the proceedings, we may describe the division as a weeding-out process which disposed of certain interests and certain people in the colonies and cleared the way for the growth of a new political organization; and there is no very significant connection be-

[3] Carl L. Becker's *The Declaration of Independence* (New York, 1922) is of course the standard treatment of the background of that document. The Declaration, as a piece of propaganda, attempted to accomplish two purposes: announce a cause which would gain the united support of the colonies and transfer the charge of colonial oppression from Parliament to King.

tween the surviving toryism and the new controversies which arose after the war.

The dissension over the Articles of Confederation and the proposals for a new constitution is almost in the same category. It has been fashionable, of course, to speak of the Federalists of the eighties as conservatives, and in so much as the term recognizes their desire to conserve the fruits of victory by making a creative effort to hold the independence they had won, it gives a just description of them. Yet the more one examines the personalities and the motives involved in the constitutional controversy, the more one is struck by the fact that the quarrel was less between radical and conservative attitudes of mind than between people with different things to conserve. The politicians who had a good thing in the existing state organizations, the speculators who held state script rather than that issued by the Continental Congress, the titleholders of real property in states that were experiencing inflation, taxpayers in states that collected custom duties on their neighbors' imports, and others who had an interest vested in things as they were—these, rather than men who held to states' rights as a matter of principle or radical believers in the direct rule of the people, formed the body of the opposition to the Constitution. Many of the men who supported the Constitution had a material interest in a strong and well-established federal government, but the extent to which economic interests can be identified with conservative or radical states of mind is yet undetermined;[4] and it would be easily possible to challenge current notions with the theory that the founding fathers were, on the whole, a rather radical group in their willingness to make a drastic revision in the existing form of American government by establishing a republic on the large scale which theorists agreed was impossible and according to a federated scheme which was wholly novel.[5]

[4] There is a verbal trap involved in any attempt to discuss this question because the terms "radical" and "conservative," in America at least, are used indiscriminately with reference to a person's temperament and his alliance with certain economic or political interests. Unless their reference is clearly indicated, their use does not contribute to a clear analysis of this period.

[5] The conventional view of such standard political theorists of the eighteenth century as Montesquieu was that a republican form of government was suitable for such small countries as Switzerland and Holland but impracticable on a large scale.

In one respect, however, the debate over the Constitution did anticipate the later controversy which violated the principles of the humanistic movement of the late eighteenth century. The often-quoted remark by Alexander Hamilton that "Your people, Sir, are a great beast" and the insistence of John Adams upon the recognition of a "natural aristocracy" indicate a general distrust of the people which led to the establishment of a mixed rather than a democratic government for the new nation;[6] and the fear of mob rule, such as that recently exhibited by Shays's Rebellion in western Massachusetts, did affect the determination to draw up a constitution and the decision to ratify it. Yet it is commonplace to observe that the rights of the people were practically forgotten in the document itself; and when that oversight was generally recognized there was no serious objection to guaranteeing their liberties in a series of amendments. The rights of man were not an issue in the first Federalist and Anti-federalist controversy.

But no sooner had the Constitution been ratified than the rights of man did become an issue in America, and the fact that they did become a matter of serious controversy is the great contradiction between the last decade of the eighteenth century and the general tenor of the age. It was a result of the French rather than the American Revolution. At its beginning American sympathies, although somewhat divided, seem to have been generally on the side of the revolutionists, whose activities in resisting a tyrant ap-

---

[6] The term "Democracy" has become such an extraordinary shibboleth in the twentieth century that it seems necessary to emphasize the fact that the government conceived for the United States neither was nor was supposed to be a democracy. On the contrary, it followed the classic pattern of "mixed" government consisting of a supreme ruler and a group of representatives of the people with a semi-aristocratic body of legislators between the two. The provision for a periodic change of personnel in the executive and upper legislative branches of the government, of course, was a democratic modification of the English pattern which included a hereditary aristocracy and monarchy; and the later provision for the popular election of these officers represented at least a superficial movement in the direction of greater democracy. To a student of literature, however, who is accustomed to viewing books and institutions alike with reference to general patterns of thought, it would seem that the Supreme Court has usurped the nonrepresentative middle position which the Senate was originally designed to fill and, consequently, that the traditional "mixed" state is now better preserved in America than in England.

peared to be a continuation and a sort of justification of the principles expressed in the Declaration of Independence. The appearance of Edmund Burke's *Reflections on the Revolution in France*, however, put the upheaval in a different light by the use of highly emotional prose which directed attention to the wrongs done to the upper classes and especially succeeded in arousing sympathy for Marie Antoinette. A democratic reaction was immediate and vehement. Thomas Paine burst into print with the *Rights of Man* in a trenchant if intemperate attack upon Burke's references to "the swinish multitude." Joel Barlow of Connecticut, who was living in France at the time, followed with his *Advice to the Privileged Orders*—advice which he gave in anticipation of "a general revolution in the principle of government" that he thought would necessarily sweep over all Europe with an "irresistible" progress.[7] "It depends not on me, or Mr. Burke, or any other writer, or description of writers," he wrote, "to determine the question, whether a change of government shall take place, and extend through Europe. It depends on a much more important class of men, the class that cannot write; and in a great measure, on those who cannot read. It is to be decided by men who reason better without books, than we do with all the books in the world."[8] After this evaluation of "the swinish multitude" and their importance to social progress, Barlow found it easy to attack the overemphasis on property which sustained the privileged orders and denounce "those Draconian codes of criminal jurisprudence which enshrine the idol property in a bloody sanctuary, and teach the modern European, that his life is of less value than the shoes on his feet."[9] And refusing to recognize "the idol property" and the

---

[7] *Advice to the Privileged Orders in the Several States of Europe, Resulting from the Necessity and Propriety of a General Revolution in the Principle of Government* (Part I, London, 1792; Part II, Paris, 1793), reprinted in the *Political Writings of Joel Barlow* (New York, 1796), from which the following quotations are taken. See p. xvi. Charles D. Hazen, *Contemporary American Opinion of the French Revolution* (Baltimore, 1897), indicates the generally sympathetic attitude of Americans during the early stages of the revolution; and Eugene P. Link, *Democratic-Republican Societies, 1790-1800* (New York, 1942), surveys the growth of self-conscious democracy during the last decade of the century.

[8] *Political Writings*, p. xv.

[9] *Ibid.*, p. xi.

distinctions it conferred, he was able to look upon the human race as "beings so nearly equal in power and capacity," characterized by so many different abilities and subject to so many schemes of classification that the legal fiction of their equality could be adopted as a practical hypothesis to be used in considering the proper order of their relationship with each other.[10] The literal application of the principles of the Declaration of Independence, in short, was first advocated as a broad social philosophy after the beginning of the French Revolution and perhaps in reaction to the exaggerated distinctions drawn by Burke.

Both Paine and Barlow, however vehement they were in the language they applied to the upper classes, were essentially humanitarian in their books of 1791 and 1792 and were thus altogether in keeping with the prevailing sentiment of their century. But with the outbreak of the Reign of Terror humanity seemed determined to betray its advocates. Neither Barlow nor Paine, however, would admit the betrayal. Barlow had already presented a disillusioned view of democracy in *A Letter to the National Convention of France*, in which he maintained that "any people, whether virtuous or vicious, wise or ignorant, numerous or few, rich or poor, are the best judges of their own wants": "A republic of beavers or monkies," he declared, "could not be benefitted by receiving their laws from men, any more than men could be in being governed by them. If the Algerines or the Hindoos were asked to shake off the yoke of despotism, and adopt ideas of equal liberty, they would that moment be in a condition to frame a better government for themselves, than could be framed for them by the most learned statesmen in the world. If the great Mr. Locke, with all his wisdom and goodness, were to attempt the task, he would probably succeed as ill as he did in his constitution for the colony of South Carolina."[11]

Paine was more enthusiastic in his support of the principles of the Revolution, writing parts of his *Age of Reason* during the Terror and publishing it after his narrow escape from the guillotine. Both men were further disillusioned when the Jacobins (with whom they had trouble enough) were succeeded by Napoleon,

[10] *Ibid.*, pp. 21-22.
[11] *Ibid.*, p. 169.

but neither, although Barlow actually dwelt for a year and a half among the Algerines, changed his principles. Paine continued actively controversial so long as he could make himself heard, but Barlow after the turn of the century was more inclined to turn philosophical, defending his republicanism in a personal letter to a friend: "I wish to live in the error if it is one, and die in it. I am too old to examine reasons for discarding a system from which I have never yet deviated."[12]

The expressions of Joel Barlow may be taken as those of a well-informed, thoughtful, humanitarian republican of the late eighteenth century whose democratic philosophy was reflected in the political actions of Thomas Jefferson. It was not particularly romantic, although when he gave it poetic license, in his philosophical poem *The Columbiad*, it took on a romantic character in its optimistic view of the future.[13] Had the humanistic movement been kept on so thoughtful a plane, it might have aroused very little controversy in a country where most material interests were opposed to any participation in European conflicts. But that was not to be. Burke's *Reflections* was only the first of many writings to present the French Revolution as a conflict between the swinish multitude and the more sensitive classes; and when the Terror broke out, when the king and queen were beheaded, and the émigrés told their tales of creaking tumbrels and a thirst for blood which ranged from Paris to the Vendée, the "people" of France appeared far worse than swine. The shock of horror brought back to apparent life all the popular ghosts that haunted the American mind: the Calvinistic belief that the mass of mankind were predestined to the flames of hell because of their inherent wickedness, the memories of mob violence which had been so general during the American Revolution and which had survived during the trying years that followed, and the fear of the Indian on the frontier or of the frontiersman himself who was currently

---

[12] Letter to Stephen Jacobs of Windsor, Vermont, April 12, 1806, in the Barlow Papers in the Harvard University Library.
[13] Barlow's earlier version of *The Columbiad*, *The Vision of Columbus*, was also optimistic in its view of the future but it did not represent mankind as eventually achieving happiness in an ideal "state of nature." I have discussed the differences between the two poems at some length in *The Connecticut Wits* (Chicago, 1943), pp. 309-326.

making trouble in Western Pennsylvania. Even the difficulty of keeping a servant was cited in evidence of the untrustworthiness of mankind.[14]

The result of this hysteria was that the imaginations of many good men shut up like excited clams. They cherished the humanity of their immediate associates and closed their eyes to any human qualities that might exist in the rest of the human race. They quit thinking of the mass of mankind as a group of individuals and dehumanized them into mobs or factions. They put the writings of the republicans under a microscope which magnified every trace of romanticism into a wild fantasy, and they condemned the distorted images they observed as the creations of the visionary philosophers in the opposing camp. Timothy Dwight, in his first baccalaureate sermon as president of Yale College, exhibited the early stages of this reaction:

In this age of innovation, visionary philosophers have . . . discovered that men are naturally wise and good, prone to submit to good government, and pleased to have their passions and appetites restrained; and that all the errors and iniquities of our species are derived merely from the oppression of the privileged and the great. From these principles, adopted in defiance of every fact, they have drawn consequences repugnant to every reason, and fraught with every folly, danger, and mischief.

In an effort to counteract this dangerously fantastic view of mankind, he called upon Yale men to open their eyes:

*You* will find all men substantially alike, and all naturally ignorant, and wicked. You will find every man pleased, not merely to be free, but to tyrannize; and to indulge without restraint, and without degree, both appetite and passion; and to be impatient of every law, which in any degree restrains either.[15]

This was relatively restrained in comparison with the extremes to which ministers and politicians alike went during the hysteria which arose at the end of the century when excitement over the

[14] By Timothy Dwight to his Yale classes, according to a manuscript notebook kept by Joshua Leavitt and preserved in the Yale University Library. Dwight's sermons, *The True Means of Establishing Public Happiness* (New Haven, 1795) and *The Nature, and Danger of Infidel Philosophy* (New Haven, 1798) provide good examples of this type of reaction.

[15] *Sermons* (New Haven, 1828), pp. 303-304.

Bavarian Illuminati swept New England and a "philosopher" was represented as a bloodthirsty advocate of atheism, communism, and free love.[16] Thomas Jefferson, as both a philosopher and the head of the republican faction, still holds the record of being the most blackguarded president in American history.

### III

The justification for referring to the late eighteenth century in America as a period of enlightenment may be found in the distinctive unity of tone which characterized the great body of its literature—even literature dealing with such subjects as the war against England and the political controversies of the time. The most effective propagandists dealt with men as reasoning creatures, capable of abstracting general truths from their common experiences and able to draw lessons from history and take thought of the future. Tom Paine, writing during the revolutionary crisis which tried men's souls, appealed directly to this reasoning man when he told his story of the Tory parent at Amboy who asked for "peace in my day." Paine's comment was that "a generous parent would have said, 'If there must be trouble, let it be in my day, that my child may have peace'"; and he significantly added that "this single reflection, well applied, is sufficient to awaken every man to duty."[17] The same appeal to "reflection, well applied" is evident in the decision of the authors of the *Federalist* papers to avoid any attempt to stir the passions of their readers and in their successful production of a classic in rational political argument. The same attitude of mind is apparent in the little satiric essays Benjamin Franklin contributed to English newspapers just before the Revolution and in various writings of other sorts both before and after.[18] Numerous direct attempts to stir up passions, of course, were made; but a general desire for the light of

---

[16] For the excitement over the Illuminati, see Vernon Stauffer, *New England and the Bavarian Illuminati* (New York, 1918) and James K. Morse, *Jedidiah Morse: A Champion of New England Orthodoxy* (New York, 1939).

[17] *The Writings of Thomas Paine*, ed. M. D. Conway (New York, 1894-96), I, 174.

[18] These may be found in volume VI of *The Writings of Benjamin Franklin*, ed. Albert H. Smyth (New York, 1905).

rational truth was sufficiently widespread and is sufficiently evident to be called a characteristic of the age.

The source of this light, however, was not a matter of common agreement. Joel Barlow (who was unusually sensitive to the qualities of his time and able to sum them up in quotable language) recognized three kinds of commonly accepted truths—those that "are as perceptible when first presented to the mind as an age or world of experience could make them," those which require the proof of "indirect and collateral experience," and those which "demand experience direct and positive." Few of his contemporaries would have quarreled with his practical classification of truth as self-evident, rational, or scientific; but within this area of agreement they disagreed vigorously concerning aspects of life which should be controlled by these different types of truth, and some of them were violently opposed to Barlow's contention "that in morals" (a subject which, to his mind, certainly embraced politics and possibly religion) we happily "have much to do with this first class of truths," less to do with the second class, and "very little to do with the third."[19] Most people, including Barlow himself, were also puzzled as to why certain truths were self-evident; but, although they advanced various theories, they were not yet ready to quarrel about them.

The demand for "experience direct and positive" as proof for all scientific conclusions was almost unanimous. The period was marked by the establishment of numerous societies for the improvement of agriculture, medical associations for protection against quackery, and other organizations to promote scientific observations of various sorts;[20] and there was already evidence of a feeling, if not precisely a belief, that the only secure truth was that achieved by observation. Before the Revolution the formal extension of that attitude was perhaps best evidenced by the popularity of William Wollaston's little textbook of ethics, *The Religion of Nature Delineated*, which taught that the criterion of virtue was

[19] *Political Writings*, pp. iv-v.
[20] For a good recent account of such organizations, see Ralph S. Bates, *Scientific Societies in the United States* (New York, 1945). An invaluable contemporary source of information about the cultural activities of the time is Samuel Miller's *A Brief Retrospect of the Eighteenth Century* (2 vols.; New York, 1803).

"conformity to the truth of things as they are" and warned against the delusions implicit in empty words and phrases.[21] Wollaston's system of morality was ridiculed by Benjamin Franklin in his youth, by Jefferson in his old age,[22] and possibly by numerous others in between; but it affected the thinking of many graduates of Yale, where it was used as a textbook,[23] and Dr. Samuel Johnson of King's College made it the basis of his *Ethics* and gave a rhapsodic summary of it as an expression of "the Genius of English America."[24] It was the sort of system that would have a strong appeal to the conservative impulse in mankind, and during the last decade of the century, when people were tired of experimenting in politics and feared the spirit of innovation generally, some early students of Wollaston fell back into his way of thinking even though they no longer consciously followed his system and utilitarianism was beginning to provide a "realistic" morality.[25]

[21] The *Religion of Nature Delineated* was originally published in London in 1725 and went through seven editions by 1750.

[22] "Ridiculed" is perhaps too strong a term to apply to Franklin's attitude in view of the mild account he gives in the *Autobiography* of the way his *Dissertation on Liberty and Necessity, Pleasure and Pain* grew out of his work as typesetter for the second edition of Wollaston's book (*Writings*, I, 277). For Jefferson, see his letter to Thomas Law, June 13, 1814, in *The Writings of Thomas Jefferson*, ed. A. L. Bergh (Washington, 1903), XIV, 138-139.

[23] Cf. *The Connecticut Wits*, pp. 10-13, 26, 48.

[24] The full extent of Wollaston's influence upon Johnson has not been explored. Herbert W. Schneider (who was one of the original editors of Johnson's works) observes in *A History of American Philosophy* (New York, 1946), pp. 31-32: "In connection with Johnson's *Ethica*, the reader should refer to William Wollaston, *The Religion of Nature Delineated* (Glasgow, 1746), the significance of which as a source for Johnson's work escaped the editors of his writings." The first part of *Raphael, or the Genius of English America* (printed by the Schneiders from a manuscript dating from the early seventies) is little more than an abstract of Wollaston's major argument put into the form of a dialogue which Johnson describes as "A Rhapsody."

[25] Professor Merle Curti has in preparation, I believe, a study of utilitarianism in eighteenth-century America which should indicate the prevalence of the concept of "the greatest happiness for the greatest number" before it became commonplace through the extensive use of William Paley's *Moral Philosophy* as a textbook. I have been particularly struck by the attempts of a former follower of Wollaston to struggle with the new philosophy as they are revealed in Timothy Dwight's sermons preached to Yale students after 1795 and later published under the title *Theology: Explained and Defended*. Cf. *The Connecticut Wits*, pp. 364-365.

Whether its use was the cause or a symptom of a state of mind, it does illustrate the use of "experience direct and positive" in forming moral judgments.

The most unilluminating controversy of the period of enlightenment was that which dealt with the kind of truth which could be demonstrated by "indirect or collateral experience" or by the use of the reasoning process. Practically everybody professed a willingness to follow "reason" and very few people agreed concerning the distance they were willing to be led. In so much as reason was thought to consist of the power to draw simple inductions or inferences from observation and the ability to reach fairly obvious conclusions from commonly accepted premises, it was an altogether admirable faculty. As soon as it was extended beyond mere shrewdness, however, it was contemplated with varying degrees of suspicion. This was particularly true in matters of religion all during the period and of politics in the last decade of the century. The "New Light" followers of Jonathan Edwards, for example, aroused more antagonism among their fellow Calvinists who objected to their elaborate logical processes than they did among the liberals who objected to their doctrines: the second attempt at novel-writing in America was a satire upon them as "mathematical metaphysicians,"[26] and a conservative objection was raised to the teaching of Edwards's own treatise on the will at Yale on the grounds that Edwards's "Scheme, in proportion as it is admitted by any Mind," might make students atheists apparently by separating man from his creator by such a long chain of logical causation that God at a distance might come to look like Fate.[27] Only the fact that the New Light theologians and the nonintellectual churchgoers alike respected the Scriptures as the revealed word of

[26] This attempt by John Trumbull, like the earlier effort by Philip Freneau and Hugh Henry Brackenridge, was not published. It was written in 1772 and was evidently supposed to be entitled *The Mathematical Metaphysician*. Four complete chapters and a sketch of their continuation exist in manuscript in the Woodbridge Papers in the Burton Historical Collection of the Detroit Public Library, and the theologians satirized are Joseph Bellamy, Samuel Hopkins, Stephen West, George Beckwith, Jacob Green, John Smalley, and Nathaniel Whitaker.

[27] Chauncey Whittelsey to Ezra Stiles in June, 1768. Quoted in *The Connecticut Wits*, p. 28.

God, directly available to the eyes of every man, kept this criticism from being a serious one.

The deists, who insisted that reason was the *only* oracle of man, sacrificed the protection of reverence for the Scriptures and consequently aroused fears that their paths of speculative reason would lead men away from God entirely. In a strict sense, these fears were unjustified. Ethan Allen, the earliest of the outspoken deists in America, actually admitted proof of the existence of God from "a sense of dependency" and brought only "the object, nature or perfections" of the divine being within the "province of reason" or the "course of ratiocination on the succession of causes and events."[28] Allen's attitude, rather than Tom Paine's extreme statement that "the only idea man can affix to the name of God is that of a first cause,"[29] probably represents the customary deistic view; for Paine himself, reasoning from nature, usually affixed an idea of benevolence to the Deity. Yet both men were denounced by normally sensible people as atheists, and deism in general was confused with infidelity.[30] The deistic argument brought out none of the fine discrimination which characterized most religious discussion in early America. It was not an ordinary theological controversy.

The serious implications of the issue were moral.[31] The prevailing humanistic impulse which had been turning men's minds from theology to politics had at the same time been undermining the old time religion by identifying it with morality. Yet this morality was not "new." Benjamin Franklin, who summarized the eighteenth-century system of practical ethics in his *Autobiography*, retained almost all of the principles which John Cotton had outlined for the guidance of the Puritans a century and a half before, removing only the element of piety and the virtue of not trying to

---

[28] See Ethan Allen, *Reason the Only Oracle of Man* (1784), chap. I, sec. II, pp. 25, 28.

[29] *The Age of Reason*, in *Writings*, IV, 47.

[30] For illustrations of the prevalence of this attitude, see the works cited in notes 14, 16, and 33.

[31] Howard M. Jones has stressed the importance of considering American intellectual history of this period as a part of a moral tradition in his essay "The Drift to Liberalism in the American Eighteenth Century," reprinted in *Authority and the Individual* (Cambridge, 1937).

get ahead in the world.³² Most of the Ten Commandments continued to represent the basic moral principles upon which human relationships were founded, and the Christian ethic was still the highest ground on which good men could aspire to stand. There was a certain practical simplicity about the familiar moral commands which the Deists lost in their efforts to simplify theology into a universal religion, and the age, on the whole, preferred an agreement on how to behave toward one's fellow man to an agreement on the nature of God and on his mysterious ways to men. Although the closing years of the century saw an aggressive deistic movement, especially among some of the more enthusiastic republicans, the so-called "republican religion" was not a vital force in American history.³³ Speculative deism, like the New Light theology, came to America a half a century or more too late to be more than a fad. The age of enlightenment was not an age of intellectuality.

The widespread suspicion of the practical value of "indirect and collateral experience" gained by an extension of the reasoning process into the field of religion, even on the part of some men such as Franklin who enjoyed the intellectual exercise,³⁴ left a gap in human knowledge which self-evident truth was called upon to fill. Much of this knowledge, of course, was self-evident in the light

---

³² This can be made evident, I believe, by an analytic comparison of the thirteen practical virtues listed by Franklin in his *Autobiography* with the seven Puritan virtues treated by Cotton in his sermon in *The Way of Life* (London, 1641) reprinted in Perry Miller and Thomas Johnson, *The Puritans* (New York, 1938), pp. 319-327.

³³ This is probably not the view most generally held by scholars, but I believe that a careful investigation would prove that the relationship between the two major "liberal" religious movements of the time—deism and unitarianism—was analogical rather than historical. Neither of the two most comprehensive surveys of American deism, H. M. Morais, *Deism in Eighteenth-Century America* (New York, 1934), and G. A. Koch, *Republican Religion* (New York, 1933), indicates the aftereffects of the movement; and although Joseph Haroutunian, *Piety versus Moralism* (New York, 1932), properly relates "The Unitarian Revolt" to a humanitarian or moral impulse, he seems to imply (p. 179) a deistic connection and does not particularly emphasize the much stronger influence of universalism.

³⁴ Franklin, it may be recalled, discussed his own interests in speculative religion in his *Autobiography* but came to the conclusion that he would refrain from expressing his opinions in public because such doctrines might be true but were not very useful.

of the habitual opinions and observations of mankind; but there was a conscious and general belief that there was some direct road toward genuine truth—particularly moral truth—which John Locke had not surveyed, and a comprehensive account of the groping efforts to discover this road would form one of the most complicated chapters in American intellectual history. Some outline of it, however, may be possible.

In the first place, there was a distinct Platonic element in Christianity itself, and this Platonic quality was emphasized by the pietism of the devout early settlers and a number of later ministers.[35] It probably survived as an unobtrusive reality in almost every church congregation, it was formally taught by the Quakers, and it appeared in a crude but very popular form in the evangelical movement. It consisted of an extrarational perception of the excellence of God as revealed by an inner light or to an inner sense. Only a fine line could be drawn between it, in its cruder manifestations, and the emotionalism characteristic of the religious revivals;[36] but such a line was drawn, and a person who possessed this inner perception of God's excellence usually professed to experience a personal revelation of God's will. The personal revelation was, of course, a "self-evident truth"; and in so much as it applied to individual moral actions its dictates were generally respected even by people who might have been skeptical concerning their source, for the belief in self-evident truth was so much more widespread than was any agreement concerning its source that people in general could not be greatly intolerant.

In the second place, there existed a similar Platonic tradition which was nonpietistic in that it was not concerned with the excellences of God but with ideas of goodness and beauty. Its most popular advocate in early eighteenth-century England had been Francis Hutcheson, and it was actively supported, in the latter part of the century, by Dr. Richard Price, whose sympathy with both the American and the French Revolution attracted favorable

---

[35] Schneider, *op. cit.*, places a considerable amount of emphasis upon the pietistic element in American philosophy.

[36] Oliver W. Elsbree's chapter on "The Second Great Awakening" in his *Rise of the Missionary Spirit in America, 1790-1815* (Williamsport, Penn., 1928) surveys the religious revivals of this period.

attention to his writings.³⁷ This tradition insisted upon the existence of an inner "sense" which spontaneously distinguished between beauty and ugliness or right and wrong and thus made aesthetic and moral truth as self-evident as the axioms in mathematics. Hutcheson is known to have directly influenced Jonathan Edwards, who found philosophical support to his pietism in *An Inquiry into the Original of Our Ideas of Beauty and Virtue*, and his followers.³⁸ But the effect of this tradition upon the lay thought of America has not been studied. Hutcheson's influence was probably considerable, and Dr. Price's certainly was. Something of this tradition, derived from Cudworth and others, may be found in Samuel Johnson's reference to "a kind of intellectual light within us" which was "a medium of knowledge" enabling man to perceive objects in their various relations and which he attributed to "the universal presence and action of the Deity."³⁹ But it is possible to distinguish between this and the pietism of Edwards only by a knowledge of the author's personality, and it is difficult if not impossible to disengage certain strains of eighteenth-century thought from the direct influence of various classical writers. From the opening pages of Euclid's geometry, too, came an incalcuable impression of self-evident truth which was fixed in the minds of every educated person.

The most important intellectual development of this sort in late eighteenth-century America, however, was the spread of the Scottish "Common Sense" philosophy which was a part of the Hutcheson tradition but which presented the notion of an inner sense in systematic opposition to the empiricism of John Locke and the skepticism which David Hume derived from it. The early writers

---

³⁷ Dr. Price is another important individual whose influence in America has not been adequately studied, although Herbert Schneider, *op. cit.*, p. 63, quotes Dr. William Ellery Channing as having said that Price had saved him from Locke's philosophy by giving him the "Platonic doctrine of ideas" and that Price's Dissertations "probably, moulded my philosophy into the form it has always retained, and opened my mind into the transcendental depth." Advertisements for Price's books appeared with some frequency in American newspapers, and he seems to have been generally admired by young Americans such as Joel Barlow who shared his political views.

³⁸ Schneider, *op. cit.*, p. 13.

³⁹ See paragraphs 13 ("Of Intellectual Light or Intuitive Evidence") and 14 ("Whence it is Derived") in chap. i of Johnson's *Elementa Philosophica*.

of this school who were widely read in America were Thomas Reid, who made a formal academic system of this philosophy, and two popularizers: Sir James Beattie, who dealt with the moral sense in his *Essay on the Nature and Immutability of Truth in Opposition to Sophistry and Scepticism,* and Henry Home, Lord Kames, who considered both the moral and the aesthetic sense in his *Elements of Criticism.* The books by Beattie and Kames were widely advertised in American newspapers, and, although the *Elements of Criticism* was used for a short time as a textbook at Yale, they made their impressions primarily upon individual readers.[40] Reid's influence was exerted through the universities—especially at Princeton under President John Witherspoon and perhaps somewhat indirectly at Pennsylvania through the stimulus of Dr. Benjamin Rush, although the Harvard students of Professor David Tappan may have been introduced to Reid as well as to Hutcheson and Price.[41] Both Kames and Beattie went far beyond Reid in the extension of their philosophy into the everyday affairs of life, but all three agreed in denying Locke's contention that the mind was

---

[40] Most of my first-hand observations concerning the influence of Beattie and Kames upon individual writers are set forth and indexed in *The Connecticut Wits,* although I made no attempt there to record the numerous indications of their popularity in the advertisements of books in eighteenth-century newspapers or in the successive editions of Kames's *Elements.* Professor Gilbert Chinard, I believe, was the first scholar to call attention to Kames's ideas in America after the period of Jonathan Edwards. See his monograph, *The Commonplace Book of Thomas Jefferson* (Baltimore, 1926), pp. 16-19.

[41] The importance of the Scottish Common Sense philosophy in America was stressed by James McCosh in the opening pages of his *Realistic Philosophy* (2 vols.; London, 1887) and re-emphasized by I. Woodbridge Riley in *American Philosophy: The Early Schools* (New York, 1907) and in *American Thought from Puritanism to Pragmatism and Beyond* (New York, 1915), but their attention was largely directed toward Princeton and went into little detail concerning its appearance in the eighteenth century. Howard M. Jones, in the essay cited above, has suggested its relevance to the study of the thought of the earlier period; Paul R. Anderson and Max H. Fisch, *Philosophy in America* (New York, 1939), p. 158, refer to the Common Sense epistomology found in James Wilson's lectures on law at the College of Philadelphia in 1790-1791, and also (p. 272) to Rush's acquaintance with the Scottish philosophy in Edinburgh; and Schneider, *op. cit.,* p. 63, has some suggestive comments upon Professor David Tappan and his influence at Harvard. The entire matter, however, has by no means been adequately studied.

a *tabula rasa* on which ideas were formed by the impressions of sensation and reflection and in asserting that every individual possessed an inner perceptive "sense" which Locke did not recognize. Because the ideas—especially the moral ideas—perceived by this sense were common to all men in all environments in all ages, the sense was called a "Common Sense"; and the Scottish school of philosophy derived its eighteenth-century name from this term.

By means of this "Common Sense"—actually in Lord Kames's intellectually weak version of it—such radically different individuals as Thomas Jefferson and the ultra conservative John Trumbull perceived the self-evident truths on which they based their contradictory responses to the world around them. It was a popular philosophy because it enabled almost everybody to avoid the compulsion to speculate in those regions in which speculative reasoning appeared futile or, for one reason or another, undesirable. The academic philosophers used it to oppose Bishop Berkeley's Idealism and consequently gave it an alternative label of "Scottish Realism."[42] The young Jefferson used it in politics. Young men of letters, such as John Trumbull, used it to justify their critical opinions and social satire; and others, such as Timothy Dwight, used it to guide their poetic descriptions of natural scenery.[43] But primarily the inner sense was a moral sense, and Joel Barlow was speaking quite correctly for his time in saying that in morals men had mostly to do with truths which were "as perceptible when first presented to the mind as age or world of experience could make them." That these "truths" were actually not common to all men or to the same men at different times—especially when questions of morals were extended to include politics—seemed to make little difference to anybody. In the Scottish Common Sense the age of enlightenment found a philosophy which was acceptable in some respects to its best minds and also teachable to under-

---

[42] Both McCosh and Riley emphasized the importance of the Scottish philosophy with reference to its theory of being rather than its theory of knowledge, and their view of its academic significance is echoed by Schneider in his chapter on "Scottish Common Sense as American Realism," *op. cit.*, pp. 264 ff., although Schneider's treatment of the school is better balanced than that of his predecessors.

[43] See *The Connecticut Wits*, pp. 48-50, 55-56, 91-92, 95-97.

graduates. It should be needless to observe that the light of this philosophy was rather dim.

These three paths—that of pious communion with the divine being, that of neoplatonic intuition, and that of a formally defined common sense—were the major intellectual ways to self-evident truth in late eighteenth-century America. There was also a fourth way which led obscurely through the emotions. Less seems to be known about this than about any other aspect of American intellectual history. The notion that human beings were naturally benevolent, of course, had long been preached in opposition to Calvinistic theories of human nature;[44] and the belief that virtue depended upon benevolent feelings, whether natural or acquired, was widely held. Even Calvinistic preachers were given to appeals to the "affections," and the recent revival of classical rhetoric placed a considerable emphasis upon the power to persuade by arousing the passions.[45] It is not necessary to cite such gross and violent stimulants as religious revivals and controversial bitterness in order to demonstrate that emotion played an important and generally recognized part in influencing men's minds. Whether it was a recognized source of knowledge, however, is another question.

The crux of the problem lies in the matter of which was supposed to exist first—the moral idea or the moral sentiment? In such lines of thought as Christian pietism and the Hutcheson tradition, in which a Platonic strain is clear, the answer obviously must be that all feelings are necessarily responses to pre-existent ideas. The same must be said of the Scottish philosophy, particularly after it was further systematized at the end of the century by Reid's leading disciple Dugald Stewart. Although these certainly represented the dominant attitude of what might be called, for the sake of convenience, the American mind of this period, there was

[44] This is demonstrated by Ronald S. Crane in his very suggestive article, "Suggestions toward a Genealogy of the 'Man of Feeling,'" *ELH*, I (1934), 205-230.

[45] One of the major studies yet to be made of this period, in both English and American literature, will deal with the effect of the return to pure classic (as opposed to neoclassic) rhetoric upon literature. In *The Connecticut Wits*, pp. 31-32, 120-122, 130-131, I have touched upon it briefly in connection with John Ward's *System of Oratory* (London, 1759) and its effect upon the poetic imagery of David Humphreys.

also abroad a somewhat tentative belief that the feelings were a source rather than a response to moral ideas. To a historian of ethics this might appear to represent a modified Aristotelian revival,[46] but in its broader cultural context it appears to be a belief that emerged from the decadence of sentimentalism during the last part of the eighteenth century.

For with Laurence Sterne and his American followers—especially among the novelists—sentimentalism had degenerated into an entirely artificial thing which had no connection with morality but took its emotion neat and cultivated tears for their own sake.[47] In doing so, however, it practically abandoned and therefore left in a state of intellectual semirespectability Shaftesbury's consideration of the feelings as a source of moral ideas which were merely shaped and made communicable by the mind. This notion may have been picked up by a few thoughtful Americans directly from Shaftesbury, whose *Characteristics* was regularly advertised by booksellers, or it may have been derived from some critics of the Scottish philosophy who thought that the Edinburgh classification of the moral sense as an "intellectual power" deprived it of any motive power in affecting human actions.[48] From whatever origins this view of the feelings was derived, it received support from an unexpected quarter at the end of the century when those

---

[46] In its English environment it seems to be so considered by C. E. M. Joad. See his *Guide to the Philosophy of Morals and Politics* (London, 1938), pp. 110, 241, 282.

[47] James Russell Lowell's essay "Rousseau and the Sentimentalists," from which these phrases are adapted, is an unusually interesting document in the history of sentimentalism because its distinction between active "sentiment" and inactive "sentimentalism" exemplifies a vigorous nineteenth-century antagonism between two attitudes toward the emotions which Crane (in the article cited above) found combined in the seventeenth-century latitudinarian divines. Herbert Brown's *The Sentimental Novel in America, 1789-1860* (Durham, N. C., 1940) provides adequate illustrations of the fruitless sentimentalism of the novelist, but the influence of Sterne in America has not been studied. Edward Niles Hooker's "Humour in the Age of Pope," *Huntington Library Quarterly*, XI (August, 1948), 361-385, brilliantly indicates the significance of Sterne in the broad pattern of eighteenth-century thought.

[48] I do not know enough about contemporary criticism of the Scottish philosophers to cite evidence in support of this suggestion, but it is the major point of Sir James Mackintosh's criticism of Dugald Stewart, and I am sure that Sir James did not think that up all by himself.

Americans who had been reading the French philosophers began to advocate the theory that man was by nature neither good nor evil but would naturally gravitate toward a condition of social welfare if he could be once freed from the superstitions and restraints of the existing society. There was a certain resemblance between Shaftesbury's Will of Nature and the Law of Nature taught by Holbach and Volney and also a quality of self-determinism implicit in each. The converging of deistic sentimentalism and atheistic materialism into a single road to self-evident truth is not the least of the ironies of this age of contradictions.[49]

IV

The formal significance of this search for self-evident truth, in American intellectual history, is that it marked the beginning of a widespread revolt against the empiricism of John Locke and thus prepared the way for the Transcendentalists and the emotionalists of the nineteenth century. For American Transcendentalism was to owe a great deal both to the pietistic and to the nonreligious Platonic tradition; and it was to grow out of Harvard College, where such students as Emerson and Thoreau were formally instructed in the Scottish philosophy of Dugald Stewart in order that they might write an essay on Locke's *Human Understanding* which would criticize his handling of certain "controverted points."[50] Although the Transcendentalists were to receive their immediate inspiration from Coleridge, Carlyle, and the Germans, they had their

---

[49] Max Savelle, *Seeds of Liberty* (New York, 1948), p. 171, suggests that materialism was a logical conclusion of deism, but it seems to me that, in this period in America, English deism and French atheistic materialism were entirely independent lines of thought which happened to coincide in so much as each released man from the particular determinations of a divine being. Dr. Benjamin Rush's interest in the material causes of mental states may have some relevance here; but, while recognizing his importance, I am not sure of precisely how or even whether he should be fitted into the pattern of this discussion.

[50] For the importance of the Scottish philosophy in the Harvard curriculum during the period of Emerson and Thoreau, see Edgeley W. Todd, "Philosophical Ideas at Harvard College, 1817-1837," *New England Quarterly*, XVI (March, 1943), 63-90; Merrell R. Davis, "Emerson's 'Reason' and the Scottish Philosophers," *ibid.*, XVII (June, 1944), 209-228; and Joseph Kwiat, "Thoreau's Philosophical Apprenticeship," *ibid.*, XVIII (March, 1945), 51-69.

cultural roots in eighteenth-century America, as also did James Russell Lowell, who derived his belief that "all thought begins in feeling" most directly from Sir James Mackintosh.[51] This does not mean that the intellectual theories of Locke were dying out during the period following the American Revolution. In fact, there is evidence that they were beginning to experience a revival after a period of distrust aroused by the "skepticism" of his follower David Hume and by the "immaterialism" of Bishop Berkeley which had reputedly flourished at Princeton until it was stamped out by Witherspoon and had certainly influenced Samuel Johnson of King's College.[52] Locke's *Essay* continued to be the standard textbook of "mental science" and was taught to an increasing number of college students. The new popular life given to empiricism, however, was supplied by the associationist psychology of David Hartley; and although one American poet seems to have adopted that psychology, the theories of Hartley did not become prevalent in America until Dugald Stewart had partially reconciled them with the Common Sense philosophy and until the influence of Hartley's followers, Joseph Priestley in science and Archibald Alison in aesthetics, began to be evident in the early years of the new century.[53]

While the prevailing attitude of late eighteenth-century Amer-

[51] The stanza containing this statement was interpolated by Lowell in a revised verson of "An Incident in a Railroad Car," apparently from a desire to clarify the philosophical implications of the poem—implications which are in accord with Mackintosh's *A General View of the Progress of Ethical Philosophy*, which he was required to study at the end of his senior year at college.

[52] See Schneider, *op. cit.*, pp. 21-26.

[53] The poet was Thomas Odiorne, whose blank verse poem dealing with the relationship of man and nature, "The Progress of Refinement," I have discussed in an article, "Thomas Odiorne: An American Predecessor of Wordsworth," *American Literature*, X (Jan., 1939), 417-436. The importance of the associationist psychology in early nineteenth-century America has been generally recognized since the publication of William Charvat's *American Critical Thought: 1810-1835* (Philadelphia, 1936); and a good illustration of the breadth of its effect may be found in Robert E. Streeter's "Association Psychology and Literary Nationalism in the *North American Review*, 1815-1825," *American Literature*, XVII (Nov., 1945), 243-254. Dr. Benjamin Rush, in his recently published *Letters* (Princeton, 1951), speaks of himself as having also "long been a disciple of Dr. Hartley" (p. 780, and cf. pp. 783, 953-954, 957).

ica was, in theory, one of serious reservations toward Locke's empirical system of knowledge, a vigorous empiricism was perhaps the outstanding practical characteristic of the general state of mind at this time. However much some Americans may have liked to speculate on the nature of God and the perfectibility of man, they were all inclined to consider that truth demonstrated by "experience direct and positive" was more desirable; and they had no hesitancy in accepting it even when it violated the logic of their self-evident philosophy. One of the best illustrations of this is their widespread acceptance of the idea of progress. The men who saw ordered settlements where there had once been only forests, who were engaged in making new laws to secure their future prosperity, and who were creating a new kind of nation in defiance of precedent and political theory knew that society changed and observed that the change was usually for the better. Even so conservative a character as Timothy Dwight, touring New England and observing with satisfaction that there was not a single log cabin in the state of Connecticut, believed that society was improving and looked forward to the time when the unprincipled pioneers of Vermont would acquire enough property to fix them in the ways of morality and perhaps make them religious men.[54] In Pennsylvania Dr. Benjamin Rush surveyed "the progress of population, agriculture, manners, and government" on the frontier and not only outlined the stages by which civilization advanced in his own state but commented upon the superiority of its method of advance over the old European method of conquest.[55] Poets in all sections of the country rushed into print to imitate and answer Alexander Pope's *Essay on Man*, and the invariable burden of their reply was that "whatever is," is to be made better.[56] Liberal and conservative agreed that their children's world would be bet-

[54] *Travels in New-England and New-York* (New Haven, 1822-1823), II, 462-463. A substantial part of the book is made up of notes on travels during the last five years of the eighteenth century.

[55] The survey was published in his *Essays, Literary, Moral and Philosophical* (Philadelphia, 1798).

[56] A survey of the imitative answers to *An Essay on Man* from 1760 to 1825 indicates that before the close of the Revolution American poets seem to have feared Pope's rationalism and that afterwards they objected to his acceptance of things as they were and therefore "corrected" him by advancing the idea of progress.

ter than their own: their own quarrel was over the manner and speed with which improvement would come. Some had more active imaginations than others and were willing to look farther into the future, but the ordinary American did not need imagination to grasp the idea of progress. If he had a memory span of a few years or an opportunity to travel about the country, he could observe it.

Although this idea of progress was so vague that it held within it the possibility of several definitions, it implicitly contradicted the concept of unchanging and unchangeable human nature which lay back of the "Common Sense" philosophy. In the next century, of course, this contradiction was to be recognized, and a division was to occur between the socially minded people who wanted to improve human nature by reforming its material environment and the Transcendentalists, who held that individuals could be brought to a better realization of their capabilities within the limits of their unchangeable nature and of a society which never advanced. But in the age of enlightenment implicit logical contradictions were not disturbing. Whether progress was self-deterministic, resulting in a sort of heaven on earth which the followers of some French philosophers considered an ideal "state of nature," or whether it was teleological, resulting in a millennium planned in advance by God's will, was a relatively minor issue of dispute which was brought into prominence only when it was connected with some other quarrel. Americans generally agreed, on empirical grounds, upon an important concept which had a vital effect upon their lives and thoughts a generation before it was widely grasped in Europe, where it was perhaps more prevalent as a romantic than as a realistic idea.

Another striking example of the appearance of Old World romanticism as New World realism may be found in the literary situation of the American Indian. It is true that to the Puritans the native savage was generally a child of the devil to whom missionaries were sent more in the hope of improving his disposition than in the expectation of saving his soul, and to the readers of captivity narratives throughout the United States at the end of the eighteenth century he played a bloodthirsty role which thrilled them because it was based upon the facts of Colonial and Revolu-

## THE LATE EIGHTEENTH CENTURY

tionary history.[57] To the readers of newspapers he sometimes appeared as no more than a dirty, drunken beggar—as a one-eyed tawny character known as "Blind Sam" did when he wandered out of his local gutter and had a considerable social success in a Pennsylvania city where the "noble savage" had become fashionable.[58] None of these representations could be called entirely unrealistic, despite the fact that the captivity narratives were often American equivalents of the "Gothic" romance, yet none of them was a serious attempt to synthesize all the information available about the "man of America" into a general idea of the Indian. Such an attempt was made, however, by the philosophical historians of the New World[59] and by some of its more philosophical explorers, who were aware of the generalizations commonly made by European naturalists and historical writers and had put them to the test of their own observations and found them false. The remarks made by the distinguished French naturalist, Count Buffon, concerning the degeneracy of all the higher forms of life in the new world were echoed and exaggerated by his followers in both France and

[57] See Roy Harvey Pearce, "The Significance of the Captivity Narrative," *American Literature*, XIX (March, 1947), 1-20.

[58] Hugh Henry Brackenridge tells this story with considerable glee in an article on the Indian wars of 1792 which was reprinted in his *Gazette Publications* (Carlisle, Penn., 1806), pp. 93-102. His observation to the effect that "An Indian chief in the hands of a good interpreter and agent, is a more profitable property, than a tame bear or a lion presented for a show" indicates his skepticism of the "man of America" discovered by the historians and observers treated in the following paragraph. The same passage is interesting because of its reference (p. 100) to a man who had "his brain turned with Jean Jacques Rousseau's, and other rhapsodies"; for references to Rousseau are so rare, in comparison to allusions to other French philosophers, during this period that one suspects his supposed influence upon early American thought of being comparable to the astrological "influences" of the stars. Persons who divide their antipathies between Rousseau and the common people, however, would be difficult to convince on this point.

[59] Those who were particularly denounced by the "wicked wits" of Hartford in the *Anarchiad* were the Abbé Raynal, the Comte de Buffon, the Abbé de Pau, and William Robertson. The more formal reaction to these and to others has been surveyed by Ralph Norman Miller in an unpublished dissertation, "The Historians Discover America: A Study of American Historical Writing in the Eighteenth Century" (Northwestern University, 1946), to whom I am indebted for a number of references in this and the following paragraph.

England.[60] The Abbé Raynal thought the Indians were "a species of men degraded and degenerated in their natural constitution, in their stature, in their way of life, and in their understandings";[61] and Lord Kames sometimes maintained that their notorious lack of sexual passion was an indication that they had degenerated into "a separate race."[62] Agreeing with Montesquieu concerning the influence of climate upon men and their institutions, most of these writers assumed that the European settlers (and the livestock brought with them) were subject to the same degenerative influences; and the assumption soon spread so far from the intellectual circles of its origin that in 1775 a British general boasted "that with a thousand British grenadiers, he would undertake to go from one end of America to the other, and geld all the males, partly by force and partly by a little coaxing." "It is plain," remarked Benjamin Franklin, who was an interested listener, "he took us for a species of animals very little superior to brutes."[63]

Such mistakes were intolerable to thoughtful and observant Americans, who were willing to argue with British generals with their swords but took up their pens against the naturalists and historians. First, however, they collected evidence. And from their evidence rather than from romantic dreams they drew their picture of the Indian who was, according to the researches of Jefferson,[64] eloquent in council, courageous in battle, and affectionate in his devotion to his family—whose constitution, according to the observations of the trader James Adair,[65] breathed liberty and equality

---

[60] Although Raynal perhaps aroused more antagonism in America, Buffon's position as a naturalist was such that his opinions carried more weight and provoked the most careful responses. For a consideration of one of the earliest of these, see Ruth Henline, "A Study of *Notes on the State of Virginia* as an Evidence of Jefferson's Reaction against the Theories of the French Naturalists," *Virginia Magazine of History and Biography*, LV (1947), 233-246.

[61] *A Philosophical and Political History of the Settlements and Trade of the Europeans in the East and West Indies* (Edinburgh, 1792), V, 246.

[62] *Sketches of the History of Man* (Edinburgh, 1788), I, 50.

[63] Miller, *op. cit.*, pp. 183-184, found this in the memoirs of Franklin quoted by Robert Walsh, Jr., in *An Appeal from the Judgments of Great Britain Respecting the United States of America* (Philadelphia, 1819), p. 192. Cf. also Walsh, pp. 189-190.

[64] *Notes on Virginia*, Query 6.

[65] *History of the American Indians* (London, 1775), pp. 406-407.

—and whose achievements, according to the poet Barlow and the historian Samuel Williams,[66] included the establishment of a monarchy more happy and benevolent than any before recorded in the history of unchristianized mankind. In short, they found or thought they found through observation a savage almost as noble as any developed in the European literary tradition which may have had a brief vogue in Philadelphia society but which generally had little effect in eighteenth-century America.

The fact that these and many other American writers evolved such reputedly romantic ideas as the idea of progress and the idea of the noble savage out of their own experiences in observation, research, and reflection indicates an empirical quality of mind which was so widespread that it was becoming a characteristic element in American literature. It existed simultaneously with an equally widespread willingness to accept something like intuitive perceptions of self-evident truth; and although there were inevitable conflicts implicit in these two attitudes, they did not develop upon purely philosophical grounds until the nineteenth century. In the eighteenth they may be found side by side, unreconciled, as another illustration of the curious contradictions of the period.

## v

The person who finds himself in the greatest difficulties of all in his attempts to generalize about this era in American life is the purely literary historian who tries to apply such terms as "romantic" and "neoclassic" to its expression in verse. Most students of English literature, if forced to give their acquiescence to a broad generalization, would agree that the Romantic period was one of revolt against heroic couplets and formal diction and of concern for such matters as physical nature, the nonclassical past, and freedom from the tyranny of a monarch and the privileged classes that support his throne. They might also want to add that it was a period of extraordinary respect for the imagination in which the poet's fancy

---

[66] See "A Dissertation on the Genius and Institutions of Manco Capac" in Barlow's *Vision of Columbus* (Hartford, 1787), pp. 77-91, and also Books II and III of the poem itself. Samuel Williams discusses the Incas in *The Natural and Civil History of Vermont* (Burlington, 1809), I, 243-249. The book was originally published in 1794.

was encouraged to roam in all sorts of unusual places from distant lands to the nooks and crannies of everyday life and be inspired with wonder at what it found there. Looking at the stiff and formal surface of most American verse at the same period, these students have often branded it as an age of neoclassicism representing the "cultural lag" of a new civilization behind its mother country.

Yet if one looks beneath this forbidding surface he may readily question whether the American versifiers were behind or ahead of their English contemporaries in their concern for literary matters which are generally considered romantic. There are more birds and beasts and plants, by actual count, in the early poems of Philip Freneau than in an equivalent amount of material from Wordsworth or Coleridge;[67] and a similar investigation would probably produce an even greater excess in the poems of Richard Alsop. Thomas Odiorne, who anticipated Wordsworth in his use of the associationist psychology of David Hartley, also anticipated him in using it to explain the delicate adjustment between the mind of man and his uncultivated natural surroundings.[68] Miscellaneous nature verse was common, ranging from Thomsonian odes and descriptive pieces on the seasons to more individual pieces such as sonnets to a violet or on a summer cloud, effusions to a spider or an owl, short descriptions of a mountain oak or a thunderstorm, and verses on the drumming of a partridge or on various rivers with Indian names strange to English poetry.[69] Timothy Dwight was reported to have introduced so many thunderstorms into his biblical epic, *The Conquest of Canaan*, that John Trumbull said he should supply every copy with a lightning rod, and David Humphreys included a glowing description of Ohio scenery in his poetic *Ad-*

[67] The count was made by Mr. Clifford B. May, of the Maine Township High School, Park Ridge, Illinois, and showed that while Wordsworth's fondness for pastoral terms placed him ahead of Freneau in the variety of his allusions to nature, broadly interpreted, the American poet led in the frequency of such allusions. Coleridge trailed them both.

[68] See "Thomas Odiorne: An American Predecessor of Wordsworth," *American Literature*, X (Jan., 1939), 417-436.

[69] For the specific examples of verse mentioned, see Joseph Lathrop, *A Miscellaneous Collection of Original Pieces* (Springfield, Mass., 1786); Samuel Low, *Poems* (New York, 1800); and Josias Lyndon Arnold, *Poems* (Providence, 1797).

*dress to the Armies of the United States.*[70] John Blair Linn, writing on "the powers of Genius" at the end of the century, was not at all exceptional in maintaining that genius found "a joy unknown" to lower minds in external nature and especially in

> the darkness of an aged wood,
> The ceaseless uproar of the restive flood,
> The sullen grandeur of the mountain's brow
> Which throws a shadow on the vales below.[71]

Nature was anything but an unusual theme in eighteenth-century American verse.

An interest in the nonclassical past was also common enough. Reports of the Ohio Mound Builders gave the "wicked wits" of Hartford, just after the Revolution, the framework for their satiric epic the *Anarchiad*.[72] The young Philip Freneau attempted a long narrative poem on Christopher Columbus,[73] and Joel Barlow made the story of Columbus, by the machinery of a vision, support his long narrative of American history including the story of the Incas of Peru. Although the use of Indian wars was mostly confined to the prose captivity narratives, Timothy Dwight wrote of the destruction of the Pequods in Spenserian stanzas,[74] and an anonymous "returned captive," two decades after the Revolution, gave the history of his own experiences in verse which included the legends he had heard of the pre-Indian inhabitants of the region about the falls of Louisville.[75] One epic and a number of shorter poems were written about the capture of Louisburg.[76] Before the Revolutionary War was over poets rushed its events into verse with all the eager-

---

[70] Cf. *The Connecticut Wits*, pp. 91-92, 95-96, 121.

[71] The *Powers of Genius* (Philadelphia, 1802), p. 94.

[72] The general title of this satire as published in the *New Haven Gazette and the Connecticut Magazine*, 1786-1788, was "American Antiquities."

[73] "The Pictures of Columbus, the Genoese." He also wrote a shorter poem, "Columbus to Ferdinand."

[74] *Greenfield Hill* (New York, 1794), pp. 93 ff.

[75] *The Returned Captive* (Hudson, N. Y., 1787).

[76] John Maylem's *The Conquest of Louisburg* (Boston, 1758) was at least designed to be epic-like, and Francis Hopkinson's "On the Late Successful Expedition against Louisbourg" is one of the shorter poems. See also Benjamin Y. Prime, *The Patriot Muse; or, Poems upon some of the Principal Events of the Late War* (London, 1746).

ness of men who had been starved for a proper literary diet and had at last found something which they could serve up to the satisfaction of themselves and of an expectant public. Much of their enthusiasm, of course, was an expression of patriotism. Some of it was evidently the result of a belief that America was at last in the process of acquiring a heroic history and a feeling of the need for heroic associations even before there developed an aesthetic which justified that feeling. Most of this search for a past was for something associated with the American continent or its English settlers and led no further afield than to the Protestant reformation and the Puritan migration or to the court of Queen Isabella; but, disregarding the many biblical poems which dealt with subjects more characteristic of the neoclassical period than the Romantic, both Freneau and Alsop wrote meditatively of the ruins of Egypt, there was some concern for Oriental antiquities, and numerous versifications of Ossian bore witness to interest aroused by supposedly Celtic history.[77]

Neither of these themes, however, produced any evidences of profound emotion on the part of the American poets who dealt with them. The emotion may have existed among men who lacked the talent to reveal it in a manner perceptible to modern readers, but it is more likely that it simply was not there. For external nature could not have the same emotional value to the country-born-and-bred American versifiers that it had to the city-dwelling poets of Great Britain. The young United States produced one imitator of Robert Burns and one of Robert Bloomfield in addition to the young poet whose literary interests anticipated those of Wordsworth.[78] But no American poet evidently turned or could turn to

[77] These were quite common. John Blair Linn's *Miscellaneous Works* (New York, 1795) included "Oithona" and "The Death of Cuthullin" done into heroic couplets; William Mumford versified six addresses and selections in his *Poems* (Richmond, 1798), pp. 107-146; and Josias L. Arnold had two in his *Poems* (Providence, 1797), pp. 36-37, 38-39. Freneau's "The Pyramids of Egypt" was written in 1769 and published in his *Poems* of 1786, and Richard Alsop's interest in Egyptian antiquities was displayed in *The Charms of Fancy* (New York, 1856), which was composed in 1788.

[78] The imitator of Burns was David Bruce, whose *Poems Chiefly in the Scottish Dialect* was published in Washington, Pennsylvania, in 1801. See Harry R. Warfel, "David Bruce: Federalist Poet of Western Pennsylvania," *Western Pennsylvania Historical Magazine*, VIII (July, Oct., 1925), nos. 3

nature as a genuine spiritual sanctuary which provided protection from world-weariness and a means of escape from the demands of ordinary life. Too many of them found their means of escape in town. Somewhat similarly, the fashion for turning to the past was also an artificial one for Americans who had little access to the history of their country, who had little conception of themselves as products of a historical process, and who were more inclined to think of themselves as the inventors of new institutions than as a new people. Although a number of historians were beginning to meditate upon the effect of America upon Americans, Crèvecoeur's essay "What Is an American?" represented the exceptional point of view of a man who was himself a foreigner and had traveled both widely and philosophically enough to be detached in some of his observations.[79] The poets had not, and the past to them was a curiosity rather than a continuity to which they themselves belonged. It was something they could contemplate with interest but not with emotion, and it consequently had the cold singularity of a historical exhibit rather than a rich vitality which they could explore with wonder. Americans were alert enough to contemporary interests to share the matter of English romanticism but were not able to be moved by it to an expression of individual emotion.

They were even less able to be moved—in the last decade of the century, at least—by the spirit of defiance against a tyrannical monarch and his supporters. Until the second year of their revolution they had been accustomed to addressing themselves to a king for protection against a tyrannical parliament in which they had no representation, and after the Revolution they had shown them-

---

and 4. Whether the anonymous poet whose work appeared in *The Untaught Bard* (New York, 1804) started as an imitator of Bloomfield is uncertain, for the preface suggests that the poems had been written some time before publication; but the title suggests "The Farmer's Boy," and the volume contains notes alluding to Bloomfield. In the first years of the nineteenth century, incidentally, there seems to have been some confusion as to whether Bloomfield or Wordsworth should be considered the founder of the new school of simple poetry and nature verse.

[79] Miller, *op. cit., passim*, indicates that an interest in the influence of the American environment upon the American character did not become unmistakably evident among the formal historians until the beginning of the revolutionary period.

selves more afraid of the tyranny of the mob than of their individual rulers. In the twelve years before 1776 and 1788 the king as a symbol of tyranny had been squeezed dry of its emotional value by propaganda based upon the Declaration of Independence, and their own ruler during most of following decade was their most respected hero who was very reserved in his grasp of power. The natural human antagonism to arbitrary force, which was so strongly exhibited by the English romantics, was consequently directed for a while against mob rule;[80] and although it produced some of the most vigorous verse in eighteenth-century America, it was not romantic verse. Later those who did versify for the democratic movement were so personally involved in the struggle that they were generally unable to see it in terms of other than personal issues.

Philip Freneau may serve to illustrate, in the experiences of one person, what happened to the romantic inclination during this period. As a young man in Princeton he possessed, to a rare degree, the roving imagination which was characteristic of the Romantic movement generally. As he described it in an undergraduate poem on "The Power of Fancy," it was a wakeful, vagrant, restless thing which had a quality of divinity in it and which led him through Europe, over Asia, into the South Seas and to the golden shore of California, and back into the past and abroad in the world of dreams. As he exhibited its operation in various youthful poems, he not only stood in awe and wonder before the ancient pyramids of Egypt and followed Christopher Columbus on his voyage to the New World but pursued Jonah into the belly of a whale and shared his sensations beneath the withered gourd, participated in the grief of Orpheus for his lost Eurydice, and prophesied the future glory of America—while incidentally, in a fragment of a novel, sending a character on a pilgrimage to Mecca. He revealed an interest in nature in his youthful work and after a visit to the West Indies in his early twenties developed a sensuous delight in it. All during his college years he had shown a concern for politics, taking an

[80] The best known expression of this is found in the *Anarchiad;* but attacks upon mobs were commonplace in the annual newsboys' addresses to their subscribers during the last twelve years of the century, in the newspapers generally, and in a substantial proportion of the volumes published by poetic Federalists.

active interest in the Whig cause and the American opposition to Great Britain. He readily accepted King George III as a symbol of tyranny, condemned the inhumanity of man to man as displayed on a British prison ship, and vigorously opposed Negro slavery. By most of the common criteria applied to the subject matter of verse he was a romantic poet.[81]

The concentration of his romantic interests appeared most definitely in "The House of Night"—a poem which looked back to Young's *Night Thoughts on Death* in its conception, to *Paradise Lost* in some of its diction and imagery, and to Gray's "Elegy" in form, yet forward for a generation or more in other elements of its subject matter. For if the poem were not dated its readers would suspect an imitation of Coleridge in the image of the black ship and the palace with the enchanted dome, of Keats in the unsnuffed candles glaring in the high chamber above the winding stairs, of Poe in the picture of Death seen through the infernal windows flaming red, of Browning in the rank and blighted garden where screams were heard from the distempered ground, and of Shelley in the winged allegories hovering about the head of a corpse and in the philosophy of mutability which substitutes physical change for death. Had "The House of Night" been written in England in 1777 it would have become an unusual document in literary history. During the decade which followed Freneau continued on his romantic career, writing of the sea and its winds, of the natural scenery in his native country and in Bermuda and the West Indies, translating a Scandinavian war song, describing the customs of the American Indians, paying tribute to the force of nature which stood between them and civilization, and even praising the mysticism of Emanuel Swedenborg.[82] Although most of his verse was in the

---

[81] The poems dealing with these subjects can be identified by title in Fred L. Pattee's edition of *The Poems of Philip Freneau* (Princeton, 1902-1907) and many of them may be found in Harry H. Clark's volume of selections (New York, 1929), which also contains an introduction discussing Freneau's romanticism. Clark treats Freneau as a transitional poet and observes the "apparent contradictions" in his work. For Freneau's fragment of a novel, see Lewis Leary, "Father Bombo's Pilgrimage," *Pennsylvania Magazine of History and Biography*, LXVI (Oct., 1942), 459-478.

[82] The revised title of the poem omits Swedenborg's name and appears as "On a Book called Unitarian Theology."

forms popular during the neoclassic period and his blank verse was generally Miltonic, these early poems provide abundant evidence of a genuine talent threatening, under the pressure of a new subject matter, to burst out into the idiom which we have come to consider characteristic of a later period.

Yet something happened to that talent. It had not developed fully according to its youthful promise during the eighties, and further development, except for some refinement of lyric expression perhaps, appears to have been suspended after the publication of a second edition of his poems in 1788. Freneau himself recognized that something was wrong and, like most of his verse-making contemporaries, blamed it on the American public, commenting without bitterness "that according to the common course of things, any particular nation or people must have arrived to, or rather passed, their meridian of opulence and refinement, before they consider the professors of the fine arts in any other light than a nuisance to the community."[83] He was not entirely right, for most original poets have been obliged to survive public indifference and critical antagonism. The reason why the romantic interests of the American poets did not find expression in their poetic idiom as well as in their subject matter must be sought elsewhere.

The most general reason was a lack of literary sophistication that the poets themselves shared with their readers. They knew the best of English poetry just as they were sensitively aware of the latest literary interests. The cultural level represented by a knowledge of the best that had been said and thought in English verse was, in fact, surprisingly high in the early United States. In a sense, it was too high. Americans knew and admired Pope and Thomson and Gray but did not know enough of their imitators to be bored by their conventions. Not being aware of how completely the florid style in verse had wilted, they were unable to appreciate the freshness of a new kind of expression. Like the later Hawthorne, Freneau undervalued his own artistic originality and failed to follow its guidance. Other poets, to a lesser degree, failed in the same way; and American verse of the late eighteenth century is full of anticipations of something new which somehow did not quite come off. There was

[83] From "Advice to Authors" (1788) as reprinted by Robert E. Spiller, *The Roots of National Culture* (New York, 1937), p. 359.

a cultural lag, if we must use the term, in the verbal though not in the intellectual sophistication of the United States; and the contrast between the two is partially responsible, at least, for the apparent contradiction to be seen in a poetry which was often neoclassic in tone and form yet implicitly romantic in its subject matter.

Another condition which affected the appearance of American verse, when surveyed as a whole, was the ease with which authors could be diverted from the purpose of self-expression or from any sort of inner motivation. The past which they considered a proper subject for literature was an immediate past. The experiences which the poet shared with the rest of the people in the new nation was a recent experience. The events that caused the most genuine excitement were current events. Such imagination as they were able to direct upon a substantial part of their subject matter had little time in which to work. The newspapers, which were their primary means of publication, encouraged hasty expression, and the vigorous controversies of the period stimulated the production of satire which agreed with the bias that every newspaper possessed. In particular, those poets who had what might be called a romantic temperament were caught up by the Jeffersonian movement in the last decade of the century and became active participants in its struggles, answering their conservative opponents in their own language and prizing a phrase that would cut to the quick more highly than one which would set thoughts to wandering through eternity. Freneau, whose literary energy was sustained for a generation after his romantic impulse was stabilized, is also a good illustration of this phenomenon; for the greater part of his later verse is directly concerned with the political controversy in which he was involved, and most of it is in the manner of the age in which personal satire flourished. The social conditions of late eighteenth-century America were like those of the times of Dryden and the Queen Anne wits, when political parties were in the process of forming in England; and despite the fact that much American verse contained romantic undertones a substantial amount of it was in the older spirit, thus encouraging, perhaps, an exaggerated estimate of the neoclassic tendencies of American writers as a whole.

The evidence, however, seems to sustain the observation that in formal literature, as in its humanism, in its enlightenment, and in its popular philosophical tendencies, the late eighteenth century in America was an age of curious but not entirely inexplicable contradictions.

## VI

Is it possible, after such an incomplete survey as this, to suggest even a hypothetical answer to the question of why these contradictions existed? The period was apparently one in which the humanistic impulse outgrew the imaginations of many men whose minds were formed under its influences and accordingly caused them to react strongly against it, thus causing a crystallization in politics of temperamental differences which still exist and are still expressed in the political division created at this time. Second, it was a period in which the spirit of enlightenment outran the rationalizations of formal philosophy and consequently left men groping for truth before a generally acceptable method of reaching it could be placed within their grasp. Third, it was a period of such intense practicality that people were more anxious to find simple solutions to their problems than intellectually coherent ones; and they accordingly had no hesitancy in applying a sort of intuitive common sense to matters of morals, which were fairly well settled by tradition, while using an empirical common sense to deal with ideas which were affected by the physical and social environment. Finally, it was a period in which the minds of literary men were sensitive to new fashions in subject matter but not sensitive enough to the decay of old fashions in poetic expression. The one generalization which seems justly applicable to all aspects of the age is that it was a period in which events were moving ahead of thought and the human mind was finding it unusually difficult to keep meditatively abreast with its practical activities.

Such a condition may have been advantageous to the establishment, in a spirit of compromise and under the pressure of necessity, of political institutions which must possess some kinship to the contradictions inherent in human nature in order to receive the mass assent necessary to their survival through successive generations. But it is not a condition favorable to the production of great literature which requires the reconciliation of many stimuli into one vigorous unity which gives a deep satisfaction to the individual who produces it and arouses a similar satisfaction in the individual who reads it. The proper conclusion for these observations, then, may be the rather commonplace suggestion that humane literature draws its enduring vitality from a quality of philosophical assurance which is novel enough to excite the mind of a talented writer yet is sufficiently familiar to be communicable to a fairly large number of readers.

This assurance may be of many sorts. When the importance of the people could be taken for granted, America could produce and appreciate the compact effectiveness of Lincoln's Gettysburg Address. When the eighteenth-century historians' notion of the American Indian was so well established that it could balance the wicked redskin of the captivity narrative, the "Leather-Stocking Tales" of James Fenimore Cooper were possible. When the intuitive road to truth became clearly visible to a man like Emerson, all the forces which went into the making of American Transcendentalism could be united in one literary movement. Or, on the other hand, when the road of observation and induction could be dispassionately followed, it became possible for an American writer to blend fantastic romance and psychological realism into the original artistic creations of Nathaniel Hawthorne. In a period closer to the eighteenth century, the acceptance of the associationist psychology in aesthetics made possible an increasingly natural treatment of the American past and the American scene in the early humorous prose of Washington Irving and in the serious verse of William Cullen Bryant. The achievement of American literature in the early nineteenth century was that of reconciling some of the conflicts that had arisen in the period before, and a genuine understanding of this achievement may be reached, perhaps, only through a recognition of some of the problems revealed in the less intrinsically interesting literature of the earlier "age of contradictions."

# The Decline of
# Neoclassicism
## 1801-1848

# The Decline of Neoclassicism
# 1801-1848

*M. F. HEISER*
THE STATE UNIVERSITY OF IOWA

I

THIS essay aims to explain, so far as space permits, the causes, immediate and underlying, for the gradual decline in America of what is called neoclassicism, from Dennie's Addisonian *Port Folio* (1801 ff.) through Cooper's Swiftian *Monikins* (1835) to Poe's Newtonian *Eureka* (1848). Professor Lovejoy has indicated that the neoclassical idea-complex is, in general, like deism, a part of a larger phenomenon in the history of ideas, the Enlightenment.[1] I should say that his characterization of the ideas associated with the Enlightenment in England and France applies in general to America with the qualification that in America neoclassical authors such as Dwight and Trumbull, and deists like Franklin and Paine, placed relatively little stress upon the ancient classics as literary models, and they were already more optimistically inclined to accept republicanism and the idea of progress. Certainly Americans, even in the eighteenth century, were much less inhibited by Old World social and economic caste systems—they were in a sense always a frontier people. And after 1765 they moved rapidly away from political dependence and thus became spokesmen for a somewhat antitraditional nationalism, which was another tendency

[1] A. O. Lovejoy, "The Parallel of Deism and Classicism," *Modern Philology*, XXIX (Feb., 1932), 281-299.

which differentiated them from British neoclassicists such as Dr. Johnson, in so far as they were devoted to traditionalism and universality. Granting, then, that neoclassicism may never have existed in full form in America, it reached its peak during the 1780's and '90's, and we are here concerned mainly with its fight for survival against ever-increasing odds and with the causes for its decline in the midst of an alien political and intellectual environment and new (or romantic?) European cultural influences.

However, the manifestations of neoclassicism in America, in whatever form, are clearly evident and are much more subject to definition than the manifestations of the various romanticisms which tended to succeed it in American literary history. Neoclassicism, in general, may be said to be a literary point of view and expression oriented in the direction of society rather than in the direction of the individual in society. This society, whether it existed or not in fact, is a construction of rational man which parallels in its enlightened standards the observed or supposed order, rule, and harmony of the universe—what the eighteenth century meant by Nature, things as they self-evidently are in general. In literature this order is found in the notorious "rules" derived from a classical body of writing which forms the base for the doctrine of imitation. The classical statement of neoclassicism is Pope's *Essay on Criticism*. In poetry, marked by an absence of the sonnet and informal lyric, the emphasis is upon urbane statement, upon correctness and ease, clarity and polish, upon wit and ethics rather than sublimity and pathos. The age is marked by conventional satire which presupposes an accepted social norm and a cultivated taste. In prose the moral and didactic essay strives for clarity, precision, perspicuity, good sense.[2]

In America the neoclassical idea that the proper study of man-

[2] For central statements of the nature of neoclassical theory and practice, see Alan D. McKillop, *English Literature from Dryden to Burns* (New York, 1948), pp. 170-173 and *passim;* Ronald S. Crane's discussion of "Neo-Classical Criticism" in Joseph Shipley (ed.), *Dictionary of World Literature* (New York, 1943), pp. 193-203; Walter Jackson Bate, *From Classic to Romantic* (Cambridge, Mass., 1946), chaps. i and ii and his incisive introductions to Dryden, Pope, and Johnson in *Criticism: The Basic Texts* (New York, 1952); and in America, William C. Charvat, *The Origins of American Critical Thought, 1810-1835* (Philadelphia, 1936), and Harry Hayden Clark's outline of "American Criticism to 1919" in Shipley, *op. cit.*, pp. 23-24.

kind is man, conceived of as a dualistic creature capable of virtue and reason but addicted to vice and folly and in need of discipline, received support and at the same time qualification in a Puritan, or ex-Puritan, country in which the stress upon morality, public and private, remained remarkably powerful. Puritans were little impressed with man's capacity for virtue and reason, except among the elect; the stress upon moral discipline was therefore perhaps even more marked than in England, further removed in time from Puritanism as a vital force in society. A corollary of this point of view is seen in the widespread acceptance in the America of this period of the neoclassical theory of the need for social subordination as a basis of ordered liberty (cf. Dr. Johnson). Such a theory received additional support among Puritans and Federalists in America after the frightening spectacle of equalitarianism run wild in Shays's Rebellion (1786-1787) and the Whisky Rebellion (1794) at home and the French Revolution abroad.

A historical commonplace, I suppose, has it that the early nineteenth century witnessed spectacular changes in the external and mechanical facts of life. The revolutions of the steam engine created, or promised, a change as dynamic as and more certain than that wrought by the American and French Revolutions. The gradual triumph of industrialism over agrarianism established a largely new social and cultural pattern. The winning of the West resulted in unlimited opportunities for the wealthy entrepreneur and the destitute small farmer alike. Horizons seemed everywhere expanding. If it appears that not enough emphasis is given here to the facts of sociopolitical history which the literature to a great extent mirrored, it is hoped that the reader will bear in mind that the present problem is not so much concerned with the contemporary observation of such facts as with the attitudes or mind-sets in which they were observed and the underlying reasons for those attitudes.[3]

Roughly speaking, the chronological configuration of neoclassical thought and expression in America may be indicated by three over-

[3] For historical orientation the reader is referred to the standard histories of the period, particularly the fine treatments of the "Age of Jackson" by the Schlesingers and others. A recent, well-written account of the everyday life of those key years is Robert E. Riegel's *Young America 1830-1840* (Norman, Oklahoma, 1949).

lapping circles, compressed between a lingering Puritanism largely hostile or indifferent to belles-lettres in the eighteenth century, and a new ferment, induced by revolution, the happily successful War of 1812, a firmly established and burgeoning democracy, and new romantic models, in the nineteenth century. The first circle contains writing neoclassical in form but not entirely so in its ideas. With the rise of belles-lettres in the eighteenth century, the verse forms of Butler, Pope, Thomson, Gray, Churchill, and Goldsmith were standard models, but the sentiments expressed by the American poets were still profoundly colored by bibliolatry, Calvinism, provincialism, and local or national interests. A good example is furnished by the writings of Timothy Dwight over a period of nearly fifty years. His master's thesis (1772) was a defense of the eloquence of the Scriptures as divinely inspired. With Trumbull and others he led the revolt against the study of the classical languages at Yale College. His "The Critics: A Fable" (written 1785) is an attack in Hudibrastic verse upon the limitations of the formal rules of criticism, and *The Triumph of Infidelity* (1788) is a theological, Edwardean *Dunciad*, denouncing many of the central tenets and figures of the Enlightenment. *Greenfield Hill* (1794), his best work, is a series of eulogies, in imitation of various English authors, of American village and rural life. As President of Yale College after 1796 he warned against infidel philosophy and Jeffersonianism, and refused to accept geological and other scientific evidence contrary to a literal interpretation of the Bible.[4]

The second circle, the central one, is neoclassical in form and thought. It encompasses Franklin and Paine, much of Freneau and Barlow, Brackenridge, Rush, the deists, Jefferson and early Unitarians, including *immigrés* like Priestley and Thomas Cooper. A typical figure is H. H. Brackenridge,[5] whose *Modern Chivalry*, written in installments between 1792 and 1815, is the most complete (800 pages) expression of the neoclassical spirit in the new nation.

Third, and most difficult to analyze, is the circle of writers whose

[4] See Leon Howard's excellent study, *The Connecticut Wits* (Chicago, 1943), especially pp. 79-111, 206-238, 342-401, and Charles E. Cuningham, *Timothy Dwight* (New York, 1942), stressing Dwight's career as president of Yale.

[5] For a study of Brackenridge, see Claude M. Newlin, *The Life and Writings of Hugh Henry Brackenridge* (Princeton, 1932).

sociopolitical ideas are readily identifiable with the Enlightenment (e.g., social solidarity, the property base, common sense, political liberalism), but whose literary forms and models either are no longer neoclassical or are not in conformity with the taste of the age. To point briefly to two examples: James Fenimore Cooper, writer of sentimental, historical, and frontier fiction, who, I believe, was in the main ideologically a man of the eighteenth century; and James Kirke Paulding, democrat and neoclassical critic of Scott who yielded to the hastily composed forms of sketch and short story, in spite of standards derived from Pope, Fielding, and Goldsmith. As America approached the end of the period under discussion, the clash between ideals of primitivism and progress is increasingly marked. Primitivism is no longer related to a classical golden age, but is either escape into a medieval past (the Scott vogue), sentimental and ineffectual lament for the vanishing American Indian (after the fashion of *The Last of the Mohicans*), praise of the wildness of nature (e.g., *Walden*), or search for Utopia (Melville and Charles W. Webber). The idea of progress [6] becomes by this time social progress and "manifest destiny" (the march of mind and the progress of public improvement). In its various aspects it means mercantile and industrial progress, progress through science (practical science), nationalism and belief in "the westward course of empire," reform movements (social romanticisms), equalitarianism, even for women (from Mary Wollstonecraft's *Vindication* . . . [1792] to Margaret Fuller's *Woman in the Nineteenth Century* [1845]). The idea of an ordered and rational progress, which is a kind of halfway station in the later Enlightenment, was modified by Jacksonian and frontier democracy in so far as these were anti-intellectual and chaotic.

No teacher or historian of literature who allows himself to speak of the differences in two consecutive periods or generations in terms of "convention and revolt" believes that he has thereby satisfactorily explained the course of literary history. He is aware of an evolutionary process; he knows that any generation, any decade, indeed any year, is to be characterized as being in transition. The state of American letters in 1848 was obviously different from that

[6] See A. A. Ekirch, *The Idea of Progress in America, 1815-1860* (New York, 1944).

of 1801. The task assumed in this chapter is the analysis not so much of the nature of the difference but of the movements or forces which caused the difference. But this is to be done in a special way. Assuming that the literary choir in 1801 sounded the clear note of neoclassicism, why is that note so faint nearly a half-century later? It may seem unnecessary to separate the causes for the decline of one movement from the causes for the rise of its successor. Nevertheless we shall be concerned with the movement away from the norms of 1801, rather than the movement toward the norms of 1848. How, and why, then, did neoclassicism decline after 1801?

## II

### FROM SOCIAL SOLIDARITY TO INDIVIDUALISM

Whatever else men of the Enlightenment believed in, or thought they believed in: the great norm of Nature, the position of man "Midway from nothing to the Deity," common sense, a fixed standard of taste, immutable laws of the universe, natural rights, the conviction that "whatever is, is right," the guiding power of reason —their thinking was dominated by the concept of social solidarity. They believed in society. They believed that the life of the individual takes its existence from the social norm and is bound by it. They held that human nature is everywhere and always the same. Their lives were moulded by conceptions of conformity to social ethics. Order was the first law of society as well as of heaven.

This does not mean that the enlightened man was always a confirmed conservative in politics, religion, and all other areas of human thought. Tom Paine was of the Enlightenment as well as Timothy Dwight, Jefferson as well as Hamilton and John Adams, Freneau as well as Fenno, if not more so. But they were not individualists. They held certain truths as self-evident, undebatable, true for you and me not as individuals but as Men in Society. We have no distinct rights of our own, but rights in common with all others as members of society.

Benjamin Franklin urged the unification of the British colonies in America in 1754 in the public interest. Not until 1775 did he begin to think of himself, or of anyone, as an American, and only then because his rights as a member of society were in jeopardy.

Tom Paine, in *Common Sense*, appealed to the self-interest of different groups of men, but he did it in the interest of the social whole. The *Federalist* essays were written to persuade reasonable men of the good of the whole under the Constitution. Classical, laissez-faire economics, although from our vantage point in history it may seem somewhat mystical, was a body of fixed laws not to be tampered with by self-aggrandizing individuals. It was not at all individualistic.

But there were two natural-rights traditions, both of the Enlightenment, in America as well as in England at the close of the eighteenth century. One, the conservative tradition, was based upon natural law and emphasized the necessity for institutions nicely adjusted to preserve the social framework which was the mirror of the harmonious framework of the physical universe. It emphasized the social contract, the property base essential for liberty, the system of checks and balances so skilfully worked into the American Constitution. The other, the radical tradition, was anti-institutional, primitivistic, a deductive assumption about the natural goodness of man. The two traditions can be seen clearly expressed in two Americans of the Enlightenment: Timothy Dwight and Philip Freneau. The former labeled natural goodness a "luscious lie"; the other believed that man, freed from the tyranny of corrupt institutions, could, by reason of his natural goodness, achieve a rational earthly millennium.[7] These two positions had their political counterparts in Federalism and Republicanism, or, not quite so accurately, Hamiltonianism and Jeffersonian Democracy. We shall discuss the declension of these two traditions, the more conservative one first.

Federalism died out rather early as an effective organized political force in America, but Federalistic ideas lingered on in several major writers of the first half of the nineteenth century. Timothy Dwight, President of Yale College, Federalist and defender of Edwardeanism in theology, is typical of the synthesis of conservative Calvinism and sociopolitical thought of the conservative wing of the En-

---

[7] *The Triumph of Infidelity* (1788), line 726 (Vernon L. Parrington, ed., *The Connecticut Wits*, New York, 1926, p. 271); Harry Hayden Clark (ed.), *Poems of Freneau* (New York, 1929), "On Mr. Paine's Rights of Man," pp. 124-125, and "On a Book Called Unitarian Theology," pp. 341-343. See, also, Barlow, *The Conspiracy of Kings* and *Advice to the Privileged Orders* (London, 1792).

lightenment. After 1800 he concerned himself chiefly with attacks upon "infidel philosophy," particularly that of the French Revolution, and with defense of the theological and social system of the tight little state of Connecticut. He advocated utilitarian education, equality of the sexes, abolition of slavery (on moral and utilitarian grounds rather than on the grounds of feeling), improvement of the social environment, religious toleration, and a stable agrarianism. He attacked deism, heterodoxy, perfectibility, natural goodness, primitivism, the conception of the noble savage, the frontier, faith in the judgment of the common man, and scientific theories contrary to the Scriptures. His Revolutionary patriotism and espousal of the cause of liberty were blunted by the course of the French Revolution and the triumph of Jeffersonianism.

In 1794, in *Greenfield Hill*, Dwight had put into verse his picture of the ideal society, village life in rural Connecticut, where in peace, harmony, prosperity, and sweet subordination, but freed from European feudal customs, men recognize that "happiness on laws depend[s]."[8]

Hugh Henry Brackenridge, although a liberal Jeffersonian in many respects, particularly in the defense of the principles of the French Revolution, pleaded the cause of the classical golden mean in his satirical survey of American social history from 1792 to 1815, *Modern Chivalry*. He was an ardent champion of the Constitution, English law, the checks and balances of Polybius and Plutarch, and he scorned frontier primitivism and the perfectibilian theories of "Walking Stewart." By "Modern Chivalry" Brackenridge means irrational democracy as well as the hereditary and propertied position of the paternalistic Federalists. Quixotism is the violation of the rational balance of society by an unenlightened and uneducated populace. Most important for our purposes the eight hundred pages of *Modern Chivalry* give a detailed picture of the beginnings of self-seeking individualism and leveling to the masses which were to supersede the conservative idea of social solidarity in nineteenth century America. Here is pictured, and satirized, one of the causes we are seeking.

Joseph Dennie, "the lay preacher," and editor (1801-1809) of the *Port Folio*, one of the first important literary periodicals of

[8] Vernon L. Parrington (ed.), *The Connecticut Wits*, p. 188.

## THE DECLINE OF NEOCLASSICISM

the century, continued throughout the administration of Jefferson the conservative, even reactionary, snobbery of a social class shocked and frightened by what Dennie regarded as an upstart, heretical, boisterous, free-thinking generation. He was openly contemptuous of democracy, French thought, and nationalism. His position, if not his nature and powers, is like that of Burke, essentially linked with the rights and privileges of property, suspicious of experiment and change, denying the mechanical nature of society and government.[9] And just as Burke with his organic principle and traditionalism in his revolt against the extension of the more radical principles of the Enlightenment prepared the way for the appearance and acceptance of Coleridge, Wordsworth, Scott, and the older romanticists of England,[10] so Dennie, thoroughly neoclassical as he was, was the first to recognize the worth of the *Lyrical Ballads* in this country,[11] seeing nothing in the volume to upset the established and beloved order of society. Conservatism became an unwitting bridge to something new in literature.

Washington Irving, who so remarkably left his literary impress upon the age, was essentially a Federalist. But the fine satire of Jefferson in Book IV of the *Knickerbocker History*, the engaging rural traditionalism of so much of the *Sketch Book* and *Bracebridge Hall* are offset by a reluctance, or an incapacity, on Irving's part to defend his principles through social criticism. In an age of tremendous social change Irving retired into antiquarianism; he became a legend hunter and a celebrity hunter. The charm of his style cast a nostalgic aura over a way of life recognizably no longer characteristic of his age.

---

[9] Dennie's ideas are set forth most clearly in his essays of *The Lay Preacher*, written between 1795 and 1801, and collected and edited most recently by Milton Ellis (New York: Scholars' Facsimiles and Reprints, 1943).

[10] For a study of Burke's influence in nineteenth-century England, see Alfred Cobban, *Edmund Burke and the Revolt against the Eighteenth Century* (New York, 1929).

[11] See Leon Howard, "Wordsworth in America," *Modern Language Notes*, XLVIII (June, 1933), 359-365. Dennie recognized the worth of the *Lyrical Ballads* soon after the volume appeared, first in his *Farmers' Museum*, then in the *Gazette of the United States*, Aug. 9, 1800, and upon several occasions in the *Port Folio* between 1801 and 1803. See I (June 13, 1801), 191.

Such is not the case with James Kirke Paulding and James Fenimore Cooper. Cooper is the archetype of the writer adhering inflexibly to fixed, inherited, and deeply felt social and political principles, in his case those of an eighteenth-century landed gentleman. He had little fixed literary theory.[12] This shortcoming allowed him to fall into the pattern of Scott's romantic fiction; he could follow effortlessly the romantic tradition in portrayal of character and use of historical and sentimental romance while insisting upon verisimilitude in situation and setting, and upon writing with didactic and social intent. His books successively proclaim the principles of American democracy as solidified in the document of the Constitution (to 1828), attack the violation of those principles under Jacksonian democracy and New England commercial "Whiggism" (1828-1841), and from then on subside into a resigned nostalgia for those principles which he regarded as lost. For example, he could defend laissez-faire economics in *Notions of the Americans* (1828),[13] but when party faction had in his opinion perverted rational democratic principles he could attack laissez faire in *Oak-Openings* (1848). His Federalism never changed. To place him with the Jacksonians is, it seems to me, to misread his use of the word "democrat."[14] Jacksonianism grows, through the substrata of elements of labor, the frontier, and small business, and the superstrata of theoretical, metaphysical equalitarianism, naturally out of Jeffersonianism; but Cooper's views, compounded of natural aristocracy and eighteenth-century Federalism, were to

---

[12] For aspects of Cooper's neoclassical literary theory, see his Preface to *The Pioneers*. He also discusses his literary theory in other prefaces, in his chapter "On Language" in *The American Democrat*, in Letter XXIII of *Notions of the Americans*, in his *Gleanings in Europe* (see index in the volumes on England and France edited by Robert E. Spiller), and in his review of Lockhart's *Life of Scott* in the *Knickerbocker Magazine*, XII (Oct., 1838), pp. 349-366.

[13] First edition, London, 1828, II, p. 448; Letter XXXVIII in the American edition of the same year.

[14] See Joseph L. Blau (ed.), *Social Theories of Jacksonian Democracy* (New York, 1947), Introduction, p. xv, on Cooper's attack on the "stake-in-society" principle. For orientation, see Joseph Dorfman's "The Jackson Wage-Earner Thesis," *American Historical Review*, LIV (Jan., 1949), 296-306. Cooper's economic ideas were much influenced by Henry C. Carey, as is shown by Harold Scudder, "Cooper's *The Crater*," *American Literature*, XIX (May, 1947), 109-126.

remain as fixed as John Marshall's. The whole movement of theoretical thought in eighteenth-century England (prior to Thomas Paine) lay behind his position, that movement which substituted the man of principle, of virtue, and of talents for the chivalric hero of feudal honor. Cooper's heroes represent a different ethic, that of conformity to natural law and Christian benevolence. The new order in America represented to him the achievement of the dignity of man, and its success proved man's rational ability in self-rule. His nationalism consists in steady devotion to these principles; his attacks upon American misrule are parallel to Burke's in *Reflections on the Revolution in France*. Neither can be properly accused of apostasy. Such a position justifies his statement that Scott is poisonous for Americans, for Scott returned to a glamourized feudalism abhorrent to Cooper's republican political ethics. Thus Leather-Stocking becomes the symbol for Cooper of the hero of virtue, the symbol of man's natural capabilities, compounded in part of Rousseau's nobleman and the ideal ethical representative of the American frontier.[15] But Cooper's social orientation remains aristocratic. In the conflict between Natty, a good man *out of* society, and Judge Temple, the good man *in* society, the judge inevitably wins. Each is in a doomed category, for Natty is in part representative of the more radical side of the Enlightenment, as Temple is of the more conservative, but Cooper sees that only *one* is doomed. Natty is what Temple would be were he not a gentleman. And the gentleman, like Burke's expert in government, is the agent of societal order, the card that steers the gale, in Pope's phrase. This is Cooper's position whether in *The Pioneers* (1823), *Notions of the Americans* (1828), *The Monikins* (1835),[16] *The American Democrat* (1838), the anti-rent trilogy (1845-1846), or *The Crater* (1847). He consistently upholds agrarian pursuits and land-holding as the only true

---

[15] This is essentially the point of view expressed in Dorothy Anne Dondore, *The Prairie and the Making of Middle America* (Cedar Rapids, Iowa, 1926). It will be remembered that Cooper, in the Preface to the *Leatherstocking Series*, says that Natty, as well as the Indian, is a poetic conception filled out by idealistic imagination. For background, see Helen T. Garrett, "The Imitation of the Ideal," *PMLA*, LXII (Sept., 1947), 735-744, where the idea is discussed as "the polemic of a dying classicism."

[16] *The Monikins*, in which Cooper also satirizes the stake-in-society theory, contains interesting parallels with Swift's *Gulliver*. See Willi Müller, *The Monikins von J. F. Cooper...* (Rostock, 1900).

source of wealth, against the sordid commercialism and industrialism of his day. But such tenets were doomed in America. When understood, he was sharply criticized. Social ideas could be ignored in his fiction, yet nowhere in this period is there a finer example of the clash of ideas of the Enlightenment with nineteenth-century trends, rightly seen. What he saw was social leveling and the wiping out of class distinctions upon which his own ideas of social solidarity must rest.

Crèvecoeur, in his famous letter, "What is an American?," had noted in the eighteenth century the distinctive independence fostered by the New World environment. The differences remarked of Americans in our history, early and late, have usually been traced to our republican institutions, which are an outgrowth of the rational dream of the Enlightenment, and to the encouragement given to individualism by the existence until recently of the western frontier. The extension of republican principles from Jeffersonian to Jacksonian democracy, and westward expansion shifting the balance of political power to the west took the reins of social control out of the hands of enlightened and large-property-owning conservatives; and industrial and commercial expansion in the North created new social classes, laborers, merchants, small businessmen, and industrial capitalists relatively unknown to the Enlightenment.

Alexis de Tocqueville, who visited America in the early 1830's, was an unbiased and unusually sympathetic observer of America as a social phenomenon. In *Democracy in America*[17] he has recorded his impressions and conclusions as to the effect upon literature of unique social convictions and conditions in America. Shrewdly observing that America as yet had, in the proper sense, no literature of its own, he pointed to the journalists as the only truly American authors.[18] Yet he predicted the rise of a native literature in America, the exact nature of which cannot be determined beforehand because of the democratic society out of which it will come. In aristocratic societies with their fixed order

[17] *De la Démocratie en Amérique* (1835); first American edition, 1838.
[18] Phillips Bradley (ed.), *Democracy in America* (New York, 1945), II, 56.

## THE DECLINE OF NEOCLASSICISM

Style will be thought of almost as much importance as thought, and the form will be no less considered than the matter; the diction will be polished, measured, and uniform. The tone of the mind will be always dignified, seldom very animated, and writers will care more to perfect what they produce than to multiply their productions.

But in a democratic society, with its mingling of ranks,

> The mind of each is . . . unattached to that of his fellows by tradition or common habits; and they have never had the power, the inclination, or the time to act together. It is from the bosom of this heterogeneous and agitated mass, however, that authors spring. . . .[19]

Therefore, he says, there will be an absence of formal rules, and frequent change will be inevitable, for "each new generation is a new people." It is impossible that any rules should ever be permanent. Form will be slighted, style fantastic, incorrect, vehement, and bold. There will be more imagination than profundity, more passion than taste. Furthermore, tradition and even concern for the present will fade as democratic poets are haunted by the vision of the future. "Democracy which shuts the past against the poet, opens the future before him."[20] De Tocqueville thus anticipates Whitman by twenty years. He also predicts the psychological probings and gropings of the Transcendentalists, of Poe, and of Hawthorne and Melville. Writers in a democracy, and particularly poets, he says, will

> search below the external surface which is palpable to the senses, in order to read the inner soul; and nothing lends itself more to the delineation of the ideal than the scrutiny of the hidden depths in the immaterial nature of man. . . . I have only to look at myself. Man springs out of nothing, crosses time, and disappears forever in the bosom of God; he is seen but for a moment, wandering on the verge of the two abysses, and there he is lost.[21]

In other words, democratic authors are concerned not with society but with themselves, for democracy breeds individualism and insularity. The democratic man has no obvious ties or debts to anyone above or below him in the social scale.

[19] *Ibid.*, II, 57, 58.
[20] *Ibid.*, II, 74.
[21] *Ibid.*, II, 75-76.

The wave of the future as a concern of American literature and its critics is seen early in the call for a national literature,[22] and the spirit of nationalism is not theoretically consistent with the principles of the Enlightenment. The emphasis upon national differences leads eventually to emphasis upon sectional, local, and individual differences. Social solidarity is a neoclassical norm which pervades the social scale, and since human nature is fixed and everywhere the same, national and sectional differences are minimized. The spirit of nationalism was, of course, rampant in America following the Revolution, and it received renewed impetus from the War of 1812. The slurs of British travelers and reviewers[23] stirred up a paper war, bringing American nationalism to the fore as a live issue, particularly after 1814.

Literary nationalism is by no means exclusively a force towards romanticism, although critics have generally made such an assumption.[24] Although nationalism may have contributed to the treatment of native themes, other factors probably had more influence. And such treatment does not lead inevitably to romanticism. The Connecticut Wits, strongly nationalistic, were also strongly neoclassical in technique in such poems as *M'Fingal, Greenfield Hill,* and the *Columbiad*. The deists and Jeffersonians, in spite of their cosmopolitanism, were in one respect nationalistic above all others, in their hatred of things British. The Federalists, less nationalistic, were more ready to accept English (and therefore romantic) critics and literature. Here again in deism we see a parallel with classicism, and yet a refusal to follow models. Nationalism was at first a classical force. What Americans wanted in a national literature was a

[22] For a representative list of articles on literary nationalism in the early nineteenth century, see Kendall B. Taft (ed.), *The Minor Knickerbockers* (New York, 1947), p. lxxx, n. 280.

[23] See Jane Mesick, *The English Traveller in America, 1785-1835* (New York, 1922).

[24] A recent example may be found in Spiller *et al.*, *Literary History of the United States* (New York, 1948), I, 121, on the catalytic effect of the American Revolution. "In this frame of mind, Americans rushed into print to proclaim their declaration of intellectual independence, grimly determined to stand and die in the literary trenches rather than submit to any return to colonial bondage in things of the spirit. Inevitably, they were led to use American scenes and materials—and thus helped prepare the way for the American Renaissance of the nineteenth century."

new and indigenous body of writing, but what they had in mind, for the most part, was another Augustan period, not a romantic age. Furthermore, as Emerson pointed out, fifty years of nationalism had produced no national literature.

National pride in America was the spur for at least two forms of literary creation which were not romantic: those derivative from classical sources, and those writings, principally satiric, which were hostile to British romanticists. Even that American writing which is most derivative from English and European romantic models lacked the little spontaneity those models possessed. The fact remains that the typical sources chosen by American poets and prose writers of the period were either neoclassical or the most nearly classical of the new school, Scott and Byron, who admired Pope and satirized Wordsworth and Coleridge.

James K. Paulding is the best example of an extreme nationalist who remained neoclassical in spirit throughout his career. At first his nationalism was negative, that is, the result of animosity to most things British. But his critical orientation remained with the eighteenth century, with Pope, Swift, Goldsmith, and Fielding. What, then, is the rationale of the occasional union of nationalism and neoclassicism in America? The latter, by its very absence of national coloring, furnishes the only sound principles upon which national and independent literary themes may be developed. Since by neoclassical theory Nature is "still the same" in every country and in all climes, a literature to be truly national must move from the general to the particular. American national literature cannot be founded upon English national literature. It is clear that Paulding showed hostility to romanticism as a predominantly English phenomenon of recent origin.[25]

To make the point doubly clear, consider that many American romantics were the least national: Irving, the cosmopolitan who attempted to remove national animosities by good humor; Poe, who founded aesthetic principles on universal laws; Longfellow, and all those Transcendentalists who revolted against American materialism. The romantic age borrowed more ideas, perhaps, from

[25] See Paulding's series of nationalistic satires of things English, *John Bull and Brother Jonathan* (1812), *The United States and England* (1815), *A Sketch of Old England* ... (1822), and *John Bull in America* (1825).

non-American sources than any other period in our literary history. America came out of its isolation in the romantic years of the "Renaissance."[26]

The problem of the influence of nationalism upon American letters and thought is, then, a particularly difficult problem. There seem to have emerged at least four distinct varieties of nationalistic feeling.[27] The first might be called the Nationalism of the Enlightenment, based upon the rational but optimistic assurance that in America, removed from the corrupting influences of unshakable custom in Europe and the Mother Country, the theories of enlightened men miraculously could come to practical test and fruition. America became in the eyes of Americans, and indeed of the whole Western World, the repository of the universal rational principles of human liberty.[28] This variety of nationalism, the result of rational pride in being "the observ'd of all observers," was strictly ideological; yet the inevitable feeling of superiority to older nations detracted from its cosmopolitan origins. In no sense a romantic protest, it was the common feeling of conservatives and radicals not yet divided into party lines by factional disputes within the nation. In this sense Dwight, Trumbull, John Adams, Washington, Hamilton, and later Cooper and Calhoun, were on common ground with

[26] A critical examination of a representative periodical, the *North American Review*, indicates that arguments against a national literature were equally balanced between writers holding neoclassical and romantic ideas. The ten most common arguments follow: (1) Good literature is based on classical models. (2) Independence produces useless "novelties." (3) America must be universal before it can be truly national. (4) There is but one republic of letters. Literature should transcend prejudice and sectionalism. (5) Classical literature is the best literature. (6) America should aspire to rival the best in English literature. (7) Intercourse with the best minds leads to great art. (8) The mind alone, man's higher and better nature, can exhibit the highest beauty. (9) The poetic imagination is universal. (10) The poet should leave the real for the ideal and appeal to the universal human heart. See Harry Hayden Clark, "Literary Criticism in the *North American Review*, 1815-1835," *Transactions of the Wisconsin Academy of Sciences, Arts and Letters*, XXXII (1940), 299-350. See, also, Robert E. Streeter, "Association Psychology and Literary Nationalism in the *North American Review*, 1815-1825," *American Literature*, XVII (Nov., 1945), 243-254.

[27] See Hans Kohn, *The Idea of Nationalism* (New York, 1944), chap. vi on America.

[28] See Gilbert Chinard's brilliant chapter on "The American Dream" in *The Literary History of the United States* (New York, 1948).

Franklin, Jefferson, Paine, Barlow, Freneau, Paulding, and William Ellery Channing.

A second kind of nationalism, an extension of the first, is more properly designated democratic nationalism. Stemming from American and French revolutionary leveling tendencies, it is a class movement, less ideological but more hypothetical and quixotic than the first, and more directly concerned with everyday actions and emotions. The assumption is made that all men, under wholesome institutions, regardless of training or other qualifications, are capable of holding the reins of government. The utopian theories of progress, natural goodness, and perfectibility came to the fore; the irrational goddess "Reason" was enthroned in the public square; belief outran reality: enter political romanticism.

> Here social man a second birth shall find,
> And a new range of reason lift his mind.[29]

Conservative thinkers were repelled by such nationalism after the evident excesses of the French Revolution, from Dwight and Dennie to Irving, Cooper, Legaré, and Poe. It was tainted in their minds with atheism, mob rule, vulgarity, and absurd literary puffing. Such manning of the barricades against the social hierarchy signalized a division in the ranks: it forced the conservative back into Christian orthodoxy, social and political Federalism, indignant didacticism and decorum in belles-lettres. On the other hand, it encouraged romantic religious sects such as free-will Methodism, spearheaded the shift from Jeffersonianism to class-conscious Jacksonianism, and encouraged amateurism in literature, particularly in the periodicals and newspapers.

Cultural nationalism, a third variety, had major obstacles to its progress in America, for the new nation lacked the first ordinary requirements, a national language and literature. Nor could Noah Webster succeed in supplying these deficiencies through spelling reform, Americanisms, or copyright laws. Nevertheless, American institutions and natural scenery, in spite of the absence of cultural traditions lamented by Irving, Cooper, and Hawthorne, offered romantic themes to Bryant, Percival, the Hudson River school, and eventually to Emerson and Thoreau. Impetus to cultural nationalism

[29] Joel Barlow, *The Columbiad*, 2 vols. (1809), I, 149.

came from Germany in the historical writing of George Bancroft.

After the War of 1812 economic nationalism, antithetical to Jefferson's cosmopolitan agrarianism, was increasingly manifest in protectivist, mercantilistic tariff laws, which further separated North and South economically and culturally. Mathew Carey was the ideological leader of this movement, which eventually took on the coloring of expansionistic imperialism.[30]

The growth of Southern sectionalism and ultimately of Southern nationalism may be illustrated in relation to these different nationalisms. The early stand of the South on slavery was not divisive. But it rebelled against democratic nationalism on religious and social grounds, and Southern ruling-class preconceptions were strengthened by the feudalistic biases of Scott and Carlyle. Culturally, until after 1830, the South demonstrated little sectional or national cohesiveness. In the tradition of states' rights, loyalties were to states rather than to the section or to the nation.[31] Cultural relations were generally closer with England than with other states in the nation. Economic nationalism, dominated by Northern commercial and industrial interests, was not in accord with Southern agrarianism. However, cotton imperialism and slave imperialism were natural products of Southern divisive nationalism just prior to the Civil War. In retreat from all these four nationalisms, the South evolved gradually a cultural nationalism of its own which was political, economic, social, and sometimes religious. Its sources were immediately economic. "The American Dream" was supplanted by the idea of the Greek state; democratic nationalism yielded to the semifeudal, paternalistic order romanticized by Scott. A kind of racial and military myth grew up, by which Southerners identified themselves with the chivalric traditions of the Normans, as opposed to the barbarous Saxon North. The economic and moral isolation forced on them by the North seemed somehow to give them kinship with the exiled and rebellious Byron.

In its literature the South as a section seems to have clung longer

---

[30] See Kenneth W. Rowe, *Mathew Carey: A Study in American Economic Development* (Baltimore, 1933).

[31] See Jay B. Hubbell, "Literary Nationalism in the Old South," in *American Studies in Honor of W. K. Boyd* (Durham, N. C., 1940), pp. 175-220.

than the North to neoclassical patterns of thought. Of course this fact may be explained in part by greater religious, economic, political, and social solidarity. Prior to about 1830, the liberal ideas of the eighteenth century, although gradually on the wane, were predominant among Southern intellectuals and political leaders.[32] Thomas Jefferson set the pattern, followed by John Taylor of Caroline, the scientific agrarian; George Tucker, the University of Virginia professor who as late as 1837 saw in slavery the economic and moral ruin of the South;[33] and the English-born scientist and religious free-thinker, Thomas Cooper, President of South Carolina College (1820-1833), who although he later thought better of his condemnation in 1787 of slavery on utilitarian and humanitarian grounds,[34] remained a rationalistic champion of free thought, free trade, and states' rights. Southern leaders of this period were liberal aristocrats who denied any aristocracy other than that of talents, education, and worth; they partook of the progressive optimism of the later years of the Enlightenment, believing in the dignity and natural rights of man. Further, they were willing to rely upon the common man to make rational decisions; they were enlightened, skeptical, and tolerant religiously and otherwise, and dismissed authority, convention, and tradition as undesirable gauges of truth.[35]

The literature of the South in the period is almost uniformly neoclassical. Wirt's *Letters of the British Spy* (1803), his contributions to "The Rainbow" (1804) and "The Old Bachelor" (1814), are imitative of Goldsmith and the *Spectator*. His partiality to Sterne and Cervantes is well known. It is to be noted that his nationalism, in spite of his exaggerated eulogy of Patrick Henry, is not a romantic trait. A brilliant orator, Wirt urged upon young lawyers a style utilitarian, masculine, and logical, disciplined by "reason and judgment." In order to avoid the "florid and Asiatic," he recommended

---

[32] See Clement Eaton, *Freedom of Thought in the Old South* (Durham, N. C., 1940), pp. 3-31. For a somewhat different opinion, see R. B. Davis, "Literary Tastes in Virginia before Poe," *William and Mary Quarterly*, XIX (Jan., 1939), 55-68.
[33] *The Laws of Wages, Profits and Rent, Investigated* (Philadelphia).
[34] *Letters on the Slave Trade.*
[35] Eaton, *op. cit.*

as models the legal and political arguments of Hamilton and Marshall.[36]

George Tucker, pessimistic about the possibilities for the development of letters in the nation and in his native state of Virginia,[37] wrote in *A Voyage to the Moon* (1827), satire in the vein of *Gulliver's Travels* and *The Citizen of the World*. The more prominent Southern periodicals of the period, such as the Baltimore *Portico*, demonstrate conclusively the continuing strength of neoclassicism in letters and antipathy to contemporary English romanticism. One critic in the *Portico* damned Scott's *Field of Waterloo* as a "contemptible production" employing an abominable style.[38] In a series of articles on "Polite Learning" the author points out that the present age has reached a peak of excellence beyond which the only way is downward. No further polish can be added to a literature boasting of Dryden, Pope, Akenside, Johnson, Swift, and Fielding, and who can "conceive an important addition to science, in which we are now defective?" "When no active principle of progression employs the mind, it will indulge in the mischievous occupation of innovating on what is established, or of corrupting what is perfect. Hence the feeble imitations, the ponderous commentaries. . . ." This is Pope's feeling in *The Dunciad*. The writer goes on to declare that "equality and freedom is wrecking literature today as the Goths destroyed Rome." Poetry is on the decline. The true course can be followed only if "genius will pursue the proper track of legitimate fame, and adhere to established principles of classic taste."[39] Of the English romanticists only Byron, whose moral blemishes were manifest, was worthy of their qualified praise as comparable to Pope. Coleridge, never a tolerable poet, by his visions and "sickening nonsense" and "derangement of intellect" succeeded only in bringing upon himself disgrace and

[36] See William Matthews, *Men, Places, and Things* (Chicago, 1887), pp. 33-35.
[37] See *Letters from Virginia* (Baltimore, 1816), "On the Low State of Polite Letters in Virginia." For discussion of this letter, see Jay B. Hubbell, *op. cit.*
[38] Feb., 1816, pp. 99-100.
[39] The *Portico*, generally neoclassical in its criticism, was nevertheless strongly nationalistic. See Marshall W. Fishwick, "*The Portico* and Literary Nationalism after the War of 1812," *William and Mary Quarterly*, VIII (April, 1951), 238-245.

general contempt. And Southey is his equal in absurdity. "No writer ever waged so fatal a war against taste and beauty."[40] Only W. B. O. Peabody later approached the extreme classical position of the *Portico*.[41]

But the liberal premises of the Enlightenment and their literary concomitant, neoclassicism, disappeared with accelerating pace under the impact of events. The South, which itself had hitherto assumed the lead in rational and enlightened proposals for the abolition of its "peculiar institution" of slavery, found itself increasingly the object of the enthusiastic and extremist attacks of Northern social romanticism in the form of radical abolitionism. The battle lines were already drawn by the Missouri Compromise of 1820. In the following decades, and particularly in the 1830's, the abolition movement struck hard at Southern institutions. In 1831 Garrison launched the New England Anti-Slavery Society and published the first issue of the *Liberator*. In 1833 the American Anti-Slavery Society in Philadelphia was established, and Oberlin College in Ohio opened its doors equally to Negroes and whites. In 1836 appeared the first antislavery novel, *The Slave*, by Richard Hildreth, a disciple of Bentham, and Lundy's *The War in Texas*, denouncing that skirmish as a slaveholder's scheme. Theodore Dwight Weld, one of the most influential abolitionists, in *The Bible Against Slavery* (1837) and *American Slavery as It Is* (1839) furnished part of the inspiration for *Uncle Tom's Cabin*. In the South the reaction set in. The theory of states' rights had already admitted of individualism in the South in such men as George Mason and John Randolph of Roanoke, a genuine aristocrat, who carried the position to the extreme of justifying the individual's disregard of government and assumption of individual sovereignty based on reason. Now Northern religious, social, and philosophical radicalism contributed to the discarding of rational and liberal ideals in the South. Cosmopolitanism gave way to intense localism. Calhoun, hitherto a unionist, became the philosopher of Southern sectionalism, evolving the prin-

[40] Sept., 1816, p. 187; Nov., 1816, p. 421; Aug., 1817, p. 99; Dec., 1817, pp. 417 ff. The *Portico* even rejects the "uniform barbarity" of Scott's poetry, and argues that Scott "embraced the most repugnant qualities" of the Middle Ages.
[41] See his articles in the *North American Review*, summarized by Clark, *op. cit.*

ciple of "the concurrent majority."[42] N. B. Tucker's violent *Partisan Leader* (1836) matched the tone of the Northern fire-eaters.

The appeal to reason was supplanted in the South by suppression of radical criticism, free speech and thought. Most Southern liberals changed with their section, and many a champion of liberalism was forced from the pulpit, the university chair, and the legislative desk. Slavery, hitherto an admitted evil, found economic excuse and sanction in the increasing value of the Negro as property with the widespread use of the cotton gin and the expansion of the Cotton Kingdom into the Gulf Coast. Economic motives thus tended to destroy the doctrine of natural rights and republicanism. Thomas Dew, professor at William and Mary College, trained in Germany, came forward in 1832 with his *Review of the Debate on the Abolition of Slavery in the Virginia Legislature of 1831 and 1832*, a defense of slavery as a "positive good." Many a religious skeptic, Unitarian, and deist embraced again the orthodox faith, usually one of the "romantic" sects, Methodist or Baptist.[43] Nowhere was the success of religious revivalism so marked as in the South, particularly on the frontier.

How much economic considerations dominated the shift away from liberalism, and how much other factors, more or less immediate, contributed, it is difficult to assay. But the economic causes seem to loom largest. Agrarianism itself, identified as it was earlier with the rational thinking of Adam Smith, Franklin, Jefferson, and the French Physiocrats, was capable of transposal to a feeling of class consciousness. Jefferson's early distrust of commerce and industrialism became for Southerners a defensive pride in a traditional and distinctive culture quite different from the pride in self-sufficiency of Northern and Western small landowners. The South felt, with justification, that protective tariffs were directed against its economic progress. Thus the Southern agrarian way of life contributed to sectionalism as opposed to strong state loyalties, and ultimately to Southern nationalism.

The South, for many reasons, seems to have had more concern with the frontier than the North. Timothy Dwight of Connecti-

---

[42] Clement Eaton, *op. cit.*, Parrington, *op. cit.*, and Joseph Dorfman, *The Economic Mind in American Civilization* (New York, 1946).

[43] Eaton, *op. cit.*, p. 30.

cut looked upon the frontier as the repository of the unfit. Men of the South looked upon it as the answer to the problem of farmers whose tobacco lands in the Tidewater were impoverished. At any rate, the Southwest and even the first states carved from the Northwest Territory were largely populated from the South. The western lands in the South furnished the necessary soil for King Cotton upon which the Southern economy thenceforth too largely rested. One major effect of the frontier, then, was to entrench agrarian pursuits, slavery, and the plantation system, and to maintain, through representation by new states, the Southern balance in the United States Senate as a protection against Northern legislation.

One effect, rather difficult to substantiate, of the plantation system may have been a general urge to escape from the idleness, isolation, and dull rounds of rural existence.[44] Such escape was found either through equally idle physical pursuits, such as military service, or through the reading of novels of action like the romances of Scott. In addition to a natural if oversensitive reaction to Northern criticism,[45] the fact that there existed, by their own once liberal standards, moral arguments against slavery led apologists to a defense of slavery on grounds of paternalism, racial inferiority, and the maintenance of blood honor and white supremacy, all of which grounds are contradictory to the principles of the Enlightenment. One authority goes so far as to trace the rise of romanticism in the South to the guilt complex over slavery and the illicit interracial sexual practices which inevitably accompanied property rights over human bodies.[46] It is certain that the institution of slavery stimulated irrational and defensive social views.[47]

---

[44] This seems to be Eaton's conclusion.
[45] Southerners cherished the military traditions of the Cavaliers, and were quick to resent aspersions on their honor, as the continued frequency of dueling and published codes of honor will attest.
[46] W. J. Cash, *The Mind of the South* (New York, 1941), pp. 54-56.
[47] Rollin G. Osterweis, in *Romanticism and Nationalism in the Old South* (New Haven, 1949), shows clearly that what he calls "the third leg of the tripod," romantic cultural nationalism, developed after 1831 as an emotional and intellectual counterpart of the other two legs, slavery and the plantation system. His book divides the South into four geographical sections which reveal diversity within an essentially unified pattern. It is to be noted that the particular and limited kind of romanticism admitted into the South (Scott, Byron, and the Greek revival) is that which aroused

The literary fruits of these transitions do not clearly appear in the South until the decade or two just preceding the War between the States, except on the levels of reading interest in romantic, chivalric fiction and poetry, and of literary criticism. The vogues of Scott, Moore, Byron, Bulwer, and later of Carlyle would not appear to be major influences toward romanticism, if the anterior influences here cited are accepted, so much as they are the corroborating effects of other influences, environmental, social, economic. But it cannot be denied that such literary favorites justified, accelerated, and confirmed existing trends;[48] they also supplied ready models for the few early Southern poets and fiction writers such as Poe, Kennedy, and Simms. Yet these and many others retained many neoclassical predilections after the dividing years around 1830.

Poe's early poetry is obviously Byronic, rebellious, and subjective. Yet "Tamerlane" celebrates the milder, more general good of love over heroic ambition, and "Al Aaraaf" presents a still more general norm in abstract beauty. It is Poe the "romantic" who makes sport of the untutored-genius theory of poetic creation, and who reveals in "The Philosophy of Composition" the mechanical pains taken in the creation of a work of art. In the thirties he turned in practice from the creation of beauty to the creation of truth, from poetry to prose, and devised the rigid rules of the short story form. The poet for whom science had been a vulture preying on the poet's heart[49] found in Newtonian science and the argument from design the models for his plots.[50] Much of his satire

---

the least opposition from critics who in the nineteenth century still used neoclassical yardsticks.

[48] Mark Twain's violent attack on Scott in *Life on the Mississippi*, in which he accuses Scott of undoing all the good done by Cervantes' satire of knight errantry, and accuses him also of having practically caused the Civil War, is indicative of an earlier attitude in the South. The subject is well-canvassed in two articles by Grace W. Landrum, "Sir Walter Scott and His Literary Rivals in the Old South," *American Literature*, II (Nov., 1930), 256-276; "Notes on the Reading of the Old South," *American Literature*, III (March, 1931), 60-71.

[49] "Sonnet to Science," 1829. Thomas Warton, in his *History of English Poetry*, 1774-1781, had indicated a similar effect of scientific knowledge upon the poetic imagination.

[50] See Margaret Alterton, *Origins of Poe's Critical Theory* (Iowa City, 1925), and Introduction to Alterton and Craig (eds.), *Edgar Allan Poe*

was directed at various romanticisms: social reform, Transcendentalism, Longfellow's sentimental moralizing, ideas of progress and perfectibility, mobocracy, the vogue of the pseudo sciences, Gothicism, the Lake poets, the vogue of affected simplicity. This of course does not make Poe any more neoclassical than Byron. Retaining the ideas of rationality, consistency, judgment, adherence to probability, he went beyond neoclassicism, particularly in his verse after 1840, seeking to explore the inner recesses of the mind and soul rather than the normative and universal aspects of life which physical science and faculty psychology had effectively removed from the province of imaginative art. He created his own logically consistent world in which the universal associations resulting from sensory experience might still operate, but only in unexpected and unusual combinations. By this is meant that his images were not unique or striking in his day. They were just those of the popular periodical literature of the time. Like Pope's satires, his tales survive over those of other writers of the period because of their greater art, not because they were unique or original. Yet Poe's romanticism is in the choice of subject matter; his themes are not from general nature, nor from the nature of Wordsworth and Bryant. They are chosen for their own sake, and for sensational effect. Poe's romanticism is often undeniably journalistic and occasional; he is a "professional romanticist." As such, he is a mirror for his period but not necessarily a part of it. His effects are as carefully and artificially contrived to fit a formula as Pope's couplets. In spite of his own theoretical position, it seems evident that his unity, his totality of effect, even his "supernal beauty," are cold and mechanical, one might say mathematical. Except, then, for his dubiously justifiable pride and prejudice in the traditions of the Southern gentlemen, Poe is not centrally to be explained in terms of the South.[51]

(New York, 1935). It should be pointed out, however, that while Poe's *Eureka* may be said to be neoclassical in the stress upon order and harmony based on Newton and Laplace, it is dedicated to Alexander von Humboldt. Floyd Stovall has also demonstrated Poe's debt to Coleridge on more than the poetic level. See "Poe's Debt to Coleridge," *Univ. Texas Stud. in Eng.*, X (July, 1930), 70-127.

[51] Poe's defense of slavery, chivalric attitude toward women, and scorn of democracy are not distinctively Southern traits.

Simms is more typically Southern than Poe, or perhaps it would be more accurate to say his work demonstrates the deteriorating influence of typically Southern social and economic romanticism. Under different environmental circumstances he might, as Parrington suggests, have been an American Fielding. Yet he was too naïve, too whole-heartedly loyal to his native state and city, too uncritical, untutored, and unrestrained in his writing ever to have achieved the ordered restraint and rationalism of the neoclassical discipline. Further, his eye was trained upon the distinctions of time and place. Thoroughly nationalistic as well as Southern in spirit, he insisted upon American individuality.[52] To be a true poet, he felt, one must sing according to the peculiar nature and needs of his time and place, not according to custom. Genius must be original as America is original. Our distinctive environment, the familiar objects which surround us from childhood, imbue the soul with "sympathies" which are subjective and not universal.[53] Pointing to his age as one of *égoisme*, he accepts the individuality, the private quality, the identity of the author's self and his writing illustrated by the chief romantic figures of the age, Byron, Wordsworth, Shelley, Keats. This *égoisme* accounts, he thinks, for the substitution of imagination for judgment, and for the characteristic attempts of the poets of the time in the direction of the vague, the mystic, the shadowy, and imperfect in literature.[54]

The strained and paradoxical nature of the position into which the antebellum South forced itself is illustrated by the writings of the scholarly Hugh Swinton Legaré. In him the mixed ideals of the South receive their most scholarly expression. The South was sorely in need of moral justification of a kind not to be found in the rational and empirical laissez-faire agrarianism of Jefferson and John Taylor of Caroline. Legaré's most representative ideas came from the study of law, from which he may be said to have derived a theory of historic rights contradictory to the natural rights theory of late eighteenth-century liberalism. Government is not the operation of a body of mechanical principles; it is rather a human

---

[52] *Views and Reviews* (1845), I, 1. This volume contains Simms's most representative literary opinions.
[53] *Ibid.*, I, 6, 8, 9.
[54] *Ibid.*, II, 148, 151.

institution built upon gradually evolving precedents. His position is similar to that of Burke.

The future, then, for Legaré, is to be sought entirely in terms of the past. The present does not provide the solution to its own problems. This kind of traditionalism carries over into the field of literature. An ardent defender of the ancients over the moderns, he finds in Greek poetry and eloquence the kind of beauty and sublimity that speak straight to the human heart, unencumbered with metaphysics and bombastic affectation,[55] and unclouded by the "undisciplined and reckless spirit" of so much of modern romanticism, particularly Byron, although he is genuinely moved by Byron's "incoherent though powerful and agitating romance," and especially by *Manfred*.[56] His norm is "Attic eloquence," which is to what he calls "Asiatic" eloquence as classical is to romantic poetry. Not approving of the bad taste of much of modern literature, he yet agrees with Schlegel that religion is the ultimate source of changing tides of taste.[57] The classical ideal in Legaré is seen to be of a piece with the borrowings of Calhoun from a conception of Greek "democracy" and with the prevalent vogue in the South for Greek Revival architecture.[58] Hellenism becomes associated

---

[55] In the *Southern Review*, May, 1828, p. 444, in a review of Percival's *Clio*, Legaré rejects the random fancies of such "poetical opium-eaters." Ossian, for example, he says, would have been taken at Athens "as an instance of absolute monstrosity." Those who consider such poetry sublime, to quote Percival, "as words Spoken in the fever of a dream Breathless and indistinct, yet full of awe High and mysterious" are taken in by "a fury in the words," but they do not understand the meaning; there is no meaning. "We profess ourselves of that old-fashioned, prosaical school, which absolutely refuses to admire in literature what it is not able to comprehend, and lays it down as its first canon of criticism that a reader has a right to see clearly what his author would be after ... what principally distinguishes the modern or romantic poetry from the classical, is, that the former is more concerned about *spiritualities* than *temporalities*—about soul than body—about the shadowy abstractions of the mind than the objects of the senses."

[56] See *Writings of H. S. Legaré*, 2 vols. (Charleston, 1845), essays on "Classical Learning," "Sir Philip Sidney's Miscellanies," "Lord Byron's Character and Writings."

[57] *Ibid.*, "Byron's Letters and Journals." For a generally romantic statement of definition of poetry by Legaré, see the passage quoted from "Classical Literature" in Edd W. Parks (ed.), *Southern Poets* (New York, 1936), p. li.

[58] See Talbot Hamlin, *Greek Revival Architecture in America* (New York, 1944), for the romantic nature of the Greek Revival.

with an older and simpler but more elevated way of life; this kind of Hellenism is readily absorbed into the romantic escapism fostered by a doomed but vigorously defensive economic order—an order by and for the leisure class.

We have seen that the rise of divisive sectionalism in the South followed the decline of economic and social solidarity in the early nineteenth century. The same is true of the other sections of the rapidly expanding and loosely knit country. The literature of the Western frontier, after slowly freeing itself from Eastern dominance,[59] took on the violent, extravagant, and unpolished coloration of that geographical section. Gilbert Imlay's *America* (1792) was one of the first books to treat the American West in glowing and poetic terms. But the West of Daniel Boone and the romantic hunters of Kentucky quickly gave way to the agrarian West of the settler-farmer. The prevailing impulse was the search for free land and economic opportunity. In the same year that Paulding wrote in Popean couplets the saga of *The Backwoodsman* (1818), the ornithologist Thomas Nuttall at the falls of the Ohio commented on the nature and intentions of Western immigrants.

> A stranger who descends the Ohio at this season of emigration, can not but be struck with the jarring vortex of heterogeneous population . . . all searching for some better country, which lies to the west as Eden did to the east.[60]

To the nationalistic impulse, then, toward westward expansion (national interest against the British seen in the Lewis and Clark expedition and the Louisiana Purchase, and later in the Oregon dispute) was added the private economic, essentially agrarian, impulse, which as far as the settlers themselves were concerned had little or nothing to do with the agrarian ideal of the enlightenment. Further, actual experience on the frontier varied sharply from the agrarian theory and ideal, and the extension of agriculture into the

[59] The criticism in James Hall's *Western Monthly Magazine*, 1830-1837 (the name was changed from *Illinois Monthly Magazine* in 1832), was to a great extent dictated by Eastern writers, particularly Dennie. See John T. Flanagan, *James Hall, Literary Pioneer of the Ohio Valley* (Minneapolis, 1941).

[60] *A Journal of Travels. . . .* (Philadelphia, 1821); quoted by W. H. Venable, in *Beginnings of Literary Culture in the Ohio Valley* (Cincinnati, 1891), p. 21.

West meant in part the extension of slavery. It also meant the extension of internal improvements, commerce, and industry into the Ohio and Mississippi valleys.

This economic fact, this often fiercely equalitarian way of life, had no literary tradition fitted for its expression. Western settlers did not live the lives of sentimental heroes and heroines; romantic fiction about the frontier had little vogue in America.[61] The vanishing Indian, the natural enemy of the settler, had his vogue in the period at the hands of Eastern writers, and was treated with varying degrees of realism by Cooper, Bird, Neal, Simms, and Snelling. Before the appearance of indigenous Western writing on any large scale the most significant aspect of the West was treated by Cooper in his portrait of Leather-Stocking.

The original hunter of *The Pioneers* (1823) clearly expresses subversive impulses. The character was conceived in terms of the antithesis between nature and civilization, between freedom and law, that has governed most American interpretations of the westward movement. Cooper was able to speak for his people on this theme because the forces at work within him closely reproduced the patterns of thought and feeling that prevailed in the society at large. But he felt the problem more deeply than his contemporaries: he was at once more strongly devoted to the principle of social order and more vividly responsive to the ideas of nature and freedom in the Western forest than they were ... the character of Leatherstocking is by far the most important symbol of the national experience of adventure across the continent.[62]

It need not be objected, I think, that Cooper did not rise above the pattern of the sentimental novel in his failure to make Leather-Stocking the romantic hero in the novels of the series bearing his name. It might be more significant to say that Cooper, himself the gentleman, had no intention of going beyond the limits of his social code. Nor was he a spokesman, after 1828, of the American ideal of progress through equalitarianism. And it was in the West that this essentially anarchic ideal reached one major form of expression. The height of individualistic primitivism is apparently reached in the romance by Charles W. Webber in *Old Hicks, the*

---

[61] Ralph Leslie Rusk, *The Literature of the Middle Western Frontier* (New York, 1925), I, 90; II, 1.

[62] Henry Nash Smith, *Virgin Land* (Boston, 1950), pp. 60-61.

*Guide* (1848), who goes so far as to identify genius with the intuitive savage or primitive frontiersman.

> They arrive at truth by much the same processes; they equally scorn all shackles but those of the God-imposed senses, whether corporeal or spiritual, and, with like self-reliance, rule all precedents by the Gospel as revealed within themselves.[63]

From Puritan times New England has been a land of separatists. New Englanders have had a traditional and superior misinformation about lesser sections of the country. The first major secessionist movement was that of the Hartford Convention of 1814. Timothy Dwight in 1815 admitted that the vilifications of America by the *Quarterly Review* were valid, except that they did not apply to New England, and certainly not to Connecticut.[64] Hostility toward New England felt by other sections of the country can be measured in the works of Cooper, Irving, and Poe. Although most men called for a national literature, they wrote usually as sectionalists.

But the growth of sectionalism is only a halfway station in the decline of social solidarity. Of more significance is the growth of individualism and the justification and defense of individualism by authors themselves. Most of the pleas for a national literature did not intend to contribute to this kind of growth; they were merely patriotic, anti-British, optimistic about the future, or apologetic about existing conditions in America (the lack of copyright, patronage, education, and native themes, and concern for more practical pursuits) which prevented the rise of a literature worthy of America's political position in the world. Most representative perhaps are the neoclassical Paulding's five volumes in the paper war against the British quarterlies, his essay on "A National Literature" in *Salmagundi, Second Series* (1819), and his salute to the *Southern Literary Messenger* in its first issue (1835) urging originality and treatment of native themes; Cooper's *Notions of the Americans* (1828) and *Letter to His Countrymen* (1834); articles on a national literature in the *North American Review* after 1815, and in the *Knickerbocker Magazine* in 1835; W. E. Chan-

---

[63] *Old Hicks*, 304-305; quoted by Smith, p. 73.
[64] See his *Remarks on the Review of Inchiquin's Letters* (Boston, 1815), pp. 15, 63, 171.

ning's "Remarks on National Literature" (1830), prophesying that freedom and liberty will give "new impulses to the human mind";[65] Verplanck's *American Scholar* (1836), critical of literary subserviency and imitation of foreign models; and Peter Duponceau's *Discourse on the Necessity and Means of Making Our Literature Independent of that of Great Britain.*[66]

The truth is, of course, that a national American expression did emerge in the nineteenth century. There is no one quite like Emerson, whom Arnold singled out as the great man of the age, or like Thoreau, Hawthorne, Poe, Melville, or Whitman in English letters. And these writers, all of them, concerned as they ultimately were with the nature of society, were first concerned with the individual. Emerson's plea for an American scholar was not a plea for a national literature so much as a plea for a kind of man who will write it. And the man must be a nonconformist. Thoreau withdrew from any and all institutions which would make him less an individual. Hawthorne, relatively unconcerned with the sins of society, must test to the quick the secret sin. Melville's Taji and Ahab and Pierre must know, must wrestle privately with the angel of the Lord, even though they lose. Poe and his characters are haunted by the secret of identity. But these authors are the masters. They were not, many of them, properly recognized in their day, not because they were removed from the human scene of their time, but because they were inside it, because they were its conscience, and the conscience though real is seldom heard, or is assuaged by external action.

In a real sense the individualism of the age is expressed by its external reform movements, by what we often call social romanticism. It is revealing to note that such movements were considered "enthusiastic" and overly emotional in the eighteenth century; in the nineteenth they were often considered superficial and mechanical by those who believed that reform must come not from social action but from within. The fact remains that the humanitarian objection to slavery, for instance, by Franklin and Jefferson is a moral objection based upon rational and uniformitarian theories of

---

[65] *Works* (Boston, 1899), p. 134.
[66] Quoted in G. Harrison Orians, *Short History of American Literature* (New York, 1940), p. 122.

natural rights; the humanitarian objection to slavery by Garrison, Whittier, and most abolitionists is a moral objection based upon a feeling, an emotion, a vicarious and sympathetic reaction against institutional injustice, a feeling symbolized by Garrison's burning of the Constitution. One exception in the abolition movement was Richard Hildreth, author of *The Slave* (1836), who like Willis Hall and a few others was a Benthamite utilitarian still talking in societal terms of the greatest good for the greatest number. But Hildreth's is not eighteenth-century utilitarianism: his solution for most problems sounds like last week's plea for greater and greater industrial production and more and more consumption, to remove tension and dissatisfaction by prosperity.[67]

The great social shift which underlies the decline of neoclassicism would appear to be the shift away from social solidarity described at some length here. Other shifts, treated more briefly in the following sections because of the limitations of space, are in many respects corollaries of this basic theorem.

### III

### From Man in Society to Man in Nature

The agrarian way of life had always been statistically typical of America in Colonial times, in spite of the fact that just prior to the Revolution New York and Philadelphia were second only to London in size in the British Empire. The Industrial Revolution tended to cause more crowding into cities, although such an effect was uniquely counteracted in America by the westward movement into the Mississippi basin and beyond. But even before the Industrial Revolution the agrarian way of life was subject to a gradual revolution of its own. This Agrarian Revolution is seen in marked form

---

[67] See Hildreth's *Theory of Morals* (1844), and *Theory of Politics* (1853). For a study of Hildreth, see Donald E. Emerson, *Richard Hildreth* (Baltimore, 1946). Utilitarianism in America is discussed in Joseph L. Blau (ed.), *American Philosophic Addresses, 1700-1900* (New York, 1946) (Willis Hall's Phi Beta Kappa address, 1844, pp. 208-230), and in C. W. Everett's "Bentham in the United States of America," in George W. Keeton and Georg Schwarzenberger (eds.), *Jeremy Bentham and the Law, a Symposium* (London, 1948), pp. 185-201.

in England after about 1720 as the result of scientific improvements in agriculture: crop rotation, better tillage, improved strains of livestock and grasses, and a consequent shift toward farming on a large scale by wealthy landowners and the displacement of the more backward peasantry by enclosure of open villages. One effect of this movement was mass emigration to America or to urban areas. Another effect is seen in the increased interest of writers in rural landscape (parallel to the Hudson River School of painters), in the life of the squirearchy, or in nostalgic, romantic, or realistic treatment of the poor peasant and his plight. In a period marked by literary club-life and urban-centered culture, there was also a growing interest in rural themes seen in Thomson, Gray, Percy, Goldsmith, Cowper, Crabbe, Burns, and Blake, and in more extreme form in Gothicism and the Ossianic poems. The interest of these writers and writings was certain to have a marked influence upon American writers dependent upon English models and at the same time products themselves of an agrarian society.

Representative American interest in the Agrarian Revolution is to be seen in Franklin, Brackenridge, Freneau, William Cobbett, Jefferson, John Taylor of Caroline.[68] Irving abroad captured the romance of country life and the lingering customs of a disappearing peasantry in *The Sketch Book* and *Bracebridge Hall*. Paulding, Cooper, and Kennedy in their novels describe at length life on the large country estate or plantation. In Paulding's *Westward Ho!* (1832) the heroine's father has moved into Kentucky to make a fresh start on the rich frontier, having left the worn-out tobacco lands of Virginia behind. Cooper in his outdoor novels pleads for the agrarian as opposed to the commercial way of life, and for the conservation of natural resources threatened by reckless and ignorant squatters.[69] These men are essentially of the Enlightenment, but they serve to indicate a trend toward the treatment of external nature, or of the man of society in contact with external nature.

[68] Brackenridge: *Modern Chivalry*, ed. Claude M. Newlin (New York, 1937), p. 696; Freneau: "The Rising Glory of America," "The American Village"; Cobbett: *The American Gardener* (1819); Jefferson: *Notes on Virginia* (1782-83); letter to James Madison, Dec. 20, 1787; Taylor: *Arator* (1813).

[69] *The Prairie* (1827), particularly, is concerned with the conservation of natural resources.

One of the most remarkable minor vogues after 1800 was that of the verse of Robert Bloomfield, English poet of the cult of simplicity, lamenting the disappearance of the simple agrarian virtues as well as the disappearance of social solidarity among peasants and landed gentry. The popularity of *The Farmer's Boy* (1800) is little short of phenomenal. Within three years of its first London appearance it had gone through five American editions. (The *Lyrical Ballads* was published only once in America before 1824.) The *American Review and Literary Journal* in January, 1801, gives us some clue to the sources of the *Farmer's Boy's* success, in contrasting Bloomfield's "neat built cottage" to Thomson's "castle," and in praising its "singular felicity and surprising originality" and "chaste morality and piety."[70] Many other reviewers sang the praises of the *Farmer's Boy*. The *Ladies Magazine and Musical Depository* in 1801 reprinted it in its entirety by installments. C. B. Brown's *Literary Magazine and American Register* had its attention arrested by this simple "child of nature."[71] *The Literary Mirror* (of Portsmouth, N. H.) printed Bloomfield's "The Miller's Maid" in 1808. Brown's *American Register* thought his *Wild Flowers* one of two productions of 1806 "likely to endure."[72] In a predominantly rural America the simple theory that God made the country and man the town had its appeal.

A second contributing factor in the shift in subject matter toward external nature is the rise of Linnaean or biological as opposed to Newtonian physical sciences. In the eighteenth century America offered a fertile field for Linnaean taxonomists questing for new species. In addition to foreign botanists,[73] there were many native or resident scientists dedicated to such pursuits. John Bartram, called by Linnaeus himself the finest natural botanist of the age, established the Philadelphia botanical gardens. His son, William Bartram, combined scientific lore and lyrical description of Southern scenery in his *Travels* (1791), which captured the poetic imagination of writers on two continents, among them Chateaubriand, Wordsworth, and Coleridge, who in turn influenced Amer-

[70] Pp. 109-117.
[71] III (June, 1805), 470.
[72] I (1806-1807), 166.
[73] For example, Kalm and Michaux. See Adolph B. Benson, *The America of 1750: Peter Kalm's Travels in North America* (New York, 1937).

ican romanticists.[74] In the nineteenth century universal scholars like Rafinesque and artist-naturalists like Alexander Wilson and Audubon tramped the western wildernesses. Audubon in his *Ornithological Biography* indicates the source of the enthusiasm of the naturalist who contemplated in the wilderness the purpose and import of the luxurious profusion of nature "fresh from the Creator's own hand."[75] Scientific interests of the naturalists extended also to the ethnology of the American Indian. Henry Schoolcraft's narratives and the *Algic Researches* (1839), and *Oneóta* (1845) stimulated further literary interest in the red man and supplied material for such poems as Longfellow's *Hiawatha* (1855).

The effects of the profound interest in external nature in the nineteenth century are obvious and everywhere apparent in the literature. The romantic treatment of landscape is discussed in Chapter IV of this book. Contemplation of lower forms of life in the external universe contributed to Freneau's lyric expressions of transiency in the poem "To a Wild Honeysuckle," to Bryant's lyrics identifying poetry and the impulses from nature,[76] to the descriptive passages in Cooper reminiscent of the paintings of the Hudson River School, to the idylls and narratives of Longfellow, to the continuation of the vogue of simplicity in Whittier, to the lyrics of R. H. Dana, Sr.,[77] and J. G. Percival. Typically extreme, Poe dwelt upon the eerie, the exotic, the melodramatically symbolic and surrealistic in his search for striking effects through the use of natural imagery.[78] The use of nature as metaphysical and exotic symbol appears in the fiction of Hawthorne and Melville. Nature for the Transcendentalists and others became also a symbol or manifestation of free development and spiritual growth on the levels of instinct and intuition. Social reforms such as Brook Farm turned to rural utopias. Extreme individualists like Thoreau found Truth in the bean patch, in the depths of Walden Pond, on

---

[74] See N. Bryllion Fagin's study, *William Bartram, Interpreter of the American Landscape* (Baltimore, 1933).

[75] *Ornithological Biography* (1831-39), I, xii; II, v.

[76] For example, "I Broke the Spell," where, speaking of the objects of nature, Bryant writes: "And these and poetry are one."

[77] See Dana's "Daybreak" and "Factitious Life."

[78] Poe's imagery is the subject of a detailed doctoral study by Hans Gottschalk, State University of Iowa, 1949, "The Imagery of Poe's Poems and Tales, a Chronological Interpretive Study."

the top of a huckleberry hill where the state of Massachusetts did not intrude, in places where he could grow wild like a flower.

In the Transcendental novelist Sylvester Judd's *Margaret* (1845), a child of nature and intuition finds no internal conflicts, only those that constantly confront the naturally good soul in its refusal to comprehend and be bound by societal institutions, including the Congregational Church. In this "one Yankee novel,"[79] Moncure D. Conway said he found revealed to him the whole spiritual history of New England.[80] Judd attended Harvard Divinity School and may have heard Emerson's 1838 address; the sermon at his ordination in Augusta, Maine, was preached by Jones Very. While at Harvard he seems to have been attracted by a trinity of ideas: man's natural goodness, the dependability of intuition, and the innate moral sense as a guide to conduct.[81] Upon these three ideas of virtue the new Christian Utopian community of Mons Christi in Judd's novel is built over the ashes of the Colonial town of Livingston. The new trinity is drawn from contemplation of and union with free and beautiful external nature. "All things are incense to me," says Margaret, "—the woods, the brooks, the birds, the fogs, the dew, the clouds, the sky; I will be incense to God; like my dear Redeemer, a sweet smelling savor. Into me the Universe flows, from me it returns back to its Maker."[82]

IV

SHIFTS IN FOREIGN AND NATIVE LITERARY INFLUENCES

Literature creates literature. The form, the ideas, the style of certain historically important literary productions have a way of appearing in the subsequent literature in the same language or in other languages. Such "vogues" may be conscious or not. They may be derivative from a single author, from a school of authors, from a dominant social, political, religious movement or idea-complex of an age.

[79] Margaret Fuller, review of *Margaret* in *New York Weekly Tribune*, Jan. 10, 1846.
[80] *Autobiography* (Boston, 1904), I, 179.
[81] See Philip Judd Brockway, "Sylvester Judd: Novelist of Transcendentalism," *New England Quarterly*, XIII (Dec., 1940), 654-677.
[82] *Margaret*, p. 457.

In American verse from 1750 to 1820 the most obvious model was Alexander Pope. He set the stamp of his style upon American verse. The heroic couplet easily predominated over blank verse, octosyllabics, odes, and stanzaic forms. Timothy Dwight, critical of Pope's moral attitudes, yet followed the master craftsman of the mock-heroic line, and even approached his skill in such passages of *The Triumph of Infidelity* (1788) as that describing contemporary infidelity:

> There stood the infidel of modern breed,
> Blest vegetation of infernal seed,
> Alike no Deist, and no Christian, he;
> But from all principle, all virtue, free.

The *Dunciad* was a model for a plethora of vituperative satires, generally political in content, among them *The Anarchiad* (1786), John Williams's *The Hamiltoniad* (1804), and Thomas Green Fessenden's "Jeffersoniad" in *Democracy Unveiled* (1805). Nearly every budding poet turned to Popean lines for his first efforts: Robert Treat Paine's "Invention of Letters" (1795), Bryant's "Embargo" (1809), Paulding's *Backwoodsman* (1818).[83] Pope's longest vogue, in spite of American reservations about his personal character, was as a moral philosopher. *The Essay on Man* ran through at least 105 American editions in the forty years between 1790 and 1830.[84] But in the nineteenth century there was an increasing reluctance to grant him first rank as a poet of genius. As early as 1805 a critic in the *Monthly Anthology* found him too artificial and lacking in the "full and unrestrained flow of imagination."[85] The Byron-Bowles controversy over Pope was fought in America as well as in England. But the majority voice after 1829 (as Agnes Sibley shows) increasingly found him without original genius.

The rise and decline of influence of other English neoclassical writers tends to follow the same pattern. Butler in the *Hudibras*

---

[83] *The Backwoodsman* was not a first poem. Paulding had earlier (1813) written a parody of Scott's *Lay of the Last Minstrel* in *The Lay of the Scottish Fiddle*, an attack upon both Scott and the British campaign on the Chesapeake in the War of 1812.

[84] See Agnes M. Sibley, *Alexander Pope's Prestige in America, 1725-1835* (New York, 1949), Appendix I.

[85] *Ibid.*, pp. 95-96.

and Charles Churchill were popular models for satire in the Revolutionary and Early National periods.[86] As late as 1835 Swift was still elaborately imitated by Cooper (*The Monikins*) and Hawthorne.[87] Samuel Johnson's reputation was little damaged by his hostility to America during the Revolution, but by the turn of the century (cf. Brackenridge's attack) his prose style and his critical judgments in the *Lives of the Poets* were subject to question. Americans began to disagree with his unfavorable judgments of Milton, Gray, and Cowper,[88] who were American favorites. Gray, particularly, would seem to have had a major influence upon Freneau and upon Bryant, who turns from Pope to Gray to Wordsworth as models. If the popularity of British authors can be based upon the number of American editions, Thomson, Young, Cowper, Burns, and Goldsmith served as transitions for Americans from the urbane polish and society wit of Pope. Perhaps their vogues can be traced to the same cult of simplicity represented by Bloomfield. Young's instructive reflections in the *Night Thoughts*, Thomson's accurate and homely descriptions, Burns's democratic sympathies and straightforward emotion, Cowper's blend of nature and pious morality, appealed to Americans and set the pattern for the imitation of their poetic styles and themes.[89]

In fiction, long retarded in America because of moral objections from the Puritans, and rational objections to their lack of utility by men like Jefferson,[90] the two great vogues were Richardsonian sentimentalism and the historical romance of Scott. Fielding was imitated only slightly here outside the pages of Brackenridge and Paulding. The sentimental novel, easier to write, could lay claim,

---

[86] See E. A. Richards, *Hudibras in the Burlesque Tradition* (New York, 1937), and J. M. Beatty, Jr., "Churchill and Freneau," *American Literature*, II (May, 1930), 121-130.

[87] See n. 16, *supra*, and Alice L. Cooke's "Some Evidence of Hawthorne's Indebtedness to Swift," University of Texas *Studies in English*, 1938, 140-162; and her "The Shadow of Martinus Scriblerus in Hawthorne's 'The Prophetic Pictures,'" *New England Quarterly*, XVII (Dec., 1944), 597-604.

[88] See Daniel R. Lang, "Dr. Samuel Johnson in America," unpublished dissertation, Illinois, 1939.

[89] For these vogues, see Frank Luther Mott, *Golden Multitudes* (New York, 1947), and James D. Hart, *The Popular Book* (New York, 1950).

[90] See G. H. Orians, "Censure of Fiction in American Romances and Magazines," *PMLA*, LII (March, 1937), 195-214.

rightly or wrongly, to the moral didacticism demanded by American readers and critics. But sentimentalism could readily descend to sensibility, the "titillation of the self-approving feelings" for their own sake;[91] it was also capable of adaptation as an instrument of enthusiastic reform programs such as abolition, temperance, and women's rights in the nineteenth century, occasionally treated fanatically.[92]

I need not trace the vogue of the romance here. Like the sentimental novel it is both the cause and the effect of major social and literary shifts in the eighteenth and nineteenth centuries. Two factors, one literary, one social, seem of special relevance. The first is related to the form of the novel and romance. The very looseness of the form, its freedom, length, and larger canvas, the opportunity it provides for description of local scene and for character portrayal outside of the narrower tension range of verse, its discursiveness, its apparent encouragement of lack of polish (the emphasis is upon the narrative or the emotion rather than on the construction of the sentence)—these factors make the prose fiction of the period less a matter of art and more a matter of actual or easily imagined experience. Secondly (the social factor), fiction and the authors of fiction reflect the rise of feminism and the female author. The sentimental novel, tending as it did in the hands of Richardson and his followers to center on the heroine of virtue, provided an opening for the real expert on female emotions and domestic life, the woman herself. Beginning with Susanna Rowson and others in the 1790's, the number and importance of female novelists rapidly increased until the 1850's and Harriet Beecher Stowe. The majority of their readers were also women. It is no accident, I think, that even in the novels of Hawthorne, who went beyond the sentimental and the romance, our attention is focused upon Hester, Hepzibah, Miriam, and Zenobia. This increased attention to women in long fiction carries over into poetry and the short story. Witness the popularity of Mrs. Hemans and the ideali-

[91] See Reginald Watters, "The Vogue and Influence of Samuel Richardson in America," unpublished Wisconsin dissertation, 1941, and Tremaine McDowell, "Sensibility in the Eighteenth-Century American Novel," *Studies in Philology*, XXIV (July, 1927), 383-402.

[92] See Herbert R. Brown's excellent *Sentimental Novel in America, 1789-1860* (Durham, N. C., 1940), especially pp. 181-280.

zation of women in Bryant's imitations of the "Lucy" poems, Longfellow's courtships in verse, and especially in Poe.

The vogue of Scott in narrative verse was succeeded by the general acceptance of the Waverley novels in all sections of the country, and particularly in the ante-bellum South. Byron's popularity, equaling Scott's in intensity, declined sooner, in the 1830's. Wordsworth's poems, less recognizably romantic, came into their own gradually and were imitated by Bryant and Dana. Keats and Shelley were relatively unknown. Coleridge's poetry was received unfavorably in the reviews but found disciples in Washington Allston and Poe.

Directly, and through Scott, Coleridge, and Carlyle, Germany and the Continent exercised an influence, philosophical, religious, social, and literary, which gradually undermined Lockean and post-Revolutionary rationalism[93] and British and Scottish "common-sense."[94] Irving was directed to Germany by Scott and later discovered the surface glamour of Moorish Spain, a country whose appeal is also mirrored in Bryant, Prescott, Ticknor, and Longfellow. German writings, particularly Schiller's *Robbers* and Goethe's *Werther*,[95] influenced the American sentimental novel. Madame de Staël and the Schlegels introduced German philosophy and literature to America in the second decade of the nineteenth century.

One important influence from Germany is seen in the new critical and national school of historical writing: Irving, Bancroft, Prescott, Motley, Parkman. These writers were concerned with tracing the unique development of a national identity and spirit and thereby tended to counteract the cosmopolitan, uniformitarian school of the eighteenth century. They were in one sense the forerunners of Taine in his emphasis upon *"la race, le milieu, et le*

---

[93] On post-Napoleonic rationalism and the dynamic conception of nature, see Howard Mumford Jones, "The Influence of European Ideas in Nineteenth-Century America," *American Literature*, VII (Nov., 1945), 241-273.

[94] William Charvat, *The Origins of American Critical Thought, 1810-1835* (Philadelphia, 1936).

[95] See O. W. Long, "Werther in America," *Studies in Honor of John Albrecht Walz* (Lancaster, Pa., 1941), pp. 86-116; John A. Walz, *German Influence in American Education and Culture* (Philadelphia, 1936); Harold S. Jantz, "German Thought and Literature in New England, 1620-1820," *Journal of English and Germanic Philology*, XLI (Jan., 1942), 1-45.

*moment."* But German historiography and literature is an integral part of German philosophy. In the second and third decade of the new century a group of *neuer Amerikaner*—Cogswell, Everett, Ticknor, Bancroft, Hedge—invaded German universities to study under Eichhorn, Schleiermacher, Hegel, and others. Bancroft seems to have returned with something more important for our study than the others. Not only did he put into practice the new educational theories of natural growth of Pestalozzi and Herbart; his *History of the United States* (Volume I, 1834) embodied the nationalistic principles of his German mentors. Bancroft's writing of history was inductive in theory but intuitive in practice. Like W. E. Channing he had an unbounded faith in mankind and inherent goodness.[96] God implanted in man reason, conscience, and benevolence (again the Unitarian position); therefore man may unerringly discover the truth through these innate attributes, of which reason is the most powerful. But reason equals intuition, not logical or rational power, but "that higher faculty which originates truth." This, says Professor Nye, is an excellent definition of precisely what Emerson, Coleridge, Hegel, and Fichte meant by "reason."[97]

Here, then, is a foreign influence not easily combated by neoclassical literary nationalists who saw the dangers for America in Scott and the immorality and enervating effect of Byronism. The chief English intermediaries for Germany were Scott, Coleridge, and Carlyle. But Bancroft went directly to the source.

One other popular vogue, particularly in the periodicals and gift annuals of the twenties and thirties, may be mentioned. Poe points to it in a letter dated April 30, 1835, to White. Speaking of the current and marketable tales typical of the day, Poe finds but four types. Most popular is the horror tale, "the fearful coloured

[96] It is true that Bancroft referred once (in *Life and Letters*, 1908, ed. M. A. DeW. Howe, II, 228), to "natural depravity," but it should be noted that this was in its contextute associated with the French elections of 1869 in a passage where he says France "never can recover from the effects of the last policy of Louis XIV." This one reference to depravity is contradicted (p. 311) by "my philosophy and my [liberal Congregationalist] theology," according to which Bancroft holds that "the work of redemption is perfectly well done, faultless, infinitely good."

[97] Russel B. Nye, *George Bancroft, Brahmin Rebel* (New York, 1944), p. 100.

into the horrible"; then "the ludicrous heightened into the grotesque," "the witty exaggerated into the burlesque," and "the singular wrought out into the strange and mystical."[98] A typical issue of the Baltimore *Amethyst*, for 1831, contains all these types, replete as it is with tales of enchanted grottoes, premature burials, phrenology, and black-tressed and pallid devotees of esoteric knowledge who could pose as models for Poe's own Ligeia. And it is to these subjects that Poe turned, perhaps seriously, perhaps with tongue in cheek, after 1831 in his own tales.

V

FROM NORMATIVE SATIRE TO LYRICISM AND HUMOR

Byron defended Pope, and rightly, as a poet. But the world of Pope and the world of Byron, and the literature they wrote and inspired, have little in common. Yet they were both satirists. But the first wrote against aberrations from a societal norm; the second was a romantic ironist concerned with society's clash with his private norms. Exit neoclassicism. This is one of the patterns of the first half of the nineteenth century in America. Satire was written, from Brackenridge to Poe, but Brackenridge drew on the whole tradition of satire from Horace to Fielding as well as the ordered principles of the Enlightenment. Poe, an individualist, devised his own principles for poetry (following Coleridge in part) and for the short story. Then he measured poetry and fiction by these private yardsticks. His satire is Poesque.

Many of the more prominent writers of the period in America began with satire and ended with lyricism and humor, good or ill. Freneau was the satirist of the Revolution. He lives by his lyrics, although he returned again and again to satire in verse and prose, reaching his peak in the *Letters* . . . (1798).[99] His nineteenth-century poems (he died, long after he was forgotten, in 1832) are

[98] John Ostrom (ed.), *The Letters of Edgar Allan Poe* (Cambridge, Mass., 1948), I, 57-59. For discussion of this letter, see Napier Wilt, "Poe's Attitude toward His Tales: A New Document," *Modern Philology*, XXV (Aug., 1927), 101-105.

[99] Harry Hayden Clark (ed.), Philip Freneau, *Letters on Various Interesting and Important Subjects* (New York [Scholars' Facsimiles & Reprints], 1943).

much milder than the thundering condemnations written during the Revolution. Bryant's little known youthful poems[100] were largely Popean and satirical. Like Freneau he turned to Gray and the graveyard school, and thence to Alison's theories of "associationalism," to Wordsworth, nature, liberal journalism, and somewhat cold lyricism which does not match his own later dictum that a poet should write with words of flame.[101] He belongs essentially to the cult of simplicity, of sympathy with the uncomplicated feelings of the universal human heart, content with simple "wonder and delight."

Irving provides perhaps the best example (and the only one treated at length here) of the transition from satire to good humor in a single author. His best work, *Knickerbocker's History of New York* (1809), is one of the finest examples of literary neoclassicism in American letters. Yet the author of *Salmagundi, Knickerbocker's History, The Sketch Book, The Alhambra,* and *Astoria* poses for the critic and literary historian a complex problem of interpretation, for Irving spanned the period of transition in America from neoclassicism to romanticism, and he was invariably involved, though not usually consciously, in the social and political crossfires of the day, at home and abroad. Irving's progress away from neoclassical satire, assured by his temperament as well as by the age in which he lived, was given impetus by the reading of Gothic novels, the plays of Schiller and Kotzebuë produced on the New York stage by Dunlap, the duties of his editorship of the *Analectic,* which reproduced the best of English and European periodical literature, the years in England at the height of the Romantic movement, the personal stimulus of Scott, the German sojourn of 1821-1823, and the years in Spain (1826-1829, 1842-1845).[102] One might add the lure of the boundless American frontier which excited Irving upon his return to America in 1832 after an absence of seventeen years. Professor McCarter points to a natural dwin-

---

[100] Many of them, published for the first time, appear in Tremaine McDowell (ed.), *William Cullen Bryant* (New York, 1935). See McDowell's "The Juvenile Verse of William Cullen Bryant," *Studies in Philology,* XXVI (Jan., 1929), 96-116.

[101] See "The Poet" (1863).

[102] See Henry A. Pochmann (ed.), *Washington Irving* (New York, 1934), Introduction, pp. lxiv-lxvi.

dling of the satiric into the gently humorous in Irving's work as he moved toward romanticism.[103] Parrington intimates that Irving's best work was written before romanticism gained predominance over, and emasculated, his neoclassical, satiric manner.[104]

The elements of Irving's writing which remain little changed throughout his career, his style, his social conservatism, his delight in aristocratic society, his antiquarianism, do not account for the progressive decline of the satiric in his work. The satire in Irving's writing is essentially the result of a literary situation with which he had nothing to do. In his later writing he was not by nature critical, but receptive. His talents did not run to the novel or the drama. At the outset of his career there was no path open but that of the Addisonian essay or the burlesque tale. McCarter, claiming for Irving more distinction as the originator of the short story than has hitherto been granted him, argues that the short story grew out of the successful combination of these two elements: the essay and the tale.[105] When this fusion was made of the two neoclassical forms, Irving's romanticism was complete. He ceased writing satire as a form, although the elements of wit and well-bred pleasantry, the half-serious denial of seriousness, a significant part of a style formed on eighteenth-century models, lingered on in his later work, particularly in the tailpieces of his romantic stories and legends.

The neoclassical elements in Irving's work to 1815 are evident: in his use of eighteenth-century models, Addison, Swift, Fielding, Sterne, Smollett, Goldsmith; in his neglect of the early romantic poetry of Wordsworth, Coleridge, and Southey; in his ridicule (with a few exceptions) of sentimentalism and the Gothic; in his clear and elegant style; in his play of wit and use of comic and anticlimactic effects; and in his attention in his satire to social manners and foibles and the delineation of character. He employs all the standard neoclassical satiric devices; nevertheless, the temper of his satire from the first has much of the romantic in it. He lacks consistency as to the objects of his attack, as if uncertain what his

[103] Pete K. McCarter, "The Literary, Political, and Socal Theories of Washington Irving," unpublished Wisconsin dissertation, 1939, p. 61.
[104] *Main Currents in American Thought* (New York, 1927, 1930), II, p. 212.
[105] *Op. cit.*, p. 182.

true norm should be. His satire usually creates an immediate sympathy for its objects. His innate and incorrigible antiquarianism casts a shadow of remoteness over his satire. The subjective element is never absent. He loves eccentricity for its own sake. His satire is not really didactic in purpose. Fancy predominates over judgment. He lacked genuine critical ability. His reading in the romances, modern and medieval, gave romantic coloring to his early efforts.

In his essay on Robert Treat Paine in 1812 and even as late as 1819 in the "Mutability of Literature" in *The Sketch Book,* Irving called for acceptance of tradition and the development of a rigorous criticism to curb the effusions of second-rate authors.[106] Twenty years later, in "Desultory Thoughts on Criticism," he flatly accepted individual taste as the last and final resort.

> The reader, therefore, should not suffer himself to be readily shaken from the conviction of his own feelings by the sweeping censures of pseudo-critics. The author he has admired may be chargeable with a thousand faults; but it is nevertheless beauties and excellences that have excited his admiration; and he should recollect that taste and judgment are as much evinced in the perception of beauties among defects, as in a detection of the blessed and blessing spirit that is quick to discover and extol all that is pleasing and meritorious. Give me the honest bee, that extracts honey from the humblest weed, but save me from the ingenuity of the spider, which traces its venom even in the midst of a flower-garden.[107]

Satire cannot live in this atmosphere. It has given way to romantic general humor and gentle good will. "The Goldsmith of our time," as Thackeray called him,[108] is no longer the Goldsmith of the *Citizen of the World;* he is the sentimentalist of the *Deserted Village.* And it must not be forgotten that a large segment of the literary world from 1820 to 1850 is "The World of Washington Irving," in which all other writers are but "Minor Knickerbockers."

Perhaps one of the most significant forms of literature coming out of the West was the humor of the southwestern frontier. In its earliest manifestations this humor created a mythical figure who

---

[106] Geoffrey Crayon Edition, p. 190.
[107] *Biographies and Miscellanies,* Geoffrey Crayon Edition, pp. 534-535
[108] "Nil Nisi Bonum," *Harper's Weekly,* XX (1860), 542.

was representative of man in nature, cut off completely from society and facing the wilderness alone—and, most important, defeating it. (Crockett, for example, averts disaster by greasing the axles of the world with bear "ile.") Davy Crockett (1834) was not the only member of this tradition; Bird of Philadelphia wrote of Ralph Stackpole and Paulding of New York presented Col. Nimrod Wildfire to the theater-going public. The romantic figure of man alone in nature appealed to both East and West, and was in a sense a co-creation. But the tradition that began with A. B. Longstreet's *Georgia Scenes* (1835) was distinctly Western in creation.

Nevertheless, Longstreet cannot be called romantic; nor can one of his followers, J. G. Baldwin, author of *Flush Times in Alabama and Mississippi* (1853). Both men write in the older essay style; Longstreet moralizes about the vices he portrays; some of Baldwin's sketches are completely devoid of humor while those which are consciously so often employ the humor of indirection. Another interesting feature of this southwestern humor is that it produced the only picaresque hero in America between Captain John Farrago and *A Connecticut Yankee*, J. J. Hooper's rogue, Simon Suggs (1845).

Strangest of all is the fact that out of this individualistic section and in this romantic era with its disregard of literary form in the neoclassical sense came a new literary form. The new form was not hidebound by rules, but it was probably the tightest one to emerge in romantic nineteenth-century America. This was the frame story, a distinctly literary phenomenon, which was devised to give some kind of adequate transcription to the oral tale. Within a frame of "author language" at the beginning and end was set the oral tale, in the exact words of the backwoods cracker or clay-eater or piney-woods tacky who was telling the tale. There is often a climactic order in the oral tale, the narrator spieling off a string of incidents, each a little more impressive than the last, until he reaches the one on which he intends to dwell. One of the finest examples of the frame story is T. B. Thorpe's "The Big Bear of Arkansas." (1841). (Granted the frame story is not, strictly speaking, a new form, it still remains that the circumstances which gave rise to it seem to have little if any relation to its earlier uses.)

It is a curious fact that after 1800 very few of those Americans who wrote satire wrote it in New England, in the South, or in the West. The middle states, the center of the Union, produced the satire, most of it emanating from the social and literary club life of New York. The South buried itself in cotton and romance, New England in Harvard and Transcendentalism, the West in mud and frontier humor. Those who took their poetry seriously began to doubt that satire is really poetry.[109] Poe went beyond doubt to flat denial: the poet does not, he said, stoop to truth and moralize his song.[110] He sings and dreams his own dreams unless science has destroyed the possibility of dreaming.[111]

VI

THE TURN FROM NEOCLASSICAL TO ROMANTIC CRITICISM

Although all generalizations on this much disputed subject are dangerous and open to exceptions, the over-all picture one gets of the differences between neoclassical and romantic literary criticism from such a recent book as J. W. H. Atkins' *English Literary Criticism: 17th and 18th Centuries* (London, 1951), somewhat biased toward the romantic, is roughly as follows. The neoclassicists sought to judge rationally, to evaluate, in the light of absolutes, of rules supposedly based on human nature regarded as always and in all ages "still the same"; the romantics as individualists guided by emotion sought to show that each work of art (in Hazlitt's phrase) was *sui generis*, different, and seldom within the realm (as Keats said) of "rule and compass vile." The neoclassicists tended to ground their values on a (Newtonian?) mechanistic, ordered and changeless cosmos; the romantics tended to stress the organic concept. For them, literature was conditioned by the literary creator's personality and to some extent social conditions which often

[109] Sibley, *op. cit.*, pp. 94-100. See, also, Dana's review of Washington Allston's *Sylphs of the Seasons, North American Review*, V (Sept., 1817), 365-389.
[110] Poe rather ambiguously maintained that a satire could not be a true poem. Yet, in a review of Park Benjamin's "Infatuation," he called for a satire from some "vigorous, original, and fearless man of genius in America" to put an end to "complaints of the American deficiency in this respect" (*Works*, Virginia Edition, XII, 108-109).
[111] "Sonnet to Science."

change and (as reformers like Shelley thought) ought to be changed. The neoclassicists usually sought in imagery what Johnson called "the grandeur of generality" and refused to "gild the streaks of the tulip"; the romantics increasingly exalted writing which supplied deficiencies in details of natural description and appealed warmly to all the five senses, as in the case of Keats. If the neoclassicists' imagination was not always associated with Hobbes's definition of it as "decaying sense," they tended to focus it on archetypes of a universal or changeless kind; the romantics, individualistic and relativistic, paved the way for emphasis on a criticism which (from the Wartons on) emphasized the historical approach, constant and desirable change, and a recognition of the "otherness" of past ages as well as the right of the contemporary age to be distinctive. Dissatisfied with a mechanical cosmos and a social caste system resting in part on outward forms, many of the romantics like the younger Wordsworth and Coleridge advocated a poetry based on the imagination considered as "creative," as "clearest insight" and "amplitude of mind" which (in I. A. Richards' words on Coleridge) "gains insight into reality, reads nature as a symbol of something behind or within nature not ordinarily perceived." Generally the neoclassicists valued social conformity while the romantics in youth valued individualism, defiance of conventions, or what Thoreau was to call "Civil Disobedience." If the neoclassicists tended to draw on earlier French principles, many of the romantics turned to German critical principles. The neoclassicists tended to stress the idea that the "kinds" of writing are distinct, while the romantics, scornful of rules, tended to think that the "kinds" might be mixed, just as the rules of unity of time, place, and action might be violated with good results. In critical practice the neoclassicists from Dryden's *All for Love* to Bentley's revision of Milton tended to think that Shakespeare and Milton with all their greatness could be "improved"; the romantics, while indifferent to judicial "constants" or critical yardsticks derived from the past, generally emphasized (as did Coleridge and De Quincey) the idolatry of Shakespeare and Milton as *sui generis* and examples of artistic individualism. One might as well admit that these generalizations are about as often honored in the breach as in the observance, and dozens of exceptions will occur to every reader; but they may be of some use as very broad frames of reference, since the conflicts in English literature were in the main imported by American critics.

Some aspects of the backgrounds and the history of American critical thought to 1835 (such as the influence of the Scottish associationalists) have been the subject of detailed and scholarly investigation.[112] Prior to about 1825, in spite of new impulses at home and abroad, the critical standards were still neoclassical. The rules were so generally agreed upon that the critic wrote anonymously, as if speaking not for himself but for society and its uniform standards of taste. Bryant, the first American critic of stature, as late as his *Lectures on Poetry* (1825-1826), and in spite of his own imitations of Wordsworth, is as yet little removed from the neoclassical position. His discussion of imagination, the emotions, and understanding must not be misunderstood to the extent of placing him within the critical orbit of Coleridge. Rather, it seems clear that these terms are closer to Pope's "spirit, taste, and sense" than to Coleridge's primary and secondary imagination. Imagination still means to Bryant the fancy, and understanding is the apprehension of those universal principles of taste which take their rise in the reason of things and are applied in criticism by the judgment. Poetry is related to the best and most universal sympathies of our nature. "Certainly it is a noble occupation to shape the creations of the mind into perfect forms according to those laws which man learns from observing the works of his Maker."[113] Here we may see the working of psychological thought in America through various strains of Locke,[114] Edwards,[115] and the Scottish school,[116] emphasizing in the senses the seat of the affections, the sources of emotional response. What Bryant does insist upon is freedom from sickly imitation of models, whether Pope, Words-

---

[112] William Charvat, *op. cit.*, and Margaret Alterton, *Origins of Poe's Critical Theory* (Iowa City, 1922).

[113] *Prose Writings*, I, 15-16.

[114] See Merle Curti, "The Great Mr. Locke: America's Philosopher 1783-1861," *Huntington Library Bulletin*, XI (April, 1937), 107-151.

[115] See Perry Miller, "Jonathan Edwards to Emerson," *New England Quarterly*, XIII (Dec., 1940), 589-617.

[116] For documentation of the influence of the Scottish aestheticians on Bryant, see William P. Hudson, "Archibald Alison and William Cullen Bryant," *American Literature*, XII (March, 1940), 59-68.

worth, or Byron. But it is clear that a new criticism is not embodied in Bryant's *Lectures*.

Bryant, however, did contribute to an important transition in theory and practice in verse, the shift from polish, correctness, and regularity of form to "organic verse," and intentional roughness. In a famous 1819 essay he defended the trisyllabic foot against the prevalent rule for regularity which "has been observed to the frequent sacrifice of beauty of expression, and variety and vivacity of numbers."[117] In his review of Solyman Brown's "Essay on American Poetry" he criticized the "balanced and wearisome regularity" of the Connecticut Wits.[118] In his own verses he was capable of surprising variety of forms and metrics, "in that day notable triumphs in the modernization of American prosody."[119]

The heroic couplet, in spite of the continuing popularity of Pope's *Essay on Man*, was apparently very difficult to write by the time R. H. Dana, Sr., published his first volume of poems in 1827. In a typical passage from "Thoughts on the Soul" the couplet rhyme is all that remains of that noble instrument of wit and precision.[120] Over half of the lines are run-on; the ideas have no internal organization in the line.

Poe was as painstaking metrically as any neoclassicist, but he was seeking for unique and indefinite effects by mechanical contrivance. He also argued somewhat absurdly for quantitative verse in English and denied the necessity of metrical regularity in successive feet of the poetic line.[121] The rhythm of "The Raven" is purposely complicated; "The Bells" is a notable experiment in tonal effects.

---

[117] Parke Godwin (ed.), *Prose Writings of William Cullen Bryant* (New York, 1884), I, 58.

[118] Tremaine McDowell (ed.), *William Cullen Bryant* (New York, 1935), p. 172.

[119] *Ibid.*, p. lvi. Gay Wilson Allen, in his important study *American Prosody* (New York, 1935), p. 53, calls Bryant "the forefather of American prosody."

[120] Richard Henry Dana, *Poems and Prose Writings* (New York, 1850), I, 85-96.

[121] See "The Rationale of Verse." Detailed discussion of Poe's prosody is to be found in Allen, *op. cit.*, pp. 56-85, and W. L. Werner, "Poe's Theories and Practice in Poetic Technique," *American Literature*, II (May, 1930), 157-165.

The Transcendentalists, as might be expected, produced the least polished, or seeming-polished, verse. Many of their metrical irregularities go back to the reading by Emerson and Thoreau of seventeenth-century devotional and metaphysical verse. They captured some of its charge and compression. The "roughest poets" of the school were Emerson, whose own metrical freedom is both exemplified and justified in "Merlin" (1847), Jones Very, the younger W. E. Channing, who according to Thoreau wrote in the "sublimo-slipshod," and Christopher Cranch, who in "Correspondences" created some of the first free verse in America.

But there is a theory that accompanies roughness. Emerson wrote for the *Dial* a little essay on "New Poetry," an apology for the private verse of Channing, who was so scathingly reviewed by Poe. Faults, and "halting rhymes," said Emerson, proclaim the man above the artist. "Men of genius in general are, more than others, incapable of any perfect exhibition." Though lacking in finish, the failures of genius seem to him better than the victories of talent.[122]

The same transition is evident from the public, polished prose of Brackenridge to the private, spontaneous, and purposefully uneven prose of Emerson and Thoreau, and the adroitly illiterate localisms of the humor writers, Lowell as well as those of the frontier. Even the best writers of the period, among them Cooper, Paulding, and Simms, were often shockingly unconcerned with the labor of the file. Poe, it is true, took great pains, not, however, in order to make his prose that of statement but to make it surcharged with dramatic effect.

Romantic criticism has its genuine beginnings in 1816 in the pages of the *North American Review* under R. H. Dana, Sr., and Willard Phillips. There had been intimations of it previously, in attacks upon rhyme, in extravagant praise of the cult of simplicity of Bloomfield, Wordsworth, and Coleridge, in admission of the charm of Scott and the exotic of Moore and Southey. A probable source (or at least a corroborating body of material) for much of Emerson's transcendentalism may be found in the articles of the *North American Review* which throughout the twenties and

---

[122] *Dial*, I (1840), 220-232. This essay is available in Perry Miller (ed.). *The Transcendentalists* (1950), pp. 375-381.

thirties called attention of its readers to German and French thought, foreign cultures, Coleridge, Wordsworth, and Carlyle.[123]

Professor Charvat has admirably shown the way in which the literary criticism of the historian W. H. Prescott turned against British criticism as blind to European historical development and as politically partisan, and then turned from the Scottish associationalists to the methods and criteria of the German critics.[124] We greatly need similarly thorough studies of transitions in the critical thinking of such men as diverse as William Dunlap, Alexander Everett, Robert Walsh, Gulian Verplanck, George Ticknor, E. P. Whipple, P. S. DuPonceau, J. G. Percival, the early Holmes (whose preface to "Poetry: A Metrical Essay" [1836] says he was trained "after the schools of classical English verse"), Edward S. Gould, James A. Hillhouse (whose "Choice of an Era in Epic and Tragic Writing" [1826] shows how the turn from the ancient classics as models to the Bible brought in different standards of sublimity), and especially O. W. B. Peabody, whose earlier neoclassical standards were greatly modified by his admiration of Scott as a novelist having the dignity of a serious historian and by his devotion shown in his 1836 edition of Shakespeare distinctive in its historical sense shown in his reconstructing the original text. Indeed, changing reactions to Shakespeare and Scott are pivotal in this whole transition. If as F. O. Galloway concludes,[125] the rise of the historical method and a recognition of the distinctive "otherness" of past ages and their relativity is a major influence on the turn against neoclassical uniformitarianism, then we need thorough studies of the history of the reviews and essays on Herder and Madame de Staël in America. Scott Goodnight has located some thirty American discussions of Herder before 1846,[126] and George Ripley's es-

---

[123] See n. 26, *supra*.

[124] William Charvat and Michael Kraus (eds.), *William Hickling Prescott* (New York, 1943), pp. lxxxviii-ci.

[125] Francis Galloway, *Reason, Rule and Revolt in English Classicism* (New York, 1940), p. 286.

[126] Scott H. Goodnight, *German Literature in American Magazines Prior to 1846* (Madison, Wisconsin, 1907), *passim*. Two especially symptomatic essays are George Bancroft, "Herder's Writings," *North American Review*, XX (Jan., 1825), 138-147, and George Ripley, review-essay on Herder's *Spirit of Hebrew Poetry* (trans. J. Marsh), *Christian Examiner*, XVIII (1835), 167 ff.

says on and use of Herder illustrate the way in which clergymen were to be inspired to much excellent critical writing as a result of their attempt to support or attack the German ideas of the "higher criticism" of the Bible and the question of whether or not it should be approached historically as having been conditioned by its time and place and its racial backgrounds, making it not absolute but relativistic. Madame de Staël not only helped introduce German ideas but in her *Influence of Literature upon Society* (translated and published in Boston, New York, and Philadelphia in 1813) emphasized the idea of progress through republican freedom and the beneficent influence of Protestant religion, and she also (presaging Taine) suggested approaching literature historically in terms of its reciprocal relation to changing religion, law, morality, and social standards. She represented an appealing transition from the Enlightenment to the individualism of Transcendentalism of the German kind. Jefferson and Ticknor were her personal friends, Theophilus Parsons praised her style, and before 1836 even the staid *North American Review* devoted five essays to her ideas.[127] In his 1834 introduction to Cousin's *Psychology* the American C. S. Henry (himself an important transitional figure) said that, with the rise of German ideas through the vogue of Madame de Staël's *De L'Allemagne*, the vogue of Locke which mainly supported neoclassicism was doomed.

The Unitarian *Christian Examiner* continued the work of romantic critics in the *North American Review* by giving general sanction to the criticism of Coleridge in the *Biographia Literaria*. James McHenry's *American Quarterly Review*, begun in 1827, although essentially neoclassical, as Mr. Charvat concludes, gave much space to German works; praised the eccentric romantic Percival[128] and Dana's probing of "the abysses and darkness of a bad

---

[127] These are summarized in Clark's article, just cited, pp. 309, 312, 314, 341, 343. See also R. L. Hawkins, *Madame de Staël and the United States* (1930), and R. C. Whitford, "Madame de Staël's Literary Reputation in America," *Modern Language Notes*, XXXIII (Dec., 1918), 476-480.

[128] In one of his editorials for the *Connecticut Herald* in 1823 Percival defined poetic genius as "a peculiarly excited and impassioned state of the mind, accompanied with nice sensibility and rapid associations, by which it is fitted to call up and unite together the materials of imagery in such a manner as shall give to the reader the most complete and commanding

mind."[129] Wordsworth and "The Lakers" suffered at the *Quarterly's* hands, because of the uninspired, unimaginative level of some of their verses. "Natural thoughts expressed in ordinary language" is a definition too tame for a critic who has tasted the stronger fare of Byron. He felt that by metaphysical abstractions and depth of learning the Lake poets sought to compensate for the absence of a poetical imagination. They "drag forth hidden resemblances," "combine forced associations," and shroud their writings in a veil of mystery. However, a commentator on English and American lyric poetry discovers the reason for the popularity of such "unintelligible poetry": "There is a wild sublimity . . . eminently calculated to excite the fancy to energy and action."[130]

By late 1836 the *Quarterly*, hitherto harshly critical of English romantic Lake poets, had escaped from the fascination of Byron and returned to Shelley and Wordsworth as England's best, because they were reformers, directed by benevolent impulses unknown to the cold philosophers of the eighteenth century. Shelley felt that "there was a power pervading and governing all things." Wordsworth, of whom the critic admits his former contempt, is now seen to be a true lover of nature and, more important, of man, who with an acute sensibility and eager imagination, "interests himself with all that is near him, and multiplies himself, and forms a part of the multitude of affections that controul and break over the souls of men."[131]

Except in the South and the West, idealistic romanticism was generally accepted critically toward the end of the third decade of the nineteenth century. Legaré in the *Southern Review* still preferred the classical "temporalities" to romantic "spiritualities,"

---

sense of reality" (Julius H. Ward, *Life and Letters of James Gates Percival* [Boston, 1866], p. 545).

[129] March, 1828, p. 115.

[130] "American Lyric Poetry" (March 1836), pp. 101 ff.

[131] Sept., 1836, p. 66. For the quarrel between Walsh's *Quarterly* and Clark's *Knickerbocker* over the competence of McHenry's reviews, see Mott, *A History of American Magazines* (Cambridge, Mass., 1938), I, 274-275. See also Sister M. Frederick Lochemes, *Robert Walsh: His Story* (Washington, D. C., 1941), for a fuller account of Walsh, a neoclassical nationalist.

while James Hall's *Illinois Monthly*, extremely nationalistic, was almost uniformly critical of contemporary British writers.

At the beginning of the nineteenth century American theories of education, although often contradictory in their attitude toward the classics, were soundly neoclassical.[132] The practical, utilitarian "modern" education advocated by Franklin, Paine, Freneau, and Rush had its opponents, as for example Samuel Knox, in his *Essay on the Best System of Liberal Education*,[133] and to some extent the classical-minded H. H. Brackenridge in *Modern Chivalry*. It is ironical that one effect of the utilitarian principle, with its emphasis upon the modern languages[134] and the functional training necessary in a republic, tended to turn readers to the romantic literature of nonrepublican countries, or to dissipate, especially among the general public, neoclassical standards of taste.

But the traditionalism of the universities was strengthened by Federalism and by general reaction against the French Revolution. John Quincy Adams, in the chair of rhetoric at Harvard, went back to classical Roman models. E. T. Channing, although he taught many of the Transcendentalists at Harvard, did not teach them romanticism. Blair's *Rhetoric*, Channing's principal text, making no distinction between poetry and rhetoric, emphasizes the faculty of taste, to be cultivated by "attention to the most approved models," and application of good sense and reason to the objects of taste.[135] The good style he considered the happy combination of perspicuity and ornament. "The general effect of his lectures on style was to encourage correctness and stiffness rather

---

[132] A. O. Hansen, *Liberalism and American Education in the Eighteenth Century* (New York, 1926). Hansen emphasizes the idea of perfectibility and progress in American educational thought of the time, an idea which leads ultimately away from rationalism. Education, however, was looked upon as the principal means of perfecting and fixing institutions which would be consistent with republican principles. Institutions are therefore considered mutable and perfectible in so far as they had not yet been devised to coincide with the natural and immutable liberties of Man. Education is ultimately a means of social control. The emphasis is generally upon society, not upon the individual, in American thought prior to 1800.

[133] Baltimore, 1799.

[134] The first university courses in modern foreign literatures were offered at Harvard by the first Smith professor, George Ticknor.

[135] Edinburgh, 1813, p. 23.

than suppleness and native idiom."[136] Yet Blair and the Scottish philosophers' emphasis upon empirical truths, upon experience,[137] strengthened Channing's desire to create a style "suited to our state of society." In the *North American Review* in an article "On Models in Literature" he spoke out against slavish imitation of the classics, which makes

> what is foreign, artificial, and uncongenial the foundation of a man's literary habits, ambitions and prejudices . . . the imitator, the man who gets his stock of thought and sentiment of beauty from books, is cautious, constrained, and modeled throughout.[138]

In his courses at Harvard he contemplated the use of Burke's *Inquiry* and Alison *On Taste*, as more directly concerned with the psychological basis of the sublime. And he seems to have believed that there is an intuitional shortcut to truth, that "the sacred and generous fountains of the heart" which produce "feeling," are very often reason itself.[139] It becomes evident how the Common Sense philosophy, relying on that very quality of reason which is in all men, makes easy the pathway to intuition and beyond it, to the creative imagination. Anyone who has seen Thoreau's student compositions for Channing's class cannot doubt the implications of his teaching.[140] The "rational individualism" of the neoclassical school becomes intuitional individualism. The appeal to the "consensus gentium" disappears, and uniformitarianism is only a goal to be arrived at through universal truths apparent to each self-cultivating individual, who puts himself passively in tune with the infinite.

[136] Charvat, *Origins*, p. 128.
[137] See Kames, *Elements of Criticism*, I, 11-12, on the psychological basis for truth rather than the authority of the ancients.
[138] July, 1816, pp. 204-206.
[139] *Lectures*, pp. 38-39: "This siren or this fury is very often reason herself, kindled and inspired. Persuasion has, indeed, little appearance of proving and convincing; but this is so, probably, because feeling makes perception so rapid that steps and processes are not recognized." This is the nineteenth-century counterpart of the "grace beyond the reach of art," familiar to but not encouraged by Pope and neoclassicism.
[140] See J. J. Kwiat, "Thoreau's Philosophical Apprenticeship," *New England Quarterly*, XVIII (March, 1945), 51-69; Merrill R. Davis, "Emerson's 'Reason' and the Scottish Philosophers," *ibid.*, XVII (June, 1944), 209-228; and E. W. Todd, "Philosophical Ideas in Harvard College," *ibid.*, XVI (March, 1943), 63-90.

In tracing the decline of a movement the violence of initial protests against the status quo illustrates not so much the spread of the new order desired as the strength of the status quo itself. Thus in the wake of the Swiss Pestalozzi's influence which began in a small number of schools in the 1820's, protests in the name of spontaneity and individuality began against authoritarianism and uniformitarianism associated with neoclassicism. (In a sense, of course, this dissociating of reason from authority was a continuation in America from Paine's *Age of Reason*, although now redirected from theological to educational channels.) Thus in 1828 a writer in the *American Journal of Education* argued, "Reason, the distinguishing attribute of our nature, should not be debased by the inculcations of authority, or the deceptions of prejudice and error." And in objecting to the mechanical kind of instruction in the United States, a writer in the *American Annals of Education and Instruction* wrote in 1831:

If it be allowable in any country, it is utterly out of place in one where men are called to *act* in government of themselves, to examine the qualifications and measure of men who are to decide their fate and that of their families. He that *gives* or *encourages* such instruction as this, is among the most *dangerous enemies of his country*, for he is undermining the very basis of its freedom, and preparing and accustoming men to obey, in blind ignorance, the dictates of those who go before them.

And the next year another writer in the same periodical insisted that "the great object to be kept in view in all our efforts for the instruction and government and education of the young, should be to lead them as early and as rapidly as possible, to *self-instruction, self-government*, and *self-education*."[141]

One way to prove the immediate effects of teaching in the universities upon literary thought is to examine the contents of undergraduate periodicals, although it must be pointed out that, then as now, the reading of literature by students occurred, for the most part, outside the classroom assignments.

The *Harvard Lyceum* of 1810 is still strongly neoclassical. "Sci-

[141] These three quotations are cited by Merle Curti in his *Social Ideas of American Educators* (New York, 1935), pp. 29-30, from the *American Journal of Education*, III (June, 1828), 370, and *American Annals of Education and Instruction*, I (Dec., 1831), 577, and *ibid.*, II (April 1, 1832), 161.

ence and literature seem to be all that is old fashioned and good that we have left."¹⁴² A national literature must be built on the past, but especially that past which is strong in "moral thought." "Do not go to the impious Briton."¹⁴³ Except for Southey, no English or German writer since the American Revolution is mentioned.

By 1835 Harvard students had changed their tone somewhat. In the *Harvardiana* (1835-1839) the value of novels is now a subject for lively debate. E. R. Hoar, in a Carlylean article on "Indifference" urges "quickness of feeling" and moral "enthusiasm" as necessary to purposeful living.¹⁴⁴ A later review (II, 329) of *Sartor Resartus* in 1836 praises Carlyle for his beauty of thought. The typical critical essay is hostile to the older romanticists, as if Harvard students were already oriented to the new American synthesis of Transcendentalism. But the language of criticism remains neoclassical. One critic quotes with approval Henry Taylor's statement that "Poetry of which sense is not the basis . . . will not long be reputed to be poetry of the highest order . . . it fails to satisfy the understanding."¹⁴⁵ H. B. Dennis in "Rural Sentimentalities" (I, 256) admits admiration for rural scenery, agrees that the charms of nature are superior to those of art, but says the effusions of poets of nature are "ridiculous and absurd." A. C. Spooner (I, 257) attributes Byron's loss of popularity to his opposition to reason and truth. Reason is man's guide on earth; "imagination gives him a foretaste of heaven."

The Amherst *Shrine* (1832-1833) is frankly romantic. Coleridge is "the most remarkable genius of the age," wild and untamed. Wordsworth's love of nature is "an intense and burning passion." American poets are measured by the yardstick of Wordsworth and Coleridge.¹⁴⁶ Bryant is too correct and without strength, Pierpont is not American at all but of the school of Pope, Halleck's society verse is "insignificant," Willis has too much glitter, Longfellow lacks "agony" and passion, but Dana resembles Wordsworth in his power, his love of nature and the human soul; Percival,

---

¹⁴² July 14, 1810, Prospectus.
¹⁴³ "Letter to a Student," Nov. 17, 1810, p. 232.
¹⁴⁴ I (1835), 46.
¹⁴⁵ I, 217.
¹⁴⁶ II (1833), 149-212.

the greatest American at present, combines imagination, power, enthusiasm, and boldness. The key to these criticisms is found in the sketch of Longfellow.

What makes descriptive poetry of real moral utility is to have every scene with its shadow of sentiment or thought, not confused and thrown up in a mass at the end, but distinct and refined, and attached to its proper object, so that the soul may catch it, at once, and be hallowed by its power.[147]

Here is the associative principle at work, demonstrating again how readily the essentially neoclassical theory of the eighteenth century can be adapted to romantic uses.

Washington Allston, as painter and poet who early absorbed cultural and ideological currents from abroad, illustrates with remarkable clarity this synthesis of accepted neoclassical frames of reference with romantic and transcendental techniques and modes of expression. The major personal influence upon his thought was Coleridge, whom he met in Rome about 1805. His first poetry, *Sylphs of the Seasons*, is Wordsworthian. The poet is said to create new forms not by reason of direct sensory appeal to his emotions, but by art, by allowing the imagination to play over emotions recollected.[148] Allston's later sonnet, "On the Late S. T. Coleridge," speaks of their looking together "on the unfathom'd deep, The Human Soul," and of Coleridge's "living Truth. . . Binding in one, as with harmonious zones, the heart and intellect." The artist does exactly what Coleridge did in philosophy; he (like Michelangelo) brings to view "the invisible Idea" whose validity is checked by his inner sense which sees the organic relationship of Art and Nature, which speaks to the heart as "life to life responding."[149]

Allston consistently emphasized in his *Lectures on Art* (*ca.* 1832) the individuality of artists as well as the individuality of the objects of art. The type (the human being) must have character; therefore the source of the type must be found in each individual. Hence the correspondence between the natural and moral orders. In art as in the free mind of man each individual is idealized, that

---

[147] II, 209.
[148] *Lectures on Art and Poems* (New York, 1850), pp. 212-217.
[149] *Ibid.*, p. 346.

is, made a whole, since it is the inner desire of man to see the whole. The four tests of great art therefore become for Allston originality, ideal (human and poetic) truth, invention (Coleridge's secondary imagination), and unity, the inevitable effect of the individual's attainment of "primeval harmony."[150] Consider the following passage, so strangely familiar to twentieth-century readers of T. S. Eliot.

> So, too, is the external world to the mind; which needs, also, as the condition of its manifestation, its objective correlative. Hence the presence of some outward object, predetermined to correspond to the pre-existing idea in its living power, is essential to the evolution of its proper end,—the pleasurable emotion.[151]

Allston's language is that of Thomas Reid and Archibald Alison, of the Scottish school. Add to this his debt to Coleridge, upon whom the influence of associationism has been made clear.[152] The problem is, are we right in attributing the decline of neoclassicism to Hartley and the essentially (in intent) neoclassical Scottish school itself, or even to the nineteenth-century interpretation of it? What complex of forces caused the use of Scottish intuitional psychology as a critical defense of a point of view already attained? The answer, or an answer, it seems to me, lies in the individual's search for truth which is more personally perceived through the heart than the unsatisfying constructions of a uniformly held rationalism. "General truth" must be impregnated with the individual mind which imaginatively creates for itself the "unseen real." Art, therefore, does not appeal to uniform reason but to the human heart whose variety, like that of Nature, is seen to be a part of the unity of God's plan.[153] Uniformitarianism is a goal to be achieved individually, not a point of departure.

Criticism, in general, then, lagged behind literary practice, but gradually moved away from the position of the guardian of correct taste to that of the rapturous impressionist, from generalities to aesthetic particulars, from spirit, taste, and sense to imagination,

[150] *Ibid.*, pp. 75-110.
[151] *Ibid.*, p. 16.
[152] Walter Jackson Bate, *From Classic to Romantic* (Cambridge, Mass., 1946).
[153] See the similarity to Poe's idea of following the perfect plots of God as represented in the cosmos (*Eureka*).

genius, and sublimity, from understanding to intuitive but absolute comprehensiveness,[154] from judgment to individual bias and predilection, through which, as in Thoreau, the eternal world is reshaped by the mind of the unique individual.

## VII

### Conclusion

James Marsh, Vermont prophet of romantic idealism, in his "Preliminary Essay" to Coleridge's *Aids to Reflection*[155] suggests an answer to the problem posed here and at the same time suggests the barriers in the way of arriving at the answer by any attempted analysis of cause and effect. In supporting Coleridge's distinction between intuitive reason and common understanding he insists upon the necessity of the belief in freedom of the will by which men transcend the deterministic operation of cause and effect and find the nature of their own being isolated within themselves. This is to deny the Lockean materialism and the uniformitarianism of the Enlightenment, the mechanical operation of the will as a rational choice in deism, as well as the spiritual validity of the Common-Sense philosophy of the mind of the anti-Lockean Scottish school. And here is the whole point: the spiritual truths of Christianity, says Marsh, are incompatible with such "easy" theories of the mind and the will; the truth must be plumbed with difficulty in the inner recesses of the individual.

The decline of neoclassicism was the result of a complex of many divergent forces at home and abroad. When some of the terms frequently used here are considered, such as nationalism, sectionalism, the frontier, racism, class consciousness, progress, the heroic, humanitarianism, utopianism, chivalry, subjectivism, originality, imagination, Gothicism, the supernatural, intuition, biological growth, transciency, sensibility——they may be seen to be aspects of a common force, the rise of diversitarian individualism.

[154] See Margaret Fuller's "Short Essay on Critics" in the *Dial*, I (July, 1840), 5-11.
[155] First edition in America, Burlington, Vt., 1829. The central part of Marsh's argument is contained within pp. xxxiii-xlv. See also Marjorie Nicolson, "James Marsh and the Vermont Transcendentalists," *Philosophical Review*, XXXIV (Jan., 1925), 28-50.

The Enlightenment, of which neoclassicism is the most central literary expression, contained in its admission of "rational individualism" the seeds of its own dissolution. With the rise of the common man, predicated by the Enlightenment, it was inevitable that the terms rational and reason should undergo transformation in order to remain inclusive. The emphasis shifted from the "rational" to the "individual" who has received the license to know the truth, truth which is not self-evident but evident to the self. Reason to men in the Enlightenment was discursive; truth was therefore readily communicable. Reason in the nineteenth century became intuitive or speculative; truth was therefore difficult of transference. Uniformity, instead of remaining a binding and limiting force, became the goal to be arrived at by every individual fulfilling the demands of his own inner reason, and hence the transition from neoclassical uniformity to romantic diversity and realistic particularity.

No doubt many causes for the shifting fortunes of neoclassical thought and literary practice in America have been left untouched in this chapter. Some of the probable influences appended here have received treatment in scholarly books and articles; others may prove fruitful suggestions for further research.

Among the forces buttressing the survival of neoclassicism were the following: Religious conservatism, strengthened by recoil from the excesses of infidelity in France and at home, tended to uphold the status quo, the old, the tried, the accepted, the conventional, and the safe. Eighteenth-century Calvinism had absorbed the rationalism of the followers of Locke and Newton and Shaftesbury; such Calvinism, in watered-down form, still dominated religious thought in the first half of the nineteenth century. The Presbyterian doctrine of means withheld from the individual the errors of private interpretation and made for adherence to the older sanctions of morality and didacticism and for a continuation of the attack upon fiction and the stage. Early Unitarians were Federalistic and neoclassical. At the same time, the survival of deism and natural religion tended in part to maintain the parallel with neoclassicism in their emphasis upon uniformity, cosmopolitanism, and rationalism.

Continuing Federalistic and orthodox control of education, the courts, and the press perpetuated doctrines of propriety, correct taste, and ordered hierarchy in society, and anti-individualistic standardization of literary style. Diversion of intellectuals to practical politics and the construction of an American economy is the factor most frequently lamented by writers who would promote a national literature. Because of lack of copyright, pensions, and patrons, America offered little financial reward for literary effort.[156] The second-rate minds, or men of independent means who did write (the least original thinkers), followed old and familiar paths. The chief body of literature with any status, in 1815, was political, religious, and social satire useful as a rhetorical weapon in factional disputes. Satire is traditionally on the side opposed to change.

Nationalism in the first two decades of the century was mainly either hostile to the British and therefore to British post-Revolutionary (romantic) literature, or contemplated (cf. Paulding) a national literature which would rival that of the Augustan Age. At the same time, concern for the Constitution and the Union, combined with an ardent but common-sense nationalism, led many writers to oppose sectional, party, and individual enthusiasms and to seek to return the country to rational reliance upon the wisdom of the spirit of the Constitution and the founding fathers.

Until after the War of 1812 the great preponderance of literary models and techniques available and congenial to Americans was neoclassical. The first English romanticists to make an impression were Scott, easily identified with political and social conservatism, and Byron, himself the champion of Pope against the school of "affected simplicity" of Wordsworth and Coleridge. The English romanticists were not at the time considered members of a single school. Emulation of the Hartford Wits and of Irving perpetuated the earlier trend toward neoclassicism.

The West and the American Indian before 1830 were generally treated with urbane satire, or as generalized subject matter. In the South new literary ideas were resisted until in the 1830's they

---

[156] Longfellow was of course an exception to this general rule, although his sales and popularity were hardly based upon superiority to other American writers. See W. S. Tryon, "Nationalism and International Copyright in America," *American Literature*, XXIV (Nov., 1952), 301-309.

served to buttress and rationalize a growing sectional stand and contribute to an old myth made new.

Among counter influences undermining neoclassicism were the following. Religious revivalism and reaction against deism and rationalism not only re-emphasized the individual's relation to a personal God and to his own sense of sin, but also spurred the growth of emotionalism and of divisive sects, especially those of a romantic and unlearned cast (Methodists and Baptists) whose ministers had little other education than that of feeling and the wisdom of the "untutored heart." The later "scientific" deists, seeking revelation and design in particular objects of nature, tended to stress either divine immanence or the fact of transciency and change. Shaftesburyan benevolence of feeling, plus orthodox, Quaker, and later Unitarian emphasis upon individual inner light and the indwelling life contributed to the very wide vogue of the cult of simplicity (Bloomfield's *Farmer's Boy*, Wordsworth, Bryant, and similar works). Channing's "Moral Argument against Calvinism" (1819) was a landmark of religious optimism, idealism, and individualism.

The idea of progress emphasizing perfectibility and "march of mind" was counter to rational primitivism, typical in general of neoclassicism, and to Scottish Common-Sense thought involving the unchangeable. The idea of the perfectibility of man is irrational and leads to theories of the heart and to social romanticisms such as the abolition and temperance movements. Nevertheless, the growing influence of the Scottish school, especially in its intuitional elements, anti-Lockean belief in innate ideas, and admission of individual differences in the associative principle (Alison, *On Taste*), gave sanction to subjectivity, originality, and treatment of particularized landscape.

Early nationalism, while often neoclassical in techniques of expression, was nevertheless divisive in effect. The aspersions of British travelers on America developed animosities which helped to arouse American individualism and self-reliance in attempts to prove the superiority of individual indigenous particulars. The surprisingly successful conclusion of the War of 1812 and the promulgation of the Monroe Doctrine established America in the minds of Europeans and Americans alike as a new, successful, and unique force among nations. But by the Missouri Compromise (1820) the lines of sectionalism between North and South were clearly drawn; the West received new attention; henceforth divisive and defensive attitudes were to promote regional and subjective political, economic, social, and literary expression.

The implications of independence and equalitarianism spread to the lower classes of society; faith in the common man led to irrational democracy and conflict between commercial and agrarian groups. The frontier experience encouraged self-reliance and individual action, and tended to disprove generalized ideas of rational primitivism, at the same time furnishing material for the realistic and romantic treatment of the Indian.

The descriptive accounts of the travels of naturalists and biological scientists (the Bartrams, Wilson, Audubon, Rafinesque) created new material and more original, particular, and rich imagery for poetry. The continuing vogue of Gothicism and the rise of pseudo sciences such as phrenology and mesmerism[157] offered fresh outlets and sensational themes for writers. Such material was particularly common in the periodical literature of the day, both native and imported, and furnished the starting point, for example, for the tales of Poe. Richardsonian sentimentality in the novel and drama mushroomed into exaggerated and self-centered, and often ardently reformist, sensibility. The war with the Barbary pirates increased interest in Orientalism already stirred by treatment of Oriental themes in Montesquieu, Goldsmith, Moore, Southey, and the Gothic writers. Such interest was developed by Royall Tyler, Irving, Knapp, Paulding, and later by Poe and the Transcendentalists. Sir William Jones's work, well known in America (cf. Percival and Noah Webster), scientific and historical interest in the languages of the Orient and of the American Indian, and especially Webster's attempt to foster a unique American language counteracted the notion that language is or should be fixed for all time and substituted a conception of indigenous naturalness, growth, and change.

Cogswell, Everett, Ticknor, Bancroft, Hedge, the *neuer Amerikaner*, studied abroad, particularly in Germany. At least the last three named brought back ideas later embodied in romantic and

---

[157] See "The Influence of Mesmerism in American Literature," by William DeGrove Baker, Jr., in *Summaries of Doctoral Dissertations*, Northwestern University, 1951, XVIII, 5-10.

Transcendental thought. Irving, abroad, was confirmed in his easy drift toward romanticism by Scott's introducing him to German tales and strengthening his love of antiquarian lore. The vogue of Byron and Byronism reached its peak in the second and third decades of the century. Publication in America of the lectures of the Schlegels, whose influence is marked in the periodicals and upon individuals such as the Transcendentalists, Legaré, and Poe,[158] opened up the study in America of foreign literatures, history, and metaphysics. The successful transplanting of Wordsworth to American soil is seen in the periodicals from 1815 on, culminating in the second American edition of his poems in 1824. The best example of his influence is Bryant's revision of "Thanatopsis," where classical melancholy is wedded, perhaps in part through Alison's influence, to the idea of the restorative powers and moral associations of external nature. In the *North American Review* Phillips and Dana brought a new note into American criticism, that of judging a work of art on its own terms. E. T. Channing's teaching of rhetoric at Harvard, his insistence upon originality, freedom from imitation, and individualism, and his belief that intuition furnishes for reason a shortcut to truth stimulated a new generation of writers to revolt against the doctrine of imitation.

Democracy, as de Tocqueville was to point out, produced a contempt for forms. In its hasty expectation of the future it was not interested in rules derived from antiquity. At the same time those who remained aristocratic in sympathies in an era of democratic leveling tended to revolt from the democratic ideal as creating mediocrity. In their escape from the uninspired they longed for what they conceived to have been the beauties of the past.

Physical science first destroyed many poetic themes and then, by reaction, suggested new, supernatural ideas to the individual writer such as Poe and the early Emerson. Biological science (Lamarck, Erasmus Darwin) provided the rationale for an idea of organic growth, and an ontogenetic theory in criticism—the idea of the creative imagination *versus* the older rational conception of understanding and judgment.

[158] On Poe's use of A. W. von Schlegel, see, particularly, George Kelly, "The Aesthetic Theories of Edgar Allan Poe," unpublished doctoral dissertation, University of Iowa, 1953.

Nationalism of a cultural variety received philosophical and historical support from the German School, as seen in Bancroft's *History*. Foreign travel and study by Irving, Ticknor, Prescott, Willis, Bryant, Emerson, Cooper, and Longfellow reduced American insularity and broadened Americans' knowledge and appreciation of foreign and romantic literatures and cultures. The struggles of various European states for national identity and independence provoked a natural sympathy in Americans: thenceforth Americans were more willing to accept national romantic literature from abroad.

The organized abolition movement in the thirties shifted the emphasis in the North from natural to human rights, and in the South from natural to historic rights, the doctrine of racial differences, and the creation of a defensive sectional heroic myth of its own. Reaction of the West and South against the financial control of the East and North created further sectional differences and identifications, breaking up the solidarity of the country. Shift in political power toward the West and division in the East between small and big business interests led to the triumph of Jacksonianism over the old order—the triumph of laissez faire individualism. Utopianism (Fanny Wright, New Harmony, Brook Farm) and theories of a classless society (Fourierism) promoted the individual's attack upon law and government as hindrances to free development.

Revolt against Locke (fostered in part by the Scottish philosophers) and the increasing vogue of Coleridge's *Aids to Reflection*, edited by James Marsh (1829), and the vogue of Cousin, edited by C. S. Henry (1834), helped turn the age from extrovertive to introvertive. And finally, the dynamic progress of America, and the absence of homogeneity of climate, geography, class, professions, even nationality, the result of successive transoceanic migrations, created the "epic of America," a heroic-romantic idea.

# The Rise of Romanticism
## 1805–1855

# The Rise of Romanticism
# 1805-1855

### G. HARRISON ORIANS
UNIVERSITY OF TOLEDO

I

THE PURPOSE of this study is to trace the forces that induced the major tendencies of American literature from 1805 to 1855, exclusive of the more extreme aspects of New England Transcendentalism.[1] The period outlined is one commonly heralded in literary texts as romanticism. Tremaine McDowell in a Macmillan anthology calls it the Romantic Triumph.[2] E. E. Leisy gives it the twin labels of Romantic Impulse and New England Transcendentalism.[3] V. L. Parrington, expanding the interval to 1800 and to 1860 calls it the Romantic Revolution. And so the labels go, in four or five histories of American literature. If such classification were a hundred per cent true, our search would narrow itself to a consideration of why European romanticism was imported here, and that alone would comprise the investigation. But there were tendencies not clearly romantic in character and the identification of this period with romanticism is by no means sanctioned by every critic and scholar. It does not appear as the descriptive label in the two latest histories of American literature, and implicitly by

[1] The place of Transcendentalism in the romantic thought of the time is the subject of another paper, by Professor Alexander Kern.
[2] *American Literature: A Period Anthology* (New York, 1933, 1949), Vol. II.
[3] Clark, Gates, and Leisy, *The Voices of England and America* (New York, 1941), Vol. III.

the use of such a term as the American Renaissance it is denied or avoided by three of the latest anthologies. This, however, is not to say that there were no traces of romantic doctrine or practice on the American literary scene, but the confusion in terminology and the inconsistency in application make descriptive generalization difficult.

To add to the confusion there is current a definition of romanticism unrelated to time or influence. H. H. Boyesen said that it seeks "to break up the traditional order of things. . . . Romantic poetry invariably deals with longing, . . . not a definite desire but a dim, mysterious aspiration."[4] James Marsh in his edition of Herder's *Spirit of Hebrew Poetry* comparably defined romanticism as a "reaching for the unknown," thus using a Schlegelian distinction, and allying it with an idealism that is boundless.[5] But this identity of the term with abstruse unreality, valid for contrasting purposes, is not one ordinarily used by major critics or historians, probably because this concept, divorced from time or place, lacks those palpable qualities which serve to tie it down and locate it within the realms of code or movement.

Even when romanticism is identified with tenets of a social or literary character, the lack of a general agreement in meaning is apparent. No critics deny the evidence of European romanticism in America, but they do question the validity of certain phases. Professor Howard M. Jones challenges the legitimacy of political liberalism as a channel of American romanticism, or as having either origin or considerable support from European phases of the movement.[6] Another area dismissed is that of crown and altar. A number of European writers turned to the support of royalty and the church as an expression of their romantic impulses.[7] With equal vigor English authors like Hunt and Shelley hated both church and state as agencies of tyranny. But in revolt English romanticists were not in hearty accord with each other or finally consistent even with themselves. Wordsworth and Coleridge for only a short period evinced liberal political enthusiasms. Southey, at one time an ardent

[4] *Atlantic Monthly*, XXXVI (Dec., 1875), 695.
[5] Boston, 1833, Introduction.
[6] *Ideas in America* (Cambridge, Mass., 1945), pp. 110-112.
[7] Romanism and religious mysticism emerged in two German romantics, Wackenroder and Novalis.

idealist, became a reactionary twenty years later. Byron proclaimed himself a freedom-loving liberal, but his rebellious spirit was partly turned against an England that censured him. If political liberalism be indeed seriously advanced as an important category of romanticism, then clearly the confusion on the English literary scene is too pronounced for anything like valid generalization or classifying certainty. That the doctrine is no more soundly applied to the literary tendencies in America will appear later. Elsewhere even the Industrial Revolution, the result of the application of English scientific knowledge to industry, has been heralded as another mark of romanticism. For this point of view there has been scant support, not only because industrialism, when referred to any literary period, has been associated with the Victorian age, but also because frequent elaborations have been made of the point-for-point differences between industrialism and romantic doctrine.

Confusion, then, has resulted from the numerous attempts to find in romanticism either consistent or harmonious elements, and critics today are still unable to assign to it a precise meaning, chiefly because romanticism as a temper and mood is not reducible to a simple formula. Several writers have declared that the movement was but a congeries of fads and impulses, lacking positive goals and compounded of error. Merle Curti remarks that the catch-all character of the word *romanticism* may perhaps be the only thing about it that is entirely clear.[8] This being the case, I shall not assume that any given set of conditions could account for the varied phases of literary art in America (1805-1855) nor contend that the literary tendencies of this period were completely identifiable with romanticism,[9] and I shall not ascribe to literary influences alone the

---

[8] *The Growth of American Thought* (New York, 1943), p. 238; see also Russell Blankenship, *American Literature* (New York, 1931), p. 196, and Grant Knight, *American Literature and Culture* (New York, 1932), p. 63.

[9] There are many definitions of romanticism. Walter Pater wrote: "It is the addition of strangeness to beauty that constitutes the Romantic character in art. ... It is the addition of curiosity to the desire of beauty that constitutes the Romantic temper. ... The essential elements, then, of the Romantic spirit are curiosity and the love of beauty; and it is as the accidental effects of these qualities only that it seeks the Middle Ages" (*Macmillan's Magazine*, XXXV, 65).

Arthur Lovejoy in *The Great Chain of Being* (Cambridge, Mass., 1942) supplies several pertinent passages, the most central of which reads: "And

larger concepts in the history of ideas which only a complex social, political, and economic milieu could bring about. Scepticism rather than assumption must be our method. Too much careless assertion has already been devoted to this thorny question of what America owed to an English and continental romantic movement, and too little attention has been paid to the literary consequences of America's form of government and America's physical environment.

In order to simplify the handling of literary tendencies in America between 1805 and 1855, it may be wise first to set down the dominant characteristics of early nineteenth-century literature so that their American pertinence can either be dismissed or expanded upon. This is done without reference to exclusive categories or systematic organization:

(1) The revolt against the literary forms and the dominant trends

<hr>

these assumptions, though assuredly not the only important ones, are the one common factor in a number of otherwise diverse tendencies which, by one or another critic or historian, have been termed 'Romantic': the immense multiplication of genres and of verse-forms; the admission of the aesthetic legitimacy of the *genre mixte;* the *goût de la nuance;* the naturalization in art of the 'grotesque'; the quest for local color; the endeavor to reconstruct in time or space or in cultural condition; the *étalage du moi;* the demand for particularized fidelity in landscape-description; the revulsion against simplicity; the distrust of universal formulas in politics; the aesthetic antipathy to standardization; the identification of the Absolute with the 'concrete universal' in metaphysics; the feeling of 'the glory of the imperfect'; the cultivation of individual, national, and racial peculiarities; the depreciation of the obvious and the general high valuation (wholly foreign to most earlier periods) of originality, and the usually futile and absurd self-conscious pursuit of that attribute. It is, however, of no great consequence whether or not we apply to this transformation of current assumptions about value the name of 'Romanticism'; what it is essential to remember is that the transformation has taken place and that it, perhaps, more than any other *one* thing has distinguished, both for better and worse, the prevailing assumptions of the mind of the nineteenth and of our own century from those of the preceding period in the intellectual history of the West. That change, in short, has consisted in the substitution of what may be called diversitarianism for uniformitarianism as the ruling preconception in most of the normative provinces of thought." One or two of these tendencies flowered a little late for our terminal date, 1855; the others in the main are quite applicable to the romantic manifestations in America of the period, 1805-1855. This central definition occurs on pp. 293, 294; others may be found on pp. 306, 307, 311, and 313.

A very interesting and pointed discussion of the question of romanticism of the Augustan period, exemplified in the work of Coleridge, Wordsworth, Byron, and Shelley; (2) the new emphasis upon the imaginative, as opposed to the purely rational aspects of literature, which led authors into a quest for the strange and the terrible; (3) the return to the nature of individual man, paralleled by an assertion of the importance of personality; (4) an interest in the ordinary as the common denominator in a democratic form of government; (5) the fresh interest in external nature, early perceptible in America in the poetry of Freneau and Hayes and the biological writings of the Bartrams and Wilson, and continued in the poetry of Bryant, the novels of Cooper, and the Transcendental sonnets of Very; (6) the treatment of the past, chiefly apparent in the search for vestiges of antiquity; (7) the cultivation of national and racial peculiarities, and the utilization of these in genre poetry, legendary tales, and regional novels; (8) the emphasis upon originality instead of standardization, and the ardent, sometimes eccentric search for the different in conduct and thought; (9) brooding concern with the consequences of industrialism.

---

in American literature is carried on by Howard Mumford Jones in *Ideas in America* (Cambridge, 1945), pp. 107-109, in which both the chronological perplexity and the ideological confusion of romantic scholars are set forth. His summation of the meanings of romanticism has special validity for the realities of the American scene. "Romanticism as Political or Economic Theory," his number five, should by readers be referred to the main title of the address, "The Drift to Liberalism in the American Eighteenth Century," for in the nineteenth century America already had an achieved democracy, a fact which prevented such forms of political radicalism as Hunt and Shelley represented from flourishing on this side of the Atlantic.

Norman Foerster, in the *Reinterpretation of American Literature* (New York, 1928), thus sums up what he regards as the features of romanticism: "For inspiration we looked to England and the Continent, as England had looked to Germany, and Germany to France (or Rousseau). We had our lovers of beauty; we were fascinated by the Middle Ages; we wrote ballads; we had disciples of nature; we turned to the national past, to the Indians, the Puritans, and the Revolution; we cultivated the sense of wonder, the supernatural, the grotesque, the ego; the genius; we were ardent in social reform, and carried out pantisocratic notions at Brook Farm and Fruitlands; we worked out new theories of poetry and art in revolt against pseudo-classicism; we were reverently appreciative of Shakespere, traveled much in the realms of Elizabethan gold, discovered or rediscovered Homer, Plato, Dante, Calderon, Rousseau, Goethe, Kant, and the Germans generally. And at length we had our decadence in Bayard Taylor, Stoddard, Stedman, Aldrich, Lanier, etc." (pp. 32-33).

How much were Americans committed to these various aspects? What ideas dominant in the age were only slightly romantic in coloring? What overseas features were neglected? These questions about the literary scene must be sketchily answered along with the larger query of what brought the tendencies about. It would be impossible in a paper of this length to do more than touch lightly upon the most basic of these matters, especially since literature is so organic in character as to defy complete analysis of causes or trends. There are, of course, some who ascribe everything in American life between 1800 and 1860 to the power of a romantic movement, suggesting influence and forces where they neither exist nor have meaning. In answer to these we can firmly contend that Americans did not invariably accept the main tenets of romantic writers.[10] They were outspoken enough against Southey's Curse of Kehamaism and Wordsworth's theories of diction (at least for many a year) and his interpretations of simple characters. They mostly ignored Keats. Only in limited circles did they belatedly welcome Shelley.[11] American acceptance of English

[10] A philosophical reason for de-emphasizing the romantic characteristics of the age is the organic nature of the social state. Many of the ideas which seem to have appeared suddenly and to have altered the whole structure of society have an illusory suddenness about them but can be traced to remote origins or to an obscure ancestry. Literary movements are not an amalgam of inanimate substances which time or circumstances have thrown into a caldron; they are organic and of a slow growth. Like a rubric thread, a force or tendency may appear for a time on the surface of life's design and then disappear for a long time on the nether side. Nor do movements stop with the suddenness of a military command. Many have lived on with vigor even after literary historians have long since sung their requiems.

[11] The reception of the important English poets before 1860 may be examined in a number of special studies. Keats was unquestionably slighted by Americans before 1840, but in the forties and fifties he had his quota of followers. See Hyder Rollins, *Keats' Reputation in America to 1848* (Cambridge, Mass., 1946). Shelley was declared relatively unknown in June, 1832 (*American Quarterly Review*, XIX, 287). For other notices see G. L. Marsh, "Early Reviews of Shelley," *Modern Philology*, XXVII (1920), 73; and Julia Power, *Shelley in America in the Nineteenth Century* (Lincoln, Neb., 1940). For Tennyson see J. O. Eidson, *Tennyson in America* (Athens, Ga., 1943). For an over-all view see Charvat, *op. cit.*, chap. i. As for Wordsworth, see the complaints over the neglect of his works in the *North American Review*, XVIII (1824), 356-371. A review of the Wordsworthian criticism is to be found in Annabel Newton, *Wordsworth in American Criticism* (Chicago, 1928), especially chaps. iv and v. Consult also William Charvat,

ideas stopped, moreover, with those safely objective phases, such as "return to the past" or devotion to national interest. There was much less slavish aping of all things English than simplified analyses have contended. Because of the variation, therefore, in the transmission of English and German romanticism, the fundamental query in our investigation must be this: Why did certain tendencies arise? Why did others, equally attractive elsewhere, fail to win followers or an audience here? As regards the romantic aspects of American literature the question may very well be: Why were certain phases of romanticism, such as the Scott variety, dominant? and why were other phases submerged?

II

Let the attention be fixed for a moment on the second phase of this query. Why, in America, were the negative phases of European romanticism—revolt against eighteenth-centry form and the flight from didacticism—so little accepted? Why did American writers turn aside from areas so alluring to European eyes and for which there was so much overseas precedent? Consider first the question of revolt. What has been called the expansion in literary form—sonnet, blank verse, Spenserian stanza, octosyllabic lines, Pindaric odes, lyrics, etc.—is frequently cited as evidence of a nineteenth-century revolt from eighteenth-centry literary standards. But American Augustan literature was so slight in bulk that it is almost folly to speak of the expanded romantic literature as written in revolt from it. Such elements of reaction as appeared were more the consequence of nationalistic pride than a profound reaction to prevailing forms. For a considerable time even mild dissatisfaction with dominant forms was cautiously voiced. At least until 1830 the American temper was rather conservative. Percival's principles as set forth in the preface to *Prometheus*, Part II, were rejected by his contemporaries. In some circles even Bryant's mild advocacy of

---

*op. cit.*, chaps. iv, v. By 1840 Wordsworth was beginning to exert considerable influence, especially on literary humanitarians, and his doctrine of the beneficence of nature fortified the Transcendental and Unitarian optimism. Charvat dates Wordsworth's acceptance in the really significant critical circles as of 1836 (*Christian Examiner*, VII [1836], 127; *Quarterly Christian Spectator*, XIX [1836], 383; *American Quarterly Review*, XX [1836], 66).

trisyllabic feet in iambic verse, only a slight deviation from neoclassic regularity, brought abuse upon his head. But such departures from standard practice as appeared were not necessarily signs of revolt.[12] Percival's motivation was more patriotism or desire for individual distinction than it was an effort to break the bounds of a fettered imagination, and Bryant did not think of himself as voicing any revolutionary sentiments. American authors were dealing with material that had undergone a sea change. Moreover, their turning of Old-World models to new uses resulted in such alterations of spirit and structure as honest workmen would naturally make. The expression of their imaginative concepts led independent Americans to modify the English forms. Domestication could scarcely have been effected without some change in the conventional patterns. Especially was this apparent in the increasingly poetic aspects of Cooper's art, and also in his later democratic reaction to the feudalistic tendencies of Scott.[13] It is obvious too in the rejection by Emerson and Thoreau of neat and gracefully uttered literary forms.[14]

Americans failed, with minor exceptions, to go along with the extreme subjectivism of the romanticists, chiefly because of the survival here of a classical temper. The breakdown of universalism, which we call romantic, led to an emphasis on the personal, the intimate, and released what Irving Babbit unsympathetically called the power "to enthrall the individual sensibility," or to release the individual imagination. In a limited way, in the informal essay, the emotional lyric, and the sentimental novel Americans did give themselves over to this nonclassical phase, but when such subjectivism became a revolt against standards in morality and art and orthodox patterns of conduct, they soon found themselves in pro-

[12] William Cullen Bryant, *Lectures on Poetry*, IV, paragraph 11. In the preceding paragraph he had declared:
"The study of poetry which should encourage the free and unlimited aspirations of the mind after all that is noble, and beautiful, has been perverted into a contrivance to chill and repress them."
[13] See his novels of the early thirties, *The Bravo*, *The Headsman*, *The Heidenmauer*, and *The Monikins*.
[14] Kathryn McEuen (in "Emerson's Rhymes," *American Literature*, XX [March, 1948], 31-42) contended that Emerson was working his way toward "free or cadenced verse," and that he consciously modified or avoided "the set patterns of his predecessors."

test. Though Melville speaks of going to sea as a substitute for ball and pistol, American romanticists did not, at least not for long, accept either pessimism or despair or profligacy as a consistent mood. America had no Leopardi or Bürger or Thomas Beddoes. In its classics it had no real *Don Juan*, no *Lucinde*, certainly no *Mademoiselle de Maupin*. American romanticists, because of the pressure of common sense or moral ideals, were decorously restrained. Many in America rejected the tenets of the romantic tradition, for they felt it represented a lack of restraint and stood for the release of pent-up emotions that had better be suppressed. They believed firmly in mental and moral discipline. They considered reprehensible the mounting impatience with all discipline in artistic products. Certain publicists attacked the morbid imagination of a Goethe, the whining sensibility of a Pinckney. The subjective fancies in *Kubla Khan* offended the fastidious, and the greater freedom of the new poets openly shocked them. James Grant Percival was censured for representing a personally oriented world, and other persons who proclaimed *weltschmerz* and adopted outer signs, in dress and look, of the Byronic hero, were declared unmanly for their deep quaffs from cups of imaginary woe. Romanticism and lack of restraint were by some used interchangeably, and it was felt that if the loss of firm moral fiber, which the movement seemed to induce, were to prevail, it would have a deleterious effect upon youth, the structure of society, and upon the very disciplines of an intellectual world.[15]

Rejection of romantic dogma is also seen in the scorn for aesthetic indefiniteness as a legitimate feature of the romantic quest. Critical leaders might recognize as reasonable the overriding of the distinction between painting and poetry, for the practice of eighteenth-century poets argued against a too rigid application of the principles expounded by Lessing in *The Laocoön*. But they were not ready to accept poetry which indulged in pure sensuousness, and their active orthodoxy conservatively objected to the Schlegelian avoidance of thought and mental structure in poetry.

[15] Gardiner's Phi Beta Kappa address at Harvard, 1834, titled "Address on Classical Learning and Eloquence," inveighs against the breakdown of restraint in romantic circles. For orientation and bibliography, see Agnes M. Sibley, *Alexander Pope's Prestige in America 1725-1835* (New York, 1949).

This is not to say there was no subscription to pure aestheticism in America, but that the view was not general. Even so moderate a critic as George Bancroft declared in 1827 that America had no advocates for the theory which regards beauty as "something independent of moral effect."[16] The critics were quick, in the name of moral idealism, to censure works in which lush details were inadequately linked to ideas.

Thus distrustful of pure form, the age insisted upon the moral and social obligations of the creative arts. Small wonder that Poe's lyrics were for a time neglected and that his aesthetic theories stirred little intelligent response until later in the century. Pure aestheticism was Poe's poetic-musical theory, and this and its mystical air led to its rejection. For Poe the poetic principle was the aspiration for supernal beauty, "the elevating excitement of the Soul," and this was attained by an indefiniteness of message.

Poe wrote in a letter in 1831:

A Poem, in my opinion, is opposed to a work of science by having, for its immediate object, pleasure, not truth; to romance, by having, for its object, an indefinite instead of a definite pleasure, being a poem only so far as this object is attained; romance presenting perceptible images with definite,—poetry with indefinite sensations, to which end music is essential; since the comprehension of sweet sound is our most indefinite conception. Music, when combined with a pleasurable idea, is poetry; music, without the idea is simply music; the idea without the music is prose, from its very definiteness.

In the same letter he said, "Of Coleridge I cannot speak but with reverence. His towering intellect: His gigantic power!" Nor should he have spoken without reverence, for Hervey Allen points out that the entire passage quoted, with the exception of the words, "In my opinion," was lifted verbatim from Coleridge's *Biographia Literaria*.[17]

---

[16] *North American Review*, XXIV (April, 1827), 444.

[17] Hervey Allen, *Israfel, or the Life and Times of Edgar Allan Poe* (New York, 1934), 512. Over a half-hundred studies have been made in Poe's sources, but among them the most fruitful have been the Coleridgean investigations: H. T. Baker, "Coleridge's Influence on Poe's Poetry," *Modern Language Notes*, XXV (March, 1910), 94-95; Floyd Stovall, "Poe's Debt to Coleridge," *University of Texas Studies in English*, X (July, 1930), 70-127; see also Killis Campbell, *The Mind of Poe and Other Studies* (Cambridge, Mass., 1933), pp. 149-154.

But whatever might have been the contemporary reaction to Poe's ethics in lifting the passage from a kindred writer, his popularity would not have been increased by any citation of Coleridge's name. Coleridge was generally condemned in American criticism, if not for his aestheticism, as was Poe, then for his supernaturalism and mysticism, although James Marsh and others exalted and popularized his religious and philosophic ideas.[18]

In his *Poetic Principle* Poe exemplified along with Coleridge and most of the English romantic poets the principle of associating music and poetry in practice. And while the relation between music and literature was not so great in England or America as it

---

[18] See an article by R. C. Waterston, *North American Review*, XXXIX (Oct., 1834), 437-458. A more significant interpretation occurs in G. B. Cheever (*North American Review*, XL [April, 1835], 299-351), who defended Coleridge's character as a poet and philosopher. At the opening of the review he paid tribute to Coleridge's intellectual stature: "We regard as a peculiar privilege, the opportunity to express our admiration of the genius, character, and writings of Samuel Taylor Coleridge. It is rarely, indeed, that God has placed such a mind as his in an earthly mould, to shed its splendor on a world in ruins. We regard him with feelings of veneration and love, which we have paid to few other names in English literature. Nor does the obloquy, by which he was pursued through life, in the least degree lessen that veneration. It was the inevitable accompaniment of his greatness. It was the appropriate testimony of an age of littleness and superficiality, towards one, who towered in such grandeur beyond the measure of all his contemporaries" (p. 299).

Coleridge's philosophic system Cheever as an ardent Transcendentalist is quick to praise: His is a system "that recognises a spiritual world to come," and a spiritual nature in man to move in it; spiritual presentiments and prefigurings; spiritual wants, and obligations, and principles; and grounds of conviction and action coeval with man's spiritual being. It recognizes God the Creator, and man made in his image; but wilfully fallen, the subject of an evil nature.

"It is not merely a history of the human understanding. It asserts the dignity of reason, as the mind's organ of inward sense, whereby it has 'the power of acquainting itself with invisible realities or spiritual objects.' It recognises 'truths that are either absolutely certain, or necessarily true for the human mind from the laws and constitution of the mind itself.' . . . It exhibits the entire difference between the two faculties; 'the legitimate exercise of the understanding, and its limitation to objects of sense; with the errors, both of unbelief and misbelief, that result from its extension beyond the sphere of possible experience. Wherever the forms of reasoning, appropriate only to the *natural* world, are applied to *spiritual* realities, it may be truly said, that the more strictly logical the reasoning is in all its *parts*, the more irrational it is as a *whole*.'"

was in Germany, it still was evident. Nor was there as much elimination of the boundaries between the arts as was demonstrated by Schlegel and Hoffmann. Poe and T. H. Chivers were perhaps the only American poets who were so completely beguiled into the vague regions of cosmic music or ineffable melodies as almost completely to lose themselves. Had Poe's lyrical mood mounted not only from prose to poetry, but also from poetry to music itself, the musical melody might have prevented the overstraining of the lyrical impulse.

If pure aestheticism offended the moral sensibilities of America's common-sense critics, they were even more repelled by scenes and characters tinged with crime. Dynamic romanticism, which gloried in the emotions and triumphs of robbers, was sharply attacked by critics and publicists. Bulwer, when he made Paul Clifford, a pickpocket, the hero of one novel and Eugene Aram, a murderer, the central character of another, not only baffled those who wished fiction to operate on a strong and consistent scheme of moral divagation, but seemed to exult in the emotions and triumphs of robbers and other fictional pariahs. Though he was widely enough read, still his formula was condemned because his characters had such attributes as would falsify the great moral truths of life. Many failed to recognize that the central character of a novel is not like a figure in an allegory in whose person matchless qualities are represented for the emulation of the readers. In consequence Bulwer became the storm center of controversy.[18a]

The critical attack on dynamic romanticism came as early as 1811 when Schiller's *The Robbers*, another test case, was reprehended on the grounds that personal motive did not justify the end when the end was a violation of social morality. Dictates of established standards and morality should prevail no matter how much an individual might seek to rationalize his position. The real, though unstated, objection in this criticism was Schiller's obvious glorification of natural impulse as opposed to public benefit. A. H. Everett in April, 1823, attacked the ascription, in the work of Schiller, of both abominable and exemplary traits to the same in-

[18a] American reaction to dynamic romanticism was apparent in the forties in the general rejection of French romanticism and what was regarded as wicked French literature. See H. M. Jones, "American Comment on George Sand, 1837-1849," *American Literature*, III (Jan., 1932), 404-407.

dividual or, as he phrased it, "the most contradictory moral qualities as existing together" in one person. Ten years later the *American Quarterly Review*, pointing to a crime wave alleged to have followed the publication of Schiller's play, proclaimed it as evidence of the antisocial nature of its central character.[19]

Criticism of dynamic romanticism extended to Byron, the most popular poet in the fifteen years after 1815. Amid copious imitations of his poetic manner there was always the protest of an articulate opposition. But his popularity was a strong shield against charges, and for a time the aspersions of moralists served as a measure of his mounting success. Aspiring poetizers imitated his verses, his rhythms and rhymes, and built up their own lines from scattered striking passages. They affected his flowing tie as well as his worldly gloom. Longfellow, discussing the heyday of Byron's popularity, remarked in 1831: every community furnished "its little Byron, its self-tormenting scoffer at morality, its gloomy misanthropist in song." The thunderings of pulpit and review, articulate enough, had little effect on so popular a literary figure.

But critical abuse was present from the first. William Tudor bracketed him with Sterne as an author who exploited sentiment for the vulgar. Byron was attacked for his world weariness and his melancholy. S. G. Goodrich referred to his dreary scepticisms, to his "gloomy, cavernous regions of thought"; Emerson held the prevalent view that Byron's mind was depraved and his will perverted; and publicists warned against his romantic excesses, his

[19] It is possible, of course, to build up almost any kind of generalization by arbitrarily selecting the evidence. The abuse was real, but despite the critical castigation, the impression should not be conveyed that Schiller lacked esteem, or that robbers were always reprehended in fiction or poetry. Scott's *Rob Roy* is a clear case of the acceptance of outlaw characters in the historical novel, and for a time Byron's early hero, as exemplified in *The Giaour*, *Lara*, and *The Corsair*, was readily acclaimed as a fashionable figure of dash, proud contempt, and bold action. Before 1820 such characters were usually accepted by critics as well as readers. The very prevalence of ballads and plays about social outcasts argues that the opposition was not restrictive in operation, however much moral objection there may have been to socially irresponsible individuals. But in both England and America Schiller was generally frowned upon for the specious reasoning and conduct of his outlaws. Obvious distrust of the ethics of Schiller's characters was apparent early and became increasingly clear after 1820 when his mode was associated with the Satanism of Byron and the whole school of guilt and passion. See A. H. Everett, "Life and Writings of Schiller," *North American Review*, XVI, 397.

selfish gloom, and reprehended him for making capital of his woes. All of which is to say that Byron was himself the Byronic hero whose Satanism and violent and wicked passions, though transitorily fashionable, were reprehended by critics and moralists of two decades.

Apart from the self-evident reasons in the attacks on Byron and Bulwer, what causes can be assigned for the opposition to unrestrained romanticism? Much of the opposition to Byronism, to aestheticism, to romantic heroes, was a consequence of the intense moral feeling that pervaded American life between 1800 and 1840 and decorously turned it from the main impulses of the continental movement. Dynamic moralism it has been called as well as Christian idealism, restrained decency, Christian ethics, and other phrases to indicate the temper of piety which frowned upon excesses that might corrupt character or lead to vice. One might simply label this attitude Puritanism and pass on to application, but actually the matter is more complex than this. The recurrent revivals, especially among Methodists and Baptists, kept the moral fervor incandescent. This was particularly true in the tramontane regions where, in scattered agricultural settlements and small villages, the fleshpots of the cities were unknown. Ruralism and homespun virtues were still the protection of American social life, and these were being celebrated by Child, Sedgwick, Paulding and others. In the intellectual centers of Philadelphia and eastern Massachusetts, American moralism likewise mounted into dynamic force. Here too revivalism came in the years after the French Revolution in all except strictly Anglican circles. While much less important in the population at large, in Boston and other Eastern cities the force of Unitarianism was highly effective, at least in its earlier, more militant days. W. E. Channing especially, having been moved to ardent philanthropy through the reading of Hutcheson, Ferguson, and Goldsmith, came not only to a state of active benevolence but to a vital moralism—and as dominant figure of the rationalists between 1815 and his death, he grafted his outlook upon the branches of the Unitarian movement.[20] After 1830 the gentle stimuli of this group were intensified by the idealism of

[20] *Memoirs*, I, 63; see also J. W. Chadwick, *W. E. Channing*, pp. 41-42. Consult also Martineau, *Types of Ethical Theory*, II, 474-523.

Kant and the eclectic philosophy of the French school, De Gerando, Cousin, and Jouffroy; but though these schools of idealism strengthened the moral arm of the Unitarians, they did not originate their commitment to the moral law.

Such moralism led to a rejection of authors who disdained "disinterested benevolence," and it prompted condemnation of those whose books tended to weaken morals. Only the hardiest spirits condoned Godwin or Smollett, and the cynics of the eighteenth century rarely came off unscorched by social judgment. Penetrating moralism may be regarded as one of the most potent of the social or literary forces affecting the production of literature in America after 1815 and in accounting for the distrust of romantic extremes, romantic weakness, and absurdity.

Reinforcing this moralism of the churchmen was the conservativism of the "commonsense" critics closely analyzed by William Charvat.[21] This school employed common-sense criteria in their measurement of literary efforts and kept firm control upon literary excesses. Wordsworth's experiments in diction called forth its ire, and the excursions into the supernatural by Coleridge were dismissed as going beyond the fanciful and legendary domains of proper poets. The heroes of the Satanic school were dismissed, not only because of their immorality, but also because their actions were unheroic, their hearts filled with self-pity, and their emotional attitudinizing unbefitting characters of worth and soul. W. H. Prescott approved romantic writers when they fell within the class of social benefactors but disliked the selfish individualism so frequently displayed. S. Gilman, staunch defender of the Scottish principles of Reid and Stewart, turned the Common-Sense attitude of the Scottish school to the egocentric phases of romanticism, concluding with disdain that they violated the rules of good art.[22] Since most critics of the period were schooled in the Scottish philosophers and in Lord Kames and Blair, the application of Common-Sense ideas was an almost inevitable phase of their criticism.

The other literary factor which gave pause to ambitious roman-

[21] William Charvat, *American Critical Thought: 1810-1835* (Philadelphia, 1936), chap. iii.
[22] See *North American Review*, XIII (Oct., 1821), 450-473; XVI (Jan., 1823), 110-123.

ticists was the existence of a fairly strong neoclassical criticism, closely related to the Scottish school though not identical with it. In periodical literature it encouraged the imitation of the Attic grace of Addison, and in poetry it attempted to maintain a conservative neoclassical tradition. Men like William Tudor, J. C. Gray, and Franklin Dexter, though hospitable to Scott, still paid allegiance to Dryden and Pope, castigated the literature of their own day as a maze of undisciplined and unchastened mental efforts, and condemned the contemporary authors as a school of "ballad-mongers and song-wrights."[23] But this neoclassic aspect has been too thoroughly covered in the preceding chapter to need emphasis here.

### III

The question before us in this study—What was responsible for the changes in the literary scene in the half century after 1805?—is therefore a complicated one, and had, as we have just seen, its strong negative aspects. We may quite properly ask: If all these rational and moral factors retarded the acceptance of sensuous romanticism, why was the country so readily deluged with its more objective forms? What was there in the literary milieu which furthered the spread of the right kind of a literary movement? What characteristics of the time-spirit were responsible for the direction which American literary activity took?

### LITERARY AGENCIES AND ATTITUDES

First to be cited are the agencies which provided outlet for the expanding literary spirit. Obviously the tendencies potential in any age develop fully and succeed in reaching the reading public only when there is a happy combination of current trends, literary talent, and agencies of dissemination and publicity. In America of the second quarter there were many new avenues of communication which served to spread the current impulses. Chief among these were new and sturdier magazines: the *North American Review* (1815), the *New York Mirror* (1824), the *American Quarterly Review* (1827), the *New England Magazine* (1831),

---

[23] See especially the *North American Review*, I (July, 1815), 275-284; III (July, 1816), 272-283; IV (March, 1817), 411; XXVIII (Jan., 1829), 1-18.

the *Knickerbocker Magazine* (1835), *Burton's Gentleman's Magazine* (1839), *Graham's Magazine* (1840), and several others. While it is not accurate to say that America was enjoying a flourishing periodical growth,[24] still, compared with facilities prior to 1814, there were agencies for the voicing of editorial policies, and there were new mediums of publication for rising authors.

Part of this expansion of magazines was a consequence of regional pride, with Charleston, Philadelphia, New York, Cincinnati vying with each other. Other journals were the consequence of theological controversy. The esteemed *North American Review*, founded in 1815, had so many Unitarian contributors that the Trinitarians, by 1819, felt the urge to establish the *Christian Spectator* as a medium for the interpretation of orthodox opinions and as an organ for examining the soundness of literary thought and philosophy. The Unitarian *Christian Examiner* followed; and came to be, by the end of the twenties, an important critical journal. Literary information was also expanded by American reprints of British periodicals, which, in the twenties and thirties, enjoyed a circulation equal to that of the more popular American publications.[25] These American magazines and reprints not only made possible the reviews of new books, but provided space for the critical evaluation of literary tendencies and the spread of knowledge about European literary developments. Moreover, many of the American authors of the period owed their total or partial support to such new magazines as the *New York Mirror* or the *American Monthly Magazine*.

The magazine, which as early as the 1790's had shown some concern for feminine readers, blossomed into a variety of literary enterprises specially designed for the enlarging circle of women readers. Especially successful in this category was *Godey's Lady's*

[24] Periodicals of the twenties had at best a precarious existence, but about 1825 there was an obvious attempt to establish magazines in America along the lines of the English publications of the time. See the *Short History*, pp. 96-98; also, Mott's *History of American Magazines, 1741-1850* (New York, 1930), pp. 299-354.

[25] E. Douglas Branch, *The Sentimental Years: 1836-1860*, p. 102, thus comments: "In the Eighteen Thirties, Theodore Foster and Leonard Scott, of New York, were reprinting British magazines without change in title or contents. A year's subscription to Foster's reprints of all four *Reviews*, the *London, Edinburgh, Foreign* and *Westminster*, cost but eight dollars."

*Book*, which included almost everything which might capture the fancy of a Victorian lady: light fiction, sentimental poems, articles of admonition, fashions and music. Atkinson's *Casket* within its eclectic folds sought to maintain the same successful appeals.

A second literary institution was the gift book,[26] which not only furnished a market for paintings and engravings but also for sketches, poems, and tales. Edited by prominent literary personages, the gift book had during its first fifteen years sufficient reputation to make it a proper outlet for ambitious young men; and thus providing a market for burgeoning authors, it kept some aspirants to fame in the ranks of competitors who might otherwise have despaired of finding publishing outlets. Though it had lost much of its actual literary influence by the mid-forties, the gift book still remained an agency for sentimental effusions, legends, and regional tales.

Third among the agencies for the dissemination of ideas was the lyceum. Established in the late twenties and by 1831 already in its thousands, it was at first primarily an agency for the collection of natural history materials and the exercise of the abilities of its members.[27] In its purely local capacity it unfolded talent and led to the discovery of otherwise dormant genius. As it moved into a national association it became more and more a kind of lecture bureau, and opportunities were opened up for the itinerant lecturer who thus secured a ready-made audience for his message. The words of the traveling orators, with their hortatory tone, could not have failed to find lodgment in the minds of many listeners. Had we a record of the programs of all the lyceums of early days we could properly measure the full place of the institution in the intellectual history of the times. All we have, actually, is the history of three of these lyceums, and from these not too

---

[26] Indication of the place and importance of the gift book in American literature may be found in Fred Lewis Pattee, *The Feminine Fifties* (New York, 1940), and in Ralph Thompson, *American Literary Annuals and Gift-Books, 1825-1865* (New York, 1936).

[27] An outline of the history of the American Lyceum may be found in Cecil B. Hayes, *The American Lyceum*, Bulletin No. 12, U. S. Department of the Interior, Office of Education (Washington, 1932). See also unpublished master's thesis of Columbia University: Paul Wakelee Stoddard, "The Place of the Lyceum in American Life" (1933); and J. S. Noffsinger, *Correspondence Schools, Lyceums, Chautauquas* (New York, 1926).

conclusive evidence. Emerson was only one of dozens of authors who wrote in part to supply the demands of these lyceums.

Further dissemination of knowledge was fostered by the spread of the railroads in the years after 1833, with the first road west of the Alleghenies constructed between Toledo and Adrian in 1837. Before 1855 thousands of miles of rails were in operation. This expansion made possible the spread of the lecture from New England to the West, and brought the messages of alarm, of information, and of inspiration to great masses of people. With the new travel facilities tours could be arranged without hopeless gaps between lectures. The hinterland, by the fifties a crucial region, saw men like Lincoln, Emerson, Ripley, Greeley, Curtis, and others; and contact with the frontier helped to reinforce Emerson's and Parker's Transcendental brand of self-reliance and optimism.

One of the causes for increased alertness to literary tendencies after 1830 was the growth of the academy throughout the nation. The Census of 1850 reported 6085 academies and other schools, though this number must have included many temporary institutions and private schools not on a secondary level. But even so, with all possible deductions, the number was still impressive and reflected the expanded demand for knowledge, an increase among those who might read and appreciate literature, and a mounting sense of responsibility for democratic leadership and individual achievement. While the offerings of such schools differed widely, they did provide cultural as well as vocational instruction, and they experimented with new methods of making their instruction effective. Not so much can be said for the free public schools, which until the revival of the forties and fifties continued in the main as pauper schools with short terms and poorly trained staffs. But in the fifth and sixth decades of the century, under the leadership of inspired, educational thinkers, such as James G. Carter, Horace Mann, Henry Barnard, Caleb Mills, and Calvin Wiley, the elementary school program was vastly improved, and the period of students' attendance was increased. Thus a new audience was being educated to appreciate democratic and indigenous literature.

More important than facilities for publication and agencies of literacy in the development of creative tendencies after 1815 were certain social and literary attitudes which prompted expression and determined the bent of authors and the coloring of products. Some of these had shown themselves in mild degree before the turn of the century and were themselves products of eighteenth-century forces, but in expanded fashion they brought their weight to bear upon literary forms, strengthening, developing, and amplifying them. These were numerous, but we may single out six.

First is the state of American reading and book-purchasing. In 1820 a large portion of the books read in the United States and on the shelves of circulating libraries were actually printed abroad. What this fact means, when one fronts it squarely, is that literary tendencies abroad, aside from positive rejections, soon prevailed here. Even for local enterprise the same truth holds: works printed here came mostly from overseas texts. Alexander H. Everett blamed native booksellers and printers for their ready republication of foreign books.[28] Granting the justice of his charge, one must not censure cisatlantic printers too severely: in a not-too-literary age the printers' desire to publish works of assured reputation cannot be charged altogether to cupidity, especially since American curiosity about European literature, seriously restricted during the Napoleonic struggle, was mounting to a lucrative sharpness. The fact that English works could be freely and profitably reproduced, without hazarding money upon untried literary ventures, could alone have explained the tremendous piratical activity in all seaboard cities of America.

The absence of international copyright can thus be held responsible in the main for the swamping of America with European works and for the relative neglect of native talent. Even the attempt to get literature recognized as property at all was without real success until the thirties, and the combination of lethargy, publishing opposition, and the demands of the reading public for books at nominal cost continued the American reliance upon transatlantic products. When one observes, therefore, the American reprinting of English works and English models, he sees American taste and American reading in more or less coincidence with that of England. All of which, aside from the inadequacy of the American publishing business (not yet fully prepared to meet native

[28] *North American Review*, XII (April, 1821), 260.

readers' demands) is merely to say that the greatest factor in determining the character of literature in America in 1820 was surviving provincialism. No new force certainly, it was still strongly operative despite national pride, War of 1812 hostility, commercial enterprise, and the ambition of authors. The existence in America of a temper which was, as Emerson declared, "timid, imitative, tame," would alone have been sufficient to account for the fact that America looked to England not only for literary innovations but also for the best examples of literary achievement. For some scholars no other cause need be sought to explain the themes and forms of American literature in the first half of the nineteenth century.

Such provincialism must have been at least indirectly responsible for the absence of a strong native literary tradition, though other causes also operated: an inadequate book-buying public, a heavily rural culture, a faulty distribution and sales system, and slight financial returns from native productions. Writers whose devotion to creative activity was perforce incidental or part time could neither develop nor sustain literature on a high productive level. Add to this real discouragement the lingering veneration for English authors, and American half-heartedness and imitativeness become entirely logical.

### Overseas Traditionalism and Eclecticism

The forces of dependency were not only sustained by the deluge of English books but quickened by travel ties with the Old World. American authors who toured or resided in Europe readily reflected current British or continental literary fads. At least three studies of Americans in Europe serve to reinforce this contention.[29] Let us instance two cases. Washington Irving in the first part of the *Sketch Book* thus voiced his aspirations:

[29] See R. E. Spiller, *The American in England* (New York, 1926). The story is carried down to 1835. See also my "Early Travelers to England," *J.E.G.P.*, XXVI (Oct., 1927), 569-581. An interesting study of young scholars who pursued their studies in foreign countries is afforded in Orie William Long's *Literary Pioneers, Early American Explorers of European Culture* (Cambridge, Mass., 1935). The scholars studied include: George Ticknor, Edward Everett, Joseph Green Cogswell, George Bancroft, Henry Wadsworth Longfellow, and John Lothrop Motley.

Europe was rich in the accumulated treasures of age. Her very ruins told the history of times gone by, and every mouldering stone was a chronicle. I longed to wander over the scenes of renowned achievement—to tread, as it were, in the footsteps of antiquity—to loiter about the ruined castle—to meditate on the falling tower—to escape, in short, from the commonplace realities of the present, and lose myself among the shadowy grandeurs of the past.

This antiquarian mood, in marked contrast to that of the *Knickerbocker History*, was the joint result of travel and residence in England and familiarity with romantic works. Washington Irving, claimed F. L. Pattee, was changed from an eighteenth-century classicist to a nineteenth-century romanticist through the reading of Scott.[30] But the effect thus produced must have been greatly heightened by the direct stimulus of Scott's personality. Shortly after its appearance Irving had read *The Lady of the Lake* with obvious delight and enthusiasm, and Scott's novels engrossed him as they came out. Then in 1815 he headed northward to Edinburgh and the Scottish terrain. Here he engaged in long conversations with Scott, at Abbotsford, upon the subject of Spanish literature, German legend, and professional authorship. Sole evidence of the talk about things German was Irving's subsequent passion for German legends and his devotion to the study of German itself shortly after his departure from the novelist's home. The intimate days at Abbotsford did much to intensify historical sensibilities in Irving and to quicken within him the stirrings of romance. After 1826 Irving moved into the glamorous world of Moorish Spain, and in the shadows of the old Alhambra his imagination took on a completely romantic, antiquarian mood. Spain completed what Scotland began.

If Irving's response to the European scene for a time resulted in an absorption in the Early Middle Ages, so did Longfellow's as he described the belfry of Bruges and other monuments of fourteenth-century Germany. The record of Longfellow's addiction to Uhland and Tieck, as he moved in a world of half-shadows, is a familiar one. If under their joint guidance he did not quite become a votary of the night, in the sense of George Chapman or Novalis, he at least walked in regions of twilight. The romantic unrealities

---

[30] *Development of the American Short Story* (New York, 1923), pp. 7-9.

of German cities bemused him and left him dreaming mystic dreams of magic realms. But for Longfellow, German residence merely intensified a tendency already apparent before he left America. He had a romantic point of view as early as 1825-1826 (*vide* his *Lay Monastery* papers), and he had lingered over Irving's *Sketch Book* and *Bracebridge Hall,* upon which he modeled his college compositions. Both the gloom of Ossian and the escapist's concept of poetry Longfellow obviously had acquired before he set foot on Europe. But his early romantic moods were intensified by Göttingen and Heidelberg, and for a half decade he was clearly nostalgic for the dim twilight of the past.

To nontravelers the overseas impact came through European masterpieces of poetry and prose carefully selected by Longfellow and others. Especially through continental anthologies a multitude of Americans joined in this humanistic triumph.[31] Ripley, Griswold, Fuller, Bryant, aided in this distribution, and every vessel which touched American shores became a supply house for more European material. Some of the imported writings were wildly assailed, as the sensational novels of Paul de Koch, but in the main, they were accepted, whether they involved the frank emotionalism of *Jane Eyre* or the clear potations of Fredrika Bremer.

Two purely external factors furthered this literary expansion. The first was the cheapening of paper about 1840, which multiplied manyfold the overseas material which the pirates printed. Willis Gaylord Clark lamented the "ten thousand pages of trash which the want of a copyright law entails upon us from England."[32] A second was the establishment of steamship lines in 1838 which not only made rapid trips to Europe possible but (after the *Great Western*) resulted in the importation of the latest books and magazines, which N. P. Willis complained of as driving American materials and themes to the wall:

*In literature we are no longer a distinct nation.* The triumph of Atlantic steam navigation has driven the smaller drop into the larger, and London has become the center. Farewell nationality! The English language now marks the limits of a literary empire, and America is a suburb.

---

[31] For a partial list of American anthologies in the 1840's, see my *Short History,* chap. x, p. 131.
[32] *The Literary Remains* (New York, 1839), p. 230.

Our themes, our resources, the disappearing savage, and the retiring wilderness, the free thought, and the action as free, the spirit of daring innovation, and the irreverent question of usage, the picturesque mixture of many nations in an equal home, the feeling of expanse, of unsubserviency, of distance from time-hallowed authority and prejudice —all the elements which were working gradually but gloriously together to make us a nation by ourselves, have, in this approximation of shores, either perished for our using, or slipped within the clutch of England.[33]

The editorial policy of *Harper's* in the fifties must have seemed a corroboration of Willis's pessimistic prophecies.

### ANTITRADITIONALISM

These forces of conservatism and imitativeness were checked by peculiarly native factors that served in part to offset them, forces such as the breadth of the Atlantic, with the resulting distance from literary arbiters, the growth of a spirit of nationalism, considerably swelled by two wars of separation, and a new and enlarging spirit of antitraditionalism. The last of these served to stimulate home production and led to American idealistic impulses.[34] Antitraditionalism was animated with the spirit of Emerson's *Divinity School Address* and Whitman's "To a Historian." In both New England and on the frontier there existed a strong vein of self-trust and nonconformity. The frontier temper, since frontiersmen had to co-operate to survive, was less a product of antisocial attitudes than a result of the winnowing of seaboard populations by the process of migration. The most self-reliant, restless spirits of the East were those in the vanguard of every westward movement. This process going on year after year established a far-flung generation which believed in itself and which turned first to its own inner impulses. But East or West the inspired leader of this sturdy independent movement was Emerson. Sharply critical of politics and political leaders, Emerson was no less critical of sycophantic individuals who asked God and the nation to do for them what they should do for themselves. Conformity to social practice, to the so-called wisdom of the past,

---

[33] *A L'Abri, or The Tent Pitch'd* (New York, 1839), p. 150.
[34] The antitraditionalism of the Transcendentalists and the subjectivism of the romanticists are so similar that it is difficult to tell them apart except for the Transcendental disposition to elevate dissent into a creed.

consistency even to what had formerly been one's own best judgment, this independent thinker of Concord decried, and sought to lead his listeners to a state of supreme judgeship where man's latest and finest wisdom, coming from his inner inspiration, would hold the measures of life and action. "We will walk with our own feet, we will work with our own hands, we will speak with our own minds," he declared. Dreaming always of the future, not of the past, he was ready at all times to encourage conduct which challenged authority and broke the molds of conventionality. But for all his seeming challenge of the fundamentals of ordinary thinking, Emerson did not possess the reformer's instinct, and was as little ready to join professional humanitarian groups as he was to leave off self-scrutiny. Equally unconventional in his own way, even to the point of being a Democrat in staunchly Whiggish New England was Nathaniel Hawthorne, who possessed a free-roving mind, easily at home in the world of conflict and speculation. He propounded liberal and fanciful queries. Though he preached against *mort main*, he was even more violently opposed to the intransigent spirit of reform which he felt destroyed men's souls through fanatic measures to better their bodies.

## Nationalism

An equally causative and stimulative force, the spirit of nationalism, which first accompanied the struggles for political independence, became after 1820 a full-fledged literary aspiration and movement. Its beginnings can be traced back to the mid-eighteenth century. Freneau and Brackenridge had in 1770 demonstrated terrestrial ambition in their feeling for the land—one land—and its destiny in "The Rising Glory of America," and other romantic bards shared this vision of a transcendent America. Unassociated with independence at first, it envisaged a nation with a glorious destiny, either within or without the British Commonwealth. Then came the Revolution to interpret the land of their dreams as an America of political independence. This fact injected a new note into the chorus of enthusiasm. Though republican in form, the government should possess the generally recognized literary accompaniments of nationality, and these should be of a caliber to go hand in hand with political achievements. With the agitation for a stronger union in the 1780's there came, therefore, from Noah Webster, Timothy Dwight, Royall Tyler, and others a demand for a national epic, a federal or national language, and a native drama. America must build up forms that would prove her membership in the family of literary nations, and at the same time provide a literature which in its merit would match the greatness of America's political experiment.

Then came the War of 1812, a second War of Independence, and its successful termination led to a twofold attempt: (1) to secure intellectual independence from Great Britain and other European countries in whose literature there were dangerous survivals of feudalism; (2) to supply peculiarly American materials for the literary forms then in fashion. For all the insistence of Edward Everett and James Kirke Paulding that the effect of republican principles should be discernible in our literature most nationalists were content to call for native materials only and for the employment of these in works of art. For them this meant American scenery, American historical events, regional atmosphere, and especially the American Indian. Critics with republican faith were insistent that a democratic society not only could encourage literary talent, but that America was rich in exactly the materials needed for the current forms. They found no encouragement from either English Tory critics or classical scholars.[35] But this did not keep the *North American* reviewers and other patriotic writers from chanting America's potential literary glories. Some of these demands for a national literature were somewhat blatant, even a

---

[35] For a summary of this controversy, see my *A Short History of American Literature* (New York, 1940), pp. 78-90; also, "The Romance Ferment after *Waverley*," *American Literature*, III (Jan., 1932), 408-431. See also the unpublished doctoral dissertation by William Herman Willer, "Native Themes in American Prose Fiction," University of Minnesota, 1944, pp. 6-64. Other important references include: R. W. Bolwell, "Concerning the Study of Nationalism in American Literature," *American Literature*, X (Jan., 1939), 405-416; Harry H. Clark, "Nationalism in American Literature," *University of Toronto Quarterly*, II (July, 1933), 491-519; W. E. Sedgwick, "The Materials for an American Literature; A Critical Problem of the Early Nineteenth Century," *Harvard Studies and Notes in Philology and Literature*, XVII (1935), 141-162; E. K. Brown, "The National Idea in American Criticism," *Dalhousie Review*, XIV (July, 1934), 133-147.

little bumptious, but they were a part of America's growing up, and the best of the demands were sober and rational.[36]

Those who wanted an American literature totally separated from all overseas roots were in the minority. Much of what was called cultural nationalism meant only an American literature which would reinforce American democracy. Not local color but political principles, contended Cooper, could insure an American product free from open or subtle reminders of feudalism. Free American letters from a devotion to rank and American literature will have expressed all that is necessary to be different.

Still there was the demand to make American literature as native as resources permitted. This led to injunctions to turn to the American Indian, to American seasonal contrasts, and to the frontier. For a generation these materials were utilized until they approached exhaustion. Long before the poverty of the resources was apparent, however, an occasional critic issued a word of warning or lamented the sad results of overzealous encouragement from reviewers, orators, ambitious patriots.

This reaction to the deluge of romantic material from 1820 to 1836 was partly responsible for turning attention of critics to a new phase of nationalism, the production of literature of merit which would have international significance. There followed the debate of the forties[37] between those who would retain strong national interests and those who would risk the obvious dangers of eclecticism.

[36] James Fenimore Cooper in a note to chap. xv of *Satanstoe* (1845) remarked of the servility that prevailed in 1800 as in sharp contrast to patriotic confidence prevailing a generation later:
"The American who could write a book—a real, live book—forty years since, was a sort of prodigy. It was the same with him who could paint any picture beyond a common portrait. The very fruits and natural productions of the country were esteemed, doubtingly; and he was a bold man who dared to extol even canvass-back ducks, in the year 1800! At the present day, the feeling is fast undergoing an organic change. It is now the fashion to *extol* everything American, and from submitting to a degree that was almost abject to the feeling of colonial dependency, the country is filled, to-day, with the most profound provincial self-admiration. It is to be hoped that the next change will bring us to something like the truth."
[37] See for the controversy about nationalism in the forties Alexander B. Meek, *Americanism in Literature* (Charleston, 1844) and William Gilmore Simms's review of this oration in his *Views and Reviews* (New York, 1845),

While mounting nationalism after 1800 was partly an index of the increasing maturity of the American republic, nationalistic ardor received a special stimulus in the Paper War which followed the conflict of 1812. The American spine was stiffened in reaction to Tory criticism of American manners, American genius, and American literary productivity. This is not a topic that can be reviewed here, but its force was so great that it must not be lost sight of.

### Faith in Progress

A third factor responsible for expanding activities in literature was the sense of optimism which followed the War of 1812. The success of America in that conflict stimulated, as has been noted, the spirit of literary nationalism, but led as well to the expansion of American dreams, to a belief in manifest destiny, and to buoyancy in American writing. The New World was to fulfil ardent prophecy, to move on to greater achievement in realms of body and spirit. Throughout the generation after 1820 this spirit of optimism was sustained by a strong though by no means universal belief in progress. Not altogether a product of American material advances and the American Dream, the idea was systematically explored in philosophical and historical speculations and voiced by editors and poets.[38] The eighteenth century with its chain-of-being and its concept of a fixed universe had partly given way before a vision of a world whose limits were constantly expanding and whose denizens had a passion for physical progress. This vision was widely followed on an open road of intuition, optimism, and faith.

It reached its peak in the forties. Though there was at the same

---

pp. 1-19; see also Rufus Griswold, Preface to *Prose Writers of America* (New York, 1847). Other works having a bearing on the subject are H. W. Longfellow, "National Literature" in *Kavanagh* (Boston, 1849), pp. 365-368, and Lowell's review of this work in the *North American Review*, LXIX (July, 1849), 196-215. See also A.S.P., "Fugitive Poetry in America," *Southern Quarterly Review*, XIV (July, 1848), 101-231. For a modern review see B. T. Spencer, "A National Literature, 1837-1855," *American Literature*, VII (May, 1936), 125-159.

[38] See for a detailed exploration of this subject the excellent study by Arthur Alphonse Ekirch, *The Idea of Progress in America, 1815-1860* (New York, 1944).

time dissent and conservatism, this faith in progress mounted to a high level and was maintained there by a variety of idealistic and material forces. Believing with the antitraditionalists in the gospel of self-reliance and the essential worth of the individual, the romanticists of that decade were ready to accept the forward thrust of a society made up of worthy personalities. The expansion in power and merit of the individual held the key for the growth of a society or a nation. Undergirding this faith in America were two obvious forces: the belief in social reform, as advanced by Sumner and others, and a full realization of man's gradual conquest of the immense forces of the American continent. Ascendent over all others, however, as a factor in sustaining the romanticist's interpretations was belief in material progress, and it was this idea, with or without subtlety, that upheld the optimism of countless Americans.

Other views, literary in character, spanned a half-century or better and served as continuing stimuli to certain kinds of domestic literary activity: intense emotionalism and antiquarianism. Almost antipodal in character, these forces were nevertheless equally strong in determining the nature of literature in the second quarter of the nineteenth century.

## Emotionalism

Eighteenth century in origin, emotionalism did not reach an American climax until 1840. Prior to 1800 America had its tribute to tears in the songs of Hopkinson, and before 1810 American fiction and popular overseas reprints had freely supplied sentimental heroes and heroines, with their weeping and swoonings, their copious sentiments and their addiction to sensibility. Brown's Clara wept and fainted her way through *Wieland,* and Eliza of *Coquette* fame, whose grave the tears of strangers watered, abundantly illustrated the current "emotions of shame, remorse, patience and regret." Equally European were other forms of intense emotionalism. Americans of the 1800's were more addicted to the unrestrained sorrows of Werther and the sorrows of Ossian than they were to the sorrows of Job. For a half generation thereafter the demand for lachrymose characters declined, but sentimentalism blossomed under the stimulus of Dickens and the cumulative emotionalism of facile women writers.[39] On one hand were the countless verses of the women's journals, and on the other the cumulative volumes of the Lamplighter school.

Emotionalism, through the mounting importance of women in the social and literary world, was responsible for much of the new quantity production. After 1840 women readers increased in number chiefly because of new and thriving women's magazines and gift books tailored for their taste. Women writers in turn began to crowd into the literary arena. Whether this audience of women was a consequence of the new emotionalism, or the emotionalism served in turn to summon up a generation of women readers is not a question one needs to answer here. The important thing is that the new sentimentalism of Lydia Sigourney and the women contributors to *Graham's* became an important factor in determining the direction which literature took and the new volume to which it swelled.

Emotionalism, however, must not be thought of merely as the twin of tears. It was a form of emancipation for the individual, an enlargement of his feelings, a freeing of his inner responses; through its elastic ramifications it widened the expression of individual thoughts and moods. As a force of literary power, it served to stimulate all literature which ranged beyond the limits of one-time classical restrictions.

### Antiquarianism

Antiquarianism was after 1815 another powerful attitude productive of the new trends in literature. Frequently it was identified with the return to the Middle Ages, but though such labeling could be applied with judgment to the English scene, it had little validity in America, where the white man's communities were less than two hundred years old. Nor could it apply to a land devoid of castles, mouldering or new. Thus the chief reliance of both the Gothic romancers and the historical novelists seemed denied American retrospective interpreters. But they quickly sought out and found

---

[39] For the emotionalism of the imitators of Dickens, see Alexander Cowie *The American Novel* (New York, 1949), chap. x; see also Herbert Brown, *The Sentimental Novel in America, 1789-1860* (Durham, N. C., 1940), Book II; and F. L. Pattee, *The Feminine Fifties* (New York, 1940), chap. vi.

substitutes for the stock antiquities of European civilization. Not enough was known of the Viking Leif Ericson to make capital of, but they could and did look with care at the Indian and recognized him as a survivor of an ancient people still in a primitive state, whose history was shrouded in legend and myth. Here at least was hope for true antiquities. Soon historian, antiquarian, and poet were trying to discover and record the imaginative residue of his history and traditions. There was also considerable interest in the prehistoric features of the Ohio valley. But before such literary pieces as S. B. Beach's *Escalala* could flourish, there had to be extensive research in a very difficult field. Daniel Drake, of Cincinnati, and Caleb Atwater led the way to wide speculation about the state of primitive tribes in various portions of the world. Atwater's theories were popularized by Chateaubriand in his *Travels in Italy and America* (1828). Chateaubriand, who had made much of the romantic Indian beside his romantic stream, could shape no tale from the mound-builders; and other writers found the subject equally intractable. Still antiquarianism as an attitude was very influential; and though it soon exhausted the small stock of legends associated with the Eastern rivers and local caves or monadnocks, it continued to exert pressure upon poetry, fiction, and folklore.

Antiquarianism as a movement had developed in mid-eighteenth-century England, was aided by multifarious researches over a forty-year period, and culminated before 1810 in the ministrelsy of Scott and the festive labors of Joseph Strutt. American antiquarianism, greatly retarded by the Revolutionary War, had produced seven state histories; and men like Ezra Stiles, Timothy Dwight, Abiel Holmes, and Jeremy Belknap kept the antiquarian spirit alive; and it was sustained in various passages of Irving's *Knickerbocker* history.[40]

### IV

These general factors in the literary and educational field served jointly to modify, change, and spread the new literary tendencies in early nineteenth-century America; and they certainly account

[40] For evidence of strong enthusiasm for American antiquities after 1810, see *North American Review*, I (May, 1815), 111-121; II (Nov., 1815), 13-32; XII (April, 1821), 466-488; XV (July, 1822), 250-282.

for much of its temper and its inner force. But the literature of the age was so little harmonious in its tendencies that no congeries of forces could impel it in any given direction or account for the particular varieties which it displayed. Any attempt, therefore, to explain the literary change, as in this present effort, must admittedly deal in generalities, without determining how each and every ism or force affected each tendency. If the treatment be cursory, in consequence, this is a weakness that cannot be helped. General causes, moreover, were joined with special ones in accounting for the particular forms utilized in the second quarter of the nineteenth century. Let us turn sharply in our inquiry, therefore, to the destinies of the more dominant forms to see what contributing factors, apart from the general ones already adduced, may be held accountable for their rise and predominance.

Since the subjective forms are less significant in this examination than the safely objective ones, and are not quite in the main line of our inquiry, let us briefly examine two of them (the familiar essay and the sentimental lyric) and move on to the main trends. The familiar essay emerged, in both England and America, as new magazines made their appearance and broke the hold which the refined Addisonian essay had upon the eighteenth century. In England, so declared Theophilus Parsons, this result was a consequence of the success of the *Edinburgh Review* and *Blackwood's Magazine*. And in America the *New York Review*, Willis's *American Monthly Magazine*, the *New England Magazine*, the *Southern Literary Messenger*, and *Knickerbocker's Magazine* were jointly successful in achieving much the same end.

But there were other factors which served to weaken the appeal of the older, didactic form. The gradual shift from the objective to the subjective in literature, the turning from wisdom and observations about life to sheer revelation of personality, to the concentration on style—these major changes in artistic outlook, product of the revolt from authority and convention, guaranteed a new and highly familiar type of essay.

Personalism, however, never became a staunchly American movement. In consequence, no magazine could have been filled with the offerings of English models, or American echoes of them. There is doubt that the personal essay would have begun or expanded here had not such American employers of the form as Nathaniel P. Willis, Lewis and Gaylord Clark,[41] and William Cox[42] been close and careful students of Christopher North[43] and Charles Lamb.[44] The examples of British essayists was the most important factor in the development of American essays in which ease of tone, private opinions, personal antipathies, ingratiating oral expression were blended. Other factors there were, too, but they registered in considerably lessened degree: the spirit of the age, its interest in personality, its attachment to minutiae, its welcoming of a candid, naïve manner, its interest in the fusion of the amusing, the spirited, and the pathetic.

An even clearer medium for the expression of personal concepts was the sentimental lyric, for the expansion of which we must seek

---

[41] The blend of Cockney and Scotch was apparent in the columns of the twin brothers Clark. Lewis Gaylord Clark, editor of the *Knickerbocker Magazine*, made frequent reference to Lamb and aped his poetic moodiness though patterning his "Editor's Table" and "Knick-knacks" after the informal column of Christopher North. At once more readable and more Elian was the miscellaneous department of the *Knickerbocker* called "Ollopodiana." A mood of editorial ease and informality pervades it.

[42] *Blackwood's Magazine*, reprinted in America and widely popular, featured the *Noctes Ambrosianae* of John Wilson, which startled and entertained American readers because of its humor and its elegantly slashing attacks. Its literary potpourri, compounded of satire, nature appreciation, literary criticism, etc., found an early imitator in the "Editor's Table" of Willis's *American Monthly Magazine*, founded in 1829, the first number of which opened with a quotation from Christopher North.

[43] See G. C. Verplanck, "Memoir of the late Robert C. Sands," *New-York Mirror*, XI (February, 1834), 251.

[44] In 1831 Nathaniel P. Willis, himself an ardent admirer of Lamb's informal methods, testified to his vogue in America among youthful writers of the third and fourth decades:

"How profoundly dull was England to the merits of Charles Lamb till he died! . . . America was posterity to him. The writings of all our young authors were tinctured with imitations of his style, when in England, (as I personally know) it was difficult to light upon a person who had read Elia" [see *L'Abri* (New York, 1839), 120]. Despite its effect on younger writers, however, the Lamb type of spontaneous, candid, and confessional essay had a slow growth, a fact which was attributed by the *American Quarterly Review* (XIX, 194) to the lack of colloquial power among American writers. This in turn was ascribed to the almost total absence in America of literary clubs, and the rarity of general and exciting association which might serve as a kind of intellectual gymnasium.

explanation.[45] Much of the lyricism of the age was a consequence of the fine correlation between the *Zeitgeist* and ever-mounting subjectivity. Recognizing fully that the two elements responsible for the cultivation of the sentimental lyric are imagery and feeling, and that the latter had to exist as much in the reader as in the poet, one can readily see how a proper and helpful social feeling was essential to lyrical development. A truly adequate age-spirit had to prevail before emotion could be converted into complex imagery to become in turn for the public a contemplated feeling expressive of individual mood. The change in society which placed the individual first in the scheme of things and glorified his personality brought about not only a concern for a political and social state, but also an interest in the peculiarities of temper and the varieties of emotional response. The expansion of lyricism was the logical result.

What chiefly developed and sustained the American lyric tradition, however, were popular authors from overseas whose works were, in the absence of copyright protection, widely published in America. How extensive such republication was even in the second decade was testified by W. C. Bryant: "the popular English works of the day are reprinted in our country; they are dispersed all over the Union; they are found in everybody's hands; they are made the subject of everybody's conversation."[46] Attractive English models stood ready as prototypes for American verses, and the spirit of imitation was strong.[47]

[45] The expansion in lyricism was not as great as desired by certain critics and readers. The *American Quarterly Review* (XIX [March, 1836], 101) sought to explain the reasons for restricted output: "The numberless projects which absorb the faculties of our countrymen, having for their ends objects of *utility*, and arising from a restless spirit of enterprise, and an unquenchable thirst of gain, are inconsistent with the attainment of that mental discipline which alone can appreciate the sublime and the beautiful, and lead man to a contemplation of things which partake not of the profitable realities of life.

"To repress the wanderings of fancy, and to deaden the aspirations of genius, which, under other circumstances, would have been abandoned to their natural inclinations, is the inevitable result of this universal prevalence of utilitarian doctrines...."

[46] Review of Solyman Brown, *An Essay on American Poetry*, *North American Review*, VII (July, 1818), 207.

[47] Certain potential forces at the beginning of the century one dismisses

THE RISE OF ROMANTICISM 197

Authors imitated included all well-known writers of the day, from the time that their verses appeared in magazines or in boards until their fame was forgotten. Successive literary figures thus paraded through the American literary world. Burns,[48] Thomas Moore,[49] the Scott of "Alice Brand" and "Harp of the North, Awake," Lydia E. Landon,[50] James Montgomery,[51] and others became successively the idol of versifiers.[52]

Most prominent among these lyrical idols, however, were Lord Byron and Mrs. Hemans. Byron's is a name previously introduced in these pages, but the concern here is with his lyrics. In his monograph on *Byron and Byronism in America*, W. E. Leonard contended that he "stood to the lyric poetry of his age—employing the word in the broadest sense of all subjective poetry—as Shakespeare had stood to the dramatic poetry of Elizabethan times."[53] Only a study of volume length could explore so broad a statement,

---

reluctantly because their popularity and reception were not sufficient to make them potent agents. Scott's *Minstrelsy of the Scottish Border* had an influence on developing antiquarianism but scarcely increased the nation's singing strength. The *Lyrical Ballads* of Wordsworth and Coleridge, though noticed favorably in early reviews, were soon swept under by the thunderings of the *Edinburgh Review* and those in America who echoed it. Not until two decades later did these models become effective forces.

[48] Early Burns enthusiasts included the Croaker wits. See Nelson F. Adkins, *Fitz-Greene Halleck: An Early Knickerbocker Wit and Poet*, pp. 23, 48, 137, and 191. Also see Frank L. Pleadwell, *Life and Works of Joseph Rodman Drake* (New York, 1935), p. 116. Halleck on his Scottish tour (1822) visited the Burns country, and pressed a rose from Alloway Kirk in Ayrshire, the sight of which early the following year prompted a panegyric on Burns's genius and popularity.

[49] Adkins, *op. cit.*, pp. 23, 112-113, 119, 190, 284; Stanley Williams, *Life of Washington Irving* (New York, 1935), I, 399; Mott, *op. cit.*, pp. 180, 190, 231, 278.

[50] Enthusiastically received were the poems of Letitia Elizabeth Landon, especially between 1824 and 1835. A representative testimony may be found in the *New-York Mirror*, II (Oct. 16, 1824), 94-95.

[51] E. T. Channing in the *North American Review* (IX [Sept., 1819], 276) charged Montgomery with possessing little talent, but he was frequently reprinted, and his *Lectures on Poetry* was brought out in the Harper's Family Library.

[52] The Brown University Library in 1936 reproduced in facsimile fifty old American Songs (before the Civil War) from original or early editions in the Harris Collection. All but six of the collection were selected from the years 1809 to 1858.

[53] (New York, 1907), p. 111.

but though an overenthusiastic judgment, it could possibly be sustained by an examination of the work of major and minor Americans between 1812 and 1835. It is almost impossible to find a poet of those years who was not touched at one point or another by Byron's lyrics of love and despair, of passion and rhetoric. More broadly, because of his introspection, melancholy, sentiment, and public unhappiness, Byron stirred almost every writer for a generation who wished to voice subjective emotions. Leonard's list of Byron's imitators from 1850 to 1860 indicates that, for all of his dismissal by the critics in the interval, Byron was continuing as a literary influence on minor American literati.

Later influence in America from overseas was exerted by Mrs. Hemans. Entry after entry in the reviews and in the newspaper corners referred to her poetry or reproduced her lines. Poetesses like Hannah F. Gould and Mrs. Sigourney sought to rival her merits and match her reputation. Her imitators numbered high in the dozens, and frequently she was heralded as the equal of Tennyson, as the nonpareil among feminine versifiers. She was almost a universal favorite.[54]

Of course, the sentimental outbursts might not have resulted had not the absence of an international copyright brought the convenient foreign models to America, backed as they were with all the weight of an assured English success, nor would Mrs. Hemans and L. E. L. have flourished had it not been for the great increase in the numbers of women readers and the number of magazines

[54] W. E. Leonard remarked (*op. cit.*, 90): "I have remarked more than once on the popularity of the Byronic Mrs. Hemans; and one has but to glance at her tales and longer historical poems, with their romanticism, gloom, and pseudo-grandeur, with their French and Italian mottoes, to note affinities with Byron on the one hand, and with our versifiers on the other. The influence of her peaceful, often 'prettily sentimental' poems of the affections belongs to another, though related, chapter of American verse, and is mentioned here only to make clear the distinction; imitation of these latter was the peculiar merit of Mrs. Sigourney and many Annualists." In 1827 her poems were favorably reviewed by George Bancroft, and in the thirties Professor Norton of Harvard edited a volume of selections. *The American Quarterly Review* (XXI [June, 1837], 270), said of her: "We have no fear about the increasing fame of Mrs. Hemans." A few pages later the reviewer placed her in the highest rank of those who "profess her beautiful art," remarking that "she depicts strongly but with truth," and that "her pathos and strength are uncommon."

which offered haven for stray verses. Add the poet's corners in the numerous newspapers as an outlet for fugitive verse and the increasing ranks of feminine versifiers were perhaps inevitable. Small wonder that American women, enjoying the freedom of verse for the first time, followed so faithfully the overseas conventions that surrounded them.

v

### Objective Forms

The other dominant literary forms of the age may be referred to as objective: historical-regional tales, the historical romance, romantic history, the legendary sketch, and the metrical romance. All of these are, properly speaking, reflections in part of the antiquarian spirit; and antiquarianism, along with nationalism, enrichment of American experience from the world of nature, and mounting American enthusiasm had much to do with their development. Their forms, moreover, were closely associated with what the age loved to term truth and morality, and they could, without too many warnings and restrictions, be safely entrusted to a new generation of readers.

But it was not the combination of these forces that was chiefly responsible for the great expansion of antiquarian activity after 1815. The greatest influence in a country not yet emancipated from the magic of great names nor from a one-time colonial subserviency was the impact of literary example. Antiquarianism, in short, came to America strongly through the stupendous labors of Walter Scott, first in his metrical romances and then in his romances of history. The retrospective mood was supported for a time by the popularity of *Childe Harold*, but in the world of the historical romance and its associated forms, Scott stood for a half generation as the great stimulating force.

The contrast between his work and the feeble efforts of his immediate predecessors not only conveyed an impression that a new and strong worker had arrived but inaugurated a complete change in the genre itself, so complete as to make possible considerable modification in the antagonistic judgment which had prevailed against it. And in opening up men's eyes to the harmlessness of fiction as such, he created a new literary audience to whom the reading of fiction was a new privilege. This in turn created a market for works of the Waverley stamp, and made possible the numerous volumes of imitation which flooded America during the second quarter of the nineteenth century.[55]

Antiquarianism in America in the 1820's owed somewhat in mid-decade to the semicentennial celebrations, but as far as poetic narrative and historical romance were concerned, there is no question that the truly prominent force for romantic narratives was the example and practice of Scott. With Scott's historical imagination, his vital interest in people, his gift for story-telling, his nostalgia for the picturesqueness of the past, many of the tendencies of the whole Romantic movement seemed to come into focus. He took part in the ballad revival, was interested in the poetic sadness of Ossian's imitators, displayed keenness for wizards and bogles, interested himself in Schiller, Bürger, and Goethe, introduced the picturesque in nature and personality. Not sharing the illusions of his contemporaries and enjoying the advantage of a century of retrospect, one can see today that Scott did not excel in all these fields and did not achieve finality in what he attempted. We can see also that though Scott was in a real sense a culmination of the romantic tendencies of his age, he represents the actual fusion of several elements that were gaining strength in the late eighteenth century. These would unquestionably have exerted their due influence in the world of letters had no Scott ever appeared, but the very fact that he so greatly outrivaled (with the exception of Byron) other claimants to fame in his generation, made his example and vogue[56] a literary

[55] Scott's influence on American literature is the subject of my forthcoming book, of which four sections have already appeared in print.

[56] Of Scott's popularity there were literally thousands of testimonies from which only representative expressions can be reproduced. Susan Cooper remarked of Scott: "every reading household . . . held these books in their hands" (Introduction to *Prairie* [New York, 1898], xxviii). Fitz-Greene Halleck remarked of the appearance of *Waverley*, *Guy Mannering*, and *The Antiquary* that they produced "a widespread enthusiasm throughout Great Britain and this country, which has probably never been equalled in the history of literature" (J. G. Wilson, *Life and Letters of Halleck*, p. 162). C. S. M. concluded that "the circulation of (Scott's) romances, and their influence on the taste of the age probably exceed anything that the world has seen for ages, if it was ever seen" (*Knickerbocker Magazine*, V, 319). "Not only in England and in America" declared the *North*

impulse of the first order, and led to more literary outpourings of the same character. To his contemporaries his éclat was so blinding that he was heralded as the master craftsman, the Wizard of the North, destined to outdistance and outclass all literary rivals.

Since the literary forms Scott helped to popularize or expand, if not initiate, had considerable complexity and their own special followers, we may turn briefly to each to see how and in what degree his influence was exerted and what in simple outline were the other forces responsible for these leading forms of the thirties and forties.

The earliest of these was the legendary.[57] Since the first important success in this literary field sprang from the imagination of Irving, the problem of cause or force must be referred to his literary career. Culmination of a developing antiquarian impulse that went back to Collins, Percy, and others, Irving's work not only breathed the time-spirit but sent the retrospective tale into literary achievement. Apart from the impulse of a tradition, the tales he wrote received a direct stimulus from the highly associative aspects of Scott's metrical romances. In Scott, especially in the colorful legends of his border tales, Irving found not only the legendary spirit but also enthusiasm for the transmutation of all such materials as native locale afforded. The legendary materials were romantic, not only

---

*American Review* in 1823, "but in Germany they [his works] meet with a reception more wide, more prompt, more superstitiously fond than could be believed possible, were it not known to be real" (XVII [Oct., 1823], 383). So very popular was Scott that publishers raced with each other in capturing a sure market, and with such industry that by 1823 over 500,000 volumes of his works had appeared" (C. J. Ingersol, *Annual Oration before the American Philosophical Society at the University of Pennsylvania*, Oct. 18, 1823; noted in the *North American Review*, XVII, 157). As early as 1817 the *American Monthly Magazine* declared: ". . . his works are in everybody's hands and his praises in everybody's mouth." And the *American Quarterly Review* declared in September, 1827, that "all those who read at all, from the highest to the lowest, devoured with unsated appetite, these fictions as they appeared with unexampled rapidity; all admired with an intensity of fashionable enthusiasm" (II, 33).

W. E. Dodd in the *Cotton Kingdom* declared that "*Marmion*, and *Ivanhoe*, and *The Heart of Midlothian* were common intellectual property in all parts of the South." U. B. Phillips, Carl Holliday, J. T. Moore, P. A. Bruce, and Francis Gaines have made similar assertions.

[57] The extent of the legendary in American letters may be studied in Willer, *op. cit., passim*.

because they selected an incident that was unusual and exciting, but because they turned the eye and attention to a happening of yesteryear. Irving in *Bracebridge Hall*, the *Sketch Book*, and *The Alhambra* worked well the mine thus opened, and let his imagination rove over details high above the harsh realities of mundane experience. But if Scott and his antecedent antiquarians provided an impetus for a writer like Irving, it was his own success which sent a whole generation searching for ingredients for new volumes of tales. It is not the purpose here to trace the tradition that followed—it lasted for at least twenty years after the *Sketch Book*, and it explored the resources of stream, village, mountain, and cave—but to suggest that the major force and model in all this tremendous activity was the achievement of Irving. He burst upon the literary world in 1820, and within twelve years he had completed his best contributions to the tale. But he went on imitating himself at the same time that countless others imitated him, too.

### The Historical Romance

The main impulse from Scott was in the direction of the historical romance.[58] Scott convinced Americans that they had a past that could be used in accordance with his pattern. He aroused the national pride, never lethargic, to create an American school of historical romance. He quickened the imagination about the life of the past, enabling writer and reader alike to perceive the drama of other days, convincing them that men possessed the same warm

---

[58]Scott's influence on the writing of historical romance may be established both by the numbers of actual imitations and by the clamor which his example raised. Upon the demands for Waverley-like romances in America we may dwell for a moment: Robert Walsh several times declared that American materials were ample for the Waverley type of novel (*American Quarterly Review*, II [Sept., 1827], 33). W. H. Prescott (*North American Review* [1827] XXV, 193) spoke of Scott as working a revolution in American as well as English fiction. The editors of the *North American Review* were the first to ask for American historical fiction, pointing out not only the richness of America in the materials needed for such fiction, but the desirability of turning the demand for national literature into this specific channel. Representative declarations will be found in XV (Oct., 1822), 319-340; XXI (July, 1825), 78-104; XXXII (April, 1831), 386-421. For a general review of the words of encouragement to those who would write American romances, see my "The Romance Ferment after *Waverley*," *American Literature*, III (Jan., 1932), 408-431.

emotions and urges in bygone times as they do in contemporary life. And Scott furnished a convenient formula. It was analyzed by W. H. Gardiner as regionalism, romantic landscape, and retrospection, but actually it fused more tendencies than these three. Scott combined within his novels the ingredients of many of the tales of the day: the portrayal of local and national legends; the stress upon dialect and national characteristics; the glamour of hills and vales and ruins where mystery and strangeness were to be found; antiquarian taste for ancient memorials; the depiction of the life and peculiarities of humble personages who displayed the typical features of an age or a civilization; and the interest in quickening the obscure life of an older period of civilized existence. To his generation Scott brought characters rooted in the soil; but more significant than all else, he brought the gift of romance which made his readers forget themselves and brought wonder into their lives.[59]

But this prose formula of Scott was not at once taken up. The earliest readers were struck wordless with admiration for his knowl-

[59] Scott's fame and genius led to unrestrained comments. The *Select Journal* remarked in October, 1832: "We have lived during the same period with one of those highly gifted men whom the world has yet produced only at intervals of centuries." Heman Humphrey called Scott "the idol of half Scotland, England, and America" (*A Tour in Great Britain, France and Belgium*, II, 90). Henry Coleman spoke of Scott having "wielded so despotic an empire over the imagination, thoughts, and affections of the whole civilized world" (*European Life and Manners* [Boston, 1849], 72). When W. H. Prescott sought to prove the popularity of Irving's *Bracebridge Hall*, he compared the number of printings with those of the less important Waverley novels.

When a yardstick was sought to prove the literary enthusiasm of the age, Scott was compared with Shakespeare. The coupling of Scott's and Shakespeare's names was frequent. See *North American Review*, XXV (July, 1827), 192-203; *Ladies Literary Museum* (March 28, 1818); *Literary Casket and Pocket Magazine*, I (May, 1821), 94; *New York Literary Journal*, IV (Nov., 1820), 1; *The Alexander Gazette* (April 5, 1819). N. P. Willis, in the *American Monthly Magazine* (Jan., 1831), remarked of Scott: "No writer since Shakespeare has obtained such dominion over the human heart, and no one has shown himself so full of the genial glow and spirit of humanity. No one has approached so near that 'myriad-minded' poet in the delineation of character, and we sometimes feel that the novelist might have drawn Iago, and that Rob Roy would not have been unworthy of the dramatist's pencil." L. F. T., writing in the *United States Magazine* for April, 1842, contended that Scott and Shakespeare are alike in character treatment, ability to feed the imagination, and the appropriation of material from every source to their use.

edge of Scottish antiquities and his vivid imagination. They regarded his proficiency in literature and history as a striking power too extensive for the lowly pen of would-be imitators. Then came James Fenimore Cooper to show the way for the domestication of the Scott romance in America.

At the time of *The Spy* (1821), his first historical romance, Cooper was more or less a novice at the business of novel-writing; and since he had full respect for the British novelists he and his wife had been reading, there was no compulsion upon him to deviate from the standard practices, however careful he might be not to follow slavishly in anyone's footsteps. Thus the sentimentalism he introduced, especially in Isabel Singleton of *The Spy*, is in a vein which had·been popular for forty years, and the employment of mystery and terror in *Lionel Lincoln* either goes back to standard practice of the Gothic novel or turns to Scott's *Black Dwarf* for a more recent example of a well-established literary practice. History and dialect and banquet scenes he could have found in the Waverleys. The same is true of the gallery of characters, high and low, of topographical features, and of the devotion ·to the picturesque. *The Spy* was a test of the Waverley formula by strictly American materials. Cooper provided in Harvey Birch a more than American parallel to Edie Ochiltree, and in Dr. Sitgreaves the equivalent of one of Scott's learned bores. The choice of the Neutral Ground proved happily adaptable for the transfusion of Scott's manner and for the duplication of the essential features of a border tale. Resemblances to the general pattern of Scott are equally apparent in *The Wept of Wish-ton-Wish* with its opening and its blockhouse attack, both redolent of Ivanhoe, and its Meek Wolf a poor caricature of Nehemiah Solsgrace. Cooper did not always deal, however, with these trappings of older societies. It was not long before he presented to the American public distinctive narratives of the Indian and the frontier and created the memorable character of Leather-Stocking.[60]

But if Cooper, in domesticating the historical romance succeeded by patriotism and genius in creating a fresh and vivid form of

[60] For an analysis of the native ingredients that helped to shape Cooper's concept of Leather-Stocking, see Gregory Paine, "Introduction" to *Deerslayer* (New York, 1933).

romance, many of his contemporaries were far less successful. Among the truly close imitations of Scott were such works as *Tales of an American Landlord*, McClung's *Camden*, Captain Murgatroyd's *The Refugee*, and McHenry's novels, *O'Halloran*, *Hearts of Steel*, and *The Wilderness*.[61] Many works which were not designed as parodies followed Scott's manner closely, including his blemishes all copied and exaggerated in extravagant fashion, especially in the numerous petty anachronisms which even the freedom exercised by Scott could not excuse. But the retrospective methods of Scott were so convenient and alluring and the historical romance so new that even writers of originality in this form sometimes unconsciously moved along in his mighty steps.

Other authors went to the opposite extreme, violently eschewing any of Scott's methods or mannerisms: men like John Neal,[62] who was nevertheless stimulated by his example; or William Gilmore Simms, who, though sometimes reminiscent of Scott, wrote so freely and with such verve, and in so many volumes, that no original could have afforded guidance over half his literary pilgrimage. James Kirke Paulding, generally heralded in critical circles as a realist and imitator of Fielding, was not without indebtedness to Scott, especially in *The Dutchman's Fireside* and *The Old Continental*. But Paulding's sharp penetration and satirical spirit led him, despite a protest from Irving, to direct his critical lance at Scott, as in *The Lay of the Scottish Fiddle* (1813). *The Koningsmarke* (1823), a quiz upon Scott's methods, purports to reveal the arcana of the novelist's art, especially of that new and striking variety known as the historical romance.

One of the events stimulative of historical fiction was the semi-centennial celebration in 1825, which spurred patriotic ambition to new heights. It led Cooper to write *Lionel Lincoln* and at least to contemplate writing a series of one each for the separate thirteen republics. It led to an outpouring of literary pieces greater in quantity than the historical romances of England at the same time. This mood of celebration was in turn heightened by the visit of

---

[61] See Arthur Hobson Quinn, *American Fiction* (New York, 1936), pp. 51-52 for a brief notice of McHenry's novels.
[62] See Neal's *Rambling Recollections of a Somewhat Literary Life* (Boston, 1869), for a glimpse of his stormy individualism.

Lafayette to the United States in 1824 and by the rousing assemblies with which he was everywhere feted.

Had Scott not appeared, the time spirit and other factors might have called for the expansion of the novel independent of overseas influence. During the Era of Good Feeling the tendency was toward an assertive freedom, and one of the avenues which this freedom took was the invasion of the novel-reading and novel-writing fields. Any novelist free from the absurdities of the Gothic novels of Lewis, the daring radicalism of Godwin, and the trifling absurdities of the sentimental tradition stood a fair chance of gaining readers. But that the novel would have taken the direction of the historical retrospective or that it would have centered so markedly about the activities and output of one man does not appear within the bounds of probability.

It was in the South that Scott had the most loyal and persistent followers. P. A. Bruce declared that there were "few libraries of importance . . . that were lacking in those splendid volumes in which he has drawn such romantic pictures of the entrenched camp, the martial council, and the sombre castle swarming to the battlements with mail-clad defenders."[63] Southern periodicals, such as the *Southern Rose*, the *Southern Literary Messenger*, the *Southern Quarterly Review*, and the *Magnolia* make clear by their direct and casual references to Scott that they were addressing readers who had the utmost familiarity with the Waverley novels.

Scott's novels may well have done much to strengthen gentlemanly qualities in the Southern gentry. His works may have led Southerners to desire a more chivalric order through his bringing before his readers visions which, once seen, were not easily forgotten; but if his influence was great in this direction, it was not because his message to the South differed from that to the West, or because in a particular area a literary work suddenly exerted a preponderant influence, but because he fitted into the Southern design for living. The outdoor life, the rural activities, the agrarian basis of life, the survival of the English ideal must have had more to do with the formation of the Southern manner[64] than all the books

---

[63] P. A. Bruce, *Brave Deeds of Confederate Soldiers* (Philadelphia, 1916), p. 169.

[64] For a fuller discussion of Scott's cultural influence, see my "Mark

ever consumed in the region, however much such literary influence may have enriched the decorative aspects of that life. And in the South the character of his literary rivals—Byron, G. P. R. James, and above all Thomas Carlyle—demonstrates that conclusions drawn from vogue alone are based on unsure and sketchy grounds.[65]

Even among his early enthusiasts the model of Scott dimmed with time. One of the reasons for this was an increasing recognition of Scott's Tory sentiments. Democratic he was in his instinctive human sympathies, and especially in the handling of the lowly characters in his novels, but he was, of course, a political conservative, and he did aspire to outward shows and titles. Cooper, by 1830, was protesting, in the name of American liberalism, against the species of danger which Scott's novels had for Americans, with their rigid caste system, their reverence for title, their occasional glorification of the medieval at the expense of the modern.

In Scott's heyday there were those who found his novels, apart from such subtle political sympathies, insufficiently informed with ideas. Those whose hearts swelled with moral idealism and whose view of life was earnest, especially followers of Coleridge and Carlyle, were disappointed with what might have been called Scott's "ease in Zion." This mounting distrust of authors who ministered primarily to pleasure was related to the suspicion against the ideal of aesthetic beauty in Poe and accounts for the serious delay in the American appreciation of the genius of Shelley. It was related also to the mounting seriousness of readers inclined toward metaphysical queries.

Finally, there were authors, like Hawthorne in *The Scarlet Letter*, who, though moving toward Scott in the appreciation of tableau scenes, could recognize that dramatic moments in the past, though proper objects of pictorial art and interesting when objec-

---

Twain, Walter Scott, and the Civil War," *South Atlantic Quarterly*, XL (Oct., 1941), 342-359.

[65] *Ibid.*, pp. 348-349; see also Grace W. Landrum, "Sir Walter Scott and His Literary Rivals in the Old South," *American Literature*, II (Nov., 1930), 256-276; Rollin G. Osterweis, *Romanticism and Nationalism in the Old South* (New Haven, Conn., 1949); and J. B. Hubbell, "Literary Nationalism in the Old South," in *American Studies in Honor of W. K. Boyd* (Durham, N. C., 1940), pp. 175-220.

tively portrayed, could but inadequately supply those inner conflicts and driving forces which made human conduct an almost unpredictable affair. Thus there was in Hawthorne and other metaphysical novelists a recognition that pageantry was not enough; there must be an intensification of mood and presentation of motive that captures the reader in the realm of his own will.

## REGIONALISM

One of the movements associated with the vogue of Scott is regionalism, and shortly after the popularity of the Waverley series, in Austria, in Italy, Spain, and France, a movement for regional interpretation went along with the retrospective. Upon the Continent this owed as much to political as to literary forces, for the destruction of Napoleon's dream of a French empire of Europe led to a renewal of strong political nationalism and the literary regionalism with which it was accompanied. In America the new temper of nationalism, also political in the sense that victory in the War heightened the native spirit of confidence, borrowed from literary impulse as well—from the Schlegels and Madame de Staël[66]—though the regional aspects of Scott's fiction (as in *Waverly, Guy Mannering, The Antiquary, The Heart of Midlothian,* and *St. Ronan's Well*) were not immediately reflected in regional stories. In Scotland John Galt, David Moir, and Susan Ferrier

[66] *The Analectic Magazine* praised the work of Mme de Staël highly (see II [1813], 177). Her place in romantic thought was thoroughly established by the publication of *De l'Allemagne,* a work studied by W. E. Channing and many other scholars of the day. Her American vogue may be traced through other works as well. Andrew Ritchie (*North American Review,* VIII [Dec., 1818], 26-63), called her "the finest genius in France," a judgment more than matched by T. Parsons' declaration that she was the "greatest female that has ever written." He condemned, however, the doctrine of perfectibility which she advanced, declaring it "directly opposed to all right reason and tolerably fair argument" (*North American Review,* XI [July, 1820], 124-140). Less sympathetically Alexander H. Everett declared that philosophy, and not poetry, was her proper department (*North American Review,* XIV [Jan., 1822], 101-128). Her *De l'Allemagne* had a great deal to do with the intensification in study of national culture and literature. She was responsible for the articulation of Schlegel's theories and for his increase in reputation. For brief notice, see R. C. Whitford, "Mme. de Staël's Reputation in America," *Modern Language Notes,* XXXIII (Dec., 1918), 467-480.

quickly seized upon this part of Scott's formula and poured out tales of low-life Scottish existence which are sometimes read today. Now American authors recognized the regional features of Scott but combined them, as he frequently did, with the purely antiquarian. Novelists like Mrs. Child, Mrs. Cheney, Mrs. Cushing and others conveyed the sense of community existence and of one-time manners, but these materials were invariably restricted to a Colonial or Revolutionary frame. The same is true to a lesser degree of John Pendleton Kennedy's *Swallow Barn* (1832), a combination of Scott's best regionalism and the spirit of Irving's *Bracebridge Hall*. Attempting to describe the life of the planter upon his acres and exhibiting the false but glamorous concept that plantation life was one of endless leisure devoted to endless romantic objectives, *Swallow Barn* represented, with W. A. Caruthers' *Cavaliers of Virginia* (1834-1835), a response in literature to the tremendous expansion of the plantation system westward to include Alabama and Mississippi. The plantation, rightly or wrongly, was regarded as a symbol of economic conditions which held the South together, and of the romantic spirit which was its pride and glory. Deeply rooted as was this tradition, its strength was in its combination of an ideal of the English gentry, an intense love of region, and above all, an addiction to a form of fiction which fitted in with the desires of authors and readers alike.

Most Southern novels were not strongly regional, however, for the adherence of Southern authors to the historical pattern was even more faithful than that of their compatriots in the North. For real evidence of Scott's impact on American regional materials one has to turn to the imported literature of the West. On the frontier Scott was widely circulated and his gallery of low-life characters was greatly appreciated. Characters like Dandy Dinmont and Edie Ochiltree had the combination of the strange and the bizarre which the Southwest humorists appreciated and which led not only to a keener observation of life about them but to the literary utilization at times of such materials.

The Southwest had been supplied with many of the literary resources of the East—almanacs, newspapers, travel books—and in these publications local types, oddities of character and manners, colorful and dramatic episodes appeared and joined to make Americans aware of native materials. These sources supplied many characterizations and anecdotes of the lower classes of society and familiarized readers with their sayings and antics. With these materials at hand the humorists found in the methods of Cooper, Christopher North, and Scott certain techniques which they could employ for the full utilization of such wealth. Thus at times there appears, in a remote following of the low-life in Scott's novels, the continuation of a tradition that began in Ireland and Scotland and was to extend to all quarters of the literary globe. This is not to declare, of course, that the humorous tradition either began in Scott or would have been essentially different had his works never made their way westward. The remoteness of America, the difficulty of transportation and communication created islands of culture which made possible the idiosyncracies the humorists celebrated; and this celebration, stemming back to bizarre Yankee types, antedated the War of 1812 and the literary modes it ushered in. The superbly rich backwoods speech, authentic localities, and colorful types would somehow have found their way into print, especially since the local-color humorists had so zealous a desire to be local,[67] autochthonous, and specific; but that the tradition they established would have developed so rapidly or that their works would have exerted so great a force without outside literary aid does not seem altogether likely.

## Romantic History

Another of the retrospective forms to be assayed is romantic history. In the period before 1830 there had stirred a general an-

[67] Apart from James Hall and others, there was a strong urge at Cincinnati and Lexington towards a purely indigenous regionalism in the West. Benjamin Drake, for instance, in his *An Address. . .* ([Cincinnati, 1831], 7, 11, 14) declared that "instead of transmontane sentiments and opinions without discrimination, to be moulded to the circumstances of this [Mississippi] valley, our literature should be the result of the political, moral, and physical conditions by which we are surrounded." Thus the true implications of Scott's regionalism, instead of its purely academic and theatrical quality, was beginning to be understood. Unfortunately, except for the work of Caroline Matilda Kirkland, Western authors did not learn the lesson Drake sought to teach. Not until Eggleston, with the Taine influence, did the theory of literary products as the inevitable result of the interplay of environment, character, and atmosphere gain its proper ascendency in the thinking of Western writers.

noyance with the kind of literary composition which ignored personality. The new freedom was releasing the powers of the individual and emphasizing their values. More and more men sought to escape the boredom of anonymity. Articulately they voiced dissatisfaction with history that was compounded of documents and dry annals. Recognizing that human passion played an important part in every historical crisis, they wished to see their history featuring human factors and warm emotions.

Insistence upon a vital, dynamic history readers were finding in the pages of Macaulay[68] and Carlyle, but how the transformation could be effected was once again disclosed in the writings of Walter Scott. The widespread praise of Scott's service to history[69] in filling the cultural gaps left by previous historians was putting the spotlight upon their defects. If historians had known how to vivify the past, they would never have stood in debt to a mere romancer. In pleasing through historical tales, Scott turned the flood of public interest into what had been a private lake. A public stimulated to read history by the charming tales of a novelist was going to demand in that history the dramatic quality which had first arrested its attention and aroused its interest. If in putting history in a place of prominence, in giving historians popular readers, the course of historiography was changed, then Scott had some influence on that change.[70]

That the historians, well-read in the Waverley novels, were swift to avail themselves of the new manner and the new techniques may be illustrated by the efforts of William Prescott. His enthusiasm sprang from the possibility he saw of combining Scott's verve with professional fact-sifting. His contentions on the subject, penned in 1839 when he was thirty-five and had his main historical works yet to write, adequately illustrated what he had learned from Scott in the matter of dramatizing history. The germ of a

[68] *Edinburgh Review*, XL (May, 1828), 362-363.
[69] The influence of Scott upon historians in general, European, English and American, has been admirably summarized by G. H. Maynadier in "*Ivanhoe* and Its Literary Consequences," *Essays in Memory of Barrett Wendell* (Cambridge, Mass., 1936).
[70] A general review of the development of history-writing in America may be found in J. Franklin Jameson, *The History of Historical Writing in America* (Boston, 1891).

new history sown by Scott's dull and unread *Life of Napoleon* came to a fine fruition in Prescott's works on the Spanish conquistadores[71]—a field giving ample opportunity for the romantic chivalry and battle pieces so dear to the heart of Scott.[72]

## THE INDIAN ROMANCE

Historical works on the Indian by Parkman and others introduce a topic of wide interest in American letters and suggest another field of literary activity in which the retrospective found imitators, though constituting only one of the common modes of expression.[73] In the 1790's the concept of the noble savage[74] flourished for a few years, especially after Mrs. Morton's *Quabi*,[75] and it was sustained in the two succeeding decades by Irving's "Philip of Pokanoket" and Campbell's *Gertrude of Wyoming*. After 1817, however, the interest in the Indian obviously mounted, and for a time he became the leading figure on the literary scene. What were the reasons for this emphasis? First was the colorful career of Tecumseh, intelligent leader of the Indians, the Napoleon of the red men. Second was the signing of the Treaty of Chicago in 1820. Official *Proceedings* of the treaty negotiations stirred interest in the red man, but books by Jedediah Morse, Dr. Jarvis, and especially John E. Heckewelder, had the same effect. These works aided Cooper and provided groundwork for Eastburn and Sands.

---

[71] *Biographical and Critical Miscellanies* (Philadelphia, 1879), pp. 263, 265.

[72] What is contended for Prescott is equally demonstrable in the career of Parkman, Gayarré, and others. See Charles Haight-Farnham, *A Life of Francis Parkman* (Boston, 1901), p. 73.

[73] For the study of primitivism the reader is referred to Montaigne (Essay "Of Coaches"), Lafitau, Mercier, Aphra Behn (*Oronooko*) and others. The savage was frequently held up to shame the civilized readers of an effete age. The outlander essays of Montesquieu, Goldsmith, and Freneau were interesting forms of satire in an age of reason, but the Samoans, the Persians, and the Algerines made way for savage heroes whose ethnological traits, heroic glories, and primitive life were the proper ingredients for new, heroic, romantic narratives.

[74] Early treatment of the Indian in poetry included: Roger Williams, excerpt from *A Key into the Language of America* (London, 1643); Benjamin Thompson, *New England's Crisis* (1676); George Cocking, *War: An Heroic Poem* (1762); Joel Barlow, *The Vision of Columbus* (1787).

[75] For Dunlap, Arnold, and Gisborne, minor poets who treated this theme, see F. E. Farley, *Anniversary Papers by the Colleagues and Pupils of George Lyman Kittredge* (Boston, 1913), pp. 251-260.

James Athearn Jones's three volumes of Indian legends, myths, and stories prepared the way for a plethora of such material even though he himself made little distinction between exciting episodes and folklore.

But the greatest factor was antiquarianism. The Indian, it was argued, constituted America's past. Here stood a race without a history, whose glory, if it existed, went back to former ages. While this concept echoed somewhat the golden age doctrine and built a contrast between what was and now is, it also had impetus from the Gothicism of the age. American students of the Gothic, thwarted by the newness of America and unable with any convincingness to transfer mouldering castles of Europe to the American scene, still clamored for ruins as an indispensable ingredient in their narratives. If they could discover no crumbling piles of brick or stone, they could fix upon the ruins of a race. Eagerly the search for forlorn Indian leaders and doomed tribes went on.[76]

It is doubtful, however, if nationalism, antiquarianism, Gothicism, and historical events could have popularized the Indian if only the literary models of the late eighteenth century had been available for the purpose. Epics and mock-epics might have fitted the Indian out with the proper virtues, but by 1815 the old-style epic was dead. Though Americans, with the defeat of Little Turtle and Tecumseh, found the Indian menace sufficiently removed for them to glamourize the race, it was not until Longfellow's *Hiawatha* in 1855 that a model was discovered that might transmute this primitive material into neo-epic form. Long before that date the sentimental graveyard poem was occasionally adopted for Indian pieces, but in that direction neither originality nor interest was found.[77] Fortunately able lit-

---

[76] Ossianism was largely responsible for the sentimental verses in which ancient chieftains lamented over the burial grounds of their race. Of such sentimental texture many of the gift-book verses were compounded. See F. I. Carpenter, "The Vogue of Ossian in America," *American Literature*, II (Jan., 1931), 405-417.

[77] While there were few directly primitivistic verses after 1810 seeking to point to the Indian as a glorification of all the human qualities lacking in white settlers, the glorification of Indian attributes common in the primitivistic writings of the eighteenth century made these same attributes readily available for the metrical novels of the nineteenth century. In novel and long verse narrative both Indian and white attributes were heightened for the sake of romance.

erary men were on hand to devise models for the effective handling of Indian materials: Cooper introduced a new and workable formula for prose narratives, and for poetic stories Scott's metrical achievements once again became the favorite objects of emulation. In 1808 *Marmion*, with its border conflict, provided a proper vehicle for the imaginative presentation of the many struggles between the white man and the red. The model was not immediately utilized, though the parallelism between border raiders and Indian bands was quickly perceived.[78] With Scott's *Lady of the Lake* new materials for comparison were available, for Rhoderick Dhu and other Highland chieftains stood in the imagination as bold, impetuous leaders whose shrewdness, intrepidity, and physical hardihood might be matched among Indian chieftains. With *Yamoyden* (1820), by J. W. Eastburn and R. C. Sands, and *Sanillac*, by Henry Whiting, the new type of metrical novel was well on its popular course;[79] and in the years to follow many tales of Indian chieftains with direct indebtedness to, occasional borrowings from, or reminiscences of, Scott were to run from the presses. Some of these were weak, puerile efforts; others like Meek's *Red Eagle*, Colton's *Tecumseh*, and Myer's *Ensinore* were able poems and furnished fitting American parallels to the Scottish models.

It should be noted, however, that Scott's *Marmion, Lady of the Lake, Rokeby*, and *Lord of the Isles* were not completed as a series before his example summoned a rival into the field in the person of Lord Byron. From the pages of Byron's Oriental romances came the traits of bold freebooters or ruthless Oriental blade-wielders, which gave a Byronic rather than a Scottish cast to certain Indian poems. *Mengive, Elsinore*, and *Mentwa* were some of the poetical narratives wherein the gloomy Indian chieftain, full of dark foreboding, stalked unsocially through pages of romance.

This mood of gloom, which was the special mark of the Byronic

---

[78] For enthusiastic voicing of romantic optimism, see William Tudor, "Miss Huntley's Poems," *North American Review*, I (May, 1815), 111-121; and "An Address to the Phi Beta Kappa Society," *North American Review*, II (Nov., 1815), 13-32; John Knapp, "National Poetry," *North American Review*, VIII (Dec., 1818), 169-176.

[79] An extended treatment of the Indian in the longer narrative poem will be found in G. H. Orians, *The Indian in the Metrical Romance* (Urbana, Illinois, 1929).

hero, whether in the roll of Mr. Gray in Cooper's *Pilot*, the undaunted and introspective heroes of Neal's novels, or in the simple little sketches of minor authors, was heightened by the deep melancholy of Ossianic verses. MacPherson's brooding heroes sitting in their foggy gloom were cousins german to Indian chieftains lamenting the destiny of their race or, at the ruins of a cherished landmark, dolefully chanting of old wrongs and former griefs. Into their profound despair was thus injected a strong note of sentimentalism little harmonious with larger philosophical implications.[80]

With Cooper's *Last of the Mohicans* (1826) and the rest of the Leather-Stocking tales the floodgates of emotion about the Indians were opened, and volume after volume idealizing their lives or fictionalizing their simple activities appeared. The Indian thus created was romantic, full of poetic speech, stalwart, stoic, generous, brave, and eloquent. That some of the representations were primitivistic is clear enough, but from another and stronger point of view, much of the nobility of the savage was simply the normal glorification of a fictional hero in a romantic pattern. Glorification of the savage in nonfictional prose is one thing; in a metrical or historical romance, the commonest expression of the nineteenth century, it becomes something entirely different.

This observation is especially true of the work of James Fenimore Cooper, who broke the bonds of the conventional romance, utilized the force of a great nature tradition, and turned loose the powers of his own mighty imagination when he formed a model for an Indian narrative in 1823 that was to provide example for scores of Indian romances. In his recording of the wiles of the

[80] Grenville Mellen remarked, in his review of Cooper's *Red Rover:* "This bronze noble of nature is . . . made to talk like Ossian for whole pages, and measure out hexameters, as though he had been practising for a poetic prize" (*North American Review*, XXVII [July, 1828], 140). John Neal, in the preface to the second edition of *Rachel Dyer* thus remarked of Cooper's Indians: "Not so much as one true Yankee is to be found in any of our native books: hardly so much as one true Yankee phrase. Not so much as one true Indian, though you hardly take up a story on either side of the water now, without finding a red-man stowed away in it; and what sort of a red-man? Why one that uniformly talks the best English the author is capable of—more than half the time perhaps out-Ossianing Ossian" ([Portland, 1828], p. xv).

Indian in pursuit, his at-homeness in the forest, his presentation of the epic sweep and grandeur of forest life, Cooper gave to the Indian theme an attractiveness that it could not have possessed in the equally romantic Gothic tradition. Then in 1826 came his *Last of the Mohicans*, with which volume he opened up an even more romantic phase of the Indian tradition and became with N. M. Hentz the originator of a tradition that did not die for forty years, though long before that lapse of time most marks of freshness, novelty, and merit had departed. But the tradition did not end before it had produced such distinctive volumes as Simms's *Yemassee* and *Cassique of Kiawah*, J. S. French's *Elkswatawa*, and D. P. Thompson's *The Doomed Chief*.[81]

Late in the forties a deluge of Indian novels, the greatest that America had seen, greeted the public eye, and this outpouring was accompanied by sixteen long rhymed romances, most of them reminiscent of Scott. But it was not exclusively a model as old as *The Lady of the Lake* which prompted this outburst. No one factor could possibly have accounted for it. Schoolcraft's *Algic Researches* (1837) and subsequent volumes, Catlin's *Letters* and *Notes* and other purely antiquarian works were reflected in the imaginative writings after 1837. Considerable impetus to Indian writing came from political events, the tribal removals of 1838 which stirred guilt-haunted interest in the Indian, and the presidential candidacy of William Henry Harrison, hero of Tippecanoe.[82] His political career stirred other poets than those in his own party, and the glory of the frontier and frontier armies appeared in novel and poem, particularly in Colton's *Tecumseh*. If these political forces were not enough, there was Cooper's return to the Indian field with *The Pathfinder*, *Oak Openings*, and *Satanstoe*, sufficient in vitality to have ushered in a new period of

---

[81] For a discussion of the theme of the vanishing American from 1826 (the date of *The Last of the Mohicans*) to 1836 (the date of French's *Elkskatawa*), see G. H. Orians, "The Cult of the Vanishing American," *University of Toledo Bulletin* (May, 1934).

[82] George Catlin, *Letters and Notes on the Manners, Customs, and Conditions of the North American Indians* (1841); anonymous, *Events in American History* (Lancaster, Pa., 1841); Benjamin Drake, *Life of Tecumseh* (1841); William Lette Stone, *The Life and Times of Red Jacket* (1841); William M. Willett, *Scenes in the Wilderness* (1842); Samuel Taylor, *Report of a Visit to Some Tribes of Indians* (1843); and several others.

Indian romance and guarantee its vitality until after the Civil War. Because of a number of factors, therefore, most of them native, the antiquarianism of the age was to turn for major emphasis, both scientific and imaginative, to the lowly red man.

## The Gothic

Earliest of the traditions associated with romantic fiction is the quest for the strange, the exotic, and the supernatural. At their peak in the last decade of the eighteenth century,[83] the "dreary phantoms of the cave and cloister," and the "malicious monks and revengeful Italians"[84] still made readers swoon for fear during the ensuing ten years. Forms of the Gothic survived, in fact, until 1850 in both tales and longer works of fiction. Terror ingredients,[85] for instance, were apparent in Cooper's *Lionel Lincoln* and Simms's *Forayers* and were widely employed in the novels of John Neal and R. H. Dana. In certain works of fiction this Gothic survival can be accounted for by the peculiarity of American retrospective materials. Salem witchcraft, cavernous recesses, the regicides, these were relatively minor materials in the affairs of nations, but they loomed large to those who sought for the unusual and dramatic in America's meager past. Their employment in historical tales quite readily invoked devices of terror popular in Radcliffe, Lewis, the German school, and Scott. It is natural, therefore, that in the handling of such material devices out of the Gothic novel should reappear.[86]

---

[83] For evidence of the extent of Gothicism in England, see E. T. S. Tompkins: *The Popular Novel in England* (London, 1932), chap. vii, pp. 243-296; Edith Birkhead, *The Tale of Terror* (New York, 1921), *passim*; and Eino Railo, *The Haunted Castle* (London, 1927), chaps. i-iv, vii-xi.

[84] The Gothic romance was assailed by Dennie in "The Lay Preacher," *Portfolio* nos. 79-82 (July 16, 23, 30, and Aug. 6, 1803). See also *North American Review*, XV (July, 1822), 252-254; III (July, 1816), 217-218.

[85] Only a few genuine Gothic romances were ever written in America. The best known was *Alonzo and Melissa* (Poughkeepsie, N. Y., 1811). See also *The Sicilian Pirate, or the Pillar of Mystery: A Terrific Romance*, cited by Birkhead, *op cit.*, pp. 196-197.

[86] That the Gothic tale was a well-known form in England down to the appearance of Scott's *Waverley* (1814) is proved by Scott's comments in the introductory chapter of that novel:
"Had I announced in my frontispiece, 'Waverley, a Tale of Other Days,' must not every novel reader have anticipated a castle scarce less than that

But the question at this point is not why Gothicism survived, but what led to its expansion and to its transformation in character after 1825. To many readers by that date Mrs. Radcliffe and Monk Lewis were unknown. The expansion of the fiction-reading world after 1820 ushered in many readers who were unconversant with the fiction printed at the turn of the century, and for them the Gothicism of Scott was as new as his special historical pattern. Thus Scott's novels, which drove the feebler Gothic pieces from the field, contained in themselves some of the Gothic materials previously banished; but, commingled in his works with the true and the moral, such extravagances seemed a legitimate part of his formula.[87]

Other factors, apart from Scott, were, however, responsible for the expansion of the Gothic in the tales of the twenties[88] and thirties, and together they brought about a transformation of the form: the temporary popularity of Maturin, after his *Melmoth the Wanderer* (1821), the acquaintance with E. T. A. Hoffmann, and after 1828 the popularization of short German romances through imitations in *Blackwood's Magazine*. Poe's indebtedness

---

of Udolpho, of which the eastern wing has been long uninhabited, and the keys either lost or consigned to the care of some aged butler or housekeeper, whose trembling steps about the middle of the second volume were doomed to guide the hero or heroine to the ruinous precincts? Would not the owl have shrieked and the cricket cried in my very title page? and could it have been possible to me with a moderate attention to decorum to introduce any scene more lively than might be produced by the jocularity of a clownish but faithful valet or the garrulous narrative of the heroine's *fille-de-chambre*, when rehearsing the stories of blood and horror which she had heard in the servant's hall? Again, had my title borne 'Waverley, A Romance from the German,' what head so obtuse as not to imagine forth a profligate abbot, and oppressive duke, a secret and mysterious association of Rosicrucians and Illuminati, with all their properties of black cowls, caverns, daggers, electrical machines, trap-doors, and dark lanterns?"

[87] For a detailed study of Gothic materials in Scott, though marshaled to support a thesis upon order of composition, see Mody Boatright, *PMLA*, L (March, 1935), 235-261. Scott's Gothicism is less generously advanced in half-a-dozen other treatments, of shorter compass.

[88] For a conception of the importance of Gothic ingredients in the novels of the third decade, see Oral Coad, "The Gothic Element in American Literature," *Journal of English and Germanic Philology*, XXIV (Jan., 1928), 85 ff.

to Hoffmann has been sufficiently insisted upon,[89] and the general impact of the German type of tale upon Americans of two decades can be traced both in Poe's early tales and in the minor authors of two decades.

Out of these three forces a new type of Gothic, the malign, gradually emerged. Hawthorne as an undergraduate at Bowdoin was a reader of Maturin's *Melmoth the Wanderer*. Here falls the long, penetrating, but evil glance that sent chills down the spine. Already in Brown the association of evil with the Gothic was pronounced, and it was reinforced by other manifestations of the time. Coleridge's "The Ancient Mariner," with his long and withering look, was of the same school and had American reflection in Dana's "Buccaneer."[90] Here, as in Coleridge, Dana furnished the punishment of the mariner through sinister power, and more important, by the utter loneliness which enveloped the hero and made him suffer.

Equally important in the expansion of the mode was the new discontent and disillusionment in Byron's witch drama, *Manfred*, with its setting in the wild, tempestuous reaches of the Swiss Alps. Manfred, the self-condemned, finds even nature affording a contrasting backdrop to the dreariness which is his own soul. Manfred's was a terror of the spirit which Poe and others made much of. Poe called the variety "the terror of the soul, not of Germany." But his phrase, for all its antithesis, points clearly to Germany as the common source for terroristic devices, and his inclusion of haunted houses, ghouls, plagues, mesmerism, demons, diabolic hatred further illustrates the time's reliance upon such ingredients. Even if all other evidence of the one-time popularity of the German tale were to vanish, Poe's burlesques of its features would serve as adequate proof of its one-time ascendency.

---

[89] Gustav Gruener, "Notes on the Influence of E.T.A. Hoffmann upon Edgar Allan Poe," PMLA, XIX (1904), 1-25; also, Palmer Cobb, *The Influence of the Tales upon Edgar Allan Poe* (Chapel Hill, N. C., 1908). Poe read Hoffman at the Baltimore Public Library (cf. Allen I, 341). For the influence of Hoffmann's *Die Elixier des Teufels* upon Poe, see Grace P. Smith, "Poe's Metzengerstein," *Modern Language Notes*, XLVIII (June, 1933), 356-359. As an influence on the same story, Stedman and Woodberry (I, cix), single out Hoffmann's *Der Majorat*.

[90] J. S. Flagg, *Life and Letters of Washington Allston* (1892), pp. 224, 355.

But Poe, like Hawthorne, eventually aimed at something beyond cold horror, and his emphasis upon the psychological and new kinds of fear stresses the fact that American authors of the Gothic were less committed to the absurdly terroristic debauch than were their overseas kinsmen. Supernaturalism when utilized by Hawthorne fitted into his allegorical or ethical pattern, and the terror of Poe attempted to reach a firm foundation in physical distress or abnormal psychology. Mere terror, when it led to a strong emotional experience, as in the "Murders in Rue Morgue," was attached to a detective interest, and this union held true for O'Brien and other Poe imitators. Poe's more climactic pieces, such as "The Fall of the House of Usher," and Hawthorne's "Earth's Holocaust" and "Ethan Brand"[91] illustrate the new variety adequately, and represent, apart from their allegorical and other phases, the final shift from the purely mechanistic to the psychological.

## ROMANTIC LANDSCAPE

The éclat of Scott was again partly responsible for a marked nineteenth-century manifestation, the romantic landscape, for the topographical sketch was not only an essential part of Scott's literary technique, but it constituted an important part of his appeal everywhere. The development of nature appreciation, however, was much broader and more complex than it appears in Scott's works. Arising in theological, sociological, and philosophical speculations after Shaftesbury, this modern poetic emotion was already a clear tradition by the end of the eighteenth century[92] and was fostered by surviving deism and primitivism. But these were forces less felt in America than more obvious ones. Here the early picturesque landscape was mostly the consequence of the retiring wilderness and popular overseas models in which poetic description, rhapsody, and vivid imagery were variously to be perceived.

[91] The fixed stares and haunting laughter of Ethan are echoes of Maturin's *Melmoth the Wanderer.*
[92] The connection of Rousseau's name with this tradition is scarcely warranted. See chap. ii, n. 58. Articles on Rousseau, such as that by A. H. Everett in the *North American Review,* XV (July, 1822), 1-21, advert to Rousseau's philosophical and political views, but have no reference to American popularity.

Scott's connection with the movement though minor is apparent in both his poems and his novels, the popularity of which not only expanded the reading public, but brought glimpses of natural beauty to readers who would not have found it in Wordsworth, Tennyson, Emerson, or Percival. Especially spirited were the Scottish scenes from the border landscapes of *The Lay of the Last Minstrel* to the scenes of desolation in *Lord of the Isles*. In *Marmion,* for instance, Scott not only graphically presents Edinburgh as seen by Marmion over Blackford Hill but sings of nature in all her variable seasons and moods. Americans could hardly have failed to fall in love with Highland scenery as they read *The Lady of the Lake*, a poem which made the area classic ground. And Scott's novels continued the description of lowland and highland in passages so set apart that their topographical significance could not be misunderstood and their service in arousing dormant or lethargic emotions about natural beauty could not be missed. Of his achievement in this direction George Saintsbury remarked: "He did what even Shakespere had been prevented by his medium of communication from doing with equal fulness—he provided a companion gallery of landscape and 'interior' such as had never been known before."

Pre-Scott forces appeared in Timothy Dwight[93] and Alexander Wilson,[94] but a potent landscape tradition really emerged with James Fenimore Cooper, who, recognizing the beauties that a prodigal nature had bestowed upon America, described with poetic feeling its streams, lakes, forests, and plains. By his own achievement Cooper became one of the principal forces in the later prevalence of the romantic landscape, in novels, short stories, and travel sketches. No reader of *The Deerslayer, The Pioneers,* or *The Prairie* could miss the magnificent scenes which the novelist unfolded, their stress upon "vastness and indefiniteness" and their discovery of majesty in the wilderness. His mind had been emancipated by the figureless sea, too, and in this uninhibted and almost

[93] *Travels in New-England and New-York* (New Haven, 1821-1822). Many of the notes for these travels were made from 1796 to 1810.

[94] Not only Wilson's description of native birds, as constituting an important romantic phase of the American scene, but his poetical description of American seasons and American topography (as in his lines on a pedestrian expedition to Niagara from Pennsylvania) constitute an important contribution to the new landscape school.

lawless way he freed his art from narrow detail and the gilded frames which restrain and hinder the imagination.

Cooper's attempt to capture the beauty of the native scene may have been stimulated slightly by James Thomson, with whose works he was conversant.[95] The great popularity of Thomson after 1800 (three editions between 1790 and 1797, and seven between 1800 and 1815) made him a model for other descriptive writers and further expanded the romantic landscape as a literary form. Thomson and Cowper, rather than Wordsworth, accelerated the development of the romantic landscape.[96]

[95] Thomson's practice was probably responsible for the use of a seasonal framework in *The Pioneers*. Cooper's merits as a landscape painter were commended in a speech by Charles King on the eve of Cooper's departure for his European tour: "He has looked with a poet's fancy and a painter's eye upon the grandeur and magnificence of our mountain scenery, the varied tints and glorious sunshine of our autumn skies and woods, our rushing cataracts, and mighty rivers, and forests coeval with nature." Quoted in Spiller, *James Fenimore Cooper*, pp. 92-93.

[96] Wordsworth exercised a stimulative influence upon the work of Bryant; R. H. Dana, writing in the preface of the reprinting of *The Idle Man* (1833), thus recalled Bryant's testimony to the stimulus which Wordsworth's example gave him:

"I shall never forget with what feeling my friend Bryant some years ago described to me the effect produced upon him by his meeting for the first time with Wordsworth's *Ballads*. He lived, when quite young, where but few works of poetry were to be had: at a period, too, when Pope was still the great idol in the Temple of Art. He said that upon opening Wordsworth a thousand springs seemed to gush up at once in his heart, and the face of nature of a sudden to change into a strange freshness and life."

This quotation probably hints Dana's own enthusiasm for Wordsworth more than it does Bryant's, but the testimony is interesting for its hint of the life which Wordsworth gave to nature rhapsody in America. Of course, in Bryant's case Wordsworth was not a model to imitate sedulously, nor did his work disclose to Bryant the aspects of nature which he should versify, but it did aid in awakening his heart and strengthening his vision of the potentialities in nature. Bryant did in three or four poems echo Wordsworth (in "Oh Fairest of the Rural Maids," "The Yellow Violet," "The Rivulet," and in his uncollected "The Early Anemone"). His "Forest Hymn" and "A Winter Piece" approximate a Wordsworthian tone; and in his "Inscription for the Entrance to a Wood," knowledge of the works of another Lake School poet, Robert Southey (especially "For a Tablet on the Banks of a Stream," and "In a Forest,") may certainly be observed as well as familiarity with Wordsworth's famous ode. But Wordsworthian influence could not have extended much beyond occasional reminiscence. Wordsworth aroused Bryant and encouraged him but did not lead him to slavish imitation. Bryant always regarded his nature poetry as belonging

Certain other eighteenth-century forces—the cult of solitude and of gloom—played an important part in the expansion of the landscape tradition. Solitude, a marked tradition through the last half of the nineteenth century, came to nineteenth-century America through a widened interest in Thomson, Beattie, and Cowper. Zimmerman on solitude, in gift-book form, contributed to the reflective mood, but the Great American Forest and the frontier were chiefly responsible for the expansion of the themes of solitude and retirement. To the quiet of a secluded grove Americans added the solitude of a primeval woods, the vast loneliness of a mountain fastness, the silence of a rolling prairie, and the imaginative vision of life sequestered in blissful seclusion. Though the cult of solitude suffered a setback in the early twenties (imitators of Byron made shade and solitude the haunts of sullen misanthropy or regions of guilt-tormented souls), the silent landscape once again expanded in countless Indian poems, especially of Hoffman, Colton, and Street, and in the pages of Emerson and Thoreau.

The parallel mood of gloom, which arose in the graveyard tra-

---

to a great tradition, of which Thomson and Cowper were major forces and Wordsworth and himself inheritors. Occasional critics, like John Wilson, Edgar Allan Poe, W. J. Snelling, and Willard Philips, were impressed not so much with the Wordsworthian tone in Bryant's work as with the fact that he belonged to the Thomson-Young-Cowper literary tradition of the eighteenth century, and several critics have contended the same thing in our day.

Bryant stood for originality and individuality as an important phase of romantic art, and he must have striven, as he viewed the wonders of the Berkshires, to give an individual cast to his own nature reflections. In his essay on American poetry he not only admonishes poets to avoid the mannerisms of others, but states the rationale for the independence of effort: "... we desire to set a mark on that servile habit of copying which adopts the vocabulary of some favourite author, and apes the fashion of his sentences, and cramps and forces the ideas into a shape, which they would not naturally have taken, and of which the only recommendation is, not that it is most elegant or most striking, but that it bears some resemblance to the manner of him who is proposed as a model. This way of writing has an air of poverty and meanness—it seems to indicate a paucity of reading as well as perversion of taste—it might almost lead us to suspect that the writer had but one or two examples of poetical composition in his hands, and was afraid of expressing himself, except according to some formula which they might contain—and it ever has been, and ever will be, the resort of those who are sensible that their works need some factitious recommendation to give them even a temporary popularity." In another section of the essay he points to the crippling effect of slavish imitation of the

dition of the eighteenth century, was heightened by the poems of Ossian[97] with their splash of rain and general mistiness. While these served admirably for writers like Chastellux who wished to stir moods of depression, gloom was not a force that had a wide appeal when presented in intense isolation. Few nature travelers were willing merely to sentimentalize over desolate scenes or bald landscapes. The same objection can be made to the undeniably strong influence of Mrs. Radcliffe,[98] one-third of whose pages were descriptive and afforded a rich source for those evoking the moods of wildness and desolation amid naked crags and storm-beaten areas. We find later travel-writers like Allen, Codman, and Carter adverting to the descriptive features of her work.

Gloom received a more complex impetus in the work of Byron, whose mood was at once more personal and majestic, full of eloquent descriptive power. Byron's rhetorical verses, the effect of

---

eighteenth-century manner: "The imagination is confined to one trodden circle, doomed to the chains of a perpetual mannerism, and condemned to tinkle the same eternal tune with its fetters."

A poet thus committed to originality was little likely to follow, except in his juvenile pieces, the manner of another or to allow another to set bounds to his own mental horizon. Bryant and Wordsworth were both writers of ballad and blank verse forms, and voiced their mutual romantic enthusiasm in the presence of streams and mountains. That there might be resemblances in tone in their work is to be expected, especially since both were in the great nature tradition that stemmed from Thomson; but one can be impressed at the same time with the independence with which they mutually pursued a common poetic end.

Bryant's success in his chosen medium, in fact, may in itself be regarded as a factor in Wordsworth's later American popularity and influence. He and Emerson, in their love of nature and concern for natural beauties, prepared an American audience for the reception of Wordsworth in an America first chilly toward and then openly repelled by the naturisms in Wordsworth's work.

Consider also W. P. Hudson's "Archibald Alison and W. C. Bryant," *American Literature*, XII (March, 1940) 59-68, which discusses his knowledge of the Scottish associational psychology as preparing Bryant for an appreciative reading of Wordsworth and as influencing his critical principles.

[97] Evidence of the vogue of Ossian is usually in unexpected places, as when Whitman labels a slight sketch in his *Specimen Days* an "Ossianic Night," and there are other passages reminiscent of the same source.

[98] Mrs. Radcliffe's influence and popularity have been frequently noted. See Montague Summers, *The Gothic Quest, passim*; also consult references to n. 83.

which was later reinforced by the rhapsodies of Chateaubriand,[99] undoubtedly exerted considerable force on both those who described challenging scenes and those who sought to combine geographical observation with poetic mood or mystic insight.

A final influence on the romantic landscape before 1825 was the foreign travel book. American travel to England and the Continent had produced the letters of Buckminster (1809), the observations of Louis Simond, and the reflections of Dr. Rusk. But after 1815, when the restrictions on travel were no longer in force, it was possible, through the new swift packet service, for Americans to go on summer transatlantic excursions. In consequence, students, practical tourists, and journalistic adventurers thronged the Old World. Most of these, regardless of the purpose which took them overseas, tramped areas of picturesque interest and eagerly set down their impressions. Subsequently printed as letters, journals, notes, their impressions helped establish a tradition of description of foreign areas, and, more important, served to awaken romantic sensibilities to landscape on the part of those unable to stir from their home communities.[100]

V

All of these romantic traditions, distinct from each other as they may seem, had in large or slight degree a relationship to the interests and practice of Scott. But certain concepts and forms were, as has been noted, not assignable to such a classification, and there were other tendencies which were either remote from or opposed to the ideals and concepts Scott championed. Most markedly

---

[99] Americans could have become acquainted with his memoirs and rhapsodies in several volumes: *The Natchez* (London, 1827); *Recollections of Italy, England, and America* (Philadelphia, 1816), and a variant title of the same work, *Travels in America and Italy* (London, 1828). The American travels along the Mississippi had appeared previously in *The Natchez*, and were excerpted from that volume, a practice much indulged by Chateaubriand. *Atala* was printed in English in London editions of 1802, 1803, and 1817, and there was a Boston edition in 1802 and another American edition in 1818. Some of his American rhapsodies had been thrown into his *Essai historique, politique, et moral sur les revolutions anciennes et modern* (1797 and 1814), anglicized as *The History of Revolutions*. See Gilbert Chinard, "Chateaubriand en Amerique," *Modern Philology*, IX (July, 1911), 129-149.

[100] See n. 29 above.

at variance with the retrospective tendencies from Scott was the romantic idealism of the generation after 1830. This concept, it has been frequently asserted, was the blend resulting from the alliance of romanticism, when transplanted to the United States, and Transcendentalism. That the two movements were related scarcely anyone will question, because they enjoyed a peak of literary activity at the same time; and the two manners, if we may so designate them, were frequently found in the same literary personages. So-called Transcendentalists, Emerson, Thoreau, Margaret Fuller, W. H. Channing, had certain beliefs in common, beliefs which it may baffle one to classify as Transcendental or romantic. That they held these beliefs as Transcendentalists rather than as romanticists, however, has never been established. As for the adjective *romantic*, when used with idealism it is employed purely in a conventional sense, for the philosophical aspects of the movement, at any rate, had applications totally unconnected with any literary period. The transcendental or the ideal had been employed even before the medieval Schoolmen to suggest concepts which went beyond the finite, and the upsurge of Neoplatonism in the seventeenth century was clearly outside the limits of a romantic classification. But the nineteenth-century movement was real enough, and in New England of the 1830's philosophical idealism made a strong American stand.

The impact upon New England had long been prepared for, even as early as the Great Awakening of the early eighteenth century. Later the Unitarian movement, involving in part the radical doctrines of the Enlightenment, opened up new concepts. It contributed to the throwing off of formal restrictions in religion. And it was not long before the more mystical members, termed Transcendentalists, were throwing off the restrictions of logic, too. Relying upon intuition and upon inner light, these thinkers became the foes of rationalism and conventional doctrine. "I do not know," said Emerson, "what arguments mean in relation to the expression of a thought." However, he held that "The laws of moral nature answer to those of matter [nature] as face to face in a glass.... The axioms of physics translate the laws of ethics."

The most important force in the movement was the introduction of idealistic philosophy from France and from Germany through Madame de Staël, Cousin, and Kant. Eventually, Hegel, Goethe, Condillac, Jouffroy, and other important thinkers were productive of a transformation in New England thinking about theology and liberal principles. Little enough of this philosophical thought from overseas came directly. Language limitations and close ties to English movements and coteries made English literature (Coleridge and Carlyle especially) the most important source.

The first transmitter of this idealistic culture was Thomas Carlyle, whose American vogue began as early as 1822.[101] Throughout the twenties, as Vance pointed out, Carlyle's reputation was on the increase, and it was primarily his early German studies that made an impact upon American thinking. At the same time idealistic concepts were making their way to America through other mediums. Schelling, a contemporary German philosopher, and Fichte, but lately deceased, became known to writers like George Bancroft; and hints of their idealistic doctrines found their way into the current issues of the magazines.[102] And here and there, directly or indirectly, the thoughts of Kant's *Critique of Pure Reason* were finding lodgment. Harry Hayden Clark has pointed out that while Emerson had dozens of other sources,[103] he could

---

[101] For Carlyle's reception down to 1833, see William Silas Vance, "Carlyle in America before *Sartor Resartus*," *American Literature*, VII (Jan., 1936), 363-375. See also Frank Luther Mott, "Carlyle's American Public," *Philological Quarterly*, IV (1925), 245-264; and George Kummer, "Anonymity and Carlyle's Early Reputation in America," *American Literature* XI, (Nov., 1936), 1-25.

[102] *North American Review*, XX (Jan., 1825), 138-149. Alexander H. Everett, writing in the *North American Review* (April, 1824), stressed the weaknesses of idealism, but at the same time, for all his lack of sympathy, he did familiarize serious students with Platonic concepts. For Americans in Germany, see Long, *op. cit., passim.*

[103] Beginning with its publication in 1826, Sampson Reed's *Observations on the Growth of the Mind* and subsequently his oration, "Genius," exerted considerable Swedenborgian influence upon Emerson. Journal entries make clear that Reed's work influenced both the form and content of *Nature*. For a detailed study see Clarence Paul Hotson, "Sampson Reed, a Teacher of Emerson," *New England Quarterly*, II (April, 1929), 249-277. Other studies by Hotson may be found in: *New-Church Review*, XXXVI (Jan., April, July, and Oct., 1929), 45-59, 173-186, 304-316, 435-448; *Studies in Philology*, XXVII (July, 1930), 517-545; *New Philosophy*, XXI (1928), 482-516; *New Church Messenger*, CXL (Feb. 3, 1932), 89-94; and *Philological Quarterly*, X (Oct., 1931), 369-383.

have found many of his early Transcendental ideas in the pages of the *North American Review* and that this journal "had done much to acquaint its readers with the ideas to which he was to give the prestige of his impressive personality." Clark further cites sixteen articles in which French (especially Gerando and Cousin), English, and German aspects of Transcendentalism appear, in some of which the merits of spiritual intuitions anticipated Emerson's keen insight.[104] By 1833 Emerson paid a visit to Carlyle himself, all the way to Craiggenputtock on a lonely moor, and in 1835, with an edition of *Sartor Resartus*, not only greatly reinforced Carlyle's American vogue, but brought his "idealism," "organic filaments," "natural supernationalism," and other transcendental chapters to the attention of the cultured young men of his generation. In consequence, Carlyle became a significant voice in the popularization of the New Idealism.[105]

Another force in the transmission of the new philosophical

---

[104] "Literary Criticism in the *North American Review*, 1815-1835," *Transactions of the Wisconsin Academy of Sciences, Arts, and Letters*, XXXII (Madison, 1940), 299-301.

[105] For Carlyle's reception in America in the ten years after 1830, see: Timothy Walker, "Defense of Mechanical Philosophy," *North American Review*, XXXIII, (July, 1831), 122-135; W. B. O. Peabody, "Croker's Boswell," *North American Review*, XXXIV (Jan., 1832), 102; anon., "Life of Friedrich Schiller," *Christian Examiner*, XVI (July, 1834), 365-392; G. H. Calvert, "Life of Schiller," *North American Review*, XXXIX (July, 1834), 1-30; A. H. Everett, "Sartor Resartus," *North American Review*, XLI (Oct., 1835), 454-482; N. L. Frothingham, "Sartor Resartus," *Christian Examiner*, XXI (1837), 74-84; J. G. Palfrey, "Miss Martineau's 'Society in America,'" *North American Review*, XLV (Oct., 1837), 418-460; anon., "Foster's Republication of the London and Westminster Review," *Southern Rose*, VI (Jan., 1838), 173; anon., "Carlyle's Essay on Walter Scott," *Southern Rose*, VI (May 26, 1838), 309-310; anon., "French Revolution," *Southern Literary Journal*, VII (Aug., 1838), 160; anon., "French Revolution," *Boston Quarterly Review*, I (Oct., 1838), 407-417; "Original Papers—Thomas Carlyle," *Hesperian*, II (Nov., 1838), 1-20; W. H. Prescott, "Scott's Histories and Novels," *North American Review*, XLIX (Oct., 1839), 342; anon., "Critical and Miscellaneous Essays," *Literary Examiner and Western Monthly Review*, I (Dec., 1839), 460-464; anon., "Carlyle's Chartism," *Democratic Review*, VIII (July 1840), 13-29; anon., "Hints for a Critical Estimate of the Writings of Carlyle," *Yale Literary Magazine*, V (Aug., 1840), 478-482; O. A. Brownson, "French Revolution," *Boston Quarterly Review*, III (Sept., 1840), 358-395.

thought was Coleridge.[106] As a poet Coleridge was neither well-known nor widely influential,[107] but in limited intellectual circles his philosophy was read and esteemed. James Marsh, trinitarian, edited Coleridge's *Aids to Reflection* in 1829 and two years later, *The Friend*. His interpretations—in long introductions to these books—did much to dispel charges of Coleridgean obscurity and made the English distinctions between *Vernunft* and *Verstand* well known and understood, at least in New England.[108] Thus the idealism of Fichte, Schelling, and Kant was delivered to an American audience.

An equally effective means for the transfer of Kantian and Platonic doctrine was through French eclecticism, especially that of Gerando, Cousin,[109] Collard, and Jouffroy, with whose works the translators were busy and who were consistently reviewed between 1825 and 1840.[110] Transcendental thought, at any rate, was much modified and inspired by the French writers of the period. Students at the Harvard Divinity School received Uni-

[106] See F. T. Thompson, "Emerson and Carlyle," *Studies in Philology* XXIV (July, 1927), 438-453; also "Emerson's Indebtedness to Coleridge," *Studies in Philology*, XXIII (Jan., 1926), 55-76.

[107] See note 18 above. *The American Quarterly Review* (XIX [March, 1836], 2) declared: "We fear, that among those called literary, and which now form an immense body, his works are little read." For a favorable exception, see R. H. Dana, Jr., *North American Review*, VII (May, 1818), 76-86; also VIII (March, 1819), 298-322.

[108] James Marsh was the first real expounder of German philosophy via Coleridge in America. For a careful study of Marsh's place in the tradition of idealism, see Marjorie Nicolson, "James Marsh and the Vermont Transcendentalists," *Philosophical Review*, XXXIV (1928), 28. See also Charvat, *op. cit.*, pp. 77-79. Marsh edited Coleridge's *Aids to Reflection* (1829) and *The Friend* (1831). The last of these was enthusiastically reviewed by George B. Cheever in the *North American Review*, XL (April, 1835), 299-352.

[109] "Cousin's Philosophy," *North American Review*, XXXV (July, 1832), 19-36. Caleb Sprague Henry had as early as 1827 written a long anti-Locke introduction to Cousin, and after 1838 Orestes Brownson was an important channel for the American interest in Cousin's Platonism and eclectic thought.

[110] The influence of the French eclectic school is clearly revealed in the *Christian Examiner* (VII [1830], 70): "We confess that we look with the deepest interest on the progress of the eclectic school in France, of which Cousin, Collard, Jouffroy, and De Gerando are distinguished representatives."

tarian doctrine from their teachers, but the periodicals of the day and editions of Coleridge and Jouffroy and Cousin afforded them food of a different character. Back of this accessibility to overseas stimulation on the part of the Transcendentalists was the heavy philosophical undergirding of Unitarianism itself, and its concern with rational thinkers and with German, French, and British thought. From the French writers, however, there was no new interweaving of conflicting arguments, but a reinforcement of the central concepts of idealism.[111]

## Reform Movements

The concept of American idealism is associated in many minds with humanitarian reform efforts, chiefly because of the activity of such Transcendentalists as Ripley and Parker, who backed with noble zeal the more prominent reform movements of the time. Combining their desire for better lives and better conditions with practical matters of everyday concern, they clearly challenged a nonhumanitarian view of society. Since, however, it was the wont of all idealists to express their inspiration in their own particular way, no strong common denominator of reform activity can be found among them.

The typical romantic idealist, first interested in ecclesiastical conditions, soon related his thinking to earthly affairs. He no longer believed that the world was wonderfully made, a world from which the Supreme Creator could safely withdraw. Thus doubting the claims of enthusiastic deists, the idealist was not indifferent to evidences of global maladministration. Always sensitively alert to the ills of life and at odds with the universe about him, he crusaded for programs professedly aimed at the public good. That these were mutually exclusive or not harmonious did not matter: he stood above the conflict of rival causes and reforms which sought to draw his attention, and his subscription to one or more clashing concepts made his temper the more characteristic. Assert-

[111] "History of Intellectual Philosophy," *North American Review*, XXIX (July, 1829), 109. Praise of Locke concerns Everett as well as attack upon idealism. For a full recognition of the place of Locke in American philosophical thought of the nineteenth century, see Merle Curti, "The Great Mr. Locke: America's Philosopher, 1783-1861," *Huntington Library Bulletin*, No. 11 (April, 1937), pp. 107-152.

## THE RISE OF ROMANTICISM

ing the inalienable worth of the individual and relying upon man's inner integrity, the idealist formulated a doctrine of excellence extended to all realms of human activity, even to those regarded as debasing and ignoble. At the center of man, when unswayed by social circumstance, there was always an innate goodness; and upon this the unflinching faith of the reformer reposed. Hence his social aspiration to elevate, to uplift, or to ameliorate.

Actually, however, Transcendentalists did not all share in reform programs whether the objective was the reshaping of the contemporary life or the elimination of specific abuses. Not all agreed that politics or society en masse was the agency for the amelioration of the ills of mankind. Like Carlyle, such idealists as Emerson and Thoreau believed that only through the regeneration of the individual could society be reformed or shaped into dreams of perfection. Thus it was that political measures were not always sought after and that communal experiments failed to hold even when they for a while attracted many able and independent thinkers.

Reform in the forties was, in fact, only slightly a product of purely idealistic leadership, and there were forces clearly anti-idealistic, in a philosophical sense, which may be held accountable for some of the observable results. Utilitarianism, as expounded first by Helvetius and then by Jeremy Bentham[112] and John Stuart Mill, introduced utility as the center of a scheme of social morality; and their American apostles, Dr. Thomas Cooper, Albert Gallatin, John Quincy Adams, Richard Hildreth, and others, made Utilitarian doctrines the mainspring of reform activity, as did John Neal, Bentham's erstwhile secretary.[113]

---

[112] After 1817 twenty-five of Bentham's books, brought to America for strategic distribution, began to exert an influence upon such reformers as William Beach Laurence, crusader for the abolishment of debtors' prisons; Edward Livingston, writer of the legal code of Louisiana; and Edwin Chapin, Universalist minister, reformer and advocate of the Principle of Usefulness as the final test of men, things, and institutions.

[113] John Neal was Bentham's secretary for a time in England. On his return to America he founded the *Yankee* magazine, across the pages of which he blazoned variations of the theme of "Utility" and "Greatest Happiness for the Greatest Number." In England Neal prepared for the press Bentham's *Judicial Evidence*, and with it a biographical sketch of Bentham. On his return to America he published a part of his translation

On the ideological level humanitarianism was advanced also by the dictates of Christian ethics, as operative among Congregationalists, Presbyterians, and other well-known church-groups of the time. This aspect of the topic is too well known to need elaboration. Alleviation of suffering, amelioration of the lot of man, elimination of obvious abuses which degrade mankind—all of these objectives flowed naturally from concepts of religious duty. Social action received support from special sects, too: from the Quakers with their brotherhood of man and stress of simplicity of living, from the Methodists with their stress upon individual experience and their concern for the spiritual heritage of the common man; and from the Unitarians with their stress upon intelligence and love as attributes of Deity.[114] Man became the Biblical focal point, Christ's example and the precepts of man's responsibility to man became milestones on the way to the regeneration of mankind—a concept to a great extent responsible for the Unitarian interest in social reform movements.

But these ideals might have remained inactive had not the new emotionalism of the age served to emphasize the human virtues, kindness, gentleness and mercy, and had not the more sensate spirits of that reform generation been readily influenced by the gentle promptings of sentimental thought. On the reform level, humanitarianism arose above such energy-draining responses as tears and platitudinous sensibility. When emotion hardened mere sentiment into muscular activity, the way for true and triumphant reform measures was open.[115]

---

of Dumont's Bentham ("Morals and Legislation") in the *Yankee*. See *Wandering Recollections of a Somewhat Busy Life* (Boston, 1869), chap. xvi. See Paul A. Palmer, "Benthamism in England and America," *American Political Science Review*, XXXV (Oct., 1941), 855-871. John H. Burton's *Benthamiana*, a one volume anthology of "extracts" along with Burton's sympathetic exposition of "The Opinions of Jeremy Bentham," made the gist of his thought readily available to Americans in 1844.

[114] O. B. Frothingham, *Boston Unitarianism, 1820-1850* (New York, 1890), pp. 63-66. Even Emerson had remarked in 1839, "I am more of a Quaker than anything else. I believe in the 'still small voice' and that voice is Christ within us" (Emerson's *Works*, Centenary Edition, VIII, 431). See F. B. Tolles, "Emerson and Quakerism," *American Literature*, X (May, 1938), 142-165.

[115] Legislative reforms for the improvement of society were justified

In the thirties and forties especially humanitarianism had an economic basis. Cities were rapidly expanding. Growing urbanism, a consequence of a changing economic structure, brought on crowded conditions, squalor, a loss of old social restraints, and a variety of social vices. Intemperance, disease, and crime were concomitant with the growth of factory towns. But cities which created the problem were the seats of wealth, and wealth provided solutions to some of the increasingly vexing complexities. Not only did urbanism necessitate humanitarian reform movements, it also initiated the demands for educational programs that could ameliorate the conditions produced by congestion. Notable also as an outgrowth of urbanism was the sustained demand for a liberalized land policy which would open up to settlers vast tracts of Western land and would tend to equalize areas of population.

A tremendous impetus to reform activity was also given by the Panic of 1837. Religious agnosticism, equal division of property, organization of trade unions, ten-hour-day laws, and crusades for the abolition of monopolies were some of the results of the economic distress. Conspicuous among the depression fruits was the movement to promote collectivistic communities, beginning with George Ripley's Brook Farm, Owens's New Harmony, Dr. Keil's Bethel community. The most flourishing were inspired by economic theories. Forty to fifty Fourieristic communities were established on the basis of joint-ownership, as a protest against the competitive profits system; but unsound management and financing led to a dissolution of many of the phalanxes with the first signs of real economic recovery.[116]

---

on purely Utilitarian grounds: crusaders against capital punishment based their criticism of the system on the essentially Utilitarian contention that the system had failed to prevent crime. The temperance leaguers, moreover, maintained that the closing of the wine shops would prevent the rabble from wasting their wages, would improve the national health, advance the standards of living, and provide a check on criminal activity. Pacifists pointed out the uselessness of wars and their inhumanity, and advocates for the abolishment of debtors' prisons relied heavily upon Bentham's arguments.

[116] In 1840 *The Social Destiny of Man* was published by Arthur Brisbane, whose popularization of Fourier's psychological, economic, and social philosophy was further promoted by such prominent men as Horace Greely of the *Tribune*, Parke Godwin of the *Post*, and George Ripley of the

Back of all the reform activity of the second quarter, however, was the belief in the potential perfectibility of man in which Transcendentalist and anti-Transcendentalist joined. It was a part of the general Victorian temperament in both England and America, and the general agitation for reform in both realms had this strong supporting sentiment. Before the Civil War, however, humanitarian movements were spectacular by reason of their variety or their unpopularity, not because they attracted great numbers. During the Civil War the strength and validity of the new reform programs had been evidenced by the success of the anti-slavery movement—but it was not until the Gilded Age that humanitarianism reached its full flowering in extensive organization and became firmly established as a feature in the American outlook.

DEMOCRATIC THOUGHT

Earlier it was contended that the idealists of New England were much interested in the doctrines of self-reliance, of divine justice, and of the glorification of the common and the lowly. The association of such doctrines with democratic thought is inevitable, but generalizations based upon this connection must not be pushed too far. The fact that Emerson preached with great assiduity and eloquence the doctrines of individualism has given rise to an all too general belief that American democracy owed much to the Romantic movement in general and to romantic idealism in particular. While such contentions are not foreign to the truth and while idealists did expound doctrines that had romantic color, these doctrines (with the possible exception of Bancroft's) were not synonymous with Jacksonianism or with the forces that were dominant in the age. Only Hawthorne, moreover, of the prominent New England novelists, was an avowed political Democrat, and the rest were scarcely known as party men. Emerson, in par-

---

*Harbinger.* For a study of the various communities, see John H. Noyes: *History of American Socialisms* (1870); Charles Nordhoff, *Communistic Societies in the United States* (1875); and Arthur E. Bestor, "American Phalanxes: A Study of Fourierist Socialism in the United States" (Yale University Dissertation, 1938): and Bestor's *Backwoods Utopias: The Sectarian and Owenite Phases of Communitarian Socialism in America: 1663-1829* (Philadelphia, 1950).

ticular, was clearly abstract when it came to political measures. But his abstraction, though scarcely representative of the idealistic movement, must not be construed as unconcern for democratic thinking. He evinced deep concern over Jackson's employment of the spoils system, and he feared his threat to stable government. Still he had faith in the wisdom of the people and in the cause of representative government. And he had traveled widely enough in the West to understand its fresh, virile spirit. For all the absence of directives in Emerson, he was followed by other idealists, Hedge, Ripley, Fuller, and Parker, who were more concrete in outlook (especially as concerned the antislavery movement) and translated idealistic concepts into special measures or crusades.

But when we come to the more specific question of what were the causes for such changes as occurred in concepts of government in the second quarter of the nineteenth century, our search takes us far from romantic idealism. Many of the factors that made for democratic thought were operative through the almost two hundred years of European life on this continent. The frontier and ruralism, especially—these, which America had from the beginning, were among the reasons why colony after colony set up forms of representative government and achieved large measures of local autonomy. These forces, potent in 1800, continued to operate through much of the nineteenth century.[117] Since our purpose here is not to analyze all the factors that led to individualistic thought in America, but rather to demonstrate what new agencies and movements came in to modify an already vigorous tradition, it is not necessary to linger longer on the prevalence and importance of these basic disposing causes.

The clearest innovation in democratic thinking was the new panegyric upon our achieved democracy, its merits and its triumphs. Bryant in his "Antiquity of Freedom" and "The Battle Field" sought to join the American cause with the vast tradition in the progress of mankind and to teach the lesson of eternal vigilance. Even more eloquently George Bancroft, uniting German idealism and Jacksonianism, made his pages of history read as paeans to the cause of democracy and thus turned historiography into an

[117] See Ralph Gabriel, *The Course of American Democratic Thought* (New York, 1940).

ideological channel. Bancroft supported his historical writing with the belief that the history of America had been marked with a progressive unfolding of the principles of liberty, and that the American record had been an achievement in majority rule. His scholarship has been challenged, not for the neglect of primary sources, but for the infusion of democratic sympathies. As Russel Nye declared, "Bancroft saw illustrated in American history the genesis of a Divine plan for man's ultimate attainment of complete and perfect social, political, moral, and spiritual liberty and happiness."[118] Whitman's very early editorial writing also supported Jacksonianism.

Apart from such praise of American democracy as the continuing bulwark of human dignity, the most pronounced democratic manifestation after 1820 was the breaking loose again of the American revolutionary concepts which had for years been damned up by prejudice aroused during the French Revolution. Some of those who had been alarmed by the Revolution to the point of conservatism began to lose their hysterical fear of popular movements, and other diehards had gone to their graves.

This in itself was of prime importance in the rise of Jacksonianism along with such factors as the gradual disappearance of class hostility, the expansion of the frontier, and the development of faith in the safety of democracy. Of course, there is a disposition on the part of many people with a natural talent for one-cause-mindedness to seek always for a simple explanation of events rather than a complex one. Schlesinger has pointed out that the change in American government and politics that took place about 1830 was

---

[118] *Abstracts, University of Wisconsin Doctoral Dissertations*, 1940. More dynamic treatment is found in Nye's *George Bancroft, Brahmin Rebel* (New York, 1944), chaps. iv-vi. See also Watt Stewart, "George Bancroft, Historian of the American Republic," *Mississippi Valley Historical Review*, XIX (June, 1932), 77-87. For an earlier evaluation, see W. H. Prescott, "Bancroft's History of the United States," *North American Review*, LII, 75. Joseph L. Blau has edited a useful collection of writings embodying *The Principles of Jacksonian Democracy* (New York, 1949). Those interested in tracing the complex development of the many minor New England idealists will find much assistance in *The Transcendentalists: An Anthology* (Cambridge, Mass., 1950), edited by Perry Miller, with useful introductions. See also Perry Miller's "From Edwards to Emerson," *New England Quarterly*, XIII (1940), 587-617.

not a sudden or impulsive revolution brought on by a ruthless, irresponsible army man,[119] but a transformation of American life through a series of forces operating in every phase of human activity. With this conclusion we may readily agree. Those factors that swept a strong, dynamic individual like Jackson into office did not in 1828 spring suddenly into existence by the magic of his personality but had been mounting with ever-increasing strength from the close of the War of 1812. Jacksonianism as a label for the movement had about the same validity as the word Rousseauistic, a convenient term but not a cause. We may turn, therefore, to a brief examination of the concepts which contributed to the new spirit and the new popular power. Politically Jacksonianism represented a natural advance in the progress of democracy. It was not only a continuation of the social revolution of 1776 interrupted by the French Revolution, but also a consequence of a shift in the American electorate. The expansion of America beyond the Alleghenies into the valleys of the Ohio, the Kentucky, and the Tennessee brought from this region, with all its growth and strength, forces not new but newly preponderant. By 1828 almost a third of Americans lived West of the Alleghenies, a change of almost 30 per cent in twenty years. Eight states, including Tennessee, Ohio, Indiana, Illinois, Kentucky, and Michigan, were carved out of the Western domain; and these exercised considerable influence on American thought. They were rural, and in the West as in the East, the independence of action and thought that came from personal management and decision made for democratic concepts. Jointly they brought for the first time a new force into the Union which Jackson's candidacy merely signalized.[120] Jackson's victory was more a recognition of the changing face of the American republic than it was a victory for a cause. It is true that during his administration he attempted to live up to certain campaign promises; but he was not able to fulfil all of these, because of Nullification, which he opposed. Equalitarian ideas were advanced, however. The expansion of the privileges of the electorate went on. Property qualifications for voting were removed. State constitu-

[119] Jackson, it must be remembered, was defeated in the campaign of 1824.
[120] Kentucky and Tennessee came into the Union as manhood suffrage states *before* Jackson's candidacy.

tions were liberalized, a process that was to go on for the rest of the century.

Literary romanticism played a small part in the movement, though in the main a decorative one; it did not, as has been claimed recently, initiate it. It led to genre studies and prompted celebration of the homespun and simple everyday subjects as the material of poetry, in the work of Paulding ("The Backwoodsman"), Whittier, Longfellow, and Whitman ("Song of Occupations," "Song of the Broad-axe," etc.). These literary men were influenced, we know, by Burns, Wordsworth, and others into introducing the near and lowly in subject matter. But as far as America was concerned, these literary manifestations were in the main rather effects than causes. Writers did much, of course, to advance the sentiment favoring abolition of slavery.[121]

Other factors in the mounting democratic spirit include the early labor movement and the emphasis upon legislative reform by American utilitarians. But more pronounced than either of these, in emphasizing individual liberty and democratic privilege, were the various crusades in thought and action with which Americans associated themselves. When lowly Greece was battling against the Turk, there were ten years of American enthusiasm for Greek liberty. Everyone from presidents on down, poets, orators, artists, song-writers, engravers, were busy with celebration of the Cause. All over America the oppression of the Greeks produced public worry, a concern which expressed itself in liberty ships and liberty cargoes, in public subscriptions and private donations.[122] The triumph of the Greeks in 1830 coincided with other struggles for liberty in that year,[123] but the other revolutions were unsuccessful, and a few of the ill-fated exiles made their way to America to strengthen belief in America as the land of freedom, and to fortify, here and there, American faith in the rightness of the cause of

[121] For an analysis of the place of the West in our changing democracy of this period, see F. J. Turner's *The Frontier in American History* (New York, 1921); A. M. Schlesinger, *New Viewpoints in American History* (New York, 1937); and R. C. Buley, *The Old Northwest: Pioneer Period, 1815-1840* (Indianapolis, 1950).

[122] See G. H. Orians' *Short History*, chap. viii, pp. 83-96.

[123] *Celebrations in Baltimore of the Triumph of Liberty in France with the Address Delivered on that Occasion* by William Wirt, on Monday, October 25, 1830 (Baltimore, 1830), pp. 10-11.

representative government. The same thing happened, but on a larger scale, in the revolution of 1848.[124] Melville speaks of the flames of Europe in his *Mardi,* and Whitman addressed the first published poem of his *Leaves of Grass* "To a Foil'd European Revolutionaire." Exiles from Germany swarmed to America and in the foreign-language press kept up not only a demand for liberty in Europe, but combated any antidemocratic tendencies in America. They rallied to the standard of Lincoln, and they constituted the nuclei for democratic movements in such cities as Cincinnati, Chicago, and St. Louis. This whole subject is now being examined more thoroughly. Suffice it to say here that the influx of overseas liberals undoubtedly exerted its influence on the cause of American freedom.

### Conclusion and Summary

After so long an excursion into the causes of literary transition, it may be well to summarize in a concluding section some of the contentions thus far made. Early nineteenth-century literature may be regarded partly as the reassertion of some of the tendencies of the Renaissance, with its freedom, its colorfulness, and its expansiveness. Both in part were rooted in the treasures of the past and looked back with appreciation to the forms and spirit of an earlier period. Both showed the exuberance of genius and the unrestrained enthusiasm for new knowledge. This reassertion of the spirit of the Renaissance was perhaps inevitable, for the forces of unity and selectivity so consistently applied in the eighteenth century could have gone no further toward concentration, and literature would not have remained static. That variety and freedom and expansion should follow was the normal order of development in art. American literature accordingly displayed along with the British an expansion in literary forms which included blank verse, the sonnet, the metrical romance, and the new historical romance. It applied the methods of Lamb and Christopher North to the random reflections of its less serious authors, and it joined with the more sensitive spirits of England and Europe in pouring forth their emotions in a torrent of lyrics and sentimental novels. Along

---

[124] For a partial study of the European phase, see Alphonse de Lamartine, *The History of the French Revolution of 1848* (London, 1883).

with the British it broke away from addiction, in history, to state papers and documents and turned to the concerns and emotions of the common and the ordinary. American literature broke away from the narrow interpretations of the picturesque, the beautiful, and the desolate to variety and freedom in landscape description and to impressionism in the response to mountains and valleys and to the vast expanse of the American wilderness. Many Americans seized upon American scenic beauty as their own demesne, voicing with Irving the belief that "on no country have the charms of nature been more prodigally lavished."

However, as previous comments have made amply clear, some of the literary manifestations of the 1805-1855 period represent no radical change in character. Because many of the tendencies of the age stemmed from the eighteenth century, many failed to recognize a shift in emphasis: political liberalism was a product of the seventeenth and eighteenth centuries; sentimentalism was at its peak in England in 1775; Gothicism, though it changed its direction, flowered at the century's end. The rupture in communications during the Napoleonic wars served to foster and continue popular fashions of the 1790's and in this way the manner of the eighteenth century lingered longer in America than in England.

Shortly after the War of 1812 there came a quickened interest in the literary developments in England and the Continent. This latter fact, operating in the absence of an international copyright, accounted for the publishers' reprinting zeal and for the generally awakened interest in continental letters. America was to be tremendously influenced for a generation by ideas from such overseas importation. In consequence, letters in America showed the wide disparity that in general marked the literature of Europe in the nineteenth century with the added complexity natural in a society at once old and new and in a republic whose political philosophy shaped movements and tendencies. In short, a whole group of causes prompted a clear following of English trends (in addition to factors just cited): (a) surviving provincialism, (b) the popularity of the reprints of English magazines, (c) cheap reprints of books, especially novels, in consequence of the greatly reduced cost of paper, (d) traditionalism and overseas travel, and (e) eclecticism.

With the tremendous impact of continental and English literature after 1817, American authors, though in despair at rivaling the merits of transatlantic productions, were not lured into mere slavish imitation. Nor were American works immediately and universally poured into romantic moulds. The *major* characteristics which marked the literature of England and France during the first twenty years of the nineteenth century were not, as far as America was concerned, romantic features at all. The ideas set afloat which altered the political and social institutions of feudal Europe had little relevance in America, because we had already *achieved* democracy. All of which makes clear that while literature in America most certainly had romantic characteristics, there was nothing like a mere reproduction of English tendencies either immediately or with a time lag of a decade or two. American writers of the first half of the nineteenth century never fully recapitulated the main trends of the English romantics, and even the dominantly borrowed features not infrequently underwent a change in the process of domestication. In a few instances, as in the case of Lamb, American appreciation of authors or forms anticipated that of England. Certain authors, like Hawthorne, had no British prototypes, although Hawthorne occasionally showed the influence of such writers as Spenser, Bunyan, Godwin, Maturin, and Scott. American curiosity about the Indian soon provided an indigenous subject, the treatment of which is not to be summed up under Nature's simple plan or under the lingering forms of primitivism. And even American treatment of the regional soon was embracing aims and objectives not to be traced in Scott's border material or in the ethnological phases of Maria Edgeworth. The forces, ardently patriotic in character, which sought, despite derivative forms and tendencies, to further an expanded American literature were: (a) the impact of the untrammeled American wilderness; (b) antitraditionalism; (c) the psychological effect of the War of 1812; (d) the mounting spirit of optimism; and (e) nationalism.

In addition to these causes, operating to increase literary expression, both dependent and independent, were other general attitudes or forces which exercised considerable influence: (a) new agencies of publicity and new publishing mediums; (b) an awakened American concern for intellectual matters (especially in the field of idealism); (c) militant sectarianism which carried emotion over into literary movements; (d) a combination of common-sense attitudes and moral dynamism which erected a successful roadblock to most of the excesses of French and German romanticism; (e) subjectivism, or the concern for the thoughts and emotions of the individual, which sustained both the informal essay and the new and vigorous lyric; and (f) the rise of a new class of women readers and writers who took over certain areas of the reading and publishing world and gave a more sentimental cast to literature in general.

More important than all these in turning literature in the direction of Scott was antiquarianism, especially in fiction and poetry. This, along with a strong national ambition to make the American literary reputation mount to the level of the political one, prompted the special direction which American letters took. It turned Americans to visions of colonial days, to founding cities and colonies; it led to earnest refurbishing of Americans legends and heroes; it led to vivid impressions of the border struggle. Antiquarianism, plus the popularity of the revived octosyllabic, led to hosts of Indian poems in which manners, customs, and achievements of Indian chieftains were celebrated, or in which romantic interpretations of Indian character were exploited. Antiquarianism led to the more extensive treatment of the Indian in fiction, both in his role as melancholic victim and protagonist in the Indian wars.

But antiquarianism, as a complex and developing literary attitude, could not supply the moulds into which its spirit could be poured; and here the most potent influence was that of English writers, heralded in newspapers, magazines, and praised by the London critics, who seemed so great that only by imitation could American literary efforts seem to thrive or impress the readers of two generations. But the influence of Wordsworth, Bulwer, Moore, and even Byron, however optimistically viewed, recedes before that of Scott. His vogue was perhaps the greatest single factor, quantitatively, in the development of American letters and culture in the pre-Civil War period; and for most of America the Scott form of romance suffered little decline until the outbreak of the Civil

War. It did encounter serious competition from two directions: (a) the sentimental novel that stemmed directly from the popularity of Charles Dickens and his numerous imitators in the late thirties; (b) the competition, especially in New England, of Carlyle and Coleridge. In the South, Carlyle served to reinforce (along with G. P. R. James) the Scott influence in shaping and reinforcing Southern thought and character in the direction of an aristocratic Toryism. In New England one might think of Carlyle and Coleridge as finally, after 1835, submerging Scott's great influence. Actually both Carlyle and Coleridge appealed to those with a theological bias, and these men did not constitute the novel's *normal* reading public, nor could fiction long have held them, once they became absorbed in matters of intellectual speculation. With the rise of an articulate Unitarianism and a free-ranging Transcendentalism, of community lyceums and Saturday clubs, an alert intellectualism was astir. Ideas were what counted in that New England atmosphere and even the appeal of Scott's novels as truth and history could not hold serious readers in competition with metaphysical queries. If for a time Scott deflected the thinkers from their orbit, it was a deflection which could not long have prevailed. Soon the Transcendentalists, at least, became absorbed in eclectic philosophy, in Carlyle, Coleridge, and Jouffroy; and this field may be thought of as their proper province.

Thus the literature of the age, developing along both subjective and objective lines, was at once an example and an effect of the prevailing complexity of literary factors. The current of inspiration before 1855 flowed through no single and strongly banked channel of creative activity, but through a delta of artistic outlets, with interlacing bayous of compromise and little inlets of eccentricity. As the literature moved away from universalism, from social conformity, to individual expression, the breakdown of general standards of what man was like, or nature, or the sublime, produced an interest in the particular and the diverse which for at least a half-century dominated literary expression. And the leading literary forms were markedly influenced by this diversification. But in addition to the influences which more or less pervaded the whole period—overseas impulse, native forces, and the attraction of literary personalities—there were factors peculiar to the various forms which in broad or subtle ways modified or abetted them. Multiple effects of multiple causes, they were still the logical results of the period which produced them, and of the blended influences which served to shape them.

# The Rise of
# Transcendentalism
## 1815-1860

# The Rise of Transcendentalism
## 1815-1860[1]

*ALEXANDER KERN*
UNIVERSITY OF IOWA

AMERICAN Transcendentalism was, it now appears, an essentially indigenous movement, which, though it showed foreign influences and counterparts, developed along independent lines in response to American needs. First appearing as "The Latest Form of Infidelity," and later recognized for the importance of its literary contributions, it was perhaps the major liberating force of its period, and as such made significant contributions to a number of areas. In philosophy it was important to the development of the pragmatisms[2] of William James, Charles Saunders Peirce, and

---

[1] Basic references for major aspects of the movement include Arthur E. Christy, *The Orient in American Transcendentalism* (New York, 1932); George W. Cooke, *The Poets of Transcendentalism: An Anthology* (Boston, 1903); Octavius B. Frothingham, *Transcendentalism in New England: A History* (New York, 1876); Harold C. Goddard, *Studies in New England Transcendentalism* (New York, 1908); Clarence L. F. Gohdes, *The Periodicals of American Transcendentalism* (Durham, N. C., 1931); Perry Miller, *The Transcendentalists: An Anthology* (Cambridge, Mass., 1950); Henry A. Pochmann, *New England Transcendentalism and St. Louis Hegelianism* (Philadelphia, 1948); Lindsay Swift, *Brook Farm* (New York, 1900).

[2] A. O. Lovejoy, "The Thirteen Pragmatisms," *Journal of Philosophy*, V (1908), 1-12; 29-39; F. I. Carpenter, "Points of Comparison between Emerson and William James," *New England Quarterly*, II (1929), 458-474; F. I. Carpenter, "William James and Emerson," *American Literature*, XI (1939), 39-57; C. S. Peirce, *Collected Papers*, ed. Hartshorne and Weiss (Cambridge, Mass., 1931-1935), VI, 86-87; John Dewey, "Emerson," *Characters and Events* (New York, 1929), I, 69-77.

John Dewey. In religion it both spiritualized a wing of Unitarianism and gave grounds for the growth of free religion. To literature it furnished a new and significant aesthetic theory and our two best writers of nonfictional prose in Emerson and Thoreau, as well as two of our major poets in Emerson and his distant disciple Whitman. Even Hawthorne and Melville were affected by it, if negatively. In the social realm, Transcendentalism provided for its time not only the most cogent criticism of commercial materialism, but it indirectly affected American education, and though it had little immediate effect on other institutions, it reinforced Gandhi's program of nonviolent resistance, which has influenced the lives of hundreds of millions of people. Consequently the development of Transcendentalism in all these several directions can fruitfully be explored.

But in order to discover how and why Transcendentalism grew, it is necessary to find out what it was. This is difficult to do, because it was a developing movement, not a static philosophy, and because the Transcendentalists were, as separate thinkers, hardly logical system-builders, while, as a group, they were radical individualists who often disagreed with each other, however much alike they may have appeared to their opponents. For these reasons no completely successful definition of Transcendentalism has ever been worked out. Take, for example, two definitions offered by men who knew it at first hand: Emerson called Transcendentalism "Idealism as it appears in 1842,"[3] yet this accurately applied only to a certain New England group, for Poe, who was certainly an idealist, was not part of the movement. Cabot's assertion that Transcendentalism was "Romanticism on Puritan ground,"[4] is also too broad, since it would fit Hawthorne, Melville, and even Henry Wadsworth Longfellow. Nor have modern scholars been much more successful.[5] Nevertheless, by pointing out the common characteristics of the members of the group and their common

---

[3] Ralph Waldo Emerson, *The Complete Works of Ralph Waldo Emerson*, ed. E. W. Emerson (Boston, 1903-1904) (hereinafter cited as Emerson, *Works*), I, 329.

[4] J. E. Cabot, *A Memoir of Ralph Waldo Emerson* (Boston, 1887), I, 248.

[5] Gohdes, *op cit.*, p. 3; H. G. Townsend, *Philosophical Ideas in the United States* (New York, 1934), p. 86.

## THE RISE OF TRANSCENDENTALISM

ideas, it is possible to set forth a model or constructed type, like Professor Wellek's "Movement,"[6] which can increase our understanding of its inception and growth.

The names of thirty-odd of the more significant Transcendentalists whose works will be considered follow in chronological order: Dr. William Ellery Channing (1780-1842), James Marsh (1794-1842), Convers Francis (1795-1863), Amos Bronson Alcott (1799-1888), George Bancroft (1800-1891), Sampson Reed (1800-1880), William Howard Furness (1802-1896), George Ripley (1802-1880), Caleb Stetson (c. 1802-1870), Ralph Waldo Emerson (1803-1882), Orestes Brownson (1803-1876), Caleb Sprague Henry (1804-1884), Elizabeth Palmer Peabody (1804-1894), Frederic Henry Hedge (1805-1890), Sophia Ripley (c. 1807-1861), William Henry Channing (1810-1884), (Sarah) Margaret Fuller (1810-1850), Theodore Parker (1810-1860), Cyrus Bartol (1813-1900), Charles T. Brooks (1813-1883), Christopher Cranch (1813-1892), John Sullivan Dwight (1813-1893), Sylvester Judd (1813-1853), Samuel Osgood (1813-1880), Jones Very (1813-1880), Ellen Sturgis Hooper (1815-1848), Charles Stearns Wheeler (1816-1843), Henry David Thoreau (1817-1862), (William) Ellery Channing (1818-1901), Caroline Sturgis Tappan (1818-1888), John Weiss (1818-1879), Samuel Longfellow (1819-1892), Charles King Newcomb (1820-1894), Octavius B. Frothingham (1822-1895), Samuel Johnson (1822-1882), Thomas Wentworth Higginson (1823-1911), David Wasson (1823-1887), Franklin Benjamin Sanborn (1831-1917), Moncure Conway (1823-1907).

Of the less familiar figures, Marsh and Reed were precursors; Bancroft, the historian, though a Transcendentalist in philosophy, was not a member of the central group; the Sturgis sisters were poets; Henry and Osgood became Episcopal rectors; Wheeler, who influenced Thoreau, died young; and Conway, Frothingham, Higginson, Longfellow, Johnson, Sanborn, Wasson, and Weiss, members of the later movement which is not the subject of this paper, will be mentioned only in connection with the antislavery movement.

Of the central group, all were New Englanders and Unitarians,

[6] René Wellek, "Periods and Movements," *English Institute Annual, 1940* (New York, 1941), pp. 90-91.

and all who attended any college attended Harvard (at least for work in divinity). All except Ellery Channing had at one time been clergymen or teachers. A number came from clerical or professional families, and most from the middle class which prized education, so that even when they were not well off, they found relatives and scholarships to support college careers. Brownson, Parker, and Alcott came from poorer families, were mainly self-educated, and significantly represent in their various ways more radical social positions. They were all serious, religious, intent on self-improvement, independent, and individualistic. Though some were more nearly mystical and others more logical, though some believed in self-reform and others more in social reform, though some remained Unitarians while others revolted against the church; they were substantially alike as intuitive idealists—moral and unworldly. With these similarities of background and temperament they produced a movement which could be identified without mistake.

Negatively they rejected the following ideas: (1) the sensationalist, anti-idealist features of Locke's philosophy;[7] (2) the associationist psychology, which denied the active shaping power of the human mind;[8] (3) the concept of a mechanical universe with a bystanding God, which derived from Newton and Paley; (4) the sensationalist and associationist features of the Scottish Common-Sense school; (5) the materialist philosophy and "pale negations" of the conservative Unitarians—their institutionalized ritual, their coolness, conservatism, and decorum illogically combined with a belief in the saving powers of Jesus and in the miracles of the New Testament; (6) the Calvinistic acceptance of total depravity, predestination, and pessimism; (7) the need to adhere to the generalized, balanced, formalized style of neoclassicism with its emphasis on fluency, structure, and careful working out of decorative details; (8) the commercial ideal of thrift, industry, profit, and "success" as attested by vulgar monetary standards; (9) the improvement of society by social legislation through the will of the majority.

Affirmatively, the Transcendentalists adopted the following concepts: (1) an intuitive idealism which accepted ideas as ultimates;

---

[7] For Locke's sensationalism, see Harald Höffding, *A History of Modern Philosophy* (London, 1924), I, 383-387.

[8] *Ibid.*, I, 447.

(2) a view of the imagination or intuition (in their language Reason) giving a direct apprehension of reality which the logical faculties (the Understanding) could not furnish; (3) the concept of an organic universe in which Nature, suffused by an immanent God, corresponded with spirit in such a way that the connections and indeed the whole could be grasped by contemplation and intuition; (4) a living religion in which miracles seemed natural; (5) the divinity of man, who consequently did not need salvation; (6) a concept of Genius which could produce works of art by recording its intuitions through the use of nature symbols; (7) a freedom and spontaneity in art to permit the creation of works liberated from the artificialities produced by talent or mechanical rules alone; (8) an individual moral insight which should supersede the dollar as the standard of conduct; (9) self-improvement as the primary avenue of social improvement; (10) individualism, i.e., reliance on God, rather than conformity to the will of a political or social majority; (11) an optimism about the potentialities of individual lives and of the universe.

With this pattern of negative and affirmative concepts in mind, it is possible now to proceed by showing in successive sections certain transitions from earlier to Transcendentalist views:

I. The philosophical shift from sensationalism and materialism to intuitive idealism—from the moral sense to the direct apprehension of reality.

II. The transformation of a mechanistic universe to a vitalistic and evolving nature which serves as a symbol of the realm of the spirit.

III. The religious development from the conservative Unitarian institutionalism which combined philosophical materialism with belief in the miracles of the New Testament to the clear insistence upon the divinity of man.

IV. The literary change from neoclassical principles of correctness to the romantic use of symbol to body forth the intuited and organic vision of the genuinely creative artist.

V. The turn in social thought from emphasis upon collective natural rights to individual integrity and the freedom of each man for maximum personal development.

In this process of plotting transitions, it will be necessary to note both the leading lines of growth and the deviations and disagreements among the members of the group. It will, moreover, be necessary to take cognizance of the factors which contributed to the changes, including both the ostensible causes of dissatisfaction with the previously accepted ideas and the reading which may have furnished some of the hints followed out in the new developments. While the Transcendentalists were such wide readers that specific literary sources cannot always be isolated with assurance, still it is worth the attempt to treat the influences as critically as may be. The developmental period will be especially emphasized as well as the contributions of Emerson as the most important if not the most typical writer of the school. By this method, it is hoped, it will be possible to appreciate how the Transcendentalists, in response to a special set of psychic needs, aroused in particular by the contradictions in Unitarianism, developed an American thought pattern which though it used materials from many philosophies, avoided the religious and political conservatism of the later Coleridge and Wordsworth, the sexual license of Goethe and Byron, and the hero-worship and disdain of the masses of Carlyle.

I

The idealism of the Transcendentalists, although of course the ultimate sources of some of the Transcendental ideas were foreign, was composed finally into a distinctive American pattern. Nor can it be said that any single strand of foreign thought was primary, because the emphasis on any particular European philosopher varied from individual to individual. The new design which emerged was not purely Platonic, nor Berkeleyan, nor Kantian,[9] but a complicated interweaving.

In this turn toward idealism the American Transcendentalists were part of the Romantic movement, which met a similar problem in similar ways. Locke's *Essay Concerning Human Understanding* and the later analysis of Hume, which held that absolute knowledge of the outer world was impossible, left the problem

[9] H. W. Schneider, *A History of American Philosophy* (New York, 1946), p. 284; H. D. Gray, *Emerson, A Statement of New England Transcendentalism as Expressed in the Philosophy of its Chief Exponent* (Stanford Univ., 1917), p. 66. Cf. W. H. Werkmeister, *A History of Philosophical Ideas in America* (New York, 1949), p. 41.

of epistemology in a state which proved emotionally unsatisfying to a large number of thinkers of whom the Transcendentalists were only one group. They, like the Scottish Common-Sense school founded by Reid, like Kant and his followers, like Coleridge, and like the French eclectics, sought for a theory which would not only make knowledge possible and would give ideas a permanent place in the universe, but would also leave room for religion. Whether or not the new philosophy preceded the religious controversy, the real issue was philosophical and ultimately epistemological. The first dissatisfaction with Unitarianism was not with what its clergy accepted on faith—that is, its belief in revelation and miracles, but with its liberal rationalism which left it with a materialistic philosophy except in the realm of morals.

For serious thinkers of a certain temperament, dissatisfaction with the emotionally cool sensationalism, mechanism, and determinism descending from Locke was increasing. The Scottish Common-Sense philosophers, Reid,[10] Stewart,[11] and Brown,[12] had offered some amelioration, both through insisting that the dictates of universal common apprehension could not be gainsaid by any logical analysis, and more particularly through claiming that man had an innate moral sense which unerringly judged right and wrong.[13] These philosophers were taught at Harvard,[14] partly to soften Locke. Yet even this was not totally satisfactory. Thus beginning in the 1820's one of the clearest issues was the need for idealism as opposed to materialism. This was true of James Marsh; it was true not only of Emerson's *Nature*,[15] but more significantly of his lecture

---

[10] Thomas Reid (1710-1796), preacher and professor at Aberdeen and Glasgow, published his principal work, *Inquiry into the Human Mind on the Principles of Common Sense*, in 1764.

[11] Dugald Stewart (1753-1858) published *Elements of the Philosophy of the Human Mind* from 1792 to 1827, and *Outlines of Moral Philosophy* in 1793.

[12] Thomas Brown (1778-1820) published posthumously *Physiology of the Human Mind* (1820) and *Lectures on the Philosophy of the Human Mind* (1822).

[13] Höffding, *op. cit.*, I, 451.

[14] E. W. Todd, "Philosophical Ideas at Harvard College, 1817-1837," *New England Quarterly*, XVI (1943), 64.

[15] Emerson's technique is here, as it is generally, affirmative rather than negative, yet it emphasizes the contrast between material and ideal (*Works*, I, 8, 47).

"The Transcendentalist,"[16] which emphasized that the new views were simply idealism; it was also true of Theodore Parker's "Transcendentalism,"[17] which sets up a long contrast between materialism and idealism. Whatever we may think now, the Transcendentalists believed that the issue was one between the old philosophy, whether Lockean or Scottish, and the new idealism.

In their various ways Joseph S. Buckminster, Edward Everett, and William Ellery Channing had begun to open the windows of Boston to new winds of doctrine. Buckminster, by establishing the Anthology Club with William Emerson, Waldo's father, and its magazine the *Monthly Anthology*, but especially by giving his large library filled with foreign books to the Boston Athenaeum, had both created interest in literature and furnished a source for new ideas. Edward Everett, the first American to study in Germany, returned in 1819 filled with eloquence and classical learning. He, however, was not influenced by German idealistic thought, and it was not until George Bancroft's return in 1821 that German romanticism was brought back to America. It was Channing who of the three did the most to let in new ideas, by the personal influence of his receptivity to new ideas, by his acceptance of Price, Coleridge, and Wordsworth, and by his undogmatic spirituality.

As Dr. Channing made the first steps, he began to chart the new path. He it was who is said, on discovering in Jouffroy that Dr. Richard Price's *Dissertations on Matter and Spirit* had influenced German idealism, to have remarked:

> Price saved me from Locke's philosophy. He gave me the Platonic doctrine of ideas.... His book, probably, moulded my philosophy into the form it has always retained, and opened my mind into the *transcendental depth*. And I have always found in the accounts I have read of German philosophy in Madame de Staël, and in these later times, that it was cognate to my own. I cannot say that I have ever received a new idea from it; and the cause is obvious, if Price was alike the father of *it* and *mine*.[18]

[16] *Ibid.*, I, 329-333.
[17] In George F. Whicher (ed.), *The Transcendentalist Revolt against Materialism* (Boston, 1949), pp. 68 ff.
[18] Elizabeth Palmer Peabody, *Reminiscences of Rev. William Ellery Channing, D.D.* (Boston, 1880), p. 368.

While he claimed that Hutcheson's *Moral Philosophy* was one of the most important books he read in college, it was Coleridge to whose mind he "owed more than to the mind of any other philosophic thinker,"[19] through both the *Biographia Literaria* and personal acquaintance in 1822-1823.[20]

Perhaps Dr. Channing most closely approached Transcendentalism in his sermon "Likeness to God" in 1828, where he said:

The divine attributes are first developed in ourselves, and thence transferred to our Creator. The idea of God, sublime and awful as it is, is the idea of our own spiritual nature, purified and enlarged to infinity. In ourselves are the elements of the Divinity. God, then, does not sustain a figurative resemblance to man. It is the resemblance of a parent to a child, the likeness of a kindred nature.[21]

Late in his life Channing seemed to think that the "new views" would tend to "loosen the tie which binds the soul to its great friend and deliverer."[22] On another occasion he said, "The danger that besets our Transcendentalists is that they sometimes mistake their individualities for the Transcendent. What is common to men and revealed by Jesus transcends every single individuality, and is the spiritual object and food of all individuals. . . . there is a danger that Emerson's followers may lapse into a kind of *egotheism*."[23] But for all his influence upon Emerson,[24] Parker,[25] Elizabeth Peabody, Channing was both too much of a Christian and too much of a rationalist to go the whole way toward Transcendentalism himself.[26] And he was more highly regarded by Emerson and Parker for his high moral sentiment and religious personality than for his

---

[19] *Ibid.*, p. 75.
[20] Goddard, *op. cit.*, p. 43 n.
[21] William Ellery Channing, *Works* (Boston, 1886), p. 293.
[22] Letter of Channing to Elizabeth Peabody, August, 1841, in Peabody, *op. cit.*, p. 432.
[23] *Ibid.*, p. 365. Though Miss Peabody quotes this from memory, it is unlikely, despite the fact that she was a Transcendentalist, that she was distorting the views of her hero, Channing.
[24] Ralph L. Rusk, *The Life of Ralph Waldo Emerson* (New York, 1949), p. 103; cf. Lenthiel H. Downs, "Emerson and Dr. Channing," *New England Quarterly*, XX (Dec., 1947), 516-534.
[25] Goddard, *op. cit.*, p. 84.
[26] Arthur I. Ladu, "Channing and Transcendentalism," *American Literature*, XI (1939), 134. Cf. Channing, *Works*, p. 297.

intellectual powers and ideas.²⁷ Nevertheless he was an attractive, liberalizing influence because of his open-mindedness, his eloquence, his high spiritual station, and his real if reluctant participation in movements of reform.²⁸

Emerson and his coevals were able to develop Transcendentalist idealism much farther than Dr. Channing and to put much farther behind them the combination of sensationalism and moral sense which was taught at Harvard in the 1820's and 1830's. The growth was slow and indistinct for a time, nor did Emerson emerge as the leader until 1838. On the other hand some of the other active members of the early band lost their prominence. Hedge, less extreme in his views, withdrew not out of timidity, but out of conviction. Brownson became a Catholic in 1844, and Ripley cut himself off after the collapse of the Brook Farm experiment. Conversely, Thoreau, who was a Transcendentalist by 1837 or 1838, did not achieve prominence except among his most perceptive neighbors until after his death.

Generally speaking, the point of departure for the new movement was the sensationalist philosophy of Locke, which Alexander Hill Everett defended from the attacks of Europeans as early as 1829, before the Americans of the New School had begun to announce their views in public. Everett, in attacking Cousin and Kant, called idealism "an unsubstantial dream, which charms the infantile period of intellectual philosophy" rather than "one of the two opinions which have nearly divided the thinking men of all ages and nations."²⁹ In 1831 Timothy Walker continued the defense against the foreign evil in a denial of the views of the still anonymous Carlyle. Walker saw little to be feared in a mechanism which smooths down mountains, gives a concept of a supreme being by deduction from the lawful universe, and shows man's mind closest

---

[27] Ladu, *op. cit.*, pp. 135-136.

[28] Letter to Lydia M. Child, March, 1842, in *Letters of Lydia Maria Child* (Boston, 1883), p. 46.

[29] Alexander Hill Everett, review of Victor Cousin, *North American Review*, XXIX (1829), 109. Fear of human skepticism had caused the new idealists, thought Everett, to throw out the baby with the bath, under the assumption that complete negation of the possibility of knowledge was a necessary consequence of Locke. But the new was "transitory," and the public would "settle down again in the conclusions of Locke and Aristotle" (*ibid.*, p. 119).

to God's in subjugating matter to laws.³⁰ Needless to say Walker thought that Carlyle's dislike of Locke's philosophy was definitely wrong.³¹

Frederic Henry Hedge, a vigorous little man, educated in Germany and a competent student of philosophy, achieved an early prominence apparently because, though it cannot be documented specifically, he was important in explaining various strains of German thought to the Transcendental Club, or the "Hedge Club" as Emerson called it, since it met whenever Hedge came down from Bangor, Maine, where he preached until 1850.³² One of Hedge's major services to the movement was his article on Coleridge in the *Christian Examiner* in 1833. This was the first public defense of the Transcendentalist philosophy, and it went much farther than its titular subject. After claiming that Coleridge was not needlessly obscure,³³ Hedge went on to say that Kant distinguished between two types of consciousness, the common, which is a passive receptor of the world, and the interior, which is active.³⁴ Transcendentalism, he says, seeks to find an unconditioned absolute as the ground of finite existence, and as a final step to establish a "coincidence between the facts of ordinary experience and those which we have discovered within ourselves."³⁵ This fine paper, commended by Emerson as a "living, leaping logos," was even approved by the Unitarian Henry Ware.³⁶

More prominent in the subsequent controversy was George Ripley, a man of fine intelligence and magnificent integrity. A good scholar, indeed something of a pedant, and possibly a dull preacher, Ripley both read and knew the European philosophers. He recognized the great differences between Kant and Coleridge,³⁷ and

---

³⁰ Timothy Walker, "Defence of Mechanical Philosophy," *North American Review*, XXXIII (1831), 123, 126.

³¹ *Ibid.*, p. 130.

³² Goddard, *op. cit.*, p. 35.

³³ Frederic Hedge, review of Coleridge's works, *Christian Examiner*, XIV (1833), 116.

³⁴ *Ibid.*, XIV, 119.

³⁵ *Ibid.*, XIV, 121.

³⁶ R. V. Wells, *Three Christian Transcendentalists: James Marsh, Caleb Sprague Henry, Frederic Henry Hedge* (New York, 1943), p. 97 n.

³⁷ George Ripley, review of Charles Follen, "Inaugural Discourse," *Christian Examiner*, XI (1832), 375.

pointed out that they seemed obscure only to certain kinds of minds. He was opposed to utilitarianism with its "selfish calculations" which were in constant danger of disagreeing with "the dictates of unchangeable justice."[38] An honest and vigorous fighter, Ripley sought in 1836 in his *Discourse on the Philosophy of Religion* to counter the public attack of Andrews Norton, the Unitarian "Pope." Ripley pointed out that in religion men are conversant with invisible objects, though this does not make men visionary or impractical.[39] Indeed, Ripley argued that "things which are unseen possess the only independent reality."[40] In thorough Transcendental fashion he insisted that the power for perceiving truth is Reason,[41] that man has a faculty for recognizing moral distinctions, that man is capable of disinterested love,[42] and that man possesses a power of conceiving perfection.[43] This was a strong statement of the idealistic position.

Certainly the best philosophical thinker in the early group, and one of the most energetic in mind, was Orestes Brownson, a self-educated farm boy with a pugnacious temperament, who was for years a seeker of answers. Born in Vermont, he became in turn a Presbyterian, a Universalist, an agnostic organizer of the Working-men's Party, a Unitarian preacher, editor of the *Boston Quarterly Review* (1838-1842), and coeditor of the *Democratic Review* from 1842. In 1844 he joined the Catholic church and henceforth attacked his own former views and associates. Though difficult to get along with, he was a particularly able writer in a number of fields, notably philosophical and social, where he showed learning, logical acumen, and generalizing ability along with a heavy dogmatism which may have resulted from a certain insecurity about his social and educational background.

When he became the Unitarian minister at Canton, Massachusetts, in 1834, Brownson was within reach of the Boston group of liberals and he began to write for the *Christian Examiner*, where he first made his weight felt in a disquisition on Constant's *De la*

[38] George Ripley, review of James Mackintosh, "A General View of the Progress of Ethical Philosophy," *Christian Examiner*, XIII (1833), 332.

[39] George Ripley, *Discourses on the Philosophy of Religion* (Boston, 1836), in Miller, *op. cit.*, p. 133.

[40] *Ibid.*, p. 135.   [41] *Ibid.*, p. 137.   [42] *Ibid.*, p. 139.
[43] *Ibid.*, p. 140.

*réligion*. In this essay he explained that religious institutions regularly crystallize or ossify while religious sentiment progresses, and that a new religious movement must tear down the old outmoded structure to permit development of the new sentiment. Then he took up Constant's point "that religion and morality rest not on the understanding, not on logical deductions, but on an interior sentiment. Here is an important recognition,—a recognition of two distinct orders of human faculties. This recognition is not always made by metaphysicians, but it never escapes popular language."[44] And this feeling which may be aroused "when contemplating a vast and tranquil sea, distant mountains with harmonious outlines, or, when marking an act of heroism, of disinterestedness, or of generous self-sacrifice for others' welfare, rises without any dependence on the understanding."[45] Thus Brownson took a position in conscious opposition to the older school of thought. "We are aware, that the philosophy of sensation will condemn this position. Be it so," he added, for while he recognized the philosophy of sensation as the philosophy of the last half-century in America, he hoped it would not be that of the future.[46]

In his early Transcendental period, Brownson was especially affected by Cousin's thought (which he preferred to that of Kant, Schelling, and Hegel[47]) as not leading to skepticism, because he thought that it could span the deplorable breach between religion and philosophy.[48] And this he felt was true because Cousin made "psychology the foundation, but not the superstructure" of his philosophy, while by his technique of empiricism he gave objective validity to his results.[49] Since the reason, though appearing in us, is not our *self* but objective, according to Cousin, it is a "legitimate authority for whatever it reveals,"[50] and what it reveals is the absolute, which is given and not deduced from the relative,

---

[44] Orestes Brownson, review of Benjamin Constant, *Christian Examiner*, XVII (1834), 70.
[45] *Ibid.*, XVII, 71.
[46] *Loc. cit.*
[47] René Wellek, "The Minor Transcendentalists and the German Philosophy," *New England Quarterly*, XV (1942), 669.
[48] Orestes Brownson, article on Cousin, *Christian Examiner*, XXI (1836), 34-35.
[49] *Ibid.*, XXI, 40      [50] *Ibid.*, XXI, 45.

which it logically precedes.⁵¹ This view, which Brownson insisted was not pantheism because according to it the universe is the effect of God and not God, permits him to hold that God appears in us as reason—a view so satisfactory to him that he recommended it to all his readers. In this way he promoted a form of Transcendentalism which insisted upon intuitive apprehension of God.

In an important pamphlet, *New Views of Christianity, Society, and the Church* (1836), Brownson moved on to a vigorous and penetrating historical analysis of Unitarianism which put both the United States and Unitarianism into the stream of Western history as a part of the Atlantic civilization. This he did by setting up two contrasting social systems, the spiritual and the material, or heavenly and worldly, which are constantly at war with each other and need to be harmonized. First one predominates and then the other, materialism under Greece and Rome and spiritualism in the Middle Ages, with materialism triumphing again in Protestantism, which "brought up the state, civil liberty, human reason, philosophy, industry, all the temporal interests."[52] As a sort of premonition of his later conversion, he continued, "Properly speaking, Protestantism has no religious character" and "is, in fact, only Catholicism continued" and watered down.[53] That Brownson really means the religion of the Enlightenment by Protestantism is indicated by his assertion that the arts showed the same tendency—the familiar marks of neoclassicism, exaltation of the material order and a patterning after the Greeks and Romans.[54] Protestantism and industrialism were by Brownson associated in terms anticipating Weber and Tawney,[55] and so also were civil and political liberty. Indeed he saw the American Revolution and Unitarianism as parts of what may be called the Enlightenment.[56] But all this materialism he saw declining with the failure of the French Revolution and the

[51] *Ibid.*, XXI, 46.
[52] Orestes A. Brownson, *The Works of Orestes A. Brownson*, ed. H. F. Brownson (Detroit, 1883), IV, 17.
[53] *Ibid.*, IV, 22.
[54] *Ibid.*, IV, 17-19, 23.
[55] *Ibid.*, IV, 17-23.
[56] *Ibid.*, IV, 39-40. Following Cousin's eclecticism as a pattern, Brownson predicts a religious eclecticism which will combine the best features of both spiritualism and materialism. Of this a prototype is Dr. Channing (*ibid.*, IV, 46).

consequent despotism of Napoleon. Despair of things on earth caused men to seek refuge in heaven. While certain oversimplifications in this picture could be pointed out, it is clear that Brownson was declaring that Unitarianism, whatever its humane virtues, was attached to a dying past, though from it must come the reconciliation of the future in terms of the spiritual philosophy. This attack on all sides is significant, but at this point it is necessary to emphasize the attack on the sensational philosophy as antiquated and outmoded.

Much more immediate reaction was occasioned by the publication of Amos Bronson Alcott's *Record of Conversations on the Gospels held in Mr. Alcott's School, Unfolding the Doctrine and Discipline of Human Culture*, December, 1836. Alcott, born at Spindle Hill, Connecticut, was reared on a farm, served a period as a peddler in the South, and then turned to school teaching. Though he had been a Lockean,[57] Alcott was by temperament inclined toward idealism of an extremely intuitional sort, a tendency which was reinforced by his friendship with Dr. Channing and his reading of Reed's *Growth of the Mind* in 1829, Cousin in 1831, Coleridge's *Aids to Reflection* in 1832, and in 1833 the *Biographia Literaria*, some Plato, Proclus, and Plotinus, *Wilhelm Meister*, some Carlyle, Wordsworth's *Excursion*, Okely's life of Boehme, and an abstract of Kant. In 1834 he opened the Temple School in Boston and in 1835 became acquainted with Emerson. By this time, as his journals show, he was a thorough Transcendentalist, and indeed he influenced Emerson's *Nature*, which apparently as a consequence goes farther in the direction of absolute idealism (that is, in reducing everything to spirit) than his writing usually does.

Though Alcott had published an article on his Cheshire School in William Russell's *American Journal of Education* at the end of 1827, it was the publication of Peabody's *Record of a School* (1835) which first made his work widely known. But it was his own *Record of Conversations on the Gospels Held in Mr. Alcott's School, Unfolding the Doctrine and Discipline of Human Culture* (Vol. I, 1836; Vol. II, 1837) which called down public denunciation upon him. This book, harmless enough in twentieth-century eyes, was vigorously attacked. "Mr. Alcott should hide his head in

---
[57] Odell Shepard, *Pedlar's Progress* (Boston, 1937), p. 133.

shame," wrote a parent to the Boston *Courier;* the editor called it "indecent and obscene" and quoted a clergyman, apparently Andrews Norton, who said the book was one-third "absurd, one-third blasphemous, and one-third obscene."[58] This response was due in part to the book's religious quality (Ripley indicated that the clergy felt their territory was invaded),[59] to its romantic assumption that children were not only naturally good but closer to God, and to its supposed frankness.[60] Properly speaking, it was, of course, a threat both to the "spare the rod and spoil the child" theory of education and to conservative Unitarianism because it assumed that "*Christianity is grounded in the essential Nature of Man.*"[61]

Another important Transcendentalist publication of 1836 was W. H. Furness's *Remarks on the Four Gospels,* in which he argued that if the world were considered and understood from a spiritual point of view which recognized that scientific knowledge was incomplete and fragmentary, then there was nothing miraculous about even the resurrection of Jesus; the supernatural was "everywhere in the natural."[62] And this rather than the sensational philosophy was for Furness the most desirable because it was the broadest position.

Though it took time for the fact to become evident, it was Emerson's *Nature* which was the great book of the year 1836, for even though it did not completely unfold Emerson's mature thought, it possessed a breadth and depth which gradually made itself felt. *Nature,* Emerson's first published work, gave the impression that its author was always a Transcendentalist, but this was of course not true; like the others, Emerson began with the older views. Indeed, despite the fact that his father had been a Unitarian minister, Emerson was brought up in an atmosphere to which his Aunt Mary Moody Emerson contributed a large supply of Calvinism with a moral though not a doctrinal effect. Moreover, Emerson was taught Locke at Harvard and in addition the Scottish philosophers of the

[58] *Ibid.,* pp. 193-195; Hubert H. Hoeltje, *Sheltering Tree* (Durham, N. C., 1943), pp. 31-32.
[59] *The Journals of Bronson Alcott,* ed. Odell Shepard (Boston, 1938), p. 80.
[60] Shepard, *Pedlar's Progress,* p. 194.
[61] *Record of Conversations on the Gospels held in Mr. Alcott's School* (Boston, 1837), Introduction.
[62] Miller, *op. cit.,* p. 128.

Common-Sense school, and the latter especially influenced his thought. It appears that Emerson had an inclination toward idealism which was not completely submerged even by his formal education, with the result often a mixture of systems or a conflict between them.

This tendency toward idealism is significantly made manifest in Emerson's college essay on "The Character of Socrates," which won a Bowdoin second prize in 1820. His subject lay outside the topics most acceptable at Harvard and met with a partial rebuke from President Kirkland, who thought Emerson should be "a better Locke, Stewart, and Paley scholar."[63] But the line of this essay lay in the direction of Waldo's future development. It is easy to see some ironical reflections on the self-satisfied state of his professors in the introduction:

The increasing notice which it [the philosophy of the human mind] obtains is owing much to the genius of those men who have raised themselves with the science to general regard, but chiefly, as its patrons contend, to the uncontrolled progress of human improvement. The zeal of its advocates, however, in other respects commendable, has sinned in one particular,—they have laid a little too much self-complacent stress on the merit and success of their own unselfish exertions, and in their first contempt of the absurd and trifling speculations of former metaphysicians, appear to have confounded sophists and true philosophers, and to have been disdainful of some who have enlightened the world and marked out a path of future advancement.

Indeed the giant strength of modern improvement is more indebted to the early wisdom of Thales and Socrates and Plato than is generally allowed, or perhaps than modern philosophers have been well aware.[64]

Emerson's emphasis upon the moral courage of Socrates in disagreeing with conventional religion[65] is also significant as a premonition of Self-Reliance; his emphasis upon Socrates' abstemious life and cheerful acceptance of poverty for the sake of cultivating his soul indicates Emerson's own ideal; his insistence that Socrates is higher in character than in intellect[66] points to his future belief that character is above intellect. Emerson's quotation:

[63] Rusk, *op. cit.*, p. 80.
[64] Edward Everett Hale, *Ralph Waldo Emerson: Together with Two Early Essays of Emerson* (Boston, 1904), pp. 57-58.
[65] *Ibid.*, p. 87.
[66] *Ibid.*, p. 73.

"Let us not, then, refuse to believe even what we do not behold, and let us supply the defect of our corporeal eyes by using those of the soul; but especially let us learn to render the just homage of respect and veneration to that Divinity whose will it seems to be that we should have no other perception of him but by his effects in our favor ... by doing his will"[67]

indicates here an approval of intuition as well as of following it, which again prepares for his later doctrine of reliance upon the Over-Soul. His emphasis upon the "moral perfection" of a man who did not enjoy the advantages of Christian "revelation"[68] shows his own boldness in religious areas. His emphasis on Socrates' view that the soul was a form of eternal beauty in the divine mind and was most nearly approached by beautiful mortals,[69] foreshadows some of his later views of both friendship and aesthetics. Thus a number of later doctrines and centers of interest are adumbrated in this early essay, which shows a certain characteristic boldness of speculation.

The Scottish Common-Sense philosophers who were taught at Harvard along with Locke, as has already been pointed out, offered a halfway station on the road to idealism. Dugald Stewart's *Elements of the Philosophy of the Human Mind* and Thomas Brown's *Lectures* were part of the curriculum,[70] but perhaps more important for Emerson was the fact that he read independently in 1820-1821 Stewart's *Outlines of Moral Philosophy*, which maintained that a moral sense was inborn in each child and was a mainspring of his mental powers. These ideas were reinforced by Levi Hedge, who Ripley thought followed the moral-sense school,[71] and Levi Frisbie, professor of logic, whose lecture notes were later published by Andrews Norton,[72] although Frisbie thought that the moral sense needed cultivation.

Emerson was, in 1821, pondering these ideas which anticipated his later views. Meanwhile, at the instance of his vigorous and influential Aunt Mary, he was reading Price's *Morals* with some perplexity and on March 14 recorded in his *Journal*, "Dr. Price says that right and wrong are not determined by any reasoning or de-

[67] *Ibid.*, p. 81.   [68] *Ibid.*, p. 59.   [69] *Ibid.*, p. 75.
[70] Merrill R. Davis, "Emerson's Reason and the Scottish Philosphers," *New England Quarterly*, XVII (1944), 214-215; Todd, *op. cit.*, XVI, 64.
[71] Rusk, *op. cit.*, p. 82.   [72] *Ibid.*, pp. 81-82.

duction, but by the ultimate perception of the human mind. It is to be desired that this were capable of satisfactory proof, but, as it is in direct opposition to the skeptical philosophy, it cannot stand unsupported by strong and sufficient evidence. I will however read more...."[73]

Beneath the apparent certainty of his senior paper, "The Present State of Ethical Philosophy," which again won a Bowdoin second prize, there is some ambivalence with reference to both Hume and the Scottish school. If Emerson were attempting to win a first award by treating a more conventionally acceptable subject, he was too honest to claim more than he actually felt, and this work is more important for its somewhat confused examination of the subject than for its positive answers. Proceeding with the logical organization which characterized his early work, Emerson briefly sketches the history of moral philosophy up to Clarke, Price, Butler, Reid, Paley, Smith, and Stewart.[74] Evidently distinguishing between the common-sense and moral-sense aspects of the school, he says that ethical science's "fundamental principles are taught by the moral sense, and no advancement of time can improve them,"[75] since only natural science and not moral intuitions are progressive.[76] "The object of these reasonings," he continues, "is to confirm the decisions of the moral faculty, which is recognized as an original principle of our nature,—an intuition by which we directly determine the merit or demerit of an action."[77] On the other hand, the common sense of the Scottish group does not seem perfect to him, since its "reasonings as yet want the neatness and conclusiveness of a system," and have not removed "the terror which attached to the name of Hume";[78] nevertheless he thinks that the first true advance must be made in the Scottish school through the use of moral maxims rather than ultimate principles. Also ambivalent is his attitude toward Hume. On the one hand, Hume's claim that happiness lies in the condition of the mind, not in an external quality, represents "sagacity,"[79] and his skepticism is "manly" and does not deserve a "*sneer*."[80] On the other hand, he calls Hume's dissolution of moral

---
[73] *Journals of Ralph Waldo Emerson*, ed. E. W. Emerson and W. E. Forbes (Boston, 1909), I, 78.
[74] Hale, *op cit.*, p. 112.   [75] *Loc. cit.*   [76] *Ibid.*, p. 115.
[77] *Ibid.*, p. 116.   [78] *Ibid.*, pp. 122-123.   [79] *Ibid.*, p. 121.
[80] *Ibid.*, p. 123.

laws an "outrage."[81] Though not satisfied completely with Reid and Stewart and not yet having developed his own solution, Emerson states (anticipating his later individualism) that the chief benefit of the science of morals which has "more permanent interest than any other,"[82] lies "in its effect on the individual,"[83] and that the idea of progress cannot certainly be believed.[84]

Thus by 1821 Emerson already showed sympathies with idealism, a serious regard for honest and rigorous skeptics like Hume, acceptance of the idea of a moral sense, and some doubt of the efficacy, so far at least, of the attempts to codify morals on a practical rather than an intuitional basis. Here his permanent interest in morals is asserted, with some indication that they will be built upon insight rather than upon classification or codes.

While he did not find permanent form for his ideas until 1836, as a young preacher Emerson was beginning to put forward the ideas which characterized his later thought, though couched in terms which included Christ and God. His very first sermon, "Pray without Ceasing," asserted the dual worlds of matter and spirit, the latter "more certain and stable,"[85] though most men err in following the law of the material, working for "bread and wine and dress and our houses and our furniture."[86] But as an idealist already, Emerson pointed out that men's minds are "ideas present to the mind of God," and only men's liberty could be called their own.[87] In 1829 he spoke of nature's "everlasting analogies,"[88] and especially after the shattering death of his wife Ellen, he emphasized the doctrine of compensation.[89]

Professor Rusk finds a similar premonition of Emerson's later ideas in his unpublished sermons:

A sermon against foolish, counterfeit pride said that "The good man reveres himself, reveres his conscience, and would rather suffer any calamity than lower himself in his own esteem." Another sermon declared that physical things were chiefly significant as symbols; another, that heaven was here and now; another, that the moral sentiment, perceiver of right and wrong and therefore the sovereign part of man's nature, existed in the mind independently of experience;

[81] *Ibid.*, p. 122.   [82] *Ibid.*, p. 135.   [83] *Ibid.*, p. 134.   [84] *Ibid.*, p. 130.
[85] A. C. McGiffert, Jr. (ed.), *Young Emerson Speaks: Unpublished Discourses on Many Subjects* (Boston, 1938), p. 1.
[86] *Ibid.*, p. 2.   [87] *Ibid.*, p. 4.   [88] *Ibid.*, p. 44.   [89] *Ibid.*, p. 209.

another, that there was a "law of progress, that on-look of human nature, which is its distinguishing and beautiful characteristic." Others asserted freedom of the will in spite of all determination from outside, or the Quaker doctrine of the inward light with its implication that "the bible has no force but what it derives from within us." Jesus, the preacher explained, had no authority as a person. The delivery of the same truths Jesus uttered would have invested the humblest created spirit with the same authority, no more and no less. . . . "A trust in yourself . . . is the height not of pride but of piety, an unwillingness to learn of any but God himself." . . . He asserted that "What you can get of moral or intellectual excellence out of this little plot of ground you call *yourself*, by the sweat of your brow—is your portion." . . .

His hearers must have been struck by his habit of regarding man as divine.[90]

The *Journals* likewise reveal a gradual advance toward a coherent pattern of idealism. As early as 1820 Emerson saw the "properties of matter as the properties of mind,"[91] and in 1822 he wrote that the Platonist was right in his view of the war of mind and matter.[92] Though he used the Common-Sense argument that the Trinity was an invalid concept because "inconceivable," he gave the argument an idealistic slant by saying, "Infinite Wisdom established the foundations of the knowledge of the mind."[93] He continued his acceptance of a moral sense which comes from a mind that is God, and which, unlike the emotions or the human intellect, never fails and is always the same.[94] By 1828 he suggested that man was "connected to God by his conscience,"[95] which thus acted as the agency of the moral sense and furnished the basis of a self-trust which he began to proclaim in the same year.[96] Moreover, as every close reader of the *Journals* knows, they indicate a crisis of increasing proportions until his resignation as minister of the Second Church in 1832 and his departure for Europe.

*Nature*, while it does not give Emerson's ideas in their final form, still is a major landmark both for Emerson's thought and for Transcendentalism. Since it is well known, but especially since a number of the points it makes will be taken up in other sections of this paper dealing with scientific, religious, aesthetic, and social ideas, only a

[90] Rusk, *op. cit.*, p. 158. [91] *Journals*, I, 60. [92] *Ibid.*, I, 148.
[93] *Ibid.*, I, 104. [94] *Ibid.*, I, 187-188. [95] *Ibid.*, II, 248.
[96] *Ibid.*, II, 242, 249.

few salient aspects will come up for comment here. Certainly this intuitive idealism is more Platonic than Kantian, though one of the statements attributed to Plato is really from Kant as quoted by Coleridge.[97] Indeed the conclusion, at least, is much more Neoplatonic in its emanation theory than is usual with Emerson, because he had been reading the *Journals* of Bronson Alcott, presumably the "certain Poet" in "Prospects," whose views reinforced those of Plotinus and Proclus. The fact that Emerson emphasizes the declining slope of the great chain of being, the "degradation" of man,[98] indicates that his optimism had not yet set without cracks, that there was the dark background of death beneath this superficial optimism.[99]

That Emerson's thought had not been completely worked out is indicated by certain confusions and certain disagreements with his later ideas. Thus, while he later most characteristically maintained a dualism of matter and spirit, he here used the triple Kantian division of the senses, understanding, and reason in handling sections II to V of *Nature;* yet the modern reader is embarrassed by Emerson's handling of the spiritual element of beauty,[100] putting it below the appeal to the intellect, which is contrary to his subsequent statements of his position. Moreover, there was in the original work no indication of the evolutionary ideas which later replaced his emanationism. Nevertheless this is the most complete, if not the clearest, of the early statements of Transcendentalism.

Thoreau's early writing must be considered here to show the development of Transcendentalism, despite the facts that he did not publish any work until 1841, and that he was not seriously considered as a major member of the group until the twentieth century.[101] His college essays written for Professor Edward Channing, the Boylston Professor of Rhetoric, show the transition not only from a balanced eighteenth-century style to a looser form of prose, but

---

[97] John S. Harrison, *The Teachers of Emerson* (New York, 1910), pp. 41-42.

[98] Emerson, *Works*, I, 70-71.

[99] *Ibid.*, I, 9, 11, 16.

[100] Henry Pochmann and Gay Allen, *Masters of American Literature* (New York, 1949), I, 678; Emerson, *Works*, I, 19-24.

[101] Neither Frothingham nor Goddard treats Thoreau in detail.

from the concepts of the Scottish philosophers to those of Emerson.[102]

In Essay XIII Thoreau accepts the sensationalist concept of Locke,[103] and in No. XII he quotes Dugald Stewart on the imagination;[104] as late as 1837 he was still using the principles of the Common-Sense school to indicate the certainty of reasoning, but by this time he had separated the thought from its emotional effect, which was the element that would influence conduct.[105] Though he had characteristically emphasized self-reliance from the start,[106] his reading of *Nature* sharpened the new views and he was soon quoting from it.[107] On May 15, 1837, Thoreau wrote on the assignment, "Speak of the duty, inconvenience, and dangers of *Conformity*, in little things and great," that duty lies in conforming "to the dictates of an inward arbiter," and that "fear of displeasing the world ought not in the least to influence my actions. Were it otherwise, the principal avenue of Reform would be closed."[108] The tone of the passage indicates that Thoreau was talking about Transcendental self-reliance rather than the Scottish moral sense, but in either case there is a conflict with the approach of common sense. This makes evident a certain shift of position.

In the later exercises Transcendentalist ideas begin to supersede the earlier Common-Sense concepts; thus Thoreau is found commending Plato,[109] taking the romantic view that "The civilized man is the slave of Matter,"[110] and that truth should be sought directly by each individual, not through imitation of others.[111] The point is clear, then, that even so confirmed a Transcendentalist as Thoreau was not born to the view, but was first influenced by the prevailing ideas of the Lockean and Common-Sense schools before finding in his home town the philosophy which was more congenial to his mind.

---

[102] Joseph J. Kwiat, "Thoreau's Philosophical Apprenticeship," *New England Quarterly*, XVIII (1945), 51-69.
[103] Frank B. Sanborn, *The Life of Henry David Thoreau, Including Many Essays Hitherto Unpublished* (Boston, 1917), pp. 117-118.
[104] *Ibid.*, pp. 115-116.   [105] *Ibid.*, p. 157.   [106] *Ibid.*, pp. 66-67; 74.
[107] *Ibid.*, p. 137. Cf. Emerson, *Works*, I, 56.
[108] Sanborn, *op. cit.*, pp. 150-152.
[109] *Ibid.*, p. 176.   [110] *Ibid.*, p. 180.   [111] *Ibid.*, pp. 183-184.

By 1836 it was clear to intelligent readers in New England that an idealistic philosophy was being unmistakably propounded by a small but articulate group who were seeking to find a firmer theoretical foundation for their religious beliefs. The wide reading of this new group made it difficult to tell certainly what the sources for these ideas were, and the emphasis by different new writers on different sources did not simplify the problem. Nor is it simple today. Often the material for the accurate estimate of different philosophers as sources is lacking. Yet the influences which are clearest can be pointed out with the aid of an extensive series of scholarly studies.

Of these Platonism is of basic import since Plato is a fountainhead of philosophic idealism, but since nearly everybody read him, his specific influence is difficult to assess. If the significant criterion is similarity of thought pattern, then Emerson is the most Platonic of the Transcendentalists, for the concept of "the one and the many" was central to Emerson's thought. And even, as has been pointed out,[112] Emerson's criticisms of Plato as being too intellectual and having no system are implied self-criticisms which indicate that his problems were the same as Plato's.

However the fact that Emerson's system was not completely Platonic is indicated by the fact that he did not habitually think in certain Platonic categories which he sometimes used. Emerson generally dealt in terms of poles and did not regularly have use for the daemonic level which he derived from the *Symposium* and used in "Initial, Daemonic and Celestial Love." Moreover, his use of the "twice bisected line" gave him four categories which his other concepts did not permit him to use systematically. It is worth noting that James Freeman Clarke was able to think in Kantian terms of pure and practical reason and pure and practical understanding.[113]

Thus, while Emerson is more of a Platonist than a Kantian, a leading historian of American philosophy believes that "Things interested him neither in terms of their universal patterns nor in terms of their natural existence, but in terms of their ability to stir

---

[112] S. G. Brown, "Emerson's Platonism," *New England Quarterly*, XVIII (1945), 325-345.

[113] John W. Thomas, *James Freeman Clarke: Apostle of German Culture to America* (Boston, 1949), p. 161.

the poetic imagination, which he and his fellow transcendentalists called reason or spirit."[114] And Emerson was more Platonic than the others; Alcott being more influenced by the Neoplatonists, while Thoreau, for example, wrote that Plato is a dogma and that "The wood thrush is a more modern philosopher."[115]

The Transcendentalists did not get their Plato pure, however; and were somewhat misled by the translations and introductions of Thomas Taylor, who colored them with his own Neoplatonism and consequently gave Plato a more mystical interpretation than the texts alone would warrant.[116] Moreover the Transcendentalists read the Cambridge Platonists Cudworth and Henry Moore, and used them also in constructing their idealistic thought.[117]

Emerson and especially Alcott, among the more mystical of the Transcendentalists, made special use of the doctrines of the Neoplatonists. (Thoreau's mysticism was reinforced more strongly by the Hindu scriptures.) Though Emerson went through several periods when he accepted their views more wholeheartedly as in *Nature* and in essays like "The Over-Soul" and "Circles," and though he liked the imagery of Proclus, Porphyry, and Iamblichus, it was Alcott who was closer to the group of Neoplatonists, whom he first read in 1833. His doctrine of Genesis or Lapse, which contended that the world was an emanation from God through man's spirit and so on through animals down to atoms, is Neoplatonic.[118] Much of Alcott's obscurity lay in the fact that he was by temperament as well as by reading an heir of the hermetic mystical tradition.[119]

In addition to Platonism, the Oriental scriptures had some effect on the Transcendentalists, though this appeared less in the ideas specifically supplied than in the imagery furnished. The impact of the Hindu and Persian writings was not in any case made very early. For Emerson, at least, though he had read scattered bits

---

[114] Schneider, *op. cit.*, p. 284.
[115] Bradford Torrey and F. H. Allen (eds.), *The Journal of Henry D. Thoreau* (Boston, 1906), I, 171.
[116] F. I. Carpenter, *Emerson and Asia* (Cambridge, Mass., 1930), p. 43.
[117] Harrison, *op. cit.*, pp. 80-83.
[118] Shepard, *Pedlar's Progress*, pp. 453-462.
[119] Austin Warren, "The Orphic Sage: Bronson Alcott," *American Literature*, III (1931), 13.

earlier, it first was outlined in De Gerando's *Histoire Comparée des Systèmes de Philosophie*,[120] which he began to read in 1830. And, though he took up the Orientals again in the late 1830's, it was not until 1841 that he encountered the Persian poets in a German translation.[121] The emphasis upon Asia in *Representative Men* and works like "Hamatraya," "Brahma," and "Illusions" shows the depth and extent of the influence on Emerson. Alcott, who first read in the *Bhagavat-Gita* in 1846, gave conversations which included the Orientals in 1851.[122] And Charles Lane brought to Fruitlands in 1843 an extensive collection of Oriental books. Thoreau, however, was perhaps most interested. He translated some of the Ethnic Scriptures for the *Dial*[123] and found in these writings a confirmation of his own somewhat mystical temperament. Because of his interest, he was presented by the Englishman Thomas Chalmondeley with forty-four volumes of oriental writings in various languages.[124] Finally the Transcendentalists' excitement over oriental writing was channeled much later into the study of comparative religions by James Freeman Clarke in *Ten Great Religions* (1871, 1883).

Other sources for the idealism of the Transcendentalists included the writings of Swedenborg, especially as interpreted by the oracular writing of Sampson Reed. His oration on "Genius," delivered in 1821 and copied from manuscript by Emerson, and *Observations on the Growth of the Mind*[125] furnished a basis, though probably not the primary one, for the doctrine of correspondence. Emerson was considerably impressed by Swedenborg's use of natural facts as symbols of the spiritual realm and seemed close enough to becoming a disciple to have been asked to become a New Church pastor, but his lecture on Swedenborg in *Representative Men*, which was critical of both the rigidity and orthodoxy of the system, caused some objection.[126] A French

[120] Emerson, *Journals*, II, 329.
[121] Carpenter, *Emerson and Asia*, p. 20.
[122] Christy, *op. cit.*, p. 246.
[123] *Dial*, III (1843), 493-494; IV (1843), 59-62; 205-210; 402-404.
[124] Sanborn, *op. cit.*, p. 305; Christy, *op. cit.*, pp. 46-47.
[125] Kenneth W. Cameron, *Emerson the Essayist* (Raleigh, N.C., 1945), pp. 3-31.
[126] Clarence Hotson, "Emerson and the Swedenborgians," *Studies in Philology*, XXVII (1930), 517-545.

disciple, G. Oegger, who wrote *The True Messiah*, was also read by Emerson in 1835 in Elizabeth Peabody's manuscript translation.[127] Swedenborg was also, as will be evident later, taken up at Brook Farm.

The German idealists were of great importance to the American Transcendentalists, particularly as interpreted by French and English intermediaries. Only a few of the New Englanders were really at home in the German language, but Frederic Henry Hedge had an excellent command of it and Brownson was also thoroughly equipped to handle German philosophy, though Emerson was neither a fluent reader of German nor an adept at the close logic of Kant or Hegel. Hedge was of special value to the Transcendental Club in explaining the meaning of the German writers, while Brownson criticized the supposed skepticism of Kant's *Critique of Pure Reason* and preferred the objective idealism he found in Cousin.[128] Some of the Transcendentalists, as will appear later, were especially affected by the writings of the German mystics and theologians.

But the German attempts to solve the epistemological problem which had been posed by Descartes were transmitted to New England principally by other thinkers. Of these Madame de Staël had an indistinct though significant effect. Her *De l'Allemagne* served mainly to interest her readers in the new German solutions since she did not give sufficient detail to do more than enliven the attention paid the Germans. Yet she performed her function well, as comments by Dr. Channing, Emerson, and Clarke, indicate.[129] More specifically important were Constant and Cousin, but especially the latter. His eclecticism had a widespread vogue among the Transcendentalists because, using the Kantian system in a way which was easily comprehensible, he rescued innate ideas while still retaining some of the empiricism from the English school. Although his mixture is singularly unpalatable to the twentieth century, it offered an easy transition to Americans who had been

---

[127] Cameron, *op. cit.*, II, 83-101.
[128] René Wellek, "The Minor Transcendentalists and German Philosophy," *New England Quarterly*, XV (1942), 669.
[129] Peabody, *Reminiscences*, p. 368; Emerson, *Journals*, II, 129; Thomas, *Clarke*, p. 73.

raised on Locke and the Common-Sense philosophers but who demanded something more. Particularly adopted by Brownson, he was translated by Caleb Sprague Henry and George Ripley,[130] taken seriously for a time by Parker, and read (rather early) in 1829 by Emerson, who was not, however, especially enthusiastic about the specific doctrine.

Doubtless of greatest value to the Transcendentalists were the English romantics, who interpreted idealism in ways which could be helpful; and of these the first to be read, though not the most important, was Wordsworth. Emerson's response was significant, if not typical. Though he was impressed by flashes of genius, he was bothered by the fact that Wordsworth was too much the poet and too egotistical for comfort.[131] Gradually he appreciated Wordsworth's abilities, still objecting to his infelicities. Strangely, in order to appreciate the poetry, it seemed necessary to accept the philosophy, yet this was taught to the Americans mainly by other writers.

Next in order of influence and importance was Carlyle, whose ideas were known by his magazine articles on German literature and by his translations as early as 1827,[132] when he was still anonymous. The story of his effect upon Emerson and of Emerson's successful efforts to get *Sartor Resartus* and *Critical and Miscellaneous Writings* published are too well known to require repetition.[133] The vigor of Carlyle's interpretation, the vivid violence of his style, and eventually the optimism of "The Everlasting Yea," all had their effect. His emphasis upon Fichte's concept of "Glauben" (which was like Kant's Reason), and his treatment of the Kantian distinction between Reason and Understanding must have impressed Emerson. And even Carlyle's failure to indicate Kant's reservations on the efficacy of reason influenced Emerson further.[134]

Of course it was Coleridge who acted most vigorously on the minds of a number of the American Transcendentalists. It is only

---

[130] "Philosophical Miscellanies from the French of Cousin, Jouffroy, Constant," *Specimens of Foreign Standard Literature*, I, II (Boston, 1838).

[131] Emerson, *Journals*, II, 232, 429-430.

[132] Rusk, *op. cit.*, p. 522 n.

[133] Frank L. Thompson, "Emerson and Carlyle," *Studies in Philology*, XXIV (1927), 438-453.

[134] Rusk, *op. cit.*, 206.

a little too strong to say that he furnished the spark which set off the intellectual reaction. The American publication by James Marsh of Vermont, with his long "Preliminary Essay," of Coleridge's *Aids to Reflection* in 1829 and of *The Friend* in 1831 was a crucial effort. Coleridge emphasized the Kantian distinction as misleadingly as did Carlyle, but unlike Carlyle he incorporated a good deal of Schelling without giving credit. It is from Schelling rather than from Kant that Coleridge's idealism derives, and it is this type of view that nature has its laws in the ground of man's own existence,[135] which is echoed by Emerson when he says in *Nature* "What we are, that only can we see."[136] The effect then of Coleridge was one of the first order, since he presented materials which were much desired by the Americans in a guise which they could recognize as good.

II

Besides changing over their philosophy from what they thought was sensualism to idealism, and besides extending the application of the moral sense from one area to the direct apprehension of reality in all areas, the American Transcendentalists also transformed the previously accepted theory of the universe. They succeeded in transmuting the mechanized universe of Paley into a vitalistic and evolutionary Nature which serves as a symbol of the spiritual world. In this again the Americans were a part of the Romantic movement, for as Professor Wellek has pointed out, "we find throughout Europe . . . the same conceptions of nature and its relation to man," as well as the same conception of "the workings and nature of the poetic imagination," and the same conception of "imagery, symbolism, and myth."[137] Probably the closest of the New Englanders to this central stream, in their attitudes toward nature, were Emerson and Thoreau, who significantly are also the writers of most lasting interest. They were able to transcendentalize the scientific universe of the Enlightenment by making it the intuitively understandable symbol of the realm of the spirit.

[135] Joseph Warren Beach, *The Concept of Nature in Nineteenth-Century English Poetry* (New York, 1936), p. 328.
[136] Emerson, *Works*, I, 76.
[137] René Wellek, "The Concept of Romanticism in Literary History," *Comparative Literature*, I (1949), 147.

Emerson always saw science as important and tried to make use of it in building his philosophy. As he looked back in 1880 upon the development of Transcendentalism, he said:

> I think the paramount source of the religious revolution was Modern Science; beginning with Copernicus, who destroyed the pagan fictions of the Church, by showing mankind that the earth on which we live was not the centre of the Universe, around which the sun and stars revolved every day, and thus fitted to be the platform on which the Drama of the Divine Judgment was played before the assembled Angels of Heaven, . . . but a little scrap of a planet, rushing round the sun in our system. . . . Astronomy taught us our insignificance in Nature; showed that our sacred as our profane history had been written in gross ignorance of the laws, which were far grander than we knew; and compelled a certain extension and uplifting of our views of the Deity and his Providence. This correction of our superstitions was confirmed by the new science of Geology. . . . But we presently saw also that the religious nature in man was not affected by these errors in his understanding.

And he continued:

> Whether from these influences, or whether by a reaction of the general mind against the too formal science, religion and social life of the earlier period,—there was, in the first quarter of our nineteenth century, a certain sharpness of criticism, an eagerness for reform, which showed itself in every quarter.[138]

This might be suspect as idle, if not senile, retrospection if it were not confirmed by his early views, for as early as 1831 he wrote, "The Religion that is afraid of science dishonors God and commits suicide."[139] Yet this again is only a reflection of still earlier views, at first half-formed, of the relationship between the world and the spirit. Thus in 1820 he wrote, "We feel . . . that eternal analogy which subsists between the external changes of nature, and scenes of good and ill that chequer human life,"[140] and in 1821 he discusses with his Aunt Mary the Swedenborgian idea "that the physical world was the basso-relievo of the moral." Furthermore he records, in 1822, "the pleasure of finding out a connection between a material image and a moral sentiment."[141]

---

[138] Emerson, *Works*, X, 335-337.
[139] Emerson, *Journals*, II, 362.
[140] *Ibid.*, I, 26.   [141] *Ibid.*, I, 105.

These are at least the germs of what was to become a unified theory of correspondence.

Of major significance was his reading of Coleridge's *The Friend* in 1829,[142] but in a particular way, since Emerson was led to read a number of the authors mentioned by Coleridge, e.g., Bacon and Hunter. From Coleridge, Emerson also received the distinction between the intuited Law of Science and the Theory of Scheme which was developed by the understanding.[143] Of especial importance, however, for Emerson was the Newtonian concept of a unified and ordered universe, for it was necessary to have a concept of a lawful whole before the immutable moral order could be seen as paralleling it. Yet "only when this structural dualism was represented psychologically . . . was correspondence, as the act of intuitive perception that spanned the gap of finite (outer) and infinite (inner) and unified them in the experience of the self, a necessary assumption of this thought."[144] Thus from these sources and his own thought, Emerson formulated the idea that nature mediates between man and God.

Emerson's sermon on "Astronomy," delivered May 27, 1832, indicates the extension of his ideas in one direction. First he admitted that this science "made the theological *scheme of Redemption* absolutely incredible," so, as a consequence, "Newton became a Unitarian."[145] But while astronomy tended to cause skepticism, it more significantly offered proofs of "beneficent design"; the voice of nature led to "higher truth."[146] This much was clear to Emerson, but there follow difficulties both in terminology and in logical connection. When he says that the discoveries of astronomy reconcile "the greatness of nature to the greatness of mind,"[147] this seems to be an early statement of his later view; but when he says they make "moral distinctions still more important"[148] this is a *non sequitur*. When he continues that astronomy commands all men to "repent,"[149] the difficulty is largely terminologi-

---

[142] Beach, *op. cit.*, p. 327.
[143] Sherman Paul, *Emerson's Angle of Vision: Man and Nature in American Experience* (Cambridge, Mass., 1952), pp. 40-41.
[144] Paul, *op. cit.*, p. 35.
[145] McGiffert, *op. cit.*, pp. 174-175.
[146] *Ibid.*, p. 177.  [147] *Ibid.*, p. 176.  [148] *Ibid.*, p. 177.
[149] *Ibid.*, p. 178.

cal: he is heading toward the idea that men should follow the moral law which they can intuit from the laws of celestial mechanics. Yet when he says that the enlarged views of the solar system "can never throw the least shade upon . . . moral truth" and that the beatitudes of the Sermon on the Mount are of permanent value and agree well with "all the new and astonishing facts in the book of nature,"[150] he is not announcing anything very significant. Faith is not confirmed because a given body of science does not controvert it. But again Emerson is on the trail of his later idea that physical and moral laws in some way correspond. As he wrote in *Nature*, "things are emblematic," and the "axioms of physics translate the laws of ethics."[151]

Thus while Newton was one of the sources for his philosophical synthesis, Emerson developed his ideas rather slowly, often encountering an idea several times, or in several different writers, before he was able to complete his imaginative transformation. This, of course, makes the specific influences difficult to pin down. Consequently to Newton must be added Butler's *Analogy*, Paley's *Natural Theology*, Wollaston's *Religion of Nature*, and even Bacon's *Advancement of Learning* and J. F. W. Herschel's *A Discourse of the Study of Natural Philosophy*.[152] And even this list is not complete.

In addition to being the heir of the theoretical science of the previous period, Emerson was delighted by the beauties of nature, through which he also saw the realities of the spirit, and in this was a thorough romantic.[153] It is significant that his first philosophical essay is called *Nature* rather than *Concerning the Human Understanding*, or *The Critique of Pure Reason*, or *How To Make Our Ideas Clear*, or *Pragmatism*. Yet more important than a further discussion of the science in *Nature* is an examination of his developing evolutionary idea, of which there is no hint at all in *Nature*. The original epigraph was the following quotation from Plotinus, "Nature is but an image or imitation of wisdom, the last

---

[150] *Loc. cit.*

[151] Emerson, *Works*, I, 20, 33.

[152] Harry Hayden Clark, "Emerson and Science," *Philological Quarterly*, X (1931), 225-260.

[153] Norman Foerster, *Nature in American Literature* (New York, 1923), pp. 37-68.

## THE RISE OF TRANSCENDENTALISM 279

thing of the soul; Nature being a thing which doth only do, but not know." But in 1849 the second edition of *Nature* had a different motto, the one which we know,

> A subtle chain of countless rings
> The next unto the farthest brings;
> The eye reads omens where it goes,
> And speaks all languages the rose;
> And striving to be man, the worm
> Mounts through all the spires of form.

The poem, of course, negates the more pessimistic aspect of the descent on the chain of being, affirms a view which is at least philosophically if not scientifically evolutionary, and illustrates the generally accepted idea that Emerson's emanation theory was transmuted into evolution.[154] The origins of this view are to be found early in Emerson's thought, though they were not to take their final form until after 1840. Again a number of influences can be pointed out as contributory to the intellectual development. As early as 1829 Emerson read in Coleridge's *Aids to Reflection*, "All things strive to ascend, and ascend in their striving."[155] He had also read some Leibniz early,[156] and had picked up some of the ideas of Linnaeus, Buffon, Cuvier, John Hunter, Erasmus Darwin, and possibly Lamarck by 1833. He was consequently prepared for his visits to the Jardin des Plantes and the Hunterian Museum in Glasgow which displayed the various types of life in an ordered array showing "the upheaving principle of life everywhere incipient."[157] In his second public lecture in December, 1833, he reproduced these generally evolutionary ideas along with those of Sir Charles Bell.[158] In 1834 Emerson became acquainted with some of the morphological ideas of Goethe,[159] and in his lecture in 1836 on "The Humanity of Science" he again sounds as if he had seized upon a philosophical approach to evolution.

Lamarck finds a monad of organic life common to every animal, and becoming a worm, a mastiff, or a man, according to circumstances. He says to the caterpillar, How dost thou brother? Please God, you

---

[154] Gray, *op. cit.*, p. 45.
[155] Coleridge, *Aids to Reflection*, Comment on Aphorism No. 74.
[156] Emerson, *Journals*, I, 298.     [157] *Ibid.*, III, 163.
[158] Cabot, *op. cit.*, I, 224. *Ibid.*, II, 329 misdates the lecture as 1832.
[159] Emerson, *Journals*, III, 293.

shall yet be a philosopher.... The block fits. All agents, the most diverse, are pervaded by radical analogies; and in deviations and degradations we learn that the law is not only firm and eternal, but also alive....[160]

Another approach to this theory of development, which is not to be confused with the specific biological hypothesis of Darwin's *Origin of Species*, indicates that Emerson as a result of the unexpected attacks upon the "Divinity School Address" put less emphasis upon self-reliance, went through a period of realistic skepticism in which he emphasized experience, and then fell back upon a dogmatic optimism and "soft determinism" which depended upon a belief in "Beneficent Tendency" and amelioration, a loosely evolutionary upward spiral.[161] By the time of "The Young American" in 1844 this tendency is strong, and from this year Emerson's *Journals* also show an evolutionary cast.[162]

Further sources for Emerson's evolutionary views included Lorenz Oken and Stallo. The former he mentioned as early as 1842,[163] in the lecture on Swedenborg, and again in "Fate," where he emphasizes the effect of environment on the development of vesicles, and he seems also to have known of Oken's evolutionary theories.[164] Between Oken and Stallo there is a curious link since it was after Alcott's discussion of his illumination that the whole world was a spine (as a result of reading Oken) that Emerson gave to Alcott the lines which now preface *Nature;* and these lines were based upon Stallo's *Principles of the Philosophy of Nature* which taught that all things mount in spirals—a negation of Alcott's view.[165]

A fairly complete doctrine of evolution was set forth in Emerson's "Poetry and Imagination" in a part first delivered in 1854,[166] except for the phrase *arrested and progressive development*, which

[160] Cabot, *op. cit.*, II, 343.
[161] Stephen Whicher, "The Lapse of Uriel: A Study of the Evolution of Emerson's Thought" (unpublished dissertation, Harvard University, 1943), pp. 401-403.
[162] Emerson, *Journals*, VII, 8-9, 26, 53.
[163] *The Letters of Ralph Waldo Emerson*, ed. Ralph L. Rusk (New York, 1939), III, 76-77.
[164] Beach, *op. cit.*, pp. 342-343.
[165] Emerson, *Journals*, VIII, 77; Alcott, *Journals*, p. 211 n.
[166] Emerson, *Works*, VIII, 358.

he attributed to Hunter, but which is really by Chambers.[167] When *The Origin of Species* was published Emerson was so used to the type of ideas it contained that he was not even excited. And afterwards he sought to adjust his views to Darwin's,[168] since evolution was easily acceptable to the Transcendentalists.

Thoreau's attitude toward science and his views of nature, though difficult to work out because he usually implies rather than states them, are equally significant. It is clear by now that as a young man he was interested in nature not as a scientist seeking accurate predictability on the physical level, but as a Transcendentalist seeking a way to unlock the secrets of the spirit. It is equally clear that in his final years he became increasingly interested in finding relationships among the great batches of facts which he recorded in the *Journals*. So much so, that he has properly been regarded by scientists as a pioneer limnologist and phenologist and as an ecologist before the name was even invented.[169]

In an early *Dial* paper, Thoreau made his attitude toward science perfectly clear when he wrote, "Let us not underrate the value of a fact; it will one day flower into a truth"—a sufficiently patent statement of the view of nature as symbol, and continued:

We must look a long time before we can see. Slow are the beginnings of philosophy. He has something demoniacal in him, who can discern a law or couple two facts. We can imagine a time when "Water runs down hill" may have been taught in the schools. The true man of science will know nature better by his finer organization; he will smell, taste, see, hear, feel better than other men. His will be a deeper and finer experience. We do not learn by inference and deduction and the application of mathematics to philosophy, but by direct intercourse and sympathy. It is with science as with ethics—we cannot know truth by contrivance and method; the Baconian is as false as any other, and with all the helps of machinery and the arts, the most scientific will still

---

[167] Beach, *op. cit.*, p. 342.

[168] Pochmann and Allen, *op. cit.*, I, 678; Stow Persons, *Evolutionary Thought in America* (New Haven, 1950), p. 440.

[169] E. S. Deevey, "A Re-examination of Thoreau's *Walden*," *Quarterly Review of Biology*, XVII (1942), 1-11; Raymond Adams, "Thoreau's Science," *Scientific Monthly*, LX (1945), 379-382; Philip and Kathryn Whitford, "Thoreau: Pioneer Ecologist and Conservationist," *Scientific Monthly*, LXXIII (1951), 291-296.

be the healthiest and friendliest man, and possess a more perfect Indian wisdom.[170]

Thus Thoreau felt certain that ultimately the meaning lay in himself, not the physical world. "Instead of being 'wholly involved in nature,' he was subservient to the spirit within. This, and not nature, was the inspirer." But as the moments of ecstasy became fewer, the agony of this deprivation increased and, despite an almost desperate optimism, nearly shattered his sanity.[171] He fell back upon the recording of fact though he recognized that it represented a falling off. "It is impossible for the same person to see things from the poet's point of view and that of the man of science. The poet's second love may be science, not his first,—when use has worn off the bloom. I realize that men may be born to a condition of mind at which others arrive in middle age by the decay of their faculties."[172] Science is then for Thoreau, as for Emerson, only a symbol of a higher truth. Yet science was apparently as high as some men could ever get, and was perhaps as high as Thoreau could attain in his later life.

Though Thoreau still thought of science in 1860 as "always more barren and mixed up with error than our sympathies are,"[173] this was not the whole story. Even if he accepted science only as a second love, it is certain that his interest in natural phenomena increased as he grew older and that he finally began to apply a more sophisticated scientific method than most of his contemporaries. In *Walden* he already gave the impression of recording many natural facts for their own sakes rather than for an ulterior meaning, and this indicated an important unconscious swing in the direction of philosophical realism.[174] The last three volumes of the *Journals* also convey the fact that Thoreau was becoming increasingly scientific in his interests, seeking relations between plants and their

[170] Thoreau, *Writings*, V, 130-131.
[171] Foerster, *op. cit.*, p. 127. For Thoreau's mental strains, see Ethel Seybold, *Thoreau, the Quest and the Classics* (New Haven, 1951), p. 68; Sherman Paul, "The Wise Silence: Sound as the Agency of Correspondence in Thoreau," *New England Quarterly*, XXII (1949), 523.
[172] Thoreau, *Journals*, III, 311-312.
[173] *Ibid.*, XIII, 169.
[174] William Drake, "A Formal Study of H. D. Thoreau," University of Iowa (1948), p. 68.

habitats, and explaining the succession of forest trees. He turned to the counting of tree rings and the examination of the age of oak roots with a gusto which belied his sneers at science.

To the other Transcendentalists celestial laws proved to be of somewhat less interest. As romantics they were inspired by nature to poetic expression, but most of them concentrated on their literary and theological positions. Certain pseudo sciences did, however, prove of considerable interest to them, particularly phrenology. Dr. Kaspar Spurtzheim's doctrine of the relation of mental faculties to cranial shapes was first popularized by the publication of George Combe's *The Constitution of Man* in Boston, 1829, and Spurtzheim himself lectured there in the early 1830's. James Freeman Clarke became quite interested in this science, as did Margaret Fuller and Horace Mann, though the latter was not a Transcendentalist. Instead of accepting the view that the theory was deterministic in the sense of showing mind related to and shaped by the cranium, the Transcendentalists accepted the interpretation that moral truths could be taught and character so trained as to minimize the defects.[175] Without necessarily accepting the doctrine, Emerson, Parker, and Margaret Fuller attested to its effects.[176]

Thus it may be said that the Transcendentalists, dissatisfied with the mechanical universe of Paley and of the materialistic scientists, moved towards a romantic view of nature which accepted facts and laws as symbols of a spiritual or divine truth.[177] Their emphasis was not upon deduction of a God from the universe, *à la* Tom Paine,[178] but upon the direct perception of divine law. The views of Emerson and Thoreau were at times tinged with pantheism, yet this was not the whole story. As Bartol pointed out, "Pantheism is said to sink man and nature in God, Materialism to sink God and man in nature, and Transcendentalism to sink God and nature

---

[175] James Freeman Clarke, *Autobiography* (Boston, 1892), p. 49; Merle Curti, *The Social Ideas of American Educators* (New York, 1935), pp. 110-112.

[176] Miller, *op. cit.*, pp. 75-77.

[177] Schneider, *op. cit.*, p. 261.

[178] H. H. Clark, "An Historical Interpretation of Thomas Paine's Religion," *University of California Chronicle*, XXXV (1933), 56-87.

in man,"[179] though he cautioned that this definition was too neat. In his major period from *Nature* through *Essays, Second Series* Emerson was not an avowed pantheist, yet it appears that as his illuminated moments became less frequent, he put more emphasis upon natural law and the beneficent tendency of evolution, he made all natural instead of supernatural, and by this change of terminology and emphasis, he perhaps reverted to a clearer pantheism.[180] But no such thing should be said of Furness, Clarke, Parker, Hedge, and Alcott, who all adhered to concepts of the personality of God. At any rate it was the greatest of the Transcendentalists, Emerson, who was able to make the greatest use of previous science and to interpret an ordered universe as the basis for correspondence between matter and mind.

### III

In the field of religion the Transcendentalists caused the first immediate excitement by substituting for institutional traditionalism and belief in the revelation of God through the miracles of the New Testament, the direct intuition of a spiritual and immanent God who was still operative in the soul of each individual man. The initial conflict arose between the apostles of "The Newness" and the conservative Unitarians who were forced to a still more conservative position in the contest which followed. Many of the Transcendentalists remained within the Unitarian church, organized as it was on the Congregational system, since it had no machinery for rejecting heretics. This combat, in which Theodore Parker came to the fore, resulted later in the Free Religious Movement, which split into two wings, the Transcendentalists and the more rationalistic Scientific Theists. But this latter development lies outside the scope of this plan of discussion.

When James Marsh published Coleridge's *Aids to Reflection* in 1829, he hoped to swing the Congregational church back to idealism. But the major effect was upon a group of Unitarians who felt that religion had become too icy. This new group of divines began to find itself chilled by the "corpse-cold" institution and emotionally starved by the "pale negations" of a rationalistic religion which

---

[179] C. A. Bartol, *Radical Problems* (Boston, 1872), p. 83.
[180] Stephen Whicher, *op. cit.*, p. 402.

was more notable for the doctrines of the sovereignty of God, providence, original sin, predestination, election, and revelation through the Bible which it rejected than for positive beliefs to which it adhered. While evangelical religion had burst forth by 1801 in the Great Revival in the West, the growth of the warmer wing of Unitarianism which emerged as Transcendentalism later supplied the need for enthusiasm in the more intellectual and more sophisticated clergy.

The Unitarianism which the young and ardent group found wanting was remarkably conservative. Its members were former Federalists who did not want to be bothered by theological and social questions,[181] and though they gave up the rigorous predestinarianism and election of Puritanism, they were not unreservedly optimistic about the goodness of the nature of man, whom the Reverend Nathaniel Frothingham called a "poor worm."[182] Whigs in politics,[183] the typical Unitarians were skeptical about the value of reform and conveniently felt that society could be improved only by the gradual influence of virtuous men, which they knew themselves to be. Consequently the laymen were able to rationalize their bourgeois interests in terms of a religion which bolstered their "social conservatism."[184] (Yet it is worth noting that even Emerson and Thoreau adhered in the main to the view that the regeneration of society could come only through the regeneration of individuals.) Thus a conservative Unitarian theologian like Orville Dewey was forced, in response to liberal attacks, to accept a belief in human depravity and to suggest that Unitarians employ the terms "Father, Son, and Holy Ghost."[185]

The generally glacial quality of the Unitarian Church after the disagreement emerged is made clear by Henry Adams, who from the age of ten attended Dr. Nathaniel Frothingham's First Church:

---

[181] Stow Persons, *Free Religion, An American Faith* (New Haven, 1947), p. 3.
[182] O. B. Frothingham, *Boston Unitarianism, 1820-50* (New York, 1890), p. 13.
[183] Frothingham, *Transcendentalism*, p. 110.
[184] G. W. Cooke, *Unitarianism in America* (Boston, 1910), p. 158.
[185] Orville Dewey, *Discourses and Reviews* (written in the 1840's) in Persons, *Free Religion*, pp. 7-8.

Nothing quieted doubt so completely as the mental calm of the Unitarian clergy. In uniform excellence of life and character, moral and intellectual, the score of Unitarian clergymen about Boston, who controlled society and Harvard College, were never excelled. They proclaimed as their merit that they insisted on no doctrine, but taught, or tried to teach, the means of leading a virtuous, useful, unselfish life, which they held to be sufficient for salvation. For them, difficulties might be ignored; doubts were waste of thought; nothing exacted solution. Boston had solved the universe; or had offered and realized the best solution yet tried. The problem was worked out.

Of all the conditions of his youth which afterwards puzzled the grown-up man, this disappearance of religion p zled him most. . . . That the most powerful emotion of man next to the sexual, should disappear, might be a personal defect of his own; but that the most intelligent society, led by the most intelligent clergy, in the most moral conditions he ever knew, should have solved all the problems of the universe so thoroughly as to have quite ceased making itself anxious about past or future, and should have persuaded itself that all the problems which had convulsed human thought from earliest recorded time, were not worth discussing, seemed to him the most curious social phenomenon he had to account for in a long life.[186]

With this background it is easy to understand why the "liberal" views of the rationalistic Unitarians hardened into conservative dogma under the impact of the Transcendentalists. Indeed the Unitarians were particularly irritated because the Calvinists' prediction that Unitarianism would result in further heresy[187] turned out to be accurate.

The break of the Transcendentalists from previous Unitarian beliefs came from two principal causes: the growth of intuitive idealism and the growth of intellectual skepticism. Of these the first, probably the crucial factor, has already been dealt with in section I, while the second deserves more attention. Together they outline the paradoxical position of the Transcendentalists, who were simultaneously more spiritual than their opponents and also more doubtful of the need of revealed or institutional religion.

The inspiration of the new group was Dr. Channing, who was both an idealist and a warm and emotional advocate of personal

[186] Henry Adams, *The Education of Henry Adams* (New York, 1931, Mod. Lib. ed.), p. 34.
[187] Clarence H. Faust, "The Background of Unitarian Opposition to Transcendentalism," *Modern Philology*, XXXV (1938), 317.

religion—a man whose loftiness of character permitted him to say things that would be attacked in others. But Dr. Channing was never doubtful of the miracles of Jesus. Consequently it is Emerson, the first of the "New School" to resign his ministry, who deserves more careful consideration. As has been suggested earlier, his philosophy was already idealistic by the time he resigned as pastor of the Second Church, but this fact alone did not bring about his change of view. He found himself increasingly restless about the institution of the church. In 1831 he wrote, "Calvinism stands, fear I, by pride and ignorance; and Unitarianism, as a sect, stands by the opposition of Calvinism. It is cold and cheerless, the mere creature of the understanding, until controversy makes it warm with fire got from below."[188] Early in 1832 he said "It is the best part of a man, I sometimes think, that revolts most against his being a minister." The difficulty was that accommodation to ready-made institutions caused a loss of "integrity and . . . power."[189] Consequently he felt that "in order to be a good minister, it was necessary to leave the ministry."[190]

In his crisis over the administration of the Lord's Supper, a rite in which he no longer believed, he retired to the mountains, where he found that his first thoughts were best; and reinforcing himself with accounts of George Fox's integrity and courage,[191] he decided, himself, to be genuine and to stand on principle. This was the most important act of his career, for it gave him the moral right to speak of Self-Reliance, that is, reliance upon the intuitions of the Over-Soul. While the break did not seem necessarily final, for afterwards Emerson often preached, it was this decision which freed him from what he regarded as bondage and gave him a larger audience.

Emerson's decision was based upon a number of factors. For one thing his skepticism of dogma and of the infallibility of religious institutions was doubtless increased by his reading of Montaigne.[192] For Emerson, skepticism was the vestibule of the Temple, the clearing away of debris before building the foundations.

---

[188] Emerson, *Journals*, II, 424.
[189] *Ibid.*, II, 448-449.   [190] *Ibid.*, II, 491.   [191] *Ibid.*, II, 497-500.
[192] Emerson, *Works*, IV, 172; Charles L. Young, *Emerson's Montaigne* (New York, 1941), p. 17.

of the new belief; so he could respect Montaigne for his skepticism as well as for his sturdy individualism and independence of judgment. Furthermore, he was considerably impressed by the doctrines and character of a number of Quakers. A part of his sermon on "The Lord's Supper," the issue which he strategically picked for his congregation, was based upon Thomas Clarkson's *A Portraiture of the Society of Friends*.[193] And immediately upon his return from Europe he preached at New Bedford, where a number of Hicksite Quakers had joined the Unitarian congregation. Here he was especially impressed by Deborah Brayton and Mary Rotch.[194] He also talked of Stubler, another Quaker he had known, and of Lucretia Mott, whom he met in Philadelphia and whose wholehearted zeal he much admired.[195]

Undoubtedly Emerson was also influenced by the experience of his older brother William, who had gone to Göttingen to study for the ministry, but whose religious doubts had caused him to turn to law instead. When William talked over his problem with Goethe, the sage told him to "preach to the people what they wanted," since "his personal belief was no business of theirs."[196] But Waldo, like his brother, felt that integrity demanded the separation. Thus he left the church for a series of reasons. Had he been trained in another type of faith, his skepticism of ritual, sacrament, and institution might not have occurred, for Unitarian rationalism encouraged the sort of questioning which beset him. Or if he had been reared in a faith which accepted enthusiasm more freely, he might also have found an avenue for his abilities within the fold.

Emerson was not alone in his dissatisfaction with conventional Unitarianism, and the differences between the New School and the old were deep. The issue around which they crystallized was the value of miracles, for, as the Transcendentalists were quick to point out, it was inconsistent of a church which followed a rationalistic or common-sense philosophy to insist on the miracle

---

[193] M. C. Turpie, "A Quaker Source for Emerson's Sermon on the Lord's Supper," *New England Quarterly*, XVII (1944), 95-101.

[194] Emerson, *Journals*, III, 258-260.

[195] *Ibid.*, III, 228; VIII, 110. Cf. Paul W. Barrus, "Emerson and Quakerism," University of Iowa (1949).

[196] Rusk, *op. cit.*, p. 113.

as the sole sanction of religion. This controversy must be briefly sketched.

Although Paine had attacked miracles earlier, among the Unitarians the issue was first raised by Ripley in 1835 in a discussion of Herder in the *Christian Examiner*. Here the point was made that Herder thought it impossible "to establish the truth of any religion, merely on the ground of miracles." A miracle may call attention to a doctrine, or give authority to the teacher, but it cannot prove the truth of the assertion.[197] Such a view was potentially serious, though both Herder and Ripley themselves believed in miracles, and, as has already been noted, Furness held a rather similar view. In November, 1836, Ripley took up the subject again and added a slightly new idea, that there was no way to tell a religious miracle from a natural power without faith in the divinity of the performer.[198]

The conservative Unitarians soon began to reply to these arguments, marshaling their strength under the leadership of Andrews Norton, who led the attack by disavowing in an insulting manner responsibility for the printing of Ripley's views in the *Christian Examiner*.[199] Ripley of course rejoined with all the arts of controversy, but made it clear that the basic issue was one of philosophy. Meanwhile Martin Hurlbut's review of Furness's *Remarks* defined the issue clearly. Hurlbut thought that it would be impossible to have revelation without miracles; and he continued, "If the miracles of the Gospel are to be regarded as 'natural facts,' capable of being reduced to natural laws, and explained by them, it does appear to us, that Christianity, as a system of revealed truth, ceases to be. We are thrown back upon *mere naturalism*."[200]

At this point Emerson's "Divinity School Address" (1838) caused great excitement on both sides. Because of his serene confidence in reason, Emerson said little in favor of historical Christianity which, because it used the understanding, misinterpreted Jesus and insisted on his personality as a divinity. Here Emerson went much further than a mere denial of specific miracles; by

[197] George Ripley, review of Herder, *Christian Examiner*, XIX (1835), 195-197.
[198] Miller, *op. cit.*, p. 131.
[199] *Ibid.*, p. 159.
[200] *Christian Examiner*, XXII (1837), 122.

saying that all men had in them the same access to the divine, he denied the entire miracle of the New Testament as it was understood by the conservative Unitarians.

These sensational views were, of course, the occasion of a vigorous exchange, though Emerson himself refused to indulge in further argument. When Henry Ware, Jr., sought to draw him into a logical discussion, Emerson simply withdrew. But there was no lack of support. Andrews Norton's *Discourse on the Latest Form of Infidelity*, which was more dignified than his immediate rejoinder in the Boston *Daily Advertiser*, drew a reply from Ripley, who insisted that "The doctrine that miracles are the only evidence of divine revelation, if generally admitted, would impair the religious influence of the Christian ministry."[201] Meanwhile Brownson had challenged Norton by saying that his position showed a lack of faith in the people.[202]

At this point Theodore Parker, who was to prove himself the most important of the Transcendentalists who remained a preacher, issued a pamphlet under the pseudonym "Levi Blodgett." Parker, a Lexington man, reared in poverty and too poor to attend Harvard as an undergraduate, though he took and passed all the examinations, showed a powerful mind and prodigious energy in all his activities. Widely read—he claimed command of twenty languages—forthright and courageous, he poured forth a constant stream of expansive rhetoric, but he was also a skilled logician and a masterly conductor of argument. Though he believed personally in the miracles of Jesus, he did not see "how a miracle proves a doctrine."[203] And by appealing to the ordinary capacities of ordinary people, he hoped to prove that the conservatives were wrong, for in his writing there were no lofty mysteries.

To such straits were the conservatives reduced that Andrews Norton, laying aside for a time the old conflict between Calvinists and Unitarians, published under the title *Transcendentalism of the Germans and of Cousin and Its Influence on the Opinion in This Country* (Cambridge, Mass., 1840), two articles by the Princeton professors J. W. Alexander, Albert Dod, and Charles Hodge from the *Biblical Repertory and Princeton Review* for January, 1839. This vigorous analysis, after ridiculing Cousin, describes "the non-

[201] Miller, *op. cit.*, p. 217.   [202] *Ibid.*, p. 208.   [203] *Ibid.*, p. 229.

sense and impiety" of the "Divinity School Address" and decides that even Deism is "to be preferred to German insanity."[204]

Probably the most cogent of the series of defenses of Transcendentalist views was Parker's famous and controversial sermon on the "Transient and Permanent in Christianity," which announced his concept of "Absolute Religion," the doctrine that the human soul can intuit the permanent part of Christianity, while churches, creeds, ritual, revelation, and secondhand beliefs all partake of the transient.[205] This was of course taking the matter farther than Dr. Channing could go. Yet Parker always personally insisted that the Christian religion was the absolute religion, and it was only after the Civil War that the final doubt of even this was raised by those men who went farther than Parker—the apostles of Free Religion such as F. E. Abbott.

Without doubt the New School employed the works of German philosophers, theologians, and Biblical scholars in developing and defending their views, and they considered the Germans a liberalizing influence. Dr. Nathaniel Frothingham, one of the staunch conservatives, was asked to one of the first meetings of the "Transcendentalist Club,"[206] presumably because he was a reader of German critical works. The parade of German authors, especially theological, read by Parker and Ripley in particular is impressive: Herder, Schleiermacher, Jacobi, Eichhorn, Strauss, Steudlin, Ammon, Gabler, Hase, Wegscheider, Bauer, and especially De Wette. Parker translated and annotated De Wette in *A Critical and Historical Introduction to the Canonical Scriptures of the Old Testament* in two volumes, while James Freeman Clarke translated De Wette's *Theodore* in two volumes,[207] and Samuel Osgood translated De Wette's *Ethics*, again in two volumes, the last two being parts of Ripley's series, *Specimens of Foreign Standard Literature* (14 volumes, 1838-1842).

But neither a listing nor a detailed analysis of the use of the German theologians should be taken to indicate that Transcendentalism depended entirely upon German sources. As Brownson asserted,

---

[204] *Ibid.*, pp. 238-240.   [205] *Ibid.*, pp. 273-281.
[206] Alcott, *Journals*, pp. 78-79.
[207] De Wette furnished the model for Clarke's novel, *The Legend of Thomas Didymus, the Jewish Skeptic* (Boston, 1881).

"The movement is really of American origin, and the prominent actors in it were carried away by it before ever they formed any acquaintance with French or German metaphysics; and their attachment to the literatures of France and Germany is the effect of their connection with the movement, not the cause."[208] When an article in the *Western Messenger* agreed that there was a New School, it also agreed that the common ground among the members was not any specific doctrine or influence, but was rather a desire for more "LIFE."[209] No one foreign theologian influenced the whole group, and no one foreign theologian was wholly accepted by any of the group. The common cause of the Transcendentalists lay in a common need that was variously satisfied in detail. In general, they all felt the necessity of moving from adherence to a cold, negative, institutionalized religion, based upon an unhappy union of materialistic philosophy and belief in certain miracles, to the positive acceptance of a spiritual philosophy of a God with whom they could come into immediate and direct contact, whether or not he was held to be personal or impersonal. Their rejection of miracles as the grounding of belief in the New Testament laid them open to the claim that they were infidels and pantheists, yet they could argue that they and not the Norton camp were the more deeply religious. At any rate they were right in contending that they were not merely conservative and defensive.

### IV

Another crucial transition involved the change from neoclassical concepts of correctness, generality, and imitation in art to the romantic or Transcendental use of symbol as bodying forth the intuitive vision of the genuinely creative artist in an organic fusion of content and form. The Transcendentalists' basically religious problem was solved by a philosophical concept of the world as symbol of the mind, and the corollary of this idea of symbol carried over into their aesthetic theories and expressions. Their replacement

---

[208] Miller, *op. cit.*, p. 243. Brownson here as elsewhere goes too far; e.g., neither he nor Parker was totally unaffected by his reading of European books. In fact this rather negative statement may need revision on the appearance of Professor Henry Pochmann's forthcoming study of the influences of German thought in America.

[209] *Ibid.*, p. 203.

of a mechanistic concept of nature by a vitalistic and creative concept was paralleled by the replacement of a mechanical and formalistic aesthetic theory by an organic concept of the unfolding of form from within outward. While some, like Margaret Fuller and John Sullivan Dwight were primarily critics, Emerson and Thoreau, though they may have thought of themselves as seers, were primarily concerned with the problems of finding expressive forms in their prose and verse to articulate their insights and ideas.

Of this development Dr. Channing's "Remarks on a National Literature" were in at least one respect prophetic. For besides claiming that democratic institutions were favorable, he said that the new and higher literature would come from a new and higher religious principle. No man, he continued, can "put forth all his powers . . . till he has risen to communion with the Supreme Mind . . . till he regards himself as the recipient and minister of the Infinite Spirit."[210] Certainly it was the consciousness of such intuitions of the divine which furnished much of the fire to the Transcendentalists' literary work. And Channing's advocacy of the use of images from nature to body forth artistically the inner life of the spirit, coming after the predominantly pictorial or surface writing of Knickerbockers such as Irving, is especially important. Channing, the friend of Coleridge, pleaded for "a poetry which pierces beneath the exterior of life to the depths of the soul, and which lays open its mysterious working, borrowing from the whole outward creation fresh images and correspondences, with which to illuminate the secrets of the world within us."

Of course the Transcendentalists were not born with the new concept of literature, and both Emerson and Thoreau had to break away from the emphasis on formalized structure which had been inculcated by their Harvard teacher of rhetoric, E. T. Channing, and from the Latinate diction, abstract vocabulary, and windy parallelisms which appeared in their Harvard textbooks. What they lost in perspicuity of argument they more than made up in vividness of expression. Thoreau, in particular, in his less successful later passages even shows reversion to the flat, balanced style of his college days.

Emerson's *Nature* contains the basis of his artistic as well as of

[210] Channing, *Works*, p. 136.

his philosophical and religious ideas, but, as has already been pointed out, some of the germs appeared earlier. In 1822 he connected a material image with a moral sentiment; later he learned from Goethe the balance between form and idea (pushed in the direction of the primacy of the idea by Emerson);[211] and from 1835 he made use of Cudworth's *The True Intellectual System of the Universe*. From the latter he gained the idea of a plastic nature, *natura naturans*, which imposed the divine will on matter, and which he equated with man's ability, when he showed genius, to do the same.[212] This idea he worked out between the two essays on "Art" (1836 and 1840): in the first he emphasized the inferiority of the art object to the beholder's intuition of the divine;[213] in the second he gave Art some of the quality of *natura naturans*.[214] The first decried modern art; the second said the best art derives from the flow of the divine spirit through the artist's passive soul. Thus Emerson put a good deal of emphasis upon an inspiration that was beyond the power of the artist, and for him poetry was not meter, but "metre-making argument."[215]

Emerson had a fairly complete theory of art in which the poet by intuition seized facts from the flux of the many to set forth the one, of which truth and goodness were aspects or parts.[216] The art thus created was organic in the sense that form and content were fused, though thought was prior to form;[217] this implies a primacy of thought which may explain why Emerson is said to have called Poe "that jingle man." Yet art was not final but only initial. The creation of man was its end. Thus the audience was to be kept in the artist's mind as well, not just the work. This explains why Emerson thought that art should cheer and ennoble, and why when he was asked about *The Scarlet Letter*, he is said to have commented, "Ghastly, Ghastly!"[218]

On the question of traditionalism as opposed to innovation, he is open to more than one interpretation. Emerson saw the moral identity of all men and felt that men do not progress in time.[219]

[211] Vivian C. Hopkins, *Spires of Form* (Cambridge, Mass., 1951), p. 74.
[212] *Ibid.*, p. 64.  [213] Emerson, *Works*, II, 356, 365.
[214] *Ibid.*, VII, 39.  [215] *Ibid.*, III, 9.  [216] *Ibid.*, I, 24.  [217] *Ibid.*, III, 10.
[218] Edwin C. Mead, *The Influence of Emerson* (Boston, 1903), p. 243.
[219] Mildred Silver, "Emerson and the Idea of Progress," *American Literature*, XII (1940), 1-19.

Emphasis upon this aspect of his thought puts him into the stream from the past, and in fact with his Yankee caution he never stepped too far out of the path of tradition. Yet it is worth noting that instead of saying, If what is true for you is of all men, then you are a genius; he actually said, "To believe your own thought, to believe that what is true for you in your private heart is true for all men,—that is genius."[220] And though it is to be admitted that Emerson's Self-Reliance he felt to be God-Reliance[221] and not romantic individualism, still he was calling for the new poet who could capture the divine meaning by using as symbols "Small and mean things" and "Bare lists of words."[222] His acceptance, however qualified, of Whitman's work would seem to bear out this interpretation.[223] Emerson was at least a theoretical rebel, as his ringing declaration in *The American Scholar* makes clear. Yet his assumption that the intuition of the Over-Soul was unconditioned by either environment or personality permitted him to apply his radical insights in a conservative manner.

The same considerations must also be applied in answering the question of how rigidly moralistic his aesthetic theories were. But here he gradually overcame some of his Puritan moral background. On the other hand Emerson sometimes seemed to be descended from a long line of moralist ministers; his worry that Shakespeare had no central view of life[224] is part of this heritage. Yet he was able to accept Montaigne despite his "semisavage indecency,"[225] and from Goethe, despite his lack of moral rigor, Emerson was able to learn that a ballet should be viewed objectively and a painting as a painting.[226]

Emerson's aesthetic ideal was a controlled insight which could give a communicable experience, an experience based upon more than association of ideas as Alison's *Essay on Taste* suggested, and communicated by symbols which are more than the mannerly

---

[220] Emerson, *Works*, II, 45.
[221] *Ibid.*, X, 65-66.
[222] *Ibid.*, III, 17.
[223] Hopkins, *op. cit.*, p. 142.
[224] Robert P. Falk, "Emerson and Shakespeare," *PMLA*, LVI (1941), 532-543.
[225] Emerson, *Journals*, II, 440.
[226] Hopkins, *op. cit.*, p. 135.

metaphors recommended by Blair's *Lectures on Rhetoric*.[227] While Emerson was not opposed to revision in order to improve the expression of the poet's insights, he did not approve of the imitation of fashionable styles. Instead of being worked up by talent, art should be organic; and if it is organic, it will be recognized by readers as the genuine production of genius.

Thoreau's ideals were not too markedly different from Emerson's, since he was also interested in conveying to others his communicable insights. He too believed in the organic concept of art,[228] but with stronger emphasis upon the effects of character and training upon the genius of the artist. He believed that some physical labor was desired,[229] that a man should write as if he held a plow in his hand, and that there should be boulders in his style. In addition, Thoreau put greater emphasis upon precise expression (for him there was no such thing as a translation), and upon concreteness of fact, for he was convinced that every fact was a potential symbol.

There was in Transcendentalist literary theory a certain amount of nationalism, which went naturally with the youthful exuberance of an expanding America in a romantic period. Thoreau was, for example, content not to go to Europe with Hecker, and instead traveled extensively in Concord. Emerson, who said, "We have listened too long to the courtly muses of Europe,"[230] was certain that America would yet produce a poet. Indeed he suggested that American literature face westward and turn out more writing with the tang of Daniel Boone and Davy Crockett.[231] One of the clear aims of a group of the Transcendentalists was to publish and encourage a nonimitative American literature. Certainly the *Dial* was set up with such an aim in mind, and the verse of Ellery Channing could hardly have appeared anywhere else.

The new group also hoped to develop society by educating it

---

[227] Sherman Paul, *Emerson's Angle of Vision*, p. 131; William Charvat, *The Origins of American Critical Thought* (Philadelphia, 1936), pp. 29-30, 48-52.

[228] Fred Lorch, "Thoreau and the Organic Principle in Poetry," *PMLA*, LIII (1938), 286-302.

[229] Thoreau, *Writings*, VI, 171.

[230] Emerson, *Works*, I, 114.

[231] Hopkins, *op. cit.*, p. 144.

through the art of criticism, an aspect of the movement which shows it at perhaps its most ambitious. Despite the fact that there was relatively little painting and sculpture in the country and that public musical performances were fairly new, an attempt was bravely made to develop a criticism. Of the general critics of the arts, Margaret Fuller deserves the most attention, as leader of the "arty" group of which John S. Dwight was second in command. Intelligent, emotional, and highly trained, partly out of place in the Boston environment, she had a remarkably warm personality attractive to many women and men, and was a wonderful conversationalist. Though she never felt completely at home in writing, she was nevertheless the critic of the New York *Tribune* from 1844 to 1846, after the failure of the *Dial*, of which she was the original editor.

Margaret Fuller made a vigorous attempt to establish an objective system of criticism based upon fixed laws, though in practice she had great difficulty avoiding impressionism of a markedly emotional variety. In "A Short Essay on Critics" she tried to work out an operating theory. The first class of critics rejected by her was the subjective group, which without knowing anything about art still judges it by preconceptions. The second class she called the apprehensive, a class which would today be called impressionistic—useful popularizers but with no standards except their own responses. The right kind she considered the comprehensive critics who could feel into a work of art, but who also maintained principles and canons of judgment.[232] Unfortunately she herself vacillated between two types, the transcendental and the naturistic romantic. In the one mood she saw art as the expression of the spiritual ideal; in the other she saw the work of art as the highest growth of nature, as the ultimate goal of man.[233] But in either she was usually emotional and impressionistic.

She accepted the theory that there was a parallel between the succession of forest trees and the succession of dominant forms of art,[234] the latter expressing the dominant spirit of the age. Thus

---

[232] Margaret Fuller, "A Short Essay on Critics," *Dial*, I (1841), 5-11.
[233] Roland C. Burton, "Margaret Fuller's Criticism, Theory and Practice," unpublished dissertation, University of Iowa (1941), pp. 148-149.
[234] Margaret Fuller, "The Modern Drama," *Dial*, IV (1844), 310.

for the Greeks and Elizabethans drama was dominant, and for other ages lyrical poetry, art, or sculpture.[235] In her own age these were of low quality, and she looked toward the ballet and especially music as the great arts. Typical of the romantic tendency, she placed music at the top because of its perfect fusion of form and content,[236] and also doubtless because it offered release to her tortured and repressed emotions. Again typically, the Beethoven of the Second, Fifth, Sixth, and Ninth Symphonies was her ideal, with Handel, Bach, and Haydn following in that order.

The most celebrated music critic of the Transcendentalists was John Sullivan Dwight, who was rather a failure as a Unitarian minister, but a success as the music and Latin teacher at Brook Farm and later as a musical arbiter. From 1852 to 1881 he edited the first long-lived musical journal in the country, *Dwight's Journal of Music*. He too was an admirer of Beethoven, the transcendental composer.

While criticism was applied to all the arts by members of the new group,[237] the major emphasis was in the long run placed upon literature. With their belief in intuition as the source for inspiration, they lacked the ability or interest to work out the complex symbols required in the structure of the novel. Sylvester Judd, who wrote *Margaret* (1845), was the only Transcendental novelist. Emerson and Thoreau, in fact, did not even regard the novel very highly as an art form.[238] But though the organic theory of art offered little means for structural analysis, Emerson, at least, worked out an aesthetic theory, including the aspects of creation, of the work of art, and of the response of the audience, which embodied the theory of correspondence with some success. This theory was a radical departure from the neoclassical standards of balance, restraint, generality, correctness, and imitation which had dominated European and American taste in the previous period.

---

[235] Margaret Fuller, "Lives of the Great Composers," *Dial*, II (1842), 150.
[236] *Ibid.*, II, 152.
[237] G. W. Cooke, *John Sullivan Dwight* (Boston, 1898), p. 150.
[238] J. T. Flanagan, "Emerson as a Critic of Fiction," *Philological Quarterly*, XV (1936), 30.

V

The Transcendentalists in the economic, political, and social sphere tended to transfer their emphasis from the natural social rights of the previous age to individual integrity and the freedom of each man for maximum personal development. As a group they showed little uniformity, however, in their ideas of how this development was to take place, varying from the early reforming zeal of Brownson through the associationism of Ripley and the emphases on education of Emerson and Alcott to the extreme individualism of Thoreau's one-man revolution. Yet for all their differences—often conscious disagreements as to methods—they were in fairly close agreement in their reasons for desiring social change and advancement. They all tended to use as the standard for measuring society their intuitions of what was best, a standard of which the existing institutions always fell short. And in light of such an ideal which showed up the deficiencies of the actual, they also tended to disregard the justifications of history, of tradition, and of the past which were often adduced by conservatives who, if they did not think this the best of all possible worlds, nevertheless argued against any vigorous attempt at change.

Transcendentalism actually offered justification for opposing tendencies in American society when different aspects of the doctrine were stressed, democracy as opposed to individualism, for example, or equality as opposed to liberty. Transcendentalism, emphasizing as it did the ability of each person to come into contact with the ultimate truth, justified democracy rather than aristocracy. In this it broke with the Calvinist concept of the regenerate "elect" and the damned, who as individuals in the eyes of New England leaders were often equated with the prosperous (who were rewarded by Providence on this earth), and the poor (who were getting as much as they deserved). When given this emphasis, Transcendentalism could be a justification for majority rule and for the rights of the laboring classes. It could be argued that if all men had access to ultimate truth, the decision of a majority legislated the closest approximation of that truth, and this is the line John Dewey was emphasizing when he called Emerson the philosopher of democracy.²³⁹ On the other hand it was fairly clear to most of the Transcendentalists that most men were not actually following the moral law or, more probably, were not permitting themselves to become conscious of it. Disagreements with a man's intuitions of the absolute tended to be proof of the error or perhaps even sin of the majority. And when looking from this angle, Transcendentalism saw that political democracy was far from ultimate and that the Jacksonians showed the evils of rule by the uneducated mass; while the Democrats had the best principles, Emerson sided with the Whigs, who had the best men.²⁴⁰

Here was an ineluctable paradox in Transcendentalist political thought, since either equality or liberty, either democracy or individualism could be emphasized, but ultimately all the Transcendentalists were for improving man; the question was how this was to be done. At least four separate and distinct techniques were suggested varying all the way from (1) legislation of improvement, through (2) voluntary association and (3) education to (4) self-reform and individual action. All four were at one time or another advocated and employed.

The Transcendentalists, as vigorous individualists, departed widely from the eighteenth-century concept of social rights and the social contract. As heirs of Boston Federalism most of them failed to recognize America's revolutionary tradition. Thus there was little emphasis upon democracy in the political sense. *The Federalist* was taught at Harvard,²⁴¹ and the majority of the group were in the Federalist-Whig tradition and opposed to Jacksonian democracy. But for individualists and conservatives alike, at the end of the period the issue of slavery assumed such proportions that all showed a willingness to take group and even legislative action.

To this general attitude Bancroft and Brownson were conspicuous exceptions. George Bancroft, as a result of his education in Germany, returned to America an adherent of the Transcendental-

---

²³⁹ John Dewey, *op. cit.*, I, 76.
²⁴⁰ See John C. Gerber, "Emerson's Economics," unpublished dissertation, University of Chicago, 1941.
²⁴¹ Merrill Davis, *op. cit.*, pp. 214-215 n.

ist philosophy.[242] After a period of proving himself an advanced educator at Round Hill and a successful popularizer of German literature, he became a New England leader of the Democratic party and a dispenser of its patronage,[243] and began to write his *History of the United States* (1834ff.), proclaiming the thesis that democracy was ordained by Providence. The proof of this thesis he thought was scientific, though a more historical view would recognize it as philosophic. In a famous passage on Kant and the early Quakers he showed his Transcendentalism.

The professor of Königsberg, like Fox and Barclay and Penn, derived philosophy from the voice in the soul; like them, he made the oracle within the categorical rule of practical morality, the motive of disinterested virtue; like them, he esteemed the Inner Light, which discerns universal and necessary truths, an element of humanity; and therefore his philosophy claims for humanity the right of ever renewed progress and reform.[244]

Bancroft really meant social reform when he used the word *reform;* for him reforms could be effected only "through the masses of the people."[245] But he was never a central member of the Transcendental group, although he repeatedly praised Emerson.

Brownson, who came from a home of poverty and who did not remain a Transcendentalist, was the most vigorous politically and the most prophetic political thinker of the group. Having been influenced by Frances Wright and the Owens, he endeavored to organize a Workingman's Party about 1830.[246] His *Boston Quarterly Review* (1838-1842) was even too closely tied to the Democratic party for the taste of the Transcendentalists, who turned down his offer to make it into an organ for the group. Convinced that the election of 1840 was of crucial importance, he wrote his celebrated two-part essay on "The Laboring Classes," which, though it stirred up a hurricane of criticism at the time, is now recognized as a brilliant piece of social thought.

[242] Orie Long, *Literary Pioneers* (Cambridge, Mass., 1935), p. 134; Russel B. Nye, *George Bancroft: Brahmin Rebel* (New York, 1944), p. 101.
[243] Arthur M. Schlesinger, Jr., *Orestes A. Brownson* (Boston, 1939), p. 72.
[244] George Bancroft, *History of the United States*, II (1837), in Miller, *op. cit.*, p. 423.
[245] In Miller, *op. cit.*, p. 428.   [246] Schlesinger, *op. cit.*, pp. 19-23.

Brownson saw the real conflict in society as between the operative and the employer, with all advantages in the latter's hands.[247] The conditions of the laborer were getting worse since, as the frontier moved west, it became more difficult economically to take up new land.[248] The evil lay in the social arrangements, not the characters of either group, and could be eliminated only by changing the institutions. His program started with the premise that the power of the priesthood must be broken. Then the "proletaries" must turn to legislative enactments, first by repealing discriminatory laws and abolishing banks and other monopolies. Then must come positive laws aiding the poor. Here he went too far for the times by suggesting the end of the inheritance of property, an idea he derived from the Saint-Simonians.[249] Having tried to demonstrate that capitalism was worse than slavery, in the second article Brownson answered his critics and pushed his views even further.[250] To the idea that the poor can rise, he correctly replied that it was possible only for a few at the expense of the many, while he demanded equality as a "natural right." And if force were needed to enforce the right, as inspection of the past would indicate, then it would be forthcoming, though force might not prove necessary.

This does not seem Transcendental doctrine, though it was no less intuited than Emerson's social restraint. It was not, however, typical, and even Brownson, disillusioned in the people by the election of the Whig Harrison (1840), retreated to the view that the people, unable to see their own interests, must be protected by the operation of a Calhoun-type system of concurrent majorities.[251]

The nature and effect of voluntary associations must be considered next, leaving the question of slavery in all its ramifications until last. Such associated groups which included informal clubs like the "Transcendental" Club, occasional meetings like the Chardon Street Convention, societies in favor of peace, temperance,

---

[247] Orestes A. Brownson, "The Laboring Classes," *Boston Quarterly Review*, III (1840), 370.
[248] *Ibid.*, III, 373-374.
[249] Schlesinger, *op. cit.*, p. 94.
[250] Brownson, "The Laboring Classes," *Boston Quarterly Review*, III (1840), 420-512.
[251] Schlesinger, *op. cit.*, p. 120.

and women's rights, lyceums, and the Associationist groups like Brook Farm and Fruitlands were a characteristic of the age. They were by no means confined to the Transcendentalists, and many of the peculiar persons whose activities gave rise to the term "Transcendental nonsense" were not members of the group. The significance of these associations lies in the fact that falling as they did between legislative action and individual isolation, they furnished an outlet for the reforming ferment of the times. Some Transcendentalists were involved in each of the above movements, but only the communitarian groups can be treated here.

Of these Brook Farm is justly the most famous. George Ripley, who became increasingly dissatisfied with preaching to his Purchase Street congregation on subjects which did not closely concern him, was convinced that some form of social action was necessary. In his letter to his church on his resignation, he wrote:

There is a class of persons who desire a reform in the prevailing philosophy of the day. These are called Transcendentalists, because they believe in an order of truths which transcends the sphere of the external senses. Their leading idea is the supremacy of mind over matter. . . . These views I have always adopted. . . . There is another class of persons who are devoted to the removal of the abuses that prevail in modern society. They witness the oppressions that are done under the sun, and they cannot keep silence . . . [and] they look forward to a more pure, more lovely, more divine state of society than was ever realized on earth. With these views, I rejoice to say, I strongly and entirely sympathize.[252]

Though these were not fire-eating words, the action based upon them was more drastic than many would take. While Emerson probably came close to consenting orally to participating in the venture, he finally withdrew, saying that there was little point in moving from a small prison to a larger one.

Brook Farm, founded in 1841 upon the idea of having the scholar do some labor and thus escape some of the evils of industrialism, never flourished economically, but its school, to which Bancroft and Brownson sent sons,[253] was excellent. However, its emphasis shifted when Albert Brisbane, who had been convinced by Fourier's

---

[252] O. B. Frothingham, *George Ripley* (Boston, 1882), pp. 85-86.
[253] John T. Codman, *Brook Farm: Historic and Personal Memoirs* (Boston, 1894), p. 57; Schlesinger, *Brownson*, p. 151.

doctrines of a highly organized phalanx,[254] used his influence and persuasion to change Brook Farm over to the new form of organization in 1844.[255] This helped seal its doom, since the school attracted fewer pupils when it became associated with the more radical system.[256] Interestingly, there was a mixture of Fourier and Swedenborg in the periodical the *Harbinger* (1845-1849), which was launched at Brook Farm. This may have been the result of a need for balancing a mechanical system with a mystical religion, or simply because the complicated gradations in each fit the other.[257]

Only a shade less well known was the tragicomic experiment at Fruitlands (1842-1843). The individualistic Alcott must have been persuaded by Charles Lane to become involved in this venture, which combined many faddisms from vegetarianism and disapproval of using animals for work (or even for wool) to nudism.[258]

These experiments are difficult to assess. Products of the depression in 1837,[259] they seem to represent an attempt to escape the evident evils of industrialism by trying to return to an earlier, semifeudalistic form of organization.[260] Brook Farm, despite its poor land, might have succeeded as a school, but the collapse of all the communities indicates how much they were going against the main stream.

Not quite like any of their other avenues of expression was the Transcendentalists' emphasis upon education, though it fitted well with the view that individual development was better than political action. Alcott applied a mixture of theories to his highly efficient teaching. As a Lockean (at first) and an associationist, he believed in improving the surroundings of his schools; as a Transcendentalist he believed in bringing out the spirit of his pupils; as a New Englander he emphasized introspection. Later in life he

---

[254] Lindsay Swift, *Brook Farm*, p. 263.
[255] *Ibid.*, p. 279.
[256] Codman, *op. cit.*, p. 214.
[257] Zoltan Harazsti, *The Idyll of Brook Farm as Revealed by Unpublished Letters in the Boston Public Library* (Boston, 1937), p. 44.
[258] Clara E. Sears, *Bronson Alcott's Fruitlands* (Boston, 1915), pp. 39-40.
[259] Harazsti, *op. cit.*, p. 11.
[260] William Charvat, "American Romanticism and the Depression of 1837," *Science and Society*, II (1937), 80.

decided perhaps too conservatively, along with Greaves, that inherited constitution was a major factor.[261] Associated with him in the Temple School in 1835-1837 was Elizabeth Peabody, who preferred the Froebel technique of developing outward activity and handicraft creativity, ideas which she later applied as the founder of the American kindergarten movement.[262]

Of profound importance in this area of education was Pestalozzi, whose works were read with interest in America. Emerson cited with approval Pestalozzi's conclusion that "the amelioration of outward circumstances will be the effect, but never can be the means of mental and moral improvement."[263] And the Emersonian belief that "Education is the drawing out of the soul"[264] seems to have had a similar basis. Moreover the teaching technique which used kindness in place of corporal punishment—a technique successfully adopted by Alcott, Thoreau, and Ripley—was taken over from or was consonant with the practices of the Swiss educator.

The Transcendentalist emphasis upon individualism had its effect in another branch of education by influencing the subsequent elective system introduced much later at Harvard by Charles W. Eliot. The New Group had found it necessary to employ their own elective system at Harvard when they gained their real education by independent reading rather than from the stagnant curriculum.[265] Emerson urged that the object of education should be to remove obstructions and let "natural force have free play and exhibit its peculiar product."[266] He was also a member of the Board of Overseers which elected Eliot to the presidency, while Eliot for his part always believed that it was the Transcendentalist spirit which was the force behind the change to free election. Emerson's statement, "I would have the studies elective,"[267] was the spirit acknowledged by Eliot.

---

[261] Alcott, *Journals*, pp. 173 n., 174 n.
[262] Louise Hall Tharp, *The Peabody Sisters of Salem* (Boston, 1950), p. 319.
[263] Emerson, *Journals*, II, 416.
[264] *Ibid.*, II, 412.
[265] Clarke, *Autobiography*, p. 38.
[266] Emerson, *Journals*, III, 416.
[267] Hazen Carpenter, "Emerson, Eliot, and the Elective System," *New England Quarterly*, XXIV (1951), 23.

Certainly no less characteristic of "The Newness" was the emphasis upon self-reform, individual action, and individualism. A logical deduction from the doctrine of direct contact with God as Conscious Law, it formed the most characteristic mode of action, though it was clearly not the only one. Dr. Channing had held to the view so completely that he believed each individual should perfect himself before attempting social activity of any sort.[268] Such an emphasis, while it might help the character of the person, could actually hinder social change. Emerson's position, though less extreme, disturbed some of his more activist associates when he pursued his separate path. As he expressed it, "the only right is what is after my constitution," and he sought to practice his individualistic principle, "Every one to his chosen work."[269] His lectures on "The Times," "The Conservative," and "The Transcendentalist" took him out of social reform activity just at the instant when his associates were taking it up,[270] yet it is difficult to say that given his personality he was wrong.

The most extreme form of individualist protest was of course that of Thoreau, who wanted a minimum of government and who came as close to seceding from the state as a person can. His signing off from the church and his refusal to pay a poll tax or to vote were no less individualistic than his advocacy of the cause of John Brown. Since he wrote about his activities and thus achieved an ultimate effect through his published works, he cannot simply be called a quixotic skulker. Without claiming more than Emerson that others should follow his example—and there is never any danger of having too many Thoreaus—he offered a cogent criticism of his society by his very extremism.

The slavery crisis finally involved nearly all the Transcendentalists, whatever their previous theories of social amelioration. Even Emerson and Thoreau were so affected that they were unable to hold aloof. For this fact their very theories were responsible. Emerson with his theoretical anarchism had claimed that it was immoral to try to bind another man to anyone's insights,[271] and

---

[268] Schlesinger, *op. cit.*, p. 78.
[269] Emerson, *Works*, II, 50; "Ode Inscribed to W. H. Channing."
[270] Stephen Whicher, "The Lapse of Uriel," pp. 393 ff.
[271] Emerson, *Works*, III, 214-215.

this seemed particularly true when the law controverted his own higher intuitions. Thus the passage of the Fugitive Slave Law (1850) came as a personal shock which jolted him out of a rather more passive objection to slavery. Since it was a moral wrong, the blot must be removed before society could be improved. He was even moved to action in the extreme form of a political speech for which he was shouted down.[272] Thoreau also felt the need of active rather than passive resistance and even helped one of John Brown's raiders to escape. Such actions were not consistent with the extreme reluctance of these men to engage in group activity, but more basic was their feeling of the need to follow the dictates of their insights in whatever direction they commanded.

The leader of the group in the antislavery movement was Theodore Parker, who clearly saw that Transcendentalism had social consequences. While Parker normally used his eloquence to call on offending groups to repent rather than to call on legislatures to pass prohibitory laws,[273] he both denounced slavery and actively opposed it. His attack on Daniel Webster for his seventh of March speech, which advocated the Fugitive Slave Law, surpassed all others in vehemence.[274] Parker also took a personal part in opposing this law. He tried to whip up a crowd to attempt the rescue of the recaptured fugitive slave Sims, and Anthony Burns was close to being freed by a mob which Parker organized. (Bronson Alcott was also there.) Indeed, the opposition attempted to indict Parker for obstructing the Fugitive Slave Act, but without success.

In economic emphases the Transcendentalists varied between the extremes of Brownson's legislative reform and Thoreau's individual protest against materialism by reducing his wants. In the midground lay the ambiguous views of Emerson, who has been variously regarded as a petty bourgeois apologist and as an outstanding critic of materialism, with some evidence to back both interpretations. The question is from what part of the essay the

---

[272] M. M. Moody, "The Evolution of Emerson as an Abolitionist," *American Literature*, XVII (1945), 18.

[273] Theodore Parker, "A Sermon of Merchants," in Miller, *op. cit.*, pp. 455, 456.

[274] H. S. Commager, *Theodore Parker* (Boston, 1936), pp. 226-231.

views are extracted, since Emerson regularly constructed his lectures by ascending from the material to the moral laws. Since he felt that the laws of both levels should be obeyed, he could on the physical level emphasize a conservative laissez faire which came close to justifying the free competition of classical economics. Thus he could say that "Gravitation is Nature's Grand Vizier and prime favorite.... In morals, again, Gravity is the *laissez-faire* principle, or Destiny, or Optimism, than which nothing is wiser or stronger."[275] And on this level of law for thing, Emerson opposed charity[276] and accepted more fully than Adam Smith the view that beneficent social laws would cause a free economy to improve.[277] But even when sounding most like *Poor Richard's Almanac*, Emerson ascended by the end of a lecture to the higher realm of spirit; and it was this that made him a sharp critic of American materialism, and made the other Transcendentalists almost equally trenchant in their discussions of American society.

The prevailing individualism, the optimism, the expansionism, the manifest destiny of Jacksonian America had its echoes in the thought of the Transcendentalists too. Though the direct effect of the frontier on Emerson's ideas has been overemphasized,[278] since his thought was well worked out before he went to the West, still in a general way he, like the rest of the group, was influenced by the American intellectual climate. The exuberance which accompanied the expanding economy was part of the atmosphere which the Transcendentalists breathed. But aside from this broad influence, their ideas had been formed before the problem of society came to their attention; and the ideas they had already developed were merely carried over into the social sphere. Here their views showed a long jump from the socially rather than individually centered theories of the eighteenth century, but their individualism was both ethical and responsible. Even the most

[275] Emerson, *Journals*, VIII, 8-9.
[276] Emerson, *Works*, II, 52.
[277] John C. Gerber, "Emerson and the Political Economists," *New England Quarterly*, XXII (1949), 340.
[278] See Ernest Marchand, "Emerson and the Frontier," *American Literature*, III (1931), 149-174; Lucy Hazard, *The Frontier in American Literature* (New York, 1927), pp. 150-162; Arthur I. Ladu, "Emerson: Whig or Democrat," *New England Quarterly*, XIII (1940), 434-437.

conservative members of the group looked radical at times to the local New England public.

## VI

The Transcendentalists of New England were not pale reflections of a European movement, but an indigenous group who met American problems in a distinctive way. While they used ideas where they found them, the minds of the abler men among them were distinguished by great imaginative ability which adapted their sources to their needs with results which were strikingly different from those of their European forebears. These rebels and idealists were New Englanders, heirs also of the moral intensity and the practical ability of the earlier era. Not for nothing was Emerson called a "winged Franklin." Even such commercially unsuccessful men as Alcott had a remarkably keen judgment of people. Even so ardent an apostle of self-culture as Margaret Fuller became an equally ardent champion of the rights of women as well as of tyrannized Italy. Far from being blind visionaries, they knew what they were combating.

Most immediately they were in reaction against the sterile repudiations and cold complacency of Unitarianism. They pierced the joints in its armor as no other group was able to do. They saw clearly that the rationalistic philosophy and the acceptance of miraculous authority did not fit; that the defense of human nature against the charges of total depravity was weak if not false, when the doctrine of the mediation of Christ between man and God was still required. The New Group also attacked the sensationalism, the scientific rationalism, the common-sense realism, and the bourgeois commercialism associated with Unitarianism, though in almost every case some part of the older beliefs was transformed into something more usable.

The intuitive Transcendentalists reacted strongly against the philosophy of the Enlightenment as symbolized by Locke's *Essay Concerning Human Understanding*. Locke was impressive but unsatisfactory. Though mentioned by Emerson in "The American Scholar" as one of the able young men in a library,[279] Locke was also held by Emerson to be one of the marks of "the decline and

---
[279] Emerson, *Works*, I, 89.

not the rise of a just philosophy. With him disappeared the class of laborious philosophers who had studied Man with Plato in the belief that Man existed in connexion with the Divine Mind...."[280] The tenderer minds of the Transcendentalists could not follow Locke, and they rejected the sensationalist theories; had they been offered no ground for a new position, they would have had to invent it.

While the Transcendentalists as idealists abandoned the Lockean epistemology, with its sensationalism and associationism, they were able to build upon the foundations rather than the ruins of the eighteenth-century faith in reason, because of the romantic character of American material progress.[281] They could use Newton's laws as the basis for correspondence; and at the same time Emerson, at least on one level, could accept the doctrines of beneficent social laws. Indeed, through his dualism between physical law and moral law, Emerson could both accept the natural basis of societal laws and reject those laws as not of ultimate validity.

The major tenets and theological dogmas of the Puritans were flatly rejected. The belief in the personal sovereign God, in predestination, in original sin, in salvation of only the elect by Divine grace, in a capricious Providence, and in the Divine inspiration of the Bible were all abandoned in favor of belief in an immanent Over-Soul, in the divinity of the individual soul which could gain contact with the absolute by an intuitive process, in freedom of the will, and in the view that nature as symbol can reveal the moral laws.

Though the relationship of Puritanism and Transcendentalism still requires further study, a number of positive influences can now be pointed out. While the Transcendentalists escaped most of the dogma and theology of Calvinism, they shared its emotional qualities. Much of the zeal, introspection, soul-searching, journal keeping, industry, distrust of fiction, and moral restraint of the Puritan tradition left its mark and set the limits which prevented the Transcendentalists from imitating the less disciplined conduct of the European romantics. While retaining the intensity and exaltation of earlier New England, the Transcendentalists cast off the sense of sin

---

[280] Rusk, *op. cit.*, p. 239.
[281] Schneider, *op. cit.*, p. 261.

and inadequacy and the terror of eternal damnation whenever they could do so. Emerson, though he did not suffer from fear of Hell, certainly felt as a young man that he was inadequate in personality —cold, mean, silly.[282] On the other hand Theodore Parker, who was terrified as a child by the doctrine of eternal damnation,[283] gave up this idea, even though he was never able to abandon the exacting regimen of the Puritans which brought him to an early grave. It has been well said of the Transcendentalists that they gave to all men what the Calvinists had reserved to the elect.[284]

But in Emerson particularly the later economic doctrines have some relationship to the Puritan views which, whether engendered by early Calvinism or by the stern necessities of the struggle for existence on a bleak frontier, emphasized the qualities of thrift, industry, and prudence.[285] On the level of law for thing he opposed charity and felt that wealth was a sign of virtue.[286] Though this was not his final position, it shows an important Puritan survival in his attitudes.[287]

Finally it is worth noting that the enthusiasm which Edwards defended against the more respectable and more nearly Unitarian Chauncey is one of the more important aspects of Transcendentalism.[288] While rejecting Edwards's philosophy, for none of the Transcendentalists returned to Calvinism, they kept his emotional warmth as intuitionists of a semimystical or super-rational type.

Moreover Transcendentalism was a part of a rebellion against the cultural dominance of Europe. Edward Everett had called for an American literature,[289] and Dr. Channing had held up the ideal of an American writing which should do more than express the utili-

[282] Emerson, *Journals*, I, 362.
[283] John Weiss, *Theodore Parker* (New York, 1864), I, 30, 38.
[284] O. B. Frothingham, *Transcendentalism in New England* (New York, 1876), p. 108.
[285] Alexander C. Kern, "Emerson and Economics," *New England Quarterly*, XIII (1940), 683.
[286] Emerson, *Works*, VI, 100.
[287] Kern, *op. cit.*, pp. 682-683.
[288] Perry Miller, "Jonathan Edwards to Emerson," *New England Quarterly*, XIII (1940), 609.
[289] Edward Everett, "The Circumstances Favorable to the Progress of Literature in America," in J. L. Blau (ed.), *American Philosophic Addresses* (New York, 1946), pp. 60-93.

tarian side of American life.²⁹⁰ Emerson not only predicted an American literature, but also in poems like "Hamatraya" broke radically not only from the neoclassical, but also from the romantic tradition. The opening lines,

> Bulkeley, Hunt, Willard, Hosmer, Merriam, Flint,
> Possessed the land which rendered to their toil
> Hay, corn, roots, hemp, flax, apples, wool and wood.²⁹¹

strike a new note in American poetry. In the *Dial,* Emerson gave space to Jones Very, Ellery Channing, and Thoreau, whose "Natural History of Massachusetts" also opened up a fresh field for development. And Emerson also brought to a boil the American poet who, in *Leaves of Grass,* was most unmistakably different from recent foreign literature.

In social theory the Transcendentalists also differed from the Enlightenment, although both rejected a society of status sanctioned by revelation. The difference can perhaps be most easily stated in terms of the greater importance given by Transcendentalism to the individual, who had within him the potentiality of direct contact with ultimate reality. Consequently the loss of individual as opposed to social rights seemed the greater danger to the Transcendentalist who talked less of social contract. This difference was due in part to the fact that the American nation was based upon natural rights which represented a triumph of the Enlightenment, and the successors were able to carry the process a step farther by claiming the extreme that no individual could properly bind another by passing a law. Nor did the groups agree on the perfectibility of the world. If, as the Enlightenment held, ideas were the results of sensations, then man could be improved by giving him a better environment. But if, as the Transcendentalists believed, men's ideas came from insights into an eternal realm of total truth, then society could improve only as individuals improve. Thoreau's statement that "The sun is but a morning star" does not imply the idea of material progress. And Parker, instead of calling upon the public to pass more stringent laws to limit business, called upon the merchants to reform themselves and turn their power to goodness. These state-

---

²⁹⁰ William Ellery Channing, *Works,* pp. 124-138.
²⁹¹ Emerson, *Works,* IX, 35.

ments indicate the direction of the revolt from the more logical and mechanical theories of the Enlightenment.

Finally, whether as individuals they believed in social reform or self-reform, the Transcendentalists reacted against a bourgeois commercial money-society where position was dependent upon wealth, and not on family or culture or the intrinsic value of the individual. Emerson understood this when he said that the same sort of thinking which falling on Roman times made Stoic philosophers, "falling on Unitarian and commercial times, makes the peculiar shades of idealism which we know."[292] And Parrington felt that the absence of a commercial mentality in the South was one of the factors which prevented the appearance of a Transcendental movement there. Moreover the Transcendentalists of the clerical group, which if Veblen is right, was a sort of vicarious leisure class attached to the older aristocracy, opposed Jacksonianism partly on the above ground and partly because they unconsciously recognized the threat to their previous position of dominance. But on the positive side Transcendentalism represented the kind of rebellion against Philistinism which is vitally needed in a commercial or industrial society if its civilization is not to die.

American Transcendentalism arose in response to domestic needs and was partly shaped by the native environment. Basically the problem solved by the "Newness" was the unsatisfying coolness, rationalism, and skepticism of the Enlightenment and of American Unitarianism. In order to work out a satisfactory set of beliefs the Transcendentalists found it necessary to make a number of shifts in thought. (1) They abandoned Lockean sensationalism and Scottish Common-Sense philosophy in favor of intuitive idealism—intuitive because they were not as a group logicians. (2) Finding a mechanical universe an inadequate expression of an immanent God, they used the harmony of nature as the basis for a theory of correspondence in which phenomena became symbols of spiritual unity. (3) In religion they substituted for formal institutionalism and sterile rationalism an insistence upon the divinity of the individual soul and the validity of its apprehension of reality as superior to the sanc-

---

[292] *Ibid.*, I, 339. The diversity of opinion produced by this individualistic emphasis on shades of idealism was expressed freely in the magazine contributions of the members. For details, see Gohdes, *op. cit., passim.*

tions of historically recorded miracles. (4) In the aesthetic realm, using seventeenth century and romantic writings as examples, they decided that the organic expression of the intuitions of the reason was superior to regular and correct expression according to codified rules. (5) During a period of increasing democracy and individualism, they emphasized the development of the potentialities of each man as he was able to perceive them with his highest capacities, without necessarily considering either material prosperity or majority will as the controlling factor of central importance. In producing this loose pattern of thought the Transcendentalists made significant contributions to American culture, in philosophy, in the interpretation of science, in religious thought, in the theory and creation of art, and in social and economic thought and application.

# The Decline of Romantic Idealism
## 1855-1871

# The Decline of Romantic Idealism 1855-1871

### ⁂

*FLOYD STOVALL*
UNIVERSITY OF NORTH CAROLINA

I

THE PURPOSE in this discussion is to indicate the direction and character of the change in American literature between 1855, the date of the first publication of Whitman's *Leaves of Grass*, and 1871, the date of the publication of Eggleston's *The Hoosier Schoolmaster*, and to suggest some of the causes that contributed to the change. The period of sixteen years thus delimited is not, obviously, a distinct age in American literary history, yet the dates are not chosen arbitrarily. The first issue of *Leaves of Grass* was epochal in importance, and if the appearance of the *Hoosier Schoolmaster* was not epochal, it was nevertheless an event which, in the retrospect, takes on an increasing significance with the passing years. Whitman cut from poetry the bonds of tradition, and Eggleston did a like service for fiction in America.[1]

The span of less than two decades is really a period of transition; all the writers who came into prominence at this time belonged to two worlds, one dying and the other struggling to be born. Because

---

[1] It may be true as Professor Quinn suggests (*American Fiction*, p. 342) that the chief characters of *The Hoosier Schoolmaster* are types and that the novel has less claim to be called a pioneer in realism than Howells's *Their Wedding Journey* or James's *Watch and Ward*, both also published in 1871; on the other hand, Eggleston's work was more widely read and represented a cruder stratum of society than that of Howells or James.

they were creatures of the declining power of romanticism, their allegiance to the new power of realism was more of the head than of the heart. As we should expect, the literature produced at this time reveals contradictory qualities. New books by writers in their middle years or older take their places alongside the works of the younger generation. Speaking in general terms, the literature of this period is characterized by the gradual decline of romantic idealism, the rapid growth of materialism in public and private life, and the beginning of the new method of realism in literature.

I will attempt to explain these terms briefly, though in doing so I run the risk of seeming to try to define meanings that are of necessity indefinite. Generally I accept the dictionary definitions as they are commonly applied to literature and art. I call that romantic in which imagination predominates over fact, feeling over intellect, or the subjective over the objective point of view. I call that realistic in which fact predominates over imagination, particularly when factual situations are presented for the sake of accurate reporting rather than for a didactic purpose. Idealism is a quality of the mind which predisposes it to prefer spiritual values over material values and to cherish a belief in the will and the power of mankind to establish more and more of these values against all obstacles. Idealism may exist in harmony with realism, as it does in the novels of George Eliot, but it is wholly incompatible with materialism. I use the phrase "romantic idealism" to describe the literary expression of spiritual values in the romantic manner, and I consider that the term is appropriately applied to the work of Emerson, Longfellow, and other major American authors whose characteristic books were written during the twenty years before 1855. Materialism, of course, is a term applied to the philosophy expressed in literature, not to the literature itself.

II

Since most of the older writers continued to publish through the years which I have designated the period of the decline of idealism, it is necessary to examine some of their work in this connection. Although they were not wholly unaffected by social change, they continued writing in the romantic tradition and maintained the ideals of the earlier time. These continuations and remainders, as they may be called, of the golden age of American literature belong chiefly to New England, although they appear also in the New York area and in the South.

Literary achievement in New England reached its height about 1850 or 1855, with the publication of *Representative Men, The Scarlet Letter, Walden,* and *Hiawatha.* Of all the New England group Longfellow was the most completely romantic, especially in his earlier work. His poetry after 1855 was less sentimental and stricter in language and in poetic form. *The Courtship of Miles Standish* (1858) and *The New England Tragedies,* which were begun in 1856 but not completed until over ten years later, come nearer to realism than anything else he wrote. The hexameters of the *Courtship* are stronger and more masculine than those of *Evangeline,* and the characters are closer to life. Miles Standish himself has the stamp of authenticity. *The New England Tragedies* present true and unpleasant scenes from seventeenth-century Boston, written in a direct style which to Longfellow's public seemed prosaic. The stories have been called dull, an opinion with which I cannot agree. *The Divine Tragedy,* which was the last part of the *Christus* trilogy to be completed, though it was in large part a verse transcription of Bible texts, was free from pious sentimentality. Longfellow outgrew the taste that made him famous, and to this day the popular mind is so filled in childhood with the charming commonplaces of his early poetry that it cannot appreciate the greater realism of his later work.

Holmes, whose most important writing was done after 1855, cannot rightly be said to have turned against the romantic spirit, for he was never in sympathy with it. He liked to think of himself as an American Dr. Johnson of the nineteenth century, the enemy of sham and false sentiment wherever found. His great antagonism, however, was for Calvinism, which was a solid enough reality in his youth, and he was willing to fight it not only with reason but with sentiment if need be. He was not afraid of the implication of the new scientific hypotheses which seemed to deprive man of many of his boasted superiorities over nature, but his pleasure in promoting these new ideas derived as much from the fact that they undermined the Calvinistic dogma as from their truth.[2] In his novels he

---

[2] In *The Poet at the Breakfast-Table* (1872) Holmes writes: "What is the

condemns as inhumane (not merely as untrue) the prejudicial opinion which would condemn as sin or crime the violence of Elsie Venner and Myrtle Hazard which sprang from hereditary tendencies over which they had no control. A few touches of local color, like Colonel Sprowle's party in *Elsie Venner,* give promise of what Holmes might have done in the direction of realism if he had taken his fiction more seriously. He also felt, with Emerson, the cheerful optimism and lofty moral idealism which were characteristic of the mid-century years, and gave them free expression in a few poems, particularly in "The Chambered Nautilus." On the other hand, his novels are marred by the sensationalism that was one of the worst features of contemporary fiction. In Holmes the spirit of the enlightenment survived and adapted itself comfortably to the changing moods of the nineteenth century.[3]

Lowell, the youngest of the group here considered, had nevertheless made a reputation before 1855 in the two fields in which he most distinguished himself: in criticism with the *Fable for Critics,* and in dialect verse with the first series of the *Biglow Papers.* His later prose essays in criticism were more cosmopolitan in taste but not more original than the *Fable,* and the second series of the *Biglow Papers,* written during the Civil War, differed from the first series chiefly in their more skilful blending of the realistic elements with sentiment by the power of imagination. In the introduction to the second series Lowell wrote: "The first postulate of an original literature is that a people should use their language instinctively and unconsciously, as if it were a lively part of their growth and personality, not as the mere torpid boon of education or inheritance."[4]

---

secret of the profound interest which 'Darwinism' has excited in the minds and hearts of more persons than dare to confess their doubts and hopes? It is because it restores 'Nature' to its place as a true divine manifestation. It is that it removes the traditional curse from the helpless infant lying in its mother's arms. It is that it lifts from the shoulders of man the responsibility for the fact of death" (*Works*, III, 304-305).

[3] For a discussion of Holmes as novelist and scientist, see especially S. I. Hayakawa and Howard Mumford Jones, *Oliver Wendell Holmes* (1939), Introduction, pp. xliv-lviii, and H. H. Clark, "Dr. Holmes: a Re-Interpretation," *New England Quarterly*, XII (March, 1939), 19-34.

[4] Introduction to the Second Series of *Biglow Papers*, reprinted in the Appendix of the Cambridge Edition of the *Complete Poetical Works,* p. 443. Lowell took an optimistic view of evolution and agreed with Emerson that

This view of language, together with his example in the verses of Hosea Biglow, has had a lasting and wholesome effect on younger writers, who have been encouraged to examine afresh the living language of their time and locality.

Readers are told nowadays that the New England Transcendentalists were merely dreamers, and yet Margaret Fuller was worldly enough to be at home in a newspaper office, and Thoreau was almost as much at home on earth as the woodchuck. Emerson, though he stood at the center of the Transcendental movement and was its ablest prophet, was keenly aware of the realities of the life about him. "I embrace the common," he said to the scholars of Harvard in 1837, "I explore and sit at the feet of the familiar, the low. Give me the insight into to-day, and you may have the antique and future worlds."[5] Referring to the ten or twelve years given to the study of Latin and Greek in the school and college curriculum, he demanded, "But is not this absurd, that the whole liberal talent of this country should be directed in its best years on studies which lead to nothing?"[6] He is not the easy optimist that his detractors would have us believe. The essays in *Conduct of Life* (1860) promise no easy mastery of the world. In the first essay of the volume, which he calls "Fate," he reminds us that nature is no sentimentalist, that the world is a rough and surly place, that a man's gifts are predetermined at birth, and that he must expect to abide by the restrictions which nature imposes. "No picture of life," he says, "can have any veracity that does not admit the odious facts."[7] Nature hits the mark once in a million throws, and a masterful man is made once in a century. We cannot even be sure of our judgments of good and evil; indeed, as he reminds us, "most of the great results of history are brought about by discreditable means."[8] Dozens

---

the laws of the moral world are no less sure than the laws of the physical world. Cf. H. H. Clark, Introduction to the American Writers Series *Lowell* (1947), p. lxxxiv.

[5] "The American Scholar," *Complete Works*, I, 111.

[6] "New England Reformers," *Works*, III, 259.

[7] "Fate," *Works*, VI, 6, 11, 19. For Emerson's knowledge of science and attitude towards scientific ideas, see H. H. Clark, "Emerson and Science," *Philological Quarterly*, X, 225-260. For Emerson's attitude toward evil, see C. E. Jorgenson, "Emerson's Paradise under the Shadow of Swords, "*Philological Quarterly*, XI, 274-292.

[8] "Considerations by the Way," *Works*, VI, 256.

of other references could be made to passages in which Emerson acknowledged the grimness of life and the limitations which nature puts upon human activities. It is not too much to assert that the seeds of a realism as somber at least as that of Howells lay undeveloped in his experience.

It is not to be supposed, however, that Emerson could have been a realist by Howells's definition of the term. He had the power which he ascribes to Plato of seeing the "intellectual values of the moral sentiment," and his own ideal, like Plato's, was " a god leading things from disorder into order."[9] The disorder of things is real enough to the senses, but to the intellect it is known to be an imperfect image of reality. Emerson chides Goethe for setting actual above ideal truth: "Yes, O Goethe! but the ideal is truer than the actual. That is ephemeral, but this changes not."[10] We must learn the language of facts, and yet the vocabulary of the imagination "does not flow from experience only or mainly, but from a richer source. Not by any conscious imitation of particular forms are the grand strokes of the painter executed, but by repairing to the fountainhead of all forms in his mind."[11] It is precisely this subordination of actual to ideal truth that makes Emerson's realism unlike that of Eggleston and Howells a generation later.

Of the two remaining major New England authors, Whittier and Hawthorne, Whittier can be passed over quickly. About 1855 he began to write poems based on local scenes and characters in a style more realistic than that in which he had written his early romantic and reform verse. His idealism, however, was in no sense impaired.

Hawthorne, too, remained unchanged; but though he had been and continued to be primarily a romanticist in mood, his matter was realistic enough, and he had never been an out and out idealist.

---

[9] "Plato; New Readings," *Works*, IV, 87. John S. Harrison in *The Teachers of Emerson* (New York, 1910) says (p. 22): "In Coleridge's *Friend* Emerson found an account of a scientific method of thought which was built partly on the philosophy of Plato and partly on the teaching of Bacon." It is his opinion (p. 23) that "owing to his acceptance of this reconciliation of Plato and Bacon, Emerson adopted, as a fixed idea in all philosophic inquiry, the correlation of matter and mind."

[10] "Thoughts on Modern Literature," *Works*, XII, 329-330.

[11] "Intellect," *Works*, II, 335, 336-337.

I should not like to overstress his skepticism. Both the idealist and the realist are justified in "The Artist of the Beautiful," and only the skeptic seems undeserving of sympathy. He had great faith in man the individual, but not much in social man. He had no faith in dreams of reform through institutional change, and he was convinced that sin is an inescapable condition of human existence. If all evils should be destroyed, he suggests in "Earth's Holocaust," they would spring up again in the human heart. In "The Celestial Railroad" he satirizes the easy optimism of the forties. New England, and perhaps all of America, is characterized in Vanity Fair, where "any man may acquire an omnigenous erudition without the trouble of even learning to read," and where there is a "machine for the wholesale manufacture of individual morality."[12] Mr. Smooth-it-away, who is one of the promoters of the railroad to the Celestial City, is a type not merely of the Transcendentalist, but of all who would make salvation easier and pleasanter. Hawthorne's last and fullest statement on the effects of sin is the *Marble Faun*, published in 1860. Perhaps the author accepted the suggestion of Miriam and Kenyon that Donatello had discovered his soul through his sin and must develop his moral nature through suffering; if so, he has drawn a picture of human life which, though optimistic in the long view, is in the immediate prospect as grim as any modern realist might require. The worst of it is that each must find his own soul through his own loss and suffering; it can be neither inherited nor ingrafted.

Except in the poetry of Bryant, who was really a New Englander, the tone of literature in the vicinity of New York was somewhat lower than it was in Boston and its environs. The old Knickerbockers were being replaced in 1855 by a heterogeneous assortment of younger writers, some of them rather superficial. Cooper had died in 1851, and Irving went in 1859.[13] Halleck and N. P.

---

[12] *Works of Nathaniel Hawthorne*, II, 226. Compare E. P. Whipple's essay "Stupid Conservatism and Malignant Reform" in his *Literature and Life* (Boston, 1849, Riverside ed. 1899), pp. 322-344. "Intemperance in the advocacy of temperance, illiberality in the advocacy of liberalism, intolerance in sustaining toleration, are now the chief signs of that strange masquerade of the passions which passes with some, who are not by instinct philanthropists, under the name of philanthropy" (p. 323).

[13] As pointed out by Leonard Beach in "Washington Irving: the Artist in a Changing World" (*University of Kansas City Review*, Summer 1948,

Willis lived on until 1867, the one inactive and the other repeating himself. Bryant was absorbed in public affairs and occasions. The ground was being cleared for the erection of a new literary structure there in the last half of the century.

   Melville remained, half of New York and half of New England, divided in his origins as in his life and mind. In his early novels he had been critical of civilized man's assumed superiority to primitive man, but of man in the abstract he had a lofty opinion. In *Moby-Dick* (1851) man's pride of power was humbled, and thenceforth Melville's estimation of the human race was much reduced. At the time he wrote *The Confidence-Man*, published in 1857, he was in a mood of bitter cynicism. The book consists mainly of a series of loosely related episodes among the passengers on a steamer going from St. Louis to New Orleans. If the author meant these passengers to be representative, he judged every man to be either a simpleton or a crook. After an interval of farming and traveling, he took up writing again and was able to regain some of his confidence in himself and in humanity. The steps of this recovery through fresh philosophical inquiry are obscurely indicated in the poem *Clarel*, which was not published until 1876. Unlike Hawthorne, Melville found it impossible to devote himself wholeheartedly to writing except in the positive mood, and since his method was largely subjective, his failure to establish a right relation between the self and the universe was a major obstacle to his continued success in literature.

   Of the Southern writers, Poe was dead, Kennedy had given up literature, and only Simms remained active and worthy of consideration here. There was little if any change in his writing, either in style or in point of view, which can be attributed to a lessening of popular taste for romantic fiction. His earliest novels, like *The Yemassee* and *The Partisan*, contained minor characters from low life whose manners and speech must be accounted realistic. His heroes and heroines are perfect creatures, after the fashion of the times, but some of his secondary characters, like Captain Porgy, are believable persons. *The Sword and the Distaff* (later called *Woodcraft*) appeared in 1854, *The Forayers* in 1855, *Eutaw* in 1856, and

---

pp. 259-266), there are numerous realistic passages in Irving, particularly in *A Tour of the Prairies* and in other notes on the West of 1832-1833.

*The Cassique of Kiawah* in 1859, besides several postwar serials not published in book form. In all these, as in the earlier novels, he carried forward the tradition of Scott and Cooper and, in his attention to unpleasant detail at least, he anticipated the realism of Caldwell, Faulkner, and other moderns. He was definitely of the antebellum South, though he lived until 1870, and his realism was no more than the faithful record of observed fact which characterizes the novel in any period.

### III

A second generation of poets, most of whom were from ten to twenty years younger than the older generation, deserves but little consideration in this study. Three of these—T. B. Aldrich, R. H. Stoddard, and E. C. Stedman—were New Englanders who sooner or later joined the New York literati and contributed to their mixed character of journalism, aestheticism, and bohemianism in the third quarter of the nineteenth century. In the poetry of Aldrich the moral idealism that gave power to the older poets was drained away. "In him," it has been said, "Puritan morality, after passing through Hawthorne, half artist and half moralist, becomes wholly artistic."[14] Stoddard was a latter-day romanticist who fancied himself a poet in the manner of Keats. Stedman retained something of the New England love of great causes, as seen in his poems to John Brown and Lincoln, and he was able sooner than his contemporaries to see the worth of *Leaves of Grass*, but on the whole his poetry counts for little. Bayard Taylor and George Boker, both Pennsylvanians, were popular poets of their time, but now, except for a few poems by Taylor and Boker's verse tragedy *Francesca da Rimini* (1856), they are unread. J. G. Holland wrote two long poems that were popular in their day; one of which, *Bitter-Sweet,* describes a New England family reunion at Thanksgiving and develops the theme that, through evil, a person may be taught the value of good. Emily Dickinson, who wrote many of her poems during the sixties but published none during those years, was also among those inheritors of Transcendentalism whose idealism had been impaired by a growing consciousness of the critical spirit of the later nineteenth

---

[14] Norman Foerster, *Cambridge History of American Literature*, III, 35.

century. In her poetry sentiment hardens into wit and the reality of daily living is illuminated by brilliant metaphor.

The counterparts of these writers in the South were Henry Timrod and Paul H. Hayne, both of whom were active during the war period (Timrod died in 1867). Their poems are smoothly written and in the conventional forms; their favorite themes are love, patriotism, and nature; and they are highly idealistic in tone. But these poems do not move readers any longer.

More important is Sidney Lanier, who was just beginning to learn to write in 1871, but had written two dialect poems on real life, "Thar's More in the Man than Thar Is in the Land" (1869) and "Jones's Private Argyment" (1870), and a fragment of a poem on the peasant rebellion in medieval France, "The Jacquerie" (1868), which has passages that get close to real problems, though drawn from books rather than life at first hand. Lanier participated in the postwar consciousness of the importance of science, which he tried to reconcile with Christian idealism, being therein faithful to the lessons of his favorite college teacher, James Woodrow.[15] What he could not accept was the materialism of modern business philosophy. Though his poems were frequently ornate, in "The Revenge of Hamish" (1878) he shows his power to present a story of cruelty and wrong without sentiment or preaching.

In a more realistic vein, but less important as poetry, are some of the verses of Bret Harte and the *Pike County Ballads* (1871) of John Hay. Harte's poems are a mixture of realism and sentiment, like his stories, but are on the whole less successful. The life of the cabin, the mining camp, and the gambling hall is there, somewhat glamorized, but real enough to be felt. Hay's Pikes are perhaps also somewhat sentimentalized for popular consumption, but they speak the dialect of the Middle West and they have the habits, not always

---

[15] After leaving Oglethorpe University in 1861, Professor Woodrow was installed as the first holder of "the Perkins Professorship of Natural Science in its Relations to Revealed Religion" at the Columbia Theological Seminary, Columbia, S. C. He said he believed the Bible "is absolutely true, in the sense in which it was the design of its real author, the Holy Spirit, that it should be understood," and that "nothing will be found inconsistent with it in the established teachings of natural science." (See Fred Kingsley Elder, "James Woodrow," *South Atlantic Quarterly*, XLVI [Oct., 1947], 487.) For the influence of Woodrow on Lanier, see Philip Graham, "Lanier and Science," *American Literature*, IV (Nov., 1932), 288-292.

polite, of the frontier. Poetry by its very nature is a less suitable vehicle for the commonplaces of realism than prose.

It may seem that the poetry of Whitman is proof to the contrary, for there is in it an indubitable adherence to the commonplace, the trivial, and the ugly that must be classified as realism. But these commonplace things remain prosaic unless transformed by the arrangement of words which creates new values of emotion or meaning. These new values are generally, though perhaps not necessarily, romantic or idealistic, or both. In the first poem of the 1855 *Leaves of Grass*, for example, we have the following lines:

> The carpenter dresses his plank.... the tongue of his foreplane whistles its wild ascending lisp,
> The married and unmarried children ride home to their thanksgiving dinner,
> The pilot seizes the king-pin, he heaves down with a strong arm.
> The mate stands braced in the whaleboat, lance and harpoon are ready,
> The duck-shooter walks by silent and cautious stretches,
> The deacons are ordained with crossed hands at the altar....[16]

Of this group of six lines, picked almost at random, the first is certainly poetry and the second prose, while the other four are in between, but all attempt to describe real and commonplace actions. The difference seems to be in the words themselves, in their rhythm, and in the associated meaning evoked by the words.

Another feature of Whitman's poetry that passes for realism in verse or prose is the use of incongruous expressions or indelicate terms. Note the incongruity of the following:

> Stout as a horse, affectionate, haughty, electrical,
> I and this mystery here we stand.[17]

Of indelicacy and poor taste there are numerous examples. Two will suffice:

> I keep as delicate around the bowels as around the head and heart,

and

> The scent of these arm-pits is aroma finer than prayer.[18]

These lines are realistic enough, but they are not poetry. The de-

---
[16] *Leaves of Grass* (1855 edition), p. 21.
[17] *Ibid.*, p. 14.   [18] *Ibid.*, p. 29.

termination to write this kind of verse is the result of holding a theory of art that requires inclusiveness rather than selectivity, or else it comes from an adolescent desire to shock the reader. Both causes operated to shape Whitman's practice, but the theory was the more lasting.

In the edition of 1867, and in all editions thereafter, Whitman put first the inscription later entitled "One's-Self I Sing," in which he expresses his intention to sing of the whole man—not "physiognomy alone," but man's "physiology complete, from top to toe." It was an intention only in the sense that it describes one of the themes of the poems contained in the volume for which "One's-Self I Sing" stands as an inscription. Actually all the physiological poems had been written eight, ten, or even twelve years before, and none were written afterwards. The catalogues of commonplace things and incidents and the frank description of the body and its functions make up the principal elements in Whitman's realistic verse, and these, including *Children of Adam*, were written early, chiefly before 1860.

There is also a good deal of satire in Whitman's early verse. In the 1855 version of "Song of Myself" are these lines:

Here and there with dimes on the eyes walking
To feed the greed of the belly the brains liberally spooning,
. . . . . . . . . . . . . . . . . . .
They who piddle and patter here in collars and tailed coats. . . . I am
    aware who they are . . . and that they are not worms or fleas.[19]

Still more bitter are passages in other poems, particularly several in the poem later entitled "Faces"; for example:

This now is too lamentable to face for a man;
Some abject louse asking leave to be . . cringing for it,
Some milknosed maggot blessing what lets it wrig to its hole.

This face is a dog's snout sniffing for garbage;
Snakes nest in that mouth. . I hear the sibilant threat.[20]

Most of the literal reporting of fact and the sharp satire were kept in Whitman's later editions, but nothing of the kind was written after 1860.[21]

[19] *Ibid.*, p. 47.    [20] *Ibid.*, p. 83.
[21] There are several good studies of Whitman in relation to the complex

*Drum-Taps* (1865) contains a few poems composed in something like the vehement style of 1855-1856 and others that give literal descriptions of hospital scenes. "Eighteen Sixty-One" and "Beat! Beat! Drums!" have a warlike spirit, and "The Wound-Dresser" fairly drips blood, but pity and sadness in these poems give them a mellow tone. Whitman's later realism, as in "The Return of the Heroes" (1871) and "Song of the Exposition" (1871)—to use their later titles—was intended to convey a sense of the nation rather than of the individual and to evoke pride more than to shock or astonish.

After 1860 Whitman's poetry tends to conform to conventional patterns and to express with lyric ardor the idealisms of democracy and liberal Christianity which earlier had been partly obscured in his poetry by the multitude of gross facts and images. There is little doubt that Whitman deliberately aimed to exemplify the qualities of the poet described in Emerson's essay "The Poet" (1844), the uniter of man and nature, the liberating god, the sayer, or that Emerson hoped, when he first read *Leaves of Grass*, that at last he had found the American poet for whom in the essay he said he had looked in vain. The idealism of Emerson does not therefore decline in Whitman but expands and seeks fulfilment in organic life. Whitman hoped that he might harmonize this earlier American idealism with the unfolding materialism of the middle and latter part of the century. One of the discouragements he had to face was the moral breakdown of the nation following the Civil War, which seemed to clear the way for unrestrained materialism. Yet though he was disappointed and angry, he did not lose faith in the people and bravely called for a race of poet-prophets who should lead them to wisdom. These hopes were somewhat confusedly expressed in *Democratic*

---

intellectual movements of his time, showing that he could see both sides of a debatable question. The following are mentioned as especially suggestive: Mrs. Alice L. Cocke, "Whitman's Indebtedness to the Scientific Thought of His Day," The University of Texas *Studies in English*, XIV (July, 1934), 89-115; Leon Howard, "For a Critique of Whitman's Transcendentalism," *Modern Language Notes*, XLVII (Feb., 1932), 79-85; Emory Holloway, "Whitman as Critic of America," *Studies in Philology*, XX (July, 1923), 345-369.

*Vistas* (1871), which is no doubt an accurate picture of the state of Whitman's mind during those distressing years.[22]

## IV

Although, as I have indicated in the foregoing discussion, the work of nearly all the major writers of the middle portion of the nineteenth century shows elements at variance with the predominantly romantic and idealistic tone of the period, we must turn to the younger prose writers, most of whom were of minor importance, for fuller evidence of progressive decline. The decline first manifests itself negatively in an increase in sentimentality and sensationalism, and then positively in the growth of humor and realism, in popular literature. I call sentimentality and sensationalism negative because they result from degrading good qualities of the ideal and the romantic, and I call humor and realism positive because they are new and valid qualities which tend to counteract the ideal and the romantic.

Sentiment is a quality inherent in all literature, and even sentimentality can generally be found on the lower levels. In the United States the excess of sentiment in fiction probably derives from the novels of Samuel Richardson, which were popular well into the nineteenth century, and had many imitators, notable among whom were Mrs. Rowson in *Charlotte Temple* (1794) and Hannah Foster in *The Coquette* (1797). In poetry, the pious effusions of Mrs. Hemans in England and Mrs. Sigourney in this country set a standard for tearful females that was widely imitated in both prose and verse. There can be little doubt, however, that in the thirties and forties the overwhelmingly popular novels of Bulwer, Dickens, and Charlotte Brontë were the principal literary influence on American writers of sentimental fiction.[23] In this country Miss Sedgwick's *Hope Leslie* (1827) and *The Linwoods* (1835), though they are historical romances, are examples also of the novel of domestic

---

[22] *Democratic Vistas* was based on two earlier essays, "Democracy," published in December, 1867, and "Personalism," published in May, 1868, both in the *Galaxy;* and on a third essay, "Orbic Literature," submitted to the *Galaxy* (see Whitman's letter to his mother dated April 28-May 4, 1868), but not published there.

[23] Cf. Alexander Cowie, *The Rise of the American Novel*, p. 415.

virtues and so were influential in preparing the way for the sentimental romance.

These literary antecedents do not, however, account for the wave of sentimental fiction that swept the country between 1850 and 1860 and continued long after the Civil War. To be sure, every age has its counterpart of this literature, but what we have to account for is the extraordinary demand for it in the middle of the nineteenth century in the United States. I believe the principal causes are local and may be stated as follows: (1) the humanizing of the old religion, (2) the excess of women over men in the population of New England, and (3) industrialization. Calvinism had never recovered from the deistic attacks upon it in the late eighteenth century, and with the spread of Unitarianism, and then Transcendentalism and all kinds of strange cults besides, the old dogmatic religion was greatly softened and humanized. Moral zeal was substituted for theology in many respects, and this soon found an outlet in reform movements of all kinds, from temperance to the abolition of slavery. At the same time, particularly in New England, there was an exodus of men from the country, some temporarily in the increasing maritime trade, and some permanently in the large-scale migrations to the Middle West and the Pacific Coast. The lonely woman waiting for her lover or husband to return from the East Indies or from California and turning eventually perhaps to the black crepe and the solace of books and pets, was a characteristic element in village society. With slavery producing more and more cotton in the South, New England found her mills always larger and more numerous, and to operate them great numbers of homesick girls were gathered from farm and village homes, augmented by immigrants from Europe, to live in boardinghouses and dream of romance and marriage that would free them from drudgery.[24] These were the conditions that chiefly accounted for the immense popularity of the sentimental and pious romance.

For years this type of reading had been supplied by the annuals and by *Godey's Lady's Book,* and even magazines like *Graham's* and *Knickerbocker* were ready markets for such wares. The book which set the pattern for the sentimental romance, Susan Warner's

[24] See Witt Bowden, *The Industrial History of the United States* (1930), pp. 201 f. See also *post* p. 362.

*The Wide, Wide World*, published in 1850, was perhaps more popular in that decade than any other novel except *Uncle Tom's Cabin*. This is the story of a pious and tearful little girl who must live unwanted with an unlovely aunt, but who becomes a paragon of virtue and wisdom and eventually marries a very superior young clergyman. Two years later Susan Warner published *Queechy*, also about a little orphan girl who is very good and clever, though abused by unsympathetic relatives. She finally marries the wealthy and brilliant English gentleman who, having first observed her virtues when she was ten years old, has been waiting ever since to marry her. Other romances in this vein are *The Lamplighter* (1854), by Maria S. Cummins of Salem, which provoked Hawthorne to make the wellknown profane comment on a "mob of scribbling women," Mary Jane Holmes's *Tempest and Sunshine* (1854), Augusta Jane Evans's *Beulah* (1859) and *St. Elmo* (1866), and a hundred other best sellers from E.D.E.N. Southworth to E. P. Roe and finally Laura Jean Libbey, whose *Little Leafie* no historian has ever deigned to mention in the chronicles of American literature. Of all these stories the sentimentalists of a century ago might say what the publishers said in an advertisement of one of Mrs. Caroline Hentz's romances: "We defy any one to read aloud the chapters to a listening auditory, without deep emotion, or producing many a pearly tribute to its truthfulness, pathos, and power."[25]

In spite of a plethora of tears and piety and the rewards of virtue, both spiritual and material, among the heroes and heroines of these romances, they sometimes contain genuine pictures of domestic life and characters that are as real as your next-door neighbor. The real people are invariably minor characters, and usually the scenes are in rural or village communities. This practice of idealizing the hero and heroine while permitting minor figures to appear real is characteristic of popular writers and can be seen in today's Hollywood productions. In a review of *Wide, Wide World* and *Queechy* in the *North American Review*, Mrs. Caroline Kirkland writes:

[25] From a leaf of advertisements of books by Mrs. Hentz bound in with the first edition of her *Planter's Northern Bride* (Philadelphia: T. B. Peterson and Brothers, 1854).

.. we must place their pictures of American country life and character above all their other merits, since we know not where, in any other language, we shall find their graphic truth excelled. When after times would seek a specimen of our Doric of this date, Aunt Fortune will stand them in stead; and no Theocritus of our time will draw a bucolical swain more true to the life than Mr. Van Brunt. Even the shadow of Didenhover is a portrait.[26]

This is high praise, perhaps too high, but it comes from one whose own early book on life in the Middle West "contained certain bitter pills of realism."[27] and who might therefore be expected to judge fairly. It may be that readers of *Wide, Wide World* and *Uncle Tom's Cabin* were not so engulfed in tears that they were blind to the real merits of these books, for even a modern reader will find some good things in them.

Not all contemporary reviewers were so well pleased as Mrs. Kirkland, however. In July, 1854, an editorial note in *Putnam's Magazine* begins:

A most alarming avalanche of female authors has been pouring upon us the past three months, nearly all of whom are new. . . . The success of Uncle Tom and Fanny Fern has been the cause, doubtless, of this rapid development of the female genius, but among these new books by ladies, we recognize the names of some familiar and popular authors.[28]

And two years later, in the same department, we read:

It is with no small pleasure that we hear, from many booksellers, the announcement of a perceptible falling off in that class of books which go among the trade by the name of 'sensation-books.' . . . Without original merit of any kind, and appealing merely to the sensibilities and not to the reason and conscience, they were a species of debauched literature, and every one must be glad that the day for their disappearance has come.[29]

Alas! the poor editor was too easily made glad, as he must have discovered before long, for the avalanche continued, and still continues.

[26] *North American Review*, LXXVI, 115.
[27] Cowie, *op. cit.*, p. 225.
[28] *Putnam's Magazine*, IV, 110.
[29] *Ibid.*, May, 1856, VII, 546. The authoritative work on this class of fiction is Herbert R. Brown's *The Sentimental Novel in America* (Durham, N. C., 1940).

Some of these ladies had a good deal of sharpness in their temperament; Mrs. Parton, for example, who wrote under the name of Fanny Fern. In her *Ruth Hall* (1855) the heroine is a much-abused young lady who, like the author, becomes a successful journalist. Mrs. Parton, who was the unappreciated and unappreciative sister of N. P. Willis, withers a good many people with her satire, including her natty brother. Already she had published a series of sentimental, pious sketches, short narratives, and brief essays emphasizing virtue and gently reproving small vices, and she had become one of the best paid journalists of the day.

Like her more famous brother Mrs. Parton pursued literature on the level of popular journalism. Others, like Donald Grant Mitchell and George William Curtis, combined gentle satire with sentiment on a higher level. Both young men were writing during the fifties in the manner of Irving, and so carried on a tradition of charming literary essays long after the Civil War. Mitchell's earliest volumes, *Reveries of a Bachelor* (1850) and *Dream Life* (1851) reflect the temperament of his mind, for he kept apart from the social and political ferment of the time. *My Farm of Edgewood* (1863), *Wet Days at Edgewood* (1865), and later writings have echoes of Emerson and Thoreau. Curtis, as a youth, was at Brook Farm; and he was thereafter active in reform movements of various kinds, including abolitionism. He too wrote much in the manner of Irving and felt the moral idealism of the Channing-Emerson lineage. His *Potiphar Papers* were made up-to-date by reflecting the manner of Thackeray as well as that of Irving, but he could not be said to equal Thackeray in realism. In his most famous book, *Prue and I* (1865), pleasures of the hearth and the imagination are shown to be more satisfying than worldly possessions. In these books one sees moral idealism in the retirement of private life, whereas in most of their New England contemporaries it was carried into the public arena.

The crusade against slavery aroused many writers to use their talents for other than purely artistic purposes. Among other famous instances, like the poems of Whittier and Lowell, I need only mention the most famous novel of the time, Harriet Beecher Stowe's *Uncle Tom's Cabin* (1852), which was followed by many others, most of them combining propaganda with the lush sentiment of the domestic romance. In some of these, as in *Uncle Tom's Cabin*, there is a good deal of realistic detail and some very good characterization. One of the best of these novels is J. T. Trowbridge's *Neighbor Jackwood*, published in 1857. The principal scene of this story is a rural community in Vermont. The best part of the novel is the Jackwood family, including Abimelech Jackwood, his wife, his wife's mother, the forlorn and inconsolable Granny Rigglesty, his daughter Phoebe, age sixteen, his son, also Abimelech, age ten, and his son's troublesome dog Rover. All these are realistically, vividly, and humorously portrayed, and the rustic dialect sounds convincing. The slave hunters are suitably brutal, and the heroine, an escaped slave, beautiful, cultured, and almost white, is too good to be true. The descriptions of the New England countryside are said to be accurate, and were based on observations made by Trowbridge on the spot in the summer of 1854.[30]

There were also, after the publication of *Uncle Tom's Cabin*, numerous novels written to show that slavery in the South was more humane than it had been painted. Perhaps the best of this group is Mrs. Caroline Hentz's *The Planter's Northern Bride* (1854). Mrs. Hentz was a Northern woman by birth, but she married a Southern man and lived in the South many years. As we should expect, the planter and his bride are perfect, and all the Negroes are perfect except one, who has been persuaded to revolt by an abolitionist posing as a minister. The abolitionist himself is altogether bad. The bride's father, a New Englander and an abolitionist, but a reasonable one, is convincingly portrayed. Although Mrs. Hentz's work belongs to the class of the sentimental romance, this particular story is less tearful than the rest.

Just as idealism easily degenerates into sentimentality in second-rate writers, so romanticism degenerates into sensationalism when the great romancers are succeeded by their imitators. It is easy to trace this decline from Scott through Cooper, Simms, and J. H. Ingraham to Sylvanus Cobb, Jr., and the dime novel. It is not necessary to dwell upon the vulgarization of romantic art. The way

[30] The story was dramatized for the Boston stage, and on the first night it was hissed by the proslavery part of the audience, but the antislavery spectators came to the rescue with such cheering that the play was a success (Trowbridge, *My Own Story*, pp. 229-230). The play also "had a considerable run" in New York in May, 1857, and was published the same year.

was prepared for sensationalism in fiction when Robert Bonner took over the New York *Ledger* in 1851 and opened its pages to writers of lurid adventure and sickly sentimentality. Pattee says, "More than any other man, Bonner put a blight on 'the flowering of New England' at the time when its richest fruitage was due to come."[31] Ingraham had indicated what might be done as early as 1836 with *La Fitte; the Pirate of the Gulf*, but Cobb's *The Gunmaker of Moscow* (1856) set the pace. With the establishment of the firm of Beadle and Adams in 1860, the success of the dime novel was assured. It has had a long and, in its fashion, a distinguished career, inheriting Buffalo Bill, Kit Carson, and other Western heroes, all of whom lived and fought according to a pattern concocted in the brain of the prolific writer, or perhaps in that of the editor.[32] The Western story had its counterparts in stories of crime and crime detection and in modifications of the sentimental romance. The two stock themes of adventure and love account for the thousands of stories that fill the pulp-paper magazines today.

At their worst, sentimental and sensational novels provide a ready means for a vicarious sensual indulgence that may lead to complete intellectual debauchery. E. P. Whipple, writing in 1870, has his Mr. Hardhack to exclaim:

Why, during the last three or four months I have been through a whole course of sensational novels, and, in imagination, have married more wives than Brigham Young, and committed more homicides than Captain Kidd; and I flatter myself I have got the whole secret of the thing. It's whiskey for the mind, sir,—the regular, raw, rotbrain fluid of the Devil's own distilling. What do you suppose is to become of the intellect and hearts of a generation which takes to such a terrible tipple?"[33]

[31] Fred Lewis Pattee, *The Feminine Fifties* (1940), p. 184.
[32] For a recent discussion of the dime novel, see Henry Nash Smith, "The Western Hero in the Dime Novel," *Southwest Review*, XXXIII (Summer, 1948), 276-284. For a full account of this type of fiction, see Edmund Pearson, *Dime Novels* (Boston, 1929), and also the monumental work by Albert Johannsen, *The House of Beadle and Adams and the Dime and Nickel Novels; the Story of a Vanished Literature* (Norman, Oklahoma, 1950), 2 vols.
[33] "Mr. Hardhack on the Sensational in Literature and Life," *Atlantic Monthly*, XXVI, 195. Professor Noah Porter (later president) of Yale College writes in *Books and Reading* (New York, 1871) that (pp. 97-98) many novels and magazine stories "are simply a reflex of the commonplace aims

Mr. Hardhack also noticed a parallel sensationalism in art, religion, and popular science. Perhaps it was symptomatic of a spiritual disease which attacked the American people about the middle of the last century and quickly became epidemic—a disease for which we have not yet found the sovereign remedy.

V

Society, like nature, usually provides a corrective for an unhealthy growth in the organism, and so it was with the romantic novel, and with the sentimentality into which moral idealism had begun to deteriorate. This corrective was humor, which began to be a popular element in American writing in the second quarter of the nineteenth century, about the time of the political ascendancy of Andrew Jackson. It seems probable, as one historian of humor suggests,[34] that newspaper humor and Jacksonian democracy were equally expressions of the rising importance of the less refined classes in American society. Generalizations of this kind, however, do not reveal the whole truth. Most of the readers of sentimental and sensational fiction are young and semiliterate, whereas many cultivated readers turn to humor as a relief from over-refinement in serious literature and for the sake of the ridicule which it casts upon the follies of the day. It is not surprising, therefore, that New England, by a kind of revulsion, turned to the humorist as early and as readily as the Southwest, where no literary traditions existed. The Middle Atlantic states and the states of the old Northwest were somewhat behind the Northeast and Southwest in the field of humor until after the Civil War.

Among Down East humorists, Seba Smith, the creator of Jack Downing, was a newspaper editor, and most of the contributions of other humorists appeared in newspapers before they were collected in books. Jack, the Yankee peddler, was widely imitated and became so famous that in many remote places his name was synonymous with Yankee. T. C. Haliburton, of Nova Scotia, created

---

and vulgar feelings of the mass of readers for whom they are written." This kind of literature, he declares, "stimulates and inflames the passions, ignores or misleads the conscience, and studiously presents views of life that are fundamentally false."

[34] Walter Blair, *Native American Humor* (1937), pp. 38-39.

Sam Slick,[35] who was also a Yankee peddler and hardly less famous than Jack Downing. Perhaps equally deserving, though somewhat less popular, was B. P. Shillaber's word-twisting Mrs. Partington, a genuine character who could have been made the heroine of a realistic novel a generation or two later. The *Life and Sayings of Mrs. Partington* was published in 1854, but most of the stories and sketches had appeared periodically in the forties.

One of the more gifted of the New England humorists writing before the Civil War was Mrs. Frances M. Whitcher, whose most famous work, the *Widow Bedott Papers* (1856), first appeared anonymously in Joseph C. Neal's *Saturday Gazette* in the forties. These are dialect sketches of a village widow of uncertain age whose sharp tongue is sheathed while she tries to catch a husband, but works with a vengeance once her case becomes hopeless. There are some good exposures of village character types and the usual gossip. Another volume, published in 1867, includes a series of letters written by the Widow Spriggins about happenings before and leading up to her marriage with Jabez Spriggins, a country school teacher. As a girl she was a great reader of romances, and especially of one entitled *Children of the Abbey*, by which she lives and judges all other persons. The humor and satire consist in the distortion of words and a fantastic imitation of the manners and speech of the melodramatic books she reads. She refused to marry Jabez until he accepted Lord Mortimer as his model.

Lowell, mentioned earlier in this essay, must be included among the New England humorists in dialect. In the earlier *Biglow Papers*, the poet's angry resentment against the war with Mexico is not reconciled with his humor. In the second series, though again aroused by a more serious war, he is sometimes able to exchange the warlike for the idyllic mood, as in "The Courtin'" and parts of "Mason and Slidell" and "Sunthin' in the Pastoral Line." His character of Birdofreedum Sawin is less convincingly real than Jack Downing and the Widow Bedott. The general tendency of the poems, however, is towards realism, and the prestige of Lowell's name helped to popularize the use of rustic dialect.

[35] The name of this hero, but not much else, was borrowed by S. A. Hammett, a New Yorker sojourning in Texas, for his *Piney Woods Tavern; or Sam Slick in Texas* (1858).

In contrast with the restraint of Down East humor, the humor of the Southwest was rude and hilarious. The fabulous exploits of Mike Fink and David Crockett are far from realistic, but the doings of one of their successors were decidedly so. This was George W. Harris's hero, Sut Lovingood, the type of a class of people all too common even yet. These stories first appeared in the New York *Spirit of the Times* in 1854, though Harris had contributed other humorous sketches to this paper as early as 1845.[36] They were collected and published in 1867 as *Sut Lovingood's Yarns*. Sut prides himself on being, next to his father, the "durnedest fool" outside the asylum, or Congress, and he admits that he is always stumbling into traps that wouldn't catch a sheep.[37] He is violent and coarse and can be cruel in his pranks, but he is not stupid or mean-spirited. Sut has been called "a unique and original character in American humor," whose "vivid imagination and Rabelaisian touch" have not been surpassed.[38] Walter Blair has said that "in *Sut Lovingood*, the antebellum humor of the South reaches its highest level of achievement before Mark Twain."[39] Sut's world of gross and loveless reality is akin to that in which the twentieth-century naturalist moves; but whereas Sut admits that he is a "durned fool," the hero of the naturalistic novel takes himself seriously.

In the South the fashion in humor was somewhat less boisterous. Longstreet's *Georgia Scenes* (1835) was written in a style nearer the Down East stories of Jack Downing than those of the Southwest.[40] The author of this book was a lawyer, and his style retains something of the flavor of eighteenth-century prose, but the incidents and characters are drawn from his own observations in rural Georgia, and where dialect is used it is authentic. Similarly Judge Baldwin, in *Flush Times of Alabama and Mississippi* (1853), writes essays on frontier life, but with more of satirical intent. His characters are chiefly lawyers and their clients, and his incidents are court trials and matters that bring men into courts of law. The satire is directed at the bombast, chicanery, and crudity of the early

---

[36] Franklin J. Meine, Introduction to *Tall Tales of the Southwest* (1937), p. xxiii.
[37] *Sut Lovingood's Yarns* (1867), p. 30.
[38] Meine, *op. cit.*, pp. xxiii-xxiv.
[39] Blair, *op. cit.*, p. 101.
[40] Yet cf. Meine, *op. cit.*, p. xvi.

settlers. Another book of Southern humor, J. J. Hooper's *Adventures of Simon Suggs* (1845), has more of the characteristics of the tall tale. Simon Suggs is a picaresque hero, a thorough rascal, very different from Sut Lovingood in character, though the world in which they move is the same. Sut is a prankster merely, whereas Simon is a rogue; in the former we see the ridiculous and in the latter the virulent aspects of frontier life. These early humorists, and others writing in their style, had discovered by 1850, as Walter Blair points out, "most of the things [America] was going to laugh at, and thereafter authors played variations on themes already announced."[41]

During and shortly after the Civil War a new group of humorists arose who became critics of politics and society in general and so shifted the focus of humor from the local region to the nation as a whole. Most of them were showmen as well as writers and won their greatest acclaim on the public platform. The first and perhaps the most famous of this group was Charles Farrar Browne, a native of Maine, who went to work at seventeen on *The Carpet Bag*, B. P. Shillaber's comic weekly, where he met many other humorists in verse and prose.[42] He soon left Boston, however, and after various engagements as journeyman printer and reporter, became a contributor to the Cleveland *Plaindealer* in 1858 and began to sign his articles "Artemus Ward."[43] His first book was published in 1862, and he died in the midst of his fame in 1867 while living in London. Ward was the first of a succession of soberfaced platform humorists whose stories, irresistibly funny to his auditors, are merely amusing when read. He was a genial critic, his comedy never made bitter by prejudice or ill temper. Chiefly he laughed at the overserious and the sentimental. In his letter on agriculture addressed to the President of the Barclay County Agricultural Society, he wrote: "To me the new-mown hay is very sweet and nice. The brilliant George Arnold sings about it, in beautiful verse, down in Jersey every summer; so does the brilliant Aldrich, at Portsmouth, N. H. And yet I doubt if either of these men knows the price of a ton of hay to-

---

[41] *Op. cit.*, p. 104.
[42] J. T. Trowbridge, *My Own Story*, pp. 181-182.
[43] Melville D. Landon, in Biographical Sketch prefixed to *Artemus Ward: His Works, Complete* (1875), pp. 12-13.

day."⁴⁴ His spelling is sometimes freakish, but he never depended on this trick of writing as much as some of his contemporaries.

Other postwar humorists may be disposed of briefly. David Ross Locke won fame during the Civil War, writing under the pseudonym of Petroleum V. Nasby, a Northern Democrat and a Copperhead. *The Nasby Papers* were published in 1864, and were said to have pleased Abraham Lincoln very much. The President is reported to have remarked to Charles Sumner in 1865: "For the genius to write these things I would gladly give up my office."⁴⁵ Nasby was in fact a scoundrel so base and vulgar that surely only the heat and prejudice of war could have made him palatable to the generous mind of Lincoln. The satire, once accepted, is very telling nevertheless, and in places, one reluctantly admits, even amusing. A Southern humorist, Charles H. Smith of Georgia, may be mentioned with Locke because they both wrote of the war, though on opposite sides, and both addressed letters to Lincoln. Smith wrote as Bill Arp, "so called," and though his satire is less effective than that of his Northern counterpart, his letters are in better taste and more amusing. Of many others who might be mentioned, I name only two: Robert H. Newell and Henry W. Shaw. Newell was only incidentally a humorist, though he is probably better known as the punster Orpheus C. Kerr (Office-Seeker) and flamboyant satirist of newspaper style than as the author of various novels and poems. Shaw, writing as Josh Billings, the typical crackerbox philosopher, carried the freaks of spelling to such an extreme that he is practically unreadable today. He did not begin to write until he was forty, but he is one of the most voluminous of the lot, having ten volumes to his credit. Many of the sayings of Josh Billings are proverbial, and if they were divested of the peculiarities of illiterate form they would be as acceptable as those of more serious philosophers.

In attacking sham, folly, pretense, and sentimentality wherever found, these humorists, their contemporaries, and their successors have done a genuine service to literature and to society. They also helped to keep the nation sane before and after the Civil War and, not least of all, encouraged the use of greater realism in serious literature. As we have seen, the sketches and stories of several of

---

[44] *Artemus Ward*, p. 96.
[45] Quoted by Jennette Tandy in *Crackerbox Philosophers*, p. 123.

these humorous writers are local and realistic in character, and may justly be called early examples of local-color fiction. Two at least of the early local colorists, Bret Harte and Mark Twain, were closely affiliated with the humorists. Both were writing for *The Californian* between 1864 and 1867, and during these years both were developing the style which later brought them fame.[46] Mark Twain's ridicule of the romantic and the sentimental, beginning in the sixties and continuing throughout his career, did much to eliminate them from serious literature.[47]

Twain's "Celebrated Jumping Frog" (1865) was but an improved version of a kind of story already current, and the anecdotal structure of *Innocents Abroad* (1869) was an adaptation and improvement of the pattern of books in the Southern and Southwestern tradition of humorous literature. The literary development of Mark Twain from burlesque comedy to the high humor of *Huckleberry Finn* and finally to the embittered satire of *The Man That Corrupted Hadleyburg* illustrates both the strength and the weakness of American idealism surviving through frontier conditions and failing under the stresses of materialism in the Gilded Age.

Bret Harte, though he did most of his writing after 1871, never

[46] For discussion and examples of the early writing of Mark Twain and Bret Harte for the *Californian*, see *Sketches of the Sixties* (San Francisco: John Howell, 1926). See also Ivan Benson's *Mark Twain's Western Years* (Stanford, 1938). Mark Twain was for a while a reporter on the San Francisco *Call*, and he also wrote for the *Golden Era* in 1863-1864 and for the *Alta California* in 1866. *Innocents Abroad* was the first of several books by Mark Twain (cf. comment of Stuart P. Sherman in the *Cambridge History of American Literature*, III, 20) in which, as in *A Connecticut Yankee*, he "debunks" the romantic past of the Old World, paralleling in this the serious histories of Henry C. Lea, beginning with *Superstition and Force* in 1866.

[47] The bibliography of books and articles on Twain's early writing is too extensive to be given here; but see an interesting pamphlet by a foreign critic, S. B. Liljegren: *The Revolt against Romanticism in American Literature as Evidenced in the Works of S. L. Clemens* (Upsala, 1945). The question of early influences on Mark Twain is too difficult to be discussed. It may be mentioned, however, that Mark Twain may have got from an early acquaintance he met in 1856 in Cincinnati, a Scotchman named Macfarlane, a suggestion of the bitter mood to be found in his later writing. He quotes Macfarlane as having said that "man's heart was the only bad heart in the animal kingdom," and that "man was the only animal capable of feeling malice, envy, vindictiveness" and various other evil moods. See *Autobiography*, I, 146.

outgrew his earlier manner; he is more representative of the years immediately following the Civil War than of the Gilded Age proper. His parodies in the *Condensed Novels*, issued in 1867 in book form, but written for periodical publication, some of them as early as 1864, attest the continuing popularity of the sentimental and romantic novel and also the willingness of readers to laugh at them. Since laughter is often the beginning of criticism, these parodies mark a trend in favor of realism in fiction. With his mingling of sentiment and realism and humor, Harte, like his master Dickens, will be recognized as a transitional figure. His first great short story, "The Luck of Roaring Camp," published in the *Overland Monthly* for August, 1868, is a compound of local color and Western humor. This story, together with "The Outcasts of Poker Plat," "Tennessee's Partner," "Miggles," and others published within the following two years, made Harte's reputation and paved the way for the success of other writers in the field of the local-color short story, which, in the meantime, had been also making progress elsewhere.

## VI

Attacks on sentiment and unreality in fiction were not confined to the humorists or to the post-Civil War period. The editors of the two new magazines founded in the fifties, *Putnam's* and the *Atlantic*, called upon novelists to write of life as it really is. We do not want, says a writer in *Putnam's*, "a monstrous assemblage of grotesquely illusive pictures of life and nature, interlarded with inconceivable sentiments, unheard-of adventures, and impossible exploits," but "veritable and veracious segments of the great life-drama, displaying Nature and Man as they are, sentiments as they are felt, and deeds as they are done."[48] The *Atlantic* printed careful reviews of each of George Eliot's books as they appeared, beginning with *Scenes of Clerical Life* in May, 1858. Says the reviewer: "Novelists recognize that Nature is a better romance-maker than the fancy, and the public is learning that men and women are better than heroes and heroines, not only to live with, but also to read of. Now and then, therefore, we get a novel, like these 'Scenes of Clerical Life,' in which the fictitious element is securely based upon a

[48] "Novels: Their Meaning and Mission," *Putnam's Magazine*, IV (Oct., 1854), 391.

broad groundwork of actual truth, truth as well in detail as in general." Soon, thinks the reviewer, "the unreal ideal" will be "confined to the second-rate writers for second-rate readers."[49] The following year a reviewer says of *Adam Bede*: "The place and the people are of the simplest, and the language is of the simplest, and what happens from day to day, and from year to year, in the period of the action, might happen in any little village where the sun shines."[50] Of George Eliot's style in her next book, *The Mill on the Floss*, the *Atlantic* reviewer writes in praise that it is "strong with Saxon words that admit of no equivocation or misunderstanding." Some critics, he suspects, will find fault with "the tedious growth of a miller's boy and girl" through so many pages, but he himself thinks this the best part of the book.[51]

It would be incorrect to conclude from the tone of these reviews that American literary taste was changed quickly from the romantic to the realistic by the novels of George Eliot. There were elements of realism in Dickens and still more in Thackeray, and both these men had been favorites in this country for years before George Eliot began to be known. Our literary fashions continued to lag behind those of England and Europe, so much so that our writers were still chiefly influenced by Bulwer and Scott through the fifties, by Dickens and Thackeray through the sixties and early seventies, finally catching up with George Eliot only in the late seventies and early eighties.

To say this, however, is but to speak a half-truth, because the American novel was subject to conditions which did not exist elsewhere and was not parallel in its development to the English novel. These conditions peculiar to the United States—New England puritanism, the frontier, emergent nationalism, and others—are too well known to need reiteration here, but it is not always admitted that

[49] *Atlantic Monthly*, I (May, 1858), 891.
[50] *Ibid.*, IV (Oct., 1859), 522.
[51] *Ibid.*, V (June, 1860), 756. Professor Noah Porter (*Books and Reading*, p. 230) thinks readers will unconsciously imitate an admired novelist. Whereas the reader of Dickens will be inclined to adopt his slang, free and easy society, and his broad caricature, the reader of Thackeray is likely to be "not a little satirical, suspicious, and dissatisfied." The admiring reader of George Eliot will "take a pensive view of our human life, sympathize hopelessly with its sorrows and its tragedies, and above all, with its moral enigmas, seeing for it no redemption and no hope."

they have helped to give American literature a distinct individuality. On the other hand, our writers were subject to many of the same determining circumstances as writers abroad, particularly the rise of the laboring classes in the social scale, the growth of industrialism, social reform, the impact of science on men's thinking, and the decline of religious authority.

Not all the stories that came out of the West were humorous or satirical; some were, even before 1855, seriously descriptive of real places and people. Mrs. Caroline Kirkland's *Western Clearings*, published in 1845, was such a book. It consists of sketches and stories of life in Michigan about 1835, and it represents some of the settlers as energetic and prosperous while others are easy-going and poor. "As to the ordinary manners of the back-woodsman," she writes in the preface, "not a word can be said in their favour. They are barbarous enough. Yet he is a gentle creature in sickness; and when death comes to the family of a friend or neighbour, his whole soul is melted, and his manners could not be amended by false Chesterfield himself."[52] Another book about the Middle West which has realistic elements is Alice Cary's *Clovernook; or, Recollections of Our Neighborhood in the West*, published in 1852. It consists of sketches of places and people remembered out of the author's past. The style is smooth and somewhat melancholy in tone. The details are not sentimentalized, but have the quiet, reflective, mild tone of things not sharply but pleasantly remembered. The experiences recorded are generally sad, sometimes even drab, not altogether unlike the *Spoon River Anthology*, but less bitter. Of one character it is said: "And Annie Heaton lived on—hopelessly, aimlessly. Few persons knew her—none loved her."[53]

One of the transitional writers of fiction in the fifties and sixties was J. G. Holland, who was for a while on the staff of the Springfield *Republican* and who in 1870 became the first editor of *Scribner's Monthly*. His first novel, *The Bay-Path* (1857) was based on the history of Springfield, Massachusetts, in the first half of the

[52] Kirkland, *Western Clearings*, Preface, p. vii.
[53] Alice Cary, *Clovernook*, p. 137. Alice Cary's novel *Hagar, a Story of To-Day*, also published in 1852, is a confused and melodramatic story of the love of a minister and a country girl. It contains some realistic scenes from boardinghouses of New York where the girl lived before her baby was born and whence her lover took their child, leaving her in poverty and misery.

seventeenth century. Descriptions of people and their manners, religion, and superstitions are true to the facts and sometimes vivid. There is a neurotic minister who stirs up the passions of the settlers with stories of witchcraft that bring two persons to trial in the General Court at Boston. Holland's second novel, *Miss Gilbert's Career, an American Story* (1860) is one of the earliest stories of life in a New England mill town. The moral seems to be that a woman's place is in the home and that she should not seek a career, even in writing. There is a good deal of moralizing and sentimental piety, but also some satire on the kind of fiction that is written by young women without experience of life. Some realistic pictures are drawn of the life of mill workers, for example this description of a sleeping room for men in a mill boardinghouse:

Arthur and Cheek entered the wood-shed, and climbed the dark stairway. On entering the hall, they found a few dim lamps burning, and the atmosphere pervaded by the stench of unclean breath and unclean clothing. Sitting on his trunk, surrounded by half a dozen boys, one foul-mouthed fellow was singing an obscene song. Another was on the floor, near the stove, greasing his boots. Others, still, were already in bed, cursing those who would not permit them to sleep. Old men of sixty, and boys of almost tender years, were crowded into this dirty hole, where there was no such thing as privacy, or personal decency, possible. All heard the same foul songs, all listened to the same obscene stories, all alike were deprived of the privilege of reading and meditation; nay, of prayer itself, had such a privilege been desired. It was a place where health of body and of mind was impossible, and where morals would inevitably rot.[54]

During the following ten years the wretched life of the mill town was to be described with increasing frequency in fiction, becoming the dominant theme in the early novels of Elizabeth Stuart Phelps, whose work will be discussed further on.

The uncertainty of a period of transition is clearly illustrated in the three posthumous novels of Theodore Winthrop, a young man of great gifts who could never direct his energies to a single purpose, and who was killed in one of the first battles of the Civil War. His first-published novel, *Cecil Dreeme* (1861), is a belated Gothic romance somewhat in the manner of Hawthorne. *John Brent*, published the same year, is of most interest to us in the present study.

[54] Holland, *Miss Gilbert's Career*, pp. 142-143.

# THE DECLINE OF ROMANTIC IDEALISM 347

The story begins in California, moves eastward across the continent, and ends in London. There is a vivid description of the Pike who has left his native cottonwood country to seek his fortune in the West.

He is hung together, not put together. He inserts his lank fathom of a man into a suit of molasses-colored homespun. Frowsy and husky is the hair Nature crowns him with; frowsy and stubby the beard. He shambles in his walk. He drawls in his talk. He drinks whisky by the tank.[55]

His description of the Mormon immigrants on the way from Lancashire to Utah has something suggestive of the meanness of life in shops and mills of England:

They were the poorest class of townspeople from the great manufacturing towns,—penny tradesmen, indoor craftsmen, factory operatives,—a puny, withered set of beings; hardly men, if man means strength; hardly women, if woman means beauty. . . ! . There were children among them already aged and wrinkled, ancient as the crone . . . for any childish gayety they showed.[56]

Other passages describing the hard-featured Mormon prophet and a craftsman's shop in England constitute the chief realistic passages in the book. The mood of the story is romantic. The third novel by this author, *Edwin Brothertoft* (1862), is a story of the American Revolution and the years preceding along the Hudson River. Edwin is a patriot and a democrat, but he is weak; his wife is selfish and vulgar but strong. There is no idealization of character but an indication at least that the author, with all his romantic machinery, is feeling his way towards the fictional manner which Henry James later developed.

At a time when old ways are becoming outmoded and new ones adopted more in keeping with the spirit of the times, a vigorous magazine editor can exert a great deal of influence. This Lowell and others in the editorial offices of the *Atlantic Monthly* did in the first ten years following its establishment in 1857.[57] Many well-known

---

[55] Winthrop, *John Brent*, p. 10. For good descriptions of the northwest, see Winthrop's *The Canoe and the Saddle* (1863).

[56] *Ibid.*, p. 96.

[57] For Lowell's encouragement of Mrs. Stowe to use more realism, see Charles E. Stowe, *The Life of Harriet Beecher Stowe* (Boston, 1889), p. 334. Oliver Wendell Holmes, a regular contributor to the *Atlantic*, may have

writers modified their style to suit the editorial policy of the *Atlantic*, notably Rose Terry Cooke and Harriet Beecher Stowe. The former modified her romantic manner, earlier adapted to the needs of *Graham's* and *Harper's*, and with "Eben Jackson," published in the March, 1858, number began a series of studies of New England village life more detailed and localized than anything done before, except in the sentimentalized versions of Susan Warner. Eben Jackson goes to sea to earn money enough to enable him to marry Hetty, who waits faithfully for him twenty years and then learns of his death. Like so many others of this period, the story begins in an uncompromising realistic vein, but ends on a romantic and idealistic note. Rose Terry Cooke begins her story "Miss Lucinda" (*Atlantic*, August, 1861) by warning the reader that she offers him "no tragedy in high life, no sentimental history of fashion and wealth, but only a little story about a woman who could not be a heroine."[58] Yet this woman who was not a "heroine" lived a useful and cheerful life in her small sphere, and, eventually, she experienced the happiness of love and marriage, though her lover was certainly not a romantic hero. Rose Terry Cooke continued to write occasionally for the *Atlantic* for many years, but she never wrote a better story of local color than "Miss Lucinda."

Mrs. Stowe was a woman of versatile talent. After winning fame in the field of sentimental and sensational fiction with *Uncle Tom's Cabin* (1852) and returning to the antislavery theme less successfully with *Dred* four years later, she turned to the life she knew, the village society of New England, which generally revolved about the minister and the church, and in 1859 produced her first really good novel, some think her best, *The Minister's Wooing*. The characters, especially Dr. Hopkins and Mary Scudder, are well drawn and have the air of real people, the pictures of life in a New England town

---

helped to liberalize the opinions of its readers on science and religion. He also participated in the movement towards greater use of local color in fiction. See H. H. Clark, "Dr. Holmes: A Re-Interpretation," *New England Quarterly*, XII (March, 1939), 28.

[58] *Atlantic Monthly*, VIII, 141. Cf. this statement in a review of *Adam Bede* in the *North American Review*, LXXXIX (Oct., 1859), 547: "The romance of common life has of late years found so many exponents, that it now maintains a fair balance against the attractions of high life and aristocratic emotions."

about 1790 seem authentic, and Puritanism is made to seem no better or worse than what we know it to be from historical sources. It may be of significance that *The Minister's Wooing* began to appear serially in the *Atlantic* in December, 1858, a few months after the publication of George Eliot's *Scenes of Clerical Life*, which was reviewed in the same magazine in May.[59]

The only other novel of Mrs. Stowe's that need be mentioned here is *Oldtown Folks* (1869), which is perhaps inferior as a novel to *The Minister's Wooing*, though it is a masterpiece in the field of local color. The sketches of village life, based it is said upon the reminiscences of her husband, Professor Calvin Stowe, who is himself identified with one of the principal characters,[60] and such inimitable characters as Sam Lawson, the village gossip, lovable Grandmother Badger, sharp-tongued Aunt Lois, the benevolent Miss Mehitable, and the soul-starved Miss Asphyxia Smith—these hardly have their equals in the pages of any other American novel. There is also a story about two orphans, who turn out to be too good and too conveniently derived from a wealthy English family, but it is not the story that makes the book important. The values of Sam Lawson were not exhausted in the novel, for two years later Mrs. Stowe brought out *Sam Lawson's Fireside Stories*, for which she had also drawn freely upon her husband's talent for story telling.[61] Her last novel, *Poganuc People* (1878), is another study in village life somewhat in the manner of *Oldtown Folks*.

If one had to name a single person as typical of the literary class in the postwar decade, surely that person would be Bayard Taylor. He early became known as a poet and writer of travel books, but he

---

[59] Mrs. Stowe and George Eliot were good friends and corresponded with some regularity. In a letter to George Eliot dated Feb. 8, 1872, she apologizes for not answering sooner a letter written by George Eliot in 1870 and adds: "Yet I have always thought of you, loved you, trusted you all the same, and read every little scrap from your writing that came to hand." In the same letter she mentions Darwin's theory of natural selection as one of the "curious studies into nature" which interest her but do not occupy her mind seriously. See *Life and Letters of Harriet Beecher Stowe*, edited by Annie Fields (1897), pp. 335, 337.
[60] Constance Rourke, *Trumpets of Jubilee* (1927), p. 135. See also the introductory note to the Riverside edition of *Oldtown Folks*.
[61] Charles E. Stowe, *The Life of Harriet Beecher Stowe* (1889), pp. 439-443.

also wrote four novels, none of them much read today, and yet they are not trivial or dull. The first was *Hannah Thurston* (1862), which he subtitled, like many other nationalistic and ambitious novelists of the period, *A Story of American Life*. The setting is a small town in New York, and the general purpose of the book is to satirize the reformers of the middle of the century—Perfectionists, Cimmerians, Spiritualists, and Feminists. The heroine, Hannah, is a strong-minded woman of thirty, a Quaker and a champion of woman's rights, who sometimes speaks at public meetings. The plot of the story is to get her to fall in love with Maxwell Woodbury, thirty-six, who believes a woman's place is in the home rather than on the public platform. The plot succeeds, they are married, and the story ends with a pretty picture of Hannah as a happy mother. The book gives an interesting account of life in an "advanced" rural community, with its sewing circles, reform associations, and New Thought advocates.

Taylor's second novel, *John Godfrey's Fortunes* (1865), also "a Story of American Life," is a first-person narrative of a young man's attempt to build a career in literature. The story ends romantically with the hero's marrying a beautiful heiress, but there is much in it that is doubtless true to the life of literary circles in New York between 1845 and 1860. As the author states in the Preface, this book, like *Hannah Thurston*, "is the result of observation. Not what ought to be, or might be, is the proper province of fiction, but what is." John Godfrey is undoubtedly the author himself, and many of the other characters have been recognized as notable contemporaries, such as FitzJames O'Brien, R. H. Stoddard, and Estelle Ann Lewis, for Taylor was essentially a reporter.[62] It is good reporting and effective satire. Note this description of the "poetess" Adeliza Choate in a frenzy of inspiration:

> I feel the approach of Inspiration in every nerve;—my husband often tells me that he knows beforehand when I am going to write, my eyes shine so. Then I go upstairs to my *study*, which is next to my bedroom. It always comes on about three o'clock in the afternoon, when the wind blows from the south. I change my dress, and put on a long white gown, which I wear at no other time, take off my stays, and let my hair down my back. Then I prance up and down the room as

---

[62] See R. C. Beatty's *Bayard Taylor* (1936), pp. 237-238.

if I was possessed, and as the lines come to me I *dash* them on the black-board, one after another, and chant them in a loud voice. Sometimes I cover all four of the boards—both sides—before the Inspiration leaves me. The frail Body is overcome by the excitement of the Soul, and at night my husband often finds me lying on the floor in the middle of the room, panting—panting! [63]

This story too has its bit of low life in a by-street filled with "a very disagreeable smell," such as may be found, the author says, "wherever the poor Irish congregate."[64] There is much in the manner of the story which suggests Howells's theory of realism. In a statement which doubtless expresses Taylor's own views, John Godfrey says:

It is no part of my plan to make of myself an immaculate hero of romance. I fear, alas! that I am not a hero in any sense. I have touched neither the deeps nor the heights: I have only looked down into the one and up towards the other, in lesser vibrations on either side of that noteless middle line which most men travel from birth to death.[65]

The third novel, *The Story of Kennett* (1866) has its setting in the Quaker community of Kennett Square, in eastern Pennsylvania, where Taylor was born and to which he returned with his family in 1859 to build a fine house and settle down—for a while. In his preface addressed to his Kennett neighbors he said: "I am aware that truth and fiction are so carefully woven together in this Story of Kennett, that you will sometimes be at a loss to disentangle them." The hero and heroine are idealized, but the hero's father, who had married in secret and refused to acknowledge his wife and son for fear of losing his inheritance, is presented as a weakling and a scoundrel. The heroine's father is about as bad. A completely sentimental novel would have uncovered some fact, hitherto concealed, which in the end would have exonerated both of them. But no such concession to sentiment is permitted.

Taylor's last novel, *Joseph and His Friend* (1870), somewhat less realistic and even melodramatic at times, does not contribute to the purposes of this study. It is well to mention in passing, however, a novel by T. W. Higginson, *Malbone: An Oldport Romance* (1869), which in its principal character comes nearer the standard

---

[63] *John Godfrey's Fortunes* (1865), p. 273.
[64] *Ibid.*, p. 300.   [65] *Ibid.*, p. 320.

of realism to be set by James and Howells than any other of this decade. A reviewer in the *Overland Monthly* has this interesting comment on Philip Malbone:

> Mr. Higginson seems to have recognized the fact that very ordinary people become interesting under analysis, and that motives are much more fascinating to the better class of romance-readers than actions; and he has preferred rather to interest us with an analysis of the character of his hero "Malbone," than by any of the ordinary cheap dramatic tricks of action. In brief, we actually have a hero, who—without being externally endowed beyond his species as we meet them in society; without doing anything very extraordinary, or saying anything extra-fine; without being preternaturally heroic, brilliant, wicked, gloomy, or eccentric, but being, in fact, a man whom we should vaguely call a good fellow—is really the central and exciting figure in a romance. One can easily conceive how, under such conditions, society may be made interesting, and even heroic; and how Mr. Higginson may fill his novels with the men who fill our drawing rooms, by simply picturing them from other than the drawing-room viewpoint.[66]

Unfortunately the novel as a whole is not equal to its hero. Aunt Jane's caustic wit and the author's occasional wry humor are in the vein of realism; but the lovely young ladies, Hope and Kate, belong to the sentimental romance, and the overdramatic plot and sensational climax were perhaps a concession to popular taste.

William Dean Howells and Henry James belong properly to a later period, but since both began to write fiction before 1871 they deserve at least a brief notice in this essay. Howells may be said to have entered the field of fiction with *Their Wedding Journey* (1871) and to have indicated therein the direction of his development toward realism in the novel. Nothing exciting happens, but the characters are remembered as if they were real people one has met and not been greatly impressed with. Commenting on this fact, Howells remarks at one point: "As in literature the true artist will shun the use even of real events if they are of an improbable character, so the sincere observer of man will not desire to look upon his heroic or occasional phases, but will seek him in his habitual moods of vacancy and tiresomeness."[67] Thus it is apparent, and his

---

[66] *Overland Monthly*, III (Sept., 1869), 294-95.
[67] Howells, *Their Wedding Journey* (Boston, 1871, 1895), pp. 86-87.

reviews and editorial policy bear out the fact, that he had already by 1871 begun to formulate the theories of realism in fiction by which he is now best known.

Henry James reprinted in his first volume of short stories and novelettes only two that had been printed before the end of 1871: "A Passionate Pilgrim" and "Watch and Ward," both of which appeared in the *Atlantic* during that year. He had written earlier for the *Atlantic*, however, about a dozen stories, long and short. His "The Story of a Year" appeared there in March, 1865. The next year another story, "A Day of Days," appeared in the *Galaxy* for June 15. Other stories appearing in the *Atlantic* include "A Landscape Painter" (1866), "My Friend Bingham" (1867), and "Poor Richard" (1867). Although these stories lack the finish of later work, they illustrate his characteristic absorption in the personal lives of people, apart from any involvement with political, economic, or social problems. In the *Atlantic* for October, 1866, he has an article reviewing George Eliot's novels. He points out that there is usually a low and a middle life in her novels; he prefers the low life. He finds her novels lacking in imagination, but not like Trollope's, totally destitute of it. "What moves her most is the idea of a conscience harrassed by the memory of slighted obligations."[68]

Along with the novels of Mrs. Stowe, Holland, Taylor, and others whose works seemed not to be greatly affected by the Civil War and the economic disruption of this period, it will be appropriate to speak briefly of two juveniles that were widely read and had enough literary excellence to enable them to last to our own times. I refer to Louisa Alcott's *Little Women* (1868), which, with all its childish tears, is yet a story of real girls, and to T. B. Aldrich's *Story of a Bad Boy* (1869), in which the boys are just bad enough to be real, but neither sweetly good nor wickedly irresponsible. In their humor they are as restrained as the local-color novel of this period is restrained in its realism.

---

[68] *Atlantic*, XVIII, 492. Professor Lyon C. Richardson says in the notes to *Henry James* (1941), p. 483, that George Eliot was the subject of eight essays or reviews by James between 1866 and 1885. Several novels by Trollope and George Eliot were reprinted in *Harper's* during the early sixties. On James's early realism, see Cornelia P. Kelley, *The Early Development of Henry James* (Urbana, Ill., 1930), pp. 82-91, 122-127.

## VII

We have seen that the decline of idealism in American literature was a gradual and irregular process and that many causes operated to bring it about, some of which have already been discussed. We have observed also that as moral idealism and romantic adventure disappeared from fiction, realism was introduced, sometimes in the form of satire and the ludicrous tall tale, and sometimes in the form of greater attention to details of place and character, or local color. At the very height of the romantic period there was a good deal of pessimism and a tendency to withdraw from the affairs of ordinary life (for example, in the works of Poe, Hawthorne, and Melville) as if it were impossible to reconcile the inner and the outer worlds. Charles G. Leland, in his *Hans Breitmann Ballads* (collected in 1868), had shown how a European might be demoralized by this ambivalence in the American temperament. His *Sunshine in Thought*, published in 1862 but written several years earlier, was, he remembered afterwards, "all directed against the namby-pamby pessimism, 'lost Edens and buried Lenores,' and similar weak rubbish, which had then begun to manifest itself in literature, and which I foresaw was in future to become a great curse, as it has indeed done."[69]

The book is in fact somewhat more than that. "I do not believe with many," he declares in his preface,

> that in this age of labor, industry and utilitarianism are killing beauty and poetry. On the contrary, I see that they form the transition stage to a higher art and poetry than the world has ever known, and that through their dusty, steam-engine whirling realism, society will yet attain to naturalism, or a living and working in nature, more direct, fresher, and braver, than history has ever recorded.[70]

Replying to those who say that life is one thing and art quite another, he says that "art, if it be anything at all, is a reality."[71] The youth in Longfellow's "Excelsior," he remarks, "would have better effected his purpose if he had accepted the hospitality offered and waited till the next morning, when he might have continued re-

---

[69] Charles G. Leland, *Memoirs* (1893), p. 250.
[70] *Sunshine in Thought*, Preface, pp. 4-5.
[71] *Ibid.*, p. 66.

freshed and under more favorable conditions."[72] He is not fearful of science or of utility.

When science—and all organization is science—shall have progressed so far as to secure rights and comforts to all, we will find that practical usefulness, or the monster Utility, so much decried by the poets of the day and by philosophers, has led us to the highest forms of beauty, and to a blending of the beautiful with the useful wherever the latter occurs.[73]

This faith in science and this optimistic expectation of seeing the useful and the beautiful in a new poetic expression are boldly announced in Whitman's preface to the 1855 *Leaves of Grass*. "Exact science and its practical movements," he declares, "are no checks on the greatest poet but always his encouragement and support." And as there is love between the father and the son, so "there shall be love between the poet and the man of demonstrable science."[74] In his first poem in that book he speaks favorably of reality and materialism and shouts "Hurrah for positive science!"[75] He by no means renounces feeling and intuition, but he is aware of no contradiction between them and the senses; the realm of fact and sensual experience conducts him to the realm of spiritual values. "The facts are useful and real ... they are not my dwelling ... I enter by them to an area of the dwelling."[76] Whitman never abandoned the position here taken.

How much the attempt by Leland, Whitman, and others to reconcile science and reality with literary art may have been influenced by the European literary critics it would be difficult to determine. Sainte-Beuve was, of course, well known to the literary guild, and

[72] *Ibid.*, p. 138.
[73] *Ibid.*, p. 147. This pragmatic view may be compared with the idealistic aesthetics of the period as represented by John Bascom's *Aesthetics; or, the Science of Beauty* (Boston, 1862). Professor Bascom does not deny the possibility of reaching the beautiful through the useful, but he emphasizes the necessity of following the ideal as a guide. "The ideal," he says (p. 74), "is but the impulse received in our movements through the real, expended in the world of thought, and there wrought into that higher conception for which alone training and discipline are given. Without this momentum of the mind which reveals itself in new ideas, all scholarship would be acquisition, all knowledge, memory, all progress, patient trudging along the one thoroughfare of thought."
[74] *Leaves of Grass*, edition of 1855, p. vii.
[75] *Ibid.*, p. 28. [76] *Ibid.*

his works were occasionally noticed in the American journals.[77] In 1858 he sent Lowell a contribution for the *Atlantic* on Beranger, and Lowell translated it himself and used it in the number for February, 1858.[78] But Sainte-Beuve was too much an individualist to accept the new positivistic theories so well championed by Taine. The latter became known in this country upon the publication of his *History of English Literature* in 1864, but was not widely influential until somewhat later. The American critic E. P. Whipple defends Dickens against Taine's criticism that he was too timid in representing the passion of love, pointing out that Dickens is frank enough in exhibiting other passions equally real.[79] Noah Porter speaks with respect of Sainte-Beuve and Taine, along with Matthew Arnold, in 1871:

> The French have also taught something in respect to criticism. The comprehensive work of H. Taine upon English Literature, and his other works of art-criticism are genial, and almost recreative. The appreciative and subtle, the acute yet always civilized *St. Beuve* has enforced by abundant and attractive examples, the impression of what criticism may and ought to become. Matthew Arnold has inculcated these same lessons in his *Essays on Criticism; Culture and Anarchy; On the Study of Celtic Literature* better sometimes by his precepts than by his own practice.[80]

One contemporary historian of ideas has said that "the world has made little intellectual progress since the two eventful decades which lie between 1850 and 1870. By then were formed the kinds of

---

[77] A brief notice of the fourteenth volume of *Causeries du Lundi* appeared in the *Atlantic* for April, 1862 (IX, 522), and the first full-length essay on Sainte-Beuve was printed in the same magazine for April, 1866 (XVII, 432-454). John Esten Cooke is said to have "speculated on the immense value that would attach to causeries modeled on those of Sainte-Beuve, which might impart tone to our critical journals" (Alexander Cowie, *The Rise of the American Novel*, p. 471). M. C. Tyler, the eminent historian of early American literature, was also a little later to come under the influence of Sainte-Beuve. (Cf. H. M. Jones, *The Theory of American Literature*, 1948, pp. 104-105.) George Ripley, according to O. B. Frothingham, an intimate friend, was so familiar with Sainte-Beuve "that on occasion of that writer's decease, he sat down and wrote an account of him without recourse to books" (*Recollections and Impressions*, p. 242). See also Robert G. Mahieu's *Sainte-Beuve aux Etats Unis* (Princeton, 1945) for a detailed study of the subject.

[78] See H. E. Scudder, *James Russell Lowell*, II, 77.

[79] "The Genius of Dickens," *Atlantic Monthly*, XIX (May, 1867), 553.

[80] Noah Porter, *op. cit.*, p. 297.

mind which are manifest in the world today. These minds are the product of two great events: the failure of democratic nationalism on the continent of Europe and the promulgation of the doctrine of evolution."[81] From the one event came decadence, and from the other naturalism, according to his theory. Yet this was not at once, if at all, true in the United States. Here democracy did not immediately fail, but was believed to be strengthened by the outcome of the Civil War; and the publication of Darwin's *Origin of Species* was hardly noticed by the layman until well after the end of the war.[82] This is not to say that Americans were unaware of all new developments in scientific thinking. Books like *Vestiges of Creation*, Sir Charles Lyell's *Principles of Geology*, and the writings of Cuvier, not to mention Agassiz, Asa Gray, and others in this country, were well known and appreciated. Lyell's *Geological Evidences of the Antiquity of Man* (1862) and his public announcement of his acceptance of Darwin's theory in 1864 had their influence on American opinion. The positivism of Auguste Comte was summarized in magazine articles and also came by way of the historian Buckle and the literary critic Taine. John W. Draper's *History of the Intellectual Development of Europe* (1862), sometimes compared to Buckle's *History of Civilization in England*, was immensely popular and, together with his *History of the American Civil War* (1867), did much to establish respect in this country for the scientific approach to history. Three articles on *The Origin of Species* by Asa Gray in the *Atlantic Monthly* for July, August, and October, 1860 informed all interested persons of the general theories of that book, though the writer did not definitely endorse the theories.[83]

[81] Oscar Cargill, *Intellectual America* (1941), p. 2.
[82] Richard Hofstadter, *Social Darwinism in American Thought, 1860-1915* (1945), p. 1.
[83] See "Darwin on the Origin of Species," *Atlantic Monthly*, VI (July, 1860), 109-116; VI (Aug., 1860), 229-239. Also "Darwin and His Reviewers," *Atlantic*, VI (Oct., 1860), 406-425. In the last-named article the writer says (p. 408) that in giving the reviewers' opinions his own do not matter. "But we may confess to an impression, thus far, that the doctrine of the permanent and complete immutability of species has not been established, and may fairly be doubted. We believe that species vary, and that 'Natural Selection' works; but we suspect that its operation, like every analogous operation, may be limited by something else." Somewhat less favorable were review articles appearing in the *North American Review* for April and Oct., 1860.

Evolution was opposed in America "less because it was thought false than because it was thought to be irreconcilable with larger universal concepts,"[84] in particular the Christian concepts of the pre-eminence of mind, or spirit, over matter and of purposeful creation. In this conflict it was Spencer more than Darwin who was in the public arena as the champion of evolution, and his ideas found an immediate response in the minds of John Fiske and E. L. Youmans, and aroused them to evangelistic ardor for the Spencerian philosophy.[85] Asa Gray accepted Darwinism eventually, but Agassiz remained firmly opposed to it. Fiske and Youmans, with some assistance from Gray and others, spearheaded a crusade after the Civil War to make evolution respectable.[86] In this they found that their way had been made easier by the inroads on orthodoxy already made by Unitarianism and Transcendentalism.[87] Emerson notes in his journal: "Calvinism rushes to be Unitarianism, as Unitarianism rushes to be Naturalism."[88] Similarly, naturalism as Emerson understood it rushed to be Darwinian naturalism, with considerable help from the Transcendentalists and liberal Unitarians who organized the Free Religious Association about 1867.[89] These radical thinkers, many of whom were evolutionists before Darwin, fell in with the Spencerian optimists, identified evolution with progress, and promoted the reconciliation of science and religion with the ultimate aim of building the perfect society.[90]

The metaphysics of Hegel, and his philosophy of history, began to be accepted in the sixties along with Darwinian evolution and

---

[84] Bert James Loewenberg, "Darwinism Comes to America, 1859-1900," *Mississippi Valley Historical Review*, XXVIII (Dec., 1941), 357 ff.

[85] In a review of Spencer's *Illustrations of Progress* in the *Atlantic* for June, 1864, the reviewer says (XIII, 776): "As far as the frontiers of knowledge where the intellect may go, there is no living man whose guidance may more safely be trusted. Mr. Spencer represents the scientific spirit of the age."

[86] Hofstadter, *op. cit.*, p. 2.

[87] *Ibid.*, p. 19.

[88] *Journal*, X, 9. Quoted by Stow Persons in *Free Religion, an American Faith* (1947), p. 18.

[89] Persons, *op. cit.*, p. 44. See also O. B. Frothingham, *Recollections and Impressions*, pp. 115-126.

[90] *Ibid.*, pp. 47, 64. The popular lectures of Robert Ingersoll, beginning in the late sixties, contributed more than a little to the decline of theology and the popular faith in science.

may have been in their ultimate effects no less important. The expansive spirit of the nationalistic American in the middle of the century found some encouragement in the grand outlines of Hegel's cosmic philosophy, as it came to them indirectly through many sources. Whitman, for example, seems to have echoed in a measure the Hegelian process of division, conflict, and reconciliation in the cosmic philosophy adumbrated in *Leaves of Grass*;[91] he also accepted science and the implications of the theory of evolution, though he understood Darwin's theory as referring to a process only, not to origins.[92] In fact, he suggests, after the Hegelian principle, that Darwin's theory may be reconciled, after all conflicts, with the Christian doctrine of origins, and that the two, blending, may originate a third theory still nearer the truth.[93] Others, like Whitman, accepted both new philosophies in the belief that they were of special relevance to conditions in America, particularly to the Civil War.[94]

Gradually Darwinism gained ground as the colleges became more liberal and substituted the study of science more and more for the study of the classics. In 1867 E. L. Youmans published a collection of essays by eminent scientists to prove the importance of science in modern culture.[95] A year or so later Charles W. Eliot was writing

[91] For studies of Whitman's debt to Hegel, see Mody C. Boatright, "Whitman and Hegel," University of Texas *Studies in English* (1929), IX, 134-140; also Robert P. Falk, "Walt Whitman and German Thought," *Journal of English and Germanic Philology*, XL (July, 1941), 315-330.
[92] See Horace Traubel, *With Walt Whitman in Camden*, III, 94.
[93] Walt Whitman, *Complete Prose Works* (1898), p. 321.
[94] David F. Bowers, *op. cit.*, pp. 159-160. H. W. Schneider says, in his *History of American Philosophy* (New York, 1946), pp. 177-178: "The impact of Hegel on democratic theory in America was greater than is generally believed, and it is scarcely an exaggeration to claim that it was primarily the Hegelian influence which . . . gave America an appropriate ideology for understanding the growth after 1880 of national socialism and economic democracy." Cf. also pp. 180f. for a discussion of the Hegelian interpretation of the Civil War.
[95] E. L. Youmans, *The Culture Demanded by Modern Life*, 1867. These are essays by Tyndall, Huxley, Faraday, Draper, Spencer, Herschel, Lyell, and Mill, besides the title essay by Youmans. In the preface Youmans says: "As man is a being of action, it is demanded that his education shall be a preparation for action." He calls for less emphasis in the college curriculum on the classics and more on the sciences. Cf. also an article of like import by John Fiske, "Considerations on University Reform," in the *Atlantic*, XIX (May. 1867), 451-465.

articles to show the need of more study of science and social science, and in 1869 he was elected president of Harvard.[96] In the meantime the idealists had seen the danger of materialism in the teachings of Spencer, Huxley, and others of their school, and they began to give ear to William T. Harris, who was a Hegelian and an active opponent of the scientific school. When the *Atlantic Monthly* refused to publish his criticism of Spencer in 1867 he founded the *Journal of Speculative Philosophy*,[97] which became the chief exponent of Hegelian ideas.

The opposition to Spencer was, of course, actively carried on by the clergy and their supporters. Even some of the more liberal thinkers balked at the veiled materialism in the Synthetic Philosophy. B. P. Bowne was one of these, although he agrees that the old idea of instantaneous creation is not acceptable and that the process of creation may be evolutionary. "All that Theism cares to know," he adds, "is that Mind is the primal cause and the eternal ruler of the universe."[98] This opposition of the idealistic evolutionists was partly the result of the publication in 1871 of *The Descent of Man*, which made it quite clear that "not merely the unity of man but also his creation was at stake, and not merely creation but teleology in general."[99]

But the enemies of evolution fought a losing fight. "Ten years

[96] Samuel Eliot Morison, *Three Centuries of Harvard, 1636-1936* (1936), p. 325.

[97] Merle Curti, *The Social Ideas of American Educators* (1935), p. 312. O. B. Frothingham (*Transcendentalism in New England*, 1876) says (p. 208): "The atomic theory of the constitution of matter, which, in one or another form, is accepted by the majority of scientific men, gives ominous prediction of disaster to every scheme that is built on the necessary truths of pure reason." He quotes several writers of the scientific school, including Mill, Fiske, Taine, Tyndall, and Lewes, to show that they do not agree among themselves on the relationship of mind and matter. He concludes (p. 213): "Should the analysis of Taine and Lewes prove successful at last, and be accepted by the authorities in speculative philosophy, idealism, as a philosophy, must disappear."

[98] *The Philosophy of Herbert Spencer* (1874), p. 10. Cf. John Bascom, "Darwin's Theory of the Origin of Species," *American Presbyterian Review*, third series, III (1871), 349-379. Cf. also Henry Adams's review of the tenth edition of Lyell's *Principles of Geology* in the *North American Review*, CVII (1868), 465-501.

[99] Schneider, *op. cit.*, p. 347. Chap. vi (pp. 319-437) is a valuable guide to the controversial thought of this period.

ago," said Whitelaw Reid in addressing the Dartmouth students in 1873, "the staple subject here for reading and talk, outside study hours, was English poetry and fiction. Now it is English science. Herbert Spencer, John Stuart Mill, Huxley, Darwin, Tyndall have usurped the places of Tennyson and Browning and Matthew Arnold and Dickens."[100] The magazines from 1864 to 1871 published more and more on the subject of evolution.[101] Henry Ward Beecher wrote Spencer in 1866: "The peculiar condition of American society has made your writings more fruitful and quickening here than in Europe."[102] Youmans reported to Spencer in 1871, shortly after the publication of Darwin's *Descent of Man:* "Things are going here furiously.... Ten thousand *Descent of Man* have been printed, and I guess they are nearly all gone."[103]

It appears, then, that by 1871 Hegelianism was making some progress in preserving idealism outside the churches, but that evolution, as interpreted by Darwin and Spencer and their American apostles was generally accepted among the intellectual classes. Even liberal clergymen accepted it with minor reservations, and the magazines made it understandable to millions. Nevertheless there is little indication that Darwinism was a depressive influence in American literature before 1871. This fact is perhaps due to the prevalence of a spirit of optimism among the interpreters of Darwin during these years and for some time afterwards, cushioning the shock for minds accustomed to Emerson and Theodore Parker. Some idealists perceived the materialism inherent in Spencer's philosophy and in Darwin's theory of natural selection, but the enthusiasts were not concerned about it then.

Much more important in their immediate effects were the Civil

---

[100] Quoted from *Scribner's Monthly*, VI, 608, by Richard Hofstadter, *op. cit.*, p. 8. However, Noah Porter (*op. cit.*, pp. 305-306) omits Darwin's books from his list of recommended scientific books and warns readers that "the press is literally oppressed by the number of superficial books in which the attempt is made to popularize science and to set forth its relations to the imagination and to faith."

[101] Hofstadter, *op. cit.*, p. 9. Two humorous literary essays on the subject in the *Atlantic* were Charles F. Sprague's "Tied to a Rope," XVII (June, 1866), 721-724, and E. P. Whipple's "Mr. Hardhack on the Derivation of Man from the Monkey," XIX (March, 1867), 300-305.

[102] *Ibid.*, p. 18.

[103] Michael Kraus, *A History of American History* (1937), p. 308.

War and its aftermath of lawlessness, political corruption, and industrial expansion, which further disturbed a social order already fluid and unstable because of the retreating frontier and the unending stream of immigrants. Before the war cotton, water power, and a surplus of population had built more and bigger textile mills in New England. Working conditions were no worse in New England than in Britain, but they were bad enough. In 1843 Massachusetts forbade the employment of children under twelve years for more than ten hours a day.[104] There were ten thousand immigrants in 1820, eighty thousand in 1844, and more than four hundred thousand in 1854; thus a laboring class in the European sense was rapidly created.[105] Many of these people went into the mills, which were concentrated in New England, particularly in Massachusetts. The consumption of cotton increased from twenty million pounds in 1820 to nearly half a billion pounds in 1860, and the average size of the factory increased tenfold.[106] The decade of the fifties was "the springtime of capitalism. . . . The potentialities of wealth and power had been revealed and tested. Their realization was affected only in an incidental way by the Civil War."[107] The characteristic traits of the frontier—coarseness, strength, and acute inquisitiveness, combined with restless, nervous energy and a masterful grasp of material things[108]—became the dominant national characteristics after the Jacksonian revolution, and after the war they were accentuated by the spirit of lawlessness, intolerance, and craving for adventure born of strife.

The moral tone of the country sank to a low mark during the ten years from 1865 to 1875. "In the rapidly growing cities of the East, politicians and financiers, railroad barons and merchant princes, were stepping wide, high and handsome. . . . Everyone was making money and . . . the clank of machinery and the clink of dollars silenced religion, letters, and the arts."[109] Darwin's theory

---

[104] Arthur Cecil Bining, *The Rise of American Economic Life* (1943), p. 259.
[105] Witt Bowden, *The Industrial History of the United States* (1930), pp. 212-213.
[106] *Ibid.*, p. 217.
[107] *Ibid.*, pp. 249-250.
[108] Frederick J. Turner, *The Frontier in American History* (1920), p. 37.
[109] Morison, *op. cit.*, p. 323.

of natural selection seemed to justify laissez-faire economics, and Spencer's philosophy paralyzed the will to reform.[110] One writer just after the Civil War complained bitterly that money had become the only criterion of value in this country.

In our age of scepticism, the excellence of accumulated capital is the one thing no man doubts; and when I take off my hat to a rich man, which I always do when I meet him, I feel I can not be mistaken in paying respect to something demonstrable, tangible, real. . . . Wisdom can be bought, generally at low prices; and virtue is always assumed to be an attribute of Fortune except in moral didactic treatises. . . . It is not surprising that young men want money, and much of it, and quickly.[111]

The American gospel of wealth, which Gabriel says was based on the Scottish Common-Sense philosophy and fostered in the colleges under the leadership of James McCosh of Princeton and Noah Porter of Yale,[112] spread to the public schools through the McGuffey readers and other textbooks. "God gives a great deal of money to some persons," says McGuffey in 1844, "in order that they may assist those who are poor."[113] The success story of the good little boy who rises from industrious poverty to virtuous riches travels in a straight line from McGuffey through Horatio Alger, Jr., to the twentieth-century magazine. The gospel of wealth was also the formula by which Christian idealism made an uneasy peace with materialism, and by which the Church was persuaded to look with indulgence upon that wealth of which it received the tithe.[114]

It is not necessary to enlarge upon the scandals of Grant's administration, the manipulations of Jay Gould, Jim Fisk, and their crowd in the shadow of the White House; the lobbying of beautiful and unscrupulous women, of whom Laura Hawkins in Mark Twain's *The Gilded Age* is an example; and the general break-

---

[110] Hofstadter, *op. cit.*, pp. 32-33.
[111] Frederick Sheldon, "Fugitives from Labor," *Atlantic Monthly*, XX (Sept., 1867), 370-371.
[112] Ralph Henry Gabriel, *The Course of American Democratic Thought* (1940), p. 147.
[113] Quoted in Richard D. Mosier, *Making the American Mind: Social and Moral Ideas in the McGuffey Readers* (1947), p. 106.
[114] Gabriel, *op. cit.*, p. 157.

down of public morality that darkened the mind of young Henry Adams with enduring pessimism.[115] Adams himself, remembering, wrote:

> The world cared little for decency. What it wanted, it did not know; probably a system that would work, and men who could work it; but it found neither. Adams had tried his own little hands on it, and had failed. His friends had been driven out of Washington or had taken to fisticuffs. He himself sat down and stared helplessly into the future.[116]

Walt Whitman was appalled by the hypocrisy everywhere, the superciliousness in literature, the depravity of business, the corruption of politics, and the flippancy in social life; and he concluded that our New World democracy, "however great a success in uplifting the masses out of their sloughs, in materialistic development, products, and in a certain highly-deceptive superficial popular intellectuality, is, so far, an almost complete failure in its social aspects, and in really grand religious, moral, literary, and esthetic results."[117] As one historian summed it up: "The day of the idealists was dead; that of the materialists had been born."[118]

### VIII

Of the novelists who drew their themes and narratives from the events of the Civil War very few looked at it from the point of view of the individual soldier or citizen. John Esten Cooke was concerned with the military aspect of the war in the manner of the historical romance, and Mrs. Stowe avoided the subject. Henry Morford wrote three novels during the war—*Shoulder Straps* (1863), *The Coward* (1863), and *In the Days of Shoddy* (1864)— in which he exposed the collusion between politicians and contrac-

---

[115] Summarized from Claude G. Bowers, *The Tragic Era* (1929), pp. 263-283.
[116] *The Education of Henry Adams* (1918), p. 280.
[117] Walt Whitman, *Prose Works* (edition of 1898), p. 204.
[118] Bowers, *op. cit.*, p. 337. In May, 1870, Parke Godwin observes that "practical legislation everywhere . . . is falling into all manner of disorder and vileness" ("Our Political Degeneracy—Its Cause and Remedy," *Putnam's Magazine*, N.S. V, 600). A good discussion of the conflict between materialistic and idealistic forces after the Civil War may be found in chap. xx, "Business and the Life of the Mind," of Merle Curti's *The Growth of American Thought* (New York, 1943), pp. 507-527.

tors who furnished the army with supplies. The best of these, *In the Days of Shoddy*, has a good deal of realistic detail and some melodrama, though the author manifests a desire to avoid the latter. The plot, which requires that the villain cheat the government on contracts for army uniforms and attempt to seduce the faithful wife of a Union soldier, is obviously a contraption to expose incompetence and corruption in the official conduct of the war. Morford failed because he lacked the literary skill to shape his materials in an effective pattern; but he anticipated DeForest, and in some respects Crane, by representing the more sordid aspects of war and by describing the confused courage and poltroonery of an individual soldier when his army is in rout. Jeremiah Clemens of Alabama published *Tobias Wilson: A Tale of the Great Rebellion* in 1865, the year of his death, in which some of the unpleasant aspects of war are presented. Already, in 1856, he had produced *Bernard Lile*, a historical romance of the Texas Revolution and the Mexican War which contains some rather unromantic battle scenes, particularly the ruthless destruction and pillage of a Mexican town in revenge for the treachery of its citizens.[119]

Rebecca Harding Davis, though she writes less of the war, is important as an early realist who received little recognition before the publication of Quinn's *American Fiction* in 1936, which has an excellent summary and criticism of Mrs. Davis's work. She wrote many short stories for the *Atlantic,* some of which, beginning with "Life in the Iron Mills" (April, 1861), are definitely realistic. She is obviously determined not to be romantic, and sometimes the reader is likely to be annoyed by her reminders that her characters

---

[119] In his preface the author says most of his characters are drawn from real life. "It is a book of life—of life not as I wished it, or thought it ought to be, but as I have found it. . . . It makes no attempt to point the author's ideal of a perfect man." The hero is nevertheless unbelievably superior. The frontiersmen are more convincing. Of his dialogue the author writes: "The reader will find in this volume no approach to the extravagances of language attributed to the South-West by almanac makers and scribblers, whose knowledge of the country and the people is bounded by a steamboat excursion down the Mississippi. The South-West *has* a language of its own; but it in no degree resembles the miserable caricatures with which the country has been flooded. . . . Born upon the frontier myself, and passing the most of my life among its rudest scenes, I know the people well, and have sought to preserve their language *exactly as it is.*"

are just ordinary people. "John Lamar"[120] and "David Gaunt"[121] are war stories in which we are shown how good people are driven to commit terrible acts under the compulsions of war. Doubtless Mrs. Davis's experience of the war affected her writing in other ways than those indicated in her war stories. In old age she recalled hearing Bronson Alcott speak of war as the "armed angel which was wakening the nation to a lofty life unknown before," whereupon she comments:

I had just come up from the border where I had seen the actual war; the filthy spewings of it; the political jobbery in Union and Confederate camps; the malignant personal hatreds wearing patriotic masks, and glutted by burning homes and outraged women; the chances in it, well improved on both sides, for brutish men to grow more brutish, and for honorable gentlemen to degenerate into thieves and sots. War may be an armed angel with a mission, but she has the personal habits of the slums.[122]

Mrs. Davis's first novel, *Margret Howth, a Story of To-Day* (1862), was written for the *Atlantic* during the first months of the war and reflects its grim mood, but it is not in its action a war novel. In her first chapter she declares her realistic purpose, describing her story as "crude and homely . . . a dull, plain bit of prose, such as you might pick for yourself out of any of these warehouses or back-streets." Admitting that the popular taste is for "idyls delicately tinted" and "passion-veined hearts," she proposes to "dig into this commonplace, this vulgar American life," which, she thinks, "has a new and awful significance that we do not see."[123] This is a story of a well-bred girl who supports her parents by clerical work in an Indiana mill just before the Civil War. Her lover, being ambitious, decides to marry the daughter of the mill owner and receive a half interest in the business, but before the marriage can take place the mill burns uninsured and the hero marries the girl he really loves after all. The narrative is sternly realistic through the first half of the book, but like most of the determined realists of this period, the author cannot resist the temptation to end her book romantically and happily. Oil is found on the farm owned

[120] *Atlantic Monthly*, April, 1862.
[121] *Atlantic Monthly*, Sept. and Oct., 1862.
[122] Rebecca Harding Davis, *Bits of Gossip* (1904), pp. 33-34.
[123] *Margret Howth, A Story of To-Day*, p. 6.

by Margret's father, so that the hero is to be a rich man after all, without the sacrifice of love.

This conclusion is surprising in view of the author's earlier comment on love: "Doubtless there are people capable of a love terrible in its strength; but I never knew such a case that some one did not consider its expediency as 'a match' in the light of dollars and cents"; and her remark about her hero that "he stopped to count the cost before he fell in love," and that "it made his fingers thrill with pleasure to touch a full pocket-book as well as his mistress's hand."[124] And yet Stephen Holmes is represented as a typical American and something of an Emersonian. "He knew what this Self within him was; he knew how it had forced him to grope his way up, to give this hungry, insatiate soul air and freedom and knowledge."[125] Unlike Emerson, however, he felt that each human soul must accomplish its purpose, as each thing in nature seems to do. "The windless gray, the stars, the stone under his feet," Holmes reflected, "stood alone in the universe, each working out its own soul into deed. If there were any all-embracing harmony, one soul through all, he did not see it. Knowles—that old sceptic—believed in it, and called it Love."[126] Dr. Knowles, like Hollingsworth in *The Blithedale Romance*, was a humanitarian and reformer who could be unscrupulous in his methods of accomplishing what he believed to be a good end. One wonders whether Mrs. Davis, having raised ethical problems she could not confidently answer, took the easy way out with her happy ending.

Mrs. Davis's second novel, *Waiting for the Verdict*, which was serialized in the *Galaxy* in 1867 and published the following year, had the makings of a great novel, but the materials are not welded together skilfully, and the attempt to use the novel as a means of influencing the nation in its attitude towards the freed Negro limits the interest of the modern reader. Her novelette "A Pearl of Great Price," published in *Lippincott's Magazine* at the end of 1868, has been called "a fine study of a woman."[127] She wrote other good fiction in later decades, and always her greatest strength is in characterization.

[124] *Ibid.*, p. 104. [125] *Ibid.*, p. 121. [126] *Ibid.*, p. 161.
[127] Arthur Hobson Quinn, *American Fiction, an Historical and Critical Survey* (1936), p. 186.

Another woman who began to write in the decade of the Civil War, but whose work was little influenced by it, was Elizabeth Stuart Phelps, later Mrs. Ward. She began to write stories at an early age and published her first book when she was twenty-four. This was *The Gates Ajar* (1868), the story of a girl whose brother was killed in the war and how she recovered from her grief through the religious counsel of an aunt. In 1869 she published a volume of short stories, some of which had been previously printed in magazines. Two or three of these stories are excellent and show the author's predilection for characters who suffer much both physically and spiritually. The best in the collection is perhaps "The Tenth of January," in which the chief character is a factory girl whose face and neck were disfigured when her drunken mother knocked her against a broken crock. The boy she loves turns from her to a pretty but shallow mill girl. The story ends pathetically when the mill burns and the heroine perishes after helping to save the pretty girl for the faithless lover. The details are stark, perhaps too stark, and the author works too powerfully on the reader's sympathies.

Mrs. Ward is best represented in this period by two novels: *Hedged In* (1870) and *The Silent Partner* (1871). *Hedged In* is a story of Nixy, an orphan, who could remember singing and beating the tambourine in the streets for a man who called himself her uncle, a woman to whom he sold her, another woman who "adopted" her and got drunk every Tuesday, beating her with the empty bottle on Wednesday mornings; she could also recall a city missionary, and ten months in an orphan asylum from which she ran away. Then she was a girl of sixteen, with a baby, living in a dirty room with a dozen other people in a slum district. There was still a stain on the wall "where a gal murdered her baby, years agone."[128] She ran away with her baby from that place, was taken in by kind people, and lived to be a good woman. There is too much moralizing in the story; yet the author indicates that Nixy's case is exceptional, for in Moll Manners (who is lifted from the gutter by the reformed Nixy and dies a few days later) she shows the miserable end that Nixy might have expected but for a lucky accident.

[128] *Hedged In*, p. 5.

# THE DECLINE OF ROMANTIC IDEALISM

*The Silent Partner*, a better book, is a novel with a purpose; namely, to point out social abuses in the textile mills and indicate how they may be remedied. The author writes in her prefatory note:

> I believe that a wide-spread ignorance exists among us regarding the abuses of our factory system, more especially, but not exclusively, as exhibited in many of the country mills.
>
> I desire it to be understood that every alarming sign and every painful statement which I have given in these pages concerning the condition of the manufacturing districts could be matched with far less cheerful reading, and with far more pungent perplexities, from the pages of the Reports of the Massachusetts Bureau of Statistics of Labor, to which, with other documents of a kindred nature, and to the personal assistance of friends who have "testified that they have seen," I am deeply in debt for the ribs of my story.

It is the story of the cotton mills of Hayle & Kelso, and of Perley Kelso, who, after her father's death, wishes to be taken into the firm as a partner. The Hayles, father and son, refuse because she is a woman, but allow her the status of "silent partner." She is engaged to be married to the younger Hayle, but when she visits the mills and the homes of the workers and proposes reforms she meets such a rebuff from her unsympathetic lover that she breaks the engagement. She throws herself into the work of educating and helping the workers by providing for social improvements, and the story ends without a happy romance. The portraits of the strong-willed Sip Garth and her afflicted sister Catty, and of Bub Mell, who was eight years old, who worked in the factory, who chewed tobacco, and who had gone to school, as he said, until "he got so old he give it up"—these are of the quality of similar types in the novels of Dickens. "It was to be noticed of these people that the girls swore, that the babies smoked, that the men, more especially the elder men, had frowns like Mr. Mell."[129] And then there was the troublesome character, Bijah Mudge, who could not get a job because he testified before a committee of the Massachusetts Legislature. He talked a great deal, and before he died in the poorhouse he said: "I say there is something out o' kilter . . . when a man ken spend forty thousand dollars on the plate-glass winders of his house, and I ken work industrious and honest all

---

[129] *The Silent Partner* (1877 edition), p. 118.

of my life and be beholden to the State of Massachusetts for my poor-us vittels when I'm sixty-six years old!"[130] Our present concern is with the elements of realism and social criticism in Elizabeth Phelps's work, as illustrated in the two novels here discussed, but she continued to write throughout the nineteenth century and contributed to the local-color movement and to other currents in fiction during that time.

In reviewing novels growing out of the Civil War we must take account of Sidney Lanier's youthful contribution, *Tiger Lilies*, published in 1867 and based on his experiences in the Confederate Army, in the Federal prisons at Fortress Monroe and Point Lookout, and as a vacationer in the mountains of East Tennessee. It is not primarily a war novel, but a hodge-podge of realism, romance, and idealistic dreaming. All that concerns us here is that the mountaineer and the soldier are true to life, and that the life itself is humorously observed, as may be seen in the following passage describing a prisoner at Point Lookout:

> For this man's clothes, those three thieves, grease, dirt, and smoke, had drawn lots; but not content with the allotment, all three were evidently contending which should have the whole suit. It appeared likely that dirt would be the happy thief. "Wash 'em!" said this man one day when the Federal corporal had the impudence to refer to the sacred soil on his clothes—"wash 'em? corp'ral! I'm bound to say 'at you're a dam fool! That mud's what holds 'em together; sticks 'em fast,—like! Ef you was to put them clo's in water they'd go to nothin' just like a piece o' salt!"[131]

The mountaineers Cain and Gorm Smallin are equally real, in character as well as in speech, but the young women and the "heroes"—young college graduates and musicians—are idealized.[132]

One of the very best of the early realists, John W. DeForest, has been neglected until recently. His first novel can be read in the pages of *Putnam's Magazine*, where it appeared in installments from December, 1856, to September, 1857. It is called *Witching Times*

---

[130] *Ibid.*, p. 177.
[131] *Tiger-Lilies, Centennial Edition of the Works of Sidney Lanier* (1945), V, 157.
[132] For a discussion of the sources, structure, and meaning of *Tiger Lilies*, consult Garland Greever's excellent introduction to the Centennial Edition of the novel.

and concerns the witch trials and executions in Salem at the end of the seventeenth century. The characters, some of them historical figures, are well developed, and the pressing to death of Giles Corey is vividly described. In contrast with Longfellow, who makes Judge Hathorne more of a fanatic than Cotton Mather in the second of his *New England Tragedies*, DeForest attributes to him a more liberal attitude. His second novel, *Seacliff; or, The Mystery of the Westervelts* (1859) develops a contemporary theme and has at least one strong character, Ellen Westervelt. He also wrote short stories regularly for the magazines, first for *Harper's* and later for the *Galaxy* and especially the *Atlantic*, most of which are less than remarkable. "The City of Brass," in the *Atlantic* for October, 1869, is an effective satire on the New Englander's enthusiasm for reform and democratic processes, and "The Taillefer Bell-Ringings," in the *Atlantic* for August, 1869, though ostensibly a mystery story, is more interesting for its account of the downward career of a beautiful and conscienceless woman. Another serialized novel, *Overland*, published in the *Galaxy* from August, 1870, to July, 1871, is very readable as a story of western adventure, and yet it also exhibits the author's skill in the delineation of character and in keeping his action clear of sensationalism.

The most important of DeForest's novels falling within the period covered by this essay (*Kate Beaumont* was serialized in the *Atlantic* in 1871 but did not appear in book form until 1872), and perhaps the best he ever wrote, is *Miss Ravenel's Conversion from Secession to Loyalty*, written just after the Civil War and published in 1867. Miss Ravenel, who grew up in New Orleans, was an admirer of Southern character and social customs and a defender of the South in secession. Her father, however, was opposed to secession, and took her early in the conflict to live in Connecticut, where she met the young Captain Colbourne, a New Englander, and the more worldly Colonel Carter, a Virginian in the Federal army.[133] The story shows how Miss Ravenel grows from sympathy with the Southern cause to sympathy with the North, and from the love of Carter to the love of Colbourne. It is a good example of the blending

---

[133] Professor Cowie points out (*The Rise of the American Novel*, p. 507) that Colonel Carter has the glamorousness and most of the unscrupulousness of Rhett Butler in Margaret Mitchell's *Gone With the Wind*.

of social criticism with romance and the development of character. The novel pictures the realities of the war more faithfully than any other work of fiction before Crane's *Red Badge of Courage*.[134]

Details of the army camp, soldiers with uniforms dirty from sleeping on the ground and marching through mud and dust many days without washing, the horrible scenes of the battlefield and the scarcely less horrible scenes of the temporary hospitals—all these are faithfully included.[135] The author is much freer in reporting the coarseness of speech and manners than others of his time.[136] But it is not merely in war reporting that DeForest shows himself a realist. There is also much ironic comment on the political aspect of the war. The ward politician Gazaway, who is able to acquire a commission from the Governor by means of chicanery, and who continues his rascality to win promotion and rake in war profits, is well described.[137] Then there is the story of Mrs. LaRue, whose illicit affair with Colonel Carter is a prominent episode in the novel, a masterly portrait of a clever and worldly woman of old New Orleans.

A few passages in the novel indicate that DeForest was aware of the new currents of scientific thought yet not master of them. Speaking of the young professors at Winslow University, Colburne remarks that they are not Puritans like the older professors. They like Paris and Vienna, where they have studied, and other European cities "that used to be so wicked"; and "they accept geology, and discuss Darwin with patience."[138] Dr. Ravenel, who was a miner-

---

[134] Cf. Howells's review of *Miss Ravenel's Conversion* in the *Atlantic* for July, 1867 (XX, 120-122) in which he says "we suspect that Mr. De Forest is the first to treat the war really and artistically." DeForest's descriptions of the war were based upon his own experiences in Louisiana and elsewhere. Cf. *A Volunteer's Adventures: A Union Captain's Record of the Civil War*, edited by James H. Croushore (New Haven, 1946), parts of which had been published in *Harper's* and the *Galaxy* between 1864 and 1868. See also *A Union Officer in the Reconstruction*, edited by James H. Croushore and David Morris (New Haven, 1948), which is a revised and expanded version, prepared by DeForest but not published in his lifetime, of articles appearing in *Harper's*, the *Atlantic*, and *Putnam's* in 1868 and 1869.

[135] See *Miss Ravenel's Conversion* (edition of 1939), pp. 244, 255, 257, 258, for examples.

[136] See *ibid.*, pp. 280 and 299, where the term "son of a bitch" is used.

[137] See *ibid.*, pp. 284, 341 ff., 377-378, 431.

[138] *Ibid.*, p. 33.

alogist and something of a student of science in general, teases his daughter (then Mrs. Carter) by comparing her baby to a hollyhock and saying he "was only a grade above one," and suggesting that the soul develops its powers like a physical organism.[139] There is some doubt whether DeForest clearly understood the theory of natural selection, for he has one of his characters remark, though in a joking manner, that because of overmuch pride from European praise, Americans of the next generation might sprout peacock-tails. "On the Darwinian theory, you know; circumstances breed species."[140] The speaker seems to be thinking of Lamarckian rather than Darwinian evolution.

*Miss Ravenel's Conversion* was too advanced for popular taste and was appreciated by few critics except Howells.[141] DeForest was not only willing to describe what he saw, but he was also inclined to say what he thought of American life and institutions, and his thoughts were sometimes not complimentary. No doubt he had been reading Thackeray while his contemporaries were still preoccupied with Dickens, but there is much in the novel that cannot be accounted for by examining literary precedents.

Edward Eggleston was more fortunate with his first novel, *The Hoosier Schoolmaster: A Story of Backwoods Life in Indiana* (1871), which I have accepted for convenience as marking the end of the transitional period in which idealism predominated over realism in literature. Obviously movements in literature do not begin and end with such precision. In fact, *Miss Ravenel's Conversion* is more advanced than *The Hoosier Schoolmaster*, though it was written four or five years earlier, and romantic idealism continued to be a major influence in American literature throughout the century. But with the publication of Eggleston's Indiana classic, the Middle West became of age in literature, and all later writers from that region felt that they owed him a debt.[142]

---

[139] *Ibid.*, p. 415   [140] *Ibid.*, p. 443.

[141] Cowie, *op. cit.*, p. 511 and pp. 829-830. Cf. also the *Atlantic Monthly*, XXIX (March, 1872), 365, where Howells says in commenting on De Forest's latest novel, *Kate Beaumont:* "With 'Miss Ravenel's Conversion' and 'Overland,' 'Kate Beaumont' forms, to our mind, strong proof that we are not so much lacking in an American novelist as in a public to recognize him."

[142] See William P. Randel, *Edward Eggleston* (1946), notes, p. 260.

Eggleston was familiar with the backwoods country above the Ohio and also with the frontier in Minnesota in the fifties. In 1866 he was writing Indian stories for children which had in them the promise of his later realism. "Even for an audience of children," says one biographer, "he refused to romanticize the Indians."[143] *The Hoosier Schoolmaster* was based on the experiences of his brother as a schoolmaster in rural Indiana, and some of the characters even have their true names in the fiction. With these events are combined what Eggleston knew of Dr. Smalley's gang of night riders in Decatur County, and Dr. Smalley became Dr. Small in the story.[144] He may have been influenced by Taine's *Philosophy of Art in the Netherlands*, which he reviewed somewhat earlier.[145] Eggleston owed something also to Dickens, and something to Lowell for authority to use the speech of the country districts;[146] but there was truth in the judgment of Howells in the *Atlantic* that he drew "a picture of manners hitherto strange to literature."[147]

The important fact about *The Hoosier Schoolmaster* is that its characters act and talk like the people they purport to be and the further fact that these people are unimportant and unexceptional. It may be that the schoolmaster, Ralph Hartsook, is not altogether free from the superiority of the romantic hero and that the reformed bully, Bud Means, is too much like an evangelist's example of the power of religion; it may be that the villains are too villainous and the unfortunate too nobly responsive to benefactions; but on the whole, the book is true and its imperfections are due rather to lack of skill than wrong principles or motives on the part of the author. There is nothing here of DeForest's satire on contemporary life or on human nature, however. Eggleston had the sincere minister's idealistic views of man and his destiny. There is one reference in the book to Darwin, but it contains no intimation that Eggleston had at this time more than a general notion of his theory of evolution.[148] He had read some scientific books before this, particularly Hugh Miller's *Footprints of Creation* and *The Old Red Sandstone* and Hitchcock's *The Connection*

---

[143] *Ibid.*, p. 96.  [144] *Ibid.*, p. 122.  [145] *Ibid.*, p. 123.
[146] See Eggleston's introduction and notes to the edition of 1892.
[147] See *Atlantic Monthly*, XXIX (March, 1872), 363.
[148] *The Hoosier Schoolmaster*, pp. 111-112.

between *Geology and Natural Religion*,[149] and it is probable that he accepted the general idea of evolution at an early date, but it was not until 1887 that he made a public acceptance of Darwin.[150]

Eggleston, who turned to writing history in his middle years, was one of the first Americans in that field as well as in the field of literature to recognize the importance of social environment in determining the course of individual development. One can do no better than quote his own words of self-appraisal, written in 1890:

> If I were a dispassionate critic, and were to judge my own novels as the writings of another, I should have to say that what distinguishes them from other works of fiction is the prominence which they give to social conditions; that the individual characters are here treated to a greater degree than elsewhere as parts of a study of a society—as in some sense the logical results of the environment.[151]

The bond between his historical writing and his fiction, he adds, is that in history, as in fiction, he is "mainly interested in the evolution of society," and that in both this interest in the history of life is "the one distinguishing trait" of all he has attempted.[152] He was confessedly less sharply aware of the significance of his first novel in 1871 than he was in 1890, and it undoubtedly helped to clarify his purposes. It may be safely affirmed that in Eggleston and in *The Hoosier Schoolmaster*, which was not his best novel but was indicative of the direction of his growth, we have the beginning of a new kind of fiction in America.

## IX

It remains to summarize briefly the principal causes which contributed to the decline of romantic idealism from 1855 to 1871 and to evaluate the results thus achieved as they stand in relation to the succeeding period of American literature. The most obvious conclusion that must be reached on the basis of the facts is that both moral idealism and literary romanticism survived through the period studied and into the later decades of the century, not only in the works of the older writers who kept on writing through the

---

[149] Randel, *op. cit.*, pp. 10-11.
[150] See "Books that Have Helped Me," *Forum*, III (Aug., 1887), 578-586.
[151] "Formative Influences," *Forum*, X (Nov., 1890), 286.
[152] *Ibid.*, p. 287. Eggleston became president of the American Historical Association for 1900 (see Randel, *op. cit.*, p. 224).

seventies and eighties, but also in the books of younger writers such as Emily Dickinson, Bret Harte, and Sidney Lanier. The decline in idealism is in part the consequence of a decline in artistic qualities of literature in the younger writers. Moral force cannot inhere in a third-rate poem or prose work. This falling off in quality after an age of great achievement is quite in keeping with historical precedent and was perhaps inevitable; yet there were circumstances and events which contributed to make the younger writers not only inferior in quality but different in their purpose.

There were three major causes of the decline of idealism in America and three closely related minor causes, each with complex manifestations. The major causes were the frontier, the Civil War, and the advance of science; the minor causes were the declining authority of the churches, the widening base of public education, and the influence of foreign writers. In the advance of science I include applied science as it prepared the way for expanding industry and internal improvements, and in the declining authority of the churches I include humanitarianism and all kinds of reform movements.

The influence of the frontier did not come from the West exclusively, but was a continuing force in areas long settled. The spirit of the frontier in the East was perpetually renewed by the cultural and commercial exchanges between East and West, and by the same means the West was fitted into the national pattern. The relative freedom of the individual from social conventions and the restraints of law in the West favored the development of new standards of ethical values. The literature which came from these raw communities reacted against the sentiment and refinement that had been overdeveloped in the East. Humor is closely allied with the frontier, even when it was written in New England, because it was generally an evocation of the rustic and crude elements that remained for the purpose of satire, as in the Widow Bedott, or of opposing political vices, as in Hosea Biglow.

Without attempting to account for the Civil War in the political, economic, and moral disagreements long standing between the North and the South, I am concerned in this essay with the great conflict as an historical fact which had social and literary consequences. It was so shocking to the national sensibilities that Whitman doubted whether the real war—the realities that touched the individual soldier—would find its way into literature, and it did not to any great extent in the years immediately following. Indirectly, through the increased lawlessness, moral corruption, and respect for force which became evident among people everywhere, it did get into the books that featured sensationalism (like the dime novel) or satire (like that of Nasby or Mark Twain). Chiefly the war gave rise to a new approach to realistic fiction in the novels of DeForest and his successors.

One of the evidences of scientific advance was the industrial expansion of New England and the building of railroads and steamboats for the economic conquest of the continent. The trains and ships drained the East of its population, but the void was quickly filled by immigrant hordes that were better adapted to the immediate demands of the cotton and woolen mills. The shipping activities of the New England coast towns were also increased, and the total effect was to change the character of the population and prepare the intellectual soil for the sentimental novel of the fifties and later. In the realm of ideas, the advance of science was equally disruptive, and no doubt partly responsible for the decline in the authority of the churches and the impairment of Christian idealism, making way for vague humanitarianism, crackpot reforms, and religious oddities. Under these conditions Hegelian philosophy, the positivism of Comte, and the evolutionary theories of Spencer and Darwin were more readily embraced than they would have been earlier.

Of the minor causes, the decline of the authority of the churches, as I have just indicated, was closely related to the advance of scientific thought. The old theology had suffered from the softening process of Unitarianism and Transcendentalism on the one hand and from the rational thrusts of minds like that of Dr. Holmes, who attacked it with the logic of science. The minister, who had been a person of authority and exalted dignity, suffered such loss of prestige that he could be laughed at by Mrs. Whitcher.

The second of the minor causes, the widening base of public education, is also connected with the advance in science, for one of the reforms in the college curriculum that had been long overdue was the reduction in the proportion of the classics in the college curriculum and the increase in the proportion of the sciences and social sciences. Moreover, the multiplication of public schools and the increasing power of the writer or compiler of texts, like Noah Webster and W. H. McGuffey, had an incalculable influence on the American mind. They helped to preserve old ideals, but they also inculcated materialistic tastes.

Foreign writers had much influence in America during this period, both in precepts and in examples. I have already mentioned Hegel, Comte, Spencer, and Darwin as thinkers whose ideas had influence. Of these it is probable that Spencer was the most influential in the sixties with his "Synthetic Philosophy," partially bridging the gap between science and faith. The later Transcendentalists found it easy to reconcile themselves to his optimistic philosophy, being helped thereto by such American disciples as Youmans and Fiske. More effective immediately were the three leading novelists of the Victorian period, Dickens, Thackeray, and George Eliot, becoming progressively more realistic in method, more critical of romanticism, and more friendly to science. Dickens was most widely imitated in this period because he illustrated the characteristic fusion of romantic sentiment and social reform. Thackeray, with his sharper edge of criticism, was not much copied until after the Civil War, and George Eliot only a decade or so later.

In conclusion, it may be said that as the result of advances made during the period of this study, the pattern of a technological society was established, the advance guard of scientific materialism had appeared, moral certainty was weakened, and the ground was prepared for pessimism. Realism as a literary method had been tried successfully. An intermediate generation of writers, most of them born chiefly in the twenties, had produced mostly second-rate works, but a new group was appearing, born in the thirties and forties, who promised to carry forward the movement from romanticism to realism in fiction and to relate literature more closely to the actualities of everyday life. As might be expected, no new voices of power, after Whitman's, spoke the language of poetry, unless the voices of Emily Dickinson and Sidney Lanier were such. The last third of the century, it appeared, was destined to be dominated by prose writing, more particularly by the novel.

# The Rise of
# Realism
# 1871-1891

# The Rise of
# Realism
# 1871-1891

*ROBERT P. FALK*
UNIVERSITY OF CALIFORNIA, AT LOS ANGELES[*]

I

FOLLOWING the Civil War, in the late 1860's, the twilight of romantic idealism became fused with early indications of a new and different literary and intellectual atmosphere. During the seventies and eighties the new tendencies slowly coalesced into a complex relationship of philosophical ideas, critical principles, and literary methods until, after 1886, Howells became spokesman for an aesthetic of American realism in the Editor's Study of *Harper's Magazine*. Between the publication of *The Hoosier Schoolmaster* in 1871 and the appearance of *Criticism and Fiction* in 1891 the earlier realism passed from a negative phase of reaction through a middle period of broadest affirmation during the 1880's, when much of its characteristic work was written. In the late eighties, altered by changes in the intellectual climate and by increased industrial strife, realism shifted its center of emphasis and moved toward social and economic criticism. Howells's aggressive championing of humanitarian causes after 1886 coincided with a decline in the artistic level

[*] I wish to express my thanks to the Rutgers University research council for a semester's leave in 1948 in which to do the work for this chapter and also to acknowledge the many valuable suggestions of Professor H. H. Clark, general editor of this volume, whose wide knowledge of American literature and thought have helped to make this a more comprehensive study than it otherwise could have been.

of his own fiction but, at the same time, helped provide a rationale for the critical realism of a younger school of writers. His repeated attacks upon the romantic novel likewise provoked a reaction toward "the old, exiled romance" and set the stage for the controversies of the 1890's between the Genteel Tradition and the proponents of a stronger sociological realism. In the twenty years from 1871 to 1891 the pattern of the earlier realism, broadly speaking, moved from the revolt and experiment of the 1870's through a period of mature artistic activity in the middle eighties toward the changing ideals of the nineties.

In undertaking a new interpretation of the phenomenon of realism one is confronted with a bewildering array of cultural interrelationships within the period itself, as well as an alarming number of preconceptions about it drawn from the twenty years of scholarship which has followed in the wake of Parrington's classic study, *The Beginnings of Critical Realism* (1930). The epithets alone which have been used to characterize American life in those years suggest a whole range of attitudes which need to be understood and evaluated: "The Gilded Age," "Frontier Period," "The Age of Innocence," "New England: Indian Summer," "The Tragic Era"—even the term "realism" itself with its many literary and pilosophical associations. All of these tend to color our thinking and present obstacles, as well as aids, to a fresh look at the thing itself.

There remains, however, the desire and renewed necessity for a portrait of the whole movement. The present essay is devoted to an exploration of that possibility. It becomes necessary, first, to distinguish the broad, intellectual character of the period from its major component elements, of which we may discern three: (1) the movement of thought behind realism; (2) the social spectacle surrounding it; and (3) the body of aesthetic principles and literary practice which comprised it. The first two of these divisions embody the major causes for the development of realism between 1871 and 1891. The third involves a definition of the literary movement itself and poses the question: What *was* realism, during those years, in its more strictly aesthetic manifestations?

This last question takes one directly into a study of the critical theories and literary methods of the leading men and women of letters whose growth and mature work coincided with the intellectual temper of the seventies and eighties. One must turn, first of all, to the periodicals where most of the fiction associated with realism first appeared and where, beginning in the middle sixties, critics and reviewers provoked a war of terms from which certain constructive doctrines gradually emerged. This aesthetic controversy, and its results in the prose fiction of the period (poetry, except for the forward-looking elements in Whitman, Emily Dickinson, and to some extent Lanier, clung to the skirts of a declining idealistic tradition) belongs in the center of the picture. American literary realism was a genuine cultural movement in itself with fairly definite chronological limits and recognizeable aesthetic principles and techniques. In other words, realism had its day. It was not simply a negative reaction against romanticism, on the one hand, nor a timid approach to naturalism, on the other.

In its intellectual and social origins, realism took shape and direction from an age of sharp conflict and change when the post-Darwinian struggle for a reorientation of American thought was in its earlier intense and indecisive phase. The critical discussions of realism, and the literature which practised its principles, were the literary aspects of a broader intellectual conflict between science and religion, idealism and materialism, teleology and natural selection. As a moment of intellectual history, realism may be regarded as part of the clash between the bright promise of democratic individualism and the darker shadows of a deterministic outlook. Between these polar extremities American thought moved hesitantly away from its earlier romantic and idealistic basis, taking color and shape from the grotesque fantasy of Gilded Age politics and business materialism.

The rapid movement after the war of social and economic forces toward industrialization and the aggregation of capital found philosophic sanction both in traditional American individualism and in the new evolutionary argument for survival of the fit. Yet this powerful swing of the pendulum toward integration, and the concentration of population in large urban centers, created the momentum for a reverse movement—labor and agrarian protests, group psychology, and a class-conscious society. Collectivism gradually developed in opposition to rugged individualism and laissez faire. In intellectual circles two basic attitudes emerged showing similarities to the older, prewar individualism and equalitarianism. Psychological and analytical individualism began to replace the ethical and transcendental exaltation of personal worth; similarly economic or sociological collectivism, based on science, took the place of the earlier philosophical and idealistic abolitionism, with its ethical concept of rights. Both the new psychology and the new sociology contained the seeds of determinism.

An understanding of realism involves the intellectual implications of these swift changes in society and thought. The problems implicit in the political phenomenon of Reconstruction; the puzzling crosscurrents of thought arising from the rapid expansion westward into new cultural and economic regions; the new rights of man which had to be integrated with the old—the rights of women, the rights of sections, the rights of labor; increasingly diversified religious and racial types entering the country to find a place beside the predominantly Anglo-Protestant strain—all these played their part in the cultural history of the seventies and eighties. The impact of such forces upon the earlier idealistic and individualistic heritage produced a climate of intellectual and social disparity. It was a confusing, and at the same time, a highly provocative age.

Against a background of controversy in philosophical and religious circles, and one of growing collectivist sentiment as opposed to the prevailing individualism of the American temper, intellectuals undertook to bring together in some kind of synthesis the widely disparate elements of an age of conflict and change. Literary critics and novelists, sensitive to both the old and the new, moved slowly toward a new stabilization largely in terms of English and French fictional models and critical methods. From the artistic controversies over naturalism and realism in the painting of Gustave Courbet, from the criticism of Taine and Sainte-Beuve, from the milder English realism of George Eliot, Dickens, and Thackeray, and the French realistic-naturalism of Balzac, Flaubert, and Zola—as well as in terms of American social, political, and philosophical thought—literature and criticism in America sought a new basis and a new justification. It is this quest, as it took shape in the two decades following the Civil War, that we shall here consider the essence of the problem of realism.

## II

In the *Atlantic Monthly* for 1871 appeared the first installments of DeForest's *Kate Beaumont*, Howells's *Their Wedding Journey*, Henry James's *Passionate Pilgrim;* three of Bret Harte's California stories; essays by John Fiske, John Hay, E. P. Whipple, Higginson, and Stedman. The same year saw the appearance in *Hearth and Home* of *The Hoosier Schoolmaster*, the publication of Mrs. Stowe's *Sam Lawson's Fireside Stories*, and DeForest's *Overland*. *Roughing It* came in 1872, and in September of that year Howells wrote enthusiastically to James: "What do you intend to do for literature in '73?—a year destined to be famous."[1] The newly appointed editor had achieved the heights of his early ambition at a young age and was anxiously in search of new material. His optimism reflected the spirit of a young and coming group of writers. Mark Twain and C. D. Warner's *The Gilded Age* appeared in 1873, James was writing such fine early short stories as "The Madonna of the Future" and "Madame de Mauves," and Howells himself completed *A Chance Acquaintance*, the first of a series of delicate penetrations into the psychology of the new American woman. A great question glowed in literary circles: What was to be the nature of the new literature?

The *Atlantic* itself under Howells expanded quickly into the rich fields and new pastures of art, music, politics, and especially of the new science. Its literary section echoed to the names of Balzac, George Eliot, Turgenev, Taine, Sainte-Beuve, Dickens, Flaubert, Thackeray; in science the *Atlantic* moved steadily away from its classical moorings into, among other things, the uncharted waters of the Darwinian controversy. The success of the indefatigable popularizers of Spencer and Darwin in America, E. L. Youmans and John Fiske, and such new scientific monthlies as *Popular Science* and *Appleton's Journal* impelled the staunch literary magazines like the *North American Review*, the *Nation*, *Harper's*, and the *Atlantic* to open their pages to natural selection, "Darwinism," and the scientific spirit. "The truth is," wrote Stedman in 1875, "that our school girls and spinsters wander down the lanes

---

[1] *Life in Letters of William Dean Howells*, ed. Mildred Howells (New York, 1928), I, 172. Hereinafter referred to as *Life in Letters*.

with Darwin and Huxley and Spencer under their arms; or if they carry Tennyson, Longfellow, and Morris, read them in the light of spectrum analysis."[2] Unquestionably the older literary ways had suffered some severe shocks. Huxley had described poetic expression as "sensual caterwauling"; Turgenev's sceptical Bazarov *(Fathers and Sons)* opined that "a good chemist is twenty-times as useful as any poet."

In society and politics the lurid career of Jim Fisk, "prince of vulgarians," was ended in 1872 by a bullet; and the era of scandal and corruption centered around the first Grant administration was revived in the public mind. The age which our historians have variously named "The Great Barbecue," "The Dreadful Decade," "The Tragic Era," or "The Age of Accumulation"—the period of Black Friday and the *Crédit Mobilier,* of unashamed public and private debauchery, of the diamond-studded, hawk-nosed Boss Tweed who defrauded the city government of three million dollars and died in disgrace pilloried by the powerful lampooning of Thomas Nast in *Harper's Weekly*—this "Chromo-Civilization," as E. L. Godkin named it, was part of the story of America in the seventies. Fisk, Jay Gould, "the-public-be damned" Commodore Vanderbilt, Oakes Ames, and a hundred more "railway wreckers, cheaters, and swindlers" for the most part—they moved through the panorama of the Age of Innocence "unlovely," "ungainly," "irreverent" amidst "pools of tobacco juice" (in Parrington's vivid language) "erupting in shoddy and grotesque architecture ... a world of triumphant and unabashed vulgarity" which was nevertheless "by reason of its uncouthness the most picturesque generation in our history."[3] Yet this is not the whole story of America in those years. Many young men and women of the seventies had intellectual interests—art, music, literature—"Mr. Hunt's classes, the novels of George Eliot, and Mr. Fiske's lectures on the cosmic philosophy."[4]

Materialism, philistinism, and the dollar added their burden to the heavy ballast of scepticism emanating from the naturalistic

[2] *Victorian Poets* (New York, 1877), p. 13.

[3] V. L. Parrington, *The Beginnings of Critical Realism in America* (New York, 1930), p. 13. Hereinafter referred to as Parrington.

[4] Howells's description of Clara Kingsbury as a girl in the seventies (*A Modern Instance* [New York, 1909], p. 469).

implications of the new evolutionary science. Nevetheless, it would have taken more than their combined weight to drag perceptibly upon the American mind during the 1870's. The ideals of the Enlightenment and human perfectibility were deeply rooted there, and scientific doubts about the supernatural origin of man could unsettle it, but not warp it wholly out of its own orbit. In New England Unitarian liberals like Moncure Conway and O. B. Frothingham carried on the individualistic idealism of Emerson; in the West Brokmeyer, Snider, and Harris countered with a democratic idealism, derived from Hegel, in which "brittle individualism" was supplanted by a broader national faith showing affinities with the earlier frontier equalitarianism; in the South a more sentimentalized kind of ideality survived as a compensation for the ravages of war. And in the mature thought of Walt Whitman these regional differences met and were suffused into an almost religious unity which preserved the dignity of "great persons" and the high hopes for the ultimate triumph of democracy and "these states."

During the 1870's public interest, as Tourgée said, turned away from the agony of strife to seek relief in lighter themes.[5] Fiction followed other trends toward realism, and left the Civil War, for the most part, to the historical romancers.[6] Even Whitman, deeply affected as he was by "that four years' war" which he discovered had become "pivotal" to the entire scheme of *Leaves of Grass*,[7] was more keenly aware of the business and political selfishness of that decade. Yet even wealth, science, and materialism, he believed, must give way before "the highest mind, and soul"; and he emerged from the sixties with an idealism stronger than before.

---

[5] A. W. Tourgée, "The Renaissance of Nationalism," *North American Review*, CXLIV (Jan., 1887), 1.

[6] Rebecca W. Smith, *The Civil War and Its Aftermath in American Fiction* (University of Chicago, 1937), pp. 20, 56. It is the author's conclusion that, although the war received realistic treatment in the fiction of the sixties, the "idealistic, patriotic tradition" prevailed from about 1870 to the nineties when Bierce, Frederic, and Crane applied new techniques to the theme. See also Merle Curti, *The Growth of American Thought* (New York, 1943), chap. xviii, "The Thrust of the Civil War into Intellectual Life."

[7] Preface to 1876 edition of *Leaves of Grass* in *Walt Whitman*, ed. Floyd Stovall (New York, 1934), p. 341.

With a few exceptions like DeForest's vigorous novel, *Miss Ravenel's Conversion*, the war would not greatly influence the growing literary realism of the postwar era until the nineties, and meanwhile "the genial romanticism of Victorian evolution" was to prevail.[8] Thomas S. Perry, one of the most brilliant as well as balanced minds of the newer generation, voiced the temper of intellectual America turning from the despondency of war to face the challenge of evolutionary science, mushrooming business, and loose public morals: "We ourselves know that even out of Civil War there may rise a grander comprehension of patriotism, fuller national growth, a broader view of a nation's duties and responsibilities."[9]

One of the characteristic things about the seventies was its response to the bustling feminist movement of the times. A reviewer in 1875 remarked not too kindly of Howells that his "tales have appeared in the pages of the *Atlantic Monthly*, and the young ladies who figure in them are the actual young ladies who attentively peruse that magazine."[10] The columns of the magazines, especially the Contributor's Club of the *Atlantic*, reverberated with discussions of women's problems in fiction. The *Nation*, always somewhat edgy about both Howells and James, grumbled that Howells's women characters smelled of clinical study and were not "the important creations they are almost universally assumed to be."[11] Both writers, it was admitted, were attempting to give us a national type which James treated with "if not especially complimentary, certainly most interesting results."[12] At any rate, the increase in feminine readers had provided the audience, scientific analysis had helped to formulate the method, and a self-conscious nationalism[13] lent purpose and direction to the "Gallery of Nervous Women" being painted largely by Howells and James.

The long and turbulent history of the femininist movement in America had during these years found new and colorful adherents

---

[8] Parrington, p. 190.
[9] *From Opitz to Lessing* (Boston, 1885), pp. 8-9.
[10] *Nation*, XX (Jan. 7, 1875), 12.
[11] *Ibid.*, XXX (July 15, 1880), 50.
[12] *Ibid.* (April 8, 1880), 265.
[13] For a thorough discussion of the relation of nationalism to the rise of realism after 1870, see B. T. Spencer, "The New Realism and a National Literature," *PMLA*, LVI (Dec., 1941), 1116-1132.

in the picturesque spectacle of the Age of Innocence. From *Charlotte Temple* to the *Female Poets of America* in the delicate forties, the eternal feminine had clung closely to the literary movements and circles of the day. It had always been associated with lady's book sentiment and lush morality. In the rise of Transcendental aspirations, however, it became colored with the tinge of liberalism, Margaret Fullerism, Fourierism, and freedom and strode like Zenobia with a challenging rose in its hair. Out of the well-known "conversations" at Boston and antislavery sentiment of the forties and fifties came the 1848 Declaration of Independence for women drawn up under the aegis of Elizabeth Cady Stanton. Woman suffrage was the most conspicuous aspect of the movement which gathered momentum after the Civil War and entered the arena of Gilded Age politics with a new and vigorous force. Outwardly, its aims were phrased by Wendell Phillips, who, in 1850, flung the challenge: "After the slave, then the woman!" Organization followed, slogans, manifestoes, speeches, but slowly as the philosophy of the movement was articulated there arose in the background the specter of further emancipations. "Freedom—they proposed to have, and something more besides." The opprobrious term, free love, attached itself to the radical wing of the party.[14]

Womanism in America had always been slightly eccentric, if not neurotic. Flowing gowns and poetry were mixed with the kind of sentimentalism which had clung to the lunatic fringe of the earlier idealism. Poe had moved among them, flirted with them, and his Madeleine Ushers and Lenores were not entirely exotic types. Now, in the phantasmagoria of the Dreadful Decade, the movement caught up some strange and colorful figures. George Francis Train, described as a "crack-brained harlequin and semilunatic" with money; Theodore Tilton, a dashing editorial Apollo, abolitionist, and radical feminist; Victoria Claflin Woodhull, given to visitations from the spirit world, a female broker, president of the National Spiritualistic Association, prophetess of "universological science, Millennial Perfection, a philosophy of Integralism, peace, love, truth, progress, purpose, and aspiration."[15] She became a candidate for the president of the United States in 1872. The

[14] Constance M. Rourke, *Trumpets of Jubilee* (New York, 1927), p. 345.
[15] *Ibid.*, p. 201.

many and obscure ways in which the feminist movement wound itself in and out of politics in the 1870's and 1880's, the front-page stories and press discussions of free-love versus Anthony Comstock, Henry Ward Beecher versus Tilton, the rivalries of Mrs. Stanton and Victoria Woodhull for control of the party—all this gave the old deistic slogan a new turn: The proper study of mankind was *woman*.

An age which vacillated between such intellectual extremes as the hard-boiled philosophy of survival of the fittest and a lush Victorian sentimentality about women could touch most of the notes in between. William Graham Sumner, one of the most tough-minded of the social Darwinists, combined the extremes in one phrase. The two chief things with which government has to deal, he said, were "the property of men and the honor of women. These it has to defend against crime."[16] Rarely did the feminism of the seventies remain unmixed with esoteric doctrines of spiritualism, free love, the religion of science, the universal progress. In 1875 Madame Blavatsky founded the Theosophy Society and the same year Mary Baker Eddy published *Science and Health*, which combined Transcendentalism with practical mental healing. Walt Whitman had mingled idealism and eroticism in his glorification of the feminine sex. He had proclaimed the complete equality of the sexes and had spoken in *Democratic Vistas* of the need for great women, the mothers of men; yet it was not forgotten that he had been dismissed from his government post for alleged immorality, and his *Leaves of Grass* only very gradually emerged from its earlier reputation as an indecent book. In the South the voice of Lanier cried out for a return to chivalry in the attitude toward women who "have redeemed the whole time." The period he described as "the epoch of the Victorian women" and felt the tendency of the time was to dethrone her from the heights on which the Elizabethan poets had placed her.[17]

In the fiction of the seventies, however, the accent began to shift from idolatry of women toward analytical investigation of the springs of feminine conduct. It was the stimulus of the new evolution-

[16] *What the Social Classes Owe Each Other* (New York, 1883), p. 101.
[17] *Complete Writings of Sidney Lanier*, 10 vols., Centennial Edition (1946), IV, 209. Hereinafter referred to as *Lanier's Works*.

ary psychology which in part turned Howells, James, DeForest, Weir Mitchell, Edgar Fawcett, and others toward the soberer methods of patient analysis in the treatment of character, especially women. While Darwinists like Chauncey Wright were investigating the naturalistic origins of mental activity,[18] other Americans went to the German behaviorists for new light on psychology. G. Stanley Hall was one of the leaders in this, bringing the studies of Wundt, Herman Lotze, Helmholtz, Fechner, Zeller, and other German founders of the new psychology to the pages of the scientific journals, stimulating the study of psychic states as a means of understanding the mind.[19] Holmes and Dr. Mitchell had written and corresponded on similar subjects even earlier, and the growing interest in them had its effect on the treatment of character in the novel. The brave hero and the virtuous heroine of earlier literature belonged to a pre-Darwinian psychology in which the origins of mind and character were supernatural. Now, the study of growth and change under environmental conditions led novelists to discover and analyze the "complex" character, the "typical" character, and especially the young American woman as a product of peculiarly national social conditions.

After Mrs. Stowe, whose *Lady Byron Vindicated* (1870) championed the cause of a woman martyr, the treatment of women in literature became less and less heroic. Howells's Kitty Ellison and Florida Vervain and Lydia Blood were all different studies of a single type—"emancipated young women begotten of our institutions and our climate, and equipped with a lovely face and an irritable moral consciousness."[20] His friend Thomas S. Perry viewed the matter in the most sympathetic, and probably the most accurate, light when he said that Howells's girls are unconventional and innocent types placed in a complicated modern society who

[18] Wright's essay "The Evolution of Self-Consciousness," *North American Review*, CXVI (1873), 245-310 helped break down the barrier between "instinct" and "reason" by showing that the rational faculties might well have developed out of lower instincts by adaptation to environmental uses. (See H. W. Schneider, *A History of American Philosophy* [New York, 1946], p. 348, and Curti, *op. cit.*, p. 557.)

[19] See Hall's *Aspects of German Culture* (Boston, 1881), esp. pp. 94-114, 121-145, 295-304. Also see his *Founders of Modern Psychology* (New York, 1912).

[20] *Nation*, XX (Jan. 7, 1875), 12.

"settle everything by their native judgment."[21] Other novelists were not as complimentary toward their women characters. Mrs. Chester and Mrs. Larue of DeForest's books, Daisy Miller and Christina Light of James's, Laura Hawkins of *The Gilded Age*, Weir Mitchell's Hepzibah Guinness and Octopia Darnell, and many others illustrate the feminine character in its role of nervous invalid, jealous lover, scheming adventuress, beautiful cynic, and innocent flirt.

In its more social aspects feminism likewise provided subject matter for novels and stories portraying the suffragist goings-on of the period in varying shades of satire and realism. Henry Adams's two feminist novels, Mrs. Davis's *Kitty's Choice*, Howells's *Undiscovered Country*, James's *Bostonians*, and Elizabeth Stuart Phelps's many novels abetting careers for women were reflections of the tremendous interest in this question which filled the magazines with articles. Almost simultaneously three novels about women physicians appeared, one by Howells—a coincidence which caused him some embarrassment.[22]

If Mrs. Stanton, Mrs. Woodhull, Julia Ward Howe, and the others proclaimed a Declaration of Independence for women, they were only expanding into an age of utilitarian politics the older ideals of the Enlightenment and the freedom of the individual. In this they were squarely in line with the trend of the 1870's. Individualism no longer wore its tie-wig, or its Transcendental cloak, or even its Byronic sword of defiance—but individualism it was, none the less, which dominated intellectual America during these years. It affected the hat and cane of a college professor or the bulging waistcoat of a railroad magnate. From William Graham Sumner to Andrew Carnegie, Americans took their cue from Spencer's sociology, from biological evolution, and the survival of the fittest to maintain that social progress should go unhindered and that a sound sociology should not violate the principle of selection by "the artificial preservation of those least able to take

---

[21] *Century Illustrated Monthly Magazine*, XXIII (March, 1882), 683. Hereinafter referred to as the *Century*.

[22] See *Life in Letters*, I, 299. The novels were Mrs. Phelps's *Dr. Zay*, Howells's *Dr. Breen's Practice*, and a third by an anonymous doctor-authoress.

care of themselves."[23] Based, as it was, on the biological variation of species, Spencer's sociology thus preserved the essential freedom of the individual. Likewise, his psychology, founded upon Locke, kept open the door to human perfectibility.[24]

These two terms, *psychology* and *sociology*, explain much about thought and expression in the Gilded Age. In one sense, they were the individualism and equalitarianism of an earlier day given new names and a different rationale. From about 1870 to 1890 the movement of intellectual America was from a strongly idealistic individualism in the seventies, to an increasing concern for the group in the eighties and nineties. In the cultured circles of New England, the inherited concern for moral problems of character held over into an age which was becoming more critical and analytical in outlook. On the Middle Border the earlier frontier spirit of self-reliance was being replaced, under economic stress, by a tendency toward co-operative activity and an interest in political reforms. Literary methods in fiction showed the gradual encroachment of analysis and satire upon the conventional solicitudes of the gushy novel. James had, in the 1860's, begun his studies of character and Howells had joined character-analysis to the travel sketch. In the West, always more closely allied with the land and with native social conditions, Eggleston studied rural schools and evangelical religion influenced by the theory of Taine and in the manner of Dickens, while Mark Twain and C. D. Warner reflected a different social interest in their satire on politics in Washington. Bret Harte fathered the local-color movement in his Dickens-like mixtures of a new environment with an old technique, burst into tremendous popular favor—then gradually settled into mannerism. And DeForest, whose point of view was broader than that of most of his contemporaries in the early seventies, helped to heal the breach between North and South in *Kate Beaumont*, dealing with sectional problems and, at the same time, bringing a vigorously

---

[23] Herbert Spencer, *The Study of Sociology* (New York, 1874), p. 346. See for discussion Richard Hofstadter, *Social Darwinism in American Thought, 1860-1915* (Philadelphia, 1945), pp. 25-30. Also the more recent and comprehensive *Evolutionary Thought in America* (New Haven, 1950), ed. Stow Persons.

[24] Parrington, p. 199.

original style to his studies of representative characters and American themes.[25]

As the decade moved through its middle years, the increasingly complex character studies of James (*Roderick Hudson, The American,* and *Daisy Miller*) and those of Howells (*A Foregone Conclusion, Private Theatricals, The Lady of the Aroostook*) began to be recognized as the most serious movement in American fiction. Local-color fiction began to appear about 1875 in the early stories of Miss Jewett and Cable, where regional types and native conditions were blended more realistically than they were in the tales and sketches of the popular Bret Harte. Eggleston's studies of Methodism, circuit riders, and local politics in the Middle West showed an increasingly firm touch and less dependence upon a Dickens-like sentimentality, and in *Roxy* he added a close study of character degeneration to his earlier interests in the dialect and social conditions of Indiana.

Meanwhile the interest in political, social, and economic problems which was to quicken in the eighties and rise to flood levels after 1887[26] gave birth to literary trends running parallel with the dominating interest in individualism and character problems. The Western humorists had already connected politics to indigenous scenes and frontier characters to establish a new literary *genre*. Arthur Sedgwick in 1866 had urged the editors of comic magazines "to use politics as much as possible; it is the great chord of harmony that runs through the country."[27] In a different direction, the new interest in sociology derived from the stress on environment and conditioning influences implicit in the concept of natural selection and the doctrine of evolving species. Richard Dugdale in *The Jukes* (1877) stimulated the new study of eugenics by emphasizing hereditary and environmental conditioning influences such as disease, pauperism, and immorality.[28] A few Brahmin voices were raised against corporate greed and chicanery—notably those of Charles Francis and Henry Adams on the Erie

---

[25] Howells wrote in the *Atlantic Monthly*, XXXIV (Aug., 1875), 229 that Mr. DeForest "so far is really the only American novelist".

[26] W. F. Taylor, *The Economic Novel in America* (Chapel Hill, N. C., 1942), p. 58.

[27] *North American Review*, CII (April, 1866), 591.

[28] Hofstadter, *op. cit.*, p. 138.

Railroad scandal, but severe economic dislocation resulted in the panic of 1873 and a lingering business depression. The early struggles of the Knights of Labor under the organizing energy of T. V. Powderly likewise affected the slow growth of collectivistic ideas. Greenbackism and the unrest of the farmers in the Middle West brought a successful political union of the Grangers and the labor unions in the elections of 1878. Whitelaw Reid in 1872 urged the Dartmouth graduates not to reject politics as a career: "The course and current of men in masses (he said)—that is the most exalted of human studies. . . ."

The literary reaction to these influences took the form of critical or satirical attacks on business and politics. Among the poets, Lanier added his voice to that of Melville in lashing out at the evils of industrialism and the vulgar excesses of democratic politics. Whitman reserved his social criticism for prose treatises like *Democratic Vistas* (1871) and later prose prefaces, while the novel responded slowly to sociological trends. *The Gilded Age* (1873) was perhaps the only novel of the decade which combined political criticism and satire with enduring literary merit, but Elizabeth Stuart Phelps linked feminist seriousness to a consciousness of the evils of the factory system in *The Silent Partner* (1871) and J. G. Holland in *Sevenoaks* (1875) moralized, in what the reviewers frankly denounced as Grade-B fiction, over the career of a rich speculator and railway king who "follows that path in which the late Jim Fisk, Jr. made himself well-known."[29] DeForest and Rebecca Harding Davis raised social criticism to a somewhat higher plane in *Honest John Vane* and *John Andross*. In DeForest's work, as one critic put it, "you have but to change the names and dates a very little and you have the Congressional Washington of 1874-75."[30] Critical opinion in the seventies was somewhat uncertain as to what line to take on this social trend of the novel. The reviewers admitted the truth of the picture, but wavered in their estimates of its literary value. Henry James put the case against it forcibly when he found Mrs. Davis's *John Andross* morally

[29] *Nation*, XXI (Dec. 9, 1875), 374.
[30] *Atlantic Monthly*, XXXV (Feb., 1875), 238. For further evidence of social criticism in the fiction of the 1870's and later, see Edward E. Cassady, "Muckraking in the Gilded Age," *American Literature*, XIII (May, 1941), 135-141.

wholesome but essentially "vulgar." The reader, James said, was overwhelmed with "the evil odor of lobbyism" and "may be excused for wondering whether, if this were a logical symbol of American civilization, it would not be well to let that phenomenon be submerged in the tide of corruption."[31]

The novel in the seventies had progressed rapidly, especially under the guiding genius of Howells and James, and it left criticism, for the time being, decidedly in the rear. George Parsons Lathrop in 1874 recognized the prevailing indolence of criticism and spoke of the need for a serious inquiry into principles upon which the various forms of the novel could be judged and upon which its further progress could be guided.[32] Lathrop felt that only Hawthorne, among American novelists, could be ranked with Scott, George Eliot, Balzac, Thackeray, and Turgenev. The serious novelist, he wrote, must achieve a reconciliation between science and a sound moral outlook. "The scientific motive is the dominant one; our fiction writers become minute and sectional investigators."[33] They must substitute for "the partial and critical view" now popular, a "unifying and creative one," avoiding a superficial didacticism and searching for deeper foundations of morality in human nature.[34] The terminology varied in the reviewers' columns of the monthlies, but the essential conflict was recognized—how to achieve a synthesis between the ideal and the real, between the imaginative and the analytical, the romantic and the actual, the larger truth and a photographic reproduction of reality.

While the literary columns of the Eastern periodicals were lamenting such things as the uncertain moral tone of native fiction, the lack of international copyright law, and the effect of the "large unlettered class constantly being transformed into the readers of books"[35] on the literary production of the period—there had been

---

[31] *Nation*, XIX (Dec. 13, 1874), 442. The *Atlantic Monthly* was more sympathetic. It felt that *John Andross* was the best political satire yet written in America (it had not reviewed *The Gilded Age*) and the fact that its characters were not pleasing was beside the point. "One feels them to be true, and that is enough" (XXXV [Feb., 1875], 238).
[32] *Atlantic Monthly*, XXXIII (June, 1874), 684.
[33] *Ibid.*, XXXIII, 695.
[34] *Ibid.*
[35] *Nation*, XXVII (Oct. 17, 1878), 244.

going on unobtrusively, but effectively, a reaction against romantic excesses and sentimental idealism which was to help transform public taste and alter critical methods. This reaction was most vigorous in the West. It can be seen in the early work of Mark Twain, Bret Harte, and John Hay at the point where Western humor and exaggeration merged with literary and social criticism to produce a kind of broadside against the overripe elements of a declining romantic tradition. The great popularity of both Harte and Clemens during these years lent added sting to their ridicule of Cooper, of the Scott-tradition of historical romance, of Coleridge, Ossianism, Byronism, and overt didacticism in literature.[36] A foreign critic has observed that Mark Twain "represented the transatlantic reaction against romanticism with more consistency, violence, and success than any of his contemporaries."[37] His early parody of the "Ancient Mariner" and his ridicule of sentimentalism, pretentiousness, Ossianism, and Byron established the point of view for his later attacks on Scott and Cooper; all contributed to the irreverent treatment of the literary past. Twain's overstrained ridicule of the South, the chivalric attitude toward women, and the "Sir Walter Disease" in *Life on the Mississippi* were a part of this early negative approach to a realistic aesthetics.

Bret Harte parodied Cooper, Dumas, Dickens, and others in his *Condensed Novels*, while in verse he burlesqued Poe's "Ulalume" and illustrated in grimly realistic detail ("Mrs. Judge Jenkins") the long connubial years of Maud Muller and the Judge. Harte's effrontery, like that of Mark Twain's notorious Whittier birthday

---

[36] Instances of this iconoclastic attitude toward the literary past in the works of Harte and Twain are as follows:

Harte parodied Cooper, Dumas, Dickens, Victor Hugo and the novelists in *Condensed Novels* (1867) and burlesqued Whittier, Poe, and other romantic poets in the *Overland Monthly* during the late sixties. Mark Twain first made fun of Cooper and the noble savage in the Buffalo *Express* August 21, 1869 ("A Day at Niagara") and parodied Coleridge in "The Aged Pilot Man," which appeared in *Roughing It* (1872). Twain's attacks on Scott were mostly in *Life on the Mississippi* (1883) and *A Yankee in King Arthur's Court* (1889). In the nineties Harte wrote his articles on the short story and local color for the *Cornhill* magazine, and Twain returned to his pet peeve, Cooper, in the *North American Review* (July, 1895).

[37] S. B. Liljigren, "The Revolt Against Romanticism in American Literature as Evidenced in the Works of S. L. Clemens," *Essays and Studies in American Language and Literature* (Uppsala, 1945), p. 51.

speech, came while Whittier's popularity was still at its height; sensing the decay of the sentimental mood which found "the saddest words of tongue or pen" to be "it might have been," Harte wisecracked:

> Sadder are these, we daily see,
> It is, but hadn't oughta be!

John Hay's Pike County *Ballads* and Mark Twain's *Roughing It* both found slang, dialect, buffoonery, irreverence, and derision to be effective weapons against the polite tradition and all kinds of pretension. Twain, like Bret Harte, used the device of the realistic sequel to blast away at conventional moral idealism—as in his belittling "About the Magnanimous Incident in Literature."[38] Although neither of them can be said to have related their critical attacks to a coherent philosophy or system of aesthetics, they contributed no little toward clearing the ground for later and more constructive theories of realism.

Farther east Richard Grant White, equally virile in his adherence to common sense and much more closely acquainted with the canons of romantic aesthetic theory, brought the attack on traditionalism into the field of Shakespeare criticism. White, one of the most independent of American critics of the period, was evolving his businessman theory of Shakespeare's genius in revolt against what he termed the "maundering mystification" and "ponderous platitude" of the wonder-seeking school of Shakespeare panegyrists—especially Coleridge and the German critics. Beginning as early as 1859 with his essay "Shakespeare's Art" in the *Atlantic* and more boldly in his *Life and Genius of Shakespeare* (1865), he found reason, sanity, and conscious art to be the mainsprings of Shakespeare's mental workings. In the process of establishing a common-sense approach to Shakespeare, White slashed away at most of the romantic theories of genius, imagination, and transcendental glorification.[39]

---

[38] *Atlantic Monthly*, LXI (May, 1878), 615-619. Twain concludes with the moral of a 'modern' fable: "Beware of the books. They tell but half the story. Whenever a poor wretch asks you for help . . . give yourself the benefit of the doubt and kill the applicant."

[39] See R. P. Falk, "Critical Tendencies in Richard Grant White's Shakespeare Commentary," *American Literature*, XX (May, 1948), 144-154.

The historical romance and the popular sensational, moralistic type of fiction provided the butt for much of this early antiromantic criticism. Henry James hinted that the vogue of Scott was at an end as early as 1864[40] and felt that in handling history the novelist should eschew a loose and free license, cultivate discipline, and subject himself to "certain uncompromising realities" and facts.[41] Likewise, James's distaste for the conventional 'female' novel of Tennysonian sentiment, its posing, attitudinizing, and its "ideal-descriptive style" found expression in 1865 when the young and untried novelist brusquely advised Harriet Prescott to leave off smothering her characters with caresses and diligently to study "the canons of the so-called realistic school."[42] Both DeForest and Howells, more by example than by theory, painted unpleasant characters, found faults in their heroines, substituted average people for monsters of virtue and vice, and used commonplace incidents in place of crime and seduction.

Individualism and the preference for character over environmental motivation revealed itself in the criticism of the seventies in the discussions of European critics, especially Taine and Sainte-Beuve. Although Eggleston's appreciation of Taine's *Art of the Netherlands* had helped turn his attention to the possibilities of the novel as an instrument of social history, he was not supported in his enthusiasm by most of his critical brethren in the East. James, in 1872, felt that Taine's emphasis on the sociological and racial factors in English literature made the book "a failure" and "ineffective as the application of a theory."[43] Howells, too, approached Taine with a "friendly distrust" and objected that his deterministic race-place-time formula "does not take into sufficient account the element of individuality in the artist."[44] John Bascom in his *Philosophy of English Literature* (1874) opposed Taine by theorizing

---

[40] *North American Review*, XCIV (Oct., 1864), 587: "Thoroughly to enjoy him," James concludes, "we must again become as credulous as children at twilight."

[41] *Nation*, V (Aug. 15, 1867), 126-127. See Ernest Bernbaum, "The Views of the Great Critics on the Historical Novel," *PMLA*, XLI (1926), 495.

[42] *North American Review*, C (Jan., 1865), 272.

[43] *Atlantic Monthly*, XXIX (April, 1872), 469-470.

[44] *Ibid.*, XXIX (Feb., 1872), 241. See also his review of Taine's *Art in the Netherlands* (*ibid.*, XXVII [March, 1871], 396).

that great men are not explained by social conditions and, in so far as they transcend the national type, remain unexplained.

Sainte-Beuve, on the other hand, appealed to James as "the better apostle of the two" because, like Edmond Scherer (another of James's favorite critics), he was undogmatic, unencumbered by theories, and had "truly devout patience" in reserving judgment. James, already strongly impressionistic in criticism, felt, even in 1865, that the critic's function was "to compare a work with itself, with its own concrete standard of truth."[45] But his severe hewing to the line of aesthetic technique and of his rejection of doctrinaire critics of whatever stripe was but one side of the eclecticism of James in his early reviews—an eclecticism which was compounded not only of his own independent nature, but of the uncertainties of the age in which fluctuation on these matters was the rule rather than the exception. To what standard should the writer cling? Was it, as T. W. Higginson advised in 1870, "a daring Americanism of subject" such as brought Cooper such success?[46] T. S. Perry took a different stand: "By insisting above all things on the novel being American, we mistake the means for the end."[47] Was it realism? But here lay the danger of sinking to the level of literal fact and police records.[48] Was it a moral standard? Yet in this path lurked the specter of obtrusive didacticism and falsification.

For most critics during these years a solution was found in compromise, although it was a compromise weighted on the side of the ideal. The characters of a work of fiction must "move on an ideal plane," wrote one contributor to the *Atlantic*, "parallel with yet above the real. . . . It is in this respect that his [the novelist's] work differs from that of the photographer and the newspaper reporter."[49] John Burroughs found the work of J. T. Trowbridge "almost too faithful . . . too literal, too near the truth, too photographic to charm the imagination. . . . for however real and truthful

---

[45] *Nation*, I (Oct. 12, 1865), 469.
[46] *Atlantic Monthly*, XXV (Jan., 1870), 63. Another proponent of nationalism in the early seventies was Emma Lazarus, whose poem "How Long?" (1871) urged the use of the frontier in American poetry and decried imitation of English models.
[47] *North American Review*, CXV (Oct., 1872), 368.
[48] See "Contributor's Club," *Atlantic Monthly*, XLII (Oct., 1878), 130-131.
[49] *Atlantic Monthly*, XLI (Jan., 1878), 132.

your story or faithful to contemporary events and characters, it must be bathed and flooded with that light that never was on sea or land to satisfy the best readers."[50] Henry James, looking back on those youthful years, perfectly described the vacillation of thought in a period poised between old dreams and new science: "It's all tears and laughter (he wrote) as I look back upon that admirable time, in which nothing was so romantic as our intense vision of the real . . . we dreamed over the multiplication table."[51]

Criticism in the seventies, groping for clear principles, found itself hesitant, self-conscious, provincial, and timid.[52] It looked abroad for assistance, but only a few men like James, Perry, Lathrop, and Stedman were widely enough read to find there clues from which to work out a genuine critical philosophy. It was out of such fluctuation that the concept of realism developed.

"Realism" (of which Howells later said, "the name is not particularly good,"[53] emerged as a conscious term in American criticism during the 1860's and was at once associated with growing interest in the novel.[54] Arthur Sedgwick, reviewing George Eliot's

[50] *Scribner's Monthly*, IX (Nov., 1874), 33.
[51] "The Next Time," in *Henry James*, ed. Lyon Richardson (New York, 1941), p. 415.
[52] See the article by C. A. Bristed "American Criticism: Its Difficulties and Prospects," *North American Review*, CXIV (Jan., 1872), 23-39.
[53] *Century*, XXVIII (Aug., 1884), 663.
[54] F. L. Pattee, *The Development of the Short Story* (New York, 1923), p. 168 says the *Atlantic Monthly* used the word "realistic" as applied to literary taste in Germany as early as 1857 and comments: "It is the first time I have found the word 'realistic' in American criticism." E. E. Hale in "The Earlier Realism," *Union College Bulletin*, XXV (Jan., 1932), 5 says the term "realism" first appeared in America in *Putnam's Magazine* for May, 1856, where a commentator on modern painters said: "Realism in art has been pushed to its last terms in our day." He adds that the term was used in European criticism during the 1850's as applied to Courbet's painting, Flaubert's *Madame Bovary*, Freytag's *Soll und Haben*, and George Eliot's *Adam Bede*. It is true, of course, that articles on fiction as far back as the 1850's had used phraseology suggestive of the association of the novel with realism. *Putnam's Magazine*, III (May, 1854), 560 had said that, rather than being the vehicle for the exposition of doctrine, the novel should "represent life and manners as they are." Again, the same periodical (IV [Oct., 1854], 390-391) demanded that novels "be veritable and veracious segments of the great life-drama, displaying Nature and Man as they are. . . ." Extravagance of sentiment, conventional characters, and excessive didacticism were frowned upon this early in the name of "verisimilitude," "truth to life," and obedience to things as they are.

*Felix Holt* in 1866, stated the essential problem of realism with a clarity quite astonishing when one realizes that Howells himself rarely used the term in his critical writing until after 1880.[55] George Eliot, wrote Sedgwick,

> still keeps the path of realistic art, studying the roadside nature, and satisfied with it. She continues to receive the great reward which every true realist longs for, that she is true to nature without degenerating into the commonplace, and the old blame, that they have not enough of the ideal, which they covet.[56]

Here was the dilemma of the early realists succinctly put. The year previous, 1865, Henry James referred to "the famous realistic system which has asserted itself so largely in fictitious writing in the last few years." Balzac, James said, belongs at the head of "the great names in the realist line" because "he presents objects as they are."[57] Yet, if we would understand James's use of the term, we must take account of the qualifications he placed upon it. He would not indiscriminately recommend the realistic system—"on the contrary," he adds, "we would gladly see the vulgar realism which governs the average imagination leavened by a little old-fashioned idealism."[58] James was thus early wrestling with the problem of the real versus the ideal in literature and searching for a new synthesis which would at once reject the cloyingly Tennysonian style of the author of *Azarian*, the narrow domestic actuality found in *The Wide, Wide World*, and even the "fidelity to minute social truths" of the indefatigable Trollope.[59] It would likewise repudiate "the injudicious straining after realistic effects" which characterized Rebecca Davis's stories of common life and

---

[55] Although Howells had termed the comedies of Goldoni "realistic" in 1877, he seems first to have spoken of "realism" (the realism of Daudet and Zola) in the *Century*, XXV (Nov., 1882), 29. And not until two years later did he speak of it in the sense of a literary movement apparent in the American novel (*Century* XXVIII [Aug., 1884], 633). A summary of Goldoni's influence upon Howells's realism may be found in James L. Woodress, Jr., *Howells & Italy* (Durham, N. C., 1952), pp. 131-147.

[56] *North American Review*, CII (Oct., 1866), 557-558.

[57] *Ibid.*, C (Jan., 1865), 272.

[58] *Ibid.*

[59] See his review of Trollope's *Miss Mackenzie* (*Nation*, July 13, 1865). Also *North American Review*, C (Jan., 1865), 276-277, where he discusses Trollope, Balzac, and Harriet Prescott.

laboring people.⁶⁰ Somewhere, on a deeper level, James's "realism" was to find its center guided by Balzac, George Eliot, Thackeray, Turgenev, and Flaubert.

James's suspicion of "schools" of literature and doctrinaire theories led him to speak with reserve of what he more than once called "the so-called principle of realism."⁶¹ He shied away from George Eliot's moralistic tendency on the grounds that "her colours are a little too bright, and her shadows too mild a gray."⁶² Yet in the conclusion to the brilliant essay on Balzac, James discovered his "serious fault" to be that, unlike Shakespeare, Thackeray, and George Eliot, "he had no natural sense of morality."⁶³ The morality must not be obtrusive, he felt, but it must, like the figure in the carpet, be present; it must be sensed "as a kind of essential perfume." If it was George Eliot's error that she excluded squalor and misery from her books, James could acclaim Turgenev's truth to life because " 'life' in his pages is very far from meaning a dreary liability to sordid accidents."⁶⁴ "We value most the 'realists,' " James wrote, "who have an ideal of delicacy and elegiasts who have an ideal of joy."⁶⁵

One of the factors in James's early training which was to become an essential of his critical vocabulary and his creative technique was his deep interest in pictorial art. Like his brother William, he had absorbed much of the controversy over naturalism in French art circles from William Morris Hunt. Hunt had brought the influence of Millet—a kind of romantic humanitarianism combined with the objective techniques of the realists—into Boston salons, and had also learned much from the more vigorously socialistic-

---

⁶⁰ See his review of Mrs. Davis's "Waiting for the Verdict" (*Nation*, V [Nov. 21, 1867], 410).

⁶¹ *North American Review*, C (Jan., 1865), 272.

⁶² *Atlantic Monthly*, XVIII (Oct., 1866), 48.

⁶³ *French Poets and Novelists* (New York, 1878), p. 113. (Originally in the *Galaxy*, Dec., 1875). The influence of Balzac on James is most fully studied in Cornelia P. Kelley's *The Early Development of Henry James* (Urbana, Ill., 1930), pp. 76-88 and in C. Cestre's "La France dans l'oeuvre de Henry James," *Revue Anglo-Americaine*, X (1922-1923), 1-13. Besides James, other critics like T. S. Perry, G. P. Lathrop, and, later, Howells, recognized the leadership of Balzac in French fiction and felt him to be the founder and best practitioner of realism in the novel.

⁶⁴ *Ibid.*, p. 283.     ⁶⁵ *Ibid.*, p. 318.

naturalism of Gustave Courbet. James admired the work of Frank Duveneck, an early American realist of the Munich school, and (especially) the painting of Eastman Johnson, Winslow Homer, and Thomas Eakins, which has been called "the closest analogy in American painting to Zola and the physiological novel." The realists in both literature and art strove for a greater scientific objectivity and detachment of viewpoint.[66] The portrait, distinguished as it is from the literal photograph by its typical and representational aspects, lay close to the center of James's aesthetics.[67] His early belief that "there is no essential difference of system between the painting of a picture and the writing of a novel"[68] helped him to reject the overstrained drama and sensational adventure of the popular novel and substitute the slower tempo and the painstaking methods of the artist whose supreme interest is the illustration of character. "What is character but the determination of incident? What is incident but the illustration of character? What is either a picture or a novel that is not of character?"[69]

James, then, was clearly a product of the sixties and seventies in his efforts to reconcile the conflicting tendencies of the time. He was typical, too, in his emphasis on the individual rather than the social or the critical in literature. He was original mainly in the subtlety of his mind and the depth of his intellectual concerns. His finely drawn synthesis between the ideal and the real, between morality and actuality, between ethics and aesthetics, between content and form rested on deeper premises than that of most of his contemporary critics. Even he, at times, despaired of reconciling the extremes of thought in his day, as they affected aesthetics and criticism.[70] And often he became self-contradictory, but it was his strength that he could hold to "the Anglo-Saxon faith," to the figure in the carpet, and to the "ideal of joy" without rejecting

[66] See *Courbet and the Naturalistic Movement*, ed. George Boas (Baltimore, 1938), pp. 117, 123, and *passim* for a complete discussion of the relation of naturalistic painting to realism in literature during the late nineteenth century.

[67] See J. W. Beach, *The Method of Henry James*, chap. ii for a discussion of the influence of art on James's creative work.

[68] *North American Review*, C (Jan., 1865), 275.

[69] *Partial Portraits* (New York, 1888), p. 392.

[70] See his essay on Baudelaire (*French Poets and Novelists*, p. 80): "Baudelaire was a poet, and for a poet to be a realist is, of course, nonsense."

science, analysis, French naturalism, and the objective presentation of fact. Much later in the Preface to *The American* he put the problem thus:

> [The artist] commits himself in both directions, not quite at the same time nor to the same effect, of course, but . . . by the law of some rich passion in him for extremes. . . . His current remains therefore extraordinarily rich and mixed, washing us successively with the warm wave of the near and familiar and the tonic shock, as may be, of the far and strange.[71]

Much has been made of Howells's apostrophe in *Their Wedding Journey* (1871) to "poor real life" with its "foolish and insipid face" and the passage in the same book where he urges the artist to "shun the use even of real events if they are of improbable character." Such pronouncements sound sufficiently advanced to tempt one to say of Howells, as James did of *Madame Bovary*, that realism there has said its last word.[72] But it is important for an understanding of Howells's later views to observe that he was almost twenty years later than his fellow critics of the seventies to use the term "realism" in his critical writing.[73] The implication of his remarks about the commonplace can be misunderstood unless they are read in the light of his literary temper of this period. Howells's temperament was always more creative than critical; philosophy and analysis were not really congenial to him. Indeed, throughout his life Howells's approach to art began on the creative level, and for the most part his criticism followed later as a rationalization of what he had already accomplished in fiction. Unlike James, he had begun his career as a poet, and his early sketches abound with flights of descriptive fancy. Above all he admired, in the early seventies, the picturesque, the charming, the quaint, and the imaginative. As late as 1882, writing of Henry James, Howells recalled with special fondness "the richness of poetic effect" in his early stories.

[71] *The Art of the Novel*, ed. Richard P. Blackmur (New York, 1934), p. 31. It is worth observing that James's final synthesis of the near and the real with the remote and romantic is not much different, if we allow for a later and more scientific age, from Emerson's reconciliation of the near, the low, and the familiar with the higher transcendental truths. In James, of course, the "romantic" is a more exclusively aesthetic term.

[72] *Galaxy*, XXI (Feb., 1876), 226.     [73] See n. 53.

It is true that Howells, in reviewing the fiction of Eggleston, Harte, Boyesen, Mark Twain, DeForest, and Henry James, was impressed by such qualities as the truthfulness to nature of their characters and conditions, their verity, lifelikeness, and accurate observation; nevertheless, he consistently preferred the term "romance," recalling Hawthorne, to "novel" when speaking of prose fiction. Boyesen's *Gunnar* he liked "because it was the work of a poet,"[74] Eggleston's *Circuit Rider* is described as a "romance." Writing to James in 1873 about his recent *A Chance Acquaintance* Howells felt that his experience had prepared him "better than ever for the field of romance."[75] And he enjoyed the latter part of James's *Passionate Pilgrim* because its "finer air of romance" revealed a high degree of imagination.[76] It was not until 1879 that Howells began to clarify in his mind the distinction between a romance and a novel. Reviewing W. H. Bishop's *Detmold: A Romance*, he pointed out that the romance "like the poem [was] at once more elevated and a little more mechanical than the novel."[77] Discussing James's *Hawthorne* he found fault with his friend's persistent use of the two terms synonymously. "The romance and the novel," Howells now felt, "are as distinct as the poem and the novel."[78]

In 1882 Howells wrote one of his explosive essays, an article on Henry James for the *Century Magazine*. Always eager to say a good word for James, he praised his early work and looked back with a certain nostalgia to the older days. Then, he thought, James had stood at the dividing ways of the novel and the romance. "His best efforts seem to me those of romance; his best types have an ideal development, like Isabel and Claire Bellegarde, . . . perhaps the romance is an outworn form and would not lend itself to the reproduction of even the ideality of modern life. I myself waver

[74] *Atlantic Monthly*, XXXIV (Nov., 1874), 624.
[75] *Life in Letters*, I, 175.
[76] *Atlantic Monthly*, XXXIV (April, 1875), 492.
[77] *Ibid.*, XLIV (Aug., 1879), 265.
[78] *Ibid.*, XLV (Feb., 1880), 283. Louis J. Budd's "W. D. Howells' Defense of the Romance" (*PMLA*, LXVII [March, 1952], 32-42), published after the above was written, corroborates my interpretation of the qualified nature of Howells's realism.

somewhat in my preference...."[79] And in 1884 Howells described Bellamy's *Miss Ludington's Sister* as a mixture of realism and romance. "There is nothing antagonistic in realism to poetry or romance," he now said,[80] and it is clear that as Howells began to recognize "the prevalence of realism in the artistic atmosphere" of the early eighties he naturally associated it with the novel, a form quite apart from his first love—romance.[81]

Indeed, it was a delicate compound of Goldoni's comedies, Irving's sketches, of Hawthorne's play of fancy and sentiment, and of George Eliot's charming commonplace which composed the special atmosphere of Howells's early travel books and experiments in character. His expressed aim in *Their Wedding Journey* was to do nothing more than "talk of some ordinary traits of American life,"[82] and he preferred not to look upon man in his "heroic or occasional phases," but "to seek him in his habitual moods of vacancy and tiresomeness."[83] Like George Eliot, who gladly turned away from angels, prophets, and heroic warriors "to an old woman bending over her flower-pot" while the softened light through the leaves "just touches the rim of her spinning wheel and her stone jug, and all those common things which are the precious necessities of life to her,"[84]—so Howells (in phrasing strikingly similar) found man in his natural and unaffected dullness to be "very precious." The "rare, precious quality of truthfulness" which George Eliot found in Dutch paintings, Howells shared in those early romances.[85]

---

[79] *Century*, XXV (Nov., 1882), 27.

[80] *Ibid.*, XXVIII (Aug., 1884), 633.

[81] Bellamy has done, Howells added, "about the only thing left for the romancer to do in our times, if he will be part of its tendency: he has taken some of the crudest and most sordid traits of our life, and has produced from them an effect of the most delicate and airy romance" (*ibid.*).

[82] 1899 ed., p. 2.

[83] *Ibid.*, pp. 86-87.

[84] *The Writings of George Eliot* (New York, 1907), III, *Adam Bede*, chap. xvii, pp. 257-258.

[85] The role of George Eliot in the early growth of realism in America can scarcely be overemphasized. She became a champion of realistic methods in fiction which rejected the excesses of the French school and yet preserved the newer scientific interest in elaborate psychological analysis. She appealed to conservative critics, too, in her strong didactic tone. Besides James, Howells, T. S. Perry, Lathrop, and others, see W. C. Wilkinson, "The Literary and Ethical Quality of George Eliot's Novels," *Scribner's Monthly*,

Their tempo is slow and the author pauses long to linger over scenes and attitudes of ordinary people—peasant women with hats of felt and straw and baskets of onions, an Indian wedding quaint and pathetic, "quiet gliding nuns with white hoods and downcast faces."[86] The figures are small and remote and picturesque, exuding the charm of Old World romance, moving as though in pantomime, presenting to the eye of the author an artistic arrangement.

In all this, of course, the analogy to painting, especially Millet and the Dutch school, is very close. It is characteristic of the avenues by which both James and Howells approached realism that they saw life through art, through the portrait. As the painter reveals character, so the novelist should bring out typical and general characteristics on his canvas. In 1877 Howells wrote Charles Dudley Warner, who had urged him to try a large canvas: "I find . . . that I don't care for society, and that I do care intensely for people. I suppose therefore my tendency would always be to get my characters away from their belongings, and let four or five people act upon each other."[87] In defense of this view Howells appealed to the example of Turgenev, "the man who has set the standard for the novel of the future" and "whom certainly you can't blame for want of a vast outlook."[88] The Russian novelist had excelled in character study, and Howells's scholarly friend Perry pointed out in his reviews that the strength of Turgenev's realism lay in his deep insight into his fellowmen and his skill in placing them objectively before the reader.[89]

---

VIII (Oct., 1874), 685-703; Edward Eggleston, "George Eliot and the Novel," *Critic*, I (Jan. 29, 1881), 9; G. W. Cooke, *George Eliot* (New York, 1883); Lanier's *The English Novel* (1881); and many other articles and reviews in the periodicals.

[86] *A Chance Acquaintance* (Boston, 1873), pp. 96-98.
[87] *Life in Letters*, I, 233.
[88] *Ibid.*, p. 232.
[89] *Atlantic Monthly*, XXXIII (May, 1874), 569, 572-574. American realists learned the technique of dramatic objectivity from Turgenev and were encouraged in their own preference for character representation and the "portrait" as opposed to a greater emphasis on social criticism and environmental determinism by his impartial studies of people. As in the case of George Eliot, it was Turgenev's "middle course" which helped James and Howells to steer away from the excesses of romanticism, on the one hand, and French naturalism on the other. See James's essay on Turgenev in *French Poets and Novelists* (originally published in the *North American*

The reaction of reviewers and critics to the literary productions of the seventies offers a kind of cross-section of the taste of the period. Realism in fiction was sometimes associated with external pictures of society and social criticism, and as such it was regarded with suspicion. Characteristic of the reviews is one in the *Atlantic* speculating on the value of such pictures of American society as were portrayed in DeForest's *Playing the Mischief* (1876). The critic discovered a danger in dealing with "the vulgar phases of American society" in fiction. These, he felt, were "so shameless, defiant, and unpicturesque" that they "must be treated cautiously,— in glimpses only; or if broadly exhibited, they should be accompanied by redress in the form of something better."[90] But, while the critical palate of the 1870's was somewhat too sensitive for strong social criticism, it does not follow that it was entirely receptive to the character studies and portraits of Howells and James. In Howells's work the *Nation* discovered great technical gifts, but "a lack of romantic imagination,"[91] and despite Howells's own theories about "romance," it declared that his society novels were "all death to romance."[92] It accused him of trying to substitute photographic detail for imaginative creation and described his methods as "too unromantic . . . to deal adequately with the large and important elements of fiction."[93] James, too, suffered the strictures of the reviewers and contributors who found his early books too inconsequential to be satisfactory. One critic even argued that *The American* violated the happy-ending conclusion of novels unjustifiably and that that convention was "a law which does not

---

*Review* for April, 1874). James found Turgenev's view of the human spectacle to be "more general, more impartial, more unreservedly intelligent than that of any novelist we know." See also Lyon Richardson, *Henry James* (New York, 1941), pp. xxx-xxxi. G. P. Lathrop in the *Atlantic Monthly*, XXXIV (Sept., 1874), 321 wrote: "Of all eminently realistic novelists, Turgenieff is, I imagine, the most vigorous, acute and delicate." See Royal A. Gettman, *Turgenev in England and America*, Illinois Studies in Language and Literature, Vol. XXVII, No. 2, Urbana, for a bibliography of the subject and a study of the influence of Turgenev on James, Howells, G. P. Lathrop, and T. S. Perry.

[90] *Atlantic Monthly*, XXXVII (Feb., 1876), 238-239.
[91] *Nation*, XXXI (July 15, 1880), 50.
[92] *Ibid.*
[93] *Ibid.*

admit of exceptions."[94] Another was similarly "defrauded" by James and felt toward his books as if "he had assisted at a vivisection from which no valuable physiological principle had been demonstrated."[95] Emily Dickinson, a rebel in her own right, wrote to Higginson about Howells and James—their "relentless music dooms as it redeems."[96] And young Hamlin Garland, who later became Howells's ardent admirer, was on first reading him "irritated and repelled" by what he called Howells's "modernity."[97]

Both Howells and James were often lumped together and reprimanded for their realism. The *Nation* summed it up in 1879 as follows:

Like Mr. James, Mr. Howells is a realist—he copies life; and realism in literature, although not so plainly a disappointment as in art, is quite as unsatisfactory. . . . What is valuable in literature is not the miniature of life, but the illumination of life by the imagination. . . . Our regret is that Mr. Howells has built in stones of the street when he might have built in more durable and beautiful material.[98]

Such pronouncements involved a misunderstanding both of realism and of what James and Howells were trying to accomplish. Neither of them was attempting to "copy life"—rather they strove to avoid the pitfalls of photographic or newspaper reproduction by representing, or typifying reality.[99] Nor were they seeking to be "analytical." Howells, pleased at Mark Twain's enthusiasm over

[94] *Ibid.*, XXIV (May 13, 1877), 325. But see also for a different view the *Atlantic Monthly*, XXXVII (Feb., 1876), 237 where "unqualified praise" is given *Roderick Hudson* for its "boldly broken end . . . which so completely lends it the air of a detached piece of life without injuring its individual completeness."

[95] *Atlantic Monthly*, XL (Dec., 1877), 749.

[96] *Letters of Emily Dickinson*, ed. Mabel Loomis Todd (Boston, 1894), II, 329.

[97] *A Son of the Middle Border* (New York, 1930), p. 227.

[98] *Nation*, XXVIII (March 20, 1879), 205. See also J. H. Morse, "Henry James Jr. and the Modern Novel," *Critic*, II (Jan. 14, 1882), 1, for similar strictures on James's realism, materialism, and scientific methods.

[99] Howells frequently makes the distinction between newspaper "facts" and artistic methods. See *A Modern Instance* (New York, 1881), p. 193: "He had the true newspaper instinct, and went to work with a motive that was as different as possible from the literary motive. . . . He did not attempt to give it form. . . . He set about getting all the facts he could. . . ." See also *A World of Chance* (New York, 1893), p. 3 for another similar distinction.

*Indian Summer,* wrote: "What people cannot see is that I analyze as little as possible; they go on talking about the analytical school, which I am supposed to belong to...."[100] Yet there were others who saw in that much belabored term "realism" a potentially fruitful and constructive critical philosophy for the novel. One of these was George Parsons Lathrop, who, in 1874, discussed "The Novel and Its Future" in the *Atlantic Monthly.* After carefully distinguishing realism from literalism, he proceeded to define it as follows:

Realism sets itself at work to consider characters and events which are apparently the most ordinary and uninteresting, in order to extract from these their full value and true meaning. It would apprehend in all particulars the connections between the familiar and the extraordinary, and the seen and the unseen of human nature.... In short, realism reveals. Where we thought nothing worthy of notice, it shows everything to be rife with significance. It will be easily seen, therefore, that realism calls upon imagination to exercise its highest function, which is the conception of things in their true relations.[101]

It was Lathrop and Perry and James and Howells who found in realism a view of life, primarily to be applied to the novel, in which the grasp upon ordinary concerns of life did not necessarily exclude the imagination, and where a scientific discipline of method did not prevent a healthy tone and even, in its best sense, an idealized view of human nature. To this group must be added two other critics who, in a different way, undertook to reconcile some of the prevailing currents of thought of the seventies as they applied to literature. Sidney Lanier and E. C. Stedman, unlike the others, were practising poets as well as critics and, as such, were less concerned with realism in its fictional uses, but their contribution to the aesthetic philosophy of the period was no less significant. They undertook, among other concerns, to bring about a synthesis between certain of the implications of Darwinian evolution and the higher concerns of literature.

Whitman, of course, had much earlier linked Hegelian evolu-

[100] Cited in *Mark Twain's Letters,* ed. A. B. Paine (New York, 1917), p. 455.
[101] *Atlantic Monthly,* XXXIV (Sept., 1874), 321-322. A full bibliographical study of critical trends in relation to the realistic novel is Helen McMahon's *Criticism of Fiction, A Study of Trends in the Atlantic Monthly 1857-1898* (New York, 1952).

tionary optimism to literary theory and had thus formulated a relativist and evolutionary philosophy of criticism. By 1880, however, Spencer and Darwin had superseded Hegel, and evolution involved a stronger hint (or threat) of materialism and naturalism. Stedman realized that "the immense energy of science has paled the fire of poetry, but that the result will be in a new adaptation of poetic expression in agreement with the accepted truths of science."[102] Thomas S. Perry in the Preface to his *English Literature of the Eighteenth Century* (1883) spoke of the possibility of progress in the realm of literature. Despite the towering example of Shakespeare, he thought that "the present interest in reality and distrust of literary conventions would provide the basis for new masterpieces." George Eliot's novels show, he said, "how far the province of literature has been enlarged."[103]

It was the work of Shakespeare and George Eliot, too, that Lanier discussed in his lectures in the late 1870's at Johns Hopkins and the Peabody Institute in Baltimore. Most of the tendencies of literary theory and aesthetic speculation of the period can be found in Lanier's *Science of English Verse, Shakespere and His Forerunners,* and *The English Novel*—the impact of Spencer and Darwin, the conflict of science and literature, the relation of the arts, the function of the novel, the quest for a science of criticism, the reconciliation of opposite poles of thought, the high regard for the individual (the latter intensified in Lanier by his temperamental idealism and chivalry). Indeed, though he did not often speak of realism as such, his aesthetic theory can be regarded as a kind of summary effort, about 1880, to weave together into a harmonious pattern all the singular elements of critical thought which were coming to be associated with that term. For his *Science of English Verse* he went to the German physiological aesthetics of Helmholtz and Heinrich Schmidt, and to Tyndall, Alfred Mayer, and Piétro Blaserna for their theories of sound and acoustics.[104]

[102] *Victorian Poets* (Boston, 1884), p. 19.

[103] Preface, pp. viii-ix. For a discussion of the problem of the evolutionist critics in reconciling the greatness of Shakespeare with a concept of progress and development in literature, see R. P. Falk, "Shakespeare's Place in Walt Whitman's America," *Shakespeare Association Bulletin*, XVII (April, 1942), 86-96.

[104] See *Lanier's Works* (Centennial Edition), II, 25 n., xxix. The MSS in

Although he seems to have rejected the theory of biological evolution,[105] he found in Darwin, Spencer, and John Fiske an evolutionary foundation for principles of criticism. Likewise, he sought inspiration in German philosophy and especially in Novalis,[106] and to Emerson he partly owed his fondness for drawing analogies between science and moral laws. Finally, Poe's *Eureka* helped him to formulate, along with Spencer's system, his view of the universe as a harmony of rhythmic motions.[107] It was Spencer, Lanier said, "who has formulated the proposition that where opposing forces act, rhythm appears, and has traced the rhythmic motions of nature to the antagonistic forces there found. . . ."[108]

Lanier understood, even more clearly than most of his contemporaries, the deeply conflicting currents of doctrine which confronted the artist and thinker in an age of science and materialism. For this reason he felt the necessity of establishing a broad philosophical basis upon which to erect his aesthetics, a system which could allow place for the ideals of the artist without denying the truths of science. His work has been accused of philosophic contradiction and loose thinking. Yet, along with James and Howells, Perry, Lathrop, and a few others whose effort was toward intelligent harmonization of philosophic extremes, Lanier (against the overwhelming physical odds of his illness which gave him only a few remaining years to do it) worked out a synthesis as comprehensive for aesthetic criticism as that achieved by any other man of his age.

Harmony among the opposing forces of the universe Lanier discovered in "that great principle" of rhythm by which "the whole universe came to present itself to us as a great flutter of motions."[109] The "fret" and "sting," the "no of death"—all evil in the world—

---

the Lanier Room at Johns Hopkins contains seven pages of notes on the flyleaves of Blaserna's *Theory of Sound* (*Works*, II, xxvi).

[105] Edwin Mims, *Sidney Lanier* (1905), p. 317.

[106] Gay Allen, "Lanier as a Literary Critic," *Philological Quarterly*, XVII (April, 1938), 121-122. See also Philip Graham, "Lanier and Science," *American Literature*, IV (Nov., 1932), 288-292. Through James Woodrow Lanier became acquainted with German thinkers. Carlyle and Ruskin were likewise influential.

[107] A. H. Starke, *Sidney Lanier* (Chapel Hill, N. C., 1933), p. 372.

[108] *Lanier's Works*, II, 193-195. Also *Works*, III, 301, 317 for similar ideas.

[109] *Lanier's Works*, III, 317.

were to him the necessary antagonism or friction of life, like the cross-plucking of the taut bowstring to bring melody and harmony out of conflict. In both the physical and the moral world "this beautiful and orderly principle of rhythm thus swings to and fro like the shuttle of a loom and weaves a definite and comprehensible pattern into the otherwise chaotic fabric of things."[110]

In his speculation on social progress, Lanier held that society had evolved upward from the primitive to the modern state, and this social progress (here he was close to Herbert Spencer's sociology in *The Man Versus the State*) centered not in the group but in the individual, in his development toward personal responsibility for his own fate. Arguing from Darwinian premises and citing Fiske's "Sociology and Hero-Worship" (*Atlantic Monthly*, Jan., 1881), Lanier found in the concept of the "spontaneous variation" of species justification for his faith that the social order existed for the highest development of the individual.[111] In *The English Novel* he traced the development of this concept of personality in literature from Aeschylus to Shelley and finally to George Eliot. The Prometheus of Aeschylus is devoid of moral responsibility in his ineffectual dependence upon a hierarchy of ruling gods. In Shelley he only partially approaches the freedom of the modern individual, but in George Eliot Lanier saw the novelist "elevating the plane of all the commonplace life into the plane of the heroic by keeping every man well in mind of the awful ego within him which includes all the possibilities of heroic action."[112] The growth of the human spirit to the present "indicates a time when the control of the masses of men will be more and more relegated to each unit thereof, when the law will be given from within the bosom of each individual—not from without."[113]

In his criticism of Shakespeare Lanier applied metrical tests to study the development of his art; he went to the German scientific

---

[110] *Lanier's Works*, II, 250.

[111] Compare Whitman's glorification of "great persons" in *Democratic Vistas*. William James likewise found justification in the concept of spontaneous or accidental variation of species for his faith in individualism and the value of character (Ralph Barton Perry, *The Thought and Character of William James* [Boston, 1935], I, 470).

[112] *Lanier's Works*, IV, 201.

[113] *Lanier's Works*, II, 275.

aesthetics of Adolph Zeising and Gustave Fechner for the concept of a developing sense of beauty and proportion in the later plays;[114] and he divided (as had Fleay and others before Lanier) the work of Shakespeare into an ascending order of idealization.[115] But it was the novel that Lanier saw as "the very highest and holiest plane of creative effort"[116]—not the novel of Zola, based as it is on exact scientific reproduction, but that of George Eliot, in which he saw the reconciliation of science in its best sense and art. "The great modern novelist is at once scientific and poetic," he said; "and here, it seems to me, in the novel, we have the meeting, the reconciliation, the kiss, of science and poetry."[117] Worlds apart from the practical experience in fiction of James and Howells, from the broad scholarship of T. S. Perry and Lathrop, and even the analytical methods of his fellow poet, Stedman, Lanier nevertheless had in common with all of them a highly serious view of art, a strong individualistic bias, a predilection for the novel, and, above all, a passion amounting to religious zeal for a system of aesthetics which could encompass the polar extremities of science and idealism as they impinged upon American culture in the seventies.

### III

Intellectual America by 1880 had sobered perceptibly from the ferment and excitement which had ushered in the 1870's. The forces at work were not essentially different—evolutionary science, the expanding frontier, the aggregation of capital in large corporations, labor unrest, women's rights—yet the national temper in ten years had become more mellow, more critical, and more settled. The nervous apprehension over Darwinism, the self-conscious Americanism which had produced the international novel, the political tension of the Reconstruction era, the social disturbances of Greenback discontent and abortive labor struggles—all this had somehow altered in character, and a youthful fretting over untried issues

---

[114] Compare Lanier's concept of beauty and proportion in *Shakespere and His Forerunners* (*Works*, III, 364) in which he uses the ideas of Fechner, a German aesthetic scientist, with the essay by G. Stanley Hall, "Is Aesthetics a Science?," *Aspects of German Culture* (Boston, 1881), p. 102.
[115] *Lanier's Works*, III, 372.
[116] *Lanier's Works*, IV, 222.
[117] *Lanier's Works*, IV, 61.

gave way to a more practical desire to do something about them. The Knights of Labor, consolidated in 1878 under Terence Powderly and provided with a philosophy and a platform, proceeded to increase its membership from 28,000 in 1880 to four times that number by 1885. Meanwhile the idealism and humanitarianism of the Knights found its counterpart in the more utilitarian trade-union under Samuel Gompers, the American Federation of Labor, which was first organized in 1881. Instead of championing a loosely emotional resistance against all corporate industry, labor was now faced with conflicting philosophies, the practical and the idealistic, within its own ranks.[118]

Utility, common sense, and scientific attitudes were applied to labor problems in such political panaceas as that of Henry George in 1879, where emphasis was placed on workable reform through taxation while sensational appeals to strikes and violence were ignored. Collectivism came of age in the first years of the 1880's in the work of George, Lawrence Gronlund,[119] Richard T. Ely, Henry Demarest Lloyd, and Lester Ward. Lloyd attacked corruption in the Standard Oil Company in 1880 in the usually conservative pages of the *Atlantic*, and Ward pointed out in 1881 that laissez faire and Herbert Spencer's individualistic sociology were behind the times in a world moving toward government intervention in social affairs. "There is no necessary harmony between natural law and human advantage," he said.[120] But until 1886 or 1887 the collectivist voices were heard only in limited circles and were less popular than the individualistic followers of Spencer. In 1883 when Ward's *Dynamic Sociology* appeared, Sumner published his *What the Social Classes Owe to Each Other*, defending capitalism on the grounds of natural selection. And in 1885 Andrew Carnegie's *Triumphant Democracy* trumpeted to British audiences "a paean of the splendid material progress wrought by free capitalistic enterprise."[121]

[118] Ida Tarbell, *The Nationalizing of Business, 1878-1898* (New York, 1936), p. 149 and n. 2.
[119] Especially his *Cooperative Commonwealth* (1884), which influenced Howells and Bellamy. See W. F. Taylor, *The Economic Novel in America*, p. 236.
[120] Cited in Hofstadter, *Social Darwinism*, p. 56.
[121] W. F. Taylor, *The Economic Novel in America*, p. 39.

Philosophers, too, were shifting their beliefs somewhat from the roseate speculations of Positivism and Cosmic Evolution to the more stable ground of the practical and functional. John Fiske, with the encouragement of Huxley and Spencer, began to apply his theories of progress and evolution to the writing of history; Eggleston gave up fiction to become a professional historian and president of the American Historical Association, and Henry Adams, too, returned to the writing of history after a brief flirtation with the novel. Charles Peirce in an article in 1878 entitled "How to Make Our Ideas Clear" first defined the elements of pragmatism, pointing out that the validity of an idea lay in our sensible understanding of its function,[122] and William James in "Are We Automata?" (1879) stated the essentials of his later psychology and of his "will-to-believe" and pragmatism.[123] James, however, differed from Peirce in his strong emphasis on individualism. While Peirce did not feel that individual reactions were the true test of the validity of an idea, James urged that emotional and semiconscious states of mind were active elements of reality. Holmes, in *Mechanism in Thought and Morals* (1871) had emphasized the automatic nature of man and dealt a blow to freedom and moral responsibility; James was attempting to reinvest individual character with dignity and responsibility by stressing the validity of desire, feeling, love, aspiration, and habit.

The decade from 1880-1890 produced (as more than one scholar has observed)[124] more good fiction than any other decade in America. From 1880 to about 1887 a greater proportion of the characteristic work of the earlier American realism was written.[125] In March, 1880, Howells, writing to W. H. Bishop, announced a change in his fictional methods. He urged Bishop not to imitate Thackeray "in those pitiful winks to the reader" with which that

---

[122] H. W. Schneider, *A History of American Philosophy*, pp. 522-523.
[123] *Ibid.*, p. 524.
[124] Carl Van Doren, *The American Novel* (New York, 1940), p. 190. See also Herbert Brown, "The Great American Novel," *American Literature*, VII (March, 1935), 11.
[125] W. F. Taylor, *The Economic Novel in America*, p. 222, says: Between 1878 and 1886 "Howells' most distinctive and widely known work was done; and in any *general* consideration of that work, the heart of the problem, the core of the critical study would no doubt be found here."

bad artist "has undermined our novelists. For heaven's sake don't be sprightly. I am now striking all the witty things out of my work."[126] Both he and James deserted international themes for a purely native subject in 1880. In 1881 *A Modern Instance* and *The Portrait of a Lady* were running serially, and the following year saw the appearance of Constance Woolson's *Anne* and Mark Twain's *Prince and the Pauper*. James, after 1881, began to place his character contrasts against a background of social issues—feminism in *The Bostonians* and the anarchist movement in *The Princess Casamassima*, both published in 1886. Howells came as close as any of the realists ever did to the later methods of naturalism in his study of the interaction of character-responsibility and environmental influence on an average man and newspaper reporter, Bartley Hubbard. A few years later came *Silas Lapham* and *Indian Summer*, the latter a throwback in theme and setting to his work of the seventies, but more incisive, subtler, and deserving of a high rank among his novels.[127]

If the period of about seven years from 1880 to 1887 did not produce a *Moby-Dick*, a *Scarlet Letter*, or a *Leaves of Grass*, it deserves to be regarded as a minor flowering of American letters for the number and quality of novels it produced. Besides the finest books of Howells and one or two of James, Mark Twain's *Life on the Mississippi* and *Huckleberry Finn*[128] belong to the early 1880's, as does Howe's *Story of a Country Town*. Woolson's *For the Major* and *East Angels* (two of her best novels) were written in this period, as well as some of the most sustained work of the local-color school: Murfree's *In the Tennessee Mountains* (1884) and *The Prophet of the Great Smoky Mountains* (1885); Cable's *The Grandissimes* and *Dr. Sevier*; Jewett's *Country Doctor* (1884) and her collection of stories called *The Mate of the Daylight* (1883); and Mary

---

[126] *Life in Letters*, I, 282.

[127] Howells himself ranked *Indian Summer* one of his best novels (see A. H. Quinn, *American Fiction* [New York, 1936], p. 266). See also Alexander Cowie, *The Rise of the American Novel* (New York, 1938), p. 673.

[128] Chapters of *Huckleberry Finn* had been written as early as 1876, then laid aside until 1880. But the final completion of it belongs to the year 1883, a period of great creative energy for Clemens. See Mark Twain's *Letters*, I, 434 and *passim* for his high spirits in these years. He wrote Howells that he was piling up manuscript rapidly for the new book: "I'm booming, these days—got health and spirits to waste—got an overplus."

Wilkins's *A Humble Romance* (1887). Henry Adams's *Democracy* (1881) and John Hay's *The Breadwinners* (1883) caused much comment in literary circles partly because of their anonymity and partly because they made bold forays into political and social criticism. Dr. Weir Mitchell's *Roland Blake*, one of his most successful realistic novels of the Civil War, was published in 1885.

In varying degrees the work of these writers was influenced by native conditions and by the intellectual atmosphere of the early 1880's, and each in his own way found the period highly congenial to some of the best elements of realistic literary production. The idealism and individualism of the seventies was tempered by the advent of a more pragmatic and objective regard for methods, but the approach of sociological determinism had not yet altered its fundamental philosophy. It was in these years that the characteristic techniques of the first generation of American realists both in the local-color stories and in the novel were given a stamp which marked them off from later and different literary attitudes. The men and women who served their apprenticeship during the seventies, mainly in the novel and the short story, and who were doing their mature work in the eighties became the leading group of American realists. Most of them wrote books into the 1890's and well beyond, but the essential spirit of realism, as it revealed itself during the eighties, prevailed in their work. Before 1887 James had not irrevocably ceased to be concerned with American currents of opinion, and Howells had not taken up the torch for economic reform; Mark Twain, in his prime during the early eighties, had not yet grown embittered, Cable and Tourgée had not turned polemical in their writing on the South. The bright Victorian skies had deepened in tone, but were not yet darkened or threatened by the mechanistic and deterministic implications of European thought and native collectivism. A firmer and less self-conscious Americanism of subject had given substance and scope to the earlier internationalism and society novels of James and Howells; both moved toward a firmer objectivity without espousing a Zolaesque "exact reproduction of life." A successful interfusion of ripe powers and sustained success belonged to the realists in these years.

The advancement in James' creative work from the seventies to the eighties is less explicable, however, in terms of native conditions or even of prevailing intellectual currents than in relation to his own techniques of fiction. *Washington Square, The Portrait of a Lady*, and such a short story as "The Author of Beltraffio," as well as his two long novels of 1886, all show a greater detachment and impartiality of method and reveal glimpses into darker and further reaches of human psychology. James's position in the realistic movement is more apparent in his criticism than in his fiction, yet underlying all of his work one may see "the union of French artistry with English soundness of thought and morality."[129] He was searching for a new kind of realism which would account for the ethical idealism of a pre-Darwinian psychology, without becoming didactic, and which would, at the same time, include the deterministic elements of the new sociology, without resorting to an inflexible naturalism. The *Nation*, reviewing *The Portrait of a Lady*, described it as a work of "romantic sociology," a phrase suggesting the two sides of James's artistic nature, and called the book an example of "the imaginative treatment of reality."[130] The earlier disapproval of James as too materialistic and scientific, lacking in the "spiritual quality" persisted; yet *The Portrait* was spoken of as "an important work—the most important work James has thus far written."[131] And of *The Bostonians* a critic remarked, "We cannot help feeling that we are in the hands of one of the first of American novelists." *The Princess Casamassima* earned its author this accolade: "His persistent desire to see the truth . . . prove[s] that he has become a 'realist' in the only significant or, indeed, intelligent sense of the word."[132] Although not all opinions of James were so complimentary (there was a growing indifference to him in the eighties); nevertheless, even where he was most disliked, his craftsmanship was recognized and a few critics made an effort to understand what he was doing and to relate his work to the larger movement which was called realism.

*A Modern Instance* pushed the realism of the eighties as far as possible without quite violating its essential spirit. Howells, whose creative work was usually in advance of his theoretical criticism, here approached a kind of mild naturalism different more in degree

---

[129] Lyon Richardson, *Henry James* (New York, 1941), p. xxxvi.
[130] *Nation*, XXXIV (Feb. 2, 1882), 102.
[131] *Ibid.*   [132] *Ibid.*, XLIV (Feb. 10, 1887), 124.

than in kind from a book like *Sister Carrie*. His unshrinking portrait of gradual decline in the character of Bartley Hubbard falls this side of Dreiser only in that no single dominating force of circumstance is accountable for the break-up of the marriage,[133] and no severely tragic outcome is the result. The book cannot quite be said to have a ruling theme, despite its bold entry into the divorce question and its sharp attack on the perversions of newspaper journalism. The objection of Firkins that there is insufficient motivation for a disastrous eventuality in the marriage of Bartley and Marcia Gaylord is probably a testimony to the skill by which Howells distributed the fault, both among the characters and their circumstances, in unobtrusive ways and by a realistic accretion of trivial particles until the cumulative effect was sufficient to bring on the final break.[134] A contemporary reviewer felt the impartial distribution of justice in the book when he described Bartley's dream of escape from his marital bondage as the action of both a corrupt mind *and* a rotten social condition.[135] Although Howells might have disclaimed all moral intent in the book, there is no doubt that the Greek chorus consisting of the high-principled Atherton and the weak but saintly Ben Halleck provides a measure by which the action of the main personages can be judged. Howells carried the objective method further than he had done before, yet the very existence in the book of the high ground taken by Atherton on the divorce problem and his merciless flagellation of Halleck for loving Marcia can be regarded as a concession to the author's principles of propriety. One cannot quite call the novel a detached

---

[133] O. W. Firkins, *William Dean Howells, A Study* (Cambridge, Mass., 1924), p. 103. His "deterioration is not explained by his circumstances," for the circumstances actually favor "uprightness," according to Firkins. This opinion, however, is not quite supported by the importance of coincidence as a factor in the final separation of Bartley and Marcia. After his desertion of her, it is the accidental loss of his money which prevents his return. Howells says: "all the mute, obscure forces of habit, which are doubtless the strongest forces in human nature, were dragging him back to her" (*A Modern Instance*, p. 393.)

[134] I am indebted here to suggestions in Alexander Cowie's *Rise of the American Novel*, pp. 666-667. Cowie compares Howells's realism to that of Arnold Bennett in *The Old Wives' Tale*.

[135] *Atlantic Monthly*, L (Nov., 1882), 712.

slice-of-life.[136] The conventional critical reaction of the period to *A Modern Instance* showed the same distrust of realism as we have seen in the reviews of the seventies. Howells was too much the scientist, too depressing, lacking in sympathy for his characters, and he was prone to stress defects and overlook virtues; he failed to comfort the good or reform the bad.[137] On the other hand, the *Atlantic Monthly* thought it Howells's greatest achievement, essentially a parable "as all great works of art are parables," and the "weightiest novel of the day."[138] Significant of the direction of Howells's realism is the now familiar letter written to him by Henry James from Europe soon after James had read the book. The passage needs to be understood in its full context. James is talking of Daudet, Goncourt, and Zola:

> . . . in spite of their ferocious pessimism and their handling of unclean things, they are at least serious and honest. The floods of tepid soap and water which under the name of novels are being vomited forth in England seem . . . to do little honor to our race. I say this to you, because I regard you as the great American naturalist. I don't think you go far enough, and you are haunted with romantic phantoms and a tendency to factitious glosses; but you are in the right path. . . .[139]

The whole interrelated story of Howells and James, of their attitudes towards each other's work, their different approaches to realism, and the prevailing critical reaction to each came to its most revealing climax in the early eighties. Howells precipitated a minor tempest of comment with his essay on James in the *Century* in which he attempted to defeat the growing critical

---

[136] A reviewer in the *Century*, XXV (Jan., 1883), 464 put the idea thus: Halleck and Atherton represent "settled social tendencies" and their presence gives the author a chance to hold up saving moral standards without taking sides himself.

[137] See reviews in the *Critic*, II (Oct. 21, 1882), 278-279; *Century*, XXV (Jan., 1883), 463-465; and *Harper's Magazine*, LXVI (Jan., 1883), 314-315.

[138] *Atlantic Monthly*, L (Nov., 1882), 713.

[139] *The Letters of Henry James*, ed. Percy Lubbock (New York, 1920), I, 105. James was not the only one who called Howells a "naturalist" in those years. The *Atlantic Monthly*, LVII (June, 1886), 855-856 reviewed *Indian Summer* and said: ". . . he is a naturalist, who makes use of the microscope. . . . The difficulty with him, as with many another naturalist, is that he is too much of a specialist, and that his specialty limits the range of his sympathy."

dissatisfaction with James's work.[140] He spoke of his early liking for James's *Atlantic* stories in the face of the lukewarm attitude of readers and editors. He emphasized the romantic and ideal aspect of many of James's characters and their likeable qualities—mentioning Claire Bellegarde, Newman, and the Touchetts. Then, without warning, he suddenly launched into his now notorious attack on Dickens and Thackeray in which he spoke of those writers as men of the past whose methods in fiction are outworn. The new school, he said, "derives from Hawthorne and George Eliot" and eschews adventure and moving accidents for a subjective study of character. "It is largely influenced by French fiction in form; but it is the realism of Daudet rather than the realism of Zola that prevails with it. . . ." Finally, Howells concluded, James is the leader of this school—"it is he who is shaping and directing American fiction."[141]

Howells pleading for James's idealism; James describing Howells as a naturalist with "glosses"; a cartoon in *Life* depicting Howells trying to hoist a rotund James up to the level of an archly elevated Thackeray; an English critic in *Blackwood's* apoplectic over Howells's cool relegation of Dickens, Thackeray, Trollope, and Reade to an outworn past;[142] an American critic echoing the prevailing view that James lacked "the spiritual quality" and overdid on "scientific analysis of character"[143] and lumping Howells roughly with him in their joint denial of heroic qualities and their "morbid analysis"[144]—such was the critical turmoil over realism in 1883-1884. James H. Morse, who represented the conventional critical distrust of the realists, discussed native novelists at some

---

[140] One cannot help feeling the strong personal factor which enters into much of Howells's criticism by contrast to the more detached and intellectual nature of James's critical work. A note of special pleading, no doubt a part of Howells's warm and friendly nature, enters into his critical defenses of his friends, James, Twain, John Hay, and others.

[141] *Century*, XXV (No., 1882), 29.

[142] *Blackwood's Magazine*, CXXXIII (Jan., 1883), 136-161.

[143] J. H. Morse, *Critic*, II (Jan. 14, 1882), 1. Morse says of James: "He is neither American nor French, much less English, in his treatment of life, but he is realistic, almost materialistic, as opposed to spiritual and imaginative."

[144] J. H. Morse, "The Native Element in Fiction," *Century*, XXI (July, 1883), 372-373.

length in 1883 and listed the following seven writers who, he said, "hold the front rank today in general estimation": Howells, James, Cable, Frances Hodgson Burnett, Constance Fenimore Woolson, Elizabeth Stuart Phelps, and Harriet Prescott Spofford.[145] Morse, who found his ideal in Hawthorne and Turgenev, and who stressed the limitations of the realists in their short-suiting of pathos, passion, virtue, and the deeper sympathies, felt that Miss Woolson showed promise of becoming our best novelist because "she is clearly absorbing what is best in the art of the new school, without altogether sinking the old nobility of the virtues in the vulgar realities of the present day."[146]

The controversy over realism continued to rage throughout the 1880's and well beyond. Charles Dudley Warner put the case against it strongly in an article in the *Atlantic Monthly* in 1883. Not mentioning names, he accused "modern fiction" of overmuch photographic fidelity, a lack of idealization, a superabundance of analysis, an artisic indifference to nobility and virtue and justice, a preoccupation with the seamy side of life, a sad neglect of stories with happy endings, and a rejection of Sir Walter Scott.

The characteristics which are prominent, when we think of our recent fiction, are a wholly unidealized view of human society, which has got the name of realism; a delight in representing the worst phases of social life; an extreme analysis of persons and motives; the sacrifice of action to psychological study; the substitution of studies of character for anything like a story . . . and a despondent tone about society, politics, and the whole drift of modern life.[147]

He pleaded that Scott had restored the balance between chivalry and realism in fiction which the followers of Cervantes had destroyed, and he based his criticism on the principle that "the main object of the novel is to entertain, and the best entertainment is that which lifts the imagination and quickens the spirit . . . by taking us out of our humdrum and perhaps sordid conditions so that we can see familiar life somewhat idealized. . . ."[148]

Warner's friend, Mark Twain, took up the Scott issue promptly in *Life on the Mississippi*, published the same year. Speaking of

[145] *Ibid.*, p. 365.
[146] *Ibid.*, p. 369.
[147] *Atlantic Monthly*, LI (April, 1883), 464-474.
[148] *Ibid.*, pp. 465, 469.

*Ivanhoe* and *Don Quixote*, he said: "As far as the South is concerned the good work done by Cervantes is pretty nearly a dead letter, so effectively has Scott's pernicious work undermined it."[149] And Henry James, also in 1883, referred to Warner's article in his discussion of Daudet in the *Century*. He felt that Warner may have had the uncompromising endings of Daudet's stories in mind in his reflections (so James says with some irony) "on the perversity of those writers who will not make a novel as comfortable as one's stockings or as pretty as a Christmas card."[150] James's position here, however, was not to take either side in the issue; while admitting that Warner's complaint was "eminently just," he differed from the principle that a novel is primarily to entertain. "I should say that the main object of the novel is to represent life."[151] This is essentially his attitude in the widely known essay of 1884 on "The Art of Fiction," and in both he is careful to distinguish the "representation" of life from mere photographic fidelity. He agrees with Warner that selection is necessary to art, but for Warner it is a selection in the interest of justice and virtue; for James it is broader and deeper than that. By 1884 James had tired of overmuch generalization and found the term "realism" less essential to his critical vocabulary, but his position was not much different from that of his earlier essays; he set down his principles in "The Art of Fiction" as follows:

Art is essentially selection, but it is a selection whose main care is to be typical, to be inclusive. For many people art means rose-colored windowpanes, and selection means picking a bouquet for Mrs. Grundy. They will tell you that artistic considerations have nothing to do with the disagreeable, with the ugly; they will rattle off shallow commonplaces about the province of art and the limits of art till you are moved to some wonder in return as to the province and the limits of ignorance.[152]

The important thing, James observed, is that the selection be made with perfect freedom—"the province of art is all life, all feeling, all observation, all vision."[153] Thus James approached within a

---

[149] *Life on the Mississippi* (Author's National Edition; New York, 1907-1918), p. 349.
[150] *Century*, XXVI (Aug., 1883), 506.
[151] *Ibid.*
[152] *Partial Portraits* (New York, 1888), p. 398.
[153] *Ibid.*, p. 399.

hair's breadth of denying that there was any selection at all, and only retreated from that position in his concluding remarks on the moral element in fiction. It was the character of the mind of the artist which was the determining factor and "in proportion as that intelligence is fine will the novel . . . partake of the substance of beauty and truth."[154]

While James was thus close to an impressionist position in aesthetics,[155] Howells began to move slowly toward a concept of realism tinged with social criticism. In 1882 he spoke of wavering between romance and realism and associated the latter with Daudet. Two years later, reviewing Howe's *Story of a Country Town* and Bellamy's *Miss Ludington's Sister,* he felt that realism was "almost the only literary movement of our time that has vitality in it."[156] Yet this did not mean that romance was no longer valid for fiction. In fact, he said, the highest realism may well be "that which shall show us both of these where the feeble-thoughted and feeble-hearted imagine that they cannot exist."[157] At almost the same time, there appeared in the *Century Magazine* a review of the anonymous and much-discussed *The Breadwinners* simply signed "W." This review was an earnest defense of Howells's close friend, John Hay,[158] against charges of a lack of sympathy with the working class. Written by Howells, it first gave expression to social ideas in connection with his theories of the novel. The novelist must realize that he will be held to account "as a public teacher . . . and must do his work with the fear of a community before his eyes which will be

---

[154] *Ibid.,* p. 406.

[155] See the conclusion of his essay on Daudet (*Century,* XXVI [Aug., 1883], 508), where James avoids "the delicate matter" of determining the rank of the French writer: "it is sufficient priority for a writer that one likes him immensely." A reviewer in the *Atlantic* (LXII [Oct., 1888], 566) speaking of James's *Partial Portraits* said James was not interested in "final criticism," but rather he conveys "an impression which he acknowledges to be individual and possibly transitory."

[156] *Century,* XXVIII (Aug., 1884), 632.

[157] *Ibid.,* p. 633.

[158] Although the review speaks of the anonymous author of the book, Howells knew it was Hay; he had written Hay in January of that year expressing his sympathy with Hay's real position and implying that he planned to write a review of the novel. The review was another instance of the strong personal element in many of Howells's critical reviews (see *Life in Letters,* I, 358.)

jealous of his ethical soundness...."[159] The author of *The Bread-winners*, he says, did not attack workingmen as a class and showed them no antipathy until they began to burn and kill. Speaking for himself, Howells defended the right of workmen to strike and would have been content to see the recent telegraph strike succeed, but he agreed with the author that, "if the telegraphers like the railroad men, had begun to threaten life and destroy property, we should have wanted the troops called out against them." We are all workingmen or the sons of workingmen in America (Howells went on), but the real mischievous elements are the idle poor, as well as the idle rich. "It is quite time," he concluded, "we were invited to consider some of them (workingmen) in fiction as we saw some of them in fact during the great railroad strike."[160]

This was two years before the now widely quoted statement of Howells urging the novelist to concern himself with "the smiling aspects of life, which are the more American," and to "seek the universal in the individual rather than the social interests." Still the individualist in 1886, Howells believed that evil in the new world "is mainly from one to another one, and oftener still from one to one's self."[161] And in his own fiction of this period, *A Modern Instance, Silas Lapham, Indian Summer*, the essential problems were ethical in nature and the conflicts were those of character, but they were broadened in scope by the parallel treatment of larger social issues. Henry James, too, remained essentially a student of character in the middle eighties. If, as one reviewer put it, "the medley of woman's rights, spiritualism, inspirationism and the mind cure" provide the backdrop of *The Bostonians*, these activities are there mainly to provide James with an opportunity to depict strange contrasts of character.[162] *The Princess Casamassima* is yet another portrait, or series of portraits, but James had learned to illuminate his people, Hyacinth Robinson, the Princess, Paul Muniment, and the rest, by placing them against the shadowy suggestiveness of the socialist or anarchist movement of the times.[163] James's personal attitude toward

[159] *Century*, XXVIII (May, 1884), 153.
[160] *Ibid.*
[161] "Editor's Study," *Harper's Magazine*, LXXIII (Sept., 1886), 641.
[162] *Atlantic Monthly*, LVII (June, 1886), 851.
[163] See the suggestive essay-introduction to *The Princess Casamassima* (New York, 1948) by Lionel Trilling, where the historical accuracy of

the woman question in America and the revolutionary movement in London in these two books ranges from amused satire to plain antipathy, but his artistic use of them is another matter. It is apparent that he responded to the mounting social awareness of the 1880's at least so far as to give his character-paintings a deeper significance and a larger meaning in terms of contemporary life. In his own way James, like Howells, reached a kind of reconciliation of the claims of psychological individualism with those of environmental sociology upon his creative work. Reviewing *The Bostonians* in 1886, the *Nation* referred to James and Howells as accurate portrayers of society: "When our descendants hereafter attempt to reconstruct the society of which we form a part and imagine what sort of a world ours was, it must be in great measure to James and Howells that they will resort for enlightenment. Each in his different way portrays American society...."[164]

While James and Howells still placed character and psychology in the foreground and steered away from the deterministic implications of a too-exclusive interest in sociological influences, the balance was partially redressed in the work of Mark Twain and the local-color writers. The path Mark Twain was traveling led clearly from the early social criticism and satire of *The Gilded Age* to the mechanistic disillusionment of his later writing. In the growth of his thought, unlike James and Howells and Lanier, he seems not to have consciously sought a balance of opposing extremes, but rather to have passed swiftly from the coarse gayety of youth to the bleak pessimism and disillusion of age. A basic materialism underlies his whole career. His deflationary sanity and healthy debunking were at first suspended in laughter (*Innocents Abroad* and *Roughing It*); yet the same inconoclasm ended in the misanthropic scorn of *The Mysterious Stranger* and *What Is Man?*

---

James's picture of the Anarchist organization in Europe during the 1880's is emphasized. Trilling says (p. xxv): "Quite apart from its moral and aesthetic authority, *The Princess Casamassima* is a first-rate rendering of literal social reality." In his later Preface to the book, however, James seems to admit to only an imaginative insight into socialistic goings-on in London, worries somewhat about his lack of authoritative information, and stresses the development of Robinson's personality in conjunction with that of the Princess as the central idea of the book.

[164] *Nation*, XLII (May 13, 1886), 408.

It is not in the role of critic or philosopher, however, that Mark Twain's relation to the realism of the eighties may best be understood, for he had little patience with critical theorizing about realism, idealism, romance, morality, photographic fidelity, and such. Literary schools, criticism ("the most degraded of all trades"[165]), novels ("I detest novels"[166]), poetry, and theology were all outside his circle of interests.[167] "I can't stand George Eliot and Hawthorne and all those people," he wrote to Howells, "and as for *The Bostonians* I would rather be damned to John Bunyan's heaven than read that."[168] He detested Jane Austen, ridiculed Scott and Cooper. Only Howells's books he enjoyed, and those with the warm fervor of a friend. His own books he wrote (so he says) with one eye on the lecture audience and the other on sales.[169]

Still, there was a period of integration in Twain's career. It came in the eighties with the appearance of *Life on the Mississippi* and *Huckleberry Finn* and some fine shorter pieces, notably "The Private History of a Campaign That Failed" which has been called one of the best things he wrote. In these books Mark Twain's work broadened and deepened through a stronger blending of plot-control, social history, regionalism, realism, and character. The caustic satire of his early work merged with the nostalgia of *Tom Sawyer* to reappear in the nice adjustment of viewpoint between the realist, Huck, and the romantic, Tom, in *Huckleberry Finn*. This greater depth and significance, for finding which (see Preface) the reader will be banished, mark the height of his achievement. *Life on the Mississippi* and *Huckleberry Finn* are fundamentally great regional portraits, and in them Twain approached an equilibrium of the variable and quixotic elements of his literary personality.[170] There, the romancer and poet, the humorist and cynic, the realist and satirist,

---

[165] *Mark Twain's Autobiography*, ed. A. B. Paine (New York, 1924), II, 69.

[166] A. B. Paine, *Mark Twain, A Biography* (New York, 1912), I, 512.

[167] His well-known comment (*ibid.*): "I like history, biography, travels, curious facts, strange happenings, and science."

[168] *Mark Twain's Letters*, II, 455.

[169] "I had made up my mind to one thing—I wasn't going to touch a book unless there was money in it, and a good deal of it" (*Letters*, I, 145.)

[170] "To know Mark Twain is to know the strange and puzzling contradictions of the Gilded Age" (Parrington, *Main Currents in American Thought*, III, 88).

the epic narrator of American scenes met in happy combination. It was in the early eighties that he found the most successful expression for his theories of localism in American fiction, his keen ear for dialect, and his understanding of character-types. In these ways he made significant contributions to the development of literary realism.

As Bret Harte observed, it was the Western story which "voiced not only the dialect, but the habits of thought of a people or locality."[171] Looking back upon his work, Mark Twain felt that it is only through years of "unconscious absorption" that a writer can report the soul of a nation—its very life and speech and thought.[172] But even this is too broad a scope for the novelist. He must not try to generalize a nation. "No, he lays before you the ways and speech and life of a few people grouped in a certain place—his own place—and that is one book. In time, he and his brethren will report to you the life and the people of the whole nation...."[173] Twain goes on to mention every section and racial type which will provide subject matter for the writer and concludes that "when a thousand able novels have been written, *there* you have the soul of the people, the life of the people, the speech of the people; and not anywhere else can these be had."[174] Here, in phrases reminiscent of Whitman, Mark Twain described the place and function of the local-color school. And in his peculiarly *co-operative* approach to the American novel he is characteristically Western; he agreed with Eggleston, who said in 1892, discussing the regional movement and its achievement in Americanizing our literature: "The taking up of life in this regional way has made our literature really national by the only process possible.... The 'great American novel' for which prophetic critics yearned so fondly twenty years ago, is appearing in sections."[175] Hamlin Garland, likewise, found localism to be the key to the realistic trend, and found the work of Cable, Harris, Eggles-

[171] "The Rise of the Short Story," *Cornhill*, N.S. VII (July, 1899), 3.
[172] "What Paul Bourget Thinks of Us," *Literary Essays*, 145.
[173] *Ibid.*, pp. 146-147.
[174] *Ibid.*, p. 147.
[175] Preface to Library Edition, 1892, *The Hoosier Schoolmaster* (New York, 1899), pp. 6-7. For this and following quotations regarding the relation of the American novel to regionalism and nationalism I am indebted to B. T. Spencer's excellent study, "The New Realism and a National Literature," *PMLA*, LVI (Dec., 1941), 1129-1131.

ton, Jewett, Wilkins, and Harte to be "varying phases of the same movement, a movement which is to give us at last a really vital and original literature."[176] The local-color movement, he thought, signaled "the advance of the democratization of literature."[177] While James and Howells were attempting to typify the American character through literary portraits, Twain and the Western regionalists preferred to reflect society through portraits of places and by local peculiarities of speech and dress and habits of thought. Both methods were a part of realism, and generally speaking, the section from which a writer took his native hue determined the relative emphasis to be placed on individual character or on social conditions. If Harte and Twain, Eggleston and Joaquin Miller, Howe and Kirkland opened up the West for realistic portrayal, they were matched by Cable and Harris and Page in the South and by Sarah Orne Jewett, Mary Wilkins Freeman, Aldrich, and Howells in New England. Local color owed as much to the accurate painting of narrow domestic horizons in town and city by the women writers, and by Howells, W. H. Bishop, and others in the East as to the masculine humor and broad canvas of the Western school.[178] Parrington's belief that local color was primarily a native growth unconcerned with European technique[179] seems to disregard such factors as Miss Jewett's high regard for Tolstoi, Flaubert, Daudet, and Thackeray,[180] for the influence of Taine and Dutch painting on Eggleston, and for the whole sociological stress on environmental influence stemming from Darwin and natural selection. At any rate, the issue between West and East in localism was by no means clear-

[176] *New England Magazine*, N.S. II (1890), 243.
[177] *Literary News*, IX (1888), 236-237.
[178] Both James and Howells apparently felt that women writers were more realistic than men in the local-color story. James said, in 1865, that "the realism of local colors" had its origins in France and that success in that branch of realism would be reserved for women writers, "for if women are unable to draw, they at all events can paint, and that is what realism requires" (see *Notes and Reviews*, p. 79). Howells, in "The Editor's Study," *Harper's Magazine*, LXXIV (Feb., 1887), 484-486, discussing the short story, commented similarly that "the sketches and studies by the women seem faithfuler and more realistic than those of the men." He mentioned Mrs. Cooke, Miss Murfree, Miss Jewett, and Miss Woolson.
[179] *Parrington*, 238.
[180] See *Letters of Sarah Orne Jewett*, ed. Annie Fields (New York, 1911), pp. 30-31, 38-39, 81-82, and *passim*.

cut in any single writer and the two methods moved closer to each other in the best works of realism; as *Huckleberry Finn* is nearly as fine a portrait of a character as it is of a region, so Jewett's *A Country Doctor* (1884), Woolson's *For the Major* (1883), and the best books of Cable, Howells, and James in the 1880's showed increasing respect for environmental influences upon character.

### IV

From about 1887 to the outbreak of the Populist Revolt in 1890 it became increasingly difficult for intellectuals in America to maintain a moderate attitude toward social problems. The intensification of labor unrest, the alarming increase of strikes, the rapid rise of an urban and industrialized economy widened the rift already made between capital and labor, creditor and debtor, to the proportions of an impassable gulf. The New York traction strike in 1886, Haymarket in 1886, and a whole chain of strikes and violence in the railroad industry intensified the growing collectivist sentiment and, at the same time, produced a wave of public reaction against anarchism which had severe repercussions on the incipient labor movement.[181] Those who were directly concerned in the battles of industry and labor, or those who studied and discussed them, were forced more and more to take sides. They saw the issue clearly in Andrew Carnegie's "gospel of wealth" preached in the *North American Review* in 1889 and in Terence V. Powderly's *Thirty Years of Labor* published in the same year; or, on a somewhat higher plane, in the rugged individualism of Sumner and the social-planning argument of Lester Ward, a dispute already clarified in the early 1880's.

Although it received a decided setback after the Haymarket riots, the cause of labor was gradually acquiring powerful intellectual leadership in the East, as well as political sympathy from the Western agrarian interests. The work of Laurence Gronlund, Richard Ely, Simon Newcomb and that of the sociologists, Charles Cooley and Jacob Riis, concentrated in the few years of the late 1880's and early nineties, did much to unsettle the American mind,

[181] The once-powerful Knights of Labor almost vanished after 1886 under the attacks of Thomas Nast and other cartoonists which encouraged the public in its association of Karl Marx, free-love, nihilism, and the eight-hour day (see Roger Butterfield, *The American Past* [New York, 1947], p. 250).

still largely sustained by the religion of individual enterprise.[182] The lines were drawn more tightly and the moderates became increasingly uneasy.

In philosophy, as in sociology, the movement away from individualism came primarily from the West. While William James was formulating his pragmatic psychology to preserve the validity of individual habits and desires, Dewey was working toward a utilitarian concept in which social ethics and group psychology were predominant; this was to become the basis for the Chicago school of instrumentalism.[183] Both Dewey and the Californian idealist, Royce, contributed to the decline of Spencerian individualism in their emphasis on a sociological rather than a biological basis for human perfectibility. "It is the State, the Social Order, that is divine," Royce said in 1886. By serving the social order and turning away from ourselves, we find our "highest spiritual destiny."[184] Denton Snider, W. T. Harris, and the St. Louis Hegelians likewise substituted the ideal of state socialism, called "monocratic democracy,"[185] for unrestrained individual freedom in the realm of politics and education. Although he frequently attacked socialistic ideas, Harris in 1893 found Spencer's theory of education too narrowly individualistic. And in his ideal of national public education, which found practical expression in the Concord School of Philosophy and Literature (1879-1888), he stressed the value of civic institutions, the family, the church, and the state in bringing a child's education to its highest fulfilment.[186]

Parallel with the rapidly intensified collectivist tendency of Amer-

---

[182] See W. F. Taylor, *The Economic Novel in America*, p. 128: ". . . the latter eighties—that time when the national thought so curiously and suddenly awakened to the social problems raised by industrialism."

[183] H. W. Schneider, *A History of American Philosophy*, p. 535.

[184] *California; a Study of American Character* (Boston, 1886), p. 501. For a comparison of the social basis of Royce's philosophy and the individualism of James, see R. B. Perry, *In the Spirit of William James* (New Haven, Conn., 1938), p. 13: "For Royce society ennobled the fragmentary individual, while for James the social waste was redeemed by its individual oases. . . ."

[185] Denton J. Snider, *Social Institutions* (St. Louis, 1901), pp. 333-334.

[186] See Harris's attack on the narrow individualism of Spencer's theory of education in a lecture at Johns Hopkins in 1893 called "The Philosophy of Education," *Johns Hopkins University Studies in Historical and Political Science* (Baltimore, 1893), pp. 266-277.

ican thought in the late 1880's, social criticism and economic fiction came of age.[187] It was not until the great popularity of Bellamy's *Looking Backward* (1887) that social criticism in the novel associated itself with a clear program of political and social reform.[188] Despite the early humanitarianism of Rebecca Davis and Emma Lazarus and the social and political satire in such books as *The Gilded Age*, Henry Adams's *Democracy*, Hay's *The Breadwinners*, and a host of others, Boyesen could say in 1887 that "politics . . . which plays so large a part in the lives of our people, is, out of deference to the ladies, rarely allowed to invade our novels."[189] A writer in the *Atlantic* for the same year said that James, Howells, and Crawford provided a release from the vexing political and social questions of the day "which we go to them to escape."[190] But after 1887 such comment was quickly reduced to anachronism by the introduction into the fiction of Howells, Keenan, Fawcett, Garland, Tourgée, and Boyesen himself of the evils of a competitive society, the social and economic problems of the farm and city, and the whole question of practical reform in a stratified civilization. The novel became polemical in these years as social problems dominated the thinking of literary men. Tourgée, whose earlier Reconstruction novels were barely distinguishable from tracts, wrote *Murvale Eastman* in 1887, a sharp indictment of capitalistic wealth and a plea for Christian socialism. Cable took up his pen to discuss social problems of the South.

The change which took place in the work of Howells about 1887 was symptomatic of the socioeconomic trend of literary America in the late eighties. It can be felt at three different levels of his thinking—his critical articles in *Harper's* "Editor's Study," his letters and private opinions, and his economic novels. The latter, beginning with *The Minister's Charge* (1887), show a dropping off in artistic

---

[187] W. F. Taylor, *The Economic Novel*, p. 59, points out that the "chief concentration" of economic novels in America came after 1888 and continued until about 1897. See also Lyle Rose, "A Bibliographical Survey of Economic and Political Writings," *American Literature* XV (Jan., 1944), 381-410 for a complete listing of such books.

[188] See, however, R. L. Shurter, *The Utopian Novel in America, 1865-1900* (Cleveland, 1936), pp. 172-176 and W. F. Taylor, *op. cit.*, p. 189 for possible indebtedness of Bellamy to John MacNie's *The Diothas* (1880).

[189] "Why We Have No Great Novelists," *Forum*, II (Feb., 1887), 617.

[190] *Atlantic Monthly*, LVII (June, 1886), 851.

excellence from his work of the early 1880's almost in proportion as his social sensitivity became more acute. Like Zola, whose writing began with the unyielding attitude of the detached scientist (*L'Assommoir*, 1879) and progressed toward a vigorous championing of liberal causes, Howells permitted his sympathy for social betterment more and more to color his judicious studies of individuals and types. *A Hazard of New Fortunes* (1889) is the single exception among his economic novels of this period in which the author achieves scope and variety and lifelike people in conjunction with an attack on the evils of a competitive capitalism. But the skilful balance of a book like *A Modern Instance*, where the objective methods of the realist are held in equilibrium with a kind of moderate ethical idealism, does not belong to any of the novels Howells wrote between 1887 and 1894.

In the hands of his younger followers, the ideas Howells now espoused were to shift rapidly toward reformist treatises or pessimistic and (partially) deterministic slices of life. In his own books, however, he never quite allowed his principles of art to degenerate into newspaper reporting, nor his Christian idealism to give way to a consistently applied sociological determinism. The novels fall well short of being fictionalized illustrations of his privately expressed opinions. By 1888 Howells had come to favor national control over railways, telegraphs, and mines,[191] and his disagreement with Garland about the single-tax came about because he thought it did not go far enough.[192] He had become almost a notorious liberal (anticipating Zola and the Dreyfus case) by his stout position regarding "the civic murder" of the Haymarket "anarchists."

Lemuel Barker of *The Minister's Charge* is the first of a line of Howells's characters who are victimized by the social order. Society is here indicted of "complicity" in allowing social inequalities to exist; the remedy however is not a change of system but increased awareness of the spiritual bond that exists between brother and brother.[193] In *Annie Kilburn* (1888) Howells, now strongly influenced by Tolstoi, explored the ethical and practical bases of charity with *The Blithedale Romance* as a model. While upperclass conde-

---

[191] *Life in Letters*, I, 408.
[192] *Ibid.*, p. 407.
[193] *The Minister's Charge* (Boston, 1887), pp. 458-459.

scension and patronage to the poor are sharply condemned and the lofty humanitarianism of the idealistic Reverend Peck is portrayed with sympathy, Howells veers away from the farther reaches of Tolstoi's program. In the coldness of Dr. Peck and his indifference toward his child, he hints at his later more open condemnation of the "eremitism" of Tolstoi in *A World of Chance* (1893).[194]

If Howells became a kind of tender socialist in these books, it was only in part owing to his personal timidity or his tendency to overlook the more profound excesses of social injustice. He had become a "soft" or "Wallace" Darwinian, feeling that the struggle for survival had become a rapacious and ugly fact, and he felt that society needed to concoct ways and means to soften the struggle and protect equality of opportunity and social justice. From Silas Lapham to Gerrish (*Annie Kilburn*) and Dryfoos (*A Hazard of New Fortunes*) the selfish businessman had received increasingly harsh treatment by the author; yet the workingman is never conceived as a knight in shining armor, and poverty and destitution are not held to be the only serious ills of our civilization. Regarded by many of his contemporaries as a dangerous liberal, Howells actually was attempting to apply the older Christian values to the new conditions of struggle and competition which were reaching a climax in the latter 1880's.

One of the major themes running through all the social books of Howells in this period is that of the chance, the hazard, the waste and confusion, and the consequent suffering brought about by uncontrolled economic individualism. Yet, if Lindau, the socialist, and young Dryfoos succumb in the struggle for survival, Shelley Ray in *A World of Chance* succeeds in the literary world by the same token. It seemed to young Ray, in the closing pages of that book, that not only the economic world, but the whole realm of man's thinking and feeling were at the mercy of blind and meaningless futility. Yet Howells cannot leave him with such a view of the universe, and he concludes the novel on a note of vague and anxious hope which is often reflected in his letters of this period: "yet somehow we felt, we know, that justice ruled the world. Nothing, then,

[194] See *A World of Chance* (New York, 1893), p. 208. It should be noted, however, that Howells felt Tolstoi to have influenced him so greatly as to change his entire ways of thinking. Cf. *My Literary Passions* (New York, 1895), pp. 250-258.

that seemed chance, was really chance. It was the operation of a law so large that we caught a glimpse of its vast orbit once or twice in a lifetime. It was Providence."[195]

Humanitarian sympathy had been a part of Howells's inheritance from his early years in Ohio, but his literary training and his distaste for romantic fiction had led him in the direction of objectivity and a strict avoidance of preaching. Now, however, his social sympathies were again put in motion by the drift of events and by his reading. Besides Tolstoi he discovered Dostoevsky, Hardy, Björnson, read the books of the Spanish liberal novelist, Valdés, and the Italian patriot, Mazzini. Ruskin and Morris, too, reinforced his utopian thinking. Although he clung to his earlier distaste for the worst excesses of Zola's writing and objected to the pessimism of *Crime and Punishment* and Tolstoi's *Power of Darkness*,[196] he rapidly became the guide, philosopher, and friend of the young liberals of the nineties. In the "Editor's Study" of *Harper's* he attempted to weld his newly awakened social conscience into an aesthetic theory which he termed realism. Yet it is one of the ironies of our cultural history of this period that in his own fiction he was moving away from the subtle equilibrium of forces which had marked his best writing during the early 1880's. His economic novels tended to end on a sermonic note, and the finely shaded characters of *A Modern Instance* or *Indian Summer* now became allegorical symbols of various social classes and attitudes. His plots move slowly and dramatic action is supplanted by long philosophical discussions and conscience-wrestling. The reformer in him came close to displacing the artist.

The critical controversy over realism continued in these years with growing intensity to debate the relative merits of the idealistic and realistic schools. The realists now found new literary gods to justify their faith in the "new" realism. Zola, who had been anathema to most American reviewers and critics until about 1886, began to be received with cautious praise in the *Critic*, the *Dial*, and the *North American Review*.[197] Boyesen and Garland championed

---

[195] *Ibid.*, 374-375.
[196] "Editor's Study," *Harper's Magazine*, LXXV (Aug., 1887), 478.
[197] W. C. Frierson and H. Edwards, "French Naturalism and American Critical Opinion," *PMLA*, LXIII (Sept., 1948), 1013. Also cf. for thorough handling of Zola in America, Albert J. Salvan, *Zola aux Etats-Unis* (Providence, R. I., 1943).

Ibsen; Kirkland asserted his intention of writing, in *Zury,* "a palpable imitation of Thomas Hardy's *Far From the Madding Crowd*";[198] and the names of Tolstoi, Dostoevsky, Zola, Ruskin, and Morris began to appear more frequently in the journals alongside of the earlier favorites, George Eliot, Trollope, Daudet, Thackeray, and Flaubert, and Turgenev. Nevertheless, neither Boyesen nor Howells nor Garland was prepared to accept the darker shades of European naturalism. Although their attacks on outworn romantic ideals became sharper and Howells grew caustic over the generally unfavorable reviews of his books,[199] American realism was not even yet materialistic or deterministic. Sternly realistic as were Garland's disillusioned stories of agrarian life in the West, and forbidding as was the realism of E. W. Howe and Frederic and Kirkland (American fiction approached European naturalism more closely in these writers in the latter eighties than in either Howells or Boyesen), the full implications of a collectivist program of critical realism disassociated from the evolutionary optimism of Spencer were not yet acceptable. In *Criticism and Fiction* (1891) Howells made certain cautious statements toward associating the novel with social criticism and humanitarian causes, but it was in his fiction, rather than in critical theory, that he gave a freer rein to his awakened social conscience.[200] Boyesen, defining realism in 1890, said:

I do not mean by realism, of course, merely the practice of that extreme wing of the school which believes only that to be true which is disagreeable, and conscientiously omits all cheerful phenomena. Nor do I confine my definition to a minute insistence upon wearisome detail.... Broadly speaking, a realist is a writer who adheres strictly to the logic of reality, as he sees it; who ... deals by preference with the normal rather than the exceptional phases of life....[201]

---

[198] Preface, *Zury, The Meanest Man in Spring County* (1887).

[199] For the acrimonious attacks by conservative critics on Howells's "Editor's Study" pronouncements, see Leonard Lutwack, "William Dean Howells and the 'Editor's Study,'" *American Literature,* XXIV (May, 1952), 195-207.

[200] Everett Carter in "William Dean Howells' Theory of Critical Realism," *A Journal of English Literary History,* XVI (June, 1949), 151-166 asserts that *Criticism and Fiction* was hastily contrived and not representative of the true extent of Howells's critical realism.

[201] *Literary and Social Silhouettes* (New York, 1894), 71-72.

Popular criticism, however, continued to insist that Howells and James belonged in the most desperate wing of the party and kept up a monotonous iteration of the conflict between realism and romanticism. "Must we," a writer in the *Critic* asked in 1888, "because we confess a liking for Mr. James and Mr. Howells, by that confession declare ourselves at war with Dumas or Stevenson?"[202] The hope of finding a peaceful reconciliation of the two schools became more forlorn, however, as the realists grew more outspoken. On the other side, idealism revived among the older poet-critics and "defenders of ideality." Such critics as John Burroughs, Maurice Thompson, and Aldrich forthrightly attacked the belittling, analyzing tactics of the realists. In his *Ethics of Literary Art*, Thompson referred to the "debauchery" of *Hedda Gabler*, called *Tess of the D'Urbervilles* a "filthy novel," attacked Howells, realism, pessimism, science, James, Whitman, Zola, Hardy, De Maupassant, and Flaubert. He praised Scott, historical romance, heroism, virtue, courage, and the romantic novel.[203] Holmes discoursed at length of Zola's coarseness in 1890[204] and Aldrich lamented, in verse, the loss of old-time romance:

> The mighty Zolaistic Movement now
> Engrosses us—a miasmatic breath
> Blown from the slums. We paint life as it is,
> The hideous side of it, with careful pains,
> Making a god of the dull Commonplace.
> For have we not the old gods overthrown
> And set up strangest idols?

The literary tendencies of the 1890's began to manifest a sharper note of social protest, on the one hand, and a return to orthodoxy and gentility, on the other. Edmund Gosse, writing in the *Century* in 1890 on "The Limits of Realism in Fiction," found the realistic-naturalistic novel (he used the terms synonymously) on the decline. Ten years earlier, Gosse felt, the school of Zola had reached its height with the publication in 1880 of *Le Roman Experimental;* but a new trend of subjectivity was apparent in European circles toward

[202] *Critic*, XIII (Oct., 1888), 181.
[203] *The Ethics of Literary Art* (Hartford, Conn., 1893). See especially pp. 16-20, 50-61, 80-85.
[204] *Atlantic Monthly*, LXV (April, 1890), 556.

psychology, mysticism, and "the old exiled romance."[205] In America the change was felt in the militant realism of Garland, whose "Veritism" contained the seeds of ardent social reform, and, like Bellamy, combined a realism of subject material with an intensified idealism for greater economic justice.

The earlier realism persisted into the nineties and well beyond in the later work of Howells (*The Landlord at Lion's Head*, 1897), Sarah Orne Jewett (*The Country of the Pointed Firs*, 1896), Mary Wilkins Freeman (*Pembroke*, 1894), and the mature novels of James. Yet a greater subjectivity, which was apparent in James, may have been partly responsible for the revival of historical romance, as well as for the penetrating psychological studies of Bierce and Crane. On the other hand, the realism of social protest, colored by utopian hopes for a better future, characterized the economic novel of the late eighties and the nineties.

## v

American realism arose, as Parrington said, out of the ashes of romantic faith. Yet it was not wholly a negative movement, but rather a compromise between the old and the new. Nor was it primarily devoted to social criticism. The essential problem of intellectual America between 1871 and 1891 was the conflict of science and materialism with the inherited ideals of the Enlightenment and the traditional American faith in the individual. The ideological effort in those two decades strove to come to terms with the menace of a mechanistic world-view without wholly yielding up the inherited idealism of the earlier nineteenth century.

If one were to summarize the major factors which helped shape the American temper during those twenty years, he might best use the language of antithesis. On the intellectual level, at least, it was a period opposing extremes. *First*, traditional American idealism and ethical individualism was being tested in the fires of Darwinism and naturalistic science. *Second*, optimism and faith in progress, at first reinforced by a roseate view of evolution, were gradually tempered

---

[205] *Century*, IX (June, 1890), 391-400. For a recent detailed treatment of the literary controversies of the 1890's, see Grant C. Knight, *The Critical Period in American Literature* (Chapel Hill, N. C., 1951).

by an increasingly mechanistic and deterministic view of civilization. *Third*, economic individualism and the aggregation of private capital were being challenged by a counter movement toward group thinking and collectivist psychology. *Fourth*, subjective and intuitive (or traditional) approaches to knowledge became more and more suspect, as a critical, analytical, and objective epistemology stimulated interest in newer modes of thought, especially the psychological and the sociological. Both attitudes were tinged with deterministic implications. *Fifth*, the widening base of democracy brought in new racial and religious strains, forcing ethical and cultural standards to more workaday, utilitarian levels. *Sixth*, the aftermath of the Civil War, Reconstruction, and the rapid extension of the Middle Border and the Western frontier established new regional points of view which came into conflict with the older ideals in the East.

In the midst of the clash between such opposing philosophies and in the setting of an America swiftly emerging from an agrarian to an industrialized, urban society, literary critics and writers were working to provide for realism an effective artistic method and an intelligent critical philosophy. Like other cultural and literary movements realism began in revolt and experiment, but slowly moved toward a positive position, seeking its philosophical center somewhere near the midpoint of idealistic and naturalistic extremes of thought. It passed through its experimental phase in the self-conscious, idealistic seventies; found a moment of stabilization during the 1880's, when many of its finest literary works were written; and showed clear signs of change after 1887, when an intensified collectivist psychology coincided with a revival of subjective attitudes to open the way for a new and younger school of writers.

As a more strictly literary phenomenon, realism worked toward a harmony between the new critical and analytical methods and the older ethical and aesthetic idealism. It approached a reconciliation of Eastern and Western cultural values, bringing to the novel both the psychological methods of Howells and James and the sociological attitudes of Eggleston, Twain, and other Western regionalists. James and Howells and their disciples also found inspiration in English and French fictional models and critical methods, trying for greater objectivity and detachment of method. As a whole the twenty-year period we have called realism (as Howells said, the term is inadequate) produced some highly influential and provocative criticism, as well as a considerable number of the near-great novels and short fiction of our literature.

# Index

Abbott, F. E., 291
Abolition, 100, 113, 159, 384; Transcendentalists' attitude toward, 307
*Adam Bede* (Eliot), 344; reviewed, 348 n.
Adair, James, *History of the American Indians*, 78
Adam, fall of, 13, 20, 40
Adams, Charles Francis, 394
Adams, Henry, 285-286, 364, 392, 394, 417; *Democracy*, 419, 434; *The Education of Henry Adams*, 286 n.
Adams, John, 56
Adams, John, man of Enlightenment, 98, 108
Adams, John Quincy, teaches classical rhetoric at Harvard, 147
Addison, Joseph, Irving's use in his tales, 136
*Advancement of Learning* (Bacon), 278
*Adventures of Simon Suggs* (Hooper), 340
*Advice to the Privileged Orders* (Barlow), 57
Aeschylus, 414
*Aesthetics; or, the Science of Beauty* (Bascom), 355 n.
Agassiz, L. J. R., 357, 358
"Age of Accumulation, The," 386

*Age of Reason, The* (Paine), 46, 58, 65, 149
"Age of Innocence, The," 382, 386, 389
Agrarianism, 110, 114, 120, 432, 438
Agrarian Revolution, 124-125
*Aids to Reflection* (Coleridge), 153, 159, 261, 275, 277, 279, 284
Akenside, Mark, polish praised by *Portico*, 112
"Al Aaraaf" (Poe), 116
Alcott, Amos Bronson, 249, 309, 366; accepts idea of personality of God, 284; accepts Neoplatonic doctrine, 271; attacked for educational theories, 262; educational views of, 262, 304-305; fails in experiment at Fruitlands, 304; idealistic influences upon, 261; influences Emerson's *Nature*, 261, 268; *Journals*, 262 n., 280 n., 291, 291 n., 305 n.; opposes slavery, 307; and the Orient, 272; *Record of Conversations on the Gospel . . .*, 261; visionary view based on Oken, 280
Alcott, Louisa May, *Little Women*, 353
Aldrich, Thomas Bailey, 325, 340, 353, 431, 439; *Story of a Bad Boy*, 353

## 444 INDEX

Alexander, J. W., 290
Alger, Horatio, Jr., 363
*Algic Researches* (Schoolcraft), 127, 216
*Alhambra, The* (Irving), 135, 202
Alison, Archibald: admits individual differences in association principle, 152, 156; emphasis upon the sublime, 148; *Essay on Taste*, 295; influence of his theories on aesthetics, 74; influence upon Bryant, 135, 141 n.
Allen, Ethan, *Reason the Only Oracle of Man*, 65
Allen, Joseph Henry, 10
*All for Love* (Dryden), 140
Allston, Washington: disciple of Coleridge, 132, 151, 152; poem reviewed by Dana, 139 n.; emphasizes individuality of artist, 151-152; defines objective correlative, 152; *Lectures on Art*, 151; *Sylphs of the Seasons*, 151; synthesis of neoclassical and romantic ideas, 151-152
Alsop, Richard: *Charms of Fancy, The*, 82; romantic elements in his verse, 80
*America* (Imlay), 120
*American, The* (James), 394, 405, 409
*American Annals of Education and Instruction*, 149
"American Antiquities" (*Anarchiad*), 81
*American Democrat, The* (Cooper), 103
American Federation of Labor, 416
American Historical Association, 417
American Indian. See Indian
*American Journal of Education*, 149, 261
*American Monthly Magazine*, as a factor in the romantic essay, 194, 195 n.
*American Quarterly Review*, 145-146, 178
*American Review and Literary Journal*, 126

American Revolution, 11
*American Scholar* (Verplanck), 123
*American Scholar, The* (Emerson), 295, 309
*American Slavery as It Is* (Weld), 113
Ames, Oakes, 386
Ames, William, 40
*Amethyst, The*, 134
*Amherst Shrine*, 150-151
Ammon, Christoph von, 291
*Analectic Magazine*, 135
*Analogy* (Butler), 278
*Anarchiad, The*, 77, 80, 81, 84, 129
Anarchism: Emerson's theoretical, 306; Thoreau's approach toward, 306; public reaction against in the eighties, 432
"Ancient Mariner, The" (Coleridge), 397
*Anne* (Woolson), 418
*Annie Kilburn* (Howells), 435, 436
Antinomianism, 35
Antiquarianism: as a force to advancing Scott's methods, 242; productive of narratives through Scott's example, 200; responsible for interest in the Indian, 213; as stimulative of new trends in literature, 192-193
*Appleton's Journal*, 385
"Are We Automata?" (James), 417
Aristotelianism, 72
Arnold, George, 340
Arnold, Josias Lyndon, *Poems*, 80, 82
Arnold, Matthew: declining interest in his poetry because of interest in science, 361; opinion of Emerson, 123; praised by Noah Porter, 356
"Artemus Ward." See Browne, Charles Farrar
Articles of Confederation, 55
"Artist of the Beautiful, The" (Hawthorne), 323
"Art of Fiction, The" (James), 425
*Art of the Netherlands* (Taine), 399
Associationism: of Fourier adopted

## INDEX
445

at Brook Farm, 303, 304; of Ripley, 299; influence upon Allston through Coleridge, 152
*Astoria* (Irving), 135
*Atlantic Monthly*, 336 n., 343, 344, 347, 348, 349, 353, 356, 357, 360, 363 n., 365, 366, 371, 374, 385, 388, 398, 400, 409, 411 n., 416, 422, 423, 424, 434
Atwater, Caleb, and the moundbuilders, 193
Audubon, John James: naturalist in search of God in nature, 127; contribution to romantic imagery, 157
Austen, Jane, 429
"Author of Beltraffio, The" (James), 420
*Autobiography* (Clarke), 283 n., 305 n.
*Azarian* (Spofford), 402

Bach, J. S., 298
*Backwoodsman, The* (Paulding), 120, 129
Bacon, Francis, 277, 278
Baldwin, J. G., *The Flush Times of Alabama and Mississippi*, 138, 339
Balzac, Honoré de, 384, 385, 396, 402-403
Bancroft, George: accepts Transcendentalist philosophy though not in group, 249; belief in inherent goodness, 133; brings German romantic thought to U.S., 25; cultural nationalism, 109-110, 158; German educational views, 133; German influence, 132, 133, 157; *History of the United States*, 133, 158, 301 n.; leader of Jacksonian Democrats, 301; sends son to Brook Farm school, 303; teaches at Round Hill School, 301; Transcendental use of term "reason," 133
Baptists, 114
Barclay, Robert, 301
Barlow, Joel, 68, 70, 81; *Advice to the Privileged Orders*, 57; *The Columbiad*, 59, 106, 109; *A Letter to the National Convention of France*, 58; neoclassicism, 96, 169; *Political Writings of Joel Barlow*, 57, 62; *The Vision of Columbus*, 51, 59, 79
Bartol, Cyrus, 249, 283; *Radical Problems*, 283-284
Bartram, John: rise of biological science, 126, 157; *Travels*, 126
Bartram, William: romantic imagery in travel novels, 157; vogue among romantic authors abroad, 126
Bascom, John: *Aesthetics; or, the Science of Beauty*, 355 n.; *The Philosophy of English Literature*, 399
Bate, W. J., xi
Bauer, Bruno, 291
*Bay-Path, The* (Holland), 345
Beach, S. B., *Escalala*, 193
"Beat! Beat! Drums!" (Whitman), 329
Beattie, Sir James, 69
Beckwith, George, 64
Beecher, Henry Ward, 290, 361
Beecher, Lyman, 41
Beethoven, Ludwig van, 298
Bell, Sir Charles, 279
Bellamy, Edward, 407, 434, 440; *Looking Backward*, 434; *Miss Ludington's Sister*, 407, 426
Bellamy, Joseph, 11, 16, 17, 18, 64; *True Religion Delineated*, 16, 18
"Bells, The" (Poe), 142
Benét, William Rose, 14
*Benevolence of the Deity, The* (Chauncey), 41
Benjamin, Park, reviewed by Poe, 139 n.
Bentham, Jeremy, American vogue, 113, 124, 124 n.
Bentley, Richard, revision of Milton, 140
Beranger, Pierre Jean de, 356
Berkeley, Bishop George, 70, 74
*Bernard Lile* (Clemens), 365
*Beulah* (Evans), 332

Bible, 3, 5, 8, 11, 28, 29, 34, 35, 36, 45, 96
*Biblical Repertory and Princeton Review*, 290
Bierce, Ambrose, 440
"Big Bear of Arkansas, The" (Thorpe), 138
*Biglow Papers* (Lowell), 320; realism of, 338
"Bill Arp." *See* Smith, Charles H.
*Biographia Literaria* (Coleridge), 145, 255, 261
Bird, Robert Montgomery: realistic treatment of Indian, 121; creator of frontier characters, 138
Bishop, W. H., 417, 431; *Detmold; A Romance*, 406
*Bitter-Sweet* (Holland), 325
Björnson, 437
*Black Dwarf, The* (Scott), 204
Black Friday, 386
*Blackwood's Magazine:* on Howells, 423; as a medium for John Wilson, 195 n.; as popularizer of short German Gothic romances, 218
Blair, Hugh, 296; *Rhetoric* neoclassical, 147; text used at Harvard, 147; emphasis upon empirical truth, 148
Blake, William, interest in rural themes, 125
Blaserna, Pietro, 412
Blavatsky, Madame, 390
*Blithedale Romance, The* (Hawthorne), 367, 435
Bloomfield, Robert: American imitators of, 82; cult of simplicity, 130, 143, 156; "The Farmer's Boy," 83, 126, 156; "The Miller's Maid," 126; popularity in America, 126, 130, 143, 156; *Wild Flowers*, 126
Blount, Thomas, 43
Boehme, Jacob, 261
Boker, George, 325
*Books and Reading* (Porter), 336-337 n., 344 n.
Boone, Daniel, 296
*Boston Quarterly Review*, 258, 301

*Bostonians, The* (James), 392, 418, 420, 427, 428, 429
Bowles, William, controversy with Byron, 129
Bowne, B. P., 360
Boyesen, H. H., 406, 434, 437, 438; *Gunnar*, 406
Boyle, Robert, 4
*Bracebridge Hall* (Irving), 101, 125, 185, 202, 209
Brackenridge, Hugh Henry, 64 n., agrarianism, 125; attack on Johnson, 130; educational views, 147; *Gazette Publications*, 77; idea of the golden mean, 100; imitates satire of Fielding, 134; Jeffersonianism, 150; neoclassicism, 96; *Modern Chivalry*, 96, 100, 147; polish of his prose, 147; *The Rising Glory of America*, 51
Brayton, Deborah, 288
*Breadwinners, The* (Hay), 419, 426-427, 434
*Brief Retrospect of the Eighteenth Century, A* (Miller), 62
Brisbane, Albert, 303
Brokmeyer, Henry C., 387
Brontë, Charlotte, 330
Brook Farm, 127, 159, 247 n., 303-304, 304 n., 334
Brooks, Charles T., 249
Brown, Charles Brockden: Gothicism of, 218 n.; magazine praised by Bloomfield, 126; sentimentalism, 191; *Wieland*, 191
Brown, John, 306-307
Brown, Solyman, *Essay on American Poetry*, reviewed by Bryant, 142
Brown, S. G., 270 n.
Brown, Thomas, 253, 253 n., 264
Browne, Charles Farrar, creator of "Artemus Ward," 340
Browning, Robert, 85, 361
Brownson, Orestes A.: approves Cousin's idealism, 259-260, 274; becomes a Catholic, 256; defines class struggle, 301-302; early career, 258; early political radicalism, 301-302; evaluates Constant,

258-259; "The Laboring Classes," 301; *New Views of Christianity, Society, and the Church*, 260; reforming zeal, 299; on Transcendentalism, 291-292; on Unitarianism, 260-261; *Works*, 260 n.
Bruce, David, *Poems Chiefly in the Scottish Dialect*, 82
Bryant, William Cullen: celebration of democracy, 235; critical position, 141-142; criticized by *Amherst Shrine*, 150; domestication of English poetic forms, 170; early Popean verse, 129; foreign travel, 159; imitativeness of the age, 196; *Lectures on Poetry*, 141; literary indebtedness, 130, 132, 135, 158; relation to cult of simplicity, 156; treatment of American past and American scene, 89; "Thanatopsis," 158; trisyllabic feet in iambic verse, 169; use of natural scenery for romantic themes, 109, 117, 127; verse techniques, 142
Buckle, Henry Thomas, 357
Buckminster, Joseph S., 254
Buffalo Bill, 336
Buffon, George, Comte, 77, 78, 279
Bulwer-Lytton, Baron Edward George: and dynamic romanticism, 174; influence on American writers, 330, 344; popularity in the South, 116
Burke, Edmund: aesthetics, 148; paralleled by Legaré, 119; prepared for Romantic movement, 101; *Reflections on the Revolution in France*, 57, 59; traditionalism, 58, 101
Burnett, Frances Hodgson, 424
Burns, Anthony, 307
Burns, Robert: American imitator of, 82; interest in rural themes, 125; popularity in America, 130, 197 n.; sentimental lyrics, 197-198
Burroughs, John, 400, 439
Business, 3, 7, 8, 9, 10, 36, 41, 47
Butler, Joseph, 265, 278; *Analogy of Religion*, 278

Butler, Samuel, model for American verse, 96, 129-130
Byron, George Gordon, Lord: Byron-Bowles controversy, 129, 134, 155; critical abuse of, 175-176; and the Gothic of the malign, 219; immorality, 133, 252; Legaré's opinion, 119; loss of popularity, 150; model for Americans, 107, 132, 146, 158, 197; Oriental romances, 175 n.; popularity in the South, 110, 112, 115 n., 116, 207; reception in America, 175; rise of the metrical romance, 214-215; romanticism, 118; sustainer of retrospective moods, 199
*Byron and Byronism in America* (Leonard), 197
Byronism: dynamic moralism opposed to, 176; dynamic romanticism related to, 174; objections to, 175-176; ridiculed by Harte and Twain, 397

Cable, George Washington, 394, 418, 419, 424, 430-432, 434; *Dr. Sevier*, 418; *The Grandissimes*, 418
Cabot, J. E., 248, 248 n., 279 n., 280 n.
Caldwell, Erskine, 325
Calhoun, John: borrowing from Greek democracy, 119; nationalism, 108, sectionalism, 113
*Californian*, 342
Calvinism, 59, 64, 71, 96, 99, 154, 331, 358; Holmes on, 319-320; relation of Transcendentalists toward, 256, 299, 310-311
Cambridge Assembly, 5
Cambridge Platform, 5, 19
*Careful and Strict Enquiry into . . . Freedom of Will, A* (Edwards), 26
Carey, Mathew, leader in economic nationalism, 110
Carlyle, Thomas, 73, 252, 256-257, 261, 274-275; American reception of, 227, 227 n., 228, 228 n.; feudalistic bias, 110; ideas spread by

*North American Review*, 144; praised in *Harvardiana*, 150; *Sartor Resartus*, 274; transmitted idealistic culture, 132, 133, 227; Toryism, 243; vogue in the South, 116, 207
Carnegie, Andrew, 392, 416, 432; *Triumphant Democracy*, 416
*Carpet Bag, The*, 340
Carson, Kit, 336
Caruthers, W. A.: *The Cavaliers of Virginia*, 209; and the plantation tradition, 209
Cary, Alice, 345; *Hagar, a Story of Today*, 345 n.
*Casket, The*, 180
*Cassique of Kiawah, The* (Simms), and the vanishing American, 216, 325
Catholicism: gains Brownson as convert, 258
*Causeries du Lundi* (Sainte-Beuve), reviewed, 356 n.
*Cavaliers of Virginia, The* (Caruthers), 209
*Cecil Dreeme* (Winthrop), 346
"Celebrated Jumping Frog, The" (Clemens), 342
"Celestial Railroad, The" (Hawthorne), 323
*Century Magazine*, 406, 422, 425, 426, 439
Cervantes, Miguel de, 424-425; contrasted with Scott by Mark Twain, 116 n.; Wirt's partiality toward, 111
Chalmondeley, Thomas, 272
Chambers, Robert, 281; *Vestiges of Creation*, 357
"Chambered Nautilus, The" (Holmes), 320
*Chance Acquaintance, A* (Howells), 385, 406
Channing, Edward Tyrrell, 268-293; opposition to slavish imitation of classics, 148; "On Models in Literature," 148; probable influence on Transcendentalists, 147, 148; teacher of rhetoric at Harvard, 147, 158
Channing, William Ellery (the elder), 23, 26, 27, 28, 35, 36, 41, 68 n., 249, 255 n., 293 n., 312 n.; accepts miracles of Jesus, 287; advocates self-reform, 306; criticizes Transcendentalism, 255; faith in natural goodness, 133; influenced by Coleridge, 254; influenced by Richard Price, 254; influences Alcott, 261; literary theories, 293, 311-312; on Mme de Staël, 273; "The Moral Argument against Calvinism," 23, 156; nationalism, 109, 122-123; precursor of Transcendentalism, 258-259; "Remarks on a National Literature," 123, 293; *Reminiscences*, 254 n., 255 n., 273 n.; *Works*, 255 n., 293 n., 312 n.
Channing, William Ellery (the younger): published in *Dial*, 296, 312; verse praised by Emerson, 143
Channing, William Henry, 249; and dynamic moralism, 176; as Transcendentalist, 226
"Character of Socrates, The" (Emerson), 263
*Charlotte Temple* (Rowson), 330, 389
Chateaubriand, François René de: and difficulties of antiquarianism, 193; influence on romantic landscape, 224; influenced by Bartram, 126; popularity in America, 225 n.
Chauncey, Charles, 35, 41, 311; *The Benevolence of Deity*, 41
Child, L. M., 256 n.
*Childe Harold* (Byron), 199
*Children of Adam* (Whitman), 328
"Choice of an Era in Epic and Tragic Writing" (Hillhouse), 144
*Christian Commonwealth, The* (Eliot), 4
*Christian Examiner*, 145, 179, 257, 258, 259 n., 289
Christopher North. *See* Wilson, John

*Christian Philosopher, The* (Mather), 21
"Chromo-civilization," 386
Chubb, Thomas, 43
Church, 3, 9
Church and state, 4, 5, 47
Churchill, Charles, model for American verse, 96, 130
"Circles" (Emerson), 271
*Circuit Rider, The* (Eggleston), 406
"Circumstances Favorable to the Progress of Literature in America, The" (Everett), 311 n.
"City of Brass, The" (DeForest), 371
"Civil Disobedience" (Thoreau), 140
Civil War, 331, 340, 376, 378; moral effect of, 329; effect of on decline of idealism, 361-362; in fiction, 364-366
*Clarel* (Melville), 324
Clark, Willis Gaylord: as informal essayist, 195; literary piracy reprehended by, 185; popularity of Lamb in America exemplified by, 195 n.
Clarke, James Freeman, 249; accepts personal God, 284; *Autobiography*, 283 n., 305 n.; criticism of Harvard curriculum, 305 n.; interest in phrenology, 283; *Legend of Thomas Didymus, the Jewish Skeptic*, 291 n.; reference to Mme de Staël, 373; translation of *Theodore*, 291; use of Kantian terms, 270; writer on comparative religion, 272
Clarkson, Thomas, 288
Classics, ancient, 93, 96
Clemens, Jeremiah, 365; *Bernard Lile*, 365; *Tobias Wilson*, 365
Clemens, Samuel Langhorne, 339, 342, 363, 377, 385, 393, 397-398, 406, 410, 418, 419, 424, 428-431, 441; attack on Scott and praise of Cervantes, 116 n.; "The Celebrated Jumping Frog," 342; *Connecticut Yankee*, 138; *The Gilded Age*, 385, 392, 395, 428, 434; *Huckleberry Finn*, 342, 418, 429, 432; *Innocents Abroad*, 342, 428; *Life on the Mississippi*, 397, 418, 424, 429; *The Man That Corrupted Hadleyburg*, 342; *The Mysterious Stranger*, 428; *The Prince and the Pauper*, 418; "The Private History of a Campaign That Failed," 429; *Roughing It*, 385, 398, 428; *Tom Sawyer*, 429; *What Is Man?*, 428
*Clis* (periodical), 119 n.
*Clovernook; or Recollections of Our Neighborhood in the West* (Cary), 345
Coates, Roger, 45
Cobb, Sylvanus, Jr., 335-336; *The Gunmaker of Moscow*, 336
Cobbett, William, interest in Agrarian Revolution, 125
Codman, J. T., 303 n., 304 n.
Cogswell, Joseph G., study in German universities, 133, 157
Coleridge, Samuel Taylor, 73, 80, 85, 252, 253, 255, 257, 261, 268, 274-275, 277, 279, 293, 322 n., 397-398; *Aids to Reflection*, 153, 159, 261, 275, 279, 284; "The Ancient Mariner," 397; attacked by *Portico*, 112; *Biographia Literaria*, 145, 255, 261; criticism accepted by *Christian Examiner*, 145; cult of simplicity, 143; edited by James Marsh, 159; and French Revolution, 164; ideas spread by *North American Review*, 144; influence on Poe, 134, 172, 172 n., on Washington Allston, 151, 152; lack of influence on Bryant, 141, on Irving, 136; praised by *Amherst Shrine*, 150; reception in America, 173, 229, 229 n.; relation to Burke, 101; satirized by Byron, 107; and theological readers, 243; theory of musical verse, 173; as thinker, 173 n.; as transmitter of German ideas, 132, 229; use of Bartram's *Travels*, 126; use of term "reason," 133
*Collected Papers* (Peirce), 247

Collectivism, 233, 234 n., 383, 384, 395, 416, 419, 432, 438, 441; Brook Farm and Fruitlands, 303-304
College of Philadelphia, 69
Colonization, 7, 9
*Columbiad, The* (Barlow), 59, 106, 109
Combe, George, *The Constitution of Man*, 283
Common Sense (Scottish School), 68-71, 74, 76, 88, 89, 132, 148, 153, 156, 363; Common-Sense critics, 177; influence on Emerson, 264-266; influence on Thoreau, 268-269; relationship to Transcendentalism, 263
*Common Sense* (Paine), 99
*Compleat Body of Divinity* (Willard), 18
Complicity, 435
Comstock, Anthony, 390
Comte, Auguste, 357, 378
Concord School of Philosophy and Literature, 433
*Condensed Novels* (Harte), 343, 397
*Confession of Faith Owned and Consented unto by the Elders and Messengers of the Churches Assembled at Boston in New England, May 12, 1680, The*, 36, 37
*Confidence-Man, The* (Melville), 324
Connecticut Wits, 106, 142, 155
*Connecticut Yankee in King Arthur's Court, A* (Clemens), 138
*Conquest of Canaan, The* (Dwight), 80
*Conquest of Louisburg, The* (Maylem), 81
Conscience, 12, 26, 30, 41
Constant, Benjamin, 258-259, 273
Constitution, 52, 55, 56, 99
*Constitution of Man, The* (Combe), 283
Conway, Moncure D., 61, 249, 387
Conybeare, John, 45
Cooke, John Esten, 356 n., 363

Cooke, Rose Terry: "Eben Jackson," 348; "Miss Lucinda," 348
Cooley, Charles, 432
Cooper, James Fenimore, 325, 335, 397, 400, 429; agrarianism, 103-104, 125; and Byronic gloom, 215; careless style, 143; *The Crater*, 103; effects of foreign travel, 159; Federalism, 102, 103, 109; formula for prose narratives, 214; hostility toward Jacksonianism, 104; imitation of Swift, 93, 130; influence on landscape tradition, 221-222; lack of literary theory, 102; "Leather-Stocking-Tales," 89; *Letter to His Countrymen*, 122; *Lionel Lincoln*, 204, 205, 207; man of the Enlightenment, 97, 102, 103, 108; *The Monikins*, 93, 103, 130; nationalism, 103; *Notions of the Americans*, 102, 103, 122; novelist of the frontier, 121; *Oak-Openings*, 102, 216; *The Pathfinder*, 216; *The Pioneers*, 103, 121, 221, 222 n.; and regional art, 210; romantic treatment of the landscape, 127; *Satanstoe*, 189 n., 216; and Scott 103-104, 125; sectionalism, 122; *The Spy*, 204; treatment of the Indian, 121, 215-216; *The Wept of Wish-ton-wish*, 204
Cooper, Thomas: attitude toward slavery, 111; Unitarianism, 96
Copernicus, Nicholas, 276
*Coquette, The* (Foster), 330
"Correspondences" (Cranch), 143
Cotton, John, *The Way of Life*, 5
*Courtship of Miles Standish, The* (Longfellow), 319
Cousin, Victor, 145, 256, 259, 260 n., 261, 273-274; edited in America by C. S. Henry, 145, 159; and idealism, 177, 227, 228, 229 n.
Couvier, Georges, 279
Covenant, theory of, 17, 36, 39
*Coward, The* (Morford), 364, 365
Cowper, William: interest in rural themes, 125; vogue in America, 130

Cox, William, and the vogue of the informal essay, 195
Cranch, Christopher, 249; "Correspondences," 143; and free verse, 143
Crabbe, George, rural themes, 125
Crane, Hart, 365
Crane, Ronald, viii
Crane, Stephen, 372, 440; *The Red Badge of Courage*, 372
*Crater, The* (Cooper), 103
Crawford, F. Marion, 434
Creation, 12, 15
Crédit Mobilier, 386
Crèvecoeur, Hector St. John de: environmental effect on independence of Americans, 104; "What Is an American?," 83
*Crime and Punishment* (Dostoevsky), 437
*Crisis, The* (Paine), 52
*Critic*, 437, 439
*Criticism and Fiction* (Howells), 381, 438
*Critical and Historical Introduction to the Canonical Scripture . . . , A* (De Wette, trans. Theodore Parker), 291
*Critical and Miscellaneous Writings of Thomas Carlyle*, 274
Criticism, the critical expression of the Transcendentalists, 292-298
"The Critics: A Fable" (Dwight), 96
Critics: Transcendentalist, 293, 297-298
*Critique of Pure Reason* (Kant), 273
Crockett, Davy, 138, 296, 339
Cudworth, Ralph, 68, 294
*Culture Demanded by Modern Life, The* (Youmans), 359 n.
Cummins, Maria S., *The Lamplighter*, 332
Curtis, George William: *Potiphar Papers*, 334; *Prue and I*, 334
Cuvier, Baron, 357

*Daily Advertiser*, 290
*Daisy Miller* (James), 394

Dana, R. H., Sr.: and beginning of romantic criticism in America, 143, 158; criticism of satirical verse, 139 n.; follower of Wordsworth, 132, 150; nature lyrics, 127; praised by *American Quarterly Review*, 145; "Thoughts on the Soul," 142
Darwin, Charles, 280, 281, 357, 358, 359, 360, 361, 362, 363, 373, 374, 378, 385, 386, 412-414, 431; *The Descent of Man*, 360-361. See also Darwinism
Darwin, Erasmus, 158, 279
Darwinism, 320 n., 349 n., 385, 415, 440; and American democracy, 357; study in colleges, 359, 361; weak influence in American literature before 1871, 361
Daudet, Alphonse, 422, 423, 425, 431, 438
"David Gaunt" (Davis), 366
Davis, Rebecca Harding, 365, 366, 367, 392, 395, 402, 434; early realism of, 365-367; "David Gaunt," 366; *John Andross*, 395; "John Lamar," 366; *Kitty's Choice*, 392; *Life in the Iron Mills*, 365; *Margret Howth, a Story of To-day*, 366; "A Pearl of Great Price," 367; *Waiting for the Verdict*, 367
"Day of Days, A" (James), 353
*Day of Doom, The* (Wigglesworth), 14, 16, 25
Declaration of Independence, 54, 84
"Defence of Mechanical Philosophy" (Walker), 257 n.
DeForest, John W., 365, 370-373, 385, 388, 391-392, 393, 395, 399, 406, 409; "The City of Brass," 371; *Honest John Vane*, 395; *Kate Beaumont*, 371, 393; *Miss Ravenel's Conversion from Secession to Loyalty*, 371-373, 388; *Overland*, 385; *Playing the Mischief*, 409; realistic description of Civil War, 372, 377; *Seacliff, or, The Mystery of the Westervelts*, 371; "The Taillefer Bell-Ringings," 371; *A Union Officer in the Reconstruction*, 372 n.;

*A Volunteer's Adventures*, 372 n.; *Witching Times*, 370-371
De Gerando, Marie Joseph, 272
Deism, 43, 93, 153, 154, 156
*De l'Allemagne* (de Staël), 145, 273
*De la réligion* (Constant), 258-259
Democracy, 11, 105; Bancroft's praise of, 236, 236 n.; forces in, 234-239; idealistic concepts of literary men, 235, 238; Jacksonianism and individualism, 236-238; panegyrics upon, 235; revolutions in Europe as stimulus to, 238-239
*Democracy* (Adams), 419, 434
*Democracy in America* (de Tocqueville), 104
*Democracy Unveiled* (Fessenden), 129
*Democratic Review*, 258
*Democratic Vistas* (Whitman), 329-330, 390, 395
Dennis, H. B., criticism of nature poetry, 150; *Rural Sentimentalities*, 150
Dennie, Joseph: antinationalism, 109; conservatism, 101; influence on James Hall, 120 n.; neoclassicism, 93, 100-101
De Quincey, Thomas, romantic criticism, 140
Descartes, René, 45, 273
*Deserted Village, The* (Goldsmith), 137
*Description of New England* (Smith), 10
"Desultory Thoughts on Criticism" (Irving), 137
*Descent of Man, The* (Darwin), 360-361
Determinism, 22, 76, 310, 383, 384, 399, 419, 435
*Detmold: A Romance* (Bishop), 406
Dew, Thomas, proslavery tract, 114; *Review of the Debate on the Abolition of Slavery*, 114
De Wette, Wilhelm Martin Leberecht, 291
Dewey, John, 247 n., 248, 300 n., 433
Dewey, Orville, 285, 285 n.; *Discourses and Reviews*, 285

*Dial*, 143, 153 n., 272, 281, 296, 297, 298 n., 312, 437
Dickens, Charles, 330, 343, 344, 356, 361, 373, 374, 378, 384, 385, 393, 397, 423; emotional imitators, 192 n.; and sentimentalism, 191, 243
Dickinson, Emily, 325, 376, 378, 383, 410
Dickinson, John, *Letters from a Farmer in Pennsylvania*, 52
Dime novel, 335, 336
*Discourse on the Latest Form of Infidelity* (Norton), 290
*Discourse on ... Making Our Literature Independent of that of Great Britain* (Duponceau), 123
*Discourse on the Philosophy of Religion* (Ripley), 258
*Discourses and Reviews* (Dewey), 285
*Discourse of the Study of Natural Philosophy, A* (Herschel), 278
*Dissertation Concerning the End for Which God Created the World* (Edwards), 26
*Dissertations on Matter and Spirit* (Price), 254
*Divine and Supernatural Light Imparted to the Soul, A* (Edwards), 30
"Divinity School Address" (Emerson), 24, 280, 289, 290
*Dr. Sevier* (Cable), 418
Dod, Albert, 290
Donne, John, 13
*Don Quixote* (Cervantes), 425
*Doomed Chief, The* (Thompson), 216
Dostoevsky, 437-438
Drake, Daniel, and antiquarian research, 193
Draper, John W.: *History of the American Civil War*, 357; *History of the Intellectual Development of Europe*, 357
"Dreadful Decade, The," 386, 389
*Dream Life* (Mitchell), 334
*Dred* (Stowe), 348
Dreiser, Theodore, 421; *Sister Carrie*, 421

Dreyfus case, 435
*Drum-Taps* (Whitman), 329
Dryden, John, 87; praised by *Portico*, 112; revision of Shakespeare, 140
Dugdale, Richard, *The Jukes*, 394
Dumas, Alexandre, 397, 439
*Dunciad, The* (Pope), 96, 112, 129
Dunlap, William, influence on Irving, 135; his critical thought, 144
Duponceau, Peter: *Discourse on . . . Making Our Literature Independent of that of Great Britain*, 123; his critical thought, 144; nationalism, 123
*Dutchman's Fireside, The* (Paulding), 205
Duveneck, Frank, 404
Dwight, John Sullivan, 249, 293, 297-298
Dwight, Timothy, 70; *America, or a Poem on the Settlement of the British Colonies*, 51; antiquarian interests, 193; as a force in landscape tradition, 221; attitude toward frontier, 114-115; *The Conquest of Canaan*, 80; "The Critics: A Fable," 96; Edwardean ideas in neoclassical mold, 96; and Enlightenment, 98, 108; Federalism, 99-100, 109; *Greenfield Hill*, 81, 96, 100, 106; imitation of Popean couplet, 129; *The Nature, and Danger of Infidel Philosophy*, 60; opposition to study of classical languages, 93; sectionalism, 122; *Sermons*, 60; *Theology, Explained and Defended*, 63; *Travels in New-England and New York*, 75; *The Triumph of Infidelity*, 96, 129; *The True Means of Establishing Public Happiness*, 60
*Dwight's Journal of Music*, 298
*Dynamic Sociology* (Ward), 416

Eakins, Thomas, 404
"Earth's Holocaust" (Hawthorne), 220, 323
*East Angels* (Woolson), 418
"Eben Jackson" (Cooke), 348

Eclecticism, 182, 185; of Cousin, 260 n., 273
Economics. See Business
Eddy, Mary Baker, *Science and Health*, 390
Education, 133, 147-149; Alcott's place in American, 261-262, 304-305; Alcott's views on, 262, 304-305; Emerson and Harvard elective system, 305; Elizabeth Peabody's career, 305; influence of Pestalozzi, 305; Transcendentalist views of, 304-305
*Education of Henry Adams, The*, 286 n.
Edwards, Jonathan, x, 16, 18, 22, 24, 25, 26, 30, 31, 34, 35, 41, 46, 47, 64, 68, 69, 311; *A Careful and Strict Enquiry into . . . Freedom of Will*, 26; *A Divine and Supernatural Light Imparted to the Soul*, 30; *The Great Christian Doctrine of Original Sin Defended*, 46; *Inquiry Concerning Freedom of the Will*, 22; *Life of Brainard*, 16; *The Nature of True Virtue*, 26; *Original Sin*, 26; psychological thought, 141
*Edwin Brothertoft* (Winthrop), 347
Eggleston, Edward, 317, 322, 373-375, 393, 394, 399, 406, 417, 430-431, 441; in fiction and tradition, 317; *The Circuit Rider*, 406; recognition of importance of social environment, 375; *Roxy*, 394
Eichhorn, Johann Gottfried, 291; teacher of Americans abroad, 133
"Eighteen Sixty-One" (Whitman), 329
Elect, privileges of extended to all mankind by Transcendentalists, 311
*Elementa Philosophica* (Johnson), 68
*Elements of the Philosophy of the Human Mind* (Stewart), 264, 353 n.
Eliot, Charles W., 305, 359
Eliot, George, 343, 344, 348 n., 349, 353, 378, 384, 385, 386, 396, 401-403, 407 n., 412, 414-415, 423, 429, 438

Eliot, John, *The Christian Commonwealth*, 4
Eliot, T. S., objective correlative, 152
Ellis, George E., 16, 23
*Elsie Venner* (Holmes), 320
Ely, Richard T., 416, 432
Emerson, E. W., 248 n., 265 n.
Emerson, Ellen, 266
Emerson, Mary Moody, 262, 264, 276
Emerson, Ralph Waldo, x, 24, 27, 35, 73, 89, 249, 252, 319, 321-322, 358, 361, 367, 387, 413; accepts evolutionism, 280-281; acquaintance with Quakers, 232 n., 288; affected by German philosophy, 273; Alcott's influence on, 261; Carlyle's influence on, 274; Channing's influence on, 255; "The Character of Socrates," 263-264; "Circles," 271; *Complete Works*, 248, 253, 254, 268, 269, 275-276, 278, 280, 287, 294-295, 296, 306, 308, 309, 312, 313; definition of reason, 133; Coleridge's influence on, 275; compared with Plato, 322; concept of beauty, 268; *Conduct of Life*, 321; criticizes materialism, 308; defines reason, 133; democratic thought, 235; defines Transcendentalism, 248; desires idealism, 253-254; develops artistic philosophy, 293-296; develops his Transcendentalism, 262-268; "Divinity School Address," 24, 280, 289, 290; edits *Dial*, 312; educational theories, 305; emerges as Transcendentalist leader, 256; "Fate," 321; "Hamatraya," 312; harmonizes science and religion, 275-281; "The Humanity of Science," 279; theory of individual regeneration, 231; influence of science, 158; "Initial, Daemonic, and Celestial Love," 270; *Journals*, 264, 265-268, 272 n., 273 n., 274 n., 276, 279-280, 287-288, 295 n., 305 n., 308, 311 n.; *Letters*, 280 n.; "Merlin," 143; names "Hedge Club," 257; nationalism, 107; *Nature*, influenced by Alcott, 261, 268; "Ode Inscribed to W. H. Channing," 306 n.; "The Over-Soul," 271; Plato's influence upon, 270-271; "The Poet," 329; popularizer of Carlyle, 228; "Pray without Ceasing," 266; "The Present State of Ethical Philosophy," 265; reads Oriental philosophers, 271-272; realistic elements in, 321-322; regards novel lightly, 298; rejection of miracles, 289-290; relation to pantheism, 283-284; *Representative Men*, 272, 319; strikes new note in poetry, 312; Swedenborgianism, 272-273; theory of individual regeneration, 231; theory of roughness, 143; "The Transcendentalist," 254; uniqueness, 123; use of nature, 109; views Locke ambivalently, 309-310; views on slavery, 306-307; withdrawal from reform activities, 306
Emerson, William, 254, 288
Emotionalism as stimulative of new literature, 191-192
*English Literature of the Eighteenth Century* (Perry), 412
*English Novel, The* (Lanier), 412, 414
Enlightenment, the, 93, 96, 97, 99, 104, 108, 111, 154
Epistemology: of German idealists, transmitted to America, 273-274; of Hume, unsatisfactory to Transcendentalists, 253
Equalitarianism, 95, 102, 384, 393
Equality, 78; Transcendentalist views on, 299-300
Eremitism, 436
*Escalala* (Beach), as antiquarian poem, 193
Essay (familiar), 194-195
*Essay Concerning Human Understanding* (Locke), 252, 309
*Essay on American Poetry* (Brown), 142
*Essay on Criticism* (Pope), 94

*Essay on Man, The* (Pope), 75, 129, 142
*Essay on the Nature and Immutability of Truth in Opposition to Sophistry and Scepticism* (Beattie), 69
*Essay on Taste* (Alison), 295
*Essay on the Best System of Liberal Education* (Knox), 147
"Ethan Brand" (Hawthorne), 220
Ethics, 3, 9, 10, 36, 41, 44, 47
*Ethics* (De Wette), 291
*Ethics* (Johnson), 63
*Ethics of Literary Art, The* (Thompson), 439
Euclid, 68
*Eureka* (Poe), 93, 413
*Eutaw* (Simms), 324
*Evangeline* (Longfellow), 319
Evans, Augusta Jane, 332; *Beulah*, 332; *St. Elmo*, 332
Everett, Alexander, 256; his criticism, 144; study in Germany, 133, 157
Everett, Edward, 254, 311; "The Circumstances Favorable to the Progress of Literature in America," 311 n.
Evolution, 357, 358, 361; accepted by Emerson, 278-281; Darwinian, 373, 385, 388, 392, 394, 411-414, 415, 417, 440; growing acceptance of, 361; identified with progress, 358
"Excelsior" (Longfellow), 354
*Excursion, The* (Wordsworth), 261

*Fable for Critics* (Lowell), 320
"Fall of the House of Usher, The" (Poe), 220
*Far From the Madding Crowd* (Hardy), 438
*Farmer's Boy, The* (Bloomfield), 126, 156
*Farmers Museum*, 101 n.
"Fate" (Emerson), 321
*Fathers and Sons* (Turgenev), 386
Faulkner, William, 325
Fawcett, Edgar, 391, 434
Fechner, Gustav T., 391

Federalism, 99, 102, 109
*Federalist, The*, 99, 300
Federalists, 52, 55, 56, 61, 84
*Felix Holt* (Eliot), 402
*Female Poets of America, The*, 389
Feminism, 131-132, 388-392, 418
Fenno, Charles, 98
"Fern, Fanny." *See* Parton, Sara Payson Willis
Fessenden, Thomas Green: *Democracy Unveiled*, 129; imitates the *Dunciad*, 129; "Jeffersoniad," 129
Fichte, Johann Gottlieb, 274; definition of reason, 133
Fiction, juvenile, 353
Fielding, Henry: model for Brackenridge, 130, 134; model for Irving, 136; model for Paulding, 97, 107, 130; praised in *Portico*, 112
*Field of Waterloo* (Scott), 112
Fisk, Jim, 363, 386, 395
Fiske, John, 358, 378, 385, 386, 413-414, 417
Flaubert, Gustave, 384, 385, 401 n., 403, 431, 438-439
Fleay, F. G., 415
*Flush Times of Alabama and Mississippi, The* (Baldwin), 138, 339
Foerster, Norman, vii
*Forayers, The* (Simms), 324; terror in, 217
*Foregone Conclusion, A* (Howells), 394
Form, Emerson's and Thoreau's theories of organic, 295-296
Forms, ix
*For the Major* (Woolson), 418, 432
Foster, Hannah, *The Coquette*, 330
Fourier, Charles, 304
Fourierism, 159, 233, 233 n., 389
Fox, George, 287, 301
Francis, Convers, 249
Franklin, Benjamin, x, 42, 61, 78; agrarianism, 114, 125; advocates practical education, 147; *Autobiography*, 63, 65, 66; deist, 93; *Dissertation on Liberty and Necessity of Pleasure and Pain*, 63; neoclassicism, 96; objection to

456     INDEX

slavery, 123; product of Enlightenment, 98, 109
Frederic, Harold, 438
Freedom, 38
Free love, 61, 389, 390
Freeman, Mary Wilkins, 431; *A Humble Romance*, 419; *Pembroke*, 440
Free Religious Association, 358
Free will, 22, 26; Transcendentalist position on, 250, 280
French influences, 56-59, 73, 76; on Transcendentalism, 258, 259
French Revolution, 95, 100, 109
Freneau, Philip, 64, 80, 82, 84-87; agrarianism, 125; "Columbus to Ferdinand," 81; educational theories, 147; "The House of Night," 85; influenced by Gray, 130; *Letters on Various . . . Subjects*, 134; lyric treatment of nature, 127; neoclassicism, 96; "On a Book Called Unitarian Theology," 85; "The Pictures of Columbus, the Genoese," 81; product of the Enlightenment, 98, 99, 109; "The Power of Fancy," 84; "To a Wild Honeysuckle," 127; "Pyramids of Egypt," 82; *The Rising Glory of America*, 51; satirist, 134-135
*Friend, The* (Coleridge), 257, 277, 322 n.
Frisbie, Levi, 264
Froebel, Friedrich, 305
*From Classic to Romantic*, xi
Frontier, 59, 75, 93, 97, 103, 104, 114-115, 120, 135, 137-138, 157, 340, 342, 344, 362, 374, 376, 415; Brownson's view of, 302; Emerson's relations to, 296
"Frontier Period, The," 382
Frontier spirit, vii
Frothingham, Nathaniel, 285, 291
Frothingham, O. B., 247 n., 249, 268 n., 285 n., 303 n., 311 n., 360 n., 387
"Fugitives from Labor" (Sheldon), 363 n.
Fuller, Margaret, 249, 321; attempts objective aesthetic theory, 297; comment on Judd's *Margaret*, 128 n.; interest in literary criticism, 153 n., 293, 297-298; interest in phrenology, 283; "Lives of the Great Composers," 298 n.; "The Modern Drama," 297 n.; "A Short Essay on Critics," 297 n.; *Woman in the Nineteenth Century*, 97
Furness, William Howard, 249, 284, 289; *Remarks on the Four Gospels*, 262

Gabler, Johann Philipp, 291
*Galaxy*, 353, 367, 371
Garland, Hamlin, 410, 430, 434, 435, 437, 438, 440
Garrison, William Lloyd: abolitionism, 113; burning of Constitution, 124
*Gates Ajar, The* (Phelps), 368
*Gazette of the United States*, 101
*General History of Virginia, The* (Smith), 10
Genius, 112, 118, 121, 143; Transcendental doctrine of, 293, 294, 295-296
Genteel tradition, the, 382
*Geological Evidences of the Antiquity of Man* (Lyell), 357
George, Henry, 416
*Georgia Scenes* (Longstreet), 138, 339
Gerando, Joseph Marie De, as influence on American idealism, 177, 228, 229 n.
German influences, shape American Transcendentalism, 257, 259, 261, 268, 273, 274
*Gertrude of Wyoming* (Campbell), 212
Gift-books, 180
Gilded Age, 382, 383, 389, 393; its materialism, 342, 343
*Gilded Age, The* (Clemens and Warner), 385, 392, 395, 428, 434
Gilden, Charles, 43
God: absolute being, 25; creator, 12, 15, 17, 19, 36; existence of, 12;

# INDEX

457

goodness of, 41, 44, 47; governor of universe, 16, 17, 19, 23, 36; as judge, 14; justice of, 15; mercy of, 15; workman, 12, 15, 16, 18, 19, 36
Goddard, H. C., 247 n., 255 n., 257 n., 268 n.
*Godey's Lady's Book*, 179-180, 331
Godkin, Edwin L., 386
*God's Determinations Touching His Elect* (Taylor), 14
Goethe, Johann Wolfgang von, 191, 252, 261, 279, 288, 295, 322; influence on sentimental novel, 132
Goldoni, Carlo, 402 n., 407
Goldsmith, Oliver: cult of simplicity, 130; imitated by Irving, 136; imitated by Wirt, 111; influence on Paulding, 97, 107; interest in rural themes, 125; orientalism, 157; verse forms as models, 96
Gompers, Samuel, 416
Goncourt, Edmond de, 422
Gosse, Edmund, 439
Gothic, 217-220; factors in the revival of, 218; in Scott, 218 n.; terror of the soul, the malign, 218 n. *See also* Gothicism
Gothicism, 117, 125, 135, 136, 157
Gould, Edward S., his criticism, 144
Gould, Hannah F., 198
Gould, Jay, 363, 386
Government, 3, 4, 7, 8, 9, 10, 11, 36, 41, 47
*Graham's Magazine*, 331, 348; as medium of sentimental female verses, 192
*Grandissimes, The* (Cable), 418
Grangers, the, 395
Gray, Asa, 357, 358
Gray, Thomas: "Elegy," 85; influence on Freneau and Bryant, 130, 135; interest in rural themes, 125; popularity in America, 86; verse forms as models for Americans, 96
"Great Barbecue, The," 386
*Great Christian Doctrine of Original Sin Defended, The* (Edwards), 46
Greaves, James Pierpont, 305
Greece, and Philhellenic fever, 238

Greek Revival, 115 n., 119
Greeks: Emerson on "The Character of Socrates," 263-264; influence on Emerson, 263-264, 268, 270-271
Green, Jacob, 64
Greenbackism, 395, 415
*Greenfield Hill* (Dwight), 96, 100, 106
Grew, Nehemiah, 43
Gronlund, Lawrence, 416, 432
*Growth of the Mind* (Reed), 261
*Gulliver's Travels* (Swift), 112
*Gunmaker of Moscow, The* (Cobb), 336
*Gunnar* (Boyesen), 406

*Hagar, a Story of To-Day* (Cary), 345 n.
Hale E. E., 263 n., 265 n.
Haliburton, T. C., creator of Sam Slick, 337-338
Hall, G. Stanley, 391
Hall, James: criticism influenced by Dennie, 120 n.; nationalism of his *Illinois Monthly*, 147
Hall, Willis, Benthamite, 124
Halleck, Fitz-Greene, 323; insignificance of his society verse, 150
Halyburton, Thomas, *Natural Religion Insufficient*, 44
"Hamatraya" (Emerson), 312
Hamilton, Alexander, 56; his prose urged as model by William Wirt, 112; product of Enlightenment, 98, 108
*Hamiltoniad, The* (Williams), 129
Hamiltonianism, 99
Handel, George Frederick, 298
*Hannah Thurston* (Taylor), 350
*Hans Breitmann Ballads* (Leland), 354
*Harbinger*, 304
Hardy, Thomas, 437, 438-439
*Harper's Magazine*, 186, 348, 371, 381, 385, 434, 437
*Harper's Weekly*, 386
Harris, George W., *Sut Lovingood's Yarns*, 339
Harris, Joel Chandler, 430-431

Harris, William T., 360, 387, 433
Harrison, William Henry, provides impetus for border poems, 216
Harte, Bret, 326, 342-343, 376, 385, 393, 394, 397-398, 406, 430-431; *Condensed Novels*, 343, 397; "The Luck of Roaring Camp," 343; "Miggles," 343; "Mrs. Judge Jenkins," 397; "The Outcasts of Poker Flat," 343; "Tennessee's Partner," 343
Hartford Convention, 122
Hartley, David, 74, 80; influence on decline of neoclassicism, 152
Harvard, 69, 73
*Harvardiana*, 150
*Harvard Lyceum, The*, 149
Hase, Karl August von, 291
Hawthorne, Nathaniel, 86, 248, 322-325, 332, 346, 367, 396, 406, 407, 423, 424, 429; antitraditionalist, 187; attention to women characters, 131; "The Artist of the Beautiful," 323; *The Blithedale Romance*, 367, 435; "The Celestial Railroad," 323; concern with sin, 123; "Earth's Holocaust," 220, 323; "Ethan Brand," 220; Gothic of the malign, 219; imitation of Swift, 130; laments absence of cultural tradition, 109; *The Marble Faun*, 323; metaphysical novelist, 207-208; overseas influence, 241; *The Scarlet Letter*, 294, 319, 418; use of nature as symbol, 127; romantic mood, realistic matter, 322, 323, 324, 325
Hay, John, 326, 385, 397-398, 419, 426, 434; *The Breadwinners*, 419, 426-427, 434; *Pike County Ballads*, 398
Haydn, Franz Joseph, 298
Haymarket, 432, 435
Hayne, Paul H., 326
*Hazard of New Fortunes, A* (Howells), 435, 436
Hazlitt, William, 139
*Hearth and Home*, 385
Hecker, Isaac, 296

Heckewelder, John E., as an influence on interpretation of the Indian, 212
*Hedda Gabler* (Ibsen), 439
Hedge, Frederic, 249, 256-257, 273, 284; German influences upon, 133, 157
Hedge, Levi, 264
*Hedged In* (Phelps), 368
Hegel, Georg Wilhelm Friedrich, 133, 259, 273, 358, 359, 378, 387, 412; his philosophy reconciled with Darwinism by Whitman, 359
Hellenism, 119, 120
Helmholtz, Herman L. F. von, 391, 412
Hemans, Felicia: 330; popularity in America, 131, 198, 198 n.; as prototype for American lyricists, 197
Henry, C. S.: editor of Cousin, 159, on rise of German ideas, 145
Henry, Caleb Sprague, 249, 274
Henry, Patrick, 111
Hentz, Mrs. Caroline, 332; *The Planter's Northern Bride*, 332 n.
Herbart, Johann Friedrick, influence of educational theories, 133
Herder, Johann Gottfried von, 289, 291; American opinion of, 144, 145
Herschel, J. F. W., 278
*Hiawatha* (Longfellow), 213, 319
Higginson, Thomas Wentworth, 249, 385, 400, 410; *Malbone: An Oldport Romance*, 351
Hildreth, Richard: author of first antislavery novel, 113; Benthamite utilitarian, 124; *The Slave*, 113, 124
Hillhouse, James A.: "Choice of an Era in Epic and Tragic Writing," 144; on use of Bible as model, 144
*Histoire Comparée des Systèmes de Philosophie* (De Gerando), 272
History, 9, 21, 45, 46
*History of New England, or The Wonder-Working Providence of Sion's Saviour in New England* (Johnson), 9

*History of Civilization in England* (Buckle), 357
*History of English Literature* (Taine), 356
*History of New York, A (Knickerbocker's History)* (Irving), 184
*History of the American Civil War* (Draper), 357
*History of the American Indians* (Adair), 78
*History of the Intellectual Development of Europe* (Draper), 357
*History of the United States* (Bancroft), 133, 158, 301 n.
Hoar, E. R., 150
Hobbes, Thomas, 140
Hodge, Charles, 290
Hoffman, Ernst Theodor Amadeus, and the revival of the Gothic, 218
Holbach, 73
Holland, J. G., 325, 345, 346, 353, 395; *Bitter-Sweet*, 325; *Miss Gilbert's Career, an American Story*, 346; *Sevenoaks*, 395
Holmes, Abiel, as antiquarian, 193
Holmes, Mary Jane, *Tempest and Sunshine*, 332
Holmes, Oliver Wendell, 47, 347-348 n., 391, 417, 439; antagonism toward Calvinism, sentiment, 319; "The Chambered Nautilus," 320; *Elsie Venner*, 320; his criticism, 144; *Mechanism in Thought and Morals*, 417; "Poetry: A Metrical Essay," 144; realism and sensationalism in his novels, 319, 320
Homer, Winslow, 404
*Honest John Vane* (DeForest), 395
Hooker, Thomas, 40
Hooper, Ellen Sturgis, 249
Hooper, J. J., 340; creator of picaresque hero, 138; *Adventures of Simon Suggs*, 340
*Hoosier Schoolmaster, The* (Eggleston), 373-374, 381, 385; beginning of a new kind of fiction, 375; realism of, 317 n.
*Hope Leslie* (Sedgwick), 330
Hopkins, Samuel, 64

Horace, use by Brackenridge, 134
"House of Night, The" (Freneau), 85
Howe, E. W., 431, 438; *The Story of a Country Town*, 418, 426
Howe, Julia Ward, 392
Howells, William Dean, x, xi, 317 n., 322, 351, 352, 373, 374; *Annie Kilburn*, 435, 436; and *Atlantic Monthly*, 1871, 385; *A Chance Acquaintance*, 385, 406; change in methods after 1880, 417-418; change in outlook after 1887, 434; critical distrust of in *Nation*, 409-410; *Criticism and Fiction*, 381, 438; criticism of in eighties, 421; distinction between fiction and newspaper writing, 410 n.; early realism of, 352-353; early travel books, 407-408; essay on James, 422-423; *A Foregone Conclusion*, 394; *A Hazard of New Fortunes*, 435, 436; *Indian Summer*, 411, 418, 427, 437; influences on, 408; James's letter to, 422; *The Lady of the Aroostook*, 394; *The Landlord at Lion's Head*, 440; letter to Clemens, 411; *The Minister's Charge*, 434-435; moderate social realism, 438; *A Modern Instance*, 418, 420, 422, 427, 435, 437; persistence of earlier realism in nineties, 439; personal element in criticism of, 423 n.; *Private Theatricals*, 394; psychological methods of, 441; realism of *A Modern Instance*, 420-421; *The Rise of Silas Lapham*, 418, 427; social criticism in fiction, 435-437; social criticism of, 426-427; spokesman for American realism, 381-382; theory of realism, 405-407; *The Undiscovered Country*, 392; use of term "realism," 402 n.; view of Taine, 399; women characters of, 388, 391-392; *A World of Chance*, 436
"How to Make Our Ideas Clear" (Peirce), 417
Hubbell, J. B., xi

*Huckleberry Finn* (Clemens), 342, 418, 429, 432
*Hudibras* (Butler), 129
Hudson River School, 109, 125, 127
Humanitarianism, 58, 59, 60, 416, 437; Christian ethics as a force in, 232; and the rise of urban culture, 233; and sentimentalism, 232
"Humanity of Science, The" (Emerson), 279
Human nature, 26, 29, 31, 46
*Humble Romance, A* (Wilkins [Freeman]), 419
Humboldt, Alexander von, Poe's *Eureka* dedicated to him, 117 n.
Hume, David, 46, 68, 74, 252, 265-266
Humor, 330, 337, 376; after the Civil War, 340-342; as contribution to realism, 342; as corrective of sentimentality, 337; in New England, 337-338; in the South, 339-340; in the Southwest, 339
Humphreys, David, 71; *Address to the Armies of the United States*, 80, 81
Hunt, William Morris, 386, 403
Hunter, John, 277, 279, 281
Hurlbut, Martin, 289
Hutcheson, Francis, 67, 69, 71, 255; *Inquiry into the Original of Our Ideas of Beauty and Virtue*, 68
Hutchinson, Ann, 33, 34, 35
Huxley, Thomas Henry, 360, 361, 386, 417

Iamblichus, 271
Ibsen, 438
Idealism, 381, 383, 387, 389, 397, 398, 402, 415, 416, 419, 420, 423, 429, 435, 439, 440-441; Dr. Channing's acceptance of, 254; in Emerson and Whitman, 329; romantic, decline of, 318; sources for Transcendentalist, 270-275; Transcendentalism defined as, 248
Ideality, 387, 406, 439
*Illinois Monthly*, 147
Imagination, 148, 150, 151, 152, 158

Imlay, Gilbert, poetic treatment of the West, 120; *America*, 120
Imperialism, 110
*Ivanhoe* (Scott), 425
"Incident in a Railroad Car, An" (Lowell), 74 n.
Indian, the, 97, 121, 127, 155, 157; chief resource in search for antiquarian material, 193; decline of epic form in handling of, 213; last of tribe tradition, 216; metrical romance for celebration of, 214; popularity of, in fiction and poetry of forties, 216-217; sentimental verses regarded as unsatisfactory for recording of, 213
*Indian Summer* (Howells), 411, 418, 427, 437
Individualism, 98-124, 148, 153-154, 159, 383-384, 392-393, 394, 399, 419, 432-433, 436, 440-441; of Transcendentalists, 300, 306, 308
Industrialism, growth of, 331, 345, 377
Industrial Revolution, 124
Industry, 354
*Influence of Literature upon Society* (Mme de Staël), 145
Influences, English, 344
Influences, French, 356
Ingraham, J. H., 335, 336; *La Fitte; The Pirate of the Gulf*, 336
"Initial, Daemonic, and Celestial Love" (Emerson), 270
*Innocents Abroad* (Clemens), 342, 428
*Inquiry Concerning Freedom of Will* (Edwards), 22
*Inquiry into the Human Mind on the Principles of Common Sense* (Reid), 253 n.
Instrumentalism, 433
International copyright, 182-183, 198, 240
*In the Days of Shoddy* (Morford), 364-365
*In the Tennessee Mountains* (Murfree), 418
Intuition, 148

"Invention of Letters" (Paine), 129
Irving, Washington, x, 89, 293, 323, 324 n., 407; *The Alhambra*, 135, 202; and antiquarianism, 183, 184; *Astoria*, 135; *Bracebridge Hall*, 101, 125, 185, 202, 209; cosmopolitanism, 107; as critic, 137; "Desultory Thoughts on Criticism," 137; Federalism, 101, 109; *A History of New York . . . by Diedrich Knickerbocker*, 101, 135, 184; legendary vein of, stimulated by Scott's poems, 201, 202; "Mutability of Literature," 137; neoclassicism, 136, 155; orientalism, 157; influenced by Europe, 132, 135, 158; romanticism, 136-137; and Scott, 184; sectionalism, 122; *The Sketch Book*, 101, 125, 135, 137, 183, 185, 202; transition from satire to humor, 135-137; treatment of agrarian themes, 125

Jackson, Andrew, 337
Jacksonianism, 97, 102, 109, 159; as advance in political liberalism, 237
Jacobi, Karl G. J., 291
Jacobs, Stephen, 59
"Jacquerie, The" (Lanier), 326
James, G. P. R., literary rival of Scott in the South, 207
James, Henry, Jr.: *The American*, 394, 405, 409; "The Art of Fiction," 425-426; "The Author of Beltraffio," 420; *Bostonians*, 392, 418, 420, 427, 428; changing technique in eighties, 418, 420; compared with Emerson, 405 n.; critical distrust of, 409-410; critical eclecticism, 400; criticism of, 420, 428, 439; criticism of *John Andross*, 395-396; *Daisy Miller*, 394; "A Day of Days," 353; depiction of intellectual tone of seventies, 401; distaste for conventional romance, 399; early character studies, 394; early realism of, 352-353; essay on Daudet, 425; Howells's critical opinions of, 405, 406, 422-423; interest in character in eighties, 427-428; interest in pictorial art, 403-404; "A Landscape Painter," 353; later subjectivity, 440; letter from Howells to, 385; letter to Howells on naturalism, 422; "Madame de Mauves," 385; "The Madonna of the Future," 385; "My Friend Bingham," 353; "A Passionate Pilgrim," 353, 385, 406; "Poor Richard," 353; *The Portrait of a Lady*, 418, 420; *The Princess Casamassima*, 418, 420, 427; psychological methods of, 441; relation to critical trend in sixties and seventies, 404-405; *Roderick Hudson*, 394; "The Story of a Year," 353; use of the term "realism," 402-403; view of Taine, Sainte-Beuve, Scherer, 399-400; *Washington Square*, 419; *Watch and Ward*, 317 n., 353; women characters, 388, 391-392
James, William, 247, 417, 433; "Are We Automata?," 417
*Jane Eyre* (Brontë), 186
Jefferson, Thomas, 59, 61, 63, 69, 87; agrarianism, 110, 114, 118, 125; objections to fiction, 130; *Notes on Virginia*, 78; neoclassicism, 96; objections to slavery, 123; product of Enlightenment, 98, 109, 111; "Jeffersoniad" (Fessenden), 129
Jeffersonianism, 96, 99, 100, 102, 109
Jewett, Sarah Orne, 394, 418, 431-432, 440; *A Country Doctor*, 418, 432; *The Country of the Pointed Firs*, 440; *The Mate of the Daylight*, 418
Joad, C. E. M., *Guide to the Philosophy of Morals and Politics*, 72
*John Andross* (Davis), 395
*John Brent* (Winthrop), 346
*John Godfrey's Fortunes* (Taylor), 350
"John Lamar" (Davis), 366
Johns Hopkins University, The, 412
Johnson, Edward, *History of New England, or The Wonder-Work-*

ing *Providence of Sion's Saviour in New England*, 9
Johnson, Eastman, 404
Johnson, Samuel (1696-1772), 74; *Elementa Philosophica*, 68; *Ethics*, 63; *Raphael, or the Genius of English America*, 63
Johnson, Samuel (1709-1784), 319; *Lives of the Poets*, 130; neoclassicist, 94, 95, 140; polish praised in the *Portico*, 112; reputation in America, 130
Johnson, Samuel (1822-1882), 249
Johnson, Thomas, 3, 15
Jones, James Athearn, and the legendary, 213
"Jones's Private Argyment" (Lanier), 326
Jones, Sir William, 157
*Joseph and His Friend* (Taylor), 351
Josephus, 10
"Josh Billings." *See* Shaw, Henry W.
Jouffroy, Théodore Simon, 254; as a source of eclectic idealism, 177, 227, 229, 243
*Journal of Henry David Thoreau, The*, 271, 281-282
*Journal of Speculative Philosophy*, 360
*Journals of Bronson Alcott, The*, 262 n., 280 n., 291 n., 305 n.
*Journals of Ralph Waldo Emerson, The*, 264, 265-268, 272 n., 273 n., 274 n., 276, 279-280, 287-288, 295 n., 305 n., 308, 311 n.
Judd, Sylvester, 249, 298; appeals to nature and intuition, 128; *Margaret*, 128
*Jukes, The* (Dugdale), 394

Kalm, Peter, taxonomist, 126 n.
Kames, Lord (Henry Home), 70; *Elements of Criticism*, 69; possible influence on E. T. Channing, 148 n.; *Sketches of the History of Man*, 78
Kant, Immanuel, 227, 253, 256, 257, 259, 261, 268, 273, 275, 301

*Kate Beaumont* (DeForest), 371, 393
Keats, John, 85; and American readers, 132, 168, 168 n.; discussed by Simms, 118; romanticism, 139, 140
Keenan, Henry F., 434
Kennedy, John P.: influenced by romantic fiction, 116; description of plantation life, 125; and the regionalism of Scott, 209; *Swallow Barn*, 209
Kirkland, Mrs. Caroline, 332, 333; *Western Clearings*, 345
Kirkland, John Thornton, 263
Kirkland, Joseph, 431; *Zury*, 438
*Kitty's Choice* (Davis), 392
Knapp, Samuel L., orientalism, 157
*Knickerbocker Magazine, The*, 102 n., 122, 331
Knickerbockers, the old, 323
*Knickerbocker's History of New York* (Irving), 101, 135
Knight, Grant, xi
Knights of Labor, 395, 416
Knowledge, epistemology, 25, 30, 44, 52-53, 61, 62, 66-73, 74-76, 79
Knox, Samuel, educational theories, 147; *Essay on the Best System of Liberal Education*, 147
Koch, Paul de, attacks upon his sensationalism, 185
*Koningsmarke* (Paulding), 205
Kotzebuë, influence on Irving, 135

Labor, Brownson's position on, 301-302; "The Laboring Classes," 301 n.
*Ladies Magazine and Musical Depository*, 126
*Lady Byron Vindicated* (Stowe), 391
*Lady of the Aroostook, The* (Howells,), 394
*La Fitte; the Pirate of the Gulf* (Ingraham), 336
Laissez-faire, 99, 102, 159, 384, 416; advocated by Emerson, 308
Lake poets, 117
Lamarck, Chevalier de, 158, 279

## INDEX

463

Lamb, Charles: influence on the American informal essay, 195, 195 n.; vogue in America, 195, 241
*Lamplighter, The* (Cummins), 332
Landon, Lydia E., her American popularity, 197 n., 198
*Landlord at Lion's Head, The* (Howells), 440
"Landscape Painter, A" (James), 353
Lane, Charles, 272, 304
Lanier, Sidney, 326, 370, 376, 378, 383, 390, 395, 411-415; *The English Novel*, 412, 414; "The Jacquerie," 326; "Jones's Private Argyment," 326; "The Revenge of Hamish," 326; *The Science of English Verse*, 412; *Shakespere and His Forerunners*, 412; "Thar's More in the Man than Thar Is in the Land," 326; *Tiger Lilies*, 370
Laplace, 117 n.
*L'Assommoir* (Zola), 435
*Last of the Mohicans, The* (Cooper), 97, 215
*Lady of the Lake* (Scott), 184, 214, 216, 221
Lathrop, George Parsons, 396, 401, 411, 413, 415; "The Novel and Its Future," 411
Lathrop, Joseph, *A Miscellaneous Collection of Original Pieces*, 80
*Lay of the Scottish Fiddle, The* (Paulding), 205
Law, Thomas, 63
Lazarus, Emma, 400 n., 434
Leary, Lewis, xi
*Leaves of Grass* (Whitman), 317, 325, 327, 329, 355, 359, 387, 390, 418; realism of, 327-328; satire in, 328
Leavitt, Joshua, 60
*Lectures on Art* (Allston), 151
*Lectures on Poetry* (Bryant), 141
*Lectures on Rhetoric* (Blair), 296
*Lectures on the Philosophy of the Human Mind* (Brown), 253 n., 264
*Ledger*, New York, 336

Legaré, Hugh Swinton: conservatism, 109; influence of the Schlegels, 158; traditionalism in literature, 118-119, 146
Legendary tale, the, as an objective romantic form, 201
*Legend of Thomas Didymus, the Jewish Skeptic, The* (Clarke), 291 n.
Leibnitz, Gottfried Wilhelm von, 279
Leisy, E. E., xi
Leland, Charles G., 354, 355; *Hans Breitmann Ballads*, 354; *Sunshine in Thought*, 354
*Letter to the National Convention of France* (Barlow), 58
*Letters from a Farmer in Pennsylvania* (Dickinson), 52
*Letters of Ralph Waldo Emerson, The*, 280 n.
*Letters of the British Spy* (Wirt), 111
*Letters on Various . . . Subjects* (Freneau), 134
*Letter to His Countrymen* (Cooper), 122
Lewis, Estelle Ann, 350
Libbey, Laura Jean, *Little Leafie*, 332
Liberalism, political, 164, 165, 234, 238; not properly classifiable as an American romantic tenet, 164-165
*Liberator, The*, 113
Liberty, 22, 38, 39, 108
*Life and Genius of Shakespeare* (White), 398
*Life and Sayings of Mrs. Partington, The* (Shillaber), 338
"Life in the Iron Mills" (Davis), 365
*Life Magazine*, 423
*Life of Brainard* (Edwards), 16
*Life on the Mississippi* (Clemens), 397, 418, 424, 429
"Limits of Realism in Fiction, The" (Gosse), 439
Lincoln, Abraham, 341; "Gettysburg Address," 89

Linn, John Blair: *Miscellaneous Works*, 82; *The Powers of Genius*, 81
Linnaeus, 126, 279
*Linwoods, The* (Sedgwick), 330
*Lionel Lincoln* (Cooper), 204, 205, 217
*Lippincott's Magazine*, 367
*Literary Magazine and American Register*, 126
*Literary Mirror*, 126
*Little Leafie* (Libbey), 332
*Little Women* (Alcott), 353
*Lives of the Poets* (Johnson), 130
"Lives of the Great Composers" (Fuller), 298 n.
Livy, 10
Lloyd, Henry Demarest, 416
Local color, 343, 349, 418, 419, 428-431. See also Regionalism
Locke, David Ross, creator of "Petroleum V. Nasby," 341; *The Nasby Papers*, 377
Locke, John, 7, 52, 58, 67, 68, 69, 70, 75, 250, 252, 253, 254, 262, 263, 264, 269, 309-310, 393; antagonism of Scottish school, 153, 156, 159; *Human Understanding*, 73, 74; influence on American philosophical thought, 141, 154; influence undermined by German thought, 132, 145, 159
Longfellow, Henry Wadsworth, 248, 354, 386; cosmopolitanian, 107, 159; *The Courtship of Miles Standish*, 319; criticized by Poe, 117; *Evangeline*, 319; "Excelsior," 354; *Hiawatha*, 123, 213, 319; interest in nature, 127, 150; popularity, 155 n.; praised by *Amherst Shrine*, 151; realism of later work, 319; realism of *The New England Tragedies*, 319, 371; romanticism, 319; sentimentality, 319; sources of romantic mood, 185; women in his verse, 132
Longfellow, Samuel, 249
Longstreet, Augustus Baldwin: relation to Southwest humor, 138; *Georgia Scenes*, 138, 339
*Looking Backward* (Bellamy), 434
*Lord of the Isles, The* (Scott), 214, 221
Lotze, Herman, 391
Low, Samuel, *Poems*, 80
Lowell, James Russell, 338, 347, 356; "An Incident in a Railroad Car," 74; *Biglow Papers*, 320, realism of, 338; "The Courtin'," 338; critical work, 320; *Critics*, 320; *Fable for Critics*, 320; humorous writer, 143; "Mason and Slidell," 338; influence on Eggleston's dialect, 374; realism, 320; "Sunthin' in the Pastoral Line," 338
Louisiana Purchase, 120
"Luck of Roaring Camp, The" (Harte), 343
Lundy, Benjamin, attacks war in Texas, 113
Lyceum, as a literary institution, 180-181
Lyell, Sir Charles, 357
*Lyrical Ballads* (Wordsworth), 101, 126
Lyricism, dominant form of subjective romanticism, 196-197

McCosh, James, 70, 363; *Realistic Philosophy*, 69
*M'Fingal* (Trumbull), 106
McGuffey, William Holmes, 363, 378
McHenry, James: close imitator of Scott, 205; neoclassicism in *American Quarterly Review*, 145
Mackintosh, Sir James, 72; *General View of the Progress of Ethical Philosophy, A*, 74
*Madame Bovary* (Flaubert), 405
"Madame de Mauves" (James), 385
"Madonna of the Future, The" (James), 385
*Magnalia* (Mather), 9, 10
*Malbone: An Oldport Romance* (Higginson), 351

# INDEX

*Manductio ad Ministerium* (Mather), 6
*Manfred* (Byron), 119
Mann, Horace, 283
*Man That Corrupted Hadleyburg, The* (Clemens), 342
*Marble Faun, The* (Hawthorne), 323
*Margaret* (Judd), 128
*Margret Howth, a Story of To-Day* (Davis), 366
Marie Antoinette, 57
*Marmion* (Scott), 214, 221
Marsh, James, 249; edits Coleridge's *Aids to Reflection*, 153, 159, 284; idealism, 253
Marshall, John: Federalism, 103; imitation urged by William Wirt, 112
Mason, George, individualism, 113
"Mason and Slidell" (Lowell), 338
Masters, Edgar Lee, *Spoon River Anthology*, 345
*Mate of the Daylight, The* (Jewett), 418
Materialism, 383, 386, 412, 428, 440; and gospel of wealth, 362-363; danger of in Spencerian philosophy, 360; defined, 318; scientific, 378; Thoreau's opposition to, 306; triumph of, 364; Whitman's attitude toward, 329
Mather, Cotton, 4, 22, 43, 45, 371; *The Christian Philosopher*, 21; *Magnalia*, 9, 10; *Manductio ad Ministerium*, 6
Mather, Increase, 4
Maupassant, Guy de, 439
May, Clifford B., 80
Mayhew, Jonathan, 11
Maylem, John, *The Conquest of Louisburg*, 81
Mazzini, Guido, 437
Mechanism, Transcendentalism a reaction against, 253
*Mechanism in Thought and Morals* (Holmes), 417
*Melmoth the Wanderer* (Maturin), 219

Melville, Herman, 248, 324, 418; *Clarel*, 324; *The Confidence-Man*, 324; *Moby-Dick*, 324, 418; primitivism, 97; psychological probing forecast by de Tocqueville, 105; uniqueness, 123; use of nature as symbol, 127
"Merlin" (Emerson), 143
Mesmerism, 157
Methodism, 109, 114, 394
Metrical romance: influence of Scott's octosyllabic upon American writers of, 214, 216; the Indian in, 214
Michelangelo, 151
"Miggles" (Harte), 343
Mill, John Stuart, 361
Miller, Joaquin, 431
Miller, Samuel, *Brief Retrospect of the Eighteenth Century, A*, 62
"Miller's Maid, The" (Bloomfield), 126
Miller, Perry, vii
Millet, J. F., 403, 408
*Mill on the Floss, The* (Eliot), 344
Milton, John: 86; finds champions in America against Dr. Johnson, 130; *Paradise Lost*, 85; revision of his works by neoclassicists, 140
*Minister's Charge, The* (Howells), 434-435
*Minister's Wooing, The* (Stowe), 348
Minor Knickerbockers, 137
*Miscellaneous Collection of Original Pieces, A* (Lathrop), 80
*Miscellaneous Works* (Linn), 82
*Miss Gilbert's Career, an American Story* (Holland), 346
"Miss Lucinda" (Cooke), 348
*Miss Ludington's Sister* (Bellamy), 407, 426
Missouri Compromise, 113, 156
*Miss Ravenel's Conversion from Secession to Loyalty* (DeForest), 371-373, 388
Mitchell, Donald Grant: *Dream Life*, 334; *My Farm at Edgewood*, 334;

*Reveries of a Bachelor*, 334; *Wet Days at Edgewood*, 334
Mitchell, S. Weir, 391-392; *Roland Blake*, 419
*Moby-Dick* (Melville), 324, 418
*Modell of Christian Charity written on board the Arrabella, on the Attlantick Ocean, The* (Winthrop), 38
*Modern Chivalry* (Brackenridge), 96, 100, 147
"Modern Drama, The" (Fuller), 297 n.
*Modern Instance, A* (Howells), 418, 420, 422, 427, 435, 437
Modern Language Association, vii, xi
Monarchy, 11, 18
Montaigne, Michael de, 287-288, 295
*Monikins, The* (Cooper), 93, 103, 130
Monroe Doctrine, 156
Montesquieu, 55, 78; use of orientalism, 157
Montgomery, James, as popular lyric model, 197, 197 n.
*Monthly Anthology*, 129, 254
Moore, Thomas, vogue in America, 116, 143, 157, 197
"Moral Argument against Calvinism, The" (Channing), 23, 156
Moralism (dynamic), 176
*Morals* (Price), 264
Morford, Henry: *The Coward*, 364-365; *In the Days of Shoddy*, 364-365; *Shoulder Straps*, 364
Morris, William, 386, 437, 438
Morse, James, H., 423-424
Motley, John Lothrop, influence of Germany, 132
Mott, Lucretia, 288
"Mr. Hardhack on the Sensational in Literature and Life" (Whipple), 336 n.
"Mr. Hardhack on the Derivation of Man from the Monkey" (Whipple), 361 n.
"Mrs. Judge Jenkins" (Harte), 397
Mumford, William, *Poems*, 82

"Murders in the Rue Morgue, The" (Poe), 220
Murfree, Mary N.: *In the Tennessee Mountains*, 418; *The Prophet of the Great Smoky Mountains*, 418
*Murvale Eastman* (Tourgée), 4
"Mutability of Literature" (Irving), 137
*My Farm at Edgewood* (Mitchell), 334
"My Friend Bingham" (James), 353
*Mysterious Stranger, The* (Clemens), 428

Napoleon, 58
"Nasby, Petroleum V." See Locke, David Ross
*Nasby Papers, The* (Locke), 341
Nast, Thomas, 386
*Nation*, 385, 388, 409, 410, 420, 428
Nationalism, 93, 103, 106-110, 122-123, 155, 156, 158-159, 187-190, 241, 344, 357; in Transcendentalist literary theory, 295, 296, 311-312
*Natural and Civil History of Vermont, The* (Williams), 79
Natural law, 99, 103
Natural light, 7
Natural philosophy, 4
*Natural Religion Insufficient* (Halyburton), 44
Natural rights, 99, 114, 118
Natural science, 4, 9, 10, 21, 27, 36, 42, 45, 46
*Natural Theology* (Paley), 278
Naturalism, 339, 357, 383, 384, 403, 412, 418, 420, 423, 438
Nature, 27, 30, 47, 80-83, 84, 85, 94, 97, 107, 124-128, 150, 151, 157, 158; corresponds with spirit, 251, 282, 283, 313; light of, 5, 28, 29; Transcendentalist concept, 275-276, 278, 281-284
*Nature* (Emerson), 27, 253, 261, 262, 267-268, 271, 278; influenced by Alcott, 261, 268
*Nature of True Virtue, The* (Edwards), 26
Neal, John: fictional methods, 205;

reform activity, 231; treatment of Indian, 121; utilitarianism, 231 n.
Neal, Joseph C., 338
*Neighbor Jackwood* (Trowbridge), 335
Neoclassicism, viii, x, 93-159; Brownson on, 260; opposed by Transcendentalists, 292, 298
Neoclassic criticism, 178; in the *North American Review*, 178 n.
Newcomb, Charles King, 249
Newcomb, Simon, 432
Newell, Robert H., creator of "Orpheus C. Kerr," 341
New Harmony, 159
Newton, Sir Isaac, 4, 45, 250, 277-278, 310; influence on Emerson, 277, 278; influence on Poe, 116, 117 n.; influence supplanted by biological science, 126; nationalism, 154
*New Views of Christianity, Society, and the Church* (Brownson), 260
*New York Mirror*, 178
*New York Review*, as stimulative of the familiar essay, 194
*Night Thoughts* (Young), 130
*Noctes Ambrosianae*, as a popular essay model, 195 n.
*North American Review*, 108 n., 122, 143, 145, 148, 158; 256 n., 257 n., 332, 348 n., 385, 432, 437; as important literary agency, 178-179; Transcendental ideas in the pages of, 228
North, Christopher. *See* Wilson, John
Norton, Andrews: attacks Alcott, 262; called less religious than Transcendentalists, 292; opposes Ripley on miracles, 289; publishes Frisbie's lectures, 264; replied to by Ripley, 258; writes *The Latest Form of Infidelity*, 290
*Notions of the Americans* (Cooper), 102, 103, 122
*Notes on Virginia* (Jefferson), 78
"Novel and Its Future, The" (Lathrop), 411
Novalis, 413

Novels on the vanishing American, 215
Nuttall, Thomas, comment on Western immigrants, 120

*Oak-Openings* (Cooper), 102, 216
Oberlin College, and abolition movement, 113
Objective correlative, stated by Washington Allston, 152
O'Brien, Fitz-James, 350
"Ode Inscribed to W. H. Channing" (Emerson), 306 n.
Odiorne, Thomas, 80; "The Progress of Refinement," 74
Oegger, G., 273
Okely, Francis, 261
Oken, Lorenz, 280
*Old Continental, The* (Paulding), 205
"Old Bachelor, The" (Wirt's contributions), 111
*Old Hicks the Guide* (Webber), 121
*Oldtown Folks* (Stowe), 16, 18, 349
"On Models in Literature" (Channing), 148
*Oneota*, 127
"One's-Self I Sing" (Whitman), 328
*On Taste* (Alison), 148, 156
"On the Late S. T. Coleridge" (Allston), 151
Optimism: of Emerson, 268; of Transcendentalists, 251, 280
Order, 98
Orientalism, vogue of, 157
*Original Sin* (Edwards), 26
*Origin of Species* (Darwin), 280, 281, 357
*Ornithological Biography* (Audubon), 127
"Orpheus C. Kerr." *See* Newell, Robert H.
Osgood, Samuel, 249, 291
Ossian, 82; attacked by Legaré, 119 n.; and Cooper, 215 n.; factor in mounting emotionalism, 191; influence on romantic landscape, 224, 224 n.; influence on Indian

death-chant, 215; influence on use of rural themes, 125; melancholy, 214; stimulus to sentimental verse, 213 n.
Ossianism, 397
"Outcasts of Poker Flat, The" (Harte), 343
*Outlines of Moral Philosophy* (Stewart), 253 n., 264
*Overland* (DeForest), 385
*Overland Monthly*, 343, 352, 371
"Over-Soul, The" (Emerson), 271

Page, Thomas Nelson, 431
Paine, Robert Treat: imitates Pope, 129; "Invention of Letters," 129
Paine, Thomas, 41, 46, 59, 61, 283, 289; *The Age of Reason*, 46, 58, 65, 149; *Common Sense*, 52, 99; *The Crisis*, 52; deism, 93; educational theories, 147; neoclassicism, 96; relation to the Enlightenment, 98, 109; *The Rights of Man*, 57
Paley, William, 250, 263, 265, 275, 278, 283; *Moral Philosophy*, 63
Pantheism, 24, 36, 47
Paper, cheap, 185
Parker, Theodore, 249, 361; advocates self-reform, 312; antislavery position, 307; characterizes Transcendentalism as idealism, 254; Dr. Channing's influence on, 255; doctrine of "Absolute Religion," 291; early career, 290; as idealist, 235; interest in phrenology, 283; reads Cousin, 274; reads German theologians, 291; as reformer, 230; rejects doctrine of eternal damnation, 311; "A Sermon of Merchants," 307; "Transcendentalism," 254; "Transient and Permanent in Christianity," 291; view of God, 284; writes as "Levi Blodgett," 290
Parker, William, xi
Parkman, Francis, German influence on, 132
Parrington, V. L., 313, 382, 386, 431, 440

Parsons, Theophilus, praises Mme de Staël, 145
*Partisan, The* (Simms), 324
*Partisan Leader, The* (Tucker), 114
Parton, Sara Payson Willis, *Ruth Hall*, 334
"Passionate Pilgrim, A" (James), 353, 385, 406
*Pathfinder, The* (Cooper), 216
*Patriot Muse, The* (Prime), 81
Pau, Abbé de, 77
Paulding, James Kirke: *The Backwoodsman*, 120, 129; careless style, 143; descriptions of plantation life, 125; and Fielding, 130; *Koningsmarke*, 205; *The Lay of the Scottish Fiddle*, 205; *The Old Continental*, 205; nationalism, 107, 109, 122, 155; neoclassicism, 97, 102; orientalism, 157; and Scott, 205; *Westward Ho!*, 125; use of frontier humor on stage, 138
Peabody, Elizabeth Palmer, 249
Peabody, W. B. O.: extreme neoclassicism, 113; need for study of his criticism, 144
Peabody, Elizabeth: edits *Record of a School*, 261; educational theories, 305; follows Dr. Channing, 255; quotes Dr. Channing, 254, 273; *Reminiscences*, 254 n., 255 n., 273 n.
Peabody Institute (Baltimore), 412
"Pearl of Great Price, A" (Davis), 367
Pearson, Norman, xi
Peirce, Charles S., 247 n., 417
*Pembroke* (Freeman), 440
Penn, William, 301
Percival, James G.: *Clio* reviewed by Legaré, 119 n.; criticized by his contemporaries, 169-171; definition of genius, 145 n.; literary criticism, 144; no index of American revolt, 170; praised by *Amherst Shrine*, 150-151; praised by *American Quarterly Review*, 145; study of language, 157; use of natural scenery, 109, 127

Perfectibility, 75
Periodicals, British, popularity in America, 179 n.
Perkins, William, 3
Perry, Thomas S., 388, 391, 400, 401, 408, 411, 413, 415; *English Literature of the Eighteenth Century,* 412
Personalism, 194
Pessimism, 378; in Poe, Hawthorne, Melville, 354
Percy, Bishop, interest in rural themes, 125
Pestalozzi, Johann Heinrich, 305; influence on American schools, 149; influence on George Bancroft, 133
Phelps, Elizabeth Stuart, 346, 368-370, 392, 395, 424; *Gates Ajar,* 368; *Hedged In,* 368; *The Silent Partner,* 368-370, 395; "The Tenth of January," 368
"Philosophical Miscellanies from the French of Cousin, Jouffroy, Constant," 274 n.
Phillips, Wendell, 389
*Philosophical Inquiry into the Sublime and the Beautiful* (Burke), 148
*Philosophy of Art in the Netherlands* (Taine), 374
"Philosophy of Composition, The" (Poe), 116
*Philosophy of English Literature, The* (Bascom), 399
Phrenology, furnishes themes for writers, 157
Physiocrats (French), relation to agrarianism, 114
*Physiology of the Human Mind* (Brown), 253 n.
"Pictures of Columbus, the Genoese, The" (Freneau), 81
Pierpont, John, criticized in *Amherst Shrine,* 150
*Pike County Ballads* (Hay), 326, 398
*Pioneers, The* (Cooper), 103, 121, 221, 222 n.
*Plaindealer* (Cleveland), 340

*Planter's Northern Bride, The* (Hentz), 332 n.
Plato, 261, 263, 268, 269, 270, 271, 310, 322
Platonism, 67, 68, 71, 73
*Playing the Mischief* (DeForest), 409
Plotinus, 261, 268, 278
Plutarch, idea of checks and balances, 100
Pochmann, Henry, xi
Poe, Edgar Allan, 85, 248, 294, 324, 397, 413; aesthetic theories, 107, 172, 173-174; "Al Aaraaf," 116; anticipated by de Tocqueville, 105; and Chivers, 174; and Coleridge, 132, 172, 173; conservatism, 109; definition of poetry, 172; *Eureka,* 93, 413; "The Fall of the House of Usher," 220; hostility toward New England, 122; importance of women in verse and tales, 132; indebtedness to Hoffman, 219, 219 n.; individualism, 127; and the malign Gothic, 220; metrical effects, 142; "The Murders in the Rue Morgue," 220; "The Philosophy of Composition," 116; polished prose, 143; "The Raven," 142; romanticism, 116-117; satire, 134, 139; and Schlegel, 158; and science, 158; sensationalism, 133-134, 157; as Southern writer, 117; "Tamerlane," 116; "Ulalume," 397
*Poems Chiefly in the Scottish Dialect* (Bruce), 82
"Poet, The" (Emerson), influence on Whitman, 329
"Poetry: A Metrical Essay" (Holmes), 144
Poetry, Transcendentalists on, 294-296
*Poganuc People* (Stowe), 349
*Political Writings of Joel Barlow,* 57, 62
Politics. *See* Government
Polybius, 10; idea of checks and balances, 100
"Poor Richard" (James), 353

Pope, Alexander, 86; and Bryant's criticism, 141; and Byron, 107, 134, 155; *Essay on Man*, 75, 129, 142; as model for American writers, 96, 97, 112, 129, 130, 150; neoclassicism, 94, 148 n.; and Poe, 117
*Popular Science Monthly*, 385
Populist revolt, 432
Porphyry, 271
Porter, Noah, 356, 361 n., 363; *Books and Reading*, 336-337 n., 344 n.
*Port Folio*, 93, 100
*Portico*, 112, 113 n.
Presbyterianism, 154
*Portrait of a Lady, The* (James), 418, 420
*Portraiture of the Society of Friends, A* (Clarkson), 288
Positivism, 417
*Potiphar Papers* (Curtis), 334
Powderly, Terence V., 395, 416; *Thirty Years of Labor*, 432
*Power of Darkness* (Tolstoi), 437
"Power of Fancy, The" (Freneau), 84
*Powers of Genius, The* (Linn), 81
Pragmatism, 417, 433; influenced by Transcendentalism, 247
"Pray without Ceasing" (Emerson), 266
Predestination, denied by Transcendentalists, 250, 310
Prescott, Harriet, 399
Prescott, William Hickling: foreign study and travel, 158; influence of Scott's methods, 211; literary criticism, 144; on Scott's fame, 203 n.; on Scott's service to American fiction, 202 n.; and Spain, 132; and Waverly technique in history, 211
"Present State of Ethical Philosophy, The" (Emerson), 265
Preston, John, 40
Price, Richard, 67, 68, 69, 254, 264-265
Priestley, Joseph, 74; Unitarianism, 96
Prime, Benjamin Y., *The Patriot Muse, or, Poems upon Some of the Principal Events of the Late War*, 81
Primitivism, 212 n., 213 n.; clash with idea of progress, 97; reaches peak in *Old Hicks*, 121
*Prince and the Pauper, The* (Clemens), 418
*Princess Casamassima, The* (James), 418, 420, 427
Princeton, 51, 69, 74, 84
*Principia* (Newton), 45
*Principles of Geology* (Lyell), 357
*Principles of the Philosophy of Nature* (Stallo), 280
"Private History of a Campaign That Failed" (Clemens), 429
*Private Theatricals* (Howells), 394
Proclus, 261, 268, 271
Progress, 412, 414, 417, 440; faith in, 190-191
Progress, idea of, 51-52, 57, 75-76, 79; attacked by Poe, 117; clash with primitivism, 97, 156; Cooper unsympathetic toward, 121; early acceptance by Americans, 93; educational theory based upon, 147 n., Emerson denies, 294; Thoreau's attitude toward, 312
"Progress of Refinement, The" (Odiorne), 74
*Prophet of the Great Smoky Mountains, The* (Murfree), 418
Prose tales featuring the romantic redman, 215, 216
*Protestant Ethic and the Spirit of Capitalism, The* (Weber), 6
Providence, 8, 9, 17, 19, 22, 42
*Prue and I* (Curtis), 334
Psychology, 384, 391, 393, 440
*Psychology* (Cousin), 145
Puritanism, 3, 11, 51, 65, 76, 82, 344, 349; connection with neoclassicism, 95; hostile to *belles-lettres*, 96, 130; influence on Emerson, 295, 311; Transcendentalist attitudes toward, 311
Puritan tradition, vii, viii, x
*Putnam's Magazine*, 333, 343, 370
"Pyramids of Egypt" (Freneau), 82

## INDEX 471

Quakerism, 67, cult of simplicity, 156; humanitarianism, 232; influences Emerson, 288
*Queechy* (Warner), 332
*Quarterly Review*, 122
Quixotism, 100

Radcliffe, Ann, née Ward, 224, 224 n.
*Radical Problems* (Bartol), 283-284
Rafinesque, and biological science, 127, 157
Railroad expansion, 181
"Rainbow, The," Wirt's contributions to, 111
Randolph, John, individualism, 113
*Raphael, or the Genius of English America* (Johnson), 63
Rationalism, 36, 132
"Raven, The" (Poe), 142
Raynal, Abbé, 77; *Philosophical and Political History of the Settlements and Trade of the Europeans in the East and West Indies, A*, 78
Reade, Charles, 423
Realism, vii, viii, x, 63, 76-77, 330, 378; Boyesen's definition, 438; characteristic work of, 417; Civil War and growth of, 387 n., 388; conflict with romanticism, 439; controversy over in 1883-1884, 423; critical distrust of, 422; direction of Howells's, 422; in eighties, 419; Garland's, 440; George Eliot's influence, 407 n.; Howells's social thought, 437; Howells's theory and practice, 351, 405-408; influence of Turgenev, 408 n.; James's practice in eighties, 420; James's theory, 402-403; James's use of term, 425; Lathrop's definition, 411; milltown life in fiction, 346-347, 369; new power of, 318; origin of term in American criticism, 401 n.; Parrington's theory, 440; poetry unsuited to, 327; portrait technique, 408; problem of in America, 381-384; reaction to Howells's and James's, 410; relation of Western humor to, 397-398; relation to nationalism, 388 n.; social protest, 440; summary, 440-441; Twain's relation to in eighties, 429-430
Realistic, definition of, 318
*Realistic Philosophy* (McCosh), 69
Reason, 11, 25, 26, 27, 28, 29, 30, 35, 36, 44, 57, 60, 61, 62, 64-65, 66, 109, 133, 150, 154; Transcendentalist definition of, 251
*Reason the Only Oracle of Man* (Allen), 65
Reasoning, 25, 27
Reconstruction Era, 384, 415
*Record of a School* (Peabody), 261
*Record of Conversations on the Gospel ...* (Alcott), 261
*Red Badge of Courage, The* (Crane), 372
Reed, Sampson, 249, 272; *Growth of the Mind*, 261
*Reflections on the Revolution in France* (Burke), 57, 59, 103
Reform, social, 230-231; expression of romantic idealism, 230; and Transcendentalism, 230, 299-309; Utilitarianism, 231
Regionalism, 208-210, 210 n.; and antiquarianism, 209; indigenous phases of in the West, 210 n.; in Scotland, 208; of the South, 209
Reid, Thomas, 69, 71, 253, 265-266; influence on Washington Allston, 152; *Inquiry into the Human Mind on the Principles of Common Sense*, 253 n.
Reid, Whitelaw, 361, 395
*Reinterpretation of American Literature* (Foerster), vii
Religion: decline of, 345; humanizing of, 331
*Religion of Nature* (Wollaston), 278
"Remarks on National Literature" (Channing), 123, 293
*Remarks on the Four Gospels* (Furness), 262
*Reminiscences of Rev. William Ellery Channing*, 254 n., 255 n., 273 n.

Renaissance, tendencies of, recapitulated in the early nineteenth century, 239
*Representative Men* (Emerson), 272, 319
*Republican* (Springfield), 345
*Returned Captive, The*, 81
Revelation, 11, 28, 32, 33, 34, 45
"Return of the Heroes, The" (Whitman), 329
"Revenge of Hamish, The" (Lanier), 326
*Reveries of a Bachelor* (Mitchell), 334
*Review of the Debate on the Abolition of Slavery . . .* (Dew), 114
Revolution of 1830, 238
Revolution of 1848, 239
*Rhetoric* (Blair), 147
Richardson, Samuel, vogue of sentimentalism, 130, 131, 157, 330
*Rights of Man, The* (Paine), 57
Riis, Jacob, 432
Ripley, George, 249; comments on *Record of a School*, 262; develops idealistic position, 257-258; *Discourse on the Philosophy of Religion*, 258; edits *Specimens of Foreign Standard Literature*, 291; essay on Herder, 144-145; founds Brook Farm, 303; reads German theologians, 291; thoughts about miracles, 289-290; translates Cousin, 274; views of education, 305; withdraws from Transcendentalist movement, 256
Ripley, Sophia, 249
*Rise of Silas Lapham, The* (Howells), 418, 427
*Rising Glory of America, The* (Brackenridge), 51
*Robbers, The* (Schiller), 132, 174
Robertson, William, 77
*Roderick Hudson* (James), 394
Roe, E. P., 332
*Roland Blake* (Mitchell), 419
*Roman Experimental, Le* (Zola), 439
Romance, Gothic, 217, 218, 219, 240
Romance, historical, 202-208

Romance, Indian, 212-216
Romantic despair, 170-171
Romantic history, 202 n., 210-212
Romanticism, vii, viii, x, 53, 54, 59, 60, 76-78, 79-89, 106, 136, 139-140, 335, 383, 397, 398, 439; as aesthetic indefiniteness, 171; confusion in terminology, 164-165; declining power of, 318; definitions of, 163-164, 165 n., 166 n., 166-168, 318; dynamic, 174-176; negative phases of, 199-225; as revolt, 169, rejection of negative phases in America, 170-173; and subjectivism, 170; tenets of, 166-167; versus idealism, 226; Transcendentalism a part of, 252
Romantic landscape, 220-225, 240; Cooper's contribution to, 221; the cult of solitude related to, 223; eighteenth-century forces productive of, 220; popularity of Thomson in, 222; Scott's connection with the movement of, 221; sources of, 220-225
Rotch, Mary, 288
*Roughing It* (Clemens), 385, 398, 428
Rousseau, Jean Jacques, 72, 77, 103
Rowson, Susanna, 330; rise of feminism and female authors, 131; *Charlotte Temple*, 330, 389
*Roxy* (Eggleston), 394
Royce, Josiah, 433
"Rural Sentimentalities" (Dennis), 150
Rush, Dr. Benjamin, 69, 73; advocate of utilitarian education, 147; *Essays, Literary, Moral, and Philosophical*, 75; neoclassical thought, 96
Ruskin, John, 437, 438
Russell, William, 261
*Ruth Hall* (Parton), 334

Sainte-Beuve, Charles Augustin, 355, 356, 384, 385, 399-400
*St. Elmo* (Evans), 332
*Salmagundi*, 135
*Salmagundi, Second Series*, 122

# INDEX

*Sam Lawson's Fireside Stories* (Stowe), 349, 385
Sanborn, F. B., 249, 268 n., 272 n.
Saroyan, William, 47
Satire, 94, 155
*Sartor Resartus* (Carlyle), 150, 274
*Satanstoe* (Cooper), 189 n., 216
*Saturday Gazette*, 338
*Scarlet Letter, The* (Hawthorne), 294, 319, 418
*Scenes of Clerical Life* (Eliot), 343, 349
Schelling, Friedrich von, 259, 275
Scherer, Edmond, 400
Schiller, Johann Christoph Friedrich von: critical attack upon, 174-175, 175, n.; influence on sentimental novel, 132; plays read by Irving, 135; work defined as dynamic romanticism, 174
Schlegel, A. W. von: religion ultimate source of taste, 119; vogue in America, 132, 158
Schleiermacher, Friedrich, 291; German teacher of *neuer Amerikaner*, 133
Schmidt, Heinrich, 412
Schoolcraft, Henry: *Algic Researches*, 127, 216; as source for *Hiawatha*, 127; and vogue of Indian themes, 127
Science, 62, 355, 376, 377; Emerson's emphasis upon astronomy, 276-278, upon biology, 279-281; impact of, 345; relation to art, 355; Thoreau's ambivalence toward, 281-283
*Science and Health* (Eddy), 390
*Science of English Verse, The* (Lanier), 412
Scott, Sir Walter, 175 n., 178, 225, 242, 325, 335, 336, 344, 396, 397, 399, 424-425, 429, 439; admired by O. W. B. Peabody, 144; American imitators, 205; American vogue, 107, 110, 130, 132, 143, 155, 200 n., 201 n., 203 n., 242; *The Black Dwarf*, 204; compared with Shakespeare, 203 n.; criticized by Cooper, 103; Federalistic bias, 110; fictional forms used by Cooper, 102; and humor of Southwest, 210; influence of, 199-212, 200 n.; *The Lady of the Lake* as model for American metrical romances, 214; literary rivals of in America, 243; lyrics as models for versifiers, 197; Mark Twain's attack, 116 n.; medievalism, 97; model for romantic history, 210-212; parodied by Paulding, 129 n.; popularity in South, 110, 115, 116, 206-207; romantic interests, 200; and romantic landscape, 220-221; stimulus to Irving, 135, 158, 184; transmission of German ideas to America, 133; verse criticized by *Portico*, 112, 113 n.
Scottish philosophy, 132, 141, 144, 148, 152, 153, 156, 159
*Scribner's Monthly*, 345
Scriptures. See Bible
*Seacliff; or, The Mystery of the Westervelts* (DeForest), 371
Sectionalism, 110, 113, 114, 120, 122, 157, 159
Sedgwick, Arthur, 394, 401-402
Sedgwick, Catharine Maria, *The Linwoods*, 330
Sensationalism, 330, 335, 336, 377
Sentiment, 71-73
Sentimental novel, popularity of, 330-334
Sentimentalism, 121, 130-131, 136, 157, 330, 335, 336, 346
"Sermon of Merchants, A" (Parker), 307
*Sermons* (Dwight), 60
*Sevenoaks* (Holland), 395
Shaftesbury, Lord, 73; benevolence, 156; *Characteristics*, 72; influence in America, 154, 156; rationalism, 154
*Shakespere and His Forerunners* (Lanier), 412
Shakespearean criticism, 398, 412-415
"Shakespeare's Art" (White), 398
Shaw, Henry W., creator of "Josh Billings," 341

Shays's Rebellion, 56, 95
Sheldon, Frederick, "Fugitives from Labor," 363 n.
Shelley, Percy Bysshe, 85, 414; American reception of, 132, 168, 168 n.; praised by *American Quarterly Review*, 146; as reformer, 140; and Simms, 118
Shepard, Thomas, 11, 12, 13, 14, 16, 18, 19, 24, 30, 32, 40; *Sincere Convert*, 12; "Treatise of Ineffectual Hearing of the Word," 30
Shillaber, B. P., creator of Mrs. Partington, 338, 340; *The Life and Sayings of Mrs. Partington*, 338
"Short Essay On Critics, A" (Fuller), 297 n.
*Shoulder Straps* (Morford), 364
Sigourney, Lydia, 330; and sentimentalism, 192; rival to Mrs. Hemans, 198
*Silent Partner, The* (Phelps), 368-370, 395
Simms, William Gilmore, 324-325, 335; careless style, 143; *The Cassique of Kiawah*, 216, 325; *Eutaw*, 324; *The Forayers*, 217, 324; idea of genius, 118; nationalism, 118; *The Partisan*, 324; realism in low-life characters, 324; sectionalism, 118; Southern characteristics, 118; *The Sword and the Distaff*, 324; in tradition of Scott and Cooper, 325; treatment of Indian, 121; use of romantic models, 116; *The Yemassee*, 216, 324
Sims, Thomas, 307
Sin, 13, 17, 21, 26, 40; Transcendentalist rejection of Calvinist views, 250, 310-311
*Sincere Convert* (Shepard), 12
*Sister Carrie* (Dreiser), 421
*Sketch Book, The* (Irving), 101, 125, 135, 137, 183, 185, 202
*Slave, The* (Hildreth), 113, 124
Slavery, 110, 114-115; crusade against, 334; novels on abolition, 335
Smalley, John, 64

Smith, Adam, 265; agrarianism, 114
Smith, Charles H., creator of "Bill Arp," 341
Smith, Captain John, *Description of New England*, 10; *The General History of Virginia*, 10
Smith, Seba, creator of Jack Downing, 337
Smollett, Tobias, model for Irving, 136
Snelling, William, realistic treatment of Indian, 121
Snider, Denton T., 387, 433
Sociology, 384, 392-393, 394, 416, 420, 433
Social solidarity, 98 ff.
Socrates, 263, 264
Solitude, cult of. See Romantic landscape
*Song of Hiawatha* (Longfellow), 127
"Song of Myself" (Whitman), 328
"Song of the Exposition" (Whitman), 329
*Sorrows of Werther, The* (Goethe), 191
*Southern Literary Messenger, The*, 122; and the new essay, 194; and the popularity of Scott in the South, 206
*Southern Review*, 146
Southey, Robert: attacked by *Portico*, 113; exotic verse, 143; mentioned in *Harvard Lyceum*, 150; oriental themes, 157
Southworth, Mrs. E. D. E. N., 332
Souvenirs. See Gift-books
*Specimens of Foreign Standard Literature*, 291
*Spectator, The*, 111
Spencer, Herbert, 358, 360, 361, 363, 378, 385, 386, 392-393, 412-414, 416, 417, 433, 438
Spiller, Robert, xi
Spiritualism, 390, 427
Spofford, Harriet, *Azarian*, 402
Spooner, A. C., gives reason for Byron's loss of popularity, 150
*Spoon River Anthology* (Masters), 345

## INDEX
## 475

Sprague, Charles F., 361 n.
Spurtzheim, Dr. Kaspar, 283
*Spy, The* (Cooper), 204
Staël, Mme de, 208, 208 n., 227, 254, 273; introduction of German philosophy to America, 144; republicanism, 145; transition to Transcendentalism, 145; use of historical method, 145; vogue in America, 144
Stallo, John Bernhard, 280
Standard Oil Company, 416
Stanton, Elizabeth Cady, 389-390, 392
State and church. *See* Church and state
Sterne, Laurence, 72; model for Irving, 136; Wirt's partiality to him, 111
Stetson, Caleb, 249
Stevenson, Robert Louis, 439
Stewart, Dugald, 71, 72, 73, 74, 253 n., 263, 264-266, 269
Stewart, John ("Walking Stewart"), theory of perfectibility scorned by Brackenridge, 100
Stiles, Ezra, 64
Stoddard, R. H., 325, 350
*Story of a Bad Boy* (Aldrich), 353
*Story of a Country Town, The* (Howe), 418, 426
"Story of a Year, The" (James), 353
*Story of Kennett, The* (Taylor), 351
Stowe, Calvin, 349
Stowe, Harriet Beecher, 16, 17, 18, 40, 334, 335, 348, 349, 353, 364, 385, 391; significance of female novelists, 131; *Dred*, 348; *Lady Byron Vindicated*, 391; *The Minister's Wooing*, 348; *Oldtown Folks*, 16, 18, 349; *Poganuc People*, 349; *Sam Lawson Stories*, 349, 385
Strauss, David Friedrich, 291
Subjective, ix
Subjectivism in literature: expressed through the lyric, 195; related to the personal essay, 194

Subjectivity, danger of in Transcendentalism, 255
Sublime, 148
Sumner, Charles, 341
Sumner, William Graham, 390, 392, 432; *What the Social Classes Owe to Each Other*, 416
*Sunshine in Thought* (Leland), 354
"Sunthin' in the Pastoral Line" (Lowell), 338
*Sut Lovingood's Yarns* (Harris), 339
*Swallow Barn* (Kennedy), 209
Swedenborg, Emmanuel, 85, 272-273, 280, 304; influence on Emerson, 227 n.
Swift, Jonathan: critical model for Paulding, 107; *Gulliver* imitated by George Tucker, 112; model for Cooper, 93, 130; model for Irving, 136
*Sword and the Distaff, The* (Simms), 324
*Sylphs of the Seasons* (Allston), 151
*Synthetic Philosophy* (Spencer), 360
*System of Oratory* (Ward), 71

Tacitus, 10
"Taillefer Bell-Ringings, The" (DeForest), 371
Taine, Hippolyte Adolphe, 356, 374, 384, 385, 393, 399, 431; anticipated by American historians, 132; anticipated by Mme de Staël, 145
"Tamerlane" (Poe), 116
Tappan, Caroline Sturgis, 249
Tappan, Professor David, 69
Tawney, R. H., 6, 260
Taylor, Bayard, 325, 349, 353; *Hannah Thurston*, 350; *John Godfrey's Fortunes*, 350; *Joseph and His Friend*, 351; *The Story of Kennett*, 351
Taylor, Edward, 11, 14, 15, 16; *God's Determinations Touching His Elect*, 14
Taylor, Henry, neoclassical criticism, 150
Taylor, John, of Caroline, scientific agrarianism, 111, 118, 125

Teleology, 76
*Tempest and Sunshine* (Holmes), 332
"Tennessee's Partner" (Harte), 343
Tennyson, Alfred, 361, 385; reception in America, 168 n.
"Tenth of January, The" (Phelps), 368
*Tess of the D'Urbervilles* (Hardy), 439
Thackeray, William Makepeace, 334, 344, 373, 378; opinion of Irving, 137
Thales, 263
"Thanatopsis" (Bryant), 158
"Thar's More in the Man than Thar Is in the Land" (Lanier), 326
*Their Wedding Journey* (Howells), 317 n., 352, 385, 405, 407
*Theodore* (De Wette), 291
Theology, 3
*Theology, Explained and Defended* (Dwight), 63
Theosophy, 390
*Thirty Years of Labor* (Powderly), 432
Thompson, D. P., *The Doomed Chief*, 216
Thompson, Maurice, *The Ethics of Literary Art*, 439
Thomson, James, 80, 86, 222, 222 n., 223; and Bryant, 224 n.; and Cooper, 222 n.; contrast with Bloomfield, 126; romantic landscape, 222, 222 n., 223 n.; rural themes, 125; verse forms as models for Americans, 96
Thoreau, Henry David, 73, 249, 282 n., 284, 306 n., 319, 321, 334; advocates self-reform, 285; attitude toward science, 275, 281-283; "Civil Disobedience," 140; contributions to *Dial*, 312; individualism, 127-128, 140, 153; interest in Oriental scriptures, 272; *Journal*, 281-282; literary theories, 293, 296, 298; nature as symbol, 127-128; opposition to slavery, 306-307; primitivism, 97; reading of seventeenth-century verse, 143; romantic themes from nature, 109; student themes for E. T. Channing, 148, 268-269; as teacher, 305; uniqueness, 123; view of Plato, 271
Thorpe, T. B., "The Big Bear of Arkansas," 138
"Thoughts on the Soul" (Dana), 142
Ticknor, George: appeal of Spain, 132; criticism, 144; effects of foreign travel, 159; first university course in foreign literature, 147 n.; friendship with Mme de Staël, 145; study in German universities, 133, 157
"Tied to a Rope" (Sprague), 361 n.
*Tiger Lilies* (Lanier), 370
Tilton, Theodore, 389-390
Tindal, Matthew, 43
"To a Wild Honeysuckle" (Freneau), 127
*Tobias Wilson* (Clemens), 365
Tocqueville, Alexis de: American disregard of rules, 105; anticipates American romanticism, 105; democracy and individualism, 105, 158; *Democracy in America*, 104; rise in native American literature, 104
Tolstoi, Leo, 431, 435-438
*Tom Sawyer* (Clemens), 429
Tourgée, Albion, 387, 419, 434; *Murvale Eastman*, 434
Thackeray, William M., 384, 385, 396, 403, 417, 423, 431, 438
Tradition, 183-186, 240; attacked by Transcendentalist social theories, 299; place in Emerson's aesthetics, 294-295
"Tragic Era, The," 382, 386
Train, George Francis, 389
Transcendentalism, vii, 105, 107, 117, 127, 139, 143, 145, 147, 150, 157, 158, 325, 331, 358, 390; aesthetic theories of, 292-298; affected by German thought, 254, 257, 273, 274, 289, 291; American sources, 226; Channing sees danger of, 255; chief American followers of, 249;

differs from romanticism, 225-226; English sources, 227-229; French sources, 229; an indigenous American movement, 247; influenced by Oriental scriptures, 271-272; influenced by Plato and the Neo-Platonists, 270-271; positive beliefs associated with, 250-251; refusal to admit depravity, 250; shaped by Swedenborgians, 272-273; views rejected by, 250
"Transcendentalism" (Parker), 254
"Transcendentalist, The" (Emerson), 254
Transcendentalists, 321, 378
"Transient and Permanent in Christianity" (Parker), 291
Travel book (sketches), as an influence on romantic landscape, 225
*Travels* (Bartram), 126
*Travels in Italy and America* (Chateaubriand), 193
*Travels in New-England and New York*, 75
"Treatise of Ineffectual Hearing of the Word" (Shepard), 30
*Tribune* (New York), 297
*Triumphant Democracy* (Carnegie), 416
*Triumph of Infidelity, The* (Dwight), 96, 129
Trollope, Anthony, 353, 402, 423, 438
Trowbridge, J. T., 400; *Neighbor Jackwood*, 335
*True Intellectual System of the Universe, The* (Cudworth), 294
*True Means of Establishing Public Happiness, The* (Dwight), 60
*True Religion Delineated* (Bellamy), 16, 18
Trumbull, John, 69, 80; *Essay on the Use and Advantages of the Fine Arts*, 51; *Mathematical Metaphysician, The*, 64; *M'Fingal*, 106
Trumbull, Jonathan: opposed study of classical languages, 93, 96; product of Enlightenment, 108
Truth, 52, 62-64, 66, 67-71, 73, 79, 88; Transcendentalist view, 251, 275, 281
Tucker, George: as satirist, 112; on slavery, 111; *A Voyage to the Moon*, 112
Tucker, Nathaniel Beverley: violent secessionist, 114; *The Partisan Leader*, 114
Turgenev, Aleksandr I., 385, 386, 396, 403, 408 n., 424, 438
Turner, Arlin, xi
Twain, Mark. See Clemens, Samuel Langhorne
Tweed, William M. ("Boss Tweed"), 386
Tyler, Royall, oriental themes, 157
Tyndall, John, 361, 412

"Ulalume" (Poe), 397
*Uncle Tom's Cabin* (Stowe), 113, 334, 335, 348
Understanding, Transcendentalist definition of, 251
*Union Officer in the Reconstruction, A* (DeForest), 372 n.
Unitarianism, 66, 85, 96, 133, 154, 156, 331, 358, 387; attacked by Transcendentalists, 262; conservatism in 1830, 285-286; objected to as mechanistic, 250; paradoxical position, 286; relationship to Transcendentalism, 230
*Untaught Bard, The*, 83
Utilitarianism, 63, 124, 354; American exponents, 231. See also Neal, John
Utility, 355
Utopianism: 97, 159; of the Transcendentalists in Associationism, 303, 304

Valdés, Armando, 437
Vanderbilt, William K. ("Commodore" Vanderbilt), 386
Veblen, Thorstein, 313
Veritism, 440
Verplanck, Gulian: his literary nationalism, 123; critical thought, 144

Very, Jones, 249, 312; connection with Judd, 128; roughness of verse, 143
*Vestiges of Creation* (Chambers), 357
Victorian temper in America, 234
*Vindication of the Rights of Women* (Wollstonecraft), 97
*Vision of Columbus, The* (Barlow), 51, 59, 79
Virtue, 13, 17, 26, 32
Vocation, 5
*Volunteer's Adventures, A* (DeForest), 372 n.
*Voyage to the Moon, A* (Tucker), 112

*Waiting for the Verdict* (Davis), 367
*Walden* (Thoreau), 97, 319
Walker, Timothy, 256; "Defence of Mechanical Philosophy," 257 n.
Walker, Williston, 5, 37
Walsh, Robert: his critical thought, 144; neoclassical nationalist, 146 n.
Walsh, Robert, Jr., *Appeal from the Judgments of Great Britain Respecting the United States of America, An*, 78
Ward, John, *System of Oratory*, 71
Ward, Lester, 432; *Dynamic Sociology*, 416
Ward, Mrs. See Phelps, Elizabeth Stuart
Ware, Henry, Jr., 257, 290
*War in Texas, The* (Landry), 113
Warner, Charles D., 385, 393, 408, 424-425; *The Gilded Age*, 385, 392, 395, 428, 434
Warner, Susan, 331, 332, 333, 348; *Queechy*, 332; *The Wide, Wide World*, 332, 333, 402
Warren, Austin, viii
*Washington Square* (James), 419
Wasson, David, 249
*Watch and Ward* (James), 317 n., 353
*Way of Life, The* (Cotton), 5, 66

Wealth, Transcendentalist view of, 307-308
Webber, Charles W., *Old Hicks, the Guide*, 121
Weber, Max, 6, 260
Webster, Daniel, 307
Webster, Noah, 378
Wegscheider, Julius August Ludwig, 291
Weiss, John, 249, 311 n.
Weld, Theodore Dwight, *American Slavery as It Is*, 113
Wellek, René, viii, ix
*Western Clearings* (Kirkland), 345
*Western Messenger*, 292
Westminster catechism, 18, 19
*Westward Ho!* (Paulding), 125
*Wet Days at Edgewood* (Mitchell), 334
"What Is an American?" (Crèvecoeur), 83
*What Is Man?* (Clemens), 428
*What the Social Classes Owe to Each Other* (Sumner), 416
Wheeler, Charles Stearns, 249
Whipple, E. P., 323 n., 336, 356, 361 n., 385; his critical thought, 144; "Mr. Hardhack on the Derivation of Man from the Monkey," 361 n.; "Mr. Hardhack on the Sensational in Literature and Life," 336 n.
Whisky Rebellion, 95
Whitaker, Nathaniel, 64
Whitcher, Mrs. Frances M., *The Widow Bedott Papers*, 338
White, Richard Grant: *The Life and Genius of Shakespeare*, 398; "Shakespeare's Art," 398
Whitman, Walt, 47, 295, 317, 324, 325, 327, 328, 329, 330, 355, 359, 364, 376-378, 383, 387, 390, 395, 411, 430, 439; "Beat! Beat! Drums!," 329; *Democratic Vistas*, 329-330, 390, 395; *Drum-Taps*, 329; "Eighteen Sixty-One," 329; faith in science, 355; idealism, 329; influence of Emerson's "The Poet" on, 329; *Leaves of Grass*, 317, 325, 327, 329, 355, 359, 387, 390, 418; realism of,

327-328; satire in, 328; "One's-Self I Sing," 328; poetry and tradition, 317; "The Return of the Heroes," 329; "Song of Myself," 328; "Song of the Exposition," 329; "The Wound Dresser," 329
Whittelsey, Chauncey, 64
Whittier, John Greenleaf, 322, 334, 397
*Wide, Wide World, The* (Warner), 332, 333, 402
*Widow Bedott Papers, The* (Whitcher), 338
*Wieland* (Brown), 191
Wigglesworth, Michael, 11, 15; *Day of Doom*, 14, 16, 25
*Wild Flowers* (Bloomfield), 126
*Wilhelm Meister* (Goethe), 261
Will. *See* Free will
Willard, Samuel, 19, 20, 21, 22; *Compleat Body of Divinity*, 18
Williams, John, political satire, *The Hamiltoniad*, in imitation of *Dunciad*, 129
Williams, Samuel, *The Natural and Civil History of Vermont*, 79
Willis, N. P., 324, 334; criticized by *Amherst Shrine*, 150; effects of foreign travel, 159; lament at literary importations, 185; student of Lamb and Wilson, 195, 195 n.
Wilson, Alexander, artist-naturalist in West, 127; effect on poetic imagery, 157; landscape tradition, 221, 221 n.
Wilson, James, 69
Wilson, John, popularity in America, 195 n., 220, 239
Winthrop, John, 4, 33, 34, 35, 37, 39; *Modell of Christian Charity* . . . , 38
Winthrop, Theodore: *Edwin Brothertoft*, 347; *John Brent*, 346
Wirt, William as essayist, 194; contributions to "The Old Bachelor" and "The Rainbow," 111; *Letters of the British Spy*, 111; and the Revolution of 1830, 238 n.
Wise, John, 28
*Witching Times* (DeForest), 370-371
Witherspoon, John, 69, 74
Wollaston, William, 278; *Religion of Nature Delineated, The*, 62, 63
Wollstonecraft (Godwin), Mary, *Vindication of the Rights of Woman*, 97
*Woman in the Nineteenth Century* (Fuller), 97
Woodhull, Victoria Claflin, 389-390, 392
Woodrow, James, 326 n.
Woolson, Constance Fenimore, 424; *Anne*, 418; *East Angels*, 418; *For the Major*, 418, 432
Wordsworth, William, 80, 82, 83, 101, 126, 167, 168, 168 n., 252, 261, 274; American reception, 168 n.; and Bryant, 222 n., political enthusiasms, 164
*World of Chance, A* (Howells), 436
"Wound Dresser, The" (Whitman), 329
Wright, Chauncey, 391
Wright, Fanny, 301; utopianism, 159
Wundt, Wilhelm, 391

Yale, 60, 63, 64, 69, 96, 99
*Yemassee, The* (Simms), 216, 324
Youmans, E. L., 358, 361, 378, 385; *The Culture Demanded by Modern Life*, 359
Young, Edward, *Night Thoughts on Death*, 85
Young, Robert, influence on American writers, 130

Zeising, Adolph, 415
Zeller, Eduard, 391
Zola, Emile, 384, 404, 415, 422, 423, 435, 437-439
*Zury* (Kirkland), 438

Kirtley Library
Columbia College
8th and Rogers
Columbia, MO. 65201